THE MATERIALIZATION OF TIME IN THE ANCIENT MAYA WORLD

Maya Studies

UNIVERSITY PRESS OF FLORIDA

Florida A&M University, Tallahassee
Florida Atlantic University, Boca Raton
Florida Gulf Coast University, Ft. Myers
Florida International University, Miami
Florida State University, Tallahassee
New College of Florida, Sarasota
University of Central Florida, Orlando
University of Florida, Gainesville
University of North Florida, Jacksonville
University of South Florida, Tampa
University of West Florida, Pensacola

# The Materialization of Time in the Ancient Maya World

## Mythic History and Ritual Order

Edited by David A. Freidel, Arlen F. Chase, Anne S. Dowd, and Jerry Murdock

Foreword by Diane Z. Chase and Arlen F. Chase

UNIVERSITY PRESS OF FLORIDA

Gainesville/Tallahassee/Tampa/Boca Raton
Pensacola/Orlando/Miami/Jacksonville/Ft. Myers/Sarasota

Copyright 2024 by David A. Freidel, Arlen F. Chase, Anne S. Dowd, and Jerry Murdock
All rights reserved
Published in the United States of America

29  28  27  26  25  24     6  5  4  3  2  1

Library of Congress Cataloging-in-Publication Data
Names: Freidel, David A., editor. | Chase, Arlen F. (Arlen Frank), 1953– editor. | Dowd, Anne S., editor. | Murdock, Jerry, editor.
Title: The materialization of time in the ancient Maya world : mythic history and ritual order / edited by David A. Freidel, Arlen F. Chase, Anne S. Dowd, and Jerry Murdock ; foreword by Diane Z. Chase and Arlen F. Chase.
Other titles: Mythic history and ritual order | Maya studies.
Description: 1. | Gainesville : University Press of Florida, 2024. | Series: Maya studies | Includes bibliographical references and index.
Identifiers: LCCN 2023006650 (print) | LCCN 2023006651 (ebook) | ISBN 9780813069807 (hardback) | ISBN 9780813070582 (pdf)
Subjects: LCSH: Maya chronology. | Maya calendar. | Maya philosophy. | Mayas—History. | Time measurements—History.
Classification: LCC F1435.3.C14 M38 2023 (print) | LCC F1435.3.C14 (ebook) | DDC 529/.32978427—dc23/eng/20230524
LC record available at https://lccn.loc.gov/2023006650
LC ebook record available at https://lccn.loc.gov/2023006651

The University Press of Florida is the scholarly publishing agency for the State University System of Florida, comprising Florida A&M University, Florida Atlantic University, Florida Gulf Coast University, Florida International University, Florida State University, New College of Florida, University of Central Florida, University of Florida, University of North Florida, University of South Florida, and University of West Florida.

University Press of Florida
2046 NE Waldo Road
Suite 2100
Gainesville, FL 32609
http://upress.ufl.edu

To Jeremy Arac Sabloff, who through his gift for scientific method, his grasp of theory, and his sense of fairness and ethics continues to inspire and guide archaeologically rigorous searches into ancient peoples' behavior.

# Contents

List of Figures    ix
List of Tables    xv
Foreword    xvii

**Part I. Landesque Cosmography**

1. The Maya Materialization of Time: An Introduction    3
   *Arlen F. Chase, Anne S. Dowd, David A. Freidel, and Jerry Murdock*

2. Landesque Cosmography: Crafting Creation-Era Time on the Maya
   Lowland Landscape    25
   *David A. Freidel, Prudence M. Rice, and Michelle E. Rich*

**Part II. Building Time into Place**

3. Spatial and Temporal Standardization in Southern Mesoamerica
   during the Preclassic Period: New Insights from the Middle
   Usumacinta Region, Mexico    55
   *Takeshi Inomata and Daniela Triadan*

4. Ordering Time and Space at Yaxnohcah: Creation and Renewal
   in a Preclassic Landscape    80
   *Kathryn Reese-Taylor, Verónica A. Vázquez López, Shawn G. Morton,
   Meaghan M. Peuramaki-Brown, Sarah E. Bednar, F. C. Atasta Flores Esquivel,
   Debra S. Walker, Armando Anaya Hernández, and Nicholas P. Dunning*

5. Domesticating Time: Quadripartite Symbolism and Founding Rituals
   at Yaxuná    107
   *Travis W. Stanton, Karl A. Taube, and Ryan H. Collins*

6. In the Shadow of Descending Gods: Monumental Posts and Solar Cycles
   in the Preclassic Maya Lowlands    131
   *Francisco Estrada-Belli and David A. Freidel*

7. Stelae, Spirits, Desecration, and Devotion: The Fate of Some Time Lords
   in the Classic Maya World    149
   *David A. Freidel and Olivia Navarro-Farr*

viii · Contents

## Part III. Chambers of Time

8. Balamkú's History House: Harkening to Primordial Rhythms of Mythic Time   187
   *Anne S. Dowd and Gabrielle Vail*

9. Scorpion Star: Constellations, Seasons, and Convergences of Meaning in a Classic Maya Entity   223
   *Franco D. Rossi*

10. Time as Ordinary Practice: A Divination Building at Chan   254
    *Cynthia Robin*

11. The Chamber of Secrets at Xunantunich   273
    *M. Kathryn Brown, Leah McCurdy, and Jason Yaeger*

## Part IV. Bridging Time

12. Imagery of the Yearbearers in Maya Culture and Beyond   299
    *Susan Milbrath*

13. Lived Experience and Monumental Time in the Classic Maya Lowlands   347
    *Patricia A. McAnany*

14. The Materialization of Time in the Maya Archaeological Record: Examples from Caracol and Santa Rita Corozal, Belize   363
    *Diane Z. Chase and Arlen F. Chase*

15. Materializing Time on Wax: The Cozumel Maya Bee Gardens   387
    *Adolfo Iván Batún-Alpuche and David A. Freidel*

16. Temporal Fusion: Mythical and Mortal Time in Maya Art   400
    *James A. Doyle*

17. "How Much May They Not Have Written?" K'atuns 11 Ajaw and the Itzá   416
    *Prudence M. Rice*

## Part V. Materializing Mesoamerican Chronoscapes

18. The Ideas and Images of Cities and Centers: Teotihuacan and the Lowland Maya   433
    *David A. Freidel, Saburo Sugiyama, and Nawa Sugiyama*

19. Epilogue: Architects of Time   460
    *Anne S. Dowd*

References   485
List of Contributors   567
Index   571

# Figures

0.1. Jeremy A. Sabloff  v

2.1. Effigy turtle performance platforms at Yaxuná  27

2.2. Nixtun Ch'ich' and crocodile  29

2.3. Polychrome painted and modeled Cosmic Crocodile  32

2.4. Shell pectoral of the Crocodile Tree with skeletal head  34

2.5. Central stairway from interior corridor to the summit at Structure 6E-53, Yaxuná  39

2.6. El Perú-Waka' site zone showing water features and El Mirador hill  42

2.7. Entrance to the subsurface chamber at El Perú-Waka' Structure P13-5  45

2.8. Subsurface chamber showing fall wall of yellow matrix, Structure P13-5  46

3.1. Locations of the archaeological sites mentioned in the text  56

4.1. Central precinct of Yaxnohcah and Brisa E Group  94

4.2. The four civic groups located within 2.5 kilometers of the Brisa E Group  96

4.3. Features of altar-hearth at the Grazia complex  98

4.4. Map of Yaxnohcah with astronomical alignments of Preclassic major complexes  101

5.1. Lidar images of the cruciform plan of Yaxuná  111

5.2. Holes in the bedrock range structure of the Yaxuná E Group  112

5.3. Original hole in the bedrock of the Yaxuná plaza and a circular fire altar  116

5.4. Incised cross on the Late Preclassic center of the Yaxuná plaza  118

6.1. West Wall mural at San Bartolo  131

6.2. Upper and lower tier masks at Cerros depicting the Principal Bird Deity and the maize god  137 x · Figures

6.3. Masks depicting the maize god at Cerros   138

6.4. Images from a mural at Cival depicting the maize god wearing a variety of headdresses   139

6.5. Stela 2 at Izapa depicting a Principal Bird/Sun Deity   139

6.6. Mask from Structure 1 combining features of the maize god, the sun god, and the lightning god   142

6.7. Rain god Chahk mask on the northern side of Structure 9 at Cival   143

6.8. Stela 3 at Cival depicting a human-like image of the rain god Chahk   144

6.9. Northern edge of the Central Acropolis at El Mirador showing rain deities and other celestial beings   145

7.1. El Perú Stela 45 planted within the staircase fronting Structure M13-Sub III   155

7.2. El Perú Stela 15   157

7.3. Fragment of El Perú Stela 9   158

7.4. El Perú Stela 16   160

7.5. Defaced Stela 10, reset in Terminal Classic times   162

7.6. Crown section of broken Early Classic Stela 9   163

7.7. Composite photograph of the fragments of Stela 43 depicting K'inich Bahlam II   164

7.8. Right-side text of Stela 44 showing the name of Lady Sak Wayis K'uhul Chatan Winik   165

7.9. Tikal Stela 26   171

7.10. El Perú-Waka' Stelae 22 and 23   176

8.1. Glyphs in column texts 1, 2 and 3, in Balamkú Structure 1A-Sub   195

8.2. Additional painted glyphs, columns 4, 5, 6, 7, 8, in Balamkú Structure 1A-Sub   196

8.3. Column texts 9 and 10, Balamkú Structure 1A-Sub   196

8.4. Glyphs in column text 11, Balamkú Structure 1A-Sub   197

8.5. Northwest view of the stucco frieze on Balamkú Structure 1A-Sub   198

8.6. Drawing 82 at Naj Tunich Cave   201

8.7. Dresden Codex page 17a   202

Figures · xi

8.8. Scenes from Drawings 21–23 at Naj Tunich Cave   204

8.9. Dresden Codex page 41a   205

8.10. Dresden Codex page 29c   206

8.11. Dresden Codex page 68b   207

8.12. Floor plan of the interior of Balamkú Structure 1A-Sub   213

9.1. Paris Codex page 24b and Casa de las Monjas frieze at
Chichén Itzá   225

9.2. Sky scorpions at Chichén Itzá   228

9.3. Scorpion-tailed deer and scorpion-tailed Chahk in the Madrid
Codex   230

9.4. Scorpion-tailed goddess and scorpion-tailed God M in the
Madrid Codex   232

9.5. Scorpion-tailed maize youth at Copán and on a Late
Classic bowl   234

9.6. Maya ruler dressed as youthful scorpion-tailed deity, Stela 2,
Naranjo   236

9.7. Detail from Los Sabios mural showing Hun Ik' Ixiim ti taaj
as the impersonated deity   237

9.8. Stela 8 and Stela 35, Piedras Negras   243

9.9. Scorpion-tailed maize god in Dresden Codex   245

10.1. Map showing topography, settlement pattern, and agricultural
terraces at Chan   259

10.2. Community center at Chan showing the location of the divination
and administrative building   260

10.3. Vaulted passageway and interior stair between Structure 6 east
and Structure 6 west at Chan   262

10.4. Structure 6 east at Chan showing six of twelve rooms   263

10.5. The two central rooms of Structure 6 east at Chan   265

10.6. Terminal deposit in room 2 in Structure 6 east at Chan   267

11.1. Calendar Round dates and Tzolk'in date from Structure A-5-2nd
at Xunantunich   277

11.2. Map of Xunantunich   282

11.3. Graffiti on north wall of the Structure A-5-2nd   285

11.4. Ballplayer (bolded), twisted snakes, and other graffiti,
Structure A-5-2nd   286

xii · Figures

11.5. Decapitation scene from Structure A-5-2nd    287

11.6. Feline heads from Structure A-5-2nd    289

11.7. Anthropomorphic profiles from Structure A-5-2nd    290

11.8. Anthropomorphic figures from Structure A-5-2nd    291

11.9. Head of Chak Xib Chahk from Structure A-5-2nd    292

12.1. Madrid Codex pages 34–36    315

12.2. Madrid Codex pages 36–37    315

12.3. Madrid Codex page 34    316

12.4. Madrid Codex page 35    317

12.5. Madrid Codex page 36    318

12.6. Madrid Codex page 37    319

12.7. Paris Codex pages 19–20    320

12.8. Dresden Codex page 25    321

12.9. Dresden Codex page 26    322

12.10. Dresden Codex page 27    323

12.11. Dresden Codex page 28    324

12.12. West Wall of San Bartolo mural    325

12.13. Detail of West Wall of San Bartolo mural    326

12.14. Stela 19 at Ceibal    327

12.15. Partial reconstruction of Codex Borgia page 49    328

12.16. Partial reconstruction of Codex Borgia page 50    328

12.17. Partial reconstruction of Codex Borgia page 51    329

12.18. Partial reconstruction of Codex Borgia page 52    329

12.19. Death god and step-eyed maize god Mayapán effigy censers    330

12.20. Paired Mayapán effigy censers representing God N as Pauahtun    331

13.1. Stela C at Quirigua    351

13.2. Stela D at Copán    352

13.3. Portion of the carved mosaic façade in the Nunnery Quadrangle
at Uxmal    358

14.1. Giant Ahau Altar 19 at Caracol    369

14.2. Shell and jadeite artifacts from the front core of Structure A6    371

14.3. Cache from Structure 213 at Santa Rita Corozal    372

14.4. Paired Postclassic incensarios from Structure 213    374

Figures · xiii

14.5. Terminal Classic incensarios from Structure A6 at Caracol 375

14.6. Postclassic incensarios in Structure 81 at Santa Rita Corozal 377

14.7. Late Classic cache containers at Caracol 379

14.8. Caracol cache sequence 381

14.9. Twin-pyramid groups from Tikal 383

15.1. Late Classic stylus from Yaxuná featuring a spatula "eraser" 390

16.1. Rollout of a codex-style vessel attributed to the Fantastic Painter 405

16.2. The Princeton Vase 407

16.3. Main scene of the Cosmic Plate 408

16.4. Rollout of a codex-style vessel attributed to the Metropolitan Painter 409

16.5. Rollout of codex-style ceramic vessel attributed to the Liner School 411

16.6. Codex-style vessel from southern Campeche, Mexico, or northern Petén region, Guatemala 412

16.7. Codex-style ceramic plate 414

17.1. Landa's "k'atun wheel" 426

18.1. Lidar map of Teotihuacan indicating location of sites mentioned in the text 434

18.2. Reconstruction drawing of Yaxuná Burial 24 441

18.3. Teotihuacan-style ceramic figurine, from Burial 24 at Yaxuná 442

18.4. The Hauberg Stela 446

18.5. Ancestor bundle mask from Burial 80, El Perú-Waka' 448

18.6. Early Classic greenstone mask from Pyramid of the Sun 449

18.7. Crocodile Tree shell pectoral from El Perú-Waka' 451

18.8. Stela 16 at El Perú-Waka' portraying Sihyaj K'ahk' 454

18.9. Vessel from tomb at El Perú-Waka' 456

19.1. Transcription from Stela 5 at Tak'alik Ab'aj, Guatemala 465

19.2. Covarrubias's sketch of a jade wing oyster-shell skeuomorph pendant/paint pot 467

19.3. Hieroglyphic signs 468

19.4. Detail from Stela D at Copán 468

19.5. The Toltec Kislak Oyohualli pendant 469

19.6. Woman scribe from polychrome vessel K6020 479

# Tables

8.1. Examples of Maya painted or incised hieroglyphic texts discussed in chapter    188

9.1. Glyphic caption on north wall niche, Los Sabios mural    239

12.1. Last date in each trecena with a 26-day interval to next set of yearbearers    310

12.2. Middle Preclassic New Year dates on 0 Pop and 1 Pop, 750–680 BCE    314

17.1. Gregorian dates (CE) of Late Classic through colonial-period ~256-year *k'atun* cycles    419

19.1. Chronological overview of the Maya area    462

# Foreword

There are many ways of thinking about time.

As with most other ancient peoples, the Maya were concerned with all aspects of time. The Maya calendar not only incorporated a count of days, it also detailed astronomical information pertaining to the moon and Venus. Some of their architectural groups were constructed in the shape of time, and many of their ritual deposits served to memorialize time. Their communities were ordered and galvanized by time. While linear aspects of time were incorporated in Maya histories, past, present, and future events and activities were also tied together in cyclical time, providing the opportunity to predict or even influence the future.

Academic interpretations about the significance of time for the ancient Maya have varied over the years. In the early part of the twentieth century, hieroglyphic texts were viewed as only being concerned with marking calendrical time and as being devoid of historical reference. The Maya were believed to have been ruled by calendar priests who were essentially time lords studying the heavens. This interpretation was largely premised on the counts of different temporal intervals that were found on the vast majority of their carved stone monuments, but it also reflected the desires of modern populations to believe that there had once been a utopian past.

Beginning in the early 1960s, breakthroughs in the translation of Maya epigraphic texts contradicted such views. Tatania Proskouriakoff firmly established the historical content of Maya texts at Piedras Negras, demonstrating that they referred to events in the lives of dynastic rulers. Other research followed her work and continued to advance our historical understanding of certain Maya people and events in the past. But as the focus turned to Maya history, considerations concerning the nature and uses of Maya time were largely set aside.

This volume infuses the field of Maya studies with a new appreciation of time and with the importance of reconsidering multiple aspects of time for these ancient peoples. It demonstrates that an overt appreciation of time existed at the very beginning of the Maya developmental sequence, how time manifested itself in many components of ancient Maya societies, and how the recording and memorialization of time continued to be important to ancient Maya societies for over three millennia.

*The Materialization of Time in the Ancient Maya World* is the second volume in a set of three works that have been and are being prepared and inspired by collaborations at the Santa Fe Institute. The institute's Maya Working Group, led by David A. Freidel, Anne S. Dowd, Arlen F. Chase, and Jerry Murdock, has been meeting in Santa Fe, New Mexico, since 2011, interrupted only by the pandemic in 2020. The initial volume that resulted from these multi-day meetings was published in 2017. The product of assemblies that occurred in 2011, 2012, and 2013, it examined a distinctive architectural complex that formed a basic building block for early Maya societies (and continues to be of interest to the working group today). The present volume was conceived in the 2013 meeting and came to fruition through meetings of the group in Santa Fe in 2015, 2016, and 2017. It seeks to establish that an ideological consideration of time was central to all Maya societies. These meetings also spawned a third volume, for which the working group has met in 2018 and 2021. The third volume is tentatively titled *Being Maya* and builds on both *Maya E Groups* and *The Materialization of Time in the Ancient Maya World*, intending to complete what should be a cohesive set of works that together will help us better understand the ancient Maya.

It is our hope that the chapters in this book will spur future scholars to focus not only on the material aspects of the past archaeological record but also on the ideological beliefs that can be inferred through careful archaeological analysis. If such is the case, then this volume will have served its purpose of ensuring that generational research transcends time.

Diane Z. Chase and Arlen F. Chase
Series Editors

# I

## Landesque Cosmography

# 1

# The Maya Materialization of Time

## An Introduction

ARLEN F. CHASE, ANNE S. DOWD, DAVID A. FREIDEL,
AND JERRY MURDOCK

### Prologue

The Popol Vuh describes a time before human beings were created, when there was only sea and sky, before there was sun and moon and before there was a calendar (Tedlock 1996). The narrator of the story tells us that human beings were eventually created by the gods and given an elevated status over animals so that they would praise and worship the gods.

Time was something independent of human beings. It was something the gods created and expressed through celestial majesty, and ultimately they gave it to human beings via the Tzolk'in, Haab, and Venus calendars. The calendars helped the Maya cultivate the land, know when to make decisions, and schedule prophecy. Most important, it assisted them in worshipping and praising the gods.

So what was the Maya materialization of time? We believe that the answer to that question was central to their civilization. Almost all architecture, from villages to citadels, was intentionally designed to fulfill the requirements of worshipping the gods and centering their world in an effort to create a sustainable future.

Having walked along ancient causeways, we often have felt a connection to the sky and the rituals that commemorated those alignments. In our modern social experience, time is linear and has one-way directionality. We use economic metaphors to describe it: it can be bought, spent, saved, lost, stolen, salvaged, and wasted. But none of these modern terms are helpful for understanding Maya cosmological and cyclical concepts of time. Because Native American views of time and temporality are often at odds with western scholarship (e.g., Killsback 2013; Reid and Sieber 2015), modern notions of time and Maya notions of time may have no common ground, with the exception of the use of bookkeeping.

Over 100 years ago Albert Einstein gave us a new way to perceive time as space-time (e.g., Rigden 2005). Perhaps as long as 4,000 years ago (or possibly much longer), the Maya created a cosmological sense of time that was interconnected with the underworld, the terrestrial world, and celestial space. Metaphorically we call their concept "Maya space-time," and like Einstein's version, we see it principally as a fusing of the dimensions of space and time in which time is not a stand-alone idea, as Newton perceived it (e.g., DiSalle 2006), but rather a medium for the flow of energy and information. Specifically, the Maya ritually bundled and unbundled space and time with objects made sacred by the process. Thus, activities such as communication with and veneration of ancestors, which involved planting intention-infused objects (such as caches, bundles, and burials) into the landscape, were aspirational seeds that could be accessed in the future or influence future events.

Maya materialization of time incorporated notions of cyclicality and expanded dimensionality into the built environment. In the world of the Maya, time had "agents" that may also have functioned as forerunners for celestial deities, such as Venus, the sun, and the moon, which at a minimum could be used to instruct about when to plant, when to express reciprocity (sacrifice), and when to harvest.

Time was something to be commemorated, to be vocationally derived through divination, or to be promulgated by leaders as prophecy. Perhaps for the Maya delineating cycles of time was a way to anticipate future change and bring useful change into the present. If so, could time have functioned as a culturally sanctioned tool for managing change that priests and leaders used to exert influence or control over the community?

Being in sync with time may also have been an aspirational activity that was part and parcel of being in balance with or centered within the universe, as exemplified by "walking in the path of the sun." Perhaps the Maya used calendrical computations as referential guides for individual or institutional decision-making to keep the community and its members on the path.

When the artist Paul Gauguin created his Tahitian-inspired art works in the period 1891 and 1901, he not only recast his own life (e.g., Mathews 2001), he also memorialized basic human questions as keys to understanding the people he painted (Thomson 2011). Time for the Tahitians, as for the Maya, may also have been expressed as "storied knowledge" that helped answer cosmological questions such as: Who are we? Where do we come from? Where are we going?

Time for the Maya, in our view, appears to be a source of contextual information that gave meaning to being Maya. Finally, Maya space-time may have been a directly perceivable attribute of the divine through its many guises and manifestations. This may have been the inspiration for the obsessive efforts of the Maya to materialize time.

The path of the sun, in which we include celestial objects that intersect and move through the ecliptic, may be synonymous with the path of life through time. Activities such as those associated with the centering of the Maya landscape may have been intended to create harmony with the night sky and specifically with the tree of life, thereby ensuring rebirth and renewal for generations.

What remains today of the formerly vast and complex culture collectively known as "the Maya" are disparate groups that are still living a myth so powerful that it has survived the collapse and abandonment of palaces, temples, kingship, and conquest to echo in the consciousness of a people as unique as the myth they created.

## Background

The prehispanic Maya civilization captured the imagination of Americans in the nineteenth century with the 1841 publication of John L. Stephens's *Incidents of Travel in Central America, Chiapas, and Yucatan*. Frederick Catherwood's (1844) *camera lucida* illustrations of carved stone monuments at the site of Copán in Honduras displayed the beautiful and enigmatic hieroglyphic writing of the Classic period (250–900 CE) Maya and inspired generations of amateur scholars to study them. By the early twentieth century, these autodidacts had cracked the code of Maya mathematics and calendar calculations (e.g., Morley 1915) and we knew that the Maya were among the ancient world's foremost adepts in the study of celestial movements in accord with a count of days carefully bundled like sacred relics into units approximating years and bundles of those years.

By the end of the twentieth century, epigraphers of glyphic Mayan (e.g., Martin and Grube 2008) had firmly established that the Classic Maya dynasts of the southern lowlands, a territory that stretched from the site of Cancuén in the south to Calakmul in the north, from Palenque in the west to Copán in the east, were writing history, embedding salient events in the lives of ruling men and women into a count of days beginning on creation day, August 11 (or 13), 3114 BCE in the famous Long Count calendar. Between the second and ninth centuries CE, over generations of observation and study, Maya courtiers situated royal policy and performance in what David Stuart (2011) felicitously has called the "Order of Days."

Perhaps because the ancient sages appeared to anchor their history in the past through calendar reckoning, modern Maya scholars have been seduced into thinking that they were primarily looking backward for inspiration about how to comport themselves instead of seeing in their study of the stars ways to inspirationally chart the future course of their realms, to anchor events on auspicious dates, and to insert themselves within the broader cosmos. Did the ancestral Maya ever aspire to the greatness they surely achieved? We think the answer is yes—perhaps sometimes modestly and incrementally but always with the potential of remarkable scale. The resilient reproduction of traditional knowledge and ritual practice among many contemporary Maya is sustained through mindful lifelong education by elders of the youth who care to listen. This has been accomplished through syncretic *costumbre,* customary negotiation between people and both the divine and the ancestral that Maya have integrated into Catholic religious tenets as they perceive them (Oakes 1951). So the past, to paraphrase William Faulkner (1951), is neither dead nor past but rather, as Markus Eberl (2017) has shown in his study of Classic Maya creativity and innovation, even now conditions how Maya people respond to challenges and opportunities in their world.

Examples of the importance of past materiality can be found in both modern-day and ancient Maya customs. Evangelicals, who despise traditional ritual practice as idolatrous, desecrated and defaced a stone effigy named Pascual Abaj on a hilltop shrine near the town of Chichicastenango in highland Guatemala (Hart 2008, 82). K'iche' day keepers, healers, and officials of the town responded by building fragments of the effigy's visage into a protective wall around the place of the god's altar. Did they know that Maya in the seventeenth century built their idols into chapels behind the Catholic altars, like the one in Mopila in Yucatán (Freidel et al. 1993)? Or that Classic Maya people of the lowlands built fragments of royal stelae that had been shattered in war into the walls of a renewed temple at El Perú-Waka' in Petén, Guatemala, or placed fragments in the cores of buildings as offerings at Caracol in Belize? Probably not. The past, however constituted and constructed, is important to all modern Maya communities; some highland K'iche' Maya travel to the lowland site of Tikal to carry out annual rituals there currently. What all Maya people generally do know is that effigies, endowed with enduring animate soul force, are not so easily exorcised by defacement or destruction (O'Neil 2013; Harrison-Buck 2016). Thus, they have, over long periods of time, reinvented and innovated new uses that help ensure their continued beneficence into the future.

## The Materialization of Time

Innovation and aspiration, a key focus of our contemplation of the Maya, mark some of the earliest collective efforts of the Maya, especially as exemplified by their construction of E Groups (e.g., Freidel et al. 2017). During the Preclassic period (1000 BCE–250 CE), lowland Maya peoples of the Guatemalan Petén and adjacent areas established E Groups as the founding buildings in their centers, no doubt originally emulating neighbors to the west (see Inomata 2017b; Inomata, Pinzón, Palomo, et al. 2017); other lowland Maya communities emulated those pioneers. But all of them were departing from previous understandings of why people gathered in centers, why they coordinated their efforts, and why—and under what—circumstances they deferred to leaders. In their local areas and in the context of their local knowledge they were all pioneers in the creation of the initial Maya centers. Lowland Maya E Groups of the Middle Preclassic period (1000–350 BCE) were solar commemorative monuments and with their construction Maya people formally materialized time in a new way. From the beginning—and throughout subsequent eras of florescence, decline, and renewal—lowland Maya peoples sought to materialize through their public buildings and places visions of their coordinated relationship with their gods, propitiating the celestial avatars traveling the sky (e.g., Aveni 2001). Maya architecture was always aspirational and sometimes it was truly innovative. In the case of discoveries Takeshi Inomata has made building on evidence of calendar intervals expressed in Group E–type complexes (Aveni et al. 2003; Dowd 2017c; Freidel et al. 2017; Inomata et al. 2020, 2021; Šprajc et al. 2023; chapter 3, this volume), early Maya architecture may have been innovative and reflective of the way that all Mesoamericans conceived of time and calendars.

Throughout the Classic period, the people who occupied the lower San Pedro Mártir and Usumacinta Rivers (Middle Usumacinta region) were lowland Maya and were likely Mayan speakers in the Preclassic period before that. In the Middle Preclassic period, as related by Takeshi Inomata and Daniela Triadan in chapter 3 of this book, they created ceremonial plazas and platforms of stunning, unprecedented size. As detected by lidar and provisionally ground-truthed through test excavation, these vast, rectangular spaces were oriented north-south, angled slightly to the east of north in a fashion later Maya cities emulated (Maya north was about 15 to 18 degrees east of north), an orientation that is probably reflective of broader cosmological principles. Over the course of the night at this latitude, the star field barrel rolls across the sky. Are these remarkable innovative monumental plazas meant to mark the north-south pivot of the cosmos? As Linda Schele has observed (1992a; see also

Freidel et al. 1993), at dawn in the second week of August (August 11–13), the Milky Way stretches across the center of the sky in a north-south alignment, angled to the east. Most of the huge rectangular Middle Formative spaces located in the lower Usumacinta River area of Tabasco, Mexico, have E Groups at their center. Early lowland Maya E Groups are generally interpreted as solar commemorative buildings originally designed in the Middle Preclassic period to observe sunrise and movement across the eastern horizon over the course of the year. As Inomata (2017b) has described, the north-south axis is important in the original E Groups of Chiapas to the west of Petén, where large monumental buildings regularly dominate the northern end of these plazas. However, in the Maya lowlands of Petén adjacent to parts of Campeche and Belize, the east-west path of the sun and of the stars and constellations along the ecliptic dominated the architecture of these complexes, even at salient centers such as Yaxuná in Yucatán (Stanton 2017). The new discoveries of Inomata's team in the lower Usumacinta River and lower San Pedro Mártir River area, with their broadly "Maya North" orientation, combine early Mesoamerican architectural groupings in an innovative and creative way.

The lower Usumacinta and San Pedro Mártir Rivers are in lowland Maya territory some distance east of the heartland of Olman, the land of the Olmecs, in present-day Tabasco and Veracruz (more than 200 kilometers west of La Venta, more than 150 kilometers northwest of Chiapa de Corzo in Chiapas). But the peoples to the west of this Usumacinta area were no doubt in contact with each other both over land and by canoe along the coast of the Gulf of Mexico (Inomata et al. 2021). We think that the sages and leaders of the lowland Maya in this cultural frontier zone (who evidently arrived at this cosmographic coordination of celestial and earthly cycles) were forward looking and aspired to portray their cosmological beliefs on the landscape (Šprajc et al. 2023). Their celestial template became influential in the Mexican highlands and in the lowlands of Mesoamerica. By the beginning of the third century CE, the "Maya North" orientation, specifically fifteen degrees, five minutes east of north, guided the layout of Teotihuacan's Street of the Dead and the grand gridded plan of that city where the Pyramid of the Sun faces the setting sun on August 12 and on April 29 (S. Sugiyama 2014). Saburo Sugiyama (1993, 2014), in accord with arguments made for Maya E Groups (e.g., Freidel et al. 2017), sees these dates as dividing the solar year into 105 and 260 days, intervals that were important to both the ritual sacred almanac and the agrarian cycle.

Sugiyama (2014) notes that August 12 is, give a day on either side, creation day in the Long Count, a calendar innovated somewhere in the lowlands before the Late Preclassic period (350 BCE–1 CE), when scribes began to carve dates on stone monuments in both Olman and the Maya area. Inomata and his colleagues (chapter 3, this volume) are justifiably cautious about the possible implications of his team's discoveries pending further field testing and ground-truthing. But we are prompted to wonder if the interval between 1000 and 800 BCE—which Sugiyama has identified as the time when people of Chiapas, Petén, and the Usumacinta–San Pedro Mártir riverine lowlands interacted intensively and first innovated E Groups—constituted a first Mesoamerican Renaissance following the collapse of Early Formative (1500–1000 BCE) San Lorenzo Tenochtitlan in Olman by 1000 BCE. To us, these broadly distributed early architectural complexes represent the materialization of time in conjunction with the adoption of maize as a staple and the planting and harvesting cycles of that grain. The analogy is appropriate, given that the San Lorenzo Olmec were surely "Classic" in their establishment of a center of political and religious power. It was at San Lorenzo between 1500 and 1000 BCE that craftspeople innovated the exaltation of rulers in monumental stone images, dragging and barging the multi-ton stones from more than 40 kilometers away and placing them on a massive effigy clay platform oriented slightly west of north (Coe and Diehl 1980). From the time of their establishment after 1000 BCE, monumental Maya centers expressed the intention of both leaders and communities of ordinary people to create places in which to materialize time. The notion of "centering," as Freidel, Schele, and Parker (1993) defined it in *Maya Cosmos,* is part of what Evon Vogt (1964) called the "genetic" cultural code of the Maya—enduring sensibilities and ways of thinking that lay behind all their efforts from the earliest times. Recently, Markus Eberl (2017) formulated arguments regarding creativity and innovation among the Maya, reviewing concepts such as structure, rules, paradigms, and schemes as the cultural frames ancient Maya agents, individuals, and collective groups used to adapt to changing circumstances and to innovate. Eberl (2017) emphasized the use of innovation, contrasting the view of structures as enduring outside agents with structures as "sticky" and subject to creative change, even as the core code remained intact. We regard the establishment of lowland Maya monumental centers as a clear example of this process.

Change implies flexibility and variability, and that is clearly evident in the ways early Maya communities designed their centers. The leaders and workers had a tendency to build E Groups out of or on bedrock when they were first constructed (see Dowd 2015b, 211; 2017b, 552 for the idea of planting E Groups in communities like planting milpas). This is true both for the sites of Cenote in the central Petén (A. Chase and D. Chase 2017a) and Cival in the northeastern Petén of Guatemala. At Cival, the people also built a massive level platform out from this central group, all placed on the highest point of a hill (Estrada-Belli 2017). Unlike the builders in the Middle Usumacinta region, the Cival platform is decisively oriented east-west, although there are remnants of a longer north-south axis. At Yaxuná, Mexico, Travis Stanton and his team are still working on the E Group and adjacent buildings, but it is clear that the east-west axis was also important from the beginning and remained important into the Late Classic period. Yet the northern side of the Yaxuná E Group is occupied by an enormous acropolis that dates to the Preclassic period. Future research at Yaxuná may be able to determine if this complex dominated the early E Group, as is the case with early Chiapas E Groups. In chapter 5 of this book, Stanton, Taube, and Collins focus on the foundation of Yaxuná and the laying out of the north-south and east-west axes of Yaxuná, demonstrating that the city materialized cruciform alignments throughout its long history.

The cruciform civic plan oriented north-south and east-west, as shown for Yaxuná (chapter 5, this volume), illustrates the penchant of the ancient Maya for centering. At Yaxuná, the monumental center and its ambient space—defined as both cultural and human—can be contrasted with the space outside the center and the community—defined as natural and wild. Stanton and his team discovered an incised cross with rectilinear arms roughly extending in the four cardinal directions that was buried within the Yaxuná E Group plaza and drawn into an early floor. This symbol, the Kan cross, is normally bound by a round or square cartouche and is a symbol for early centering, already expressed on the famous Olmec-style Humboldt Celt (Campbell 1992). This celt is framed by four "ground lines," possibly toponymic symbols according to David Stuart (2015) and Kent Reilly (1996). A royal crown surmounts one of the symbols.

The use of the Kan cross at Yaxuná clearly has symbolic significance. While the binding of the cross in a cartouche might reflect the two distinct spaces Stanton and Taube are proposing, it is likely that a broader meaning is implied. In Classic Mayan glyphic writing, *k'an* means yellow, ripe, precious. These latter connotations can refer to ripe maize, which was central to Maya iconographic portraiture (Taube 1985, 2009). In the corpus of Classic period Maya painted ceramics, a turtle carapace that the maize god resurrects from is also marked with the Kan cross (e.g., Schele and Miller 1986; Taube 2009, fig. 5e). At Yaxuná, at the far eastern end of the east-west axis, there are two remarkable performance platforms with quatrefoil plans. Dating from the transition between the Middle and Late Preclassic periods, they appear to be effigy turtles designed to facilitate emergence during resurrection from trap doors in their summits (Stanton and Freidel 2003, 2005).

Explicit depictions of origin narratives start in the Maya lowlands with the

Late Preclassic Pinturas building murals at San Bartolo (see chapter 5, this volume). On the west wall of this building, four young lords offer sacrifices before four trees and the maize god offers a sacrifice at a fifth tree. A convincing argument has been made that this scene represents the establishing of the four quarters and center of the Maya cosmos in linear form—rolled out in the absence of the principle of perspective in the drawing (Taube et al. 2010). Indeed, this scene probably presages the New Years' pages of the Postclassic (900–1519 CE) Dresden Codex, which refers to four Year Bearers. These are the days in the cycles of Maya calendars that rotate to start the New Year. The point here is that Maya centering, performed in the San Bartolo narrative by the human-form divine youths, not only crafts human space but also fixes the reckoning of calendar time. The cruciform symbol, whether it is Kan (as at Yaxuná) or a quincunx (as represented linearly at San Bartolo), is also found in the Middle Preclassic southern lowlands, carved as pits in the plazas of Ceibal and Cival that contained cached offerings (Estrada-Belli 2011). In actuality the quadripartite conception of the cosmos is a central belief that is pervasive throughout the Maya and Mesoamerica region (e.g., Mathews and Garber 2004; chapter 5, this volume).

At the site of Yaxnohcah in Campeche, Mexico, Kathryn Reese-Taylor and her team (chapter 4, this volume) have shown that some of the largest structures date to the Middle Preclassic, including the E Group, triadic groups, and a massive acropolis at the northern end of the community's quadripartite design. In terms of its civic-religious buildings, this city is five times as large as Yaxuná to the north of it. It dwarfs Nakbe, the city south of El Mirador that is a Middle Preclassic harbinger of the Late Preclassic Mirador realm. The northern acropolis at Yaxnohcah rivals the size of buildings at El Mirador. All of these early sites manifest the enormous social energy inspired by innovative ideas that were apparent in the Usumacinta–San Pedro Mártir area at the beginning of the Middle Preclassic. Skewed east of north, Yaxnohcah presents a quadrilateral ground plan. The center has a formalized north-south axis in which one causeway links the central monumental architecture to a southern concentration of buildings. A second iteration of the north-south axis occurs in two other massive complexes farther south. Finally, monumental building complexes to the east and west of the site center form an east-west axis. Using lidar data, Reese-Taylor and her team (chapter 4, this volume) have shown that the two axes extend far beyond the center to tie into large building complexes at the outer edges of the Yaxnohcah community, defining jurisdiction more than community.

Freidel has used the term "landesque cosmography" to describe this kind of polity integration where outlying religious edifices mark the four quarters and define the ambient territory as belonging to the community, its ancestors, and its gods. Reese-Taylor and colleagues (chapter 4, this volume) show how this schema served to materialize time at Middle Preclassic Yaxnohcah and was used in later eras to chart the processional routes of calendar festivals. Freidel, Rice, and Rich have provided further details on the concept of landesque cosmography in chapter 2 of this volume. Rice (2018, 2021) has previously identified the layout of the extraordinary early site of Nixtun Ch'ich', which is situated on a western peninsula jutting into Lake Petén Itzá, as representing a great effigy cosmic crocodile. Freidel and colleagues combine this example of landesque cosmography with Freidel's interpretation of El Mirador hill at the site of El Perú-Waka' as an effigy cosmic turtle to argue that in both cases, gods of the Maya creation era were materialized as centers to provide an enduring basis for the prosperity of their communities.

In northeastern Petén, Guatemala, a Middle Preclassic E Group was established on top of an enormous platform at Cival. An estimated 1.4 million cubic meters of earth and stone were quarried and deposited to create that structure (chapter 6, this volume). The innovation and aspiration employed in the founding of Maya centers often required massive social commitment. This early platform was apparently roughly square in shape and aligned to the cardinal directions. Its cosmic orientation was subsequently reinforced by the centered E Group focused on the sun path. So it is not an emulation of the Middle Formative Usumacinta centers but rather its own distinct pattern that nevertheless referenced the sky and hence materialized the passage of time. Into the Late Preclassic period, the people of Cival added structures on the north, south, and west sides of the platform through construction and rebuilding. Additionally, a large acropolis covered the eastern range of the E Group.

Thus, the quadripartite plan at Cival continued to materially manifest the community's relationship with the cosmos through centering and materializing calendar time in a pivotal place that people of the community and realm would regularly convene. In the case of Cival and its ambient realm, lidar hillshades have permitted the identification of newly discovered E Groups along the escarpment at some distance west of the center. These and the many other E Groups centered on Cival (Estrada-Belli 2017) likely helped people coordinate calendar time and processional movement. This is another good example of "landesque cosmography" that demonstrates investment in the engineering and construction of a sacred landscape to define the larger community.

As in the case of the E Group plaza at Ceibal, the E Group plaza at Cival contains elaborate buried—or "planted"—offerings. One recovered Cival offering was in a pit carved into bedrock that was cruciform in shape and contained

The Maya Materialization of Time: An Introduction · 13

jadeite celts and water jars that surely referenced maize and the agrarian cycle of the rains. Directly above this bedrock deposit, a large posthole was found that might have originally held a large wooden post. The people placing this offering were likely guided by the same centering belief seen in the incised cross in the center of the Yaxuná E Group plaza but with the significant variation of a centered post and a central recessed pit in the shape of a quinqunx. Estrada-Belli (2007, 2011) identified this innovation as a symbolic World Tree, making it a Middle Preclassic concept that presaged the Late Preclassic mural scene of five trees on the west wall of the Pinturas building at San Bartolo north Cival. Additionally, the central post may have functioned as a gnomon; its shadow perhaps marked the solar zenith at other times in the year. The Late Preclassic people of Cival later set three large posts that formed a triangle into a floor immediately above the earlier post and offering. Estrada-Belli (2007) has observed that tall posts were raised in centers in many parts of Mesoamerica for flying and descending performers attached to the top with cords, suggesting that perhaps these three posts had been used in this way. The triangular pattern of the postholes at Cival forms a striking contrast to the four trees defining the perimeter of the cosmos in the San Bartolo scene and the quinqunx arrangement of the earlier Cival deposit. However, the three postholes likely manifest the "three-stone place" or "hearth of creation" that can also be seen in hearths built into the torsos of sacrificial animals in the San Bartolo murals.

Freidel et al. (1993, 65–75) proposed that the three-stone hearth is celestially represented by a triangular arrangement of stars attached to the constellation of Orion. On creation eve, August 11–13, the three-stone hearth stars and the belt stars of Orion (which represent the cosmic turtle out of which the maize god emerges in resurrection) converge with the center of the Milky Way at dawn, when it is in its north-south configuration. While one might suppose that this referencing of creation day constitutes a backward look to a legendary past, we suggest that it celebrates the perpetual return of the human world to a state of harmony with the divine world, with the aspiration that this state should always endure. Estrada-Belli's exegesis on the remarkable Classic period preserved temple and its frieze that his team discovered at nearby Holmul (Estrada-Belli and Tokovine 2016), which depicts a king apotheosizing as the sun, affirms this hope and the notion that immortality of the soul can be human as well as solar.

The plazas and buildings of lowland Maya centers were regularly renewed to enhance the ability of the people who built them to situate themselves within their cosmos and carry out rituals, many of which constituted calendar-scheduled performances associated with public spectacle. For the most part, participants in these ceremonies are now long absent from their stages. However, some are still present in the form of the famous carved stelae, called "banner stones" in Mayan, that portray rulers who often materialized time. As Stephen Houston and David Stuart (1996; Stuart 1996) showed in landmark papers, these remarkable carved sculptures were not cenotaphs but embodiments of the animate essence of the portrayed. The presence of stelae on plazas, in front of or on grand stairways, made the rulers' materializations of time a future-oriented perpetual presence, a promised immortality such as that envisioned on the Classic temple at Holmul mentioned above. The extension of the principle of historical animation into buildings became a widespread innovation in the southern lowlands. The Classic Maya, who inscribed stones with the portraits and histories of rulers, built these carved monuments into stairways, doorway jambs, and lintels, thereby endowing those buildings with the spirit and soul force of the rulers. In regions of the Maya lowlands where people raised few stelae, they seemingly went to great lengths to make animate beings out of their buildings, constructing great masks surrounding doorways and rulers floating in great nimbus cartouches. While the deeds inscribed or depicted on buildings were fixed in historical calendar time, the presence of animate personas guided future events.

David Freidel and Olivia Navarro-Farr (chapter 7, this volume) segue from the theme of plazas, buildings, and communities to that of historical time in their study of stelae raised in front of, and eventually built into, the principal city temple at El Perú-Waka' in the northwestern Petén of Guatemala. El Perú-Waka' was a citadel city founded on a steep 100-meter-high escarpment overlooking a strategic river, the Rio San Juan, 5 kilometers east of its confluence with the San Pedro Mártir, the same river discussed earlier but in this case deep in the interior of Guatemala's Petén. At 600 CE a Wak (centipede) dynasty king, whose name is not preserved, declared himself to be the twenty-fourth ruler in the dynastic succession. Calculating the likely average lengths (ca. 20 years per ruler) of individual reigns, the Wak dynasty was likely founded in the second century CE, making it the second-oldest dynasty known after that of Tikal (also founded in the first century CE, see Martin and Grube 2008). The present count of stelae at El Perú-Waka' is forty-five. All but a few were carved with portraits and inscriptions that date between 416 CE and 801 CE. Because the city played a strategic role in regional geopolitics of the southern lowlands, its rulers were valued vassals and allies to hegemons.

El Perú-Waka' was repeatedly attacked and its stelae shattered, scattered, defaced, and erased. Freidel and Navarro-Farr (chapter 7, this volume) argue that the intention of the desecraters was to ruin the animate power of the monuments and to intervene in the forward projection of the historical trajectory that their original "planting" promised. Freidel and Navarro-Farr offer explanations for perplexing features of the stelae and their contexts in relation to a central temple. Historical inscriptions play a key role in this study, as they do elsewhere in the archaeology of the southern lowlands (e.g., A. Chase and D. Chase 2020a; Martin 2020). Not all lowland Maya regularly wrote on stones, although it is very likely that literate elite lived throughout the lowlands. But writing, in association with calendar calculations, made the Classic period royal materialization of time in the Maya southern lowlands (including adjacent parts of Chiapas, Campeche, Quintana Roo, Belize, and Honduras) distinct in the pre-Hispanic western hemisphere.

Scribes emerged toward the end of the first millennium BCE in several parts of Mesoamerica, including the Oaxaca Valley, Olman, Chiapas, and the Pacific Slope of Guatemala (to list areas where they wrote calendar names). The discovery of very early Maya inscriptions at San Bartolo in Petén radiocarbon dated to around 400 BCE puts the lowland Maya innovators in this same era (Saturno et al. 2006). Although bar-and-dot numeration does not accompany the texts, it is very likely that the Maya individuals who wrote these texts were numerate as well as literate. As William Saturno and colleagues (Saturno, Rossi, et al. 2017) have described, these inscriptions were painted on the walls of a demolished building that was part of the eastern range of an E Group at the site. Writing and portraiture on walls and more broadly materializing time inside the rooms of buildings constitutes a major theme in this book, particularly during the Classic period, when stela erection proliferated in the southern lowlands after 300 CE. But even where no writing or portraits on walls appear, the materialization of time can be discerned.

Chan is a small agrarian community in Belize with a history of quotidian hard work and modest ceremonial activity. Its occupation spans 1,200 years from the Middle Preclassic through the ninth-century era of social chaos in the southern lowlands. Cynthia Robin and her team have focused on what she calls "ordinary life" there (Robin 2012) as part of a larger challenge to her colleagues in Maya archaeology to expand their epistemological inquiry into the lives of what we today would term "the 99 percent" (Sabloff 2019), the people who do not figure in written history. In chapter 10 of this volume, Robin describes in detail the vaulted community building made of masonry on the south side of the E Group at Chan that has an extraordinarily well-preserved and complex interior. The back room of this building was divided into three parts and each section had a different elevation and different features and artifacts. The western room had a quincunx pattern of holes cut into its plaster floor, an explicit reference to centering, as discussed above. A patolli board was incised in the high bench area in the western room. Patolli was played with tokens and various kinds of dice across Mesoamerica; it was likely used in divination (e.g., Smith 1977; Walden and Voorhies 2017). Finally, vertical and horizontal lines were incised into the south wall. We will return shortly to the matter of incised patterns and images on walls—"graffiti." The central room had a pile of 550 jute snail shells on a low bench area along with other artifacts suggesting divination. While jute snails were no doubt eaten (Healy et al. 1990), the concentration of shells here possibly points to their use as calculating tokens, as is documented elsewhere in ritual settings. Thousands of olive and other shell tokens were discovered in a ninth-century royal tomb at Ek' Balam in Yucatán, for example (Vargas de la Peña and Castillo Borges 2000). Jute shells have shown up in other ritual contexts in Belize, particularly in Middle to Late Preclassic contexts in the Belize Valley (e.g., Chase 2020, 202). Researchers with the Cerro Maya project in the Corozal district also discovered thousands of jute shells in a test excavation at the center of a Terminal Preclassic (0–250 CE) pyramid summit plaza in the 1970s. This kind of snail shell is the home of an important aged god called Mam, a grandfather or ancestor—or Bacab, first of the land. The use of jute as both a comestible and as a possible divinatory tool is significant. Much like the highly symbolic contents of early caches (A. Chase and D. Chase 2006; D. Chase and A. Chase 1998), it is likely that such shells were used to calculate time and to divine. Robin (chapter 10, this volume) cogently suggests that the elders of the community sat on benches in the front room to hear the prophecies being conjured in the back room. Like elites using texts and calendar inscriptions, ordinary people looked to the future and aspired to balance their lives with the divine forces of their local places. Robin compares the Chan building to another modest Classic Maya community, Joya de Cerén in El Salvador (Simmons and Sheets 2002), that has a similarly designed shaman's room and building. Archaeologists should be on the alert for more examples.

The case of the shaman's room at Chan moved our consideration of the materialization of time from exterior to interior space, from sky-gazing and public performance to contemplation, discussion, numerical calculation, divination, and prophecy based on calendar cycles, counting, and casting. The Los Sabios building at Xultun in northeastern Petén reveals how a Late Classic ruler collaborated with members of a priestly sodality of bookmakers, mathematicians, and astrologers called Tah, or "obsidian" (chapter 9, this volume). We know that the Maya, like other Mesoamericans, gazed into mirrors made of obsidian, hematite, and pyrite in order to see themselves, the sky, and, presumably, the supernatural otherworld. Painted Late Classic vases show rulers gazing into black mirrors accompanied by their adepts and scribes (Reents-Budet 1994). Obsidian artifacts—chipped eccentrics in the shape of gods and animals, small bifacially flaked pieces with the moon goddess, the maize god, the rain god, and other deities etched or painted on them—were ultimately placed as offerings under stelae and in other caches (Moholy-Nagy 2008; Hruby and Ware 2009). At Xultun, specialists made lunar count calculations on the walls of the Sabios building. A mural in the same building depicts the king and his close Tah advisers.

Additionally, a female member of the sodality was buried under the bench in the building. Rossi (chapter 9, this volume) shows how these specialists may have not only observed the sky and reflected on the past but also shaped their interpretations to address the patterns of time and deal with issues of importance to the ruler and to the future of his realm.

While the Los Sabios rooms were at some distance from the center of Xultun, another building with writing on its walls existed in the very center of its city. An Early Classic public building that has evidence of writing on the walls of its interior rooms was wonderfully preserved by ritual burial in antiquity at the center of Balamkú (north of Calakmul) in Campeche, Mexico, a site of imposing pyramids and plazas. Anne Dowd has been studying the façade of this building—a celebration of the rebirth of kingship, triumph over underworld supernatural beings, and divine communion of kings with the sun god—for many years. In Chapter 8, Dowd and Vail focus on the priestly sodality members who worked and perhaps lived in such places. The writing is not well preserved like the writing in the Xultun building, but its very presence shows that what the Tah adepts were doing was not unique. More examples will likely emerge (Freidel 2000). The activities of the Balamkú sages took place in a very important central place: the building was a cosmogram (Dowd 1998a). On the building at Balamkú, four rulers resurrect out of frogs or toads, another Maya metaphor for rebirth, as the Maya words for birth and frog are near-homophones. The four rulers thus set out the four quarters of the human world. In the heavenly center and in the building interior, sages and perhaps their ruler contemplated the past, present, and future.

In chapter 11, M. Kathryn Brown and her colleagues describe excavations in a suite of buried rooms in the colossal pyramid-palace complex at Xunantunich in Belize known as "the Castillo." This building anchors the southern end of a north-south primary axis for the monumental constructions of the Classic center. A palace complex with a throne room anchors the northern end. Intriguingly, the axis is west of north in alignment with the Milky Way when it is the World Tree at sunset on August 13 (Schele 1992a). There is independent reason to think that the people who designed and built this center had cosmology in mind: the summit of the Castillo was at one time decorated with an elaborate modeled stucco frieze depicting rulers seated inside rectilinear spaces whose uprights and horizontal beams are decorated with woven knots of royal majesty and twisted cords. Virginia Fields (2004) interpreted the portraiture in this frieze as an axis mundi representing the creation of the world, a depiction of what Linda Schele (1992a; see also Freidel et al. 1993; Villela and Schele 1996) identified as "Nah Ho Chan," the Five Sky place—the womb of the cosmos where the maize god and other gods destined for rebirth gestate before emergence. Whatever way one might interpret the symbolism, the Castillo was deeply sacred space for the people of the realm. The rooms Brown and her colleagues (chapter 11, this volume) report about are on the northeastern end of the complex and had an obscured entryway. Once Brown and her team removed the carefully packed construction material inside these ritually interred interior spaces, they discovered an amazing proliferation of incised graffiti on the walls. While the meaning of the graffiti is still elusive, Brown and her team argue that there is so much of it that these places must have served to teach neophytes to both envision and inscribe images as part of their training in the calculating arts. Incising as a means of writing and calculating numbers is attracting the attention of other researchers, especially as they discover evidence of writing boards that may have been coated with wax and written on with bone styluses (chapter 15, this volume). In chapter 6, Estrada-Belli and Freidel describe an elegant text that was inscribed in wet plaster along the base of the Holmul apotheosis building.

Classic period interior spaces were often designed with cord holders for curtains, perhaps to make activities in them even more distant and private from spectacles found in public plazas, but a room may also have been darkened for purposes of communion with the gods and ancestors. Sometimes contemporary Maya shamans practice this way. An elegant ancient Maya trope for conjuring gods can be glossed as "his (her) creation (in) his (her) darkness" (Houston and Stuart 1998, 88; see also Knowlton 2012). Conjuring gods and materializing agentive time are closely related concepts, as Diane and Arlen Chase point out in chapter 14 of this volume. But light and dark are also part of this process of materialization. The Pinturas Shrine at San Bartolo would have seen the light of dawn sweep into it, illuminating both the death and resurrection of the maize god declared in the rotation of the Milky Way and the first centering of human-form gods sacrificing before the world trees. As Susan Milbrath (chapter 12, this volume) notes, all of the activities in these Preclassic murals are occurring in the heavens, as denoted by the sky band that frames their baseline. This is a celestial story translated beautifully in painting to celebrate the future of divine rulership.

The mural scene of the four sacrificing lords before four trees on the west wall at San Bartolo is remarkably similar to a codex New Year scene from the

Postclassic period. Susan Milbrath (chapter 12, this volume), acknowledging David Stuart's identification of a Year Bearer date on that mural, 3 Ik', boldly argues that the calendar pattern of four Year Bearer days manifested in the sacred 260-day calendar and coinciding with the inauguration of the 365-day year (approximating the solar year) was innovated in the first millennium BCE to mark the 260-day agrarian season of subsistence maize. This builds on Milbrath's (2017b) previous arguments regarding the function of E Groups to commemorate the agrarian year as linked to the solar year. In chapter 12, Milbrath proposes that the Year Bearers were important in the Preclassic era, faded from view in the Classic (when the focus was on Long Count inscriptions on stelae and other public monuments), and then resurfaced in the Postclassic.

In these oscillating patterns, we see two Maya ways of thinking about time. The first aspires to create and sustain harmony between the long-term calendric materialization of time (and cosmic forces witnessed in the celestial cycles) and the shorter-term seasons that were vital to farming success (and were apparent in human life cycles). Milbrath (chapter 12, this volume) cogently shows how contemporary K'iche' plan their agrarian cycles and the inauguration of the 365-day year through the appearance of the full moon, an exemplary symbol of human fertility and fecundity. It is no coincidence that the 260-day Tzolk'in also marks human pregnancy from first identification to birth. The second way of thinking about time manifests in the famous Maya Long Count of days, established on a creation day and ultimately cyclical but for all intents and purposes linear with the potential for the reincarnation of events. In posthispanic (after 1492 CE) Maya culture (and likely also present in prehispanic belief systems), this cyclical reincarnation was analogous to the reincarnation of human souls. For Classic period Maya peoples whose rulers regularly installed historical monuments in public places and in buildings—for example, in the southern lowlands between Palenque's realm on the west, Copán's to the east, Cancuén's to the south, and Calakmul's to the north—this second temporal sensibility dominated public discourse and policy.

It is probable that all ancestral Maya understood and acted on these two modes of thought regarding time. In 1991, anthropologist Robert Carlsen and poet Martin Prechtel published a benchmark discussion about these ways of materializing time, articulating the luminous philosophy that was inherent in the beliefs and practices of contemporary Ateteco sages in highland Guatemala. Their Ateteco informants explained that there are two kinds of change that they together call *jalolkexol*. *Jal* denotes the generational cycle from birth to death and back to birth. It is the cycle manifest in the Tzolk'in. *K'ex* is the manifestation of succession, of substitution, what Carlsen and Prechtel (1991, 26) call "making the new out of the old. At the same time, just as a single plant produces multiple offspring, *k'ex* is change from one into many. Together *jal* and *k'ex* form a concentric system of change within change, a single system of transformation and renewal." *K'ex* is the principle we see as intrinsic to the Long Count, a means not just of anticipating the cyclical return of events and conditions but also of acknowledging and celebrating innovation and a future different from the past, one worth aspiring to achieve.

The present-day fame of Maya calendar calculations as materializations of time is largely attributable to the practice of including the Long Count on many carved monuments during the Classic era, although the Postclassic codices are also remarkable for their temporal calculations. Following the social chaos of the ninth century, the southern lowland Maya stopped raising stelae and in many cases abandoned their cities. When this happened, the use of the Long Count largely disappeared along with the institution of dynastic kingship and the many court sodalities that sustained governments (Okoshi et al. 2021). But as Prudence Rice ably argues in chapter 17, Maya who were resilient continued to flourish and kept a Short Count of katuns, units integral to the Long Count composed of twenty approximate years of 360 days. They also kept a count of 260 tuns (through tagging each katun with its associated numbered ajaw day), merging a pattern from the Tzolk'in cycle into historical accounting. The Short Count is predicated on this innovative "single system." Rice (chapter 17, this volume) proposes that in 771 CE, the Itzá nation founded new realms in a Katun 11 Ajaw in the center of the Petén to the south and at Chichén Itzá in the north (see also Boot 2019). In Rice's view, Chichén Itzá fell at the beginning of a Katun 11 ajaw and the post-conquest books of Chilam Balam underscore the historical power of Katun 11 ajaw in the destiny of the Itzá. The overlap between how the Maya thought about and acted upon their materializations of time and how we as scientists can detect and evaluate its impact on the material record is terrain we are now collectively exploring in this book. It is especially challenging and worthwhile when addressing great events in their history such as the founding and fall of Chichén Itzá. But this materialization can also be seen in a variety of venues in the southern lowlands, where increasingly robust calendar-anchored text-based chronicles and advancing field discoveries require us to address how the Maya thought about cyclicality in their historical trajectories.

Diane and Arlen Chase (chapter 14) have had a career-long preoccupation with the materialization of time, first at Santa Rita Corozal, Belize (D. Chase 1985a, 1985b; D. Chase and A. Chase 1988, 2008), and then at Caracol, Belize (A. Chase 1991; D. Chase and A. Chase 2004, 2011, 2017; A. Chase and

D. Chase 2013a; A. Chase et al. 2020). They have also written about their thoughts on Tikal, Guatemala (A. Chase and D. Chase 2020a; A. Chase et al. 2022). Their programmatic marshaling of archaeological evidence for Maya time practice affirms the premise of this book that all Maya people actively materialized time, always moving their quotidian rhythms of work into the sacred craft of "nurturing the gods." Creation was their collective enterprise and remains so among living Maya. The Chases (chapter 14, this volume) show how the 20-year Maya temporal unit of the katun was an armature of thought and practice for both the great Classic city of Caracol and the prosperous and cosmopolitan Postclassic capital of Santa Rita Corozal. Significantly, they amplify Prudence Rice's work on the impact of katun prophecy relating to the Short Count by demonstrating the importance of this unit of time in the Classic era. The theme of katun celebration is found at Tikal, Guatemala, in the form of twin-pyramid complexes, a Late Classic innovation of that powerful city. Katun celebrations were of great importance to the rulers and courtiers of Caracol with their giant ajaw altars. Those celebrations were also carried out by family units in most residential groups at the metropolis of Caracol through the deposition of special cache containers in association with residential shrines. They show how paired incensarios were used to manifest time in public buildings and later in residential units at Postclassic Santa Rita Corozal. Timekeeping coordinated and integrated the scales of Maya complex society. Ritual integrated Maya communities both internally and externally, as illustrated in the prospect that the two greatest kings of Caracol are actually entombed at Tikal in its most sacred ancestor shrine, the North Acropolis (Chase and Chase 2020a).

In chapter 14, the Chases make a philosophical and epistemological proposition that time and its apparitions were sentient and agentive. We have well-known examples of time personified in beautiful full-figure calendar glyphs on Stela D at Copán in Honduras. But these are metaphors of the burden—and the responsibility—that timekeepers, like kings and queens and their sages, have to know the past and to discern the best way to the future for their peoples. Gods and their effigies are associated with particular calendar cycles and jubilees. They are of time and in it, as James Doyle argues in chapter 16. Could the Maya adepts negotiate destiny with the days manifest in the sun? Or remember creation stories that were manifested in the moon and stars? We think it was likely the case, especially as sun, moon, and stars are incarnated, and materialization was always a matter of conjuring time and not just counting it but also negotiating with it through its godly forms. Clearly some Mesoamericans, most famously the Aztec, regarded their relationship with a sentient sun as critical to the survival of the world (e.g., Pérez Aguilera

2017, 216). Divine death and resurrection are not syncretic contributions of Christianity to post-conquest (1519 CE) Maya notions of godhood. They were fundamental and pervasive prehispanic tenets that are well documented in ancient Maya art, including the San Bartolo murals. The gods thus experienced generational time, in Carlsen and Prechtel's (1991) terms.

James Doyle's (chapter 16, this volume) study of the codex-style Late Classic vases that were interred with the dead in the old Mirador-area heartland of Preclassic civilization show episodes of myths recounting the birth, death, and resurrection of gods. The codex style is a beautiful innovation by artists living in the shadowed ruins of some of the largest sacred centers ever built in Mesoamerica. Their choice to make their homes among the spirits and memories of those buildings was no doubt quite deliberate. In the famous colonial-era (1519–1697 CE) Book of Council of the K'iche', it is the combined efforts of successive generations of human-form gods, fearless in the face of death and trusting in the reality of resurrection and rebirth, that defeats the deadly denizens of the otherworld (Tedlock 1996). It seems likely that the artists who painted these vases (and perhaps the individuals who used them) displayed their stories, recounted them to each other, celebrated the resiliency of the gods, and hoped for their own ability to trick fate and forge destiny despite the future reality of death.

Patricia McAnany has been contemplating evolving Maya beliefs about ancestors, the generative cycle, rebirth, and resiliency for most of her career. In chapter 13, she argues that it is not the gods or the stars but rather the people who manifest the pivotal cycles of time. She shows that for the Maya, the future is not shaped by the finality of death but rather by the transcendence of memory and the certainty of renewal, pointing to cycles of reincarnation of souls in contemporary Maya communities of Chiapas, the careful memorialization of the deceased in Preclassic and Classic Maya southern lowland practices in anticipation of their agency in the otherworld and their rebirth into this one, and the renewal of the saint in the Yucatec community of Tahcabo, where she now works. Now that she is working in the northern lowlands, McAnany finds herself wondering why the Long Count was never popular there. The great expert scholar of Maya stelae iconography, Tatiana Proskouriakoff (1950), noted that Classic period inscribed stelae are relatively rare above the eighteenth parallel north. In recent years, more inscribed stone stairways and eroded carved monuments have been discovered in the central lowlands of Campeche and Quintana Roo (e.g., Tsukamoto et al. 2015; Šprajc 2020), but the use of stelae to identify and celebrate dynasts in succession is not readily apparent in this central area or to the north of it (but see Graña-Behrens 2009).

Freidel (2018) has concluded that the Maya of the central and northern lowlands elected their divine rulers from qualified elite candidates and initiated them into a brotherhood and sisterhood of divine beings. While the northern and southern lowlands of the Classic period shared many gods and beliefs—and the 365-day calendar, the 260-day sacred almanac, and in the Terminal Classic (800–900 CE) and Postclassic a penchant for katun calendar calculations converted to a semblance of the sacred almanac writ large—the northerners did not use the Long Count very much. Freidel (2018) has suggested that this is because the Long Count served particularly to anchor successions of rulers counting from dynastic founders and to legitimate them by pedigree more than by initiation. Thus, ancient Maya northerners differed from Maya southerners in their focus on generational time over lineal succession. McAnany argues that the architectural monumentality in northern centers focused on groups, whereas southern monumentality focused on dynastic lineages. That difference may have taken on the dimensions of a religious schism in the minds of many, fueling protracted episodes of warfare.

In chapter 18, David Freidel, Saburo Sugiyama, and Nawa Sugiyama consider the theme of materializing time in light of alliance building and factional disputes involving the rulers of Teotihuacan and those of lowland Maya kingdoms spanning the Early Classic period (200–550 CE). On the basis of Saburo Sugiyama's (1993, 2014) identification of the calendar-bound design of Teotihuacan's monumental core, his and Nawa Sugiyama's documentation and analyses of the complex offerings in buildings there (Sugiyama and López Luján 2007; N. Sugiyama, S. Sugiyama et al. 2013; N. Sugiyama et al. 2014), and Freidel's hypotheses regarding the origins of the Classic calendar-recording stelae of the lowland Maya, they propose that Teotihuacan and Tikal collaborated in the innovation of lineal-descent dynastic government. Whatever the eventual fate of this proposal, it is now clear that both the New Order southern lowland kingdoms of the late fourth through early sixth centuries, partisans of Kaloomte' Sihyaj K'ahk' and the Dzibanché-based rulers of sixth-century Kaanul, had allies in Teotihuacan. In their summary thoughts, they argue that the principles of dynasty and sodality played out across Classic Mesoamerica. In Freidel's (2018) view, some great historical leaders of the Late Classic period (550–800 CE) strove to bridge the differences between kinds of Maya governmental systems but eventually failed, leaving the wide swaths of the Maya world to descend into chaos. Whether or not this view is empirically sustained, the materialization of time was central to the destiny of the Classic Maya and ultimately key to their resilience and cultural survival.

In the epilogue, Anne Dowd reviews the concept of zero or null in Maya conceptual thought and numeration as a theme. Notions of absence and totality are brought into a discussion of architecture and spatial planning in the design of cosmograms. The contributions of the Santa Fe Institute working groups over the last decade have conclusively shown that communities came together to materialize calendar and timekeeping well before cities developed in the region, likely even before sedentism was fully established. Religion was one way disparate groups were brought together, resulting in the emergence and increase of monumental constructions oriented with the sun, moon, and stars.

## Summary

The participants in this volume have challenged themselves individually and now collectively to address and rethink the most famous intellectual feature of ancestral Maya civilization. The eminent twentieth-century scholar of the Maya, J. Eric S. Thompson (1950), devoted an entire book to the proposition that the Maya worshipped time. Reflecting on the past of our discipline, the archaeologists assembled here aspire to chart some new paths forward into the future of considering the nature and use of Maya time. We see time as having infused almost all aspects of ancient Maya being, and thus this volume concerns itself with accounting for the manifestation of a Maya space-time that defined their interconnected worldview and cosmology. We believe that this book forms a coherent whole that begins with regional interaction; then focuses on public places of gathering, spectacle, and ceremony; moves closer to interior spaces of practice and learning; proceeds to the outward manifestation of mind in writing words, numbers, and calendars; and, finally, considers the inward manifestation of human beings in spirit as the source of renewal. Other archaeologists and Maya scholars are also charting new paths. Like the Maya, those who study their world with them aspire to an illuminated future.

# 2

## Landesque Cosmography

### Crafting Creation-Era Time on the Maya Lowland Landscape

DAVID A. FREIDEL, PRUDENCE M. RICE,
AND MICHELLE E. RICH

In the spring of 1972, David Freidel explored remote parts of northeastern Cozumel Island alone, locating and mapping features and sites for Jerry Sabloff and Bill Rathje's Harvard University–University of Arizona Cozumel Archaeological Project (Freidel and Sabloff 1984). Freidel found that after a while he could accurately calculate what time it was within fifteen minutes from the angle of the sun and keep precise track of his location relative to the coasts and other landmarks without relying on his compass. Observant ancient and modern Maya, like sages and outdoors people everywhere, have always known the temporal and spatial orienting properties of the sun and other celestial bodies and crafted their understandings of time into space accordingly.

This is true of Maya E Groups (Freidel et al. 2017). These complexes were predicated in part on the innovation of and investment of labor in crafted places founded on bedrock that functioned in the beginning as solar annual clocks. The notion of landesque capital (Håkansson and Widgren 2014) usefully conceives of laborious modifications of land (i.e., the creation of fields, terraces, and irrigation ditches) to make it arable as paying forward, endowing future generations with agricultural success. Cynthia Robin (2013, 2017) shows how collective effort in the small Maya community of Chan to establish formidable terraces through ordinary work helped offset risks of soil erosion on slopes and ensured the enduring prosperity of its people for centuries. In a recent essay on the concept of sustainability applied to ancient cities, Monica Smith (2015, 225) suggested that as urban communities grew in scale, their risk-buffering range of institutions widened and that "the accumulative effects of landscape-scale interactions can be described as 'landscape capital'" (see also A. Chase and D. Chase 2016, 364). Here, we use the term "landesque cosmography" to talk about the enduring impact of cosmographic landscape modification (see Ashmore 2002; Ashmore and Sabloff 2002; Stanton and Freidel 2005; and Stanton and Magnoni 2008 for related ideas). Travis Stanton has focused on this issue since his doctoral research at Yaxuná, integrating the themes of the World Tree, the Cosmic Hearth, and the maize god in the context of the large E Group at Yaxuná, performance platforms that are posited to be early Late Preclassic (ca. 350 BCE) effigy turtles, and intrasite causeways defining a Kan cross urban design that endured a millennium (Stanton and Freidel 2005). The effigy turtle platforms had sloping slabs on their sides, subsurface corridors forming quadripartite portal designs, subsurface chambers, and interior stairways leading to evident trap doors for emergence that simulated the rebirth of the maize god (fig. 2.1). Michelle Rich's (2011) dissertation on El Mirador hill at El Perú-Waka' evinced an interest in sacred landscape and social memory derived from Wendy Ashmore (2002, 1178), who clearly anticipated the notion of landesque cosmography deriving from landesque capitalism:

> Places marked by individual buildings and other discrete architectural features acquire histories as they are built, occupied, maintained, modified, partly or wholly dismantled, or allowed to fall to ruin. Each of these diverse acts can carry profound, potent social and symbolic meaning. Interment of the dead is frequently recognized as a powerful means for claiming land tenure and identity with a place (e.g., McAnany 1998; Buikstra and Charles 1999). In a similar manner, repeated construction on a spot, especially involving direct superimposition of buildings, is often taken by archaeologists as defining an *axis mundi*. (Eliade 1959)

These themes resonate with those we return to in our discussion of the San Bartolo murals below. Stanton's (chapter 5, this volume) further research subsequently discovered an incised Kan cross in the center of the E Group, presaging the urban design. Lowland Maya E Groups were, in our view (Freidel and Reilly 2010; Freidel 2017; Freidel et al. 2017) originally landesque facilities established, among other things, to buffer the risks of maize farming through scheduled marketplace exchange and the storage of surplus "in the system" rather than in the ground or in a crib. James Doyle (2012, 2013b, 2017) has observed the orderly distribution of early E Group viewsheds as an accumulative effect of landscape interactions. Francisco Estrada-Belli (2017) has documented E Groups near Cival as the means of integrating a larger community around it. Like the urban and hinterland features Smith (2015) lists—roads, waterworks, marketplaces—E Groups constituted landesque capital as much as the terraces, raised fields, canals, and stone roads of the lowland Maya world. Like

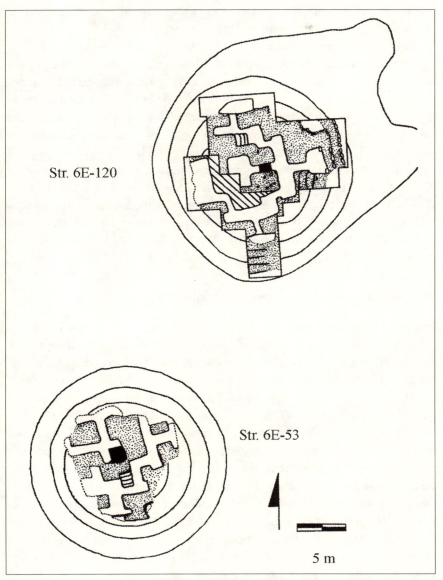

Figure 2.1. Effigy turtle performance platforms at Yaxuná. Courtesy of the Selz Foundation Yaxuná Archaeological Project. Drawing by Charles K. Suhler.

Smith's (2015) instances, they were centered in communities and were parts of urban landscapes, and as Freidel (2017) has argued, they were parts of cosmographic expressions of a kind that were enduringly typical of Maya centers (see Stanton and Freidel 2005; chapter 5, this volume).

As mentioned, early Yaxuná had performance platforms fashioned as effigy turtle carapaces. David Stuart (1987) has demonstrated that the ancient Mayan word for mountain, *witz*, depicted a living mask with clefted fontanel. This term described many kinds of human-made buildings, including pyramids and temples. It is clear that Maya centers were living landscapes, and we suggest that in some cases whole communities and massive landmarks in communities were effigies of animate creatures. Here we explore two such cases in which cosmographic animals can be discerned, the community of Nixtun Ch'ich' in central Petén and a massive terraformed hill in the city of El Perú-Waka' in northwestern Petén. The former has the appearance of a crocodile, while El Mirador hill at the latter was shaped into a huge turtle marked with the three in-line summit localities that are stars in the Classic Maya constellation of the belt stars of our Orion (Freidel et al. 1993, fig. 2:15).

### The Crocodile as Creation-Time Cosmograph

Preclassic (1000 BCE–350 CE) lowland Maya civilization (Brown and Bey 2018) is a source of many recent field discoveries that include E Groups, such as the ceremonial centers on the lower Usumacinta and San Pedro Mártir Rivers described by Takeshi Inomata and his colleagues (chapter 3, this volume). One of the most astonishing is the Middle Preclassic nucleated city of Nixtun Ch'ich' on Lake Petén Itzá (Pugh and Rice 2017; Rice and Pugh 2017; Pugh 2018; Rice 2018, 2019). Timothy Pugh and Prudence Rice (2017, 576) have proposed that the grid design allowed leaders to organize and control a newly urbanized population and that "the planned city was also likely a governmental conceit and a proclamation of social order." Recently Rice (2018) suggests that the grid design of Nixtun Ch'ich' manifests an effigy cosmic crocodile facing east with its snout extending into the waters of the lake. The city looks like a crocodile, and its grid design is better explained as an example of landesque cosmography than as a utopian vision of social order (fig. 2.2a, b). The peninsular projection of the gridded town and its salient mounds is readily observable from the flanking shorelines even today and would have been impressive when maintained and occupied. Among the coeval Olmec to the northeast, the cosmic crocodile was a metaphor for divine kingship. Here there is no material evidence of that institution, but if the place was conceived as such an animal it may have materialized the body politic.

# Landesque Cosmography: Crafting Creation-Era Time on the Maya Lowland Landscape · 29

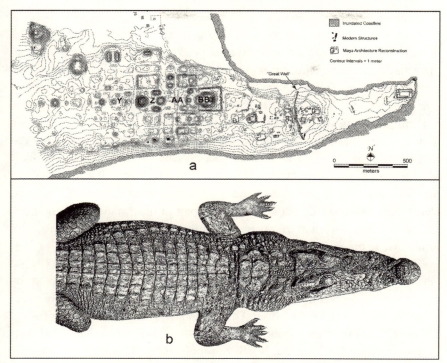

Figure 2.2. Nixtun Ch'ich' (*a*) and crocodile (*b*). Source: Rice (2018).

Our model infers an anonymous charismatic leadership at Nixtun Ch'ich' that was characteristic of governments with strong collaborative or collective political institutions (Pugh and Rice 2017; Rice 2018). Later in Classic Maya history, as Karl Taube (2010) has shown, building on arguments of David Stuart (2005b), the architectonic and rectilinear cosmic crocodile presides over the Six Sky house, the Eight House of the creator sun One Tooth Person (GI), and the Temple of the Cross at Palenque, an exemplary royal accession place. We do not propose that any royal government in the Late Preclassic era was dynastic, as it was to be in the southern lowland region during the Classic period. On the contrary, Freidel (2018) has recently argued Late Preclassic Maya divine kingship was likely based on sodality selection and initiation simulating death and resurrection. Such a sodality organization would have been predicated on institutions of collective decision-making such as appears to have been operative in Nixtun Ch'ich'.

As Rice (2018) shows in a review of the literature on cosmic and natural crocodiles the Middle Preclassic (1000–400 BCE) Olmec had such a cosmic crocodile (Reilly 1987), as did the Late Preclassic (350 BCE–1 CE) people of Izapa, where the crocodile is presented as a World Tree. Indeed, crocodile imagery is far more widespread in early lowland Mesoamerica than is commonly realized because references to the creature have not been well synthesized. For example, the Middle Preclassic Olmec motifs dubbed "flame-eyebrow" and "paw-wing" do not symbolize a "were jaguar" or avian. Rather, they are pars pro toto indicators of a crocodile: the flame-eyebrow is drawn from the prominent supraorbital ridge of an aged male crocodile's cranium and the paw-wing is the reptile's "hand" or foot (Flannery and Marcus 2000, fig. 10b). Both are present in Middle Preclassic burials at Copán, Honduras (Fash 1991, 69–70). A late (500–400 BCE) Middle Preclassic altar at Nakbe has a "celestial band with alligator-like creatures" carved around the edge (Hansen 2001, fig. 73) and the Late Preclassic Stela 9 (ca. 300–100 BCE) at Cahal Pech depicts a male standing in the maw of a crocodilian (Awe et al. 2009), part of a broader pattern of crocodilian royal symbolism at the site (Brown et al. 2018).

The crocodile emerged as a major icon of Maya royalty through the Classic period. The great royal capital of Tikal, 45 kilometers northeast of Nixtun-Ch'ich', exhibits several ties to crocodilian creatures. Its pivotal Early Classic (250–550 CE) ruler Yax Nuun Ahiin I (First/Blue-Green Knot Crocodile; 379–404 CE; Martin and Grube 2008, 32) is thought to have been buried deep under Structure 5D-34 in the North Acropolis there (Coe 1990, II:479–487; Wright 2005). As Lori Wright observes (2005), if Yax Nuun Ahiin I is the deceased in Burial 10, then he was raised in Petén, quite possibly in the lake district where Nixtun Ch'ich' is located. His lavishly furnished tomb includes a carved jadeite crocodile head and a crocodile skeleton (probably *Crocodylus moreletii*), and his residence in life might have been Structure 5D-58 in the Central Acropolis, which has a mosaic façade mask of a crocodile (Harrison 2008, 112, 114, fig. 9). The main sign of Yax Nuun Ahiin I's name glyph is a crocodile head displaying a curled snout with *yax* crenulations (as on the Maya glyph for *yax*: blue/green/first), maxillary teeth, dotted patches on the head, a two-part eye, and a curving—sometimes tripartite—supraorbital ridge. Another significant tie is seen in rare "animate" allographs of the main sign of Tikal's emblem glyph, which resembles a "bundled feathered" crocodile or crocodile head (Montgomery 2001, fig. 9; Tokovinine 2008, 5–6, fig. 3b). Given the multiple debated interpretations of these glyphs, this sign may be "the ancient name of Tikal is the place of this tied alligator (or the place where it abounds)" (Tokovinine 2008, 6).

Late Classic (550–800 CE) or Terminal Classic (800–900 CE) Maya images of thrones often show a bound "feathered alligator" (probably an effigy) draped over a skyband with the ruler seated on top (e.g., Piedras Negras Stela 11, 731 CE; Naranjo Stela 32, 820 CE). Similar scenes appear in the Postclassic

(900–1519 CE) Paris Codex: new *k'atun* lords (priests) are seated on crocodile skyband thrones for their installation at the turning/renewal of 20-year *k'atun* periods. This imagery reflects a "widely shared mythical narrative that was re-created in every accession ritual" from Late Preclassic through Postclassic times (Tokovinine 2008, 6) in which the ruler presides over a new political and cosmic order. The Paris Codex may be a copy of a Late or Terminal Classic manuscript (Vail 2006, 504).

What was this "mythical narrative"? We believe it was a creation myth, a myth in which the gods deep in the primordium sacrifice a crocodile by slitting its throat or decapitating it (Knowlton 2010; Taube 2010; Vail and Hernández 2013). Variations hold that the crocodile ascended to the heavens (a celestial "monster") and sent down a deluge or sank into the primordial waters, emerging as the terrestrial surface (an earth "monster"). The sacrifice brought about the creation of not only space but also time (Houston et al. 2006): the thirteen days of the Mesoamerican 260-day sacred almanac, their signs were said to drip with the sacrificial blood (Martin 2015, 222n66). Related to this genesis, the first day of the Classic lowland Maya almanac is Imix (water lily) or a variant, the characteristic vegetation of crocodiles' freshwater habitats; in Tojolab'al (Chiapas) the day name is Ain (crocodile) (Edmondson 1988, fig. 15b). Glyphs at Piedras Negras and Palenque show the Imix sign above a reptilian head (Doyle 2012, 130).

An early version of this myth of the sacrificed crocodile inspired the Middle Preclassic sacred landscape of Nixtun-Ch'ich': a crocodile emerging from the waters of Lake Petén Itzá, head to the east and body comprising the mainland (fig. 2.3). In particular, the landscape reproduces a sacrificed creature described in a text on the south face of a platform in Palenque Temple XIX as "hole-backed" and "painted-backed" (Stuart 2003, 2005b, 60–77). This creature has been called a "Starry Deer Crocodile," but its stellar and cervid embellishments are not evident at Nixtun-Ch'ich'.

We have only a few glimpses of the beginnings of this landscape design. The earliest pottery at the site, the late Early Preclassic K'as complex (Rice 2009a; South and Rice, forthcoming), which has calibrated radiocarbon dates of 1300–1100 BCE, was recovered in a small, single-component deposit on the tip of the Candelaria Peninsula (the snout of the crocodile) but only as scattered sherds on the mainland (its back). In what became the civic-ceremonial core of Nixtun-Ch'ich' (grid sectors Y, Z, AA, and BB), these traces of the earliest occupation were mixed with Terminal Early Preclassic (ca. 1500–1000 BCE) to Middle Preclassic transitional Ch'ich' complex pottery (ca. 1100–900 BCE) in constructions built on bedrock (Rice 2019; Rice et al. 2019).

Figure 2.3. Polychrome painted and modeled Cosmic Crocodile, Structure 6B, Cerro Maya. Photo by James F. Garber.

Sector Y is of particular interest. It consists of two contiguous substructural platforms, Y1 (west) with an E Group and Y2 (east) with a large depression, Fosa Y. Fosa Y was probably originally a small sinkhole or cenote, given that seven-meter-deep excavations never reached bedrock, and it may have held water at one time. This cavity, an entry to the watery underworld and home of the rain gods, may have been the centering point of the site's east–west *axis urbis*, which crosscuts the four core sectors (Rice and Pugh 2017). Moreover, Fosa Y is the "hole" in the back of the "hole-backed" mythical sacrificed crocodile. The Y2 platform, constructed around the fosa, began to be built during late Ch'ich' times; Platform Y1 supporting the E Group was begun slightly later. The pairing of E Groups and reservoirs is notable farther north in the Mirador Basin (Reese-Taylor 2017, table 15.2) and the mountain-pond duo is part of Mesoamerican sacred landscape ideology at least by the Early Formative (1600 BCE–300 CE) in the Olmec region (Ortíz and Rodríguez 2000). We will return to the water-mountain theme below.

Excavations in the east-west and north-south corridors of Nixtun-Ch'ich' suggest that the grid was put into place between 800 and 400 BCE during the Middle Preclassic period (Pugh and Rice 2017; Pugh 2018). The construction of the grid and adjacent structures appears to have begun with removal of surface soils down to bedrock, an activity confirmed by analysis of lake sediments in a core extracted from waters off the southern margins of the site (Obrist-Farner and Rice 2019). A wall-and-ditch defensive complex was also created at the base of the Candelaria Peninsula (Rice 2009a). This slash represents the sacrificial cut through the mythical creation crocodile's throat.

## Landesque Cosmography

For the Maya inhabiting Nixtun-Ch'ich', these numinous surroundings they had built and in which their descendants dwelt compellingly communicated the royal power of their leaders by placing it in time (see Salazar Lama 2017). The residents would have experienced the awe of this city as they walked along their avenues and streets, but they could not have seen the complete body of the mother/monster world. Its crocodilian form would have been apparent only from outside the city, for example to traders on paths approaching western Lake Petén Itzá from the cliffs of the north shore. Nevertheless, whether for inhabitants or visitors, this landscape allowed the powerful forces of primeval times to "be felt again in the present" (Bierhorst 1988, 13), especially during the orations and dancing at the great feasts affirming collective memory building and place making (Canuto 2016, 505). Thus Nixtun-Ch'ich', its early gridded layout preserved through nearly three millennia of occupation into the present, is a materialization of Maya creation time. We will elaborate this argument for landesque cosmography in the context of other lowland Maya sites.

At Late Preclassic Cerros (hereafter Cerro Maya) in Belize (chapter 6, this volume), a modeled and painted crocodile with a crenelated conch-shaped upturned snout (Taube 2005) or *yax* (first, green), seems to carry a monumental mask on the lower east panel of Structure 6B (fig. 2.3b; Freidel 1986). This image confirms our view that the cosmic crocodile was already part of the lowland Maya Preclassic material symbol system. Unfortunately, the mask being borne by the crocodile has been destroyed, but the idea of a supernatural creature carrying a deity head is well attested in the Late Preclassic sculpture on buildings, as in the case of a saurian creature framing a great mountain (*witz*) mask on Structure H X-Sub-3 in Group H at Uaxactun (Valdés 1988; Schele and Freidel 1990, fig. 4.7; Freidel et al. 1993, fig. 3.11).

In this case, the serpentine creature penetrates the frontal mountain mask and carries the profile head on its tail. In the Cerro Maya (Cerros) instance, the creature is evidently carrying the frontal monumental mask, now destroyed down to the armature (fig. 2.4). We should note that this composition is sufficiently ruined as to allow variable interpretations. James Garber and colleagues (2007, fig. 9) identify a "head in bowl" iconographic design in a Late Preclassic mask façade on Structure B1 at Blackman Eddy in Belize.

Figure 2.4. Shell pectoral of the Crocodile Tree with skeletal head, Burial 80, El Perú-Waka'. Photo by Juan Carlos Pérez and the Proyecto Arqueológico Waka'. Courtesy of the Ministry of Culture and Sports, Guatemala.

While it is possible to perceive the 6B monumental mask as resting in such a bowl—and the presence of a possible brow over the body/bowl suggests that it was very likely animated (like the Quadripartite Badge bowl of the Classic Maya; Robertson 1974)—we still argue that the crocodile is carrying this burden. The twisted band and knot motifs above the crocodile head frame the ruined earflare of the monumental mask as components of the earflare assemblage. They signal that the crocodile head is not part of the earflare assemblage but rather part of the main mask design.

An important feature of the Cerro Maya Structure 6B crocodile is that it is facing west on the east-west path of the sun. Jeffrey Vadala and Susan Milbrath (2014) have demonstrated that the previous main northern (and, southward-facing) temple at Cerro Maya, Structure 5C-2nd, was carefully oriented to the zenith passage of the sun. We suspect that Structure 6, which has the same orientation as 5C-2nd, was similarly designed for the zenith hierophany of the sun and that the crocodile here represented the path of the sun in the sky and through the earth. Significantly, Kathryn Reese-Taylor and Debra Walker (2002, 93, fig. 4.3) have identified Structure 6 as a Preclassic version of the Eight House of the North (GI) recounted in the Panel of the Cross inscriptions at Palenque because it has eight secondary substructures on its summit. The crocodile association strengthens this identification. The Nixtun Ch'ich' crocodile effigy is necessarily facing east, while the Late Preclassic Cerro Maya crocodile and later Classic period lowland Maya representations of the crocodile—which Linda Schele and others refer to as the Cosmic Monster (Schele 1992a; Freidel et al. 1993) and David Stuart (2005b) refers to as the Starry Deer Crocodile—face west on the east-west path of the sun. This sky crocodile represents Linda's Schele's interpretation of the Milky Way on the ecliptic. As Karl Taube (1989, 2010) has shown, the cosmic crocodile as an earth creature, Itzam Kab Ayiin, represents a monster slain in the primordium to make the land through which the sun must travel at night. Facing east to the rising sun, it is very likely that the Middle Preclassic people who built Nixtun Ch'ich' had this earth crocodile in mind (Rice 2018).

The city is on an enduring trade route west–east across the Maya lowlands. In the present context, Nixtun Ch'ich' is a paradigmatic example of landesque cosmography and the materialization of solar time in the Maya lowlands in the period when centers and complex society emerged (see also Freidel et al. 2017; Inomata 2017b; chapter 3, this volume).

One of the exemplary features of this gridded city is that it challenges its investigators to devise plausible explanations for the institutions that mobilized people to establish and maintain it. There is no evidence from the fieldwork to date that might directly shed light on how governance worked at Nixtun Ch'ich', so Rice (2018) notes the possible Middle Preclassic manifestations of the cosmic crocodile as a primordial myth guiding the city's effigy design and turns to general theoretical precepts, selectionist theory, and costly signaling to make sense of the situation. But the presence of the E Group solar commemorative design prominently integrated into the grid's east-west centerline allows a possible segue to coeval emergent centers elsewhere—in Petén and even in the northern lowlands (Stanton and Freidel 2005)—that evince precursors to later expressions of this landesque cosmography. As William Saturno and his colleagues (Saturno, Beltrán, et al. 2017) demonstrated, the pyramid of the Pinturas Building at San Bartolo covers a Middle Preclassic E Group. The western radial structure here is decorated with early maize god masks borne by reptiles and expressed as balustrade masks facing east, like Nixtun Ch'ich'. The eastern range of the buried San Bartolo E Group had a largely destroyed superstructure, but a fragment of mural from its walls depicts the maize god. These earlier murals may have presaged the Late Preclassic north wall mural of the Pinturas Building on the eastern side of the pyramid, which depicts a primordial Creation Mountain with a red reptile emerging from it and heading east. While this creature lacks legs, the up-curling snout, clearly a crocodile motif by Late Preclassic times, as seen at Cerro Maya, suggests that it is the cosmic crocodile. It has regular scutes depicted on its back. Crocodiles at rest in water do not show their limbs.

This living landscape in the San Bartolo murals is the ground line upon which several divine figures sit and stand. Painted footprints on it heading west underscore its status as landscape. The maize god stands in the center holding a sprouting gourd. He is framed in a triangle by three goddesses: one in the origin cave in the mountain offering a basket with three loaves of bread, one on the other side of him with an in-line triad of three flowers ornamenting her hair and with her arms outstretched in propitiation, and a third floating above while praying. The in-line triangle headdress harkens to the design of the eastern range of the E Group with its range of sun rise positions, to the belt stars of Orion that the Maya saw as a womb turtle constellation (Schele 1992a; Freidel et al. 1993), and to the moon goddess (Ux Uh, or Three Moon) at Classic period El Perú-Waka' and at Early Classic (300–600 BCE) Teotihuacan, (chapter 7, this volume). The triangle may refer to the stars of the creation hearth. The entire scene is situated in the heavens, as shown by the sky motifs that frame the base of the mural (Taube et al. 2010). Striding toward this performance is a maiden wearing the shell girdle later worn by both the Classic maize god and the moon goddess and their royal personifications. Taube and colleagues (2010) identify the maiden as a maize goddess. She leads two youthful heroes bearing royal mortuary bundles. The bundles wear funerary masks surmounted by both Maya- and Olmec-style royal crowns. These may be destined to be placed in the cave in anticipation of resurrection, for on the far side of the mountain is a scene of resurrection accompanied by child sacrifice carried out by Chahk, the rain god.

There is a watery baseline reptile on the mural on the west wall at San Bartolo. This creature's head is emerging into the first land, as defined by the five-tree scene on the surface, and its snout is upturned with five loops attached to it. This reminds us of the dots ornamenting the crenelated crocodile snout on Structure 6B at Cerro Maya (fig. 2.4), so this could be another crocodile. In contrast, the snout of the cosmic turtle depicted on the west wall of the Pinturas building curves sharply down, so snout shape on these landscape-defining creatures was not generic but specific. Notably, the maize/sun god masks on Structure 5C-2nd at Cerro Maya are emerging from basal masks with down-turned snouts that may symbolize the cosmic turtle.

Nixtun Ch'ich' is an example of landesque cosmography in the era of the first Maya lowland centers that resonates with other examples of this cosmography focused on the maize god, the world trees, and the sun as avian avatar of the old creator. We will continue to expand on this hypothesis.

Rice (2018) observes that Nixtun Ch'ich' was never emulated in the lowlands where "low-density" urbanism (e.g., A. Chase and D. Chase 2016; Fletcher 2019) was the norm in all ensuing eras. But as Inomata and Triadan (chapter 3) describe, the center of Aguada Fénix on the lower San Pedro Mártir also manifests very early orthogonal design—of causeways and reservoirs instead of streets and avenues, but nearly overlapping in time with the earliest foundation of Nixtun Ch'ich'.

It seems possible that these Maya knew about each other and regarded such design as an expression of creation in their world. The Aguada Fénix design does not obviously manifest an animal, but that is not out of the question either. The local uniqueness of Nixtun Ch'ich' in the southern Maya lowlands contrasts with the pervasive embrace of E Groups oriented to the path of the sun in the Middle Preclassic (A. Chase and D. Chase 2017a) and the subsequent pervasiveness of in-line triadic and triangular triadic designs in Late Preclassic central architecture (Freidel 1979, 1981a; Hansen 1998). As Richard Hansen (1998) makes clear, the Late Preclassic triadic designs are associated with divine rulership; the existence of Late Preclassic divine rulership was established in the 1980s (Freidel and Schele 1988b). William Saturno (2009) elegantly showed that the central message of the preserved murals at the Pinturas building was the accession of a human being to the status of divine king in emulation of the death, gestation/rebirth, and accession of the maize god. This accession took place in a cosmographic landscape on the west wall defined by the cosmic turtle (Great Turtle, the belt stars of Orion, see Freidel et al. 1993, fig. 2.15), the cosmic crocodile, the world trees, the young heroes, the maize god, and the old creator god in his guise as the solar bird (the Principal Bird Deity). Saturno and his colleagues (Saturno, Beltrán, et al. 2017) also showed continuous development of the maize god cult at San Bartolo from the Middle to Late Preclassic periods. Francisco Estrada-Belli (2017) shows how the E Group at Cival took on the symbolic trappings of rulership between the Middle and Late Preclassic periods, associated with world trees and the avian avatar of the sun (see also chapter 6, this volume). We suggest that if Nixtun Ch'ich' was established as an urban effigy of the cosmic crocodile with an E Group in its body, this Middle Preclassic effort was carried out by sodality collectives whose organization anticipated the sodality rulership that was in place elsewhere in the lowland Maya world by the Late Preclassic.

Rice (2018) thinks some kind of institutionalized leadership and robust collective or cooperative institutions must have founded and sustained Nixtun Ch'ich'. Inomata and Triadan (chapter 3) surmise that the evidence in hand suggests that Aguada Fénix had collective leadership. Saburo Sugiyama (2017a; chapter 18, this volume) and George Cowgill (2015) also argue that strong rulership and grid plans go together at Classic (300–900 CE) Teotihuacan, although they also see collective leadership institutions there. Our argument for sodality governance at Nixtun Ch'ich' as a harbinger for sodality rulership elsewhere in the Preclassic lowlands (Freidel 2018) builds on Rice's (2018) discussions of the cosmic crocodile and supplements them with Karl Taube's (2005) arguments regarding the crocodile, the World Tree, and the maize god. Taube reviews the Middle Preclassic archaeological record to show how Classic period jadeite images of Maya acrobat maize gods derive from Olmec rulers depicted as maize god crocodile world trees—as first proposed by Kent Reilly (1987)—with the maw of the crocodile forming the roots and maize tassels on the crown forming the leaves.

Crocodile world trees continued in the Late Preclassic at Izapa on Stela 2 where, as in the west wall world trees at San Bartolo, the Principal Bird Deity is featured (Guernsey 2006). At El Perú-Waka', Burial 80, which dates to the early fourth century CE (Freidel et al. 2017; Reilly and Freidel, forthcoming), contained a Crocodile Tree shell pectoral with a skeletal head of the Late Preclassic maize god (Garber and Awe 2009) depicted on its tail (fig. 2.4). This last example of the ruler as a crocodilian maize god World Tree is reiterated in mid-sixth-century CE Burial 37 at El Perú-Waka' (Freidel et al. 2013; Meléndez 2019, 245, fig. 4.28), where the ruler is adorned with a jadeite diadem depicting the maize god emerging from a crocodile-snout bib. A second jadeite jewel of a crocodile head adorned the chest of this king. At his feet was a plate painted with the Waterlily Monster, which is named the "precious pool maize tree" according to David Stuart (2005b). As Taube (2005, fig. 4) notes, King K'inich Janaab Pakal was buried with a jadeite carving in his groin depicting the head of the maize god on a downward-facing crocodile head. He has a jadeite carving of the Pax god that can read *te'* (tree) at his left foot. In our view, the groin position registers birthing (Tiesler et al. 2017, 165–189; see also chapter 7, this volume). Finally, Taube (2005) shows that a well-known codex style plate (K1892; Schele and Miller 1986) depicting the emergence of the maize god from a cracked open turtle carapace names the god One Maize Crocodile. The maize god here wears a pectoral of a human face

Figure 2.5. Central stairway from interior corridor to the summit by means of a trap door, Structure 6E-53, Yaxuná. Credit: Selz Foundation Yaxuná Archaeological Project. Photo by Charles K. Suhler.

surmounting a downward-facing crocodile head. Taube (2005) argues that this iconographic confluence marks the maize god as a crocodile World Tree and we agree.

Emergence also features in the cosmography of Nixtun Ch'ich'. Fosa Y is a natural sinkhole directly east of the E Group that Rice (2018) links to the cosmic crocodile (fig. 2.1) which, in its Classic period Starry Deer Crocodile manifestation, has a hole in its back (Stuart 2005a, 2005b). Rice argues that this is a place of emergence of the sun in a hierophany that occurred on the autumn equinox, when the dawning sun appears to rise out of Fosa Y as observed from the west (Rice and Pugh 2017). This is the height of the rainy season and a time of intense maize cultivation in Petén (Milbrath 2017b). Stuart (2005b) identifies GI in the Palenque texts of Temple XIX as the eastern dawning sun and as the rain bringer Hun Yeh Winik, One Tooth Person, whose name is conflated with that of the rain god Chahk. This is the same GI who manifests in the creation text on Palenque's Panel of the Cross and who establishes the cosmic crocodile house.

In the Late Preclassic, the maize god and the sun god appear to be conflated in some cases, as in the lower masks of Structure 5C-2nd at Cerro Maya. The maize god apparently sacrifices the avian avatar of the sun on the west wall of the Pinturas building (Taube et al. 2010) and in so doing harnesses the power of the solar year to the agricultural cycle of maize (Freidel 2017). In light of the association of the maize god and the crocodile World Tree discussed above—and the prospect that Nixtun Ch'ich' is a crocodile effigy—Fosa Y might have been the site of another hierophany, that of the solar zenith in May at the outset of the rainy season. Milbrath (2017b) suggests that the Preclassic Maya understood the principle of the gnomon and may have had tree posts set up for the purpose of witnessing the solar zenith (see also Pineda de Carías et al. 2009; Dowd 2015b, 57; Pineda de Carías et al. 2017). Estrada-Belli and Freidel (chapter 6, this volume) build on this hypothesis with their discussion of monumental posts in the E Group of Cival and on top of Structure 5C-2nd at Cerros. As mentioned, Vadala and Milbrath (2014) show that Structure 5C-2nd was aligned to the solar zenith. At Nixtun Ch'ich', that zenith might have transformed Fosa Y into an inverted gnomon, a deep hole into which the sun shone directly and without shadow (zenith sun-sighting "tubes" or observatories; see Dowd 2015b, 61).

Rice (2018) reports that a substantial feasting midden dating to the Middle Preclassic period was discovered in Fosa Y and that it was formally rimmed with plastered bench areas formed of large rocks. Among the excavated materials was a large red platter containing charcoal and human bone surrounded by what is interpreted as deliberately deposited turtle shell. As early as the beginning of the Late Preclassic at Yaxuná in the north-central lowlands, effigy turtle performance platforms designed to show the emergence of maize god kings were associated with a cache that included Olmec-style royal regalia, a jadeite celt, and a mirror (Stanton and Freidel 2005). This example is elaborated below. The cosmic turtle as a womb of emergence was manifest by the beginning of the Late Preclassic period. The aperture on the back of the cosmic crocodile, featured in Classic and Postclassic iconography, is anticipated in the fosa at Nixtun Ch'ich'. Whether or not the bottom of Fosa Y ever held a World Tree post like the one at Cival (Estrada-Belli 2017; chapter 6, this volume), the zenith passage of the sun would manifest the axis mundi World Tree seen in the lighting of the solar bird on the World Trees on the west wall of the Pinturas building in the Late Preclassic (when shadow disappears on these gnomons). As Taube (2005: fig. 4c) has shown, the Classic Maya maize god manifests as the crocodilian World Tree (see also Reilly and Freidel, forthcoming). It is not coincidental that the reptile head we identify as crocodilian on the west wall has a World Tree growing directly out of it. Nor is it coincidental that the sacrificial offering before it is a great fish with fire in its belly surrounding five (not three) hearthstones. Those stones form the quincunx, the ordering of the world that unfolds in the rest of that scene.

## A Cosmic Turtle Mountain and the Landesque Frame of History

While the Nixtun Ch'ich' crocodile effigy is remarkable and unique in its gridded plan, it is possible that we have not been looking enough at the landscape of ceremonial centers from the vantage of animal effigies. Michael Coe (1989a, 80) has speculated that the Olmec center of San Lorenzo might be a massive headless bird flying east. Even with the new identification of the rectangular plaza there (see chapter 3, this volume) it is still possible that it was an animal effigy. Kent Reilly (personal communication to David Freidel, November 2019) notes that Ignacio Bernal's (1969, fig. 2) map of La Venta island has nubbin appendages and the snout and tail of a crocodile. Lorraine Williams-Beck (personal communication to Prudence Rice, November 2017) suggests that the Late Preclassic moated fortress at Edzna in Campeche (Matheny et al. 1983, fig. 122) has a central mound that looks like a turtle carapace effigy and is certainly a water mountain.

The Maya created other animal effigies in urban landscapes that have cosmographic significance. If Stanton and Freidel (2003) are right, the in-line triadic design of the eastern range structures of E Groups generally manifests the Great Turtle constellation of the Maya Linda Schele discussed in *Maya Cosmos: Three Thousand Years on the Shaman's Path* (Freidel, Schele and Parker 1993, figs. 2.16, 2.17), and hence these ranges are turtle effigies. As discussed above, there are also two effigy turtle carapace performance platforms at Yaxuná, dating to the late Middle Preclassic period, that were designed to facilitate descent into the underworld and then resurrection. A jadeite celt and mirror, royal insignia jewels, were cached in the inner sanctuary of Yaxuná Structure 6E-53 under a large white limestone sphere that we take to be an effigy hearthstone (Suhler 1996; Stanton and Freidel 2005; Stanton et al. 2010), although it might be an effigy turtle egg. These are on the E Group axis to the east of the range structure and apparently form two points of a triangle for the Cosmic Hearth.

There are many depictions of performance in the painted vase corpus of the Classic Maya in which the maize god emerges from a turtle carapace platform. Freidel and Charles Suhler (1999) reviewed the architectural designs of emergence places and royal accession in the Maya lowlands with reference to the Yaxuná platforms. The cosmic turtle is referenced widely in the Maya area, both in texts and images, and likely was perceived in both the natural and shaped landscape in many urban settings. Here we explore the prospect that the ideas of a creation mountain and a cosmic turtle were combined in the landscape of El Perú-Waka' in northwestern Petén.

El Perú-Waka' is a very dense city situated on an escarpment overlooking the San Juan River, a tributary of the San Pedro Mártir River (Navarro-Farr and Rich 2014; fig. 2.6). At the eastern end of the city is a large promontory called El Mirador hill that has been the subject of sustained inquiry by Michelle Rich (2011, see also Rich et al. 2007; Rich et al. 2010; Rich and Matute 2014; Freidel and Rich 2018) since 2003. It has been clear since the first reconnaissance in 2001 that El Mirador hill was shaped by terracing and that it has three ritually charged and significantly modified localities on top. The southwest locality is known as the summit plaza, a leveled natural area that supports a group of Late to Terminal Classic structures oriented to the north. Rich (2011, fig. 6.13) discovered a Late Preclassic dedicatory offering in the center of this summit plaza sealed beneath seven plaster floors and cut into an even earlier floor. Thus, the last buildings were likely not the only ones there. Two localities to the east and northeast built out onto an adjacent ridge constitute large pyramidal platforms. A raised causeway connects these platforms to each other; initial construction dates to the Late Preclassic period (Rich 2011, 199–200). Rich (2011, 190–192) determined that the summit plaza was accessed by a broad stairway on its northern side that rises from a leveled surface it shares with the two pyramids. These, in turn, are apparently accessed by

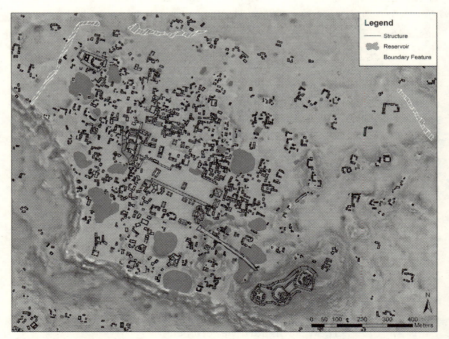

Figure 2.6. El Perú-Waka' site zone showing water features and El Mirador hill. Credit: Lidar-enhanced image courtesy of PLI, Damien Marken, and Proyecto Arqueológico Waka'.

a stairway on the northern side of the central locality, Structure 014-04, and by the causeway linking this pyramid to Structure 014-2, the largest building on El Mirador hill.

It is now clear from lidar-enhanced imagery of the city that the summit plaza promontory is directly above the main stairway that gave access to El Mirador hill from the city center. A causeway runs from the base of this stairway over an intervening hill to the plaza in front of the main temple of the city. This causeway crosses a reservoir at the foot of the hill, making this feature a water mountain, a fundamental cosmographic principle in Mesoamerica and in the Maya lowlands (Dunning et al. 1999; Freidel, Navarro-Farr et al., forthcoming). Rising 45 meters above the city plazas and dense array of compounds, El Mirador hill was a visually dominant presence where the sun rose each day. Terraced all around, it was for all intents and purposes a massive pyramid acropolis. The tops of its two certain pyramids on the ridge have a viewshed that extends to the Sierra del Lacandón to the west and that would have been visible for tens of kilometers to canoe travelers advancing up the San Pedro River toward the heartland of Petén. This was a regional landmark, not a local one, and Rich's (2011; see also Rich et al. 2007; Rich et al. 2010; Rich and Matute 2014) research confirms its historical importance. It appears likely to us that El Mirador hill at El Perú-Waka' was a cosmic animal effigy. The summit plaza was dedicated by a sealed offering dating to the Late Preclassic period and was in use through the Terminal Classic period. Excavations by Rich in the causeway linking the two adjacent pyramids show that this feature was also present in the Late Preclassic. Thus, the basic plan for El Mirador hill was in place during this era. That plan is an in-line triad, the plan of the cosmic turtle.

Northeast of the largest of the pyramids on El Mirador hill is a lower terrace that constitutes an extension of the original natural ridge, which might have been leveled artificially. This surface supports a substantial group of buildings that are unexplored and a distinctive platform that Rich (2013) has investigated. This platform was looted sometime before 2001, and there were bones and very early Early Classic ceramic vessels on the spoil heap of the looter's trench. In typical fashion for Petén, the looters had opened trenches at each end of this rectangular platform. In the other trench, looters exposed a masonry subsurface chamber with elaborate corbel-vaulted roofing for a passageway leading into it. Initial inspection of the chamber showed it to be completely empty. Rich (2013) documented that this masonry platform was used and abandoned early in the history of the city, during Late Preclassic to Early Classic times. It was built over a complex bedrock formation of flowstone, suggesting the possibility that this was originally a spring emerging from a rock shelter. Rich's excavation in 2012 of the access to the subsurface chamber revealed remains of a north-south passage leading to an elaborate sloped corbel-vaulted section that eventually opens to the chamber (fig. 2.7). That chamber had a leveled northern wall of yellow matrix rich in crystalline calcite (fig. 2.8). The wall was framed by bedrock and had flowstone emerging from the top.

The sloping vaulted entrance into the subsurface chamber is remarkable. It is made of a distinctive red-hued stone that so far has not been found elsewhere on the site, and its elaborate multi-block construction makes it look like the gullet of a living being. We propose that it was intended to look like the maw of the cosmic turtle mountain. Instead of being a completely cleaned out tomb, this subsurface chamber may have functioned as another performance sanctuary like those discovered at Yaxuná. The looters who exposed it left debris they found in their other trench all around the burial but none here. We suggest that this is the head of the turtle mountain and that it may have been used for death and resurrection rites like those discussed above.

The royal title Ahk, turtle, features regularly in the texts of Early Classic kings at Waka' (Guenter 2014, fig. 9.2). We propose that it alludes to the turtle place that was El Mirador hill. Waka' and its temple acropolis were established in the era of the Mirador state, and Mary Jane Acuña (2013; Freidel et al. 2022) discovered another Late Preclassic turtle place at the town of El Achiotal, located up the San Juan River from El Perú-Waka', heading in the direction of Mirador (accessible by canoe during flood tide). El Perú-Waka' adopted a dynasty after the fall of El Mirador and became a strategic realm in the struggles between the Kaanul regime and the Tikal-allied kingdoms in the Classic period. In 378 CE, Kaloomte' Sihyaj K'ahk' worshipped at a Wiinte' Naah Fire Shrine at El Perú-Waka' before proceeding to establish Tikal as the headquarters of his entrada (Stuart 2000; Freidel 2018). Evidently Kaloomte' Sihyaj K'ahk' founded the Waka' Fire Shrine in the place that became the city temple. Early Classic Wak dynasty kings and queens were proud of this affiliation and of their Fire Shrine. After 564 CE, Kaanul vassal kings and queens of the Late Classic continued to celebrate the exploits of Sihyaj K'ahk' on El Mirador hill into the eighth century (Rich 2011; Rich and Matute 2014). Rulers vying for control of El Perú-Waka' fought over this hill for centuries. Why? Because, we suggest, Sihyaj K'ahk' went to El Mirador hill and established his *altepetl* there, his Water Mountain (see chapter 18, this volume, for more on water mountains). While the Maya had water mountains as variants on the Flower Mountain, the true Mountain of Maize, Snake Mountain, and Turtle Mountain are all symbolically conjoined in the Aztec notion of *altepetl*. In Classic Teotihuacan, the term *altepetl* was used to denote the Pyramid of the

Figure 2.7. Entrance to the subsurface chamber. Structure P13-5. Photo by Michelle Rich. Courtesy of the Proyecto Arqueológico Waka' and the Ministry of Culture and Sports, Guatemala.

Figure 2.8. Subsurface chamber showing fall wall of yellow matrix, Structure P13-5. Project codirector Juan Carlos Pérez is in the foreground. Photo by Michelle Rich. Courtesy of the Proyecto Arqueológico Waka' and the Ministry of Culture and Sports, Guatemala.

Moon and concepts of dominion (N. Sugiyama 2014). Subsequent Maya kings and queens saw this Turtle Mountain that way; it was not regional rather than local landesque cosmography.

In her team's excavations of Structure O14-04, the middle of the three sacred localities on El Mirador hill, Rich (2011; see also Rich et al. 2010; Rich and Matute 2014) discovered a remarkable mid-seventh-century CE royal tomb, Burial 39. The offerings included an assemblage of figurines that appear to celebrate the resurrection of a human ruler as the maize god (Freidel et al. 2010; Rich et al. 2010; Rich and Matute 2014; Freidel and Rich 2018) under the aegis of another king and a queen. The timing of this tomb is right for it to be the predecessor of the Wak king K'inich Bahlam II, namesake of the Wak king who was vassal to Sihyaj K'ahk' in the fourth century CE. In front of this temple is El Perú Stela 1 (Castañeda 2011), dedicated in 657 CE as the first stela of K'inich Bahlam II (based on a distinctive jaguar head-in-sun nimbus diadem jewel that identifies him) (Guenter 2005, 2014; Castañeda 2011). Sihyaj K'ahk' went to war against Tikal immediately after establishing his authority and his Fire Shrine at Waka'. Presumably he took K'inich Bahlam I with him, as that king is memorialized by later entrada-era (378–520 CE) Wak dynasts. He conquered Tikal in 378 CE, a week after he established power at El Perú-Waka', and, we argue, made his *altepetl* dominion place on El Mirador hill. K'inich Bahlam II was placed in power by Kaanul king Yuhknoom Ch'een the Great, as related on El Perú Stela 33 (Guenter 2005), very likely on the same summit hill, judging by Stela 1. Yuhknoom Ch'een conquered Tikal in 657 CE, the same year Stela 1 was dedicated. It seems possible that he was quite deliberately striving to repeat history. If so, it is a notable display of landesque cosmography as historical time-crafting.

## The Waka' Palace as the Cosmic Turtle

Kaanul king Yuhknoom Ch'een the Great gave a royal princess from his house, very likely his daughter, in marriage to Wak king K'inich Bahlam II, probably when he presided over K'inich Balam II's accession. Queen K'abel was the superior of her husband; she used the title of Kaloomte' like her father. Together this royal couple participated in conquest wars that culminated in 679 CE with the decisive defeat of Tikal and an ensuing era of imperial peace in southern Petén. Yuhknoom Ch'een II, the closest thing the Classic Maya would experience to a true emperor, elevated himself to the title of *k'awiil* (Grube 2005), spirit of majesty, and his probable son and heir Yuhknoom Yich'aak K'ahk' to the status of Kaloomte', like his sister. The latter succeeded his father in 686 CE, and K'inich Bahlam II was his loyal vassal. To celebrate the power of the Kaanul regime and its new emperor on the occasion of the 692 CE period ending, K'inich Bahlam II and Queen K'abel built an enormous new gallery palace along the eastern side of the palace acropolis in Waka' (Freidel, Pérez, and Pérez 2018.)

The palace acropolis, located at the western end of the city, was a prominent landmark above the San Juan River. Established in the Late Preclassic period, the royal palace complex was originally at the level of the plaza to the west of it. It was still a group of plaza-level platforms when a young king died and was buried in one of them in the early fourth century CE, El Perú-Waka' Burial 80 (Pérez et al. 2019; Freidel et al. 2018). Retrospective history of the Wak dynasty on El Perú Stela 15 (Guenter 2005, 2014) shows that a King Leaf Chan Ahk presided over the period ending in 317 CE. We think this is the king in Burial 80. The name is undeciphered, but the royal appellative is Sky Turtle. This king was buried with a shell pectoral carved as a crocodile facing downward with a frontal face on its tail (fig. 2.5).

This frontal face is the sagittal-crested round-eyed skeletal royal insignia that is common on Late Preclassic jadeite diadem jewels of the Maya that James Garber and his colleagues (2007) identify as the head of the dead maize god in a sequence of jewels denoting death and resurrection in Cache 1 at

Cerro Maya. In our view, this pectoral marks the king as the crocodile maize god who emerges from the turtle carapace. By the seventh century CE, the palace acropolis was a large artificial hill, the accumulation of the construction efforts of more than twenty-four dynastic successions (Guenter 2005). Queen K'abel and K'inich Bahlam II excavated a large notch in the eastern side of this acropolis and built their massive new gallery palace close to plaza level. It was visually accessible from the plaza, symbolically harkening back to the early days of the dynasty. Evidently they reentered Burial 80 at this time, for the tomb chamber was certainly reentered from the eastern end before the construction of the gallery palace according to Griselda Pérez (Pérez et al. 2019), who directed excavation of the tomb. A new hieroglyphic inscription was set in the first tread of the new six-step stairway (see chapter 6, this volume) for the palace gallery; it related a ritual ballgame between K'inich Bahlam II and Yuhknoom Yich'aak K'ahk', his new overlord (Lee and Guenter 2010; Lee 2012). The palace gallery had a magnificent superior molding frieze of brightly painted modeled stucco. In 2017, Juan Carlos Pérez and Griselda Pérez excavated the central room of the gallery, where they discovered a small back room behind it with a stairway leading up to the flat roof area (Freidel et al. 2018). Thus, the gallery was a performance place for traveling from the underworld into the sky, like the performance platforms at Yaxuná. This was appropriate, for we think that with this gallery, the palace acropolis was transformed into an effigy of El Mirador hill, another turtle mountain for the resurrection of rulers as holy lords.

The identification of the palace acropolis as Turtle Mountain depends on two monuments, Stela 33 and Altar 6. Stelae 33 and 34 were the last to be set at the eastern end of the city, on Plaza 1, in conjunction with Stela 35. Stela 34 portrays Queen K'abel at the height of her powers in 692 CE. Sawn up and stolen in the 1960s by looters, it is the most famous stela of El Perú-Waka' and one of the most famous in the Maya world. Stela 33, which was also dedicated in 692 CE, portrays K'inich Bahlam II, who is positioned on the left facing his queen. Stela 35, dedicated in 711 CE, also portrays K'inich Bahlam II. Here, he faces to the right, also toward his queen. We think that K'abel died after 702 CE, when she is probably portrayed on badly eroded Stela 6 in front of the city temple; in 711 CE she did not raise a stela. In the case of Stelae 6 and 8 in front of the city temple, which were dedicated in 702 CE (the date of Stela 8 and 43), K'inich Bahlam faces to his left and his queen faces to the right. They flank a very large ruined Stela 7 that depicts a ruler dancing while wearing a massive backrack (Castañeda 2014). The presence of a Kaanul glyph in the accompanying text makes it very likely that this is Kaanul king Yuhknoom Ti'? K'awiil, who came to power in 697 CE.

This same pattern of Queen K'abel on the right facing left and K'inich Bahlam II on the left facing right is present on Stelae 11 and 12, dedicated in 672 CE. On the basis of this analysis of positioning monuments, K'inich Bahlam II moved Stelae 33 and 34 from their original placement to create the triad of himself on both sides framing his deceased queen as a memorial to her. We think that Stelae 33 and 34 must have originally formed a pair in the most important location in the city, in front of the palace gallery. The inscriptions on the two stelae celebrate both K'inich Bahlam's accession under Yuhknoom Ch'een the Great, very probably in 656 CE, and the accession of Yuhknoom Yich'aak K'ahk' in 687 CE. In this way, they harken back to El Mirador hill and the launching of the campaign against Tikal in 657 CE, where Stela 1 portrays the young Wak king at that momentous time and celebrates the Kaanul regime's new emperor.

Stela 34 depicts Lady K'abel standing on the mask of the Principal Bird Deity and a crescent that may depict a profile mirror bowl. Stela 33 depicts K'inich Bahlam II standing on a turtle carapace with the turtle head preserved on the right-hand side. This is the same curved-snouted turtle seen as the basal mask of the Preclassic masks from which the maize or sun gods emerge on Structure 5C-2nd at Cerro Maya. The crossed bands indicate that he is in or on that turtle. The king is either on El Mirador hill or at the palace acropolis. The latter is more likely, given the elaborate palace gallery they had established there. If our arguments are correct regarding the historical significance of Mirador Hill as a cosmic turtle effigy that marked the conquests of Tikal by Sihyaj K'ahk' and Yuhknoom Ch'een the Great, naming the royal seat of the Wak kings as a turtle mountain would have underscored the vital role of these vassal lords in those campaigns.

Altar 6 shows K'inich Bahlam seated inside the cosmic turtle; the text declares that K'inich Bahlam is in the heart of the turtle (Freidel et al. 1993, fig. 4.27). The monument only has a Calendar Round date, but the plausible date is 801 CE (Guenter 2005). If that is the case, then it says that the king had been in the turtle since 728 CE, making him 92 years old when he died. The altar is on the plaza in front of the palace acropolis. King Aj Yax Chow Pat, the last known Wak king, probably dedicated the altar. The text implies that K'inich Bahlam II was buried in Turtle Mountain, either on El Mirador hill or in the palace acropolis. David Lee and Laura Gámez (2006) discovered the palace gallery in 2005 while excavating below the final stairway to the palace acropolis. The gallery had been violently destroyed. The roof of the chamber, north of the central room, had been removed and blocks had been thrown into the room along with shattered fragments of the superior molding and hammerstones. Excavation of the southern wall produced even more

50 · David A. Freidel, Prudence M. Rice, and Michelle E. Rich

elaborate evidence of terminal ritual deposits, including shattered ceramic drums. Griselda Pérez reopened this central gallery room in 2016 and continued work there in 2017. Pérez (Pérez et al. 2019) found that the ruined gallery had been infilled and covered over. Subsequently, people had dug back down into the room from the southern end and cleared out the north section of the room, which had a partially intact roof. Elaborate shattered ceramic offerings and the remnants of fire rituals were found in the room that date to Terminal Classic times. The back room had been reentered and an ancient tunnel reopened that led northward to an empty tomb chamber. That chamber was built against the wall of the Early Classic platform that held the tomb of the fourth-century king discussed above. The Terminal Classic people refilled the tunnel, blocked it off, refilled the back room, and blocked up the doorway. They then built a small fire altar on its threshold and placed two sacrificed individuals in holes cut through the galley floor. They layered shattered stucco over their ceramic offerings and fire rituals, refilled the gallery room, and sealed the ruined palace gallery.

The successor of K'inich Bahlam II, King Bahlam Tz'am, was the last vassal of the Kaanul regime. He went to war against Tikal in 743 CE and was decisively defeated. Stelae from his reign were shattered or erased, indicating that Tikal forces sacked the city. Tikal king Yik'in Chan K'awiil boasted that he captured the Akan god of Waka' (see chapter 7, this volume). We think it highly likely that these warriors destroyed the palace gallery and sacked the tomb behind it. The plausible ruler placed in that tomb was K'inich Bahlam II or his son (he may well have outlasted several generations of heirs). The thorough removal of its contents would have been an attempt to erase him or his kind—and all memory of the turtle mountain seat of Wak kings—from history. Aj Yax Chow Pat remembered. He set the last stelae of the dynasty in front of the palace acropolis. We think he reentered the gallery to carry out the fire rituals of reverence in the presence of a royal spirit (Stuart 1998a), make the proper sacrifices, and reseal the mountain. Altar 6 was his defiant declaration that the great king was still there and that the turtle mountain of majesty endured. He also apparently dug down through the slope to reenter the tomb of Leaf Chan Ahk, the fourth-century king. The bones and offerings in this chamber were covered with cinnabar, possibly by him or by K'inich Bahlam II before him. While he may have been trying to revitalize the dynasty, he may also have been taking his leave of Waka'. Olivia Navarro-Farr (personal communication to David Freidel, November 2018) believes that the reentry rituals may have been part of a general leave taking by the royal court. Other royal tombs were reverentially reentered in the same period. As Keith Eppich (Eppich and Haney 2017) has documented, El Mirador hill remained a place of worship for another century, ministered to by a priesthood that lived on the road between it and the city temple, but the palace acropolis turtle mountain of the dynasty faded into obscurity.

## Final Thoughts

The Maya materialized time through the cosmographic shaping of their landscapes. The crocodile of Nixtun Ch'ich' now resonates with massive horizontal ceremonial centers of the Early Preclassic and Middle Preclassic described by Inomata and Triadan (chapter 3), including Aguada Fénix and Buenavista. These are orthogonally designed patterns that take Nixtun Ch'ich' out of the category of the unique and into a new category of astonishing early horizontality. And many are anchored in time materialization through the presence of E Groups, including both Aguada Fénix and Nixtun Ch'ich' (where there are three). Was the Nixtun Ch'ich' variation on the theme of orthogonality a harbinger of collective organization and political institutionalization, undergirding and reconciling with the divine rulership that manifested the monarch as an expression of the crocodile tree in Olmec, Epi-Olmec, and Classic Maya symbolism? We have reached the limits of our evidence to date; time will tell. Each generation left a legacy to the next of the awesome responsibilities involved in sustaining the history of creation and of their own people. While the history and peoples who once occupied Nixtun' Ch'ich' have faded into the shadows of time, the same is not true for El Perú-Waka'. The Maya people who work at Waka' today, discovering the past and defending the future, and those who come to worship there in the spring when the fields are planted and the rains are due, still feel the presence of the gods and ancestors who embody that land and those mountains.

# II

## Building Time into Place

# 3

# Spatial and Temporal Standardization in Southern Mesoamerica during the Preclassic Period

New Insights from the Middle Usumacinta Region, Mexico

TAKESHI INOMATA AND DANIELA TRIADAN

There is growing evidence that standardized ceremonial complexes spread across southern Mesoamerica during the late Early Preclassic and early Middle Preclassic periods (the late Early Formative and early Middle Formative in the terminology used outside the Maya area; 1400–700 BCE). This period was probably when maize agriculture was established and some Maya groups made the transition from mobile lifeways to full sedentism. Standardization in architectural forms may have been accompanied by formalization in people's practices and perceptions, including their concepts of time. The Middle Usumacinta region was a significant gap in archaeological data about these processes (fig. 3.1). Our recent work in the region has begun to fill this gap by revealing numerous standardized ceremonial complexes that were previously unknown. These buildings are closely related to the issues of temporal concepts, changing subsistence practices, and the process of political centralization.

## Foraging, Agriculture, and Time

The concept of time is tied to the daily and seasonal rhythms of life. Experiences of the natural cycle and social life significantly shape people's perception of time. Different subsistence practices, such as hunting, fishing, gathering, and cultivation, entail different rhythms in daily and seasonal activities. Thus, an important question is whether foragers and agriculturalists had fundamentally

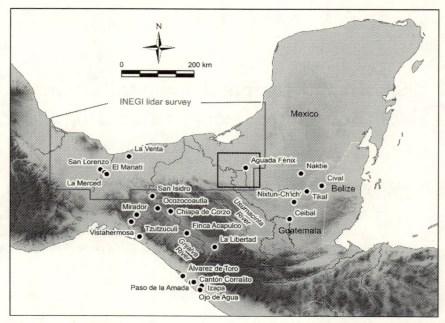

Figure 3.1. Map of southern Mesoamerica with the locations of the archaeological sites mentioned in the text. The black rectangular box indicates the Middle Usumacinta region. The gray polygon indicates the 85,000-square-kilometer area of the INEGI lidar survey.

different concepts of time. Following the Structural Marxist theory of Claude Meillassoux (1972), Richard Bradley (1998) argued for the existence of such differences, suggesting that the emergence of monuments in Neolithic Europe marked a break in worldviews. Mesolithic hunter-gatherers, according to Bradley, did not consider themselves to be separate from the natural world, and their rituals involved objects and practices directly tied to nature. The erection of monuments in the Neolithic meant new ritual practices and the creation of a landscape that was different from the natural one. Meillassoux theorized that the underlying issue was the property right over lands: unlike hunter-gatherers, who typically do not have exclusive notions of property, agricultural societies are characterized by property rights in which kin groups or fictive kin groups commonly serve as the primary units of ownership. Agriculture requires investments of labor and materials a long time before harvests come. To ensure the gains from their investments, agriculturalists need to claim exclusive rights over the patches of land they have worked on and to the crops planted in them. In this system, both the notion of the ancestor and the concept of time continuing from the distant past help legitimize a group's claim to agricultural lands. Along the same line, Ian Hodder (2007) emphasized the change in people's relation to time and history as one of the conditions that made agriculture possible. In her influential work, *Living with the Ancestors,* Patricia McAnany (1995) also has discussed the relations between agriculture, the notion of the ancestor, and land ownership in Preclassic Maya society.

There are, however, growing criticisms of the views that essentialize differences between hunter-gatherers and agriculturalists. These debates focus mainly on the questions of inequality and property ownership rather than on the concept of time. Nonetheless, as the aforementioned model of time is based on assumptions about social groups, property rights, and inequality, the roles of temporal concepts are of central importance. In this regard, it is helpful to recognize the distinction between the delayed-return and immediate-return systems among hunter-gatherers (Woodburn 1980; Barnard and Woodburn 1988). Delayed-return groups invest labor in planned manners for yields in the future, and notions of property rights are not uncommon among them. The Native Americans of the northwest coast of North America, who harvest salmon and other aquatic resources, developed hereditary hierarchy with elaborate rituals and concepts of property ownership. Examples of the immediate-return system include !Kung, Hadza, and other foragers, who gain food immediately after the labor of hunting or gathering. Among these groups, food storage, social inequality, and notions of property rights are generally undeveloped. Some levels of territoriality, property rights, and social inequality, however, can be found even among immediate-return hunter-gatherers; Australian Aboriginal people present one of the best examples (Layton 1986). By combining archaeological and historical data, Edwin Wilmsen (Denbow and Wilmsen 1986; Wilmsen 1989) contends that even the !Kung, who are often seen as quintessential immediate-return foragers, do not represent a pristine, timeless social condition. According to Wilmsen (1989), the !Kung developed their egalitarian, open social system as a result of historical processes, including contacts with hierarchical agricultural societies.

The recognition of the social complexity of hunter-gatherers can be extended to prehistoric contexts. Peter Rowley-Conwy (2001) has reviewed archaeological cases of hunter-gatherers to demonstrate that sedentism, social inequality, and ancestor veneration emerged in various places and periods in prehistory without directly leading to agriculture. Kenneth Sassaman and colleagues (Sassaman and Heckenberger 2004; Sassaman and Holly 2011), who have examined archaeological data on North American hunter-gatherers, argue that diverse social organizations and settlement systems, including power disparity and monumental constructions, emerged among those groups (see also Ames 2012). Zedeño et al. (2014) have shown that the ancestral Plains

Indians invested labor in substantial landscape engineering for bison hunts and established both ownership rights over hunting grounds based on kinship and social differentiation involving the ownership of esoteric knowledge, rituals, and associated objects. Drawing on the observation that Nambikwara in Amazonia (Lévi-Strauss 1967), Inuit, and Plains Indians (Lowie 1948) seasonally alternate nonegalitarian and more egalitarian organizations, David Graeber and David Wengrow (2021, 98–111, 456–481) suggest the possibility that such shifting organization existed during the Paleolithic period (see also Wengrow and Graeber 2015).

These studies show that hunter-gatherers should not be viewed as a starting point of cultural evolution leading toward agriculture and complex societies but should instead be understood in their own historical processes. If land ownership and ancestor veneration are not exclusively tied to agricultural societies, we also need to question the assumption about fundamental differences in the notions of time between foragers and agriculturalists. A continuum exists among hunter-gatherers, horticulturalists, and more established agriculturalists, and we need to examine diverse processes that may have existed in different contexts.

## Concepts of Time

To further examine this question, we should review the more general issue of time in anthropological studies. Theoretical debates on this issue help reveal problems underlying the simple categorization of temporal concepts among various societies. Certain traditional societies, including the Maya, are sometimes characterized as having cyclical concepts of time, which are contrasted with the linear concept of time in western society. Mircea Eliade (1959), in particular, argued that rituals at certain times of the year in traditional societies re-create events told in myths and refer back to the mythical age. Temporal conceptualizations of any society, however, combine cyclical and linear elements to varying degrees, and simplistic categorizations of them are misleading. Various scholars have questioned the applicability of Eliade's theory to historically and ethnographically known cases (Kirk 1970). Many societies, including those in the western world, employ lunisolar calendars that combine the cyclical nature of the moon and the movements of the sun. These lunisolar calendars as well as solar ones are closely tied to the cycles of seasons and agricultural activities. Moreover, even in modern societies, certain calendrical events, such as Christmas and the New Year, highlight the cyclicality of time by referring back to the distant past.

In his critique of the simplistic categorization of temporal concepts, Maurice Bloch (1977) has argued that two notions of time coexist in Bali.

One is cyclical ritual time, which is tied to ritual activities related to the legitimization of political authority. The other is linear mundane time, which is based on daily routines and has a universal character because it is related to the experience of seasons and other natural phenomena. Richard Bradley (1991), for example, has adopted those concepts of ritual and mundane time for the archaeological case of Neolithic Britain. However, this differentiation of temporal concepts within one society has also been subjected to criticism. Various scholars have indicated that both ritual and mundane activities may simultaneously incorporate repetitive and sequential elements and thus integrate cyclicality and linearity in one concept (Howe 1981; Gell 1992; Munn 1992). At the same time, the experience of natural phenomena does not simply result in a universal concept of time. These observations do not mean that there were no differences in temporal concepts among various societies. Instead, they direct our attention to the complexity in temporal concepts, which defies simplistic categorizations. They compel us to examine how different elements of time merge together, how those concepts condition social activities, and how people's practices construct concepts of time. We need to analyze these issues by placing them in specific historical contexts.

Another question concerns the issue of standardization in the measurement and conceptualization of time. The standardization of measurement systems, including those of time, length, and weight, is a common process in states and other centralized polities (Morley and Renfrew 2010; Schon 2015). In those contexts, the process of standardization is usually established and promoted by political authorities to facilitate economic activities and control by governmental institutions (Scott 1998). This process may be accompanied by the regimentation of rituals and other ceremonial activities. In contrast, immediate-return hunter-gatherers are often characterized as lacking formalization of cultural concepts. Rules of behavior may not be stated clearly and rituals can be highly variable (Gardner 1972, 436; Morris 1976, 544; Morris 1982, 39; Brunton 1989). Diverse opinions on religious matters may exist even within one kin group or family (Turnbull 1966, 246). The lack of formalization in social and ritual practices may be tied to the open social systems of such societies. Boundaries for various social groups are generally not well defined and are highly permeable (Lee 1979, 335; Woodburn 1982, 448; Ingold 1999).

Such characterizations of certain groups, however, should not be simply extended to other hunter-gatherers, as discussed above. In particular, various delayed-return hunter-gatherers, such as northwest coast Native Americans, tend to have more formalized systems of ritual and clear boundaries of corporate groups. Again, while we can observe certain tendencies among various groups, we need to examine the social dynamics of specific groups in their own historical contexts. When certain levels of formalization in notions of time and cultural concepts exist among certain hunter-gatherer groups and horticulturalists, such regulations may not be imposed by central authorities or by elites, unlike some examples found in states. We need to consider the possibility that such formalizations are sustained through the practices and discourses of many individuals.

Such processes may be akin to Michel Foucault's (1977, 1978) concept of power. Foucault discussed how decentralized forms of power, mobilized through space and social institutions, shape people's perceptions and behaviors. Some of these processes are regulated by specific temporalities, such as the work hours of office and factory workers and the synchronized movements of parading soldiers. Following his argument, Judith Butler (2011) has discussed how recursive utterances and practices create social norms and regulated ideas. Standardized buildings can play a significant role in this process because formalized spaces can elicit regulated behaviors. In addition, specific architectural forms may communicate specific symbolic values (Alonso 1994; Rabinow 1995; Love 1999; Low and Lawrence-Zúñiga 2003). As we examine Early and Middle Preclassic Maya society, which most likely lacked well-established dynasties, we need to pay attention to such social processes.

## Early Monuments and Subsistence

If standardized ceremonial complexes in southern Mesoamerica emerged in the transition from mixed subsistence to agriculture, the study of them can be contextualized in light of the growing understanding in various parts of the world that formal and substantial ceremonial complexes developed before the full establishment of agriculture. Some of these monuments were built by hunter-gatherers without any domesticated species, and others were made by mixed subsistence groups or horticulturalists. An important early study in this regard was the excavation of Kotosh in the Peruvian highlands in the 1960s (Izumi and Sono 1963; Terada and Onuki 1988; Onuki 1995). People who practiced mixed subsistence and retained residential mobility built the Temple of Crossed Arms around 2000 BCE, during the Preceramic period. Since then, even older examples of monumental constructions by hunter-gatherers or mixed subsistence groups have been found in the Andes and other parts of the world. On the Peruvian coast, monumental constructions at Sechín Bajo and other sites date to around 3500 BCE, when the inhabitants of the region practiced mixed subsistence through the use of marine resources and domesticated plants (Fuchs et al. 2006; Fuchs et al. 2009). Even larger constructions were built at Caral between 2600 and 2000 BCE, and numerous others followed in various parts on the Peruvian coast (Shady Solis et al. 2001; Burger and Salazar 2012).

Other striking examples include Göbekli Tepe and related Neolithic remains that feature elaborately carved stone monuments built during the tenth millennium BCE during the Pre-Pottery Neolithic A period (PPNA) (10000–8700 BCE) in Southwest Asia (Schmidt 2010; Watkins 2010; Banning 2011; Dietrich et al. 2012). Although the process toward the development of agriculture was beginning during this period, clearly recognizable domesticated plants do not appear until the Pre-Pottery Neolithic B period (PPNB) (8700–6800 BCE). The lack of residential structures around Göbekli Tepe suggests that it was built by mobile foragers for seasonal gatherings.

In the lower Mississippi area of the American Southeast, monumental mounds at Watson Brake that measure up to 7.5 meters in height and were arranged in an elliptical shape that measured 370 × 280 meters were constructed around 3400–3000 BCE. Evidence of domestication and sedentism is absent, and the builders were seasonally mobile foragers who consumed a wide range of resources gained through fishing, hunting, and gathering (Saunders et al. 1997). Importantly, these constructions did not lead to agriculture or political centralization. Mound building in the southeast is not well documented during the subsequent period, but such activity probably continued, leading to the constructions of Poverty Point and other sites around 1500 BCE (Kidder 2011). The builders of Poverty Point, including its Mound A, which is 22 meters tall, were also hunter-gatherers. In Florida and other parts of the southeastern coast, shell mounds of monumental proportions were created mainly between 4500 and 3000 BCE. Although their nature is still debated, these features have ringlike shapes measuring up to 250 meters in diameter, suggesting that they are not simple accumulations of food refuse but symbolic constructions intentionally built by hunter-gatherers (Sassaman 2004). Comparable monumental shell mounds are also found in Brazil (Fish et al. 2013).

The timing of the emergence of monumental construction in Mesoamerica is debated. John Clark and John Hodgson (2021) suggest that Álvarez de Toro and other shell mounds found on the Pacific coast of Chiapas, dating as early as 5000 or 6000 BCE, represent the earliest monumental buildings in Mesoamerica (fig. 3.1). According to Clark and Hodgson, these elliptical- or circular-shaped shell mounds, which measured up to 11 meters in height and 290 × 145 meters in horizontal dimensions, were intentionally built monuments, as in the case of Floridan examples. Other scholars, however, argue that they represent accumulations of discarded shells after their consumption and processing (Voorhies 2004, 2015; Voorhies and Kennett 2021). We are inclined to agree with Clark and Hodgson, given the presence of well-prepared surfaces, although the nature of these structures needs to be further examined with more extensive excavations. If they are intentionally built monuments, abundant marine resources possibly enabled such large-scale collective activities, as in the cases of the American Pacific and southeast coasts, the Peruvian coast, and other littoral regions.

Monumental constructions in inland areas of Mesoamerica, however, emerged significantly later than many of the examples from other parts of the world; they date to the second millennium BCE. There appears to have been a process unique to Mesoamerica in terms of the relation between subsistence change and ceremonial constructions. Maize was domesticated long before the initial construction of monuments in inland Mesoamerica, probably by 6700 BCE (Piperno et al. 2009; Ranere et al. 2009). However, maize appears to have remained a relatively small part of the diet for millennia, and in many parts of Mesoamerica people retained certain levels of mobility and a heavy reliance on wild resources.

Until recently, a common view was that a low reliance on maize continued through the Early Preclassic period (1900–1000 BCE) and that its consumption increased significantly during the transition to the Middle Preclassic around 1000 BCE (Blake et al. 1992; Clark and Cheetham 2002; Chisholm and Blake 2006; Clark et al. 2007; Webster 2011; Clark Rosenswig 2015; Rosenswig et al. 2015). In this view, Early Preclassic developments at the Olmec site of San Lorenzo—including the construction of a monumental plateau, the erection of colossal head sculptures, and political centralization—may have occurred while most populations practiced mixed subsistence (Arnold 2000, 2007, 2009; Taube 2000; Borstein 2001; Symonds et al. 2002; Wendt 2003; VanDerwarker 2010; Cyphers and Zurita-Noguera 2012; VanDerwarker and Kruger 2012; McCormack 2012; Killion 2013), although opposing perspectives have persisted (Coe and Diehl 1980; Pope et al. 2001; Coe 2013). In addition, various scholars have suggested that mobile lifeways continued or that sedentary and mobile populations coexisted in various parts of Mesoamerica during the Early Preclassic period (Arnold 1999; Lohse 2010; Rosenswig 2010, 2011; Lesure and Wake 2011; Inomata et al. 2015).

New data, however, are forcing us to reconsider this interpretation. The view that maize was consumed at low levels during the Early Preclassic period was based mainly on carbon and nitrogen stable isotope data on human bones excavated from the Soconusco region (Blake et al. 1992; Chisholm and Blake 2006). Nevertheless, only 14 samples from the Late Archaic (~3000–1900 BCE) through Middle Preclassic appear to have sufficient levels of collagen preservation judged from C:N ratios (Moreiras Reynaga 2013; Blake 2015, 196). Among these samples, four or five individuals from the Early Preclassic show bone collagen $\delta^{13}C$ values greater than −15, whereas three from the same period have values smaller than −15 (Lesure et al. 2021; Moreiras Reynaga 2013). In other words, the consumption of maize may have increased more gradually starting in the Early Preclassic than was previously thought. In the Olmec area of Mexico's Gulf Coast, the survey by Joshua Borstein (2001, table 8.1) showed that sites dating before the San Lorenzo phase (1400–1000 BCE) are concentrated in the lowland areas near rivers and wetlands, indicating a heavy reliance on aquatic resources. Settlements expanded to upland areas suited for maize cultivation in the San Lorenzo A phase (1400–1200 BCE) to San Lorenzo B phase (1200–1000 BCE) and the Middle Preclassic period, suggesting that the consumption of maize increased gradually during the Early Preclassic period.

Keith Prufer has presented particularly important data about the isotope analysis of the Archaic period human remains excavated in southern Belize. In this area, some individuals began to consume maize in considerable amounts between 2700 and 2000 BCE and maize became an important staple after 2000 BCE (see Kennett et al. 2020). In addition, well-preserved maize remains from El Gigante rockshelter in Honduras show that productive maize with large cobs was cultivated at least by 2300 BCE (Kennett et al. 2017). The genetic analysis of maize suggests that productive maize developed in South America and then spread to Mesoamerica (Kistler et al. 2018, 2020). If so, the inhabitants of Honduras and the southeastern Maya area may have begun a heavy reliance on maize earlier than inhabitants of Mexico. The development of maize agriculture needs to be further investigated, but diverse levels of maize consumption may have existed in Mesoamerica during the period 3000 to 1000 BCE. As suggested by the stable isotope data from the Soconusco region, groups practicing different subsistence strategies may have coexisted within small areas. This observation also implies that groups with different degrees of residential mobility may have coexisted. Around 1000 BCE, maize agriculture became well established in various parts of Mesoamerica, including the Maya lowlands. Nonetheless, some groups appear to have retained certain levels of mobility during the centuries that followed (Lohse 2010; Inomata et al. 2015).

## Study of Standardized Complexes before the Middle Usumacinta Project

In 2017, we started the Middle Usumacinta Archaeological Project to examine the development of early ceremonial complexes in the western Maya lowlands, building on our previous research at Ceibal, Guatemala. Prior to this project, the study of Preclassic standardized ceremonial complexes focused on what John Clark (Clark and Hansen 2001) named the Middle Formative Chiapas (MFC) pattern. Gareth Lowe (1977, 1989) and Andrew McDonald (1983) originally pointed out that these standardized ceremonial complexes spread across Mexico's southern Gulf Coast and Chiapas during the Middle Preclassic period. The MFC pattern consists of an E Group assemblage (a western mound and an eastern long platform), large supporting platforms arranged along the north-south axis, and in some cases, a northern pyramid. Sites with this arrangement include La Venta (Lowe 1989) on the gulf coast of Mexico; Mirador (Agrinier 1975, 2000), Chiapa de Corzo (Hicks and Rosaire 1960; Lowe and Agrinier 1960; Mason 1960; Lowe 1962; Bachand and Lowe 2012), Finca Acapulco (Lowe 1977, 2007), San Isidro (Lowe 1981), Ocozocoautla (McDonald 1999), La Libertad (Miller 2014), and possibly Vistahermosa (Treat 1986) in the Chiapas Grijalva River region and nearby areas; Tzutzuculi (McDonald 1983) and possibly Izapa (Rosenswig et al. 2013) on the Pacific coast of Chiapas; and Ceibal in the southwestern Maya lowlands (Inomata et al. 2013; Inomata 2017a, 2017b; Inomata, Pinzón, Palomo et al. 2017; Triadan et al. 2017). At San Isidro, Chiapa de Corzo, and Ceibal, archaeologists uncovered deposits of greenstone axes along the east-west axis of the E Group assemblage, similar to those found at La Venta and the Early Preclassic sites of El Manatí, La Merced, Paso de la Amada, and Cantón Corralito (Blake 1991; Ortíz C. and Rodríguez 1999; Rodríguez and Ortíz 2000; Cheetham 2010; Inomata and Triadan 2016; Aoyama et al. 2017). These caches suggest that the builders of MFC complexes did not simply imitate architectural forms but shared common ritual practices and concepts.

Lowe (1977, 1989) originally assumed that the MFC pattern originated at La Venta and that its spread into other regions reflected the expanding influence of this Olmec center. However, we have documented that the MFC complex at the Maya site of Ceibal, which features caches of greenstone axes, dates back to 950 BCE (Inomata et al. 2013; Inomata and Triadan 2016; Aoyama et al. 2017; Inomata, Pinzón, Palomo et al. 2017; Inomata, Triadan, and Aoyama 2017; Triadan et al. 2017). The complexes at Finca Acapulco and Tzutzuculi may be roughly contemporaneous. Based on analysis of published radiocarbon dates, we have argued that the growth of La Venta as a dominant center occurred around 800 BCE—that is, after the initial development of the MFC pattern at Ceibal (Inomata et al. 2013). Clark (2016) also suggests a late date for the MFC complex of La Venta, mainly from his evaluation of ceramics. If that is the case, La Venta cannot be the source of the MFC pattern.

The MFC complex at Ceibal was constructed at the beginning of this community when the use of ceramics had just started. The paucity of durable residential structures around the ceremonial complex has led us to argue that a substantial portion of the population in this region retained a certain level of mobility (Lohse 2010; Inomata et al. 2015). The use of lidar in a 470-square-kilometer area around Ceibal has revealed nine additional E Group assemblages and seven eastern winged pyramids that probably derived from the architectural format of the E Group (Inomata, Pinzón, Ranchos et al. 2017; Inomata et al. 2018). The results of excavations and surface collection suggest that these complexes spread outside the Ceibal center between late Middle Preclassic Escoba 2 and Late Preclassic Cantutse 1 phases (600–300 BCE). During this period, durable residential remains with platforms increased in the Ceibal center. Most residents of the region probably adopted full sedentism during this period, and the construction of these ceremonial complexes outside of Ceibal may have symbolized local groups' claim to agricultural lands.

The abundance of E Group assemblages, the central element of the MFC pattern, in the Maya lowlands (see A. Chase and D. Chase 2017a) has led some Mayanists to argue that this ceremonial configuration was a Maya invention (Valdés 1995; Estrada-Belli 2011). However, these complexes spread in the Maya lowlands outside Ceibal after 800 BCE (Inomata 2017b). The finds from Ceibal and a review of relevant data have led us to contend that Preclassic ceremonial complexes developed through complex interactions across Mexico's southern Gulf Coast, the Grijalva River region and the southern Pacific coast of Chiapas and spread to most parts of the Maya lowlands somewhat later (Ricketson and Ricketson 1937; Rosal et al. 1993; A. Chase and D. Chase 1995; Laporte and Fialko 1995; Hansen 1998, 2016; Estrada-Belli 2001, 2006, 2017; Stanton and Freidel 2003; Stanton and Arden 2005; Aimers and Rice 2006; Freidel et al. 2017; Inomata 2017a, 2017b). In their initial development, the inhabitants of the Pacific coast of Chiapas may have played an important role. There, the site of Ojo de Agua, which dates to 1200–1000 BCE (Hodgson et al. 2010), appears to show a prototype of the MFC pattern, including a complex similar to the E Group and pyramidal buildings (Inomata 2017b).

The contribution of San Lorenzo to this process was not clear. This early Olmec center did not have substantial mounded constructions or pyramids, although its spatial arrangements probably included plazas (Coe and Diehl 1980; Cyphers 1997; Cyphers and Di Castro 2009; Cyphers and Murtha 2014). Although the specific chronology of San Lorenzo at the transition from the Early to the Middle Preclassic is still not clear, its major development occurred around 1400 BCE and its influence on the Grijalva River region and the Pacific coast in Chiapas weakened around 1200 or 1150 BCE (Lowe 2007;

Cheetham 2010; Inomata et al. 2013). Today, the artificial plateau built over the naturally raised area shows a complex shape with gullies and ridges. Michael Coe (Coe and Diehl 1980) proposed that the San Lorenzo plateau was an effigy monument representing the shape of a giant bird. Ann Cyphers (1997; Cyphers and Murtha 2014) and others, however, have argued that the gullies and ridges are the results of erosion. Either way, prior to our research, the site plan of San Lorenzo had been seen as unique and disconnected from later standardized formats, and the presence of standardized complexes in the area west of La Venta had not been reported.

In the study of this process, the Middle Usumacinta region located between Mexico's southern Gulf Coast and the Maya lowlands should be another key area. Preclassic sites in this region were not well known. To fill this gap in our knowledge, we started the Middle Usumacinta Archaeological Project in 2017.

## Middle Usumacinta Archaeological Project

John Clark directed Inomata's attention to an early map of El Tiradero (Andrews 1943; John Clark, personal communication, 2016), which showed a spatial arrangement resembling the MFC pattern. In July 2016, Inomata and Triadan visited the area with Rodrigo Liendo Stuardo and Keiko Teranishi Castillo, who have been conducting research at Palenque and in the Middle Usumacinta region, to evaluate the feasibility of a new project. This trip convinced us of the importance of this region, and we initiated the Middle Usumacinta Archaeological Project. Our research in 2017 started with a lidar survey of areas around the site of La Carmelita and El Tiradero; the National Center for Airborne Laser Mapping (NCALM) of the University of Houston collected lidar data on May 6, 2017. Lidar covered areas of 93 square kilometers around La Carmelita and 16 square kilometers around El Tiradero. The NCALM scientists produced one-meter horizontal resolution digital elevation models and digital surface models. The high-resolution lidar data of NCALM were effective for detecting archaeological features for areas under tree canopies (A. Chase et al. 2011; A. Chase et al. 2012; A. Chase et al. 2014; Fernandez-Diaz et al. 2016, Hutson 2015; Reese-Taylor et al. 2016; A. Chase and D. Chase 2017b), and in our areas, which include broad spreads of pasture, feature visibility is even better.

The lidar image of La Carmelita clearly shows a northern pyramid, platforms, and an E Group assemblage in an arrangement similar to the MFC pattern of the Grijalva River region. Although the northern portion of the eastern platform of the E Group was damaged in modern development, this site presents an important difference. Its rectangular delimitation, defined by a series of small mounds along the site perimeter and measuring 900 meters north-south and 160 meters east-west, is not found at Grijalva sites. We call this spatial format, which is characterized by a rectangular arrangement and an E Group, the Middle Formative Usumacinta (MFU) pattern. In contrast, lidar reveals a typical MFC formation without a rectangular delimitation at El Tiradero, closely resembling that of Chiapa de Corzo. This similarity points to close contact with the Grijalva River region of Chiapas.

To expand our understanding, we also analyzed lidar-derived 5-meter-resolution digital elevation models and digital surface models for the entire study area and adjacent regions that the Instituto Nacional de Estadística y Geografía (INEGI) produced (http://inegi.org.mx). In forested areas, the INEGI digital elevation models do not show many ground-level features. Despite this limitation, we found the INEGI lidar useful for detecting archaeological sites located in pastures. A remarkable find was the site of Aguada Fénix, which was partially visible to the northeast of El Tiradero in the NCALM lidar. The INEGI lidar revealed a formal rectangular artificial plateau (Main Plateau) measuring 1,400 meters north-south, 400 meters east-west, and 10 to 15 meters in height. On the western side of the platform was a series of artificial reservoirs separated by parallel causeways. The rectangular form of the platform indicates that this site exhibits the MFU pattern. Its size rivals the plateau at San Lorenzo and surpasses the ceremonial area at La Venta.

To better understand this site and related ceremonial complexes, we conducted a lidar survey of 1,015 square kilometers in collaboration with NCALM. Data acquisition flights were carried out from June 9 to 17 in 2019. The resulting 0.5-meter-resolution digital elevation model revealed a large E Group in the center of the Main Plateau of Aguada Fénix with two western pyramids and an eastern platform measuring 400 meters in length (Inomata et al. 2020). It also showed that the northwest avenue extended 6.3 kilometers, connecting multiple complexes along the way. Surprisingly, archaeologists had never before recorded the central part of Aguada Fénix, including the large plateau. This shows that for researchers standing on the ground, features with large horizontal dimensions can be more difficult to recognize than smaller ones. Lidar is particularly effective in documenting this type of site. Our excavations showed that the Main Plateau of Aguada Fénix had a substantial size by 1000 BCE, although we do not have reliable radiocarbon dates from the initial construction layer of the plateau.

In other parts of the Middle Usumacinta region, we identified multiple MFU sites. Most of them were previously unknown. Anaya Hernández (2002) visited one site, Crisóforo Chiñas, but the published map does not show its rectangular arrangement. This example again indicates the difficulty of recognizing such horizontally large arrangements in a ground survey. These finds encouraged us to analyze lidar data of a broader area to examine the distribution of MFU complexes and related sites.

In 2019 and 2020, we analyzed the INEGI lidar data for 85,000 square kilometers that cover the western Maya lowlands and the Gulf Olmec region. The area corresponds to the modern state of Tabasco, southern Veracruz, and parts of Campeche, Chiapas, and Oaxaca (Inomata et al. 2021). We identified 478 standardized ceremonial complexes, including Aguada Fénix, other MFU and MFC sites, and their variants. A significant number of them were not known previously. These results show that those closely related complexes are distributed across the western Maya lowlands and the Gulf Olmec area.

An important understanding emerged from the analysis of the INEGI lidar data of San Lorenzo. For this study, Juan Carlos Fernandez-Diaz reprocessed the INEGI lidar point clouds and created a digital elevation model with a horizontal resolution of 2 meters which showed surface features more clearly than the INEGI's original 5-meter-resolution digital elevation model. Using this model, we recognized previously undetected platforms along the western and eastern edges of the plateau (Inomata et al. 2021). The traditional maps depicted those features as slightly elevated areas with amorphous or roundish shapes. Coe and Richard Diehl (1980) called these areas that extend in north-south directions ridges. The refined digital elevation model shows that these edge platforms have rectangular shapes. Their well-designed forms indicate that these elevated features were not unintended results of continuous occupation and rebuilding but were built intentionally according to specific designs. The edges facing the central part of the plateau, in particular, formed well-defined straight lines that demarcated a leveled area, which was probably an extensive plaza of a rectangular shape measuring 1030 × 280 meters with a small eastern wing. The excavation data Coe and Diehl (1980) reported suggest that these edge platforms were formed at least by the San Lorenzo B phase (1200–1000 BCE) and were 1.0–2.5 meters higher than the plaza surface. The architectural complex in the center of the plateau was added during the Villa Alta phase of the Classic period (Coe and Diehl 1980; Cyphers 1997). Ann Cyphers and Timothy Murtha (2014) note that lagunas (water-holding depressions) were constructed in modern times as cattle tanks, but otherwise there are no clear indications of significant terrain alterations during the modern period.

The San Lorenzo plateau has ten edge platforms on the western side and ten on the eastern side, making a total of twenty platforms. They probably represent a meaningful number, most likely the base unit of Mesoamerican calendars. In our analysis of the lidar data, we found a previously unknown

MFU complex south of the San Lorenzo plateau (Inomata et al. 2021). The rectangular formation of this complex is roughly half the size of the San Lorenzo plateau, but it also has twenty edge platforms, which define a rectangular plaza with an eastern wing. A difference is that it has an E Group and a northern pyramid, features that are lacking in the San Lorenzo plateau. The Main Plateau of Aguada Fénix probably replicated this format. It also appears to have had twenty edge platforms, although two of them were covered by the Southwest Platform, which was likely added later. Other MFU complexes at Buenavista and El Macabil also have twenty edge platforms surrounding a rectangular plaza with an eastern wing. However, many smaller MFU complexes do not have twenty clearly defined edge platforms.

Other similarities between San Lorenzo and Aguada Fénix are found in their access ways. Coe and Diehl (1980, 297) noted that the Southeast Ridge of San Lorenzo provided ramp-type access to the plateau and connected with a causeway in the area below. The digital elevation model of San Lorenzo also shows two possible corridors to the south of the plateau connecting with the Southeast and Southwest Ridges. It is likely that the Southwest Ridge, Northwest Ridge, and Northeast Ridge also provide similar access ways from the south and north. Likewise, the Group D Ridge and Group C Ridge were main entrances from the west. At Aguada Fénix, the two North Avenues, the two South Avenues, and the two main West Avenues were likely modeled after this access pattern at San Lorenzo.

We can summarize the common characteristics of MFU complexes and related sites. First, the rectangular formations of MFC complexes commonly measure 400 to 1,000 meters north-south and 100 to 200 meters east-west, but there are also a substantial number of smaller complexes. Most MFU sites appear to have been constructed during the period 1100 to 700 BCE. They are generally oriented in a north-south direction, but some variations exist. In mountainous or hilly areas, the orientations of complexes vary more widely. In nearly all cases, the rectangular forms are defined by lines of small mounds. Aguada Fénix is the only case that has a substantially raised rectangular plateau. Complexes in southern Veracruz tend to have continuous linear mounds along the rectangular plazas and prominent western wings. We call them Veracruz Ceremonial (VC) complexes, which probably represent a variant of the MFU pattern. There are also square complexes defined by continuous low earthworks that measure 150 to 350 meters wide. They are reminiscent of those found in Amazonia (Erickson 2000; Heckenberger et al. 2008; Pärssinen et al. 2009; Carson et al. 2014), but their functions are not clear.

Second, MFU complexes share the common features of the MFC pattern, including an E Group assemblage and associated supporting platforms. In some cases, northern pyramids are also present. A variant, which we call a rectangular complex, consists only of low mounds in a rectangular arrangement without an E Group. These patterns indicate that the MFU pattern was closely related to the MFC pattern of La Venta, the Grijalva River region, and nearby areas. The similarity of MFU complexes to the newly recognized form of San Lorenzo indicates that the MFU pattern developed out of the prototype established at San Lorenzo. The MFC pattern and the E Group assemblage may have developed initially on the Pacific coast of Chiapas, as indicated by the configuration of Ojo de Agua. The builders of MFU and MFC complexes likely had close contact; these complexes exhibit common or similar features. In particular, La Venta and the closely related site of Pajonal show similarities to both the MFU and the MFC patterns. While La Venta was originally classified as an MFC complex, its edge platforms are aligned tightly separated by narrow alleys like those of MFU complexes, which differs from the more dispersed placements of platforms at other MFC sites. We use a new category to identify it, the Middle Formative Gulf (MFG) pattern, as a variant of the MFC pattern. While the active use of MFU complexes may have declined around 750 or 700 BCE, the use of MFC and MFG complexes continued until 400 BCE. Some MFC and MFG sites, such as La Venta and La Libertad, were abandoned around 400 BCE. Occupation continued at other sites, such as Chiapa de Corzo, during the Late and Terminal Preclassic periods, but the original use and meaning of the MFC pattern may have been lost.

Third, most MFU sites are located in uplands above floodplains, and areas around them appear to have been fairly open without many residential structures. It is possible that the inhabitants of the Middle Usumacinta region still retained a certain level of mobility and that they lived in ephemeral structures that are difficult to detect in lidar. If that is the case, many inhabitants of the region may still have relied to varying degrees on wild food sources, particularly aquatic resources. Large MFU centers, such as Aguada Fénix, possibly had relatively small permanent populations; substantial numbers of individuals may have gathered there periodically for constructions and ceremonies. Thus, some MFU sites may be characterized as "vacant centers," which were used mainly for collective rituals and did not have large permanent populations. The presence of numerous small complexes suggests that each small local group had its own ceremonial location, but these groups traveled, in some cases long distances, to attend large ceremonies held at important centers.

Fourth, there are a small number of MFC complexes in the Middle Usumacinta region, including the sites of El Tiradero, El Mirador, and Rancho Zaragoza. El Tiradero probably dates to the Terminal Preclassic periods

(100 BCE–250 CE). The occupation of Rancho Zaragoza began during the Middle Preclassic period and continued into the Late and Terminal Preclassic, although the date of the beginning of its MFC complex is not clear. The presence of numerous mounds around these sites indicates that their residents had adopted a more sedentary way of life and had a stronger commitment to maize agriculture. Although Hernández Ayala (1981) reports that excavations in the residential areas near El Tiradero revealed materials dating to the Early, Middle, and Late Preclassic, we suspect that the Early Preclassic occupation predates the construction of the MFC complex at El Tiradero and was associated with Aguada Fénix.

## Discussion

### Spread of Standardized Complexes

These data fill a significant gap in our knowledge about the distribution of ceremonial centers in southern Mesoamerica during the Early and Middle Preclassic periods. The spread of those complexes indicates that an interregional interaction network extended across a broad area, including Mexico's southern Gulf Coast, the Grijalva River region of Chiapas and southern Pacific coast of Chiapas and Guatemala, and the western Maya lowlands. Inomata (2017b) refers to this area as the Isthmian Interaction Sphere. These regions shared standardized ceremonial complexes and possibly associated ritual practices, but there were some variations among them, as shown in differences between MFU, MFC, MFG, and VC patterns. The builders of San Lorenzo probably established a prototype of the MFU pattern and the architectural representation of calendrical symbolism based on the number 20. The E Group assemblage may have developed initially on the Pacific coast of Chiapas. Then, it may have been formalized mainly in central and southern Chiapas, and the southwestern Maya lowlands, where Ceibal is located. The inhabitants of the Middle Usumacinta region incorporated those elements from their neighbors and probably played an important role in formalizing the MFU pattern.

The occupants of the Maya lowlands outside Ceibal came into this network of interaction later. The site of Nixtun Ch'ich' on the shore of Lake Petén Itzá in central Petén may have been an important point for the transmission of ideas associated with standardized complexes. Probably around 800 BCE, the members of this community began to build a gridlike layout with multiple E Groups and access patterns similar to those of Aguada Fénix (Pugh and Rice 2017; Pugh 2019; Pugh et al. 2019; Rice 2019). In contrast to the importance of the north-south axis of the MFU pattern, the layout of Nixtun Ch'ich' emphasized the east-west axis. Later lowland Maya communities adopted the E Group assemblage without other elements of the MFU and MFC patterns and retained a loose emphasis on the east-west axis. Aguada Fénix probably was a major hub for the exchanges of these ideas across broad areas. It was connected with Campeche to the northeast through the avenues, with the Petén to the southeast through the San Pedro River, and with Mexico's southern Gulf Coast to the west through the Usumacinta River.

MFU complexes strongly emphasized horizontal monumentality. The monumentality that is expressed in terms of horizontal dimensions is also found in constructions that some hunter-gatherers or mixed subsistence groups made, such as the ancestral Plains Indians and the inhabitants of Amazonia (Brumley 1988; Erickson 2000; Heckenberger et al. 2008; Pärssinen et al. 2009; Carson et al. 2014; Zedeño et al. 2014). The horizontal monumentality of the MFU pattern contrasts with later ceremonial complexes with tall pyramids in Mesoamerica, which were closely tied to social hierarchy and political centralization. We did not find any clear evidence of social inequality in the Middle Usumacinta region for the period 1100 to 700 BCE. The horizontal forms of MFU complexes built during this period possibly facilitated interaction among the participants of ceremonies, who did not have marked social inequality.

This observation implies that during the transition from the Early Preclassic to the Middle Preclassic, the political organization of inhabitants around Aguada Fénix and other sites in the Middle Usumacinta region was different from that of San Lorenzo. It is indicative that we did not find any Olmec-style sculptures associated with MFU sites in the Middle Usumacinta region. The only stone sculpture found at Aguada Fénix shows a naturalistic depiction of a peccary (Inomata et al. 2020). We suspect that the El Mirador stela, acrobat-figure sculptures, and portable objects with Olmec iconography reported from the Middle Usumacinta region date to 800–400 BCE, contemporaneous with La Venta and mostly postdating the construction of MFU complexes. During the transition from the Early to the Middle Preclassic, the inhabitants of the Middle Usumacinta region adopted the spatial template originally established at San Lorenzo but probably did not accept the hierarchical organization of the Olmec center or the iconography representing symbols of political authority. They may even have actively resisted hierarchical organization and associated symbols. This pattern may have changed gradually after 800 BCE, when Olmec iconography spread in the Middle Usumacinta region.

Although we agree with the interpretation that San Lorenzo had hierarchical organization with rulers represented by colossal head sculptures, we also think that the level of social inequality at this Olmec center may have often been overemphasized. Cyphers (Cyphers and Di Castro 2009, 23; Cyphers and Murtha 2014; Cyphers 2016, 96; Arieta Baizabal and Cyphers 2017), for example, suggests that the summit of the San Lorenzo plateau was used primarily by elites while low-status groups lived in surrounding areas. Her excavations do show that elaborate complexes were built along the western edge of the plateau. One example is the Red Palace on Edge Platform 5, and another is Group E (an architectural compound associated with a throne and an aqueduct, which should not be confused with the E Group assemblage) on the southern part of Edge Platform 6 and the northern part of Edge Platform 7. The presence of some red floors in the flat area in the center of the plateau led Cyphers (Cyphers and Murtha 2014; Arieta Baizabal and Cyphers 2017) to argue that elite residential complexes occupied this area. Given the similarity between San Lorenzo and Aguada Fénix discussed above, however, we may need to consider the possibility that this area was an extensive plaza comparable to that of Aguada Fénix, as Diehl (2004) has suggested. Such an open plaza could have had sections with different floor preparations used for various ceremonial purposes. Some of these areas may have had low platforms or have been used for temporary ceremonial structures but may not have had permanent residences. If so, the San Lorenzo plateau may have been an inclusive space for gatherings of numerous participants that included lower-status individuals rather than an exclusive one reserved for elites.

In a similar vein, although we agree that San Lorenzo likely had a larger permanent population than that of Aguada Fénix, it is possible that a significant number of groups that participated in the construction of San Lorenzo retained certain levels of mobility (see Arnold 1999; Rosenswig 2010, 2011; Lesure and Wake 2011). Groups living away from San Lorenzo may have gathered on certain occasions to build the San Lorenzo plateau and to participate in ceremonies held there.

## Temporality of Monument Building

The construction of MFUs and other standardized complexes after 1100 BCE marked a profound social transformation in the Middle Usumacinta region. We also suspect that there was a tradition of practices that provided a basis for monument building. We have little data on the society of this region before the construction of those complexes, but the area was possibly occupied by mobile groups who relied heavily on wild resources along with small-scale maize cultivation. Like many ethnographically known groups, they may have commonly lived in small groups but gathered in larger groups in certain periods of the year. As with the case of the Plains Indians, the time of aggregation was probably the occasion for large communal rituals. Those groups of the preceding period may have built ephemeral ceremonial structures that did not leave archaeologically recognizable traces. After 1100 BCE, the inhabitants of the region transformed these ceremonial buildings into larger and more permanent landmarks.

This practice of residential mobility and seasonable gathering probably continued when MFU and other standardized complexes were constructed although some builders were slowly becoming more sedentary. We have little information on the demographic trend of this period, but we suspect that the significant increase in the number of sites reflects not only the change from ephemeral buildings to larger permanent ones but also rapid population growth. In his review of early monumental constructions in various parts of the world, Charles Stanish (2017, 185–195) suggests that their emergence corresponds with the periods when populations began to increase rapidly. That was probably also the case in southern Mesoamerica.

We have emphasized the lack of marked inequality at Aguada Fénix and related sites to highlight the contrast with San Lorenzo, but this does not mean that the builders of those sites had egalitarian societies. We suspect that there were some individuals with high authority who played a leading role in organizing construction projects and public ceremonies. These individuals may be characterized as emergent elites. We should recall the suggestion Graeber and Wengrow (2021) made that some ethnographically known societies had shifting power structures according to the seasonal cycle of aggregation and dispersal. It presents the intriguing possibility that the builders of Aguada Fénix may also have had seasonal fluctuations in political organization in which stronger power and authority structures may have emerged during periods of collective building activity and festivals. Moreover, although the rulers at San Lorenzo most likely had greater power than the leaders at Aguada Fénix, we may need to consider the possibility that the extent and strength of their power may have changed in a similar cycle.

The spatial arrangements and orientations of the MFU sites and related complexes may reflect the timing of communal rituals. The presence of twenty edge platforms at Aguada Fénix, San Lorenzo, and other sites suggests that those complexes were closely tied to calendrical concepts. The connection of E Groups to the movements of astronomical objects has long been discussed. Some E Group assemblies were oriented to the directions of sunrise on the solstices and quarter days (the midpoint days between the solstices. These days likely served as important calendrical markers rather than equinoxes; identifying equinoxes would have required the identification of the earth's equator or the precise measurement of daytime) (Šprajc 2021b). Others may be associated with the sunrise directions associated with a 260-and-105-day division of a year or intervals of multiples of twenty days from the sun's zenith passage (when the sun passes directly above the observer), but a considerable number of them do not have clear connections with specific astronomical phenomena (Aveni and Hartung 1989; Aveni 2001; Aveni et al. 2003; Freidel et al. 2017; Šprajc 2021a).

Ivan Šprajc, Inomata, and Anthony Aveni (2023) have shown that many of the Formative complexes that we identified in the INGEI lidar were designed to represent concepts associated with the 260-day calendar. This calendar represents a cycle of $20 \times 13$ days and continued to be used in various Mesoamerican societies in later periods. For example, the MFU complex of El Macabil has twenty edge platforms, and its E Group is aligned with sunrise on February 11 and October 29, separated by 260 days. Another MFU complex, Aguada Fénix, also has twenty edge platforms, and the axis of its E Group corresponds to sunrise on February 24 and October 17, separated by 130 days, half of the 260-day cycle. These complexes represent the earliest evidence for the use of the 260-day calendar in Mesoamerica, centuries before these calendrical concepts were written down in texts.

Some scholars have proposed that the 260-day calendar served as an agricultural calendar focused on maize cultivation (Milbrath 1999, 15, 59, 2017; Aveni et al. 2003; Rice 2007, 35–36). For example, referring to the 260-day agricultural calendar of the modern Ch'orti' that Raphael Girard (1962) described, which begins on February 9, Susan Milbrath (1999, 2017a) suggests that Maya E Groups concern similar agricultural scheduling. However, it is questionable whether the agricultural calendars of modern times, which are based on intensive maize agriculture involving two or even more crops a year, can be applied to these early days. The fact that many Mesoamerican groups share the 260-day calendar suggests that this calendrical system originated before the period of MFU complexes, possibly during the Early Preclassic or Archaic periods (Rice 2007, 47, 57; Stuart 2011, 36–37). While some groups in Mesoamerica began to consume significant amounts of maize during the Early Preclassic, many others, including the San Lorenzo Olmecs, appear to have continued to rely heavily on wild resources. If so, the 260-day calendar may have originally been associated with the practices of mixed subsistence rather than with intensive maize agriculture.

In mixed economies or nonintensive maize cultivation, significant labor investment in maize cultivation probably started with burning fields sometime before the beginning of the rainy season. Although clearing primary forests to make cultivation plots can take a long time, we assume that early farmers often chose areas of secondary growth that could be cleared more easily. Burning debris from clearing or previous harvests may have been done between the beginning of April and early May, followed by sowing in May (Nations and Nigh 1980). Even in the intensive agricultural system of the Classic period, the dry season from January through April appears to have been the time for activities other than agriculture, such as construction and war. The epigraphic data that Simon Martin (2020, 224–227, fig. 53) has compiled show that war was more frequent during the dry season. In the famous episode of the Caste War in 1948, the Maya abandoned their attack on Mérida at the beginning of the rainy season to return to their agricultural fields (Reed 2001, 110–111).

Given these observations, we need to consider the possibility that the alignments of many complexes with the sunrise during the period January 20 to April 1 indicate the time when mobile groups left their cultivation fields and gathered around ceremonial complexes for public events. In addition, the height of the dry season in February and March is the best period to catch fish and shells in oxbow lakes and narrowed streams after the water levels of rivers drop (Cyphers and Zurita-Noguera 2012). Since the period before standardized ceremonial complexes were built, these groups had possibly been gathering in those months in locations near rivers, such as Aguada Fénix. This period for gathering was probably the time for ceremonies. Participants in these public events probably began to return to their settlements in April in order to prepare fields for cultivation.

The connection of time reckoning with public ceremonies is suggested by the word *k'in,* which means "day" but also refers to "festival" in many Maya languages (León Portilla 1988, 17–20; Hull 2017). Aguada Fénix and El Macabil, both of which have twenty edge platforms and lines of mounds defining specific directions tied to the 260-day calendar, must have been particularly important places for time reckoning and ceremonies. As various scholars have suggested, these buildings and the E Groups of later periods more likely served to commemorate important calendrical dates and to provide spaces for rituals associated with astronomical cycles than to function as astronomical observatories for the purpose of precise observation (Aveni et al. 2003; Aimers and Rice 2006). It is probable that the organizers of those public ceremonies were also responsible for astronomical observations and time reckoning. Their esoteric knowledge must have been an important basis of their authority and power. These emergent elites provided a prototype for later Maya elites, who were the keepers of time, the organizers of public events, and the protagonists in theatrical performances (see chapter 7, this volume; chapter 9, this volume).

In sum, the orientations of MFUs and related complexes built during 1100–700 BCE possibly expressed the timing of public ceremonies that reflected the general rhythm of life for diverse populations, including incipient maize agriculturalists and practitioners of mixed subsistence. In this sense, those complexes are comparable to early monumental constructions found in other parts of the world. Stanish (2017, 232–264) notes that many of those buildings served as astronomical markers. Astronomical alignments are not limited to complexes built by agriculturalists; they are also found in those made by hunter-gatherers. For example, Poverty Point, which was built by mobile hunter-gatherers, shows alignments with sunset on the solstices and equinoxes (or more likely quarter days) (Brecher and Haag 1983; Aveni 2003, 173). Stonehenge and related sites nearby exhibit alignments with sunrise and sunset on the solstices (Parker Pearson et al. 2006, 239). Remarkably, the constructions of Stonehenge correspond with the period when the Neolithic occupants of Britain almost abandoned cereal cultivation and emphasized the collection of hazelnuts (Stevens and Fuller 2012; Graeber and Wengrow 2021, 105). These examples suggest that the practices of time reckoning through astronomical observation tied to public ceremonies in various parts of the world were rooted in long traditions involving hunter-gatherers, mixed subsistence groups, and early farmers. A comparable tradition probably also existed in Mesoamerica.

## Conclusion

The increasing data on early monumental constructions across the world indicate that it is misleading to assume a fundamental divide in the concepts of time between hunter-gatherers and agriculturalists. Although subsistence practices significantly shaped the rhythms of life, the astronomical alignments expressed at Poverty Point suggest that foragers can develop practices of time reckoning comparable to those of many agricultural societies. As important as the effect of subsistence practices were on the temporality of people's lives, we need to consider other factors, including certain characteristics of languages, such as grammatical tenses, available methods of measuring time, and occurrences of catastrophic events, including natural disasters and epidemics. Various examples of early monumental constructions suggest that sociality, or the mode of social interaction, is particularly important in this regard, including the intensity and extent of interaction among different individuals and the degree of standardization of such behavior—that is, the level of conformity to collective norms. Collective activities require and create temporal coordination among multiple individuals. Such coordination is shaped to a certain degree by the shared practices of subsistence activities and daily routines, but it is also a product of social processes rooted in human agency situated in specific historical contexts. In other words, groups that have similar subsistence practices may develop different concepts of time and different ways of time reckoning. It is also possible that those that have different subsistence practices may possess similar notions of time.

The recent discovery of standardized ceremonial complexes in the Maya lowlands and on Mexico's southern Gulf Coast may provide significant insights about relations between subsistence and temporal concepts. Except for the possible monumental constructions made of shells located on the Pacific coast of Chiapas, monumental complexes in southern Mesoamerica were built when the inhabitants of the regions began to rely significantly on maize cultivation. Before the emergence of those unequivocal monumental buildings in Mesoamerica, there was a long period of mixed subsistence. This makes the distinction between non-agriculturalists and farmers extremely vague. This period, the Archaic, was characterized by the coexistence of groups with diverse subsistence strategies (Rosenswig 2015; Lohse et al. 2021). Like various ethnographically known groups, the Archaic populations of Mesoamerica possibly had traditions of seasonal gathering and public ceremonies. The builders of early ceremonial complexes in southern Mesoamerica still included diverse populations, including mobile mixed subsistence groups, more sedentary agriculturalists, hierarchically organized groups in the Gulf Olmec area, and those without prominent social inequality in the Middle Usumacinta region.

The persisting coexistence of groups with different levels of mobility implies that they followed diverse rhythms of life, creating different temporalities within one region. Ceremonial complexes possibly provided occasions when diverse groups that gathered from distant places could share similar experiences of time. The standardization in spatial configurations and ritual practices also served to regulate people's behavior and concepts. These shared aspects of temporality may have been tied to the cyclicality of the movements of celestial bodies, which were expressed by certain alignments of buildings. These ceremonial spaces, now formalized with durable mounded constructions, probably gave participants the impression that the temporal regime they experienced in ceremonies had perpetual continuity.

These experiences of shared time and the calendrical concepts expressed by ceremonial architecture may have been precursors of the more formalized calendrical systems of later periods, but it is probably misleading to assume that the ethnographically known agricultural calendars of the later Maya are directly applicable to these early periods. Maize agriculture during the transition from the Early to the Middle Preclassic must have been less intensive than that during colonial and modern times. Groups that relied significantly on wild resources must have invested even less labor and resources in maize cultivation. Moreover, the concepts of time associated with the early ceremonial complexes at Aguada Fénix and other early Mesoamerican monuments possibly had deep roots in periods when maize was only a small part of the diet for the majority of people. We need to examine how people's concepts of time and their relations to subsistence practices changed from the Preclassic to the Classic period and then into the Postclassic and colonial times.

The early monumental constructions in southern Mesoamerica, which emerged during a period of profound social changes in terms of subsistence, the degree of sedentism, and political organization, are distinct from some examples from other areas, such as Watson Brake, which did not directly lead to an agricultural or hierarchical society. The relation between social changes and monumental constructions in southern Mesoamerica was likely recursive. While ongoing social transformations provided a condition for the emergence of those buildings, we suspect that construction projects also contributed to further social changes. Despite the persisting diversity in temporal experiences, public gatherings and the construction of ceremonial spaces opened the possibility for further homogenization in temporal concepts in later periods, when most community members followed similar temporalities that were shaped by common agricultural practices and more formalized ritual calendars.

Although the emergent elites of the Early-to-Middle Preclassic transition may have played a leading role in coordinating construction projects and public ceremonies, they probably did not have the power to coerce people to participate in those events. However, the sharing of temporal concepts promoted by such ceremonies and architectural compounds potentially set a stage for the later development of stronger political authorities who came to exert a significant influence on people's experience of time through the royal sponsoring of public rituals, the elaboration of calendars, and taxation at specific points of the year.

## Acknowledgments

Our research in the Middle Usumacinta regions was carried out under a permit granted by the Instituto Nacional de Antropología e Historia with support from the Alphawood Foundation and the National Science Foundation (BCS-1826909). We thank Rodrigo Liendo Stuardo and Keiko Teranishi Castillo for their help.

# 4

## Ordering Time and Space at Yaxnohcah

### Creation and Renewal in a Preclassic Landscape

KATHRYN REESE-TAYLOR, VERÓNICA A. VÁZQUEZ LÓPEZ,
SHAWN G. MORTON, MEAGHAN M. PEURAMAKI-BROWN,
SARAH E. BEDNAR, F. C. ATASTA FLORES ESQUIVEL,
DEBRA S. WALKER, ARMANDO ANAYA HERNÁNDEZ,
AND NICHOLAS P. DUNNING

The intricate cosmovision of the Maya embodies the beliefs and values that underlie daily practices and provide guidance for all aspects of social interactions. One enduring tenet of this philosophy is the temporality of landscape (Broda de Casas 1987; Ashmore 2015). The cultural material, imagery, texts, oral traditions, and public events of the Maya in both the past and the present attest to a fundamental conviction that time and space are intrinsically linked in what Chase and colleagues (chapter 1, this volume) refer to as Maya space-time. Actions of people—and supernatural beings—interweave time and space, akin to the fusing of time and space put forward by Timothy Ingold. Actions literally establish time and space as innate in the carrying out of events (Ingold 1993, 158, 162; Soja 1996, 57).

The fusion of time and space is widely expressed in Maya communities. For example, among the pre-Hispanic Maya, the creation of temporal landscapes via the acts of people and supernatural beings was vividly depicted in the San Bartolo murals. Events such as sacrificial offerings, the rebirth of the Maize lord, and the accession of a ruler on the West Wall and the procession of the Maize lord, the fertilization of the gourd, and the birth of the gourd babies on the North Wall create a series of landscapes, and the narrative sequence of the scenes, which move from one place and event to another, evokes the passage of time (Taube et al. 2010). The seamless juxtaposition of supernatural and earthly episodes emphasizes the parallel processes of creation.

During the postconquest colonial period (1521–1810 CE), Yucatec Maya carried out acts within a ritual cycle involving ordering and movement that gave rise to temporal landscapes. William F. Hanks (1988, 354) draws an equivalence between ritual acts of ordering and the act of "giving birth to the earthly world" (*sih*—to be born, given as a gift), implying that creation is implicit in ritual acts of ordering. Likewise, the Ch'orti' of highland Guatemala believe that as the sun moves through the sky, it creates a temporal landscape in which time and space are irrevocably entangled (Hull 2011).

In this chapter, we draw on archaeological, ethnohistoric, ethnographic, and linguistic studies to understand the entanglement of time and space that animates Maya civic landscapes (Soja 1996). Specifically, we discuss the generative acts of ordering that integrated and shaped the Preclassic city of Yaxnohcah. We hypothesize that acts of ordering, conducted primarily within a ritual context that included processions and acts of burning, created and maintained social and political integrity in the emergent kingdom during the Late Preclassic (300 BCE–200 CE).

## The Temporality of Landscapes among the Maya

In the following sections, we provide a brief overview of studies focused on the creation of landscapes—both ideological and realized—among the Maya (Knapp and Ashmore 1999). We purposefully include an array of data from the Late Preclassic to the present day to demonstrate the enduring constructs that shape space and time among the lowland Maya.

### Directional Almanacs

The relationship between time and space is clearly exemplified in the directional almanacs of the Postclassic (1000–1521 CE) and colonial periods (see chapter 12, this volume). Images in directional almanacs portray schema that consistently involve the 260-day ritual calendar. Most commonly, these calendars are organized into groups of 13 days (*trecenas*). When depicted in a maplike format, the 260 days are presented as an uninterrupted circuit that progresses from one direction to another in a counterclockwise order.

Many painted directional almanacs in central Mexico commonly refer to only four directions in a specific order: east, north, west, and south. The Codex Fejérváry-Mayer and the Codex Tudela are excellent examples of four-directional almanacs (Boone 2007). While graphically similar to the Fejérváry-Mayer, the Aubin Manuscript No. 20 presents five directions: east, north, west, south, and center (Boone 2007). The flow of time is not regularly punctuated by *trecena* days but instead is marked by five-day names. Two hundred and four red dots (spacers) interrupted by four-day names frame the calendar (fifty-one red dots between each day name). The center is encircled by one day name and fifty-one red dots. Together the 255 red dots and the five-day names represent the 260-day ritual calendar. The directions are specific locations with place signs that ground the image in a physical landscape (Boone 2007).

While the directional almanacs described above emphasize cardinal directions, Paxton (2001, 16) argues that the primacy early Maya scholarship gave to the four cardinal directions was misplaced. According to Paxton, the precolonial Maya organized the world into five sectors that corresponded to large swaths of space lying in the east, north, west, south, and center. This five-part division is demarcated by the intercardinal directions, not the cardinal directions, and is plainly referenced in both the Madrid and Dresden codices.

On pages 75–76 of the Madrid Codex, black dots outline the paths between the intercardinal directions and the center. These dots are organized into a series of twenty *trecenas,* dividing the 260-day count into units of 65 days, each of which corresponds to one of the pathways. While it is clear that the smaller black dots on Madrid pages 75–76 represent the passage of days in the 260-day ritual cycle, the symbolism of the 365-day calendar is also present, although less prominent. Footprints leading from the corners to the center are rendered between the outlines of black dots. The southwest, southeast, and northeast paths have four footprints, while the northwest path contains six footprints, for a total of eighteen footprints. Paxton (2001) reasons that each footprint equates to one *winal* (month of 20 days) and that therefore the four paths leading to the center represent one *tun* (year of 360 days). The 5-day *wayeb* (remaining 5 days of the year) is depicted by a row of small dots painted in the southeast corner.

In many contexts, footprints symbolize both the passage of time and movement from one location to another. Paxton (2001) specifically argues that the footprints on pages 75–76 of the Madrid Codex represent the movement of the sun during the tropical solar year, from winter solstice to summer solstice. The black dots representing the individual days of the 260-day calendar also convey a sense of movement. The larger black dots surround the footprints and guide their path, and day signs depicted at either end of each column of black dots show the passage of time as the circuit is followed. Moreover, within contemporary Yucatec Maya ritual discourse, "the day, state of being and destiny of the individual" are said to be that individual's "road" (Hanks 2000, 243). Therefore, the concept of human movement along a circuit is implicit in the directional and temporal ordering depicted in the Madrid Codex.

Paxton (2001) suggests that the 260-day ritual circuit begins in the southeast and moves in a counterclockwise direction. Movement between intercardinal nodes takes thirteen days, while processions from periphery to center and back are conducted in each intercardinal direction, each taking twenty-six days. Concurrently, the solar year is ordered, as indicated by footprints representing *winals*. These footprints proceed from the periphery to the center, following the same path as the days in the 260-day calendar. In the center are depictions of both the sun and the moon deities, which are argued to represent both the 365- and the 260-day calendars and serve to center both the temporal and the spatial order (Paxton 2001).

## The Five-Part Ordering of Space and Time

Paxton's (2001) discussion of the five-part ordering of space delimited by the intercardinal directions resonates well with principles of spatial ordering seen among the ancient Maya. The quincunx, which is an expression of five-part directional ordering emphasizing the intercardinal directions, has been produced using various materials on multiple scales since the Middle Preclassic (900–300 BCE). In the Late Preclassic, caches from Cerros (Freidel et al. 2002) and Caracol (A. Chase and D. Chase 1995, 96) exemplify this ordering principle in small portable artifacts, and the gourd babies' scene in the San Bartolo murals (Saturno et al. 2005; van Akkeren 2006; Taube et al. 2010) exemplify it in larger architectural embellishments. Ruud van Akkeren (2006, 42) suggests that the five-part arrangement of the babies exploding from the gourd represents the birth of the first people, the Sons of Sunrise (dawn), from Tzuywa, the Place of the Gourd, a primordial place of origin. The location of four individuals attached to umbilical cords in the intercardinal directions clearly refers to the solstices, while the individual in the center wears a belt, ear spools, and a headdress, marking him as more significant. Accordingly, the image may reflect the nexus of mythic and historical time—the spatial ordering of the world at the moment of creation—and the social ordering of a civil society with social groups centered by a political or religious order (Saturno 2009; van Akkeren 2006).

During the Early Classic period (200–550 CE), the five-part intercardinal ordering is seen in both artifacts and textual accounts. One of the most striking examples is found in the calligraphic tomb murals of Rio Azul (Stuart 1987; Acuña Smith 2014). With two notable exceptions, all murals depict the quadripartite order: either mountains or directional glyphs mark cardinal points, while the tomb's occupant anchors the center (Stuart 1987; Acuña Smith 2014). In contrast, Tomb 12 contains glyphs depicting both the cardinal and intercardinal directions. Each glyph block in the cardinal direction contains a color correlated with a specific direction and the name of an associated lord or patron. Interestingly, each of the intercardinal glyph blocks contain a toponym associated with a mythic place, suggesting a close connection with an idealized landscape. The glyphs in the southeast direction read AYIIN? CHAN-na (Cosmic Crocodile Sky), the glyph block in the northeast contains the signs WAK NAHB NAL-la (Six Aguada Place), and the glyphs to the southwest are WAK PALAW-wa NAL-la (Six Ocean Place) (Kettunen and Helmke 2013). The most enigmatic glyphs are located in the northwest corner of the tomb; they read YAX ???-le NAL-la (First/Green Watery?? Place; Stuart 1987; Acuña Smith 2014).

Examples of the five-part ordering of the quincunx abound in Late Classic (550–850 CE) architectural layouts, artifact patterns, and textual references. Of note is the stelae program of K'ahk' Tiliw on Platform 1A-1 at Quirigua, which emphasized the intercardinal directions in a sculptural arrangement with the sun as its center. Looper (2014, 178–179) argues that the monuments (Stelae A, C, Zoomorph B in the northwest, and Stela D in the northeast, Stela F in the southeast, and Stela E in the southwest) mark the solstitial points of the sun's movement and partitions the two-dimensional plane along east-west and north-south axes, unifying both time and space. This layout of a public plaza in a quincunx arrangement is also seen at Copán. The stelae program of the Late Classic Copán ruler Waxaklahun Ubaah K'awiil anchored the intercardinal directions in the Great Plaza, reflecting the quadripartite division of the cosmos with the great king at its center (Newsome 2001a).

An emphasis on intercardinal directions is also apparent in non-elite contexts, as indicated by the layout of a Late Classic residential group near the site of Blue Creek in northwestern Belize (Zaro and Lohse 2005; see also Dowd and Milbrath 2015, 41). In this arrangement, cut limestone blocks coated with fine plaster formed the large structure in the center, Structure 1. It measured 11 by 7 meters and contained four rooms: three large chambers in the north, south, and east and one smaller room in the northwest corner. A large entrance in the south room and a smaller door in the east room granted access to the three principal rooms. The outlying mounds consisted of low circular cobble platforms. Archaeologists also recovered features such as a posthole in Structure 1 and a large stone in Structure 2. Among the structures, scholars discovered an astronomical alignment that highlighted the annual passage of the sun, and they conducted an experiment to confirm this alignment. As the sun rose on the morning of the summer solstice, a shadow was cast over the large stone in Structure 2, the southwest platform, from a stadia rod placed in the Structure 1 posthole. Zaro and Lohse (2005, 91) suggest that a post only 3 meters high would have been sufficient to cast a shadow across the large stone in Structure 2. Moreover, this alignment appears to have been maintained in Structure 1 through five construction episodes, including at least one major expansion.

Contemporary practices highlight the continuing importance of the quincunx in Maya cosmology. For example, among the Ch'orti' Maya of southeast Guatemala, mid-twentieth-century accounts of a new-year world-renewal ceremony describe a ritual practice in which priests place five specially selected stones in a quincunx pattern on an altar to create the sacred cosmogram (Girard 1962, 40). The stones are specifically placed in counterclockwise order beginning in the northeast, which is said to be related to the summer and winter solstices (O'Neil 2012, fig. 2.26). Girard (1966) states that this ceremony is a commemoration and repetition of the primordial act of world creation.

## The Social Landscape: Processions, Burning Ceremonies, and Cycles of Time

In the examples discussed above, the ordering of space and time is materialized as an idealized model of actual practices. These practices are inherent in ceremonies past and present, particularly rituals that include processions and burning. This is particularly highlighted in the Madrid Codex with its implied movements through space according to a calendrical cycle.

In the following section, we outline various ritual practices that order space and time with a focus on those in the lowland Maya region. These acts create, animate, and endow coherence to the social landscape, which embodies the web of relationships among people, places, and times. Generative acts shape a shared sense of identity among members of a community, a kingdom, or a territory. For example, by demarcating boundaries both physically and conceptually, people draw a clear distinction between us and not us. In addition, boundaries result in segmentation and places and significant points in time emerge.

## Processions: Ordering the Country

The *tzol peten* is a Postclassic ceremony recorded in *The Book of Chilam Balam of Chumayel*. Hanks (1988, 351) translates *tzol peten* as the "counting out, ordering, explaining (the) country, island, region." Hanks (1988, 354) links the ritual, which involves naming locations, to the causative formation of *sih* (to be born, given as a gift), implying that an underlying generative nature is implicit in the act of ordering. Hanks also suggests that according to the Chilam

Balam, the *tzol peten* is the same act that the Christian God engaged in when he created the world.

The *tzol peten* consisted of a series of visits by members of the nobility to named locations. The *Chilam Balam of Chumayel* names approximately 171 locations that form a regional landscape. The movement of the nobles through the landscape was initially counterclockwise, beginning at P'ool, moving along the north coast past Mérida, then south to Uxmal and finally east to Valladolid, constituting an almost complete loop. The form eventually changed; a second counterclockwise cycle began with Tzóoc, continued to Muxu P'ip', and then became clockwise.

In addition to verbally naming locations, nobles engaged in actions that were encoded in the toponyms. For instance, the place-name Panab-Ha was derived from the act of digging for water that the nobles performed upon their arrival in this location. Paxton (2010, 21) points out that the *tzol peten* is the only known ritual pertaining to the naming of geographic features and settlements.

The *tzol pictun* (counting boundary marker) was another ritual involving boundary maintenance. It was described in the *Chronicle of Yaxkukal* in 1554 (Barrera Vásquez 1984, 10–11). This ordering ritual entailed a sequence of ceremonial visits to stone markers on the perimeter of a generally rectangular pattern. The ritual procession was undertaken by the governor, Ah Macan Pech, accompanied by a retinue of nobles from each territory. For instance, the Nolo people accompanied Ah Macan Pech on his journey eastward, but at the Chen Chac Hil boundary marker, the Nolo people left and the Euan people began to accompany the governor.

In the *Chronicle of Yaxkukal,* the order of events was as follows (Hanks 1987, 674–675, 680; Hanks 1989, 98–101):

A) State the directional phrase.
B) Arrive at the destination point.
C) Name the marker.
D) Leave off one set of neighbors.
E) Pick up the next set of neighbors.
F) Continue pair wise.

One transaction recorded in the *Yaxkukal* document defines the perimeters of the land being sold by referencing the *tzol pictun* (Hanks 2010). In this example, the peregrination was counterclockwise: it began in the northeast corner, moved west to the northwest corner, moved south to the southwest corner, moved east to the southeast corner, and finally moved north to the corner in which the recounting of the survey began (Hanks 2010, 312).

While Hanks (1989) asserts that the *tzol peten* descriptions in the *Chilam Balam of Chumayel* and *tzol pictun* of the *Chronicle of Yaxkukal* were strongly correlated to calendrical cycles, he does not specify which cycle. Paxton (2010, 141), however, argues that the *tzol peten* was explicitly linked to the 260-day count based on what she calls the solar cartography present in the Madrid Codex.

## Processions: New Year Ceremonies

Coe (1965) was the first to note the important relationship between calendrical cycles and spatial layouts of Maya communities in the Yucatán during the Postclassic and colonial periods. In his seminal article, "A Model of Ancient Community Structure in the Maya Lowlands," he specifically linked the Wayeb (New Year) ceremonies to community organization. Coe (1965, 103) argued that the ethnohistoric account of the Wayeb ceremonies by Landa (Tozzer 1941) and in *The Book of Chilam Balam of Chumayel* (Roys 1933) were models of a

> quadripartite division of the ancient Maya community, arranged according to the cardinal directions and with color associations; for the shifting of ritual power among these divisions in a counterclockwise fashion through a cycle of four years; and for the holding of this power by a different principal each year.

For example, during the ceremony preceding a Kan year, a hollow clay image of Kan u Wayeb was installed on a stone platform at the southern entrance to the community. Immediately before the Wayeb, officiants traveled to the southern entrance to collect the statue, which then was placed on a standard and carried to the house of the sponsor, where it remained for the five days of the Wayeb. At the end of this period, the Kan u Wayeb was taken to the eastern entrance, where it stayed for the year. Similar ceremonies were conducted during Muluk, Ik, and Kawak New Year's ceremonies. All cardinal directions were traversed in a counterclockwise progression and the connection between the four corners of the community and the center was renewed (Tozzer 1941, 139–143; Reese-Taylor 2002, 152–153). It is likely that these processions were full sensory experiences and that the movement was also accompanied by incense, dance, music, singing, and speeches, as depicted in the Bonampak murals (Reese-Taylor 2002).

In addition to the New Year's ceremonies Landa recorded, similar practices were recorded elsewhere in Colonial Mesoamerica. Ángel Julián García Zambrano (1994, 219) points out that the political foundation of a community was commonly expressed through the cosmological act of creating the four directions and the center of the world. For instance, a quadripartite patterning was established during the rotation of the *regidor* offices through the four wards of Tekanto, Yucatán, during the late colonial period (Thompson 1985).

Rogelio Valencia Rivera (2019) has identified a Classic period (250–900 CE) processual circuit that involved carrying an image of K'awiil to stations located on the four cardinal points of a city. For instance, Stela K from Quirigua specifically references the rest of K'awiil at a station during ritual peregrination (Valencia Rivera 2019, 131). This circuit seems to share many of the features of the New Year's ceremonies, although it was scheduled according to the 819-day count cycle. Like other cycles of time, the 819-day count had spatial significance. Cycles of 819 days were bundled into groups of four totaling 3,276 days and each cycle of 819 days in the bundle was associated with one of the four cardinal directions (Pharo 2014, 349).

A variety of cultural material attests to the time depth of the New Year and similar ceremonies. One Late Postclassic (ca. CE 1450) cache deposit from Santa Rita Corozal in northern Belize contained a group of figurines that included four yearbearer figures standing on the backs of turtles letting blood from their genitals (D. Chase 1985a; D. Chase and A. Chase 1988, figs. 24 and 25; D. Chase and A. Chase 2008; chapter 14, this volume). Another configuration of four God N turtle effigies was found in a Late Postclassic cache deposit in a colonnaded building at Mayapán in northern Yucatán, Mexico (Taube 1988b, 186). The west wall of Las Pinturas at San Bartolo also strongly parallels the New Year's ceremonies depicted in the deposit from Santa Rita Corozal and on pages 25–28 of the Dresden Codex. In the San Bartolo murals and the Dresden Codex, the same series of four sacrifices are offered beneath a World Tree set in each of the cardinal directions (Taube et al. 2010). The same individual makes the sacrificial offerings under each tree and in each scene he is practicing genital auto-sacrifice, like the figures on the backs of turtles from Santa Rita Corozal. Harrison-Buck and colleagues (2018) suggest that blood sacrifice, particularly by young men, is essential for renewal in New Year's ceremonies among contemporary Maya, just as it was in the distant past, while Christensen (2016) points out that during Wayeb ceremonies recorded by Landa, participants, especially boys, drew blood and anointed the stone on which the effigy was placed. These examples demonstrate both a marked consistency and community renewal in Maya ritual practices related to the New Year and other significant cycles of time from 200 BCE to 1500 CE.

## Fire Rituals: New Fire Ceremonies

The ceremony that celebrates the beginning of a new 52-year cycle[1] is known as the New Fire ceremony or the Binding of Years (*xiumolpilli* in Nahuat). The ceremony commemorated world renewal and was the reenactment of the sun's birth from a divine turquoise hearth. Sahagún (1982) retrospectively recorded the Binding of Years in 1507. It commenced when the Pleiades, known as the fire-drill constellation among the Mexica people, reached zenith in the night sky. The heart of a sacrificial victim was extracted and fire was drilled in the empty chest cavity by priests. Once lit, the fire was taken from the hill (chest?) and distributed to the people. In the Codex Borbonicus, which depicts the New Fire ceremony of the Mexica, four priests are shown carrying a bundle of sticks signifying years. These priests serve a similar function as the Ah Toks of the burner ceremonies: lighting and tending the New Fire.

Fash et al. (2009) have convincingly argued that at Teotihuacan, the *adosada* of the Pyramid of the Sun was the location of the New Fire ceremony, based on the sculptural program placed inside the temple on the summit of that platform. Three of the four carvings depicted bundles of years (*xiumolpilli*). During the Classic period in the Maya lowlands, fire drilling was performed in the Wiinte' Naah, a structure first identified by Stuart (2000). This building, which has been identified at a number of cities, is associated with Early Classic dynastic founders and with Teotihuacan symbolism (Nielsen 2006; Fash et al. 2009). The cross-torch bundles found in the Late Classic glyph naming this type of structure reference the building as a place of fire ritual and burning (Stuart 2000; Taube 2004a). This suggests that world-renewal ceremonies involving fire drilling and associated with the 52-year cycle may have been conducted by the late fourth century in the Maya lowlands.

## Fire Rituals: Burner Ceremonies

Burning incense appeared to be a crucial act in ceremonies that created or ordered space. According to Landa, the smoke from the incense cleansed the ritual area, while Hull and Carrasco (2004) note that the contemporary Ch'orti' cense the four corners of their communities with copal each year for protection. Other scholars (García Zambrano 1994; Rice 1999; Limón 2001) maintain that the smoke from the incense established the boundaries of the ritual space. Vogt (1993), however, argues that the censing of "ordered" space asserted the exclusive rights of the inhabitants over their territory.

One specific ritual known as the "burner ceremonies" marked the 65-day burner periods of the 260-day calendar in a less-well-known ritual cycle.

These periods appear to have been celebrated among contemporary male and female religious specialists of Momostenango in highland Guatemala (Tedlock 1983), among the Postclassic and Colonial Maya of the northern lowlands (Taube 1988b, 178), among the Postclassic and Colonial Nahua people of highland Mexico, and among the Zapotec people of Oaxaca (Durán 1971, 396–397; Alcina Franch 1993, 181–183). Among the Zapotec, the 65-day periods (*cociyo*) are associated with the 260-day calendar and each *cociyo* is associated with a particular quarter of the world (de la Cruz 2002; Justeson and Tavárez 2007; Lind 2015). Stuart (2011, 144–146) has also suggested that the Classic Maya of the southern lowlands observed burner ceremonies.

According to Colonial documents, burner ceremonies were conducted in a circuit, incorporating places associated with the cardinal directions (Craine and Reindorp 1979, 20). Exact timing of events and movements in a counterclockwise pattern from location to location were carefully choreographed within a widespread landscape. Burner ceremonies consisted of five fire ceremonies conducted during four discrete days within the 65-day burner periods (Craine and Reindorp 1979). The ceremonies served to subdivide the burner periods into three 20-day periods and one five-day period. Each fire ritual was performed by one of the four Ah Toks (he of the fire).[2] Both the 65-day period and the intervals of twenty days and the one-time unit of five days could begin only on one of four days. Chicchan was identified with the east and the color red, Oc with the north and the color white, Men with the west and the color black, and Ahau with the south and the color yellow (Thompson [1962] 1991, 100).[3] The day numbers (10, 4, 11, and 3) remain consistent throughout the ritual cycle (Craine and Reindorp 1979, 20n3, 178):

On 10 Chicchan, 10 Oc, 10 Men, and 10 Ahau

1) the burner (*ahtoc*) brings forth the fire (*u ch'a k'ak*) and
2) lights the fire (*u hopal u k'ak ahtoc*)

On 4 Chicchan, 4 Oc, 4 Men, 4 Ahau

3) the burner runs (*y alcaba ahtoc*)

On 11 Chicchan, 11 Oc, 11 Men, 11 Ahau

4) the burner extinguishes the fire (*u tup k'ak ahtoc*)

On 3 Chicchan, 3 Oc, 3 Men, 3 Ahau

5) the burner takes the fire (*u dcha k'ak ah toc*)

Many sixteenth-century texts from New Spain recorded the burner ceremonies. Several of the directional almanacs found in books from the central highlands, such as the Codex Borgia, the Codex Vaticano B, and the Codex Fejérváry-Mayer, depicted the 65-day burner periods. Burner ceremonies were also recorded in books from the Yucatán, including the Codex Pérez and the Book of Chilam Balam of Maní, two of the books Don Juan Pérez, the mayor of Peto, Yucatán, collected in 1835 (Crane and Reindorp 1979). They are also documented in *The Book of Chilam Balam of Chumayel* (Roys 1933), the Chilam Balam of Tizímin, the Dresden Codex, the Madrid Codex (Rice 2004), and the Kaua (Craine and Reindorp 1979, 21). The almanac in the Dresden Codex (D. 31b–35b) includes four sets of dates, which include both yearbearer and "burner" fire rituals. The sets of dates are separated by a thirteen-year period; this results in a Calendar Round cycle (Vail and Looper 2015). Finally, Landa (Tozzer 1941, 162) recorded a festival and a fire ceremony called Tupp Kak, whose main purpose was to ensure sufficient rainfall for a good harvest. R. C. E. Long (1923; Rice 2004, 246) suggests that the Tupp Kak ceremony is synonymous with *u tup k'ak ahtoc* (the burner extinguishes the fire) in the burner ritual cycle.

Rice (2004) has proposed that burner ceremonies may have origins deep in Mesoamerican prehistory. The burner days, Chikchan, Ok, Men, and Ajaw, were also yearbearers in the Olmec calendar (Edmonson 1988, 21, 231). Although yearbearer days changed several times during the course of Maya calendrical history, this particular set seems to have been venerated through burner ceremonies for more than 2,000 years.

## Other Fire Rituals

While burner ceremonies are well documented for the Late Postclassic and later periods, evidence from the Classic period indicates that other fire rituals were common. Grube (2000) has identified a "fire sequence" associated with Initial Series inscriptions in texts from various sites. The sequence consists of three glyphs between Glyph A of the Initial Series and the solar year day sign. The first sign is a verb that connotes fire manipulation, such as lighting, burning, or dousing (Grube 2000, 96). The middle sign reads *u k'ak'il* (his fire), which is followed by a deity head, most commonly consisting of various forms of the sun god, or God N. Different verbs appear to be associated with specific deities: *puuk* (scatter fire) is associated with the jaguar god of the underworld; *joch* (drill fire) with the God N opossum; *til* (burning) with Chak Xib Chahk; and *jatz* (lightning or hitting stones) with the sun god.

More recently, Bernal Romero (2014; 2016, 111) has identified other instances of fire drilling associated with an aspect of God N, Pawaaj Sahb'in, a personification of Saturn. In several examples—from the sites of Palenque,

Yaxchilan, Motul de San José, Laxtunich, and Ek' Balam—the fire-drilling ritual occurred on the sixth day of the seven-day cycle and the first day in the nine-day Lords of the Night cycle, with GI as the patron deity. The distances between the dates recorded for this ritual among the various sites all coincide with multiples of a 63-day cycle (Bernal Romero 2016, 116).

Bernal Romero (2014) suggests that the event could be associated with the "light the fire" (*tihl k'ak'*) act in Grube's fire sequence and the second event in the burner ceremony sequence. The 63-day cycle does not align with the 65-day cycle set by the burner ceremonies, but was associated with the 378-day cycle of the synodic period of Saturn as well as the greater 819-day count, which may have been used to calculate the synodic orbits of both Saturn and Jupiter (Milbrath 1999).[4] Therefore, it seems likely that similar rituals involving fire were used to commemorate multiple cycles of time during the Classic period.

In addition to burning rituals that are tied to calendrical cycles, several scholars (LeFort 2000; Eberl and Graña-Behrens 2004; Sheseña Hernández 2015) have proposed that processions and fire offerings were a part of royal accession ceremonies. In this instance, the cycles of time followed were generational in duration, as a succession of kings was ordered.

Rituals involving fire and incense burning were important in Preclassic society as well. Imagery from Izapa and the Olmec region shows people holding torches and sitting facing each other over a fire or incense burner (Rice 2004, 248). The Late Preclassic murals at San Bartolo (West Wall) depict the importance of the fire ritual, the three-stone hearth, and the four directional corner trees in relation to one of the fundamental duties of the ruler: establishing and maintaining the cosmos and the territory (Taube et al. 2010, 21–25). Hearth and fire ceremonies may also have been intrinsically linked to creation. As Stuart (1998b) points out, placing fire within a new structure figuratively makes it a home by creating a hearth. Likewise, placing fire throughout a landscape may also figuratively create a home at large—in other words, a kingdom.

## The Civic Landscape of Yaxnohcah

We now assess the material correlates of spatial and temporal ordering in the Preclassic landscape of Yaxnohcah in Campeche, Mexico. We specifically seek to identify the generative practices of ordering the inhabitants of Yaxnohcah enacted during the Late Preclassic that supported the emergence of an integrated social and political landscape, a kingdom.

Yaxnohcah is situated in the heart of the Central Karstic Uplands, an area in the center of the Yucatán Peninsula with an elevation of between 180 and

430 meters above sea level. The settlement extends over 40 square kilometers throughout an upland expanse punctuated by two wetlands (*bajos*), the Bajo Laberinto to the north and the smaller Bajo Tomatal to the south of the central precinct. A total of twenty-three civic complexes—including buildings with religious, administrative, or communal functions and large accessible plazas ideal for public gatherings—have been identified to date, and excavations by the Proyecto Arqueológico Yaxnohcah have revealed an occupation spanning from the Middle Preclassic through the Late Postclassic period (900 BCE–1450 CE).

Since 2011, project researchers have investigated the factors that contributed to the establishment, growth, and success of this urban landscape through lidar prospection, ground verification, and archaeological excavations (Reese-Taylor and Anaya Hernández 2013; Anaya Hernández et al. 2016; Anaya Hernández and Reese-Taylor 2017). The lidar survey, which was conducted in 2014, has been crucial for identifying the magnitude and plan of the settlement. The most imposing of Yaxnohcah's architectural groups consists of four large civic complexes in the central precinct and four additional civic complexes, each larger than 8,000 square meters in area, located at the intercardinal directions. In addition, smaller civic complexes, marketplaces, roads, water reservoirs, and agricultural features are scattered over 42 square kilometers (Reese-Taylor et al. 2016). The dispersed, radial layout of Yaxnohcah is similar to that of other settlements in the Maya lowlands, particularly Caracol and Coba. One important difference between Yaxnohcah and these two sites, however, is that the bulk of Yaxnohcah's civic architecture was constructed in the Preclassic period.

**Description of the Civic Plan of Yaxnohcah: The Central Precinct**

The Yaxnohcah central precinct is composed of four civic complexes. The Alba, Carmela, and Esma complexes each contain triadic arrangements, while the Brisa complex houses an E Group. Alba 1, the northernmost complex, is the largest architectonic compound by height and volume. It consists of a triangular triadic grouping with the apex structure in the north (Alba 1a). Alba 1b is the western structure and Alba 1c is the eastern structure in the triad. Alba 1 faces south with an orientation of 14° east of north (fig. 4.1a).

Alba 1 measures roughly 25 meters in height from the base of the truncated platform, which is 3,087 square meters in area. The complex platform on which Alba sits is massive, measuring 52,957 square meters in area and 10 meters in height on its eastern edge, which overlooks the Bajo Tomatal. It is clear that the builders took advantage of the escarpment to emphasize the imposing nature of this complex.

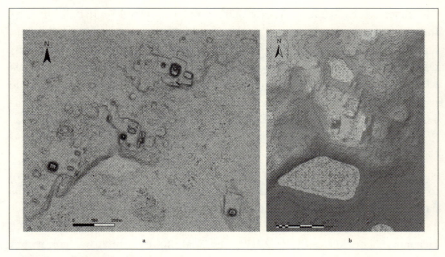

Figure 4.1. (*a*) Central precinct of Yaxnohcah, (*b*) Brisa E Group. Image 4.1a created by Kathryn Reese-Taylor using lidar data, image 4.1b created by F. C. Atasta Flores Esquivel using lidar data, © Proyecto Arqueológico Bajo El Laberinto (PABEL).

Carmela 1 is the triadic arrangement situated on the southwestern corner of the Carmela platform. Carmela 1's layout consists of an in-line triad constructed on a low platform that covered the southern half of the plaza atop the truncated platform. Carmela 1a is the center platform of the triad, Carmela 1b is the western platform, and Carmela 1c is the eastern platform. Carmela 1a is located 938 meters to the southwest of Alba 1a.

Carmela 1 is 26 meters in height from the base of the truncated platform and faces north at an orientation of 18° east of north. The base of the truncated platform of Carmela 1 measures 2,350 square meters in area. The complex platform on which Carmela 1 and its adjacent ballcourt sit measures 36,800 square meters in area and rises 8 meters from the floor at the edge of the Bajo Tomatal.

The Esma triadic group (Esma 1) is a triangular arrangement that sits at the south end of the platform. Esma 1 consists of a larger apex structure in the south, Esma 1a, and two very low-lying platforms: Esma 1c on the east and Esma 1b on the west. Esma 1c consists only of a single course of stones and is not distinguishable in the lidar data. Esma 1a is situated 1,096 meters east of Carmela 1a and 938 meters southeast of Alba 1a.

Esma 1 is 16 meters in height from the base of the truncated platform, 20 meters from the base of the platform on which the complex sits, and 23 meters from the floor at the edge of the Bajo Tomatal that surrounds the complex on three sides. Like Alba 1, the triadic group is oriented 14° east of north. In addition, the orientation from the top of Carmela 1a to the top of Esma 1a skews 14° south of east. The overall area of the Esma civic complex is 14,780 square meters.

The Brisa complex is an E Group that lies in the center of this vast dispersed settlement, which stretches over 42 k square kilometers. Massive platforms with ramps that segue seamlessly into sacbes surround the E Group. A long sacbe links the platform of the Alba complex to a ball court adjacent to and immediately north of the Brisa complex, establishing a strong north-south orientation for the main civic precinct. Triadic groups and other elaborate civic structures are situated on these platforms (fig. 4.1b).

The Brisa complex sits on a platform that rises above the surrounding ground surface by 13 meters on the east side, 6 meters on the north side, and 8 meters on the west side but by an astonishing 30 meters on the south side. The E Group has a cenote-style eastern structure (A. Chase and D. Chase 1995, 2017a) that measures 9.5 meters in height from the plaza surface and a western structure that is 16 meters in height from the plaza (Reese-Taylor 2017). The E Group is oriented 11° south of east and commemorates dates in the 365-day calendar (Reese-Taylor 2017).

To the north lies a large multiroom residential structure 6 meters in height above the plaza; in the south, a smaller civic structure rises 5.5 meters in height above the plaza. There is no doubt that the E Group would have seemed very imposing when viewed from the south, which provides the most unobstructed vantage point; it towered above the surrounding landscape by as much as 46 meters.

The Brisa Reservoir lies immediately south of the E Group. This water storage feature appears to have been constructed between 900 and 700 BCE, based on the exclusive presence of early Middle Preclassic ceramics in the defining berm. It is one of the largest and earliest reservoirs known to date in the Maya lowlands. The reservoir is enormous with a surface area of over 28,000 square meters and a capacity exceeding 84,000 cubic meters, but it was somewhat rudimentary. It was created by walling off a section of the Bajo Tomatal adjacent to an angled quarried limestone scarp lying below the Brisa E Group. No floor was added to the reservoir, which relied on the slow permeability of the underlying *bajo* clay soil to retain water.

### Description of the Civic Plan of Yaxnohcah: Intercardinal Civic Groups

The intercardinal civic groups—Fidelia, Jacinta, Grazia, and Leonora—are situated in a zone that is 1.7 to 2.5 kilometers from the center of the Brisa E Group. Each consists of a large architectural complex with accessible plazas for public gatherings (fig. 4.2a–d).

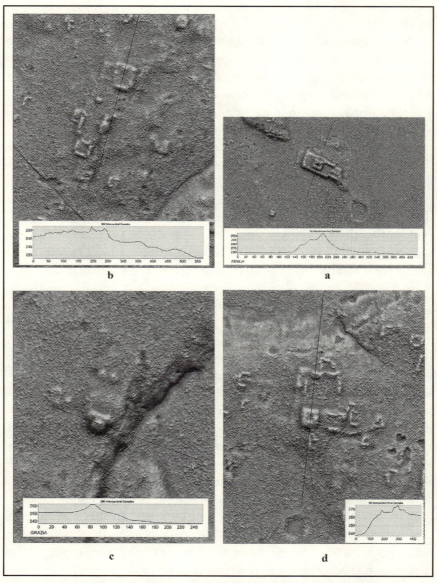

Figure 4.2. The four civic groups located within 2.5 kilometers of the Brisa E Group: (*a*) Fidelia complex, (*b*) Jacinta complex, (*c*) Grazia complex, (*d*) Leonora complex. All images created by Kathryn Reese-Taylor using lidar data, © Proyecto Arqueológico Bajo El Laberinto (PABEL).

*Northeast.* The massive Fidelia platform and its superstructures constitute the northeastern civic complex (fig. 4.2a). The truncated platform atop the Fidelia platform supports eight smaller structures in an arrangement known as the Eight House of the North (Reese 1996; Reese-Taylor and Walker 2002; Šprajc 2008). This arrangement consists of an apex structure in the north center of the truncated platform surrounded by seven smaller platforms in the cardinal and intercardinal directions. The apex structure in the Eight House of the North arrangement faces south. The Fidelia civic complex, including the Eight House of the North, is oriented 24° east of north.

Fidelia rises 25 meters from the surrounding terrain. The basal platform is 11 meters in height, while the truncated platform rises an additional 6.5 meters from the surface of the Fidelia plaza. The apex superstructure adds another 8.5 meters of height to the complex. The Fidelia platform is large: 285 meters east-west, 118 meters north-south, and 28,389 square meters in area. It is the largest civic construction outside of the central precinct at Yaxnohcah.

*Northwest.* The Jacinta complex comprises the northwest intercardinal group (fig. 4.2b). A total of eighteen medium to small structures were built atop a low-lying, elongated platform. The three small shrines along the northern edge of the complex argue for a civic function for the group, although it is likely there were also residences within this complex. This group also seems to function as a sacbe terminus. The northwest sacbe ends at a platform immediately to the southeast of the Jacinta complex.

The outcropping on which the Jacinta complex is constructed rises sharply from the Bajo Laberinto, located directly to the north, and the builders took full advantage of the natural escarpment. From this perspective, the architectural complex appears to tower 20 meters above the edge of the *bajo*. In reality, however, the platform is only 2 meters tall and the structures themselves are quite modest. The tallest structures are only 4 meters above the plaza surface, while the majority of the structures rise 1–2 meters above the plaza surface. The Jacinta platform measures 236 meters northeast-southwest and 90 meters northwest-southeast at its widest point. The area of the complex is 15,966 square meters.

*Southwest.* The Grazia complex consists of a triadic arrangement (Grazia 1) on the southern elevated section of a low-lying platform (fig. 4.2c). A small ball court lies directly to the north of the triadic complex in a lower section of the platform. Grazia 1a is the apex structure of the triad and sits on the southern edge of the truncated platform. Grazia 1b is the western platform and Grazia 1c is the eastern platform in the triad. The triadic arrangement faces north. The orientation of the triadic group is 14° east of north. A sacbe lies 0.62 kilometers to the northwest and would have facilitated movement from this zone to the central civic precinct.

Grazia 1 is 8 meters in height above the plaza floor and 12.5 meters in height from the surrounding terrain at its lowest point. Like other complexes at Yaxnohcah, the builder also took advantage of the bajo margins to create a more impressive vista. Grazia is perched on an escarpment overlooking the Bajo Laberinto to the east and, as a result, rises 24.5 meters above the bajo floor. The overall area of the complex is 8,415 square meters, the smallest of the intercardinal complexes.

We encountered a complex feature embedded in the plaza surface along the centerline of the Grazia triadic complex that consisted of a hearth and an adjacent cache (fig. 4.3a). The oval-shaped, slightly concave hearth is defined by layers of burned stones that measured 10–15 centimeters in length; its dimensions were approximately 80 centimeters east-west and 50 centimeters north-south. Inside the feature, we encountered sherds and a dark gray sediment with large charcoal inclusions. The charcoal inclusions increased in frequency under the upper layer of stones. The dark gray sediment, burned stones, and the high amount of charcoal suggest repeated burning activities (Vázquez López 2017, 18, 20–21).

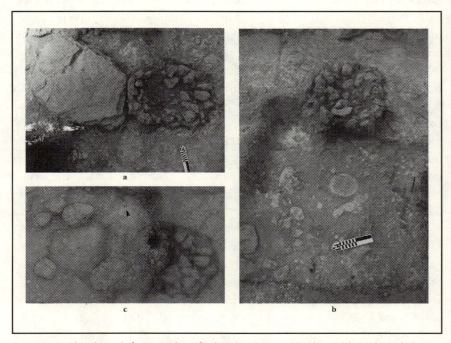

Figure 4.3. Altar-hearth feature identified at the Grazia complex: (*a*) hearth and altar, (*b*) hearth and cache under altar, (*c*) hearth and three stones supporting altar. Photo by Verónica A. Vázquez López, © Proyecto Arqueológico Bajo El Laberinto (PABEL).

The hearth was placed in the plaza surface after the construction of Floor 2. The builders cut into the surface of Floor 2 and through Floor 3 and its fill, constructing the hearth directly atop Floor 4, a compacted sascab surface.

The cache was located directly west of the hearth and was capped with a very hard, plain limestone block. This block was an asymmetrical oval shape; one half is more rounded than the other and measures $1 \times 0.67 \times 0.15$ meters. The block rested on three medium-sized stones—all approximately 30–40 cm in length and set in a triangular pattern—and most likely served as an altar. Beneath this altar, in the center of the triadic stone arrangement, we encountered a complete Sierra Red bowl that was deposited upside-down within a light gray matrix (figs. 4.3b, c). No material was recovered from within the cache vessel.

Two carbon samples were taken from the hearth and the ceramic cache. The sample from the cache returned a date of 70 BCE–20 CE, while the sample from the hearth returned a date of 70–220 CE. The evidence from the ceramic analysis and the radiocarbon dates suggest that while both the cache and the hearth were placed during the Terminal Preclassic (200 BCE–200 CE), they may not have been contemporaneous. It is possible that the hearth was constructed after the cache was placed but it is also possible that both the hearth and the cache were constructed during a single ritual act and that the hearth continued to be used in repeated burning activities.

Due to the strategic location of the hearth, which is situated on the plaza and aligned with the center of the main structure of the triadic group, we suggest that the hearth and the altar constitute a single ritual tableau associated with burnt offerings. The association of the triadic architectural arrangement, the triadic stone arrangement, and the hearth is a very compelling argument for the symbolic equivalency of Late/Terminal Preclassic triadic groups with the three primordial hearthstones.

*Southeast.* The southeast civic complex, Leonora, is known only from lidar prospection; ground verification is pending. The Leonora complex consisted of a low-lying platform with a truncated platform in the southwest corner and several long, low rectangular structures around the perimeter (fig. 4.2d). There is also a low rectangular platform placed 11 meters east and parallel to the west edge of the platform.

The truncated platform has three superstructures: an apex structure in the center of the southern edge, one platform on the eastern edge, and one platform on the northern perimeter. If there was a western structure forming a triadic group, it would have been very low and would not be easily discernible on the lidar, perhaps similar to Esma 1c, which is formed by a single course of stone blocks.

The apex structure of the truncated platform rises 8 meters from the surface of the platform, 12 meters from the immediately surrounding terrain, and 38 meters from the surface of the Bajo Tomatal immediately to the north. The view of this complex from the north, an area that included the central precinct, would have been striking. The Leonora complex covers 12,600 square meters in area and is oriented 8° east of north.

## The Civic Plan

The three main architectural complexes in the central precinct of Yaxnohcah form an isosceles triangle: Alba to the north, Carmela to the southwest, and Esma to the southeast (Flores Esquivel and Šprajc 2008). The E Group complex (Brisa) lies in the center of that triangle. The triadic arrangement of the central precinct is embedded within a four-directional spatial arrangement. Each of the four intercardinal directions corresponds to a civic complex located at a distance of 1.7 to 2.5 kilometers from the center of the Brisa E Group. The overall plan of Yaxnohcah emphasizes a quadripartite segmentation of the settlement that has a triadic arrangement of civic architecture at its center, a five-part ordering of space (fig. 4.4).

The plan appears to have been conceived early in the history of the city. Excavations in several of the complexes suggest that the design may have originated in the Middle Preclassic but was not fully realized until the Late Preclassic. Investigations in the plazas of Alba, Brisa, Grazia, and Fidelia have revealed Middle Preclassic platforms in each. Subsequent construction during the Late or Terminal Preclassic resulted in their final form, with the exception of Brisa, which continued to be expanded throughout Yaxnohcah's history. Test excavations and documentation of looters' trenches at Carmela 1 also indicate a final construction phase during the Late Preclassic.

The precision of the layout is genuinely remarkable. The orientation and dimensions of the central isosceles triangle are exact. Alba 1 is oriented 14° east of north and the sight line between Carmela 1a and Esma 1a has an alignment of 104°. This skews the entire triangle to 14° east of north. The distance between the centers of Alba 1a and Carmela 1a and the centers of Alba 1a and Esma 1a is exactly 938 meters. The distance between the centers of Carmela 1a and Esma 1a is 1,096 meters. At Tikal also, there is a triangular arrangement in the epicenter formed by raised causeways that connect complexes in the north, south, and west. However, this layout appears to lack the precision of the Yaxnohcah plan (Wagner et al. 2013, 21; Stavrakis-Pulston 2015). In addition, two of the three complexes, Alba and Carmela, appear to have been built during the Terminal Preclassic, around 100 BCE, indicating that the final plan was completed at this time. Esma is unexcavated. However,

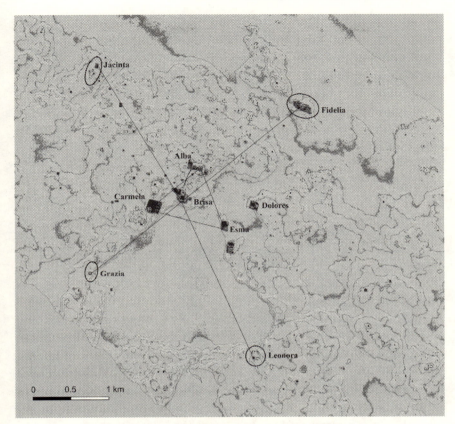

Figure 4.4. Map of Yaxnohcah with astronomical alignments of Preclassic major complexes. All images created by Kathryn Reese-Taylor using lidar data, © Proyecto Arqueológico Bajo El Laberinto (PABEL).

based on ceramics recovered from excavations, we know that Eva, located directly south of Esma, was constructed prior to 100 BCE (Uriarte Torres 2016; Kupprat et al., forthcoming). It is plausible to suggest that the Maya shifted the location of the temple platform on this peninsula to the north during the Terminal Preclassic to accommodate the formal triadic layout of the civic center.

Additionally, the apex structures of Grazia 1, Brisa 1, and Fidelia 1 are arranged in a straight line of sight, along an angle of 50° east of north. This covers a distance of 3,830 meters. The preciseness of this alignment could only have been achieved if the builders had intentionally sighted to the other two structures as they planned and constructed the third. No such alignment exists for the Jacinta and Leonora complexes.

## Description of the Civic Plan of Yaxnohcah: Alignments

While it is clear that the spatial layout of Yaxnohcah closely adheres to the trope of the quincunx, the temporalization of the landscape is cloudier. After all, we do not have the advantage of being able to speak with the architects, planners, and residents of ancient Yaxnohcah. Moreover, because Yaxnohcah has no texts or imagery, our window into the temporality of the landscape is even more limited. Yet the architecture of Yaxnohcah is rich in astronomical alignments and orientations that provide insights.

The 365-day solar year cycle is denoted in alignments and orientations that mark the summer or winter solstices. The Brisa E Group faces east-west with an alignment of 101° between Brisa 3 and Brisa 1.[5] I have argued previously that E Groups with this alignment commemorate the 365-day solar year calendar (Reese-Taylor 2017). Šprajc (2008, 2018) contends that the 11° azimuth demarcates the sunrise on February 22 and October 20, representing periods of 120 days on either side of the summer solstice and implying a correlation with the 365-day solar year.

In addition, two of the intercardinal nodes have distinct associations with solstice azimuths. The orientation of the Fidelia platform, the northeast node, is 114° (Šprajc 2008), which falls within the range of error (±2°) for the azimuths of the winter solstice sunrise (115° to 116°10′) and the summer solstice sunset (294° 50′ to 296°) in this latitude. While the alignment from Grazia 1a to the Dolores 1a is 66° 25′, which falls within the range of error (±2°) for the azimuths of the summer solstice sunrise (64° to 65° 50′). The alignment from Dolores to Grazia 1a is 246° 25′, which marks the winter solstice sunset (243° 50′ to 245°) (Tichy 1991; Milbrath 1999, 19; Aveni and Hartung 2000; Aveni 2001; Šprajc 2001, 2009; Aveni et al. 2003; Rice 2004).

The 260-day ritual cycle is also observed in the alignments of Yaxnohcah. Alignments and orientations of 14° are common in the main civic precinct.[6] Alba 1 and the Grazia 1 triadic group are oriented 14° east of north. The alignment between Carmela 1a and Esma 1a is 104° east of north, offset by 90° from 14° east of north. The azimuth 14° east of north records sunrises on February 12 and October 30, an interval of 260 days, and is commonly interpreted as marking important days within the sacred calendar (Aveni and Hartung 1986; Šprajc 2008). Furthermore, given the prevalence of triadic arrangements associated with this azimuth, it is possible that the 14° azimuth is associated with the celestial triangle in Orion called the "three hearthstones," which is closely linked to the maize agricultural cycle (Love 1994; Looper 1995; Taube 1998; Bricker and Bricker 2007; Vail and Hernández 2013, 388). Beginning in 500 BCE, Orion was invisible in the night sky from April 23 to

June 12; it disappeared as maize was first planted and reappeared as the new maize plants were sprouting (Milbrath 1999, 2017a). In fact, Milbrath (1999) equates the 260-day calendar beginning in February with the duration of the agricultural cycle in Maya region.

Timekeeping, then, seems to be embedded within the placement of structures in the Yaxnohcah landscape and is particularly prominent in the spatial relationships between complexes. Temporal cycles, including the 365-day calendar, the 260-day calendar, and the life cycle of maize, among others, were commemorated in the built environment, giving birth to civic order. Our analysis of alignments and azimuths further demonstrates that the concept of the Calendar Round was present by 200 BCE at Yaxnohcah (cf. Milbrath 2017a, 2017b, 2019).

## Generative Acts of Ordering in the Landscape of Yaxnohcah

By itself, the presence of astronomical alignments associated with the 260- and 365-day calendars does not create a dynamic social landscape. As previously discussed, it is a palimpsest of actions that endows coherence and meaning to space and time and frames relationships among groups of people, intervals of time, and distinct places that develop as social landscapes mature.

One prominent class of generative acts involves movement. Processions progressed from locale to locale according to a specific calendar, segmenting space and time and establishing places and significant points in time. In the *tzol peten,* both the boundaries of the countryside and places along the way are identified. Places are named and people are linked to them through their participation in the processions. The identity of the kingdom is (re)established, as well as that of the specific communities that make up the larger political body. Likewise, the boundaries of the city were reaffirmed and the relationship between the political center and the constituent groups that reside in each quadrant was reinforced each year during the New Year and other ceremonies (Coe 1965).

We hypothesize that a processual circuit involving the central civic precinct and the four intercardinal architectural complexes was present at Yaxnohcah during the Late Preclassic. The alignments and orientations of early structures at Yaxnohcah, including Brisa E Group, Fidelia, and Grazia, were related to the solstices, and it is probable that early ceremonies involving movement were scheduled according to the 365-day calendar. While it is impossible to know with certainty how the route was initiated, we suggest that movement from the Brisa E Group to Fidelia is a likely beginning because of Fidelia's orientation to the winter solstice and its location in the northeastern sector of the city.

Although we cannot determine the meaning of Late Preclassic rituals, which are culturally (and temporally) contingent, based exclusively on Postclassic, Colonial, or even Classic period data, we can draw attention to regularities across time when they exist and present possible interpretations. The initial movement from a station in the northeast is consistent with other patterns of movement or primacy seen in rituals associated with the quincunx through time. Girard's (1962, 40) description of the order of stone placement in Ch'orti' cosmograms suggests the primacy of the northeast in the twentieth century. Hanks (2010, 312) also notes that a survey associated with a land transaction recorded in the *tzol pictun* during the colonial period also commenced in the northeast and proceeded counterclockwise. In addition, the architectural design of Fidelia 1a is striking and consists of a complete directional circuit. Eight small platforms were constructed atop the truncated basal platform in the cardinal and intercardinal directions, evoking the layout of the directional murals in Tomb 12 at Rio Azul as well as diagrams of the cosmos in directional almanacs such as the Codex Fejérváry-Mayer and the Madrid Codex. These structures are known in the literature as the Eight House of the North (Reese 1996; Reese-Taylor and Walker 2002; Šprajc 2008).

While the 260-day processual route in the Madrid Codex commences on day 1, Imix, in the southeast, we do not know the starting date for the circuit at Yaxnohcah. Fidelia's azimuth aligns with the setting sun during the winter solstice. The northeastern intercardinal direction is associated with the summer solstice and the southeast with the winter solstice in most Maya cosmograms (Girard 1962). Therefore, if the circuit commenced with movement from Brisa to Fidelia, then it may have commenced on a solstice date.

If movement through the circuit at Yaxnohcah paralleled that of the Madrid Codex, then after a procession from the center to the northeast, the movement would have continued in a counterclockwise direction to the northwest civic node, the Jacinta complex. At least one circuit to the Brisa complex and back to the Jacinta complex would have ensued. A movement to the southwest, involving the Grazia complex, would have followed. The movement from center to periphery would have taken place in this quadrant and would have been followed by movement to the final northeast node, the Leonora complex. The pattern of procession from periphery to center would also have taken place at this node.

While the 365-day calendar may have been more prominently expressed in the landscape before 200 BCE, after that time features correlated with the 260-day calendar were constructed within the urban landscape. Several prominent civic buildings were modified and new alignments were created to emphasize the sacred calendar. The final renovations of the three central triadic complexes—Alba 1a, Carmela 1a, and (presumably) Esma 1 that form the isosceles triangle at the center of Yaxnohcah—date to this period, as well as those for the Grazia fire altar and hearth complex. The creation of the hearth, the three-stone altar, and the triadic group at Grazia replicates the nested triads seen in the center. These nested triangles serve as a striking visual metaphor for the supernatural first "three-stone" place (*yax ? nal*) (Looper 1995; Carrasco 2010; Stuart 2011). This mythic place may have been affiliated with the constellation Orion, whose disappearance and reappearance in the night sky is associated with the maize cycle and the 260-day calendar (Milbrath 1999, 2017a). In addition, twenty day names (Imix to Ahaw) form a perimeter around the central image in the Madrid Codex (pages 75–76), indicating that activities of the two deities in the center were scheduled according to the 260-day calendar. Likewise, we suggest that activities such as processions that took place in the isosceles triangle at the center of Yaxnohcah may have been scheduled according to the 260-day count.

Burning or fire rituals were common during: New Year ceremonies that celebrated the 365-day calendar; 65-day burner ceremonies that celebrated the 260-day calendar; 63-day fire sequences that possibly commemorated the 819-day count; and new fire ceremonies that celebrated the commencement of a new 52-year cycle. Moreover, the four scenes between the intercardinal directions in the Madrid Codex feature two deities seated on either side of an incense burner, suggesting that burned offerings were also an integral component of the processions depicted.

Triadic complexes evoke a symbolic affiliation with hearths and fire ceremonies, and the thirteen triadic complexes at Yaxnohcah, which presumably were built during the Late Preclassic, were placed throughout the city. Even more explicitly, the hearth and fire altar complex recovered from Grazia provides direct evidence of fire rituals conducted in a three-stone place. Like the Classic, Postclassic, and early Colonial examples, movements within a fire ritual circuit may have been carefully choreographed in a counterclockwise pattern that transitioned from locale to locale according to a predetermined timeline. Therefore, we suggest that the fire ritual from Grazia and ceremonies conducted in triadic complex hearth places throughout Yaxnohcah united people from dispersed areas and created a sense of shared identity based on membership in the kingdom.

To conclude, the generative practices discussed above reflect essential tenets of spatial and temporal ordering in Maya philosophy. With each ritual performance, coherence and meaning were inscribed into Maya landscapes. We argue that specific acts of creation and renewal can be reconstructed from the layout, architectural orientations, and material remains at Yaxnohcah and that these ritual practices were crucial to the emergence of kingdoms during the Late Preclassic. Processions that consisted of counterclockwise movement set within a prescribed timeline in both the 260- and 365-day calendars to locations in the center and the four intercardinal directions created and maintained the conceptual and political boundaries of the Late Preclassic kingdom. Fire rituals in public hearth places were analogous to initiating fire in a household hearth, an act that created a home (Stuart 1998a). Accordingly, initiating fire in triadic complexes throughout Yaxnohcah following a scripted temporal cycle would have inaugurated and regularly renewed a sense of group membership within the kingdom—a civitas.

These acts of spatial and temporal ordering established and maintained the physical and social integrity of the Yaxnohcah kingdom. Moreover, abiding tenets of ordering within Maya philosophy continued to provide a foundation for conceptual and political identities for over 1,500 years.

## Notes

1 Both the 365-day calendar and the 260-day calendars are incorporated in a 52-year cycle, commonly known as the Calendar Round.

2 The Ah Tok was a religious specialist who conducted the fire ceremonies within the 260-day calendar (Edmonson 1982). The Ah Tok is sometimes also referred to as a Chac.

3 When describing the burner ceremonies, we have elected to use the colonial spellings for day names, as they were the ones in use when the ceremonies were recorded in the various colonial documents.

4 Six cycles of 63 days equals 378 days and 13 cycles of 63 days equals 819 days.

5 This azimuth belongs to the 11° azimuth group, as 101° is offset by exactly 90° (Šprajc 2018).

6 The 104° azimuth is equivalent to the 14° south of east azimuth, which is commonly referenced in lowland Maya architecture.

# 5

# Domesticating Time

## Quadripartite Symbolism and Founding Rituals at Yaxuná

Travis W. Stanton, Karl A. Taube,
and Ryan H. Collins

This work of creating centers, of marking off their corners, of encircling them in order to "bind" them up, of moving in and out of them, has an effect on the shape of time as well as space.

(Freidel et al. 1993, 131)

The transition to settled life during the early portion of the Preclassic (1000 BCE–800 CE) had a tremendous impact on peoples' lifeways across Mesoamerica. While the Archaic period (7500–1000 BCE) origins of many Preclassic behaviors are unclear due to the paucity of concrete data prior to settled life, it is apparent that as early permanent settlements were established, widely shared views of space and time were materialized in the built environment that were particularly visible during founding events. By the time the early Maya began settling down at the end of the Early Preclassic, the Mesoamerican quadripartite "shape of time" (Coggins 1980) guided peoples' behaviors related to founding the sacred spaces that community identities coalesced around. We contend that early centers were founded as ordered, domesticated spaces structured by time that set them apart from the wild, timeless, and chaotic spaces that surrounded them. Foundational events relied on the creation of ordered quadripartite spaces that established early centers around symbolic, four-sided maize fields where calendrical rituals associated with the agrarian year were practiced. We contend that for Maya people, these rituals helped maintain the moral order of the human world.

As maize was gradually adopted as a staple crop during the Middle Preclassic (800–350 BCE), emerging elites who leveraged their ability to access sacred knowledge and perform rituals into increasingly powerful social clout presented themselves as the original workers and bearers of the burden of time. Their moral behavior and spiritual wellness maintained the balance, juxtaposing the ordered human world with the timeless wild world beyond. In this chapter we discuss the significance of the material manifestations of quadripartite symbolism in the founding of early Maya centers, using the site of Yaxuná as a case study. We argue that the quadripartite symbolism present in site planning principles throughout the Preclassic—from the establishment of the E Group at the beginning of the Middle Preclassic to the expansion of the monumental zone during the Late Preclassic (350 BCE–1 CE) to the construction of triadic groups and causeways in a crosslike plan—represent a sustained commitment to celebrating the agrarian calendar by an emerging elite who shared the burden of time.

## Founding of Centers

Essentially, Mesoamerican migrants searched for an environment with specific characteristics that consisted of several symbolic levels. Finding such a site preceded all founding rituals. Such a place had to recall the mythical moment when the earth was created: an aquatic universe framed by four mountains with a fifth elevation protruding in the middle of the water. The mountain at the core had to be dotted with caves and springs, and sometimes it was surrounded by smaller hills. A setting like this duplicated and would forever freeze the primordial scene when the waters and the sky separated and the earth sprouted upward (García Zambrano 1994, 217–218).

In his treatment of founding rituals, García Zambrano (1994) identifies enduring and widespread ritual practices associated with the founding of community spaces through a careful analysis of early Colonial period (1519–1697 CE) documents. Establishing important centers as reified places of primordial creation was a widely accepted charter across Mesoamerica that provided "the cosmogonic referents that legitimized the settlers' rights for occupying that space and for the ruler's authority over that site" (García Zambrano 1994, 218). While founding rituals were complex, they centered on practices that established a quadripartite time-space frame, variably using existing natural features and built space that extended outward from the central mountain. Smaller mountains marked the four directions emanating from the central mountain. Prior to the selection (or creation) of the central mountain, music, including the playing of drums and flutes and the blowing of conch trumpets, accompanied the establishment of the center and served as a prelude to the "shouting" in all directions to gather kinship groups. The central mountain or cave or water hole was then selected or created and processional groups set out in the four directions to measure and delimit the territory. This activity is reminiscent of Hanks's (1990, 299; Freidel et al. 1993, 130) description of modern Yukatek shamans "opening the path" when laying out the cardinal directions of an altar. García Zambrano (1994, 218) describes the limits of the territory as *rinconada,* which are often depicted in a horseshoe valley shape in toponyms from western Mesoamerica. The *rinconada,* or what effectively constituted the community limits, separated the ordered human world of structured time from the wild, timeless, and chaotic world of the *monte.* We see the practices associated with founding rituals as a way to "domesticate" space-time from its wild origins and make it a singularly human phenomenon that would remain so as long as moral behavior was maintained, especially by the ruler and the four directional wardens of a center.

After the community limits were established, people held a feast at the central mountain, conducted a fire ritual symbolizing solar movement, and enacted another directional ritual involving arrows. García Zambrano (1994, 220) notes that during contact and in early Colonial period central Mexico, shooting arrows was involved in the creation of both the cosmos and public statements of political territory—that is, the reenactment of the original founding rites: "The arrowing of the cardinal points was reminiscent of the time when the ancestors, helped by the deities, settled on earth." García Zambrano (1994, 220) further mentions that "arrowing" commonly referred to the establishment of a new community: "A metaphorical phrase conveying all the meanings attached to the arrowing of the cosmos was often used by Náhuatl-speaking groups when taking possession of a new site: . . . *y se fueron de flecha* (and they went off arrowing)." According to the chronicler Ixtlilxochitl (1975, 295), creating new fire and shooting arrows to the four directions were the ritual means by which the Chichimec took possession of a region. The reference to arrows in relation to the creation of territory probably relates to the Mixtec term for conquest, "to put an arrow in the lands of another person" (Smith 1973, 33). Clearly enough, conquest is a basic, militaristic means of creating a political domain.

Among the contemporary Huichol of Nayarit, the mythic creation of the world is described as the setting of five sacred arrows, basic symbols of the hunt, in the four directions and the world center. At the dawning of the first sun, the aged earth goddess Takutsi Nakawe told the ancestral gods to take four arrows and thrust them into the four corners of the earth, with her fifth arrow placed by the gods at the center where the first corn emerged (Negrín

1975, 38). The directional arrows recall both the world trees and the four sharpened branches wielded by the youthful kings on the West Wall of the Pinturas Shrine at San Bartolo (Taube et al. 2010). They could also relate to what García Zambrano (1994, 221) describes as "the daily path of the sun and the yearly displacement of this astral body on the horizon marked by mountains" (Ixtlilxochitl 1975, 1:295–296).

After the rituals to define the community limits had been completed, an additional set of rituals defined the community's core. East-west (heliacal) and north-south (commonly associated with caves and waterholes) coordinates were sighted from the central mountain, dividing the center into four wards. Arrows were then shot into the water holes, the most symbolically important of which was the one directly associated with the central mountain. Finally, the central core was measured and delimited in the four directions, which were assigned to important members of the community (García Zambrano 1994, 221). Although García Zambrano (1994) does not emphasize the point, we focus on the importance of directions in the definition and delineation of community space, including annual celebrations of the 365-day calendar, shrines defining the borders of communities, and internal wards, or barrios.

## Directionality and Foundation

When comparing founding events at Yaxuná to the rituals García Zambrano discussed (1994), we must turn to the E Group, where the earliest evidence of human occupation occurs at the site (fig. 5.1). While a few scattered pre-Mamom materials have been found across the site center, the only sealed contexts with these materials come from the lowest three floors in the E Group plaza, which we tentatively date to the period 900–700 BCE based a series of twenty-six radiocarbon samples from across the entire plaza sequence (see Stanton et al. forthcoming for a discussion of the ceramic dating). In our reconstruction of the civic zone of Yaxuná (Stanton and Collins 2017, 2021), we argued that the E Group was the only public architecture constructed during the founding event. While excavations have not explored underneath the western radial structure (where we believe a bedrock antecedent substructure is buried), investigations in the plaza uncovered what appears to be the first version of the range structure, which, like examples at Cenote, Cival, and Ceibal (Chase and Chase 2017a, 47; Estrada-Belli 2017; Inomata 2017b), is a modified bedrock outcrop about 1 meter high (Collins and Stanton, forthcoming).

The limestone outcrop contains a natural cave in the center axis of this first version of the range structure. Although an entrance was not discovered during excavations (locals report that a modern road next to the western

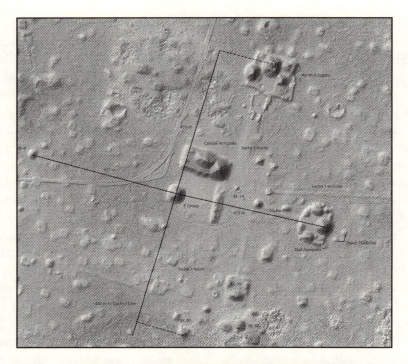

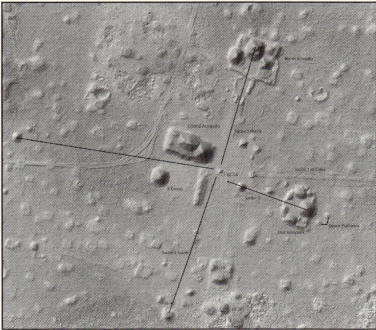

Figure 5.1. Lidar images of the cruciform plan of Yaxuná: (*a*) in the Middle Preclassic; (*b*) in the Late Preclassic. Images by Travis Stanton.

face of the radial structure paved over an entrance to a large cave), a series of natural and probably human-modified or humanmade holes penetrate from the bedrock surface to the cave, which, at least in this chamber, seems to have been filled with loose rock in antiquity (fig. 5.2). All of the holes are roughly circular with similar dimensions, a general diameter of 25 centimeters. Three are located at the outer edge and it is likely that the fourth was not uncovered in the excavated unit. We acknowledge that our interpretation of this feature remains tentative until we can test for this hypothesized final hole. At the center there are three additional holes arranged much like a flattened triangle. It is noteworthy that the middle pit is at the center of the entire grouping of holes and that it contained a Chel burnished short-necked jar (see Boucher and Palomo Carillo 2005 for type description). A natural drain leads to this central modified hole, suggesting that the vessel may have received rainwater runoff. The entire composition strongly indicates a cosmological plan. The holes at the corners pertain to the intercardinal points that frame the central pit containing the water jar, thus forming the basic cosmological quincunx model of the Mesoamerican world (see Estrada-Belli 2017 for centering with water jars at Cival).

This four-sided model is closely related to socially constructed human space, especially the rectangular maize field and a house with its four corner

Figure 5.2. Holes in the bedrock range structure of the Yaxuná E Group leading into a cave feature where an early jar (*inset*) was found. Photos by Ryan Collins.

posts (Vogt 1976; Freidel et al. 1993, 127; Taube 2003a, 2013). In Mesoamerican thought, the four supporting house beams conceptually overlap with directional trees that can be placed at the cardinal or intercardinal points (for recent discussion, see Taube 2017). Although at this point it is impossible to determine, it is conceivable that four beams may have been placed in the corner holes with the center hole left open for the water jar. This interpretation is supported at Yaxuná by the fact that the northeast hole did not perforate into the cave, thus approximating a posthole. The intentionally placed rubble filling the void space could have supported the base of possible posts placed in the holes that did enter the cave (see chapter 7, this volume).

Including the one in the center with the jar, the three holes inside the reconstructed four sides probably also pertain to the cosmic house model, in this case the hearth in the middle of the house floor. The concept of the three-stone hearth is well attested in Classic (250–900 CE) Maya epigraphy and art, including in texts pertaining to the 4 Ajaw 8 Cumk'u event of August 13, 3114 BCE (Freidel et al. 1993, 80–85; Taube 1998). The three hearthstones have also been documented for the Late Preclassic Maya and can be found in the West Wall mural at San Bartolo, Guatemala (Taube et al. 2010). In addition, the radial pyramid forming the western portion of the E Group at Uaxactun had a lip-to-lip vessel cache containing three stones placed on the floor of Structure E-VII-Sub (Taube 1998, 441), an open-summited structure with four large postholes in the corners. A large limestone sphere (an effigy hearthstone) was cached in the subsurface sanctuary floor of a late Middle Preclassic performance platform to the east of the Yaxuná E Group. Stanton and Freidel (2005) suggest that it was one of three such platforms, two of which have been documented. Mound Group B at the roughly contemporaneous site of Izapa, Chiapas, has three large stone spheres elevated on columns that form a flattened triangle, recalling the three-hole grouping at Yaxuná (Taube 1998, 439). Still earlier, a recently discovered Middle Preclassic cache from Ceibal contained three spherical stones laid out in a triangular arrangement (Inomata and Triadan 2016, 86). It is noteworthy that for the Classic period, the main sign of the emblem glyph of Ceibal was the three-stone hearth and the same site contains one of the most developed architectural statements of directions and centrality known for the Classic Maya, the radial pyramid referred to as Structure A-3 (Smith 1982, fig. 17). In addition to four stelae at the base of each stairway, Structure A-3 has a stela standing in the very center of the temple chamber (which also exhibits evidence of extensive burning). Beneath this stela, three large jade cobbles were discovered, clearly referring to the three hearthstones at the world center (Smith 1982, fig. 188; Taube 1998, 441).

The quincunx constitutes a basic symbol of the maize field in Mesoamerica, and among the contemporary Tzeltal Maya of highland Chiapas even the act of planting in the maize field replicates this basic composition: they use the dibble stick to create four corner holes and one in the center (Berlin et al. 1974, 126). In addition, planting ceremonies pertaining to the dedication to the new milpa field often include offerings to the four corners and in the center of the field, as in the case of the Ch'orti' Maya:

> At sunrise the milpa owner goes to his cleared milpas and digs a small hole in each one of them. In each, he buries one fowl, preferably a turkey. . . . This is done at each of the four corners. He then digs a small hole in the center of the same milpa and the throws into it an olla of unsweetened *chilate*. (Wisdom 1940, 439–440)

The placement of the olla in the center of the quincunx recalls the central vessel and quincunx pattern at Middle Preclassic Yaxuná, although the olla, or water jar, is also symbolic of the valley represented by the *rinconada* in western Mesoamerica. In fact, the cave or well at the center of town could be substituted in some cases for an olla; some cave openings in codices are actually abstract olla symbols. García Zambrano (1994, 222) wrote that "within the natural *olla*[,] the cave of origin marked the center of town." We suggest that the olla was not just a symbol of the center of towns, but, as in the case of the Ch'orti', was a material symbol that was used to domesticate space as real or imagined maize fields—the limits of which served to delimit human from wild space. However, the placement of ollas was not the only way to mark the center, and there is variability in the material patterns archaeologists might find.

Before cutting down the trees and brush, a devout Yukatek farmer will make offerings at the center of his field. His field has four corners and four sides like the original order established at creation. The farmer centers the field by piling up stones to mark the center—properly a layer of three followed by a fourth and then a fifth one stacked on top. This centering transforms the land from wild forest to cultivated land (Freidel et al. 1993, 130).

The concept of the four-cornered maize field was certainly present among the Middle Preclassic Olmec. Their basic symbol of the cosmos was the bar and four dots motif, a central vertical bar flanked by four elements at the corners, essentially the same as the quincunx model but with a horizontal central point, or axis mundi. By this arrangement, the bar and four dots motif approximates the human body with the bar as the central trunk and the four dots as the limbs. According to Taube (2004a, 13): "For the Olmec, the human body was both a reflection and expression of the cosmos." A number of

Middle Formative incised celts portray a more elaborate form of bar and four dots motif: the Olmec maize god is the central "bar" and celtiform maize ears are the four corner "dots" (Taube 1996, 44, fig. 6). These celts depict the maize god as the central axis mundi and denote the maize field as the four-sided world. We believe that E Group plazas were imagined as symbolic maize fields and that the rituals to claim these spaces from the timeless wild paralleled those performed in real milpas (Doyle 2013a, 2013b).

In the center of the original plaza to the west of the range structure (the center prior to the expansion of the plaza at the end of the Middle Preclassic), there is a natural circular feature (about half a meter in diameter) in the bedrock that was capped by a flat stone. The cut fragments of a single eroded vessel were recovered inside this feature along with two limestone blades and a possible limestone pendant—together constituting the original central plaza offering that may have included acts of bloodletting when it was deposited. The cap was left exposed on the first floor (Floor 11) of the plaza and was continually marked by circular rings of stone, in one case three courses high, on subsequent floors (fig. 5.3). This feature was probably a fire altar, the first of a superimposed series correlating with subsequent floors. Although there was no carbon or ash in the first altar, the later circular altars have remains of carbon and/or clean ash. They also resemble round fire altars known among the K'iche' and other contemporary Maya of highland Guatemala (see chapter 4, this volume, for a related argument regarding fire altars and centering community). As with the quincunx plan on the range structure, this feature probably also pertains to concepts of centrality and dedication, in this case a ritual feature symbolizing the pivotal symbolic hearth of the community and by extension the cosmos. In Postclassic highland Mexico (after CE 1000), the making of new fire constituted a ritual act of dedication (Elson and Smith 2001) and echoes the fire rituals associated with founding events García Zambrano (1994) discussed. Although the Codex Chimalpopoca is missing part of an initial account of hunting animals of the directional world colors, it begins with the setting up of three hearthstones (Bierhorst 1992). In addition, the Aztec making of new fire at the beginning of a 52-year cycle was probably a replication and reaffirmation of the founding of Tenochtitlan (Elson and Smith 2001).

While we have limited data about the creation of a first public ritual space at Yaxuná due to the depth of the early deposits, the data suggest that the E Group was the place where founding rituals occurred. Several important elements of such rituals, based on the early colonial period described by García Zambrano (1994), suggest that a quadripartite ordering of space-time was present. The central ancestral mountain is likely to be represented by the

Figure 5.3. Yaxuná plaza: (*a*) original hole in bedrock in the center facing south; (*b*) circular fire altar on a subsequent floor facing southeast corner. Photos by Ryan Collins.

probable bedrock version of the radial structure. The bedrock feature of the range structure is clearly associated with water; the water jar in the central hole of a probable quincunx was fed water by a natural drain. The cave is present in this same range structure feature, but locals report that a separate or even the same cave feature appears to be associated with the radial structure. Thus, the triad of mountain/cave/waterhole is associated with the Yaxuná E Group. Further, we have a central fire altar feature that likely represents the original fire, which was rekindled during subsequent phases of the E Group, likely in association with calendrical events (see chapter 4, this volume). As with most Maya E Groups, the east-west orientation of the plaza invokes associations with helical movement and the rectangular shape marked by quadripartite symbolism established the plaza as a symbolic four-sided maize field.

Thus, Yaxuná was established as a sacred gathering place at a time when the northern lowland Maya began to settle down and adopt a more sedentary, agricultural lifestyle, following the canons of E Group quadripartite space-time arrangement common in the southern lowlands. The community limits were also likely established at this time, as were the wardens of the four directions, but we have yet to locate evidence from this early period to support this supposition. Perhaps relevant data are located under the large monumental groups organized in a quadripartite arrangement that are discussed below. In any event, the shape of time appears to have been materialized in this sacred space from its very beginning.

## The Expansion and Recentering of the E Group

The Yaxuná E Group went through several modifications during the centuries after 900 BCE, all of which involved raising the plaza and building upon existing architecture. The bedrock range structure was eventually covered by the first of a series of masonry versions after several tamped-earth flooring events in the plaza. At the end of the Middle Preclassic, however, a much larger modification was undertaken and the plaza was extended to the east, where a larger version of the range structure was constructed. The first version of the range structure continued to be modified and visible in the plaza, but the center point of the plaza moved farther east with the expansion. In this new central point, a large cross was incised on the packed sascab floor to mark the central axis (fig. 5.4). Although this could suggest the Classic Maya k'an cross, it probably had another meaning. Among the Classic Maya, the k'an cross appears in a cartouche and signifies yellow and preciousness. In contrast, the Yaxuná cross more likely denotes the directions and center of the world, reinforcing the directional symbolism associated with the founding events (see chapter 4, this

Figure 5.4. Incised cross on the floor of Late Preclassic center of the Yaxuná plaza. Photograph facing northwest corner. Photo by Ryan Collins.

volume, for related arguments). In this regard, it probably relates to Middle Preclassic cruciform caches cut into plaza floors in the central axis of E Groups at Cival (Estrada-Belli 2017) and Ceibal (Inomata 2017b).

At the earliest and largest E Group at Cival, which is located on the highest hill at the site, an elaborate cruciform cache was dug into bedrock along the eastern edge of the group (Estrada-Belli 2006, 2017). This centerline cache contained four large water jars placed in the arms of the excavated cross and a fifth water jar was placed in the middle of the cross. Below the central pit, five vertical jade celts were also oriented to four directions and the center, as was a lower bed of alluvial jadeite pebbles. The directional placement of these greenstone celts recalls Middle Preclassic caching practices known for the Olmec site of La Venta in Tabasco, and at San Isidro in Chiapas. Mound 20, the principal structure in the center of San Isidro, contained a cruciform dedicatory centerline offering consisting of ear spools and celts oriented to the four directions around a central ceramic bowl (Lowe 1981).

After the celt offerings at San Isidro and La Venta, the Cival cache is most similar to cruciform pits on the centerline of a Middle Preclassic E Group at Ceibal (Smith 1982; Inomata and Triadan 2016; Aoyama et al. 2017; Inomata 2017b). The first excavated example at Ceibal, a cruciform pit excavated into the marl bedrock, contained five ceramic water jars. Four were located at the ends of the cross and one was closer to the center on the eastern extension of the pit, as were jadeite celts and an Olmec-style jadeite bloodletter (Smith 1982, 119, fig. 189). At Cerro Maya (Cerros) in Belize, Late Preclassic (ca. 100 CE) Cache 1 in Structure 6B featured a quincunx of four drinking cups surrounding a central bucket with a dish lid (Freidel 1979; Freidel et al. 1993, 242–244; see also chapter 2, this volume, on Structure 6 at Cerro Maya). Inside the bucket was another quincunx of royal jewels made of jade. Late Preclassic centering involving jadeite jewels is also featured in the main E Group at Caracol (Chase 1988, 89–90; Chase and Chase 1998, 316; chapter 14, this volume).

Although the cruciform caches excavated since 2012 at Ceibal do not contain five ceramic vessels, they have greenstone celts and other offerings, including a jadeite perforator in Cache 171 (Aoyama et al. 2017, 711, fig. 7). The presence of perforators in two of the cruciform caches strongly indicates that sacrificial bloodletting constituted part of the offering, quite possibly as an act that provided life-giving blood to the earth, as indicated by the cruciform pits oriented to the four directions. This would be very similar to ritual bloodletting known for Late Postclassic Yucatán, where penis perforation was performed atop turtle sculptures representing the earth (Chase and Chase 1986, 11; 1988, 50; Taube 1988b; chapter 14, this volume). Within the centerline of the Ceibal E Group, an even more striking example of Middle Preclassic sacrifice is the burial of five infants in the four directions and the center (Aoyama et al. 2017, 714). The burial of infants recalls the findings of infant sacrifices in the spring at the site of El Manatí, a context strongly suggestive of rain and water ritual and the Aztec offering of infants to the rain god in Late Postclassic central Mexico. For the Aztec, one of the primary places where infants were sacrificed was atop Mount Tlaloc, due east of Tenochtitlan. The mountaintop shrine contains boulders at its four corners and one boulder in the center, thereby making the quincunx cosmogram. In addition, the Aztec *Primeros Memoriales* contains a probable scene of this shrine: a sacrificed child within a walled enclosure containing a directional mountain god, or *tepictoton* (Taube 2004b).

The greenstone celts and water jars in cruciform directional offerings at the E Groups at Cival and Ceibal strongly suggest ritual and symbolism pertaining to rain and maize. Celts and axes widely identified with lightning in ancient and contemporary Mesoamerica, but it is also clear that they symbolize maize ears among the Olmec, as evidenced by the images of the Olmec maize god incised on jadeite celts (Taube 1996, 2000). In addition, Early Classic caches from Copán in Honduras feature offerings placed at the cardinal points and jade images of the maize god in the center. As Estrada-Belli

(2017, 298) has noted for the Cival cache, the ollas probably pertain to directional rain deities and the celts to growing maize: "These vessels likely symbolized the four directional and central Chahk rain gods invoked to fertilize the sprouting maize/axes symbols with the life-giving substance." Estrada-Belli (2017) notes that the Cival water jars were ritually smashed, probably to release the water into the pit. This recalls an Aztec account in *Historia de los Mexicanos por sus pinturas* that describes the house of Tlaloc as composed of four chambers surrounding a court that included four cisterns of water containing types of rain. By striking these cisterns with staffs, the rain gods released the rains and created thunder (Garibay Kintana 1979, 26). Estrada-Belli (2017, 298) compares the Cival cache and ollas to the directional placement of water jars at Early Classic (CE 100–550) Teotihuacan and the Late Postclassic (CE 1350–1521) Aztec Templo Mayor. Burial 2 from the Pyramid of the Moon at Teotihuacan, which dates to the third century CE, is a complex offering with Tlaloc water jars at the four corners and a fifth in the center, forming a quincunx (Sugiyama and López Luján 2007). The same composition occurs with the so-called Cocijo pages in the Late Postclassic (1200–1519 CE) Codex Borgia and the Codex Vaticanus B. Based on the division of the 260-day calendar into four quarters, the pages feature four Tlalocs at the corners and a fifth in the center. It is important to note that in these scenes, the directional Tlalocs are all on maize fields, indicating the basic agricultural significance of the quincunx. The Cocijo pages also concern the quartering of another calendrical cycle, the division of the 52-year cycle into four 13-year periods.

The fact that the Yaxuná cross marks the central portion of the plaza suggests that as the plaza was expanded, it was important to recenter the space, marking it with directional symbolism instead of the fire altar that had marked the center of the original plaza space (Stanton and Collins 2017, 2021). Versions of that fire altar had continued in the same spot where the original altar and associated offerings had been placed. The importance of the elaborate offerings at some of the earliest E Groups—those of Cival and Ceibal—cannot be overestimated, as they provide the clearest perspective on the meaning of these groups at their original inception in addition to being the Middle Preclassic founding of farming communities. These elaborate centerline deposits demonstrate a clear ritual and symbolic focus on directional cosmology based on the milpa, corn, and rain—here in the very tangible form of ceramic water jars placed in the center and at the cardinal points.

This, of course, pertains directly to the basic nature of E Groups as architectural markers of the annual solar cycle. Maize farming was the most important and most essential aspect of the vague solar year, as is so richly documented in the eighteen 20-day-month ceremonies of the contact-period Maya and Aztec.

In the contact-period Popul Vuh of the K'iche' Maya, the original moments of creation are referred to as the "sowing and the dawning." They concern the measurement of and creation of the earthly maize field out of the primordial sea. James Doyle (2013b) suggests that the original E Group plazas relate to the concept of the primordial maize field, and, in the Popol Vuh, the final creation of humans who inhabit this cosmic milpa are the people of corn. As the first major architectural constructions at many Maya sites, the E Group plazas denote humanly created social space based on maize and the annual solar cycle. Given the prominence of the radial pyramid to the west and the long platform to the east in E Groups, it would not be unreasonable to think that in such groups, the daily dawning replicates the original moment of the earth mountain rising from the primordial sea, and below, a drying place steadily becoming the fecund field as the sun slowly rises.

While the Yaxuná cross lacks some of the other material markers found at other E Groups, the emphasis of this cross symbolism in the center of the plaza references these same concepts and serves to recenter the plaza as a maize field. Just as the work to prepare a milpa domesticates it from the primordial wilderness and defines it as human space, the work to create communities around symbolic maize fields accomplishes the same task by extricating them from the wilds. Taube (2003a, 463) notes that the Yukatek word for work, *meyah*, "can apply to preparing the milpa, sweeping a house or courtyard, or purifying a space by a shaman or *hmen*" (Hanks 1990, 229). Both Sosa (1985, 243) and Hanks (1990, 306) document the cutting of perimeters, known as *hol ch'ak* in Yukatek, around both milpas and towns. According to Hanks (1990, 339), "Without its perimeter, a place has no unity and is potentially dangerous." Clearly, the activities involved in founding communities and creating milpas are connected to the practice of creating human, domesticated spaces out of the chaotic wilderness (Stone 1995, 15).

Slightly after the expansion of the Yaxuná E Group plaza, two low circular platforms, alluded to earlier as performance platforms, were constructed in a line directly east of the E Group, near where a Late Preclassic triadic group would be constructed (Suhler 1996; Stanton and Freidel 2005). Both the triadic group and the platforms mark the end of the monumental zone and this area may have been the original limit of the central core delimited during the founding ritual. In fact, the largest structure of the monumental groups delimiting the north, east, and west sides of the Late Preclassic quadripartite plan are all equidistant, approximately 475 meters (fig. 5.1) from the E Group radial structure when measurements are taken from the original axis, indicating that they were measured out from the central mountain following García Zambrano's (1994) model. The southern side is about 440 meters distant and the north-south Late Preclassic axis is offset slightly due to a later recentering event discussed below. Interestingly, this alignment mimics the quadripartite plan of Ek' Balam in northeastern Yucatán, which is also marked by causeways with much shorter south sides than the relatively equidistant east, west, and north sides. Both of the platforms at Yaxuná contain elaborate systems of passages and chambers and it is quite possible that they constitute symbolic caves within humanly constructed hills. The Early Classic Sa'atun Sat structure at Oxkintok to the west of Yaxuná also has a mazelike system of interior passages and could also have been intended to evoke a cave network, much like the massive cave nearby at Calcehtok.

The Yaxuná platforms presage the Early Postclassic circular dance platform in the Initial Series Group at Chichén Itzá, 20 kilometers to the north, which is in the form of a turtle with a head, limbs, and a tail (Stanton and Freidel 2005; Schmidt 2007; Taube et al. 2020). Although the Yaxuná platforms do not have any overt turtle traits, the quatrefoil corridors and cavelike sanctuaries are consistent with Late Preclassic and Classic Maya turtle imagery in which the carapace contains the quatrefoil cave motif (Taube 1998, 441; Stanton and Freidel 2005; Taube et al. 2010; Freidel et al. 2020). They are round, as is the example from Chichén Itzá. At Machaquilá, the central plaza contains a large quatrefoil—a probable dance court—and a massive turtle altar (Graham 1967), alluding to the same kind of associations.

## The Shape of Time in Urban Yaxuná

Yaxuná underwent a transformation to an urban center in the Late Preclassic period (Stanton and Collins 2021). While the E Group continued to be the central locus of the center's monumental core, several triadic acropolis groups were built in the site proper. Domestic settlement appears to have extended to about 1.5 kilometers from the site center, past the acropolis groups, and two peripheral triadic acropolis groups were connected to the Yaxuná center via causeways to the east (Hutson et al. 2012). During the Late Preclassic period, a new axis at Yaxuná was constructed, still farther east and slightly to the north. The new north-south axis lines up with a cave system running under the North Acropolis that may have provided the impetus for the shift.

This new symbolic center of the site featured a small central radial pyramid associated with three causeways, or *sakbeho'ob* in Yukatek Maya, whose lines of sight converge on or are very near to the radial structure (Freidel et al. 1993, 126). The only cardinal direction that lacks a causeway headed toward this new radial structure is the west, where the terminus is not a triadic acropolis group. However, the area between Structure 4F-4 and the new radial structure is mostly covered by *chich* and there is a direct line of sight, indicating that the area was paved and open, serving as the western side of a cruciform. Cruciform site plans have been reported at other sites such as Xunantunich (Keller 2006), Ek' Balam, and Ucanhá, and at some sites, such as Yaxha (Hellmuth 1972), the cruciform is not marked by a causeway on the western side.

As with the E Group, this new axis and directional symbolism at Yaxuná may relate to cosmic founding acts; the roads may refer to the primordial quartering of the world. According to the Aztec *Historia de los Mexicanos por sus pinturas,* after the flood, four gods and four directional roads were created to form four cosmic quarters and Tezcatlipoca and Quetzalcoatl became two great trees that raised the sky (Garibay Kintana 1971, 32). Page 1 of the Codex Fejérváry-Mayer portrays a version of this creation myth: the image is broken into directional quarters with associated world trees. The diagonal lines from the center to the corners constitute symbolic roads as they concern the passage of the 260-day calendar around the entire page, along with the four yearbearers with birds at the outmost edge of the corners. In the well-known cognate scene in the Codex Madrid (see chapter 4, this volume), the reference to intercardinal roads is explicit, as human footprints lead into the central scenes from all four corners of the scene.

In a similar creation episode known for colonial Yucatán, after the slaying of Itzam Kab Ayiin, the flood crocodile, five directional trees with associated colors and birds were created to lift the heavens, four at the cardinal points and one in the center (Taube 2017, 270; see chapter 2, this volume). Dedicated to the 365-day year and the 52-year cycle, the Dresden New Year pages prominently portray four directional trees with specific colors and offerings. The accompanying texts describe these trees as being erected (*tz'apah*), indicating that rather than being static, these world trees concern the moment of creation when they were set up, much like the Yukatek myth of the world trees made to raise the sky.

Although our understanding of Classic Maya calendrics has focused almost entirely on the roughly 20-year *k'atuns* and the Long Count, this has presented a very skewed perspective on the pre-Hispanic calendar, especially the vague solar year of eighteen 20-day months and an extra five days to constitute a vague solar year of 365 days—in other words, the *ha'ab*—despite the fact that this was the basic calendrical system for Mesoamerica from the Preclassic to the contact period for the Aztec and Maya.

Groundbreaking research by David Stuart (2004a) demonstrates that although they are rare, there are Classic Maya monumental references to New

Year celebrations, including a text from Naranjo Stela 18 that mentions the dedication of a stela, or *lakamtun,* on the day 1 Ik' and the seating of the first month of the year, 0 Pop (Stuart 2004a, 1–2). The dedication term is precisely the same as in the Dresden New Year pages, *tz'apah.* As Stuart (2004a, 1–2) notes, "The year bearer calendar was ritually important for the Classic, and possibly even the Preclassic Maya, and that indications of it do indeed appear from time to time in the earlier textual record" (see chapter 12, this volume).

In contrast to the Long Count, the annual succession of the fifty-two 365-day years has a direct relation to the world directions. Due to the sequence of the four yearbearers naming the year, the years proceed in a counterclockwise motion from east to north to west to south because each of the twenty names of the 260-day calendar has a specific direction. The first day name, Imix, is east, the second day, Ik', is north, and so on. The poorly understood 819-day cycle that appears in Classic Maya inscriptions indicates not only that the same day names and directions occurred for the Classic period, but also that the same directional colors are known for contact period Yucatán (Berlin and Kelley 1961). For both the pre-Hispanic Dresden Codex and Paris Codex New Year pages, the yearbearers are Ben (east), Etz'nab (north), Ak'bal (west), and Lamat (south), which are equivalent to the highland Mexican yearbearers of Reed, Flint, House, and Rabbit, a series that can be readily traced to Xochicalco in the Late Classic (CE 600–800). David Stuart (2004a), however, notes that the Classic Maya yearbearer series was one position before, in this case not 1 Pop as the first of the year but 0 Pop, that is, the *seating* of Pop. This has important implications in terms of the concept of governance in relation to the year, as the Classic Maya logograph for the seating of the year as well as the 20-day months is the "rear end" *chum* glyph that is also used in Classic Maya references to royal accession. As Stone and Zender (2011, 63) point out, "The same metaphoric construct [accession] was applied to the calendar in that the seating verb also stood for what numerically was the zero day of the month. The seating or beginning of a month denoted its official 'reign' over a 20-day period." For the Classic Maya, the yearbearer days were Ik', Manik', Eb, and Kaban. These names were used by the ancient Zapotec of Oaxaca and are still used today by the K'iche, Ixil, and other contemporary Maya of highland Guatemala.

In his essay on Classic Maya New Year dates, Stuart (2004a) calls attention to the fragmentary Pomoná Panel 1, a Late Classic monument that appears to have portrayed four seated subordinate *sajal* lords personified as the strongly quadripartite deity commonly referred to as God N. Typically portrayed as an aged craggy being, he often appears as a cosmic skybearer and in relation to directional mountains. Only two of the series of the Pomoná panel are largely intact. They have the dates 4 Ik' and 4 Kaban. Not only do these dates correspond to two of the Classic period yearbearers, they also strongly imply that the other two now largely missing figures held the corresponding dates of 4 Manik and 4 Eb. When the four yearbearers share the same numerical coefficient, this divides the 52-year cycle into four great quarters of 13 years. This is still observed among the Ixil Maya, who quarter the cycle by yearbearers who have the coefficient of 1 (Lincoln 1942, 115). Stuart (2004a) notes that in the Early Classic Tomb 2 at Rio Azul in Guatemala, the same dates of 4 Ik' and 4 Kaban appear as quarters of the 52-year cycle, in this case in relation to directional mountains. Although a Late Preclassic mural fragment from the Ixim temple at San Bartolo does not refer specifically to yearbearer dates, it bears a text that reads *kan haab witz,* which could be glossed as the "four year mountains," possibly relating to the contemporary concept of four direction yearbearer mountains among the K'iche and other highland Maya peoples.

In his *Relación de las cosas de Yucatán,* Diego de Landa describes the New Year rites celebrated in sixteenth-century Yukatek Maya communities, which concerned the placement and movement of god images of the four yearbearers from the houses of public officials, or *principales,* to pairs of rock shrines at the four directional entrances to the towns (Tozzer 1941, 135–150). As Michael Coe (1965, 102) writes:

> Ideally, there was a road leading in from each of the cardinal points to the center of the community. We are told that each road led directly to the *principal's* house, implying that the town was in some way divided in four quarters associated with the cardinal directions, and making it certain there were four different *principales* through a cycle of four years. (Coe 1965, 102)

Although Coe's seminal study does not discuss the pre-Hispanic Dresden New Year pages, they also illustrate this quadripartite organization. Each page not only illustrates a directional tree but also a god occupying a temple, clearly referring to the patron deities of the four quarters who are equivalent to the four community gods the *principales* cared for.

Coe (1965, 108) notes that there is ethnohistoric evidence of this ceremonial quartering of communities among the lowland Maya. Thus, the Chilam Balam of Chumayel describes Chichén Itzá as having four quarters oriented to the directions and another passage mentions four directional entrances to the city (Roys 1933, 69, 139–140, 169). In fact, there are four main *sacbehs* for the site center; these may well relate to the symbolic quartering of the site, with the Castillo constituting the pivotal center. The Chumayal also describes Mayapán as being divided into four quarters (*tzukul*), and Coe (1965) mentions that this was also the case for Tayasal, to the south, which was divided into four quarters, each presided over by a *batab* (see also Rice and Rice 2018). Coe (1965, 109) also mentions that the sixteenth Chantal community of Itzamkanac was formed of four barrios, each with a specific god. This description is strikingly similar to both Landa's account and to the Dresden New Year pages, which mentions specific gods in each of the four temples (Coe 1965, 109).

Although the Indigenous 365-day calendar is no longer used in the contemporary Maya lowlands, the planning activities of native communities are often strongly quadripartite. For example, they often include four entrances marked with crosses, a feature that has been compared to the four shrines Landa described for the New Year celebrations (Taube 1988b, 279–280; Bricker and Bricker 2011, 121). As was probably the case for the ancient entrances, the crosses serve as a protective barrier between the ordered world of the community and chaotic "primordial" realm beyond. Redfield and Villa Rojas (1934, 111) note that in the well-known Yukatek town of Chan Kom, "the most important protective crosses of all are those four pairs of large wooden crosses that stand at the four entrances to the village." John Sosa (1985, 343–344) notes that in Yalcobá in Yucatán, during the town purification ceremony known as *loh cah,* offerings are made at the borders of the community, especially to the crosses known as the "four corners of the town." Charles Wisdom (1940, 421) describes a very similar use of protective crosses for Ch'orti' in eastern highland Guatemala: "Four important roads head out of Jocotán toward the four cardinal points, and each of these has its cross at the point where it leaves the pueblo. . . . They are stood up at the center of the trail so that the spirits, who theoretically could enter the pueblo only by way of the four trails, as people do, would be forced to pass over the crosses to gain entrance, and this would be impossible" (421). These four directional crosses can be considered as cosmic world trees, as they "are of living *palo jiote* trees" (422). Among the Ixil of Nebaj, where the Indigenous New Year ceremonies are still performed, there are four shrines with crosses to honor the yearbearers during a given year: "In Nebaj, there are four Year Bearer crosses associated with the four Dominical [yearbearer] days. All are on or near archaeological mounds, are in an unvarying order of rank, and are associated with the 'four corners of the world'" (Lincoln 1942, 110). Although the contemporary Yukatek and Ch'orti' directional crosses are no longer identified with the yearbearers, the Ixil still used them to demarcate the corners of the created world.

According to Michael Coe (1965), in the contact period, the counterclockwise succession of yearbearers through the four quarters of Maya communities may have related to a political system of governance in which a principal member of one quarter served as the "governor" of the entire town for a given year. Thomas Hinton has documented a virtually identical system for the contemporary Cora of Nayarit:

> The Cora village of Jesús María is composed of four *barrios* (divisions resembling a ward) each with a name a patron saint. The *gobernadora* (Cora: *tatuan*) is the nominal chief of the pueblo and as highest officer directs the rest of the officials. He can most precisely be termed the formal agent of the *principales*. The *gobernador* serves a term of one year beginning New Year's day, with the office rotating in a counterclockwise direction around the four *barrios*. (Hinton 1964, 48)

The large introductory scene in the *Lienzo de Tlaxcala* depicting the colonial founding of the city may refer to this annual sequence of governance through the four quarters. Along with the pre-Hispanic quarters with their four governing lords at the corners, the center of this scene depicts the center of Tlaxcala as a hill with the church at its base, marking the symbolic axis mundi of the community. At the base of the hill, a sign for a succession of four years is carefully depicted and could well relate to the succession of Indigenous governance between the four *barrios*. Painted in strongly native style, a sixteenth-century portrayal of Xochitepec, Oaxaca, with four roads at the cardinal points and the church displaying mountain features in the center recalls the central scene from the *Lienzo de Tlaxcala*. In each of the town quarters there is a cross marking the barrios, which are demarcated by the four roads. Given the early date of this manuscript, it is more than likely that the Indigenous 365-day calendar and the counterclockwise succession of the four yearbearers was still present, as it was at the time of Landa's account of sixteenth-century Yucatán.

This pre-Hispanic kind of annual office holding directly relates to the civil-religious hierarchies known as the *cargo* for Indigenous communities of colonial and contemporary Mesoamerica. In Yucatán, the individual responsible for a specific division or ward of a community was termed the *ah kuch kab*; *kuch* refers to the burden, or "cargo," and *kab* signifies community (Coe 1965, 104, 106). The Yukatek term for the calendrical yearbearers related to the four directional quarters of the pre-Hispanic community was *ah kuch haab*, or bearer of the year—and essentially cognate terms can be found in other Maya languages, including Chuj and Jakaltek (Thompson 1950, 214). The concept of public authority also appears in other contemporary references to yearbearers. The Ixil refer to the four yearbearers as the *alcaldes del mundo* (*alcalde* is the Spanish term for "mayor") (Lincoln 1942, 106). This is also true for the K'iche' of Momostenango, where the four yearbearers are considered to be old men (*mam*) and directional mountains, paragons of authority and permanence (Tedlock 1983, 100). The Classic period Pomoná Panel 1 portrays youthful *sajal* lords holding up yearbearer dates pertaining to 13-year quarters of the 52-year calendar, each pertaining to a specific direction. Their waterlily headdresses denote them as impersonators of God N, an aged and frequently quadripartite deity who is often portrayed bearing the sky and sometimes as a mountain god, much like the contemporary yearbearers of Momostenango. The Palace Throne at Palenque also portrays two young men wearing the headdress of God N; they serve as the throne supports for the king. This pair of figures also lifts waterlily plants in their upraised hands, quite possibly alluding to the original mythic act of raising the sky out of the primordial sea. Clearly, the concept of public office as burden was fully present among the Classic Maya and it also related to the yearbearers of the 365-day year, as it did with the contact-period Maya.

The concept of time as a burden also relates to the theme of travel, as Thompson (1950, 125) has noted: "Each year has its burden with which he traverses his course to pass it at journey's end to his successor." In the case of the yearbearers, this relates to a counterclockwise movement from east to north to west to south. In Xochicalco and Tula portraiture, a tumpline strap denotes specific years, much as if the year is a merchant's cargo (Taube et al. 2010, fig. 13). The New Year pages of the Codex Dresden portray opossum figures carrying gods of specific years on their back. They hold fans as well as staffs; fans are a common marker of merchants in ancient Mesoamerica. According to Coe (1965, 104), the Yukatek *ah kuch kab* were "said to have been rich men" and it is quite possible that they were successful merchants.

Much like carrying a burden, traveling implies work and effort, which of course also ties directly into roads, including *sakbeh*. In Yukatek, the term *toh* signifies not only "straightness" but also concepts pertaining to proper human behavior and moral rectitude, in contrast to the primordial wild forests (Taube 2003a). As human-constructed raised roads often extend for many kilometers, *sakbehs* are architectonic statements of straightness and direct paths that might have had important implications for social order and harmony. In Mesoamerica, the sun's journey from east to west is the preeminent force that follows a straight path, guiding the seasons and the solar year. Among the contemporary Tzotzil Maya, Gossen (1974, 30) reports that the world is created through the movement of the sun: "Day and night, the yearly agricultural and religious cycles, the seasons, the divisions of the day, most plants and animals, the stars, and the constellations—all are the work of the creator, the life force itself."

The striking similarity between the organization of the principal Late Preclassic causeways at Yaxuná and the quadripartite division of the burden of time is probably not coincidental. The fact that the sacred center was organized in a quadripartite pattern with three of the directions marked by straight causeways emanating from a central precinct marked by a radial structure is highly suggestive of movement along straight lines and could very well be a material representation of the division of the burden of time among Late Preclassic wardens of the site. The importance of movement in association with the radial structure is echoed during the Classic period with the construction of the *sakbeh* from Cobá to Yaxuná. This causeway, the longest in the Maya area, ends at a building directly in front of the east staircase of the radial structure, demonstrating that this *sakbeh* leads to the heart of Yaxuná. Given its east-west orientation, it could have had strong ceremonial solar significance; movement and time seem to be part and parcel of the spatial order of the center of Yaxuná. In the words of Freidel and colleagues (1993, 131): "Because centering the world requires movement to, from, and around the designated center point, the processional route humans use to define the center is as important as the center itself." Yaxuná appears to be a clear example of the importance of movement to maintaining space-time boundaries set out during founding rituals.

## Discussion

It is necessary to consider space in order to understand time in ancient Mesoamerica. The two concepts were inseparable in the cosmovision of peoples such as the Preclassic Maya and were integrally linked with ideas of creation. However, we must be careful to view the founding rituals described in this chapter—and their continued reenactments at centers such as Yaxuná—as commemorations of the original creation story. The performance of creation was a continual process that defined and maintained the boundaries between the human world of ordered space-time and the wild timeless chaotic world of the *monte* (Freidel et al. 1993; Taube 2003a). Performances actively maintained those boundaries by binding and ordering time. Perhaps it is fitting to think that the early Maya and other Mesoamerican peoples used an ideology of domesticating wild space-time during the same period when they were adopting a sedentary life and agriculture—transitioning and distancing themselves from a lifestyle that was formerly embedded in the wild environment as they began to cut down the forest in earnest and adopt domesticated crops for sustenance. The ideological differences between domesticated and wild space-time continued to permeate Maya culture long after an urban way of life had developed, leaving material markers throughout the entire cultural sequence.

## Acknowledgments

We wish to thank Jerry Murdock, Murray Gell-Mann, and Jerry Sabloff for sponsoring the Santa Fe Institute workshops that led to this volume, as well as our colleagues who participated in the fruitful discussions that molded all of the chapters. We also thank the Consejo de Arqueología of the Instituto Nacional de Antropología e Historia for granting the permits to conduct this research, which was generously supported by the Fundación Roberto Hernández, Fundación Pedro y Elena Hernández, the Selz Foundation, Jerry Murdock, and the National Science Foundation (#1623603). This chapter benefited from comments from the editors of the book and from two anonymous reviewers, although the final product is the sole responsibility of the authors. Finally, we thank the community of Yaxuná for allowing us to conduct research in their *ejido*.

# 6

# In the Shadow of Descending Gods

## Monumental Posts and Solar Cycles in the Preclassic Maya Lowlands

Francisco Estrada-Belli and David A. Freidel

The ancient Mayan word for stela, *lakamtun* (Stuart 2005a), means banner stone, and indeed these materializations of Maya time lords (see chapter 7, this volume) like the wooden banners with their feather panaches and god images lofted by Classic warriors and diplomats (Freidel et al. 1993), were shining declarations of the divine powers. But before the age of stelae came into full flower in the first millennium CE, Preclassic Maya were raising and celebrating monumental wooden posts. The West Wall mural of the Pinturas Shrine at San Bartolo (Saturno 2009; Taube et al. 2010) depicts a monumental post, a living tree being, perhaps allspice (Weiss-Krejci 2012), growing out of the scaffold throne of rulership at 100 BCE (fig. 6.1). Five different trees (Landon 2011) frame the creation-ordering scene on that

Figure 6.1. West Wall mural at San Bartolo, ca. 50 BCE. Illustration by Heather Hurst. Reproduced here courtesy of the artist.

wall: four trees, probably marking the cardinal directions, associated with a descending avian deity called the Principal Bird Deity (PDB; Guernsey 2006) and a fifth and likely central one crowned by a realistic bird while the maize god stabs something with a javelin, probably the PDB. The descending PDBs are solar avatars of the creator, Itzam (Taube et al. 2010; Guernsey 2006; Bassie-Sweet and Hopkins 2021). Another PDB in the scene descends from rain clouds that a duck-billed devotee calls to.

These are not the only four-part world-framing monumental posts in the Late Preclassic era. Structure E-VII-sub at Uaxactun (Ricketson and Ricketson 1937, fig. 22), the western radial structure of the original solar commemorative E Group (Aveni and Hartung 1989; Coggins 1980; Freidel et al. 2017) has four holes on the open summit suitable for wooden posts. These holes are approximately 63 centimeters in diameter and 1.32 meters deep. While it is impossible to know how tall the wooden posts were, it is clear that they were intended to provide visual access to people in the plaza below. The excavators say the following: "The fact that these holes had been sealed over in ancient times is also an indication that they had been dug for some temporary purpose, such as the erection of a shed or of wooden standards upon the occasion of some festival, with the knowledge that they would afterward be removed. The normal function of Pyramid E-VII sub., therefore, seems to have been that of an enormous altar, open to the air" (Ricketson and Ricketson 1937, 90). As Coggins (1980) argues, this solar commemorative building had the shape of time. We would further note the total of eighteen stucco masks adorning it, the number of months in the approximate solar year, and the distinctive avian cast of the two masks flanking the open summit with its posts. The zenith passage here, when such posts if planted would have cast no shadow, would have been a harbinger for the rains (Milbrath 2017b).

At Cerro Maya in Belize, Late Preclassic Structure 5C-2nd was situated precisely to observe the solar zenith passage in mid-May (Vadala and Milbrath 2014). Although the passage would have come in at an angle to the north-south orientation of the building, celebrants on the plaza below would still have observed this hierophany. The summit structure had postholes 1.2 meters in diameter and 3.5 meters deep. The three preserved holes suggest that there were four altogether, widely positioned in the intercardinal directions (Schele and Freidel 1990, figs. 3.8–3.10). The size of these masonry-lined holes, which were constructed as the pyramid was being raised, suggests that they were designed to hold massive poles that ascended through the perishable roof of the building (Freidel 1986; Schele and Freidel 1990, 107–109, 435n19). If this were the case, then observers would have witnessed the disappearance of the shadows of the four posts during the zenith passage. Like the trees/posts in the West Wall mural at San Bartolo, these posts were integral to royal ritual and deity veneration (Schele and Freidel 1990; Reese 1996; Vadala and Milbrath 2014). We now turn to a triadic variation on the Preclassic materialization of time through wooden posts at the site of Cival in Petén, Guatemala.

## Telling Time with Posts

In the early 2000s, Estrada-Belli (2006, 2011) discovered a hole suitable for a monumental post built over an astonishing Middle Preclassic (850–350 BCE) cruciform ritual deposit of jade celts and pebbles and offering vessels from around 800 BCE (fig. 6.1) at Cival in northeastern Petén of Guatemala. This led him to conclude that this hole held a symbolic World Tree (Estrada-Belli 2006, 2011). Maya peoples have raised such trees—often, but not always, shaped as crosses—into the present time (Oakes 1951; Vogt 1976; Freidel et al. 1993). This first monumental post at Cival was located on the east-west centerline of an E Group complex designed to observe the equinoxes and the zenith passage of the sun on or about May 10, the beginning of the rainy season in Petén (Estrada-Belli 2011).[1] At the zenith passage, the posited monumental post would have functioned as a gnomon, a sundial whose disappearing shadow would have marked the zenith. Did the people who created this elaborate World Tree know about this disappearing shadow? It is hard to imagine that they were unaware of this potent visual performance by the sun, which they considered to be a living being that even today is worshipped and conflated with the crucified Christian god who brings the rains to the Maya area (Bricker 1981). Susan Milbrath (2017b, 96), citing Aimers and Rice (2006, 80, 92) and Rice (2007, 87, 147), declares that Preclassic Mesoamericans, including the Maya, did see the gnomon effect. Thus, time was (and continues to be [Freidel et al. 1993, 55–57]) materialized in the shadow of the ascendant god who descends from heaven to bring the rains.

The post-raising tradition at Cival persisted into the Late Preclassic period (350 BCE–250 CE), when three monumental postholes were built over the earlier World Tree offering place and the original hole in the earth (Estrada-Belli 2011). The holes form a west-pointing triangle, the pattern of the three stones of the Cosmic Hearth in the Maya creation stories of the later Classic period (250–850 CE). Linda Schele (Freidel et al. 1993, 79–80), following Dennis and Barbara Tedlock (Tedlock and Tedlock 1985, 261), suggested that the K'iche' Maya identification of three stars as the hearth was deeply ancient. The Maya believed that these stars and the belt stars of the constellation of Orion were the cosmic turtle womb place of the resurrected maize god. They rose on the solar path in the Preclassic period (Milbrath 2017b) and would have performed a nighttime zenith passage, complementing the solar zenith passage.

The gnomon function of the monumental World Trees in this Late Preclassic version at Cival would have been even more important to observers at the solar zenith passage, for by this time, the eastern range of the E Group had been supplanted by a massive triadic structure associated with solar deities and rulership (see below). The sunrise could be observed only as it came up over this great building, which made it harder to track the solar cycle. However, the original E Group eastern structure was enlarged and a new pyramid was built farther to the west. From its summit one could observe the sunrise free of obstructions through the eastern buildings. This time, the corners of the eastern structure marked solstice days. On quarter days, the sun could be seen rising behind the central peak of the triadic complex as well (Estrada-Belli 2011, fig. 4.1; see Šprajc 2021b for quarter days). After that enlargement, the zenith day sunrise could still be observed in two ways: on the horizon (over the corner structures of the triadic complex) and in the plaza (by observing the posts' shadows). This phenomenon would have been especially impressive when the pivot of the three shadows cast by the posts ended in their disappearance. The posts were about 1 meter in diameter and were set 1.5 meters into the bedrock. They are much larger than the original post on the top of the jade offering and were more similar to full-size trees. They were set on a 50-centimeter-high platform, which enhanced the visibility of the shadow phenomenon from the far reaches of the plaza as well as from the stairs of the surrounding buildings. Dance platforms with at least one large posthole were also found in the nearby E Groups of Hamontun (Estrada-Belli 2009, 2012) and Holmul in the same centerline position (Estrada-Belli 2007), suggesting that these ceremonies were common at smaller centers in this region and perhaps elsewhere in the Maya lowlands (see Freidel et al. 2017). We believe these platforms were used for dance performances in connection with solar hierophanies of the kind featured on Preclassic relief monuments such as Kaminaljuyu Stela 11 (Parsons 1986, fig. 169) and Izapa Stela 4 (Norman 1973, fig. 3.5).

## A Sun-Bird King

The Late Preclassic plaza of Cival featured a stela in the same platform in the plaza's centerline, above the pit where the first World Tree post was set and in front of the steps of a new version of the eastern structure. Stela 2 was framed by the three World Tree cosmic stones (Estrada-Belli, Bauer et al. 2003; Estrada-Belli, Grube, et al. 2003; Estrada-Belli 2006). The ruler was depicted with open arms in a striding pose, reminiscent of a spinning dance pose seen on Stela 4 at Izapa, the Late Preclassic city on the Pacific coast of Chiapas, Mexico (Norman 1973; Guernsey 2010a). On that monument, a principal bird deity is shown diving from the sky, symbolized by a sky-maw motif. Below the deity is a dancing ruler in avian costume. The avian deity's wings bear the signs for day and night, as do the dancing ruler's winged arms. It would appear that the deity descends from the sky upon the ruler/impersonator. These images could be a representation of ritual in which the solar deity was evoked during the midday zenith passage ceremony by the Cival ruler (and presumably by rulers across the Mesoamerican world) to petition the deity for the onset of the rainy season and the sprouting of maize from the earth as cosmological metaphors of life renewal. The frequent appearance of avian imagery in Late Preclassic and Classic period royal costumes also suggests that these agrarian rituals may have coincided in time and had shared meaning with secular events, including political accessions, probably as early as the Late Preclassic period, by around 200 BCE, judging from the Cival monument.

While Cival's Stela 2 is fragmented, it shows the outline of a ruler who is wearing a royal pectoral mask ornamented with the typical triple jade plaques. The image is that of a latch-lipped profile head, the Principal Bird Deity. As Taube and Saturno and colleagues suggest (Taube et al. 2010; Freidel 2017; Saturno, Beltrán et al. 2017), in the West Wall murals of the Pinturas Shrine at San Bartolo, this bird, the solar avatar of the old creator god, alights on four World Trees that, while depicted in a line, no doubt represent the four quarters and the center of the world, as in the cruciform ordering of jade celts in the Middle Preclassic cache at Cival. Just as the shadows of the World Tree posts disappear at the solar zenith, so too the bird loses its shadow when it lands at the top of a tree. In this interpretation, the scene represents the sun at zenith when the shadows cast by the World Trees disappear, a harbinger of the coming rains in the southern Maya lowlands. As William Saturno, Boris Beltrán, and Franco D. Rossi (2017) have shown, the Late Preclassic Pinturas Shrine is a morning sun shrine on the eastern side of a pyramid covering the eastern range structure of an E Group. Its stories are still in significant measure the stories of the role of the sun in creation (Taube et al. 2010) and as the symbol of divine authority.

Before each tree, a young creation-era hero lets penitential blood, piercing his penis with what Taube sees as a branch but which might actually be a javelin. Offerings of sacrifice in the form of fish, bird, deer (each with a fire started in its body) and a flower (a symbol of the soul) (Freidel et al. 1993, 183; Freidel and Guenter 2006; Fitzsimmons 2009; Scherer 2015), rest before the World Trees of the quarters. In a scene that punctuates this rolled-out world, another solar bird descends in a rain cloud, called down by a duck-billed primordial Wind god impersonator (Taube et al. 2010), arms raised in a gesture of petitioning and seduction. The fifth tree of the center completes this story. It is partially ruined, but enough is present to show that it depicts a real bird at the top of the tree, while below a maize god thrusts downward with his javelin, sacrificing the solar avatar bird. That bird as prey is also pictured on the back of a belt in another fragment of the murals at the Pinturas Shrine (Taube et al. 2010).

Sacrifice did not result in permanent death, for the bird as a living being continued to be displayed universally in the Late Preclassic lowland Maya tradition and into the Classic period, both before and after sacrifice (Freidel et al. 1993, 365). But the sacrifice must represent the covenantal connection between the maize god and the sun cycle that is made explicit in the design and orientation of lowland Maya E Groups of the Preclassic era (Aveni and Dowd 2017). Freidel (2017, 196–197) discusses the conflation of the Sun god and the maize god in the anthropomorphic lower main masks of Structure 5C-2nd at Cerro Maya, which has been dated to about 100 CE in the Late Preclassic (we will return to this building below). The coming of the rains is vital to the sprouting of planted seeds, especially maize. As Milbrath (2017b) underscores, the zenith passage of the sun in the Maya lowlands is the harbinger of the return of the rains. The sun's path across the sky marks the seasons as well as the time of day and thus represents a structured world order. At Cival the Late Preclassic ruler has the head of the solar bird on his chest, exemplifying the ritual power of Late Preclassic Maya kings to evoke the power of the sun and rain to give life to the maize god, the ultimate harbinger of life and world order, at the beginning of the agricultural season.

**Posts and Gods**

As described in the introduction, several excavated Late Preclassic buildings have yielded evidence of four monumental World Tree posts. Structure 5C-2nd at Cerros (Cerro Maya) on the coast of Corozal Bay in northern Belize is such a building (figs. 6.2, 6.3). Jeffrey Vadala and Susan Milbrath (2014) have demonstrated that the elaborate façades of this south-facing building at Cerro Maya were designed to celebrate the solar zenith passage of the sun. If the World Tree poles were indeed set to tower over the thatched roof of the superstructure temple, their shadows would have swung across the waters of the lagoon north of the temple every day over the course of the dry season, when fields were being prepared. But they would have gotten shorter and shorter as the sun approached the day of the zenith passage, finally disappearing on or about May 15 at this latitude. Then, when the sun was

Monumental Posts and Solar Cycles in the Preclassic Maya Lowlands · 137

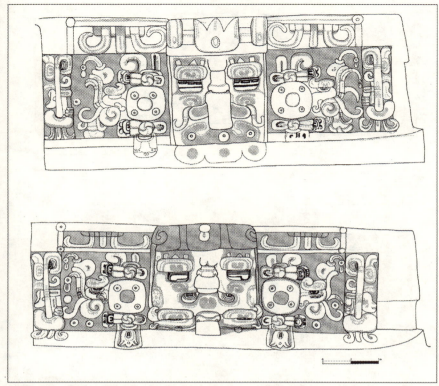

Figure 6.2. Cerros (Cerro Maya) Structure 5C-2nd upper and lower tier masks depicting the Principal Bird Deity and the maize god on the eastern side of the pyramid's central stairways. Drawings by Kathryn Reese-Taylor for the Cerros Project.

shining, the tree shadows would swing down across the stairway, connecting the temple to the plaza in front of it. Ideally, by the time the tree shadows crossed the central dance platform in the stairway, the seasonal rains would be obscuring them by midafternoon and soaking the king. These shadows would have marked the days of sprouting and intense cultivation demanded of maize farmers.

The masks on the front of 5C-2nd have been subject to numerous interpretations (fig. 6.4; Freidel 1979, 1985; Schele and Miller 1986; Schele and Freidel 1990), which is fitting for symbols of rich complexity in the context of a disciplinary investigation of material symbol systems that is always changing. That said, it is clear that Karl Taube (personal communication to David Freidel, November 1986) was correct some time ago when he identified the two upper monumental masks as images of the great bird called the Principal Bird Deity (Kathryn Reese [1996] also identified the upper masks as birds). The

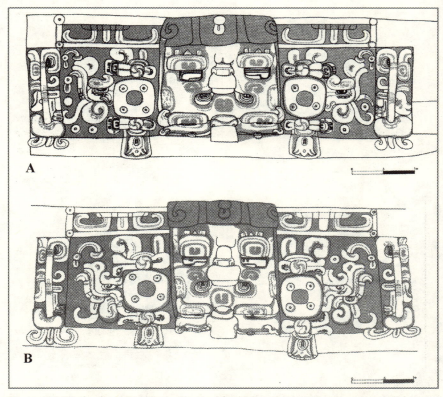

Figure 6.3. Masks depicting the maize god from the eastern (*A*) and western (*B*) lower tier of the Cerros (Cerro Maya) Structure 5C-2nd, ca. 50 BCE. Drawings by Kathryn Reese-Taylor for the Cerros Project.

masks on the lower terrace of 5C-2nd depict the Preclassic Maya maize god with (at least certainly on the eastern side) painted *k'in* glyphs on its cheeks, making it a sun-faced (K'inich) maize god (Freidel 2017). This combination of solar bird and maize god resonates with the roughly contemporary painting from the eastern shrine of Triadic Group at Cival in which several figures of the maize god were depicted wearing several headdresses, including the tri-foliated crown and head of the solar Principal Bird Deity (fig. 6.5; Estrada-Belli 2011, 22–24). These types of headdress frequently appear in Late Preclassic and Classic Maya art as symbols of rulership, suggesting that this shrine was used for rituals to the sun god and the maize god as archetypes of Maya rulers as early as in the second century BCE.

Several images of the maize god wearing the headdress of the avian god appear on the West Wall of the Pinturas Shrine, dated to the first century BCE. The theme of the bird alighting on the World Trees on Structure 5C-2nd at

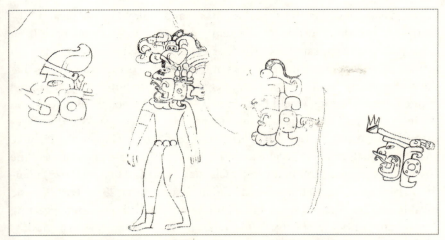

Figure 6.4. Images of the maize god wearing a variety of headdresses, including the avian solar deity's. Mural painting on the walls of the main temple room atop Cival's triadic complex, ca. 200 BCE–1 CE. Drawing by Heather Hurst for the Holmul Archaeological Project.

Figure 6.5. Stela 2 at Izapa depicting a Principal Bird/Sun Deity diving from the sky toward a World Tree flanked by two figures with arms raised. Drawing by Ajax Moreno after Norman (1973). Courtesy of the New World Archaeological Foundation.

Cerro Maya signaled in the upper tier masks and, following Vadala and Milbrath's (2014) identification of the zenith passage there, would have been evident in the disappearance of the four great pole shadows on that day. An intriguing feature of the upper masks of the solar bird at Cerro Maya is that the eastern mask has three circles of beige plaster surrounded by broad red painted bands forming what I discern to be flowing blood scrolls below it on the inferior molding, suggesting that the head has been severed and is a sacrifice (Helmke and Nielsen 2015; Freidel 2022; fig. 6.2). Christophe Helmke and Jesper Nielsen (2015) argue persuasively that there are depictions of the Great Bird's severed head in the Early Classic period and Freidel (2022) identifies a ceramic image of this severed head in Yaxuná Burial 23, an Early Classic royal tomb. The western mask has a human neck and shoulders, suggesting that it represents the creator in his avian mask. That the western mask is descending is made clear by the framing snake images of the terrace panels. While all of the panels have such snakes, representing the homophony of snake and sky in Mayan languages, the other three panels have J-scroll and bracket motifs in the upper registers that are replaced with inward-facing profile polymorphs in the western side. In this way, the upper west mask is descending out of the mouth of the sky. It is not surprising that the beak of the creator's bird mask is marked Ak'bal, darkness, as that is what will follow sunset when the creator's descent is complete.

## Birds and Gods Descend Like Rain

On the other side of the lowland Maya world in Chiapas, Mexico, the solar bird descends from the sky toward a World Tree on Izapa Stela 2 (fig. 6.5; Norman 1973; Guernsey 2006). Here, as in the case of the West Wall mural of the Pinturas Shrine at San Bartolo, small human figures raise their arms in invocation or perhaps celebration. In the case of Structure 5C-2nd, it seems plausible to us that this descent of the sun from its zenith marks the creator's gift of the coming rains. All the panels feature framing descending snake heads. The descending maize god on the West Wall mural of the Pinturas Shrine is surrounded by water and snakes (Taube et al. 2010). While this is clearly "entering the water," a metaphor for death preceding rebirth, it is also the return of the rains to water the maize kernels, "little skulls," that have been planted in anticipation of them (Carlsen and Prechtel 1991).

The descending snake heads framing the god masks at Cerro Maya likely also convey the return of the rains. All of the upper framing panels in the 5C-2nd composition have mouth symbols, the "J-scroll and bracket" motif, except for the monumental bird mask on the upper west panel. This Principal Bird

Deity mask is clearly worn by a person, as the neck and shoulder are indicated in paint below it. Its eastern counterpart is a severed bird head with plumes of red gore, the bird as sacrificed by the maize god on the West Wall mural at Pinturas. The western masked bird person on the Cerro Maya composition is framed above not by "J-scroll and bracket" frontal mouths (Quirarte 1973) but by two inward-facing snake heads in profile. The bird-masked personage is being disgorged from these snakes, a clear signal of descent. Arthur Miller (1974) convincingly showed that snakes as cords pervade the iconographic record of southeastern Mesoamerica from Izapa to Tulum. Here, we propose, is a masked bird dancer embodying the old creator in his solar bird avatar, performing the rope descent from the World Tree poles that is the essence of the Danza de los Voladores performance still important to Indigenous Maya today (Bassie-Sweet 2008, 297). Thus, it seems likely to us that the descending gods of Maya material symbolism, depicted as late as the Late Postclassic in the central shrine at Tulum in Quintana Roo, Mexico (see Miller 1974; Vadala and Milbrath 2014), register the performance of versions of the Danza de los Voladores in the Preclassic lowland contexts described above. That famous dance generally celebrated the quadripartite world and was closely connected to the petitioning of the rains to end the dry season.

Additional pieces of evidence are relevant to this line of reasoning regarding solar gnomon celebrations, rain rituals, and kingship in the Maya lowlands. The Triadic Group at Cival, which towered 30 meters above its plaza, stood directly in line with the axis of where the stela and posts were located along the path of the rising sun. The three temples were positioned to form a triangular pattern, and their eastern orientation was mirrored by the gnomon posts on the plaza. The eastern pyramid (Structure 1) was decorated with two identical masks of an anthropomorphic deity (fig. 6.6; Estrada-Belli 2006). Its black-painted L-shaped eyes and the bracketed U signs on its eyelids and earflares identify it as a solar deity. The sun god and maize god masks at Cerro Maya also have L-shaped eyes. The U-shape motif is also quite common in Preclassic Maya iconography. For example, it is found on the eyebrows of the Cerro Maya masks (fig. 6.4), it is frequently worn by the Principal Bird Deity, and it may be the symbol for the "brilliance" of both the sky and solar deities (see Stuart 2010 on "shiner"). Another important attribute of this visage is the *k'in* sign on each cheek. However, the deity's mouth is rendered as the buccal mask of the maize god (Taube 1992a) with a single tooth that ends in a bifid tongue. The latter elements leave little doubt as to its identity as a sun-faced maize god. There are incised circles on the forehead and a so-called exclamation point sign—a raindrop symbol in Middle Preclassic iconography, a droplet worn as an insignia on the sun and maize god masks at Cerro Maya (see

Figure 6.6. Mask from Structure 1 combining features of the maize god (mouth), the sun god (eyes), and the lightning god (shiner motifs on eyebrows and earflares). Triadic Group 1, Cival, ca. second century BCE. Photo by Francisco Estrada-Belli.

Freidel 2017, 190), and bracketed circles below the eyes on the Cival masks. These are known as water symbols in early Mesoamerican iconography. They set this being apart from more common images of the sun god as Lord Sun, K'inich Ajaw. Symbols of liquids dot the 5C-2nd panels at Cerro Maya as well. And the monumental masks there are flanked by profiles of centipede heads, the living orifice of the world from which the sun daily emerges (Taube 2003b); exclamation-point droplets drip from their fangs. It is clear that the Late Preclassic programs at Cival and Cerro Maya both have a clear focus on the maize and sun gods at the time of the return of the rains.

Given that the pyramid stands on the eastern side of the Cival E Group plaza, we suggest that it once supported a temple dedicated to the rising sun. The raindrops would indicate that this particular sun god was associated with the coming of the rains, as they also originate in the eastern sky and are brought into the Maya lowlands by the trade winds during the summer months. The figure of a rain-bearing sun deity in Classic Maya art was first identified by David Stuart (2005b) at Palenque in the context of the creation stories of King K'inich Ahkal Mo' Nahb III, named Hun Yeh Winik, One Tooth Person. The name of this creator-era god, following the reasoning of

David Stuart (2005b), was conflated with that of Chahk, the rain god, and was registered through the sprocketed *Spondylus* shell earflares of that god. Both the Cerro Maya and Cival sun and maize gods have the prominent protruding tooth of this deity, in the case of Cival, a bifid tongue attached to the single tooth. Therefore, we suggest that the Cival and Cerro Maya masks were referencing a Preclassic version of this rain-bringing sun god who remained important throughout the Classic period.

At the opposite, western end of the Cival plaza stood an 18-meter-tall radial pyramid (Structure 9). Excavations on the eastern and northern façades in 2014 revealed the remains of large stucco masks flanking the central stairway (fig. 6.7; Estrada-Belli 2014). The carvings were associated with the last phase of construction of the pyramid in the first to second century CE and have been severely affected by erosion. There were also signs that each of them had been set on fire, presumably during the final act in the history of Cival during the third century CE. In spite of all this, enough of the northern mask was preserved to reveal a shell-shaped ear, sprocketed as *Spondylus* in the Classic depictions of GI One Tooth Person, the rain-bringing sun (Estrada-Belli 2017). Again, this is a diagnostic element of images of the rain god Chahk and also of Hun Yeh Winik GI, the rain-bringing sun god (Stuart 2005b). That god descends and touches the earth at the time of creation in the text of King Kan

Figure 6.7. Rain god Chahk mask on the northern side of Structure 9 at Cival, a radial pyramid in the E Group of the Main Plaza, ca. first century CE. Photo by Francisco Estrada-Belli.

Bahlam on the Panel of the Cross at Palenque (Schele and Freidel 1990, 246). In the case of the Cerro Maya sun and maize god masks, the GI *Spondylus* shells are shown as dangles on the earflare assemblages.

Another early image of the descending sun and rain god is carved on Cival Stela 3 (fig. 6.8), which was recovered 400 meters east of the plaza, out of context, as it was likely in the process of being looted in 2014 (Estrada-Belli 2014, 2017). This stela probably originally stood in the central E Group plaza. It depicts a human figure with an upward-facing body and a downward-facing head, as if dropping from the sky. The blunt-snouted being (compared to the latch-beaked Principal Bird Deity images) has flamed eyebrows and a bifid tongue attached to his single prominent tooth. The figure wears a rope that emerges from the top of his head and is tied around his head. Given his diving/flying god pose, it is possible that this signals the rope of a *volador* flying performer, an individual who would have dived off a pole attached to ropes, a ritual performance that pervaded ancient Mesoamerica (Kirchhoff 1943). On his belt is a U sign. While this appears to be a complete monument, it is possible that it was part of a composition made of similar carved slabs that formed a lengthier frieze or wall decoration. Stylistically, the carving can be securely placed in the Late Preclassic period and was almost certainly in view in the plaza at the same time as the masks on the western and eastern pyramids.

Descending gods are also signaled on the frontal façade of the Late Preclassic structure discovered by tunneling inside Structure 2 at Calakmul (Carrasco Vargas 2012, 92–93), where a god impersonator in the act of descending is central to a preserved stucco façade on the roof of a building

Figure 6.8. Stela 3 at Cival depicting a human-like image of the rain god Chahk, ca. 200 BCE–1 CE. Drawing and photographs by Alexandre Tokovinine.

in an early quadrangle buried inside Structure 2. The so-called swimmers (Hansen et al. 2011; Doyle and Houston 2012) on the relief discovered in the Central Acropolis of El Mirador were thought originally to be on the side of a rainwater drainage reservoir (Argyle and Hansen 2016). However, upon closer inspection they appear to decorate the upper register of a pyramid's façade-framing sun god masks that are very similar to the ones discussed above (fig. 6.9).

Doyle and Houston (2012) had cogently suggested that these are rain god impersonators, as they wear god headdresses. One of them, who is visible only on the front half, has the L-shaped eye and shell earflare of the god images we have discussed above. We also believe it probable that these are descending gods and *volador* dancers. In fact, the fully preserved figure has what appears to be a rope extending from the waist area behind a mask on the back of his belt. Angled-profile god masks frame these performers as possible allusions to the celestial saurian profile heads that frame the Cerro Maya masks (fig. 6.2) and the sky bands at Izapa. Finally, the upper frieze on this roof depicts undulating clouds framing water birds and large Chahk heads with the prominent single tooth of GI Hun Yeh Winik. Thus, the descending god

Figure 6.9. Northern edge of the Central Acropolis at El Mirador, Late/Terminal Preclassic period (1–250 CE), showing rain deities and other celestial beings. Photo by Francisco Estrada-Belli.

motif is evidently widespread in the Late Preclassic lowlands. And while direct evidence that poles were used for *volador* performances is not accessible, we think that the iconographic evidence is persuasive.

The descending god motif is linked to the themes of death, resurrection, and royal accession in the murals of the Pinturas Shrine at San Bartolo. Freidel thinks that the Pinturas Shrine was a place for the display of royal bundles, one of numerous Late Preclassic royal shrines that served as bundle houses and accession places; Structure 5C-2nd at Cerro Maya is one example. Estrada-Belli observed that monumental masks on the El Mirador Central Acropolis façade discussed here have the mouth mirrors similar to the ornament masks on royal bundles in the Pinturas Shrine and elsewhere. The cycling of solar time, the descent of divinity down the paths of the great tree/posts into royal bundle houses, and the accession of rulers charged with that divinity is a theme worthy of sustained inquiry going forward.

## Concluding Remarks

In essence, the main focus of the Cival plaza, like that of many other E Groups, would have been the celebration of solar-related calendar events and the sun god as a primordial rain-bringing deity for the birth of the maize god since the beginning of the Middle Preclassic period (850–350 BCE; Aveni et al. 2003; Estrada-Belli 2017; Freidel et al. 2017). The combination of the contextual evidence buried in the Cival plaza and the embedded meanings of artifacts and buildings therein, however, may provide a more nuanced understanding of the cosmological vision that inspired it. In Late Preclassic times (350 BCE–250 CE), the plaza functioned as a place to celebrate the morning sun as it rose on the eastern horizon, setting the stage for the coming of the rains. The gnomon posts set on the plaza floor marked the zenith passage of the sun on two separate occasions every year, coinciding with the first and second wave of monsoons, which were separated by a brief dry period, each of which had special implications for the growing season. Towering on either side of the plaza were the pyramids, the manmade sacred mountains and residences of the gods. The western one was identified with the rain god Chahk, the eastern one with the sun god. In the Late Preclassic period, these deities presided over rituals ultimately invoking the birth of the maize god as a World Tree and as the essence of human life and earthly royal powers. The impromptu images painted in the interior of the Cival sun god temple pyramid only offer a few glimpses of the rituals performed by early rulers as they celebrated the world order by wearing the symbols of the maize and sun gods.

This complex interplay of cosmic meanings is but a latter-day manifestation of the meanings embedded in the Middle Preclassic jade cache at Cival, where the rain gods are represented by the five directional jars and the maize god is evoked by the jade axes as seedlings for World Trees supporting the sky. What was not expressed by this Middle Preclassic (ca. 800 BCE) metaphor for world order are explicit references to the figure of the ruler as a World Tree.

However, the presence of a ruler as the main agent of this early ritual, which began as the plaza was founded and its functions were established, may be implicit in the massive amount of jade (20 pounds) deposited in it that reveals a level of craftsmanship, long-distance trade connections, and wealth that rivaled the richest offerings in Classic period royal burials. At Cival, the fortunate state of preservation of the buildings' stucco decoration and of the founding ritual deposits offer a rare glimpse into what may be a set of cosmological references that perhaps were more widely associated with early E Group plazas across the Maya lowlands. These might be the residues of the first materialization of a cosmological construct that persisted well beyond the Preclassic period. We see a version of this construct again in the Late Classic twin-pyramid complexes at Tikal (Carr and Hazard 1961; chapter 14, this volume). There, the western and eastern pyramids framed the plaza where stone monuments commemorated the ruler's performances on calendar events. Temple I and Temple II in Tikal's Great Plaza (the vision of Tikal's greatest Late Classic ruler, Jasaw Chan K'awiil) face one another, forming a triangular pattern with Temple 5D-33. This may have been a direct reference to the eastern-focused architectural layout of Preclassic centers such as Cival, Mirador, Nakbe, and San Bartolo, evoking the powers of the sun, the rain, and the maize gods to maintain the world order and provide sustenance to the people.

The sun and rain gods were the main deities associated with world order, military might, and secular authority throughout the ages in Mesoamerica. These concepts were materialized in the most monumental way on buildings that evoked the forces, structures, and places of that ordered Mesoamerican universe. The materializations of this worldview were regenerated in varied detail by each succeeding state or empire. For example, at Classic period Teotihuacan, the Pyramid of the Sun and the Feathered Serpent Pyramid stood on the eastern side of the Avenue of the Dead as shrines dedicated to the sun and the rain deity. The Pyramid of the Sun's *adosada* structure was decorated with fire symbols, confirming colonial period accounts of New Fire ceremonies performed here. The Pyramid of the Feathered Serpent was decorated with the heads of the rain god, Tlaloc, carried by the feathered serpent, a celestial supernatural that Karl Taube (2005) associates with cloud-making.

Fragments of blue-painted stucco found on the summit of the pyramid also suggest that it supported a structure dedicated to the blue rain god (S. Sugiyama 2005).

The significance of Teotihuacan art and architecture as symbols of ritual authority throughout Mesoamerica was such that their iconography was embraced by Classic period rulers for centuries after Teotihuacan's demise as a place of great political power. To the Maya, the Pyramid of the Sun's *adosada* platform may have been the Wiinte' Naah, the place for fire rituals associated with the accession ceremonies of several known Maya kings and with those of later central Mexican rulers so often referred to in ancient texts (Fash et al. 2009). The significance of the sun god in central Mexican symbolism related to war was matched in Classic Maya iconography by the frequent appearance of sun god images with weapons or in other types of references to war or authority. The Tlaloc and war symbolism of the Feathered Serpent Pyramid may have been the source of inspiration for much Teotihuacan-style war insignia that were eagerly evoked by Maya architecture and rulers' insignia in the Classic period (S. Sugiyama 2005). A notable example is the recently discovered Teotihuacan-style pyramid at Tikal, which is decorated with talud-tablero and is associated with deposits of Tlaloc censers (Houston et al. 2021).

Much later in time, the association of solar and rain symbolism with war and royal power was emblematically materialized in the red and blue twin temples of the Templo Mayor at Tenochtitlan, the center of the Late Postclassic Mexica empire (Matos Moctezuma 1988). There, within each successive construction of the temple pyramid were the latest manifestations of the Mesoamerican worldview we see at Cival, not only in the form and orientation of the structures but also in the multilayered offerings of elements from the various domains and forces of the universe: the watery underworld and the plentiful earth and sky, framed by quadripartite rain god effigy jars. By then, the Mexica worldview had been materialized in the plazas of Mesoamerican cities for over 2,000 years.

## Note

1 According to the National Oceanic and Atmospheric Administration's calculator, the zenith is observable on May 6–9 and again on August 2–5 at Cival (17° 21′ 30″N, 89° 14′ 59″W). See "Solar Position Calculator" at https://gml.noaa.gov/grad/solcalc/.

# 7

# Stelae, Spirits, Desecration, and Devotion

## The Fate of Some Time Lords in the Classic Maya World

### DAVID A. FREIDEL AND OLIVIA NAVARRO-FARR

As I have argued here and elsewhere (Stuart 1996), many Maya stelae were manufactured to embody particular time periods, not just to commemorate them, and I am tempted to think that the significance of such flashing stones was related to this temporal aspect of their function. Just as a day or moment of time passes in human experience, so too does the flash of a god who brings rain and sustenance to the earth. The axes of Chahk in this way came to be thrust into the earth as sacred monuments, carrying multifaceted meanings of time, world renewal, and of rulers' active roles in those processes.

(Stuart 2010, 296)

## Architecture, Agency, and Stelae in Maya Timekeeping

An earlier work on Maya E Groups concluded that these solar commemorative buildings and plazas initially served to materialize time for people of lowland Maya communities in the context of emergent complex social institutions, increasing sedentism, and the adoption of maize as a subsistence staple (Freidel et al. 2017; see also Dowd and Milbrath 2015). E Groups served to standardize time reckoning around an agrarian calendar tied to the solar year. This emergent pattern of complexity is reviewed theoretically and comparatively in this book (chapter 3, this volume) with particular attention to the prospect, indicated by a paucity of residential aggregation in the vicinity of the first such centers, that many of the participants in the construction and use of these earliest centers in southwestern Petén and in the lower reaches of the Usumacinta and San Pedro Mártir Rivers were still mobile horticulturalists and not fully farmers. As Inomata and Triadan (chapter 3, this volume) have suggested, horticulturalists and farmers may have made, quite literally, common ground in their distinct understandings of the passage and reckoning of time through the innovation of the first centers. Other chapters (e.g., chapter 14, this volume) build on the premise of centers as places that materialized time and as places where time-transcendent portals between the world of the living and the world of the unborn, human-form gods and ancestors, were established, maintained, and periodically opened (see Freidel et al. 1993, 131). These and other supernatural sentient agents were brought into being and consigned back to latency by human agents who conjured them in the context of aggregate celebrations (see Inomata and Coben 2006 for a discussion of Maya spectacle), tying them to time manifest in celestial cycles of the sun, moon, stars, and planets. How diverse groups of ordinary people—guided by kin elders, local sodalities, village shamans, and war leaders—came to agree among themselves to do this and to defer to the charismatic and prophetic among them remains very much an open question, one that Cynthia Robin has addressed analogically at Chan (chapter 10, this volume). Here, we will focus on how exalted leaders, whom we have dubbed time lords in honor of David Stuart's conception of them, may have performed to materialize time in the Classic period (250–900 CE), when we have tangible representations of them in public space—and how their people may have thought about them and acted on their images. But we first continue to outline how some Maya got to that kind of representation through performance based in architectural settings.

The scale of the emerging Preclassic (1000 BCE–250 CE) ceremonial centers in the Maya lowlands is sometimes astonishing, as at Yaxnohcah in Campeche, for example (see chapter 4, this volume), and by the middle of the first millennium BCE some communities throughout the lowlands had constructed large public buildings. Archaeologists often infer that when people build at a large scale they are led to do so (but see Carballo and Feinman 2016 on collective action). Architectural innovation at scale is not inevitable or anonymous at the time of its successful launching. In motivating and gathering people to do the work, teaching them the craft required to do it, and sustaining interest in the collective effort, we must assume that the Maya had such leaders, sages, and traditions of teaching—of initiation into the wisdom distilled from observation and reflection over generations. In contrast to most of the leaders of the Pacific Slope of Guatemala, of Chiapas, or of the Gulf Coast heartland of the Olmec with their monumental sculpture (Coe and

Diehl 1980), leaders in the Maya lowlands have registered almost nothing of their existence beyond the centers themselves (the earliest leaders of the Izapa kingdom were similarly anonymous; see Rosenswig et al. 2018). There are Middle Preclassic (1000–350 BCE) royal tombs at La Libertad (Miller 2014) and Chiapa de Corzo (Bachand and Lowe 2012) in Chiapas, Mexico, and one at Tak'alik Ab'aj (Schieber de Lavarreda and Orrego Corzo 2013) in the Pacific Slope region of Guatemala, but nothing like them in the Maya lowlands to date (burials yes, royal tombs no).

The earliest evidence for royal tombs in the Maya lowlands is still Late Preclassic (350 BCE–150 CE) (Hansen 1998), limited to looted tombs in a large triadic structure at Wakna in the Mirador area of Petén and documented tombs in the North Acropolis at Tikal (Coe 1965). The Tikal tombs are Cauac phase (200 BCE–150 CE; Culbert and Kosakowsky 2019, 154) and likely date to the first century CE at the end of the florescence of Preclassic civilization in the lowlands. Freidel (Freidel and Suhler 1998; Freidel 2018) and Simon Martin and Nikolai Grube (2000) have proposed that the individual in Tikal Burial 85 is Yax Ehb Xook, the founder of the dynasty. Indeed, Freidel (2018) thinks that he was the innovator of dynastic succession among the lowland Maya. Dynasty as an institutional form of divine kingship manifest in stone kings was innovated in the Classic period southern lowlands (Freidel 2018). By the end of the third century CE, a Tikal king had planted a stela, Stela 29, and the advent of the Classic time lords of the southern lowlands was at hand.

But surely there were powerful rulers before the time of that stela raising—during the centuries of elaborately decorated modeled and stuccoed buildings with great masks of the sun, the rain god, the maize god, the solar bird, other human-form gods, and anonymous rulers (cf. McAnany 2019a, who suggests that these were efforts of collectives rather than rulers).

There are rare stelae, such as one at Nakbe, that, even though it is in Late Preclassic context and stylistically Late Preclassic, exhibit a resemblance to the rulers on Stela 3 at La Venta in the Olmec heartland (Hansen 1998). Another Preclassic stela is at Cival in the center of the E Group (Estrada-Belli 2017). Yet another is at Actuncan in Belize in association with a triadic group (McGovern 2004). These are certainly Preclassic rulers, harbingers of what would come. But while regal, these people remain anonymous and the practice remains decisively rare in the Maya lowlands. It is not an obvious emulation of Olmec Gulf Coast ideas about kings of stone to the west but rather a tradition circuitously related to Maya practices in the highlands and along the Pacific coast to the south. Takeshi Inomata and colleagues (2017) make a similar argument regarding the diffusion of royal practice.

Why the Classic time lords emulated neighbors and yet in important ways innovated the tradition of raising portrayals of themselves in the context of calendar jubilees and planting their stelae as enduring actors in the materialization of time is a question that has been previously addressed (Freidel and Suhler 1995; Freidel 2018). In the opening quote, David Stuart (2010) has an important part of the answer, but even more important for this particular medium anchored in Long Count time is that these southern lowland Maya committed to dynastic succession from founders, a practice not obviously of interest to their neighbors to the north and south (Freidel 2018; chapter 13, this volume). From our perspective, the main function of Classic period lowland Maya stelae was to declare the legitimate pedigree of divine rulers as scions of dynasties. The earliest known stela in the southern lowlands, Stela 29 at Tikal, depicts a probable ancestor floating above the king (Martin and Grube 2008). As the tradition of raising stelae was established, these and other monuments addressed other aspects of rule, such as alliance and warfare, but pedigree remained paramount.

In this chapter, we focus on some of the consequences of that innovation and its repercussions for many aspects of royal practice and for the practices of ordinary people as collective agents in their world. What happened when Maya rulers materialized time not only in performance but also in engendered images of themselves in stone? How did this change the conception and use of public architecture? Linda Schele and David Freidel (Freidel and Schele 1988b) addressed the transition from Preclassic to Classic as a manifestation of a major social and cultural structural transformation in lowland Maya society. Since then, Freidel has come to see the pervasive use of stelae as a distinctly southern lowland innovation, but no doubt a major trajectory-setting one. To answer our rhetorical questions, we suggest that carving kings and queens in stone and stucco changed the conception of ceremonial space significantly, not only by emphasizing time-conjuring as an intensely personified act of royalty but also by consequently encouraging the conception of royal corpses as enduring abodes of animate soul force that inhabited the buildings in which they rested. This is how Francisco Estrada-Belli (chapter 6, this volume) thinks of the Holmul king he discovered, a man entombed and then again depicted apotheosizing as a sun god in the façade of the building above.

Previous research on Late Preclassic kingship has attempted to analyze architectural design from the perspective of the performance of individuals (Schele and Miller 1986; Freidel and Schele 1988a). It was not by accident that early illustrations of kingship (Schele and Miller 1986; Schele and Freidel 1990) focused on the individual on the Hauberg Stela (see Stuart 2008) as a stand-in for the Cerro Maya king on the stairway landing of Structure 5C-2nd. The individual on this pocket stela was our earliest Maya performing king (Freidel 1988); he is gesturing toward the accompanying text to his right. Leading off to the right, counterclockwise, was the correct direction for processing around something. The gesture of the Hauberg king activated his declared words, which, in turn, must be read from left to right, circling around the king to come back to the front of him. Thus, the stela depicts the performance of the king, activated by the reader of the text. This was the extension of the ideas regarding performance and processing Freidel and Schele (1988a) have detailed (Freidel and Schele 1988a), which Freidel and colleagues (Freidel and Suhler 1998, 1999; Suhler and Freidel 1998; Stanton and Freidel 2005) later explored at Yaxuná through architecture. There was recognition, however, that monuments, other artifacts, and places could be ensouled (Freidel et al. 1993).

Our project at El Perú-Waka' in northwestern Guatemala began in 2003 and we became squarely engaged in the archaeology of a dynastic royal capital with many monuments on the plazas attesting to history from the perspective of the rulers (Freidel et al. 2007; Freidel and Escobedo 2014; Navarro-Farr et al. 2020). Those monuments, with the exception of two that were carefully sawn and looted in the 1960s (El Perú-Waka' Stelae 33 and 34; Graham 1988), were for the most part severely damaged, presumably by ancient enemies who had intentionally defaced, erased, shattered, and scattered them. Ordinary people also had moved many of the stones and their fragments around reverentially in the nondynastic era during the Terminal Classic (800–1000 CE; see Navarro-Farr et al. 2020). Many of these were subject to selective sawing destruction by modern looters in the 1960s. This complex taphonomic behavior has provided a challenge and an opportunity in attempting contextual analysis of the sequence of manufacture and use, leading from our interpretation of the portrayed performer as commissioned and dedicated to the ultimate disposition of the ensouled monument or its relic pieces.

Stephen Houston and David Stuart (1996; Stuart 1996) have compellingly marshaled textual evidence in their exploration and definition of the notion of stelae as spiritually charged portraits of performers, of stela as "kings of stone." Stuart (1996, 2011) reinforces the active and agentive qualities of these artifacts with a special focus on the status of "rulers of time," segueing from the Maya term *tun,* stone (also the 360-day unit of time), to the term *lakam-tun,* banner stone or big stone (the term for stela that he deciphered). Here we build on this conceptual foundation, accepting the earlier arguments that are based on epigraphic data and analyses. How did the ancient Maya come to see these monuments as living fractions of the people portrayed, as materializations of time, and how can we infer such understandings? The task here is to discern bridging arguments in the archaeological record through contextual analysis of what the Maya did with these great stones.

To anticipate some of the arguments below, we propose that stelae at El Perú-Waka' could stand as living proxies of kings who were alive or dead, present or not. Stela fragments, like bone relics, likely also had such an animate presence. Following desecration, shattering, and scattering, the aggregation of stelae fragments may well have recharged their soul force.[1] Monuments then, in our view, were not just materializations of a given moment in time or even reflections of a past but were also potential agents of a future in which they were revitalized. Inevitably, engagement of the relationship between ancient Maya histories, as Maya people experienced them and thought about them, and the stones that they made to declare them would take us down a temporal version of Alice in Wonderland's rabbit hole into a world in which we must appeal to Maya rules of reason to make sense of the observable record. Hopefully, such audacious conjecture (following Popper 1962) will prove worthwhile.

## The Rulers of Stone in Context

A now-anonymous ruler of the Wak (centipede) dynasty reckoned that he was the twenty-fourth "in order" on Stela 28 at El Perú-Waka'. That badly ruined monument left on Plaza 1 of the site has no dedicatory date, but Stanley Guenter (2005, 2014) has suggested that it was commissioned around 600 CE. We have no named kings preserved on any monuments between the middle of the sixth century (573 CE retrospective) and the middle of the seventh century (657 CE). It is possible that no ruler raised a monument in this period, but it is more likely that the damaged remains of other monuments from this era also lie on Plaza 1. Because of the dynastic count, however, we can reckon average lengths of reign and place the founder of the Wak dynasty in the second century CE (Guenter 2014). In 2017, Griselda Pérez Robles and Juan Carlos Pérez (Freidel et al. 2018; Pérez Robles et al., 2019) discovered an interred Wak king from the early fourth century, Burial 80 in the Palace Acropolis. This individual is nearly as old as the one on Tikal Stela 29 (Jones and Satterthwaite 1982). Assuming that we are dealing with real historical dates and not mythic founders, at the present time the Wak dynasty is the second oldest in the Maya lowlands after Tikal and its founder King Yax Ehb Xook, who lived in the first century CE. The tradition of carving stelae at Waka' can be documented back to 416 CE on Stela 15, and there are two other documented fifth-century monuments at the site. The people of Waka' embraced the innovation of carving Classic stelae of time lords early and enthusiastically. In contrast to the sculpting tradition at Tikal, where early stelae often have prismatic cross-sections with slightly more than 2 meters of carved surface, early Waka' stelae are rectangular in cross-section, are much wider, and can have 3 to 4 meters of carved surface (Guenter 2014).

The El Perú-Waka' corpus of stelae was first inventoried and documented by Ian Graham (1988). While the monuments were ably photographed and drawn by Graham in the 1970s and 1980s, there have been many advances in photographic documentation of Maya monuments since then. Stanley Guenter (2005, 2014) served as project epigrapher from 2003 to 2017, and his provisional readings of texts from Stela 44, drafted by current project epigrapher Mary Kate Kelly (2019, 2020), form the basis for the textual analysis in this chapter.

## The Wiinte' Naah Fire Shrine and Rulers in Stone

The principal temple of the city, Structure M13-1 (fig. 7.1), served as a Wiinte' Naah fire shrine. This locality, along with funerary pyramid Structure M12-32 and the Palace Acropolis, have been presented elsewhere in more detail (Freidel et al. 2013). Both Structure M13-1 and Structure M12-32 are also named as sacred mountain places. This chapter focuses on the monuments

Figure 7.1. El Perú Stela 45 planted within the staircase fronting Structure M13-Sub III. Photo by Mary Kelly. Images courtesy of Proyecto Arqueológico Waka' and the Ministry of Culture and Sports of Guatemala.

memorializing the Wiinte' Naah fire shrine, named K'ahk' Witz, or Fire Mountain, and addresses surprising and perplexing recent discoveries in tunnels within Structure M13-1. We argue that stelae were living aspects of rulers and maintained that identity through all uses of them—once a living time lord, always a living time lord.

The working hypothesis of the Proyecto Arqueológico Waka' is that Structure M13-1 is the locality of a succession of buildings that served as commemorative Wiinte' Naah fire shrines (for the Wiinte' Naah building at Teotihuacan, see Fash et al. 2009; for the Copán Structure 10L-16 Wiinte' Naah locality, see Taube 2004c and Stuart 2004b). At this locale, people of Waka' focused intense and sustained contemplation on the history of the realm and acted to effect potential trajectories in time through appealing to gods and ancestors. The earliest reference to this place or to an object associated with the Wiinte' Naah is on Stela 15 (Fig 7.2). Royals and later ordinary people and their shaman-priests (Tedlock 1992) planted and moved stelae and stelae fragments as living agents in the creation of (and the contestation of) prophetic futures (Navarro-Farr et al. 2020; see also chapter 14, this volume). We have identified the final phase of Structure M13-1 as a fire shrine. When King K'inich Bahlam II was in his late 60s or early 70s, he commissioned this building sometime after 702 CE to honor Queen K'abel, his wife of some forty-five years, whom he buried in the stairway of an earlier version of the shrine (Navarro-Farr et al. 2020). This final building has a uniquely monumental hearth built into a central room that is so wide that it was certainly open to the sky and not roofed.

The Wiinte' Naah buildings have been identified on the *adosada* (frontal platform) of the Pyramid of the Sun at Teotihuacan (Fash et al. 2009), as the Feathered Serpent Pyramid (S. Sugiyama, personal communication, March 2022), and in the 10L-16 locality at Copán (Taube 2004c). They refer to fire ceremonies; the final version of Structure M13-1 building has an actual fire place. A stela that refers to a king who is known only by his titles as Chan Yopaat referred to an earlier version of the Wiinte' Naah in the same locality. Chan Yopaat is portrayed on the shattered fragments of El Perú Stela 9 (fig. 7.3), which was dedicated around 500 CE. We cannot know where this large stone was originally planted or where its pieces were dumped following enemy attack, but people of the city dragged large fragments of this monument to the base of Structure M13-1 sometime later and the building was transformed into a place of worship during the last two centuries of occupation (Navarro-Farr et al. 2008; Navarro-Farr 2009). Wak kings and queens probably turned their backs on the fire shrine after a disastrous defeat at the hands of Tikal in 743 CE, when one of the gods of the fire shrine

Figure 7.2. El Péru Stela 15, dedicated in 416 CE when Sihyaj K'ahk' arrived. The stela records prominent reference to a Wiinte'? object or place in 378 CE. Photo by Philip Hofstetter. Image courtesy of Proyecto Arqueológico Waka' and the Ministry of Culture and Sports of Guatemala.

(and of the realm) was stolen and transformed into a Tikal god (Guenter 2014; see also Martin 2000 and Baron 2016a for a discussion of this catastrophic defeat). Probably at that time, the monumental hearth was sealed with finely carved white slabs of stone and turned into an altar.

Subsequently, ordinary people carried out individual votive fire offerings along the base of this triadic structure comprising the Fire Mountain, generating a massive ritual midden.

Figure 7.3. Fragment of El Perú Stela 9. King Chan Yopaat stands on a misty fire mountain. Wiinte' Naah is referenced in the incised text next to his leg. K'inich Ajaw, one of Waka's patron gods, emerges from the fire mountain. Photo by Philip Hofstetter. Image courtesy of Proyecto Arqueológico Waka' and the Ministry of Culture and Sports of Guatemala.

The Fate of Some Time Lords in the Classic Maya World · 159

Their shaman-priests built small masonry shrines and carried out rituals on the flanking terraces of the triadic structure and on top of the central fire shrine. There was, then, a whole new trajectory of use of this fire shrine following its desecration in the mid-eighth century (Navarro-Farr 2009).

Earlier than the performance of King Chan Yopaat memorialized on Stela 9, in 416 CE a son of Wak king K'inich Bahlam I wrote retrospective history on Stela 15 (fig. 7.2), declaring that in 378 CE Sihyaj K'ahk', whose name means Fire Born, carried out a ritual in a Wiinte', a place or object pertaining to a Wiinte' Naah, almost certainly at Waka'. Stela 15 is a large and completely glyphic stela. Its dedication in 416 CE is the earliest public reference to a Wiinte' Naah, although there is a private monument, the Marcador, at Tikal that refers to a Wiinte' Naah in the same year that celebrates the famous entrada of Sihyaj K'ahk' in 378 CE (see Stuart 2000 and Guenter 2005 for discussions of the epigraphy of Stela 15; see also Freidel et al. 2007, 2013). It seems that Sihyaj K'ahk' established Wiinte' Naah fire shrines in some Maya lowland capitals and that the first one was placed at Waka'.

The all-glyphic carving on Stela 15 (fig. 7.2) raises a fundamental question: If lowland Maya stelae were designed to engender historically important rulers in stone, who is engendered in Stela 45 (fig. 7.1), which was formally replanted in the stairway of Structure M13-1 Sub II and is devoid of portraiture? Here we turn again to David Stuart (2010), who asserts that stelae embody time, implying that time is agentive. While we certainly agree with that deduction, as do others (chapter 14, this volume), we would go further and say that this innovative and at the time of its carving unique variation on stela crafting embodies the human agent, Kaloomte' Sihyaj K'ahk', as the materialization of a historical event of far-reaching consequence. This way of thinking about agency and history in carved stone stelae did not remain unique. At Copán in Honduras, King Waxaklahun Ubaah K'awiil raised an all-glyphic stela, Stela J, in 702 CE to commemorate his accession to rule in the previous ten-year Lajuntun calendar period. The text was woven as a royal mat symbol. The other side of the monument was carved in the likeness of the divine being Lem, a name that David Stuart (2010) glosses as "lightning" or "shiny." In the text, the king links his accession to the celebration of a great baktun calendar jubilee, 9.0.0.0.0, by the founder of his dynasty, King K'inich Yax K'uk' Mo'. The materialization of time by the founder at Copán was, like the arrival of Sihyaj K'ahk' and the establishment of the Wiinte' Naah fire shrine at El Perú-Waka', a momentous event that set the trajectory of the future, and the words of later kings aspired to sustain those timelines.

A generation later, another Wak dynasty king commissioned a literal portrait of the same statesman. Stela 16 (fig. 7.4) portrays Sihyaj K'ahk' carrying

160 · David A. Freidel and Olivia Navarro-Farr

Figure 7.4. El Perú Stela 16. Kaloomte' Sihyaj K'ahk' carries the fire bundle of the Winte' Naah (Structure M13-1) and wields the raptor-headed throwing stick that symbolizes the name of his liege lord Jatz'oom (Eagle Striker). Photo by Philip Hofstetter. Image courtesy of Proyecto Arqueológico Waka' and the Ministry of Culture and Sports of Guatemala.

the fire bundle. The accompanying text declares the conjuring of the three tutelary gods of the city: the death god Akan Yaxaj, the jaguar-eared paddler god, and the moon goddess, presumably by King Tapir Chan Ahk, since his accession in 458 CE is announced on this side of the monument. This king dedicated Stela 16 in 470 CE; he was very likely the great-grandson of K'inich Bahlam I. Although his lineage is not preserved on the monument, a passage does name "Dragon" Jaguar as a son of K'inich Bahlam. This is probably part of a genealogy that ties King Tapir Chan Ahk to his forebearers.

The Wiinte' Naah fire shrine hypothesis for Structure M13-1 is based in part on the Terminal Classic (800–900 CE) arrangement of stelae fragments as improvised altars (Guenter and Rich 2004) along the western side of Structure L13-22, an open-summited platform facing Structure M13-1 across the east-west oriented grand plaza in front of the city temple. These fragments of Stelae 14, 15, and 16 date to the entrada era of the fifth century CE. While Structure M13-1 is oriented to true east-west, perhaps reflecting the orientation of the original shrine established by Sihyaj K'ahk', Structure 13-22 is oriented to Maya north like the rest of the city. However, excavations on the eastern side of the platform demonstrated the existence of a stairway onto the plaza of the Wiinte' Naah fire shrine and a midden from ceremonies in the Terminal Classic period adjacent to that stairway on its northern side (Eppich and Mixter 2013, 38–39). This platform and its improvised altars of stela fragments were certainly part of the same program of late reuse that is seen on Structure M13-1.

Stela 10 (fig. 7.5) links these altars of repurposed stelae fragments at the eastern and western ends of the fire shrine plaza. Stela 10 was reset vertically in the Terminal Classic along with its own small stone altar in front at Structure M13-1. Stela 10, which stylistically is early fifth century, depicts an unknown Wak ruler—possibly Dragon Jaguar—who is dressed as a Teotihuacano and carries a bundle (likely another effigy fire bundle). This stela was reset at the base of the north terrace of Structure M13-1. It was already badly eroded and the face of the ruler had been completely removed, probably by enemies in antiquity during an attack on the city (perhaps in the early sixth century CE).

Fragments of Stela 9 were also used as altars embedded in massive quantities of Terminal Classic ritual offerings at the base of the north terrace of Structure M13-1 (Navarro-Farr 2009; Navarro-Farr et al. 2020). The upper third of Stela 9 (fig. 7.6) was actually built into the final Terminal Classic wall of the frontal building of the fire shrine by people of the Terminal Classic city (Navarro-Farr et al. 2013, 41). This fragment displays the Principal Bird Deity, solar avatar of the creator god. Stela 9 explicitly shows the king standing on a fire mountain, and an incised text next to the leg of the king mentions a Wiinte' Naah.

The text of El Perú Stela 15 (fig. 7.2) implies that this Wiinte' ? was established by Kaloomte' Sihyaj K'ahk' in 378 CE. It is certain that he carried out an event in or with this Wiinte' ? upon his arrival at El Perú-Waka' (Stuart 2000; Guenter 2005, 2014). The original El Perú-Waka' Wiinte' Naah that Stela 15 refers to is no doubt deeply buried inside the *adosada* and the main pyramid of Structure M13-1, which was the last and most explicit expression of the Wiinte' Naah fire shrine. The eighth-century final version included an exceptional monumental fire hearth within the superstructure (Navarro-Farr et al. 2020). The main seventh-century version, M13-1 Sub II, is buried inside this building. It would have been used for performance by Queen K'abel and her husband. This building has a superstructure with two doorways. It was decommissioned, partially dismantled, and covered over with the death and interment of Queen K'abel in its stairway.

The tomb of Queen K'abel (Waka' Burial 61) cut through the stairway of Structure M13-1 Sub II (Navarro-Farr et al. 2013). This interment marked the end of that building's use life and its replacement by Structure M13-1 Sub I,

Figure 7.5. Defaced Stela 10, which was reset in Terminal Classic times in front of Structure M13-1. Photo by Olivia C. Navarro-Farr. Image courtesy of Proyecto Arqueológico Waka' and the Ministry of Culture and Sports of Guatemala.

Figure 7.6. Crown section of broken Early Classic Stela 9, which was reset in the Terminal Classic wall of the *adosada* of Structure M13-1. Photo by David Coventry. Courtesy of the Proyecto Arqueológico Waka' and the Ministry of Culture and Sports of Guatemala.

which was soon modified as a subsurface artificial cave in Structure M13-1. A set of three stelae, probably originally placed in front of M13-1 Sub II, were reset in front of M13-1. The triad of El Perú-Waka' Stelae 6, 7, and 8 includes a badly eroded portrait of a Late Classic (550–800 CE) queen on Stela 6; fragments of Stela 7 that portray a dancing Kaanul regime king that was shattered (no doubt at the time Tikal conquered Waka' in 743 CE) and then aggregated in the Terminal Classic (Freidel and Castañeda 2015); and the lower fragments of Stela 8. Stela 8 was likely the bottom half of El Perú Stela 43. Well-preserved fragments of the upper part of this monument were thinned and built into the terrace wall of the last, Terminal Classic, version of the fire shrine wall after the royal dynasty abandoned it (Navarro-Farr et al. 2020).

Stanley Guenter (2014) determined that King K'inich Bahlam II dedicated Stela 43 (fig. 7.7) in 702 CE. Guenter also discovered an inscription on the side of a fragment of Stela 43 that refers to the accession in 697 CE of Yuhknoom Ti'? K'awiil, the last of the Kaanul kings with imperial aspirations. K'inich Bahlam II and Queen K'abel had raised a pair of stelae in 692 CE that celebrated the accession in 686 CE of the previous Kaanul king, Yuhknoom Yich'aak K'ahk'. Very likely the Wak king and queen are also depicted on a pair of stelae raised in 672 CE. One of those monuments, the Wak king's

Figure 7.7. Composite photograph of the fragments of Stela 43 depicting K'inich Bahlam II in 702 CE. Fragments were thinned and built into the Terminal Classic *adosada* of Structure M13-1. Photographs by Juan Carlos Pérez. Images courtesy of Proyecto Arqueológico Waka' and the Ministry of Culture and Sports of Guatemala.

Stela 12, also honors the Kaanul king Yuhknoom Ch'een the Great. Both of these monuments were gathered by Terminal Classic people as shattered fragments and placed nearby. The queen depicted on Stela 11 wears a small mask in the headdress that is framed by little carved bones. This insignia jewel was found on the queen's headdress in Burial 61 (Meléndez 2019). Based on the temporal frame, we also think the royal couple raised a pair of stelae flanking the new emperor in 702 CE and that K'abel is the queen on the eroded Stela 6. Again, originally these stelae would have stood before Structure M13-1 Sub II. In 711 CE, K'inich Bahlam II broke tradition and raised a single stone. We surmise that Queen K'abel died between 702 and 711 CE and that K'inich Bahlam II survived her by almost two decades and built Structure M13-1 Sub I and Structure M13-1.

In 2013, a new centerline tunnel was excavated into Structure M13-1 to access existing tunnels coming down from above. This work was designed to facilitate access to the Burial 61 tomb chamber and to complete research and tunnel stabilization in this locus. Stela 44, which dates to the sixth century CE, was cached as an offering on the centerline of Structure M13-1 (Kelly 2019).

This discovery demonstrated that the manipulation of stelae originated in the period of royal power at Waka' and was not an innovation of the post-royal inhabitants or their shaman-priests.

## Uprooting and Replanting a Stone King

The glyphic texts on Stela 44 recorded a Wak dynasty king, Chak Tok Ich'aak, and referred to a great woman, very likely his queen and the mother of his heir (fig. 7.8). This queen was a woman who bore the Sak Wayis title, a well-established epithet of the Kaanul regime (Grube 2005), so we infer that she came from a Kaanul regime vassal kingdom. These royal ancestors were of great historical importance to King K'inich Bahlam II, particularly Queen Sak Wayis, further named Ikoom, whom he honored on Stela 43 in 702 CE on the occasion of celebrating the accession of the latest Kaanul regime overlord, King Yuhknoom Ti'? K'awiil (Kelly 2019).

Queen Ikoom is recalled as having presided over a calendar jubilee in 573 CE in a text that originally was above the king's head to his left. The Terminal

Figure 7.8. Right-side text of Stela 44 showing the name of Lady Sak Wayis K'uhul Chatan Winik, probably the ancestress commemorated on Stela 43 in 702 CE. She was likely the wife of King Chak Took Ich'aak of Waka' and the mother of King Wa'oom Uchab Ahk, the heir who acceded in 564 CE. Photo by Juan Carlos Pérez. Courtesy of the Proyecto Arqueológico Waka' and the Ministry of Culture and Sports of Guatemala.

Classic people, who cut up pieces of El Perú-Waka' Stela 43 and reset it into the frontal platform wall of the last Wiinte' Naah fire shrine (Navarro-Farr et al. 2020, fig.10.02), positioned the text of Ikoom next to the end of the bundle of the king to show the conjuring of this great priestess of the fire shrine as an ancestress and deity.

Structure M13-1 buried Structure M13-1 Sub II, and the king shifted the centerline of the *adosada* supporting the fire shrine to the north. Stela 44 was cached on this new centerline, basically set along the north wall of the main stairway of Structure M13-1 Sub II. The butt of the stela was placed through a rough cut in the 10-centimeter-thick plaster floor of the plaza associated with Structure M13-1 Sub II. It was angled to the east so that the top of the monument was just beneath the third tread of a short stairway leading from a western landing eastward to the doorway of a two-room sanctuary underneath the floor of the final fire shrine. We interpret this sanctuary as part of a version of the final superstructure of the fire shrine. It started as a single-room small sanctuary, then a second room was added to the western side, building out onto the platform where old King K'inich Bahlam II would have stood over the stela of his predecessor. The south wall of this front room never had the outer masonry of a freestanding superstructure. Instead, its masonry walls were tailed into surrounding construction fill. If this western room was below the surface, it is likely that it was built as an expansion of an already subsurface single-room shrine chamber, part of the larger final building complex.

Stela 44 both signaled continuity in history between Chak Took Ich'aak of Wak and K'inich Bahlam II and served as an offering to Kaloomte' K'abel, who was buried in the stairway of Structure M13-1 Sub II. However, it was only one component of a complex ritual deposit. In 2014, we discerned that a rough masonry crib had been built around Stela 44 on the west, south, and east sides, banked against an existing and better made mason's wall that extended from the side of M13-1 Sub II west. This feature had mud mortar between the stones, which was characteristic of tomb walls at Waka', and we explored it with that similarity in mind.

Over a period of eleven days, we excavated a tunnel into the side of this wall (Freidel et al. 2016). The mud mortar between the stones was fine and moist in some places and included a significant amount of sherd material and other artifacts such as lithics. Behind the wall, we found dirt-packed construction fill that was very different from the loose rubble fill above this rough platform. As we tunneled, we followed the well-preserved plaster floor of the plaza associated with Structure M13-1 Sub II. This floor had been pierced to loosely foot Stela 44. Next, we exposed another corner of rough

The Fate of Some Time Lords in the Classic Maya World · 167

masonry. This was the southwest corner of a rectilinear platform of unknown dimensions. We followed this corner to both the east and the north. A flat stone lay underneath the corner. We thought that it might be a vault stone, so we removed the corner. The distinctly yellow mortar from this corner contained highly unusual artifacts that included broken fragments from many different small and well-made greenstone beads as well as flakes of obsidian and chert. This was a new ritual pattern, but flakes of obsidian and chert are often associated with tomb deposits, usually in large quantities.

The stone under the corner was small and rectangular, and a second rectangular stone lined up with it to the south. We hypothesized that these stones were part of an outline of a place where the floor had been removed to install a tomb and cut a small test through the plaster floor. The floor had not been refurbished at any time in its use life. We then repaired the corner with cement-mortared stone, stabilized other parts of the tunnel wall, and excavated north along the inner platform to what appeared to be another corner. We penetrated the inner platform, tunneling eastward roughly in its center. The thick plaster floor had been chopped away underneath the inner platform wall and the wall had been raised over this cut in the floor. The level of the plaster floor within the platform was clearly marked with a 10-centimeter-thick layer of burnt earth and charcoal, evidence of intense fire rituals. We also encountered several finely dressed blocks that seemed to be well above floor level in the middle of a concentration of hard yellow mortar and rubble. We excavated around this concentration, following the level of the plaster floor.

When we were past this yellow mortar concentration, we started digging down into this ritually charged deposit. After the burnt layer, we encountered a level of fine, dry brown dirt and then extremely hard brown clay. Normally such clay is finely sorted material that accumulates in bodies of water. This clay was on a natural elevation, and while it was devoid of artifacts, it contained a consistent sprinkling of white crushed limestone. This clay deposit, which was more than 1.5 meters thick, was evidently artificial construction and not a natural deposit. In front of the Palace Acropolis at the eastern end of the city, excavations revealed that the elevation of that plaza employed vast quantities of clay that was mottled and contained a marbling from many different deposits. In the Structure M13-1 location, the clay was a uniform color and consistency all the way to bedrock.

When we continued excavation inside the rough platforms in 2015, we discovered that the plaster floor had been cut over a wide area inside the inner platform. Within the cut, we found only more clay. On the level of the plaster floor, however, the earth was intensely burnt in several places and additional small stone features or altars had been built, only to be buried by the two encasing platforms. This behavior of cutting away a large area of floor and not placing anything in the cut was perplexing. This floor cutting was evidently part of the elaborate and complex rituals accompanying the planting of the historically pivotal monument—pivotal because the king depicted on it was not only a hero of the realm but also a known conjurer of gods. In retrospect, it is clear that the fine brown clay underlying this platform had been laid down on a bedrock that had been prepared by first cleaning off all-natural sediments. This kind of cleaning to bedrock is preparation for the earliest known ceremonial buildings in Petén, E Groups dating to the Preclassic (Freidel et al. 2017). Our excavations suggest that the M13-1 locality was established as the city temple in the Late Preclassic period, quite possibly even as an E Group. The western radial pyramid may have been demolished when the locality was transformed into a Wiinte' Naah in 378 CE. Building the stela platform of El Perú-Waka' Stela 44 on ground consecrated through the exposure of this original foundation clay and burning ritual fires makes sense for the powerful conjurer invoked in the monument.

The uprooting of Stela 44 from its place of original planting in a prepared masonry stela platform on the plaza in front of Structure M13-1 Sub II, its removal south to the centerline of Structure M13-1 Sub I, and its resetting as a cached offering allowed King K'inich Bahlam II—and perhaps his heir designate—to stand over the valiant hero-ancestor. At the same time, the resetting honored Lady K'abel and her predecessor patroness of the fire shrine, Lady Sak Wayis Ikoom. Karen Bassie-Sweet (personal communication to David Freidel, November 2012) was the first to suggest that the Kaanul queens of Waka' were priestesses of the Teotihuacan-inspired cult. Such a role is documented on La Corona Panel 6, where a queen of the sixth-century Kaanul regime poses with the regalia of this office: a Teotihuacan-style turban with the goggles and fangs of the storm god, a serpent staff, and a great war beast representing the Feathered Serpent of Teotihuacan (Freidel and Guenter 2003; Martin 2008).

## Replanting a Captive Image of an Enemy King

In 2015, the flayed remains of El Perú-Waka' Stela 45 (fig. 7.1) were found. They had been carefully entombed standing in place in a specially made floating plaster floor in a vertical masonry crypt underneath the landing of Structure M13-1-Sub II and under the front of a doorway leading into the shrine's superstructure. When we say flayed, we mean that the front carved surface of the monument below the erased peak at the top had been entirely sheared off to a depth of about 4 centimeters. While faint outlines of the square divisions that once held glyphs on the sides can be discerned, the glyphs themselves had also been erased. The stela was not cached like Stela 44. Rather, again, it was set into a well-made plaster floor. The floor lipped up to Stela 44, having been created around it. Originally, we thought that the stela had been planted in front of an earlier version of the temple, M13-1 Sub III, and had its carved surfaces effaced while it stood in place. But further tunneling in 2019 through the southern corner of the wall adjacent to the stairway of M13-1 Sub II documented an entirely novel and unique stela context. The frontal platform of M13-1 Sub III had been built just behind the side wall of M13-1 Sub II. The stairway of the platform was next to the vertical side panel of the wall of M13-1 Sub III. This stairway, which was smaller than the stairway of M13-1 Sub II, was fashioned of well-carved large blocks of fine yellow stone that were not found elsewhere at the site (but are typical of La Corona to the north); there were six steep steps to the summit of the platform. The center of this stairway had been torn out. In this gaping hole, people had built a floating plaster floor with Stela 45 planted in it. This activity was certainly part of the process of burying M13-1 Sub III under M13-1 Sub II. In the course of building the new stairway over the desecrated one and planting Stela 45 in the hole in the middle of it, the builders constructed a corbelled vertical cache chamber around Stela 45. This chamber was positioned under the threshold of the southernmost of two doorways in the superstructure temple that once stood atop M13-1 Sub II.

Stela 45 (fig. 7.1) at El Perú-Waka' is a Tikal-style monument in shape and size, completely different in shape and size from other Waka' stelae of the era (Guenter 2014, 153–154). Tikal's Early Classic monuments are generally small, often less than 2 meters in exposed height and quadrangular in cross-section. Stela 45 is 2.2 meters tall and almost square in cross section. Early Classic stelae at El Perú-Waka', such as Stela 15 (416 CE), Stela 51 (435 CE), and Stela 16 (470 CE)—among others—are very large with 3 to 4 meters of carved surface and a rectangular cross-section. Tikal and El Perú-Waka' were likely allies in the New Order period (378–520 CE) Sihyaj K'ahk' established, so a monument with Tikal-style dimensions would not be unexpected at Waka'. The famous pyrite mosaic mirror back discovered in Bagaces in Costa Rica was inscribed as a gift from Sihyaj K'ahk's vassal king, K'inich Bahlam I, to that king's counterpart, the king of El Zotz (Garrison and Houston 2019, 24–25). El Zotz is on the route linking El Perú-Waka' to Tikal, and the sculptors of these courts surely knew about their distinctive styles.

## Perpetual Captive on the Six-Step Stairway

Why was Stela 45 carved and planted, then uprooted, desecrated, and flayed, and then ceremonially planted in the desecrated stairway fronting the Sub III version of the Waka' Wiinte' Naah? Why was it painted red like a deceased ruler following reverential reentry of a tomb and entombed under the threshold of the next incarnation of the Wiinte' Naah? This unconventional context requires considerations beyond existing expectations of stelae functions and meanings. Stela 45 surely depicted someone of central importance, both when originally carved and planted and when uprooted, erased, and replanted. We conjecture that an important Tikal ruler had a Tikal-style stela carved and planted in front of the Waka' Wiinte' Naah fire shrine. He would have been an ally and overlord to the Wak rulers, one who was later regarded as an enemy, one whose engendered being in the stone had to be dealt with in a novel way. It was not sufficient to uproot the stone, smash it into pieces, and dump it. It had to be subjected to flaying like the face of a war captive, shearing the image off and erasing the inscribed words and only then replanting the monument.

We suggest that Stela 45 may originally have depicted Tikal king Chak Tok Ich'aak II, the last of the great New Order kings of that city and the father of King Wak Chan K'awiil, the ruler who was defeated (and presumably sacrificed), under the aegis of Kaanul king K'ahk' Ti' Chi'ch'. This is Sergei Vepretskii's 2017 reading of Altar 21 Caracol that he communicated to Simon Martin (2020, 248), that king K'ahk' Ti' Chi'ch' had defeated Tikal in collaboration with Caracol king Yajaw Te' K'inich II. Stanley Guenter (2014) has persuasively argued on epigraphic and paleographic grounds that it was King Chak Tok Ich'aak II who planted Tikal Stela 26 (fig. 7.9), not Chak Tok Ich'aak I, as Martin and Grube (2008) had previously suggested. Guenter (2014) places the dedication of this monument in 507 CE, less than a year before Chak Tok Ich'aak II died (perhaps in battle or as a sacrifice in western wars; his death is noted only at Tonina in the far west, see Martin and Grube 2008).

In our scenario, King Chak Tok Ich'aak II of Tikal imposed himself on Waka' at a crucial time in the struggles between the Tikal alliance and the Kaanul regime. Kaanul's King Tun K'ab Hiix was very likely pressing south along what would become the Kaanul royal road in the west, placing a daughter, Queen Ek' Naah, in power at La Corona Sak Nikte' in 520 CE (Freidel and Guenter 2003; Martin 2008). La Corona is only some 30 kilometers north of El Perú-Waka'. The kings of Waka' had founded a dynasty in the same century as the first dynasty Yax Ehb Xook declared at Tikal. They were allies of Tikal at the time of the founding of the first Wiinte' Naah, vassals to Sihyaj K'ahk'.

The Fate of Some Time Lords in the Classic Maya World · 171

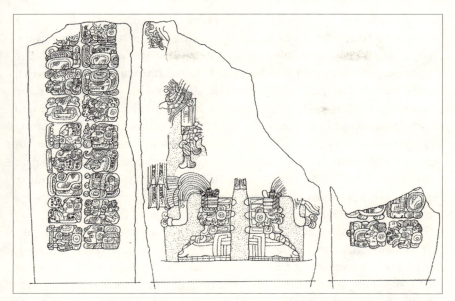

Figure 7.9. Tikal Stela 26. Drawing by Linda Schele, copyright David Schele. Photo courtesy Ancient Americas at LACMA (ancientamericas.org).

Chak Tok Ich'aak II and his father, "staff kings" of Tikal (see Schele and Freidel 1990), portrayed themselves wielding what Stephen Houston and David Stuart (1996) have identified as ceremonial drill sticks for drilling fire. While Tikal lords refer to a Wiinte' Naah (and no doubt some buildings served a fire shrine function there), current evidence indicates that the first Maya lowland Wiinte' Naah shrine was established at Waka' by Sihyaj K'ahk' in the first public event of his entrada in the late fourth century (Freidel et al. 2007). This was part of Kaloomte' Sihyaj K'ahk's declaration of dominion in the southern lowlands, not as a conqueror but rather as a liberator of dynastic kingdoms from Kaanul regime rulers who were imposing themselves from the north (Freidel 2018).

The regional wars between the Kaanul regime and the Tikal alliance that would embroil core lowland kingdoms from the mid-sixth to mid-eighth centuries were already under way at the end of the fifth century CE, if the early sixth-century turmoil in the succession at Tikal is any guide (Martin 2014). Had the Wiinte' Naah fire shrine at El Perú-Waka', which is associated with the glories of Sihyaj K'ahk's New Order hegemony, been taken by Kaanul regime lords, it would have been a serious blow to Tikal and its allies in their protracted struggle against Kaanul. We propose that King Chak Tok Ich'aak II of Tikal defended Tikal's claim and asserted authority over Waka' and its Wiinte'

172 · David A. Freidel and Olivia Navarro-Farr

Naah—much as his son, King Wak Chan K'awiil, would assert authority over King Y'ajaw Te' K'inich II of Caracol in 553 CE (Martin 2005)—in two ways. First, he had a Tikal-style stela portrait of himself raised in front of the Waka' Wiinte' Naah fire shrine of Wak king Chan Yopaat (Structure M13-1 Sub III). Second, in this historical working model, sometime just before 508 CE, he oversaw the establishment of the son of King Chan Yopaat Ajaw as heir and gave him the regnal name Chak Tok Ich'aak of Waka', unequivocally declaring to all his status as a vassal to Tikal. If Stela 45 depicted the Tikal king, he not only materialized the moment of his domination of a strategic ally as vassal on a key communication and transport route in the context of a famous temple, representing the advent of the New Order in Petén, but also projected forward into the future his living presence in front of the Wiinte' Naah of Waka'.

One reason that we think this hypothesis has potential is that he may have further demanded art tribute from King Yopaat Chan of Waka'. In this instance, art was a means of materializing soul force in time. Stanley Guenter (2014) has proposed that Stela 26 at Tikal—a monument whose style was innovative for that city—portrays and was dedicated by Chak Tok Ich'aak II of Tikal in 507 CE. In pose and costume (but not in scale), this stela is much closer stylistically to Stela 9 at El Perú-Waka', which dates to around 500 CE, than it is to any fifth- or early sixth-century stela at Tikal. It also features depending tassels from the ceremonial bar like the sixth-century stelae at El Perú-Waka'. Stela 16 depicts Sihyaj K'ahk' posthumously in 470 CE in full frontal pose with his feet splayed out. Stela 10 at El Perú-Waka', which is of an earlier date, displays a Wak dynasty king in the same pose. Stela 51 at El Perú-Waka', which dates to 435 CE, also has the same pose (Kelly 2020). Another Early Classic stela at El Perú-Waka', the massive Stela 25, also has this frontal pose on the preserved upper part. The pose on Stela 26 at Tikal is a fifth- and sixth-century Waka' pose, not the typical Tikal pose of that era (see Jones and Satterthwaite 1982). Stela 26 at Tikal is stylistically a significant departure from the profile pose of the fifth-century Tikal kings, which feature wraparound compositions or flanking parents, or the staff stelae that were characteristic of the reigns of Chak Took Ich'aak II of Tikal and his father, K'an Chitam. On both Stela 9 at El Perú-Waka' and Stela 26 at Tikal, the king is portrayed in a frontal pose with splayed feet, carrying a ceremonial bundle that has yawning masks; in the case of Stela 9, the bundle has gods emerging from it. In both cases, tassels are associated with the ends of the ceremonial bar. Stanley Guenter (2014) has noted that several sixth-century El Perú-Waka' stelae—specifically 22, 23, and 44—depict the ruler carrying a rigid bundle with rosettes, probably scrying mirrors, and depending tassels. He attributes this El Perú style to emulation of Petén style to the east of Waka'

The Fate of Some Time Lords in the Classic Maya World · 173

in this period of time, but in actuality this is better viewed as a Waka' style conveyed to Tikal on Stela 26. Guenter (2014, 14) quotes Tatiana Proskouria-koff's (1993) observation that the glyphs on Stela 26 are beautifully squared and carved, in contrast to other Early Classic inscriptions at Tikal.

Following our scenario, when Tikal's King Chak Tok Ich'aak II commissioned Stela 45 at Waka', he had the Waka' artists come to Tikal and carve Tikal Stela 26. This may have occurred around 507 CE, just before this king died. Tikal Stela 26 is called the red stela because its shattered lower fragments were found reaggregated, painted red with cinnabar like the bones of a deceased ruler, and deposited in and around the chopped surface of an altar inside the summit temple of Structure 5D-34 in the North Acropolis (Shook 1958). The upper part of this stela, we surmise, was completely erased like Stela 45 at El Perú-Waka'. It was designated Tikal Stela P1 (as in plain; Coe 1990, 501) and was discovered on the plaza before this Tikal temple. We posit that this masterpiece stela of King Chak Tok Ich'aak II of Tikal was at some point killed through shattering of the base and flaying of the top in the violence of the great wars of the Classic era. (Kaanul's King K'ahk' Ti' Chi'ch' conquered Tikal in conjunction with Caracol's King Yajaw Te' K'inich II in 562 CE, Yuhknoom Ch'een II conquered Tikal in 657 CE, and the Kaanul regime did so again in 679 CE under the auspices of vassal king Balaj Chan K'awiil of Dos Pilas). Subsequently, the basal relic fragments of Tikal king Chak Tok Ich'aak II's Stela 26 were painted red and placed in a temple on Structure 5D-34 as an elaborate dedication for a new construction phase that included in the offerings an heirloom Preclassic oracle's scrying mirror of volcanic hematite on mother-of-pearl backing (Schele and Freidel 1990, 201, 463n67), projecting into future time his soul force at Tikal in the form of revered remains.

Unlike the exquisitely carved Stela 26 at Tikal, with its preserved inscription declaring a conjured triad of Tikal gods and name of the ruler, Stela 45 at El Perú-Waka' was completely erased. We posit that a ruler of Waka' commissioned this desecration and carefully removed his visage and his words, disabling the capacity of the Tikal king's spirit to perform. When the monument was reset in the torn-out stairway of M13-Sub III, the disappeared visage rendered the king a captive and a sacrifice presented before this powerful shrine. We suggest that this desecration was carried out by Queen Ikoom Sak Wayis when as regent she planted El Perú-Waka' Stela 44, a posthumous portrait of her husband, King Chak Took Ich'aak, in front of the building in 564 CE.

One of the contextual features of El Perú-Waka' Stela 45 that supports this scenario is the fact that it was formally replanted in a ruined six-step stairway. The stairway of Structure M13-1 Sub III was distinctive not only for its fine yellow masonry blocks but for its six steep steps. Six-step stairways are special in Maya cosmology (Freidel et al. 1993; Nolan 2015) and famous because of their depiction on stair-tread panels on Hieroglyphic Stairway 2 at Yaxchilan (Tate 1991). In those panels, bound captives are depicted in contorted positions within large balls on six-step stairways. Ballplayers on Hieroglyphic Stairway 2, notably the Yaxchilan king Bird Jaguar IV, are shown on the plazas below these stairs preparing to hit the ball captives. Susan Nolan (2015) emphasizes that the individuals are likely being presented as captives rather than being killed by rolling down stairs. The actual six-step stairways are not so steep or long as to cause a fatality if someone fell (or was pushed) down them.

We can be sure that the people of Waka' knew the myths and the rituals of six-step stairways. The great palace gallery constructed in the seventh century by King K'inich Bahlam II and Queen K'abel at the western end of the city (Freidel et al. 2018; Pérez Robles et al. 2019) had a six-step stairway in which carved panels in the lowermost tread depicted Kaanul regime king Yuhknoom Yich'aak K'ahk' playing ball in 692 CE with King K'inich Bahlam II (among other ballplayers; Lee and Guenter 2010). The carved blocks of the palace's six-step stairway were torn out and scattered when the palace gallery was sacked and desecrated, probably by Tikal warriors in the catastrophic defeat of Waka' in 743 CE. Many of those carved blocks were later built into an adjacent display stairway (Piehl and Guenter 2005, 232), but one of them—which depicted Queen K'abel as a *kaloomte'* and a Kaanul regime lord—was found on the southern slope of the Palace Acropolis.

Kaloomte' K'abel was the most powerful ruler the Wak realm ever had. She was depicted in her magnificence in 692 CE on El Perú-Waka' Stela 34 (Graham 1988). That monument, paired with Stela 33 depicting her husband, K'inich Bahlam II, may have originally stood in front of the palace and six-step stairway. We think this because these monuments celebrate the Kaanul regime king Yuhknoom Yich'aak K'ahk', who had recently ascended to the throne. Because the six-step stairway celebrates Yuhknoom Yich'aak K'ahk', we think it likely that the palace gallery and the stelae were all part of a grand celebration of the Kaanul regime hegemony in Petén following the defeat of Tikal's King Nuun Ujol Chaak in 679 CE. Stelae 33 and 34 were later placed on Plaza 1 at the eastern end of the city, reset with Stela 35, the last monument of King K'inich Bahlam II dedicated in 711 CE. Queen K'abel did not plant a monument in that year. She had died sometime after 702 CE and her husband had buried her in the stairway of her Wiinte' Naah fire shrine, Structure M13-1 Sub II. Stela 35 shows the king facing to his right toward his queen, while Stela 33, more normally for him, shows the king facing left to her. Facing right was evidently the pose of higher authority.

The association of the palace's six-step stairway is important because, as Susan Nolan (2015, 25–36) has underscored, royal women are clearly implicated in the ballgame rituals of the Hieroglyphic Stairway 2 six-step stairways at Yaxchilan. As she observed, the ballgame is a metaphor for warfare, and through their associations with sacrifice and regeneration through menstruation and fecundity, the women at Yaxchilan were linked to the themes of sacrifice and regeneration in the six-step stairway mythos and the ballgame. Their magic also charged weapons of war with power. Finally, they were associated with the moon and the moon goddess. The six-step stairway of the seventh-century palace surely resonated historically with the earlier six-step stairway of the sixth-century Wiinte' Naah fire shrine. That earlier stairway was likely the place where Queen Ikoom Sak Wayis displayed captives. We argue that she replanted and engendered Stela 45 as a perpetual captive, very likely in revenge for the mortal wounding of her husband, Chak Tok Ich'aak of Wak, at the hands of Tikal warriors in a battle in 556 CE.

## Stone Images of Wak King Chak Tok Ich'aak

While the text on Stela 44 shows that Wak dynasty king Chak Tok Ich'aak died in 556 CE, the badly ruined El Perú-Waka' Stela 22 (fig. 7.10) was dedicated by an unknown king in 554 CE. On this stela, the ruler is in the same frontal pose as seen on Stela 44, with splayed feet and, in this case, with the panache on the sandals that was seen on Tikal Stela 26. His ceremonial bar is practically gone, but it has the rosettes and depending tassels seen on Stela 44. It is possible that this was just a costume preference of sixth-century Wak kings (e.g., Guenter 2014), but the death of King Chak Tok Ich'aak just two years after the dedication of this monument suggests that it was he who dedicated Stela 22 and then suddenly died unexpectedly.

There is good reason to think that Chak Tok Ich'aak of Waka' was in power for some time before the dedication of Stela 22. El Perú-Waka' Stela 23 (fig. 7.10b), which is anonymous but is generally better preserved than either Stela 22 or Stela 44, appears to be another portrait of this king as a young man in 524 CE, a period-ending jubilee. The pose and costume on this monument are virtually the same as on Stela 44, including the rosettes and tassels on the ceremonial bar, the frontal pose, the large earflares, and the splayed feet. But additional shared details include a cut-out giant limpet shell pectoral (a jewel that becomes part of standard Kaanul regime regalia in the seventh century), a wide ballplayer's belt, and a short apron or skirt (also ballgame regalia). Later, King K'inich Bahlam II would favor a distinctive jaguar and sun disc headdress diadem on three stelae that spanned his long career, so it

Figure 7.10. El Perú-Waka' Stela 22 (*a*); El Perú-Waka' Stela 23 (*b*). Photographs by Philip Hofstetter. Images courtesy of Proyecto Arqueológico Waka' and the Ministry of Culture and Sports of Guatemala.

(b)

178 · David A. Freidel and Olivia Navarro-Farr

is plausible that an earlier Wak dynasty king favored a distinctive costume in his portraits as well.

A person named Chak Tok Ich'aak Sak Wayis has been recently identified on Altar 5 at La Corona, located 30 kilometers north of El Perú-Waka' (Stuart et al. 2018). This altar was dedicated in 546 CE. It very likely portrayed the Wak king Chak Tok Ich'aak, who was married to Queen Ikoom Sak Wayis K'uhul Chatan Winik (see Stuart et al. 2018 for an alternative scenario). La Corona, ancient Sak Nikte', was certainly a vassal of the Kaanul realm at that time (Martin 2005). In 556 CE, Wak Chan K'awiil of Tikal was actively imposing himself on old allies as the forces of Kaanul gathered to the north and penetrated into Petén to encircle Tikal and cut it off from trade partners and military allies. Caracol Altar 21 (Martin 2005) gives retrospective history that declares that Caracol king Y'ajaw Te' K'inich II came to the throne under the supervision of King Wak Chan K'awiil (see also Grube 1994b, 106) and then in 556 CE the Tikal king attacked Caracol. After that, Caracol allied with the Kaanul regime against Tikal. It would make sense that Wak Chan K'awiil would also attack El Perú-Waka' in this 556 CE regional struggle to try to force this famous shrine center and strategic citadel back to his side. We argue that Tikal forces entered Waka' and desecrated the stelae celebrating Sihyaj K'ahk's establishment of the Wiinte' Naah there (Stelae 14–17) and also desecrated the shrine itself, including the six-step stairway. Queen Sak Wayis Ikoom and her son would have escaped northward. After Tikal warriors eventually withdrew from Waka', she returned to bury her husband in the old funerary pyramid, Structure M12-32 (see Meléndez 2019, 132–134, for the contextual identification of the deceased as Chak Tok Ich'aak of Waka' in Burial 37) and to rebuild the Wiinte' Naah fire shrine, Structure M13-1 Sub II.

The appropriate combination of events would have been effacement of Stela 45 when Queen Sak Wayis Ikoom commissioned another stela, Stela 44, and set it on a prominent platform in front of the shrine she rebuilt as regent of her young son, Wa'oom Uchab Ahk (Structure M13-1 Sub II). That the dead king, Chak Tok Ich'aak, presided over the Wiinte' Naah fire cult is indicated in his spiritual presence during the conjuring of the three gods of the realm under the aegis of his son. Stela 44 would have been a satisfying declaration of revenge for Queen Ikoom. In 562 CE, between the time of the death of her husband in 556 CE and the raising of this posthumous portrait, Kaanul king K'ahk' Ti' Chi'ch' (who presided over the accession of her son in 556 CE) and Caracol king Yajaw Te' K'inich II had defeated Tikal king Wak Chan K'awiil, sacrificed him, and conquered Tikal (Martin 2020).

In 2017, Mary Kate Kelly (2020) drafted the text on El Perú Stela 44, interpreting and transcribing the text as follows:

## Transcription

. . . 29 13-Pax **tz'a-[pa]-ja u-LAKAM-TUUN-li WAK-CHAN-na** ?
**CHAK-TOK-ICH'AAK WAK-AJAW u-BAAH u-CH'AB ya-AHK'AB-**
**li tu-K'UH-li AHKAN** (GI) ? (GII) ? (GIII) **u-\*K'AB-\*ji yu-ne wa-\*o-**
**\*ma u-\*CH'AB \*AHK?** . . . **i-yi-AJ IX-SAK-WAYIS**
**K'UH-"cha"-TAHN-WINIK 10–12-WINAL 7-HAAB-**
**ya 7-Oc 18-ka-se-wa CHUM-?la/?LAJ**[2] **ji-ya ta-AJAW-li wa-o-ma**
**u-CH'AB AHK? ya-AJAW-wa K'AHK'-TI'-CH'ICH'/K'IK' K'UH-**
**\*KAAN-\*AJAW** . . .

## Transliteration

. . . *bolon winak uxlajun pax tz'a[h]paj ulakamtuunil wak chan chak tok*
*ich'aak wak ajaw ubaah uch'a[h]b yahk'baal tuk'uhuul ahkan ? ? uk'abjiiy*
*yune[n] wa'oom uch'ab ahk . . . ? ix sak wayis k'uh[ul] 'cha' tahn winik*
*lajun lajunchan? winal huk haabiiy huk ook? waxaklajun kasew chumla-*
*jiiy ta ajawil wa'oom uch'ab ahk yajaw k'ahk' ti' ch'ich'/k'ik' k'uh[ul] kaan*
*ajaw . . .*

## Translation

*On *9.6.10.0.0 *8 *Ahau . . . A9 13 Pax [January 30, 564] it was erected
the stela of Wak Chan ? Chak Tok Ich'aak, the Wak Ajaw. It is his image?
his penance, his darkness,[3] for his gods, GI, GII, and GIII, he oversaw
it, his son, Wa'oom Uch'ab Ahk . . . ? Ix Sak Wayis K'uhul "cha"tahn person. It had been 10 days, 12 winals, and 7 years since, on 7 Oc 18 Sek
(9.6.2.5.10, June 30, 556) he sat in lordship, Wa'oom Uch'ab Ahk, the
vassal of K'ahk' Ti' Ch'ich'/K'ik', the holy Kaan lord.

Commissioning and planting Stela 44 honored Chak Tok Ich'aak of Waka'
with perpetual performance as conjurer of the gods. By effacing the stela of
the enemy of the same name, Queen Sak Wayis Ikoom bound his spirit forever as a war captive in stone without the possibility of declaring his words or
performing his actions.

The complex feature discovered to the north of Stela 44 represents the ritual uprooting of the monument from its original location on a sacred platform.
That platform was prepared by carefully cutting away the plaza floor, burning
the ancient clay, leveling the deposit below, and placing offerings of jade, obsidian, and chert into the distinct yellow mortar of the platform.

The stela was moved in order to reset it directly on the centerline of the
final phase of the Wiinte' Naah when it covered the tomb of Kaloomte' K'abel.
It was also set directly under the third tread of a stairway leading to the inner

sanctum of that version of the building. A ruler standing on that tread would be metaphorically rebirthing Chak Took Ich'aak. The deliberate erasure of the face and lower part of Stela 44 may have been done while the monument was standing on its platform in front of the Wiinte' Naah by warriors of Tikal that "burned" Waka' in 673 CE, according to Stanley Guenter's (2003) reading of Dos Pilas Hieroglyphic Stairway 2 history. It is a place that ends in Ka'; Waka' is the right place for Tikal king Nuun Ujol Chaak to have burned. King K'inich Yook of La Corona fled to Calakmul to seek refuge at this time (Stanley Guenter, personal communication to David Freidel, November 2014). Clearly Kaloomte' K'abel and K'inich Bahlam II returned and recovered their city and their realm, no doubt aided by Kaanul king Yuhknoom Ch'een the Great. But El Perú-Waka' Stelae 11 and 12, which had been dedicated in 672, may have been smashed in this attack.

Why erase Stela 44? Because that is what Queen Sak Wayis Ikoom of Waka' had done to Chak Tok Ich'aak II of Tikal depicted on Stela 45. In our scenario, this partly erased stela then stood in front of Structure M13-1 Sub II—the Wiinte' Naah fire shrine Queen Ikoom Sak Wayis built after the desecration of the six-step stairway fire shrine—until it was ceremonially and reverentially uprooted and moved to the centerline position of K'inich Bahlam II's final Wiinte' Naah fire shrine. This "uprooting" interpretation makes sense of the extraordinarily ritualized nature of the Waka' stela platform: cutting away the thick plaster floor, creating fires on the dirt layer below, and then marking out the cut-away area with small masonry blocks before building the low platform. Shattered fragments of jadeite beads and fragments of obsidian and chert blades and flakes (including Pachuca green obsidian) were built into the mortar of the wall of the stela platform. After the uprooting of El Perú-Waka' Stela 44, King K'inich Bahlam II had a second, larger mason's construction platform built around the stela platform. This platform buried the stela platform and was connected to the new positioning of Stela 44 by wall extensions. The mason's platform was not a simple construction pen; it was rather a burial. Its stones were set in fine brown clay mortar, the building technique for royal tombs in this city.

What this interpretation leaves unsatisfactorily explained is the selective desecration of Stela 44. Why was the lower text destroyed and the upper text preserved? The whole lower zone of carving around the monument was significantly more erased than the upper part. One possibility is that Tikal warriors wished to do to Chak Tok Ich'aak of Waka' what Queen Ikoom had done to Tikal's Chak Tok Ich'aak II by systematically erasing the monument in place in front of the Wiinte' Naah. In this back-and-forth war of stone kings, the basal fragments of Tikal Stela 26 were shattered and its top, Stela P1, was completely erased, probably in 657 CE when Yuhknoom Ch'een the Great conquered the city. In 673 CE, the Tikal warriors of King Nuun Ujol Chaak, who "burned" Waka', were possibly in the midst of destroying El Perú-Waka' Stela 44 when they were driven away when Kaloomte' K'abel and King K'inich Bahlam II returned. Such a history would have made the monument even more poignant as a memorial to the resilience and ultimate success of Waka', especially when faced with attack from Tikal. Unlike Stela 45, with its imprisoned image and words, Stela 44 still declared the conjuring of the Waka' gods of the city by the spirit of Chak Tok Ich'aak Wak Ajaw, overseen by his son and successor Wa'oom Uchab Ahk; his wife Ikoom Sak Wayis, the queen regent; and the Kaanul king K'ahk' Ti Chich (Martin and Beliaev 2017; Martin 2020). The monuments embodying kings and queens remained active agents of the Waka' Wiinte' Naah, as did their earthly remains. In the early eighth-century, Kaloomte' K'abel was laid by her husband K'inich Bahlam II in Burial 61 as such an agent in the same stairway that held the flayed and passive Chak Tok Ich'aak II of Tikal. She perpetually birthed from the *Spondylus* womb shell placed on her groin the image of the Waka' war and death god Akan Yaxaj carved from a tooth-shaped stalactite fragment. Tikal would capture and enslave that god in 743 CE when it attacked Waka', but that is another story (Freidel et al. 2018).

Stela 44 was not formally replanted when it was moved. The butt of the monument was placed through a cut in the floor and it was steeply angled to the east. This cannot be a simple matter of convenience, as K'inich Bahlam II's masons were building the new Wiinte' Naah around the monument and could have designed it to stand vertically had they chosen to do so. The masons designed this offering so that the hero-king moved eastward toward the rising sun (as did his body in Burial 37); the head and crown of the stela portrait were directly under the third tread of a short stairway leading into the sanctuary (fig. 7.9). When K'inich Bahlam II stood on that landing, as he surely did in dedicating the building, he would have been symbolically sprouting from his ancestor's head like the maize god from the skull of his sacrificed previous self. In this way, Chak Tok Ich'aak's spirit, transposed into his descendant, could once again conjure the gods of the Wiinte' Naah, materializing a defiant future of victory in the face of (especially at the beginning of the eighth century) another dark era of struggle with Tikal, the enduring enemy.

## Materializing History

In ancient Maya history, as in history elsewhere, some places stand out as being pivotal in great geopolitical struggles and are remembered for that. The

North Acropolis of Tikal was surely such a place, as was the center of Calakmul. Caracol's center was such a place with its magnificent central complex of Caana (Chase and Chase 2017c); its Caana pyramid had the magnificent stairway of King K'an II with its sweeping history of the rise of Kaanul's greatest king and his capital (Helmke and Awe 2016a; see A. Chase and D. Chase 2020a for a different interpretation of this stairway). The Great Platform of Chichén Itzá was intentionally designed to be such a place in history with its murals of battle, its scenes of accession, its great ballcourt, and its Kan Cross–shaped pyramid adorned with feathered serpents. The citadel of Waka', with its great sculptured hill rising more than 130 meters above the level of the San Pedro Mártir River and a viewshed of more than 40 kilometers to the west, became such a pivotal place when Kaloomte' Sihyaj K'ahk' arrived there and proceeded to establish dominion in the southern lowlands. During the fourth and fifth centuries, the rulers of Waka' celebrated their relationship to him, maintaining the Wiinte' Naah fire shrine and the temples on top of the great hill in honor of his memory. In the protracted struggles between the Kaanul regime rulers and Tikal and its allies in the southern lowlands, Waka' was a prize representing regional dominion successfully proclaimed, a particularly ambitious example of landesque cosmography (see chapter 2, this volume). The kings and queens of Waka' materialized history in their great stones, which were larger and more impressive than the stones of Tikal. By the sixth century, Kaanul was striving to capture Waka' and turn its kings to its dominion through royal intermarriage. Why? Part of the answer no doubt lay in the practical location of this citadel in a position to command the San Pedro Mártir and its tributaries and to be a crossing place for a north-south passage that connected Kaanul realms in the north to sources of jadeite and other prized commodities in the southern highlands. But the intense focus on the rulers of Waka' as agents in and of time is displayed in the long-term practice of erasing, defacing, shattering, reassembling, and repurposing their stone beings. These rulers, especially the great queens such as Ikoom and K'abel, materialized history in a place where history was prophesized and given direction. The archaeology of El Perú-Waka' certainly addresses many aspects of the patterns generated by this prospect.

## Acknowledgments

The Proyecto Arqueológico Waka' has been made possible by the support and cooperation of the Ministry of Culture and Sports of Guatemala, the National Institute of Anthropology and History, the National Museum of Archaeology and Ethnology and our many Guatemalan professional colleagues. The research has been supported by Jerry Glick and the Jerome E. Glick Foundation, the Alphawood Foundation, the Hitz Foundation, the US Department of the Interior, the GeoOntological Development Society of San Francisco, the National Geographic Society, the Foundation for the Cultural and Natural Patrimony of Guatemala, and generous private benefactors.

## Notes

1 See Harrison-Buck (2016) for a nuanced argument that stela desecration irreversibly killed the animate in the monuments and O'Neal (2013) for relevant discussion of breakage and reuse of Maya monuments at Piedras Negras.

2 Stuart (personal communication 2019) has suggested that this hand holding three horizontal leaflike objects is either the syllable **la** or a logogram **LAH/LAJ** and is likely related to the term for *chichicaste* (nettle).

3 Stuart (personal communication 2017) translates the phrase *ubaah uch'ahb yahk'baal* as "His 'persona' is his engendering-and-darkness."

# III

## Chambers of Time

# 8

# Balamkú's History House

## Harkening to Primordial Rhythms of Mythic Time

ANNE S. DOWD AND GABRIELLE VAIL

Only a few Maya codices have survived. The best preserved are the Postclassic period (900–1519 CE) Dresden Codex, the Códice maya de México (formerly Grolier), the Madrid Codex, and the Paris Codex, and tiny fragments of other poorly preserved excavated examples from the Classic period (250–900 CE). For this reason, hieroglyphs painted or incised on architectural walls are an important addition to the corpus of Maya writing. Such codical texts can also show where books were composed, suggesting that calendrical problem-solving was undertaken in the context of workshops where codices were produced or in classrooms overseen by a daykeeper or ritual specialist. These "books on walls" provide evidence for the materialization of time, as different texts were used to calculate calendar units, compute historical and astronomical events, teach students, and schedule the content, pace, and flow of ritual activities, including those that enabled dynastic rulers to connect with their ancestors.

Recent analyses of hieroglyphic texts written on walls of Maya buildings show that some are rendered in a style that is comparable to those painted in bark-paper folding-screen books. Fragmentary hieroglyphs that are examples of diminutive written texts painted on walls of building interiors were discovered inside Structure 1A-Sub at Balamkú, Mexico. Such wall inscriptions, which have a palimpsest of overwriting, imply works in progress intended to function as composition, training, reference, practice, or as mnemonic devices for aiding memory. The Balamkú texts and the context in which they were found are potentially comparable to finds at many other Maya sites, including those showing content pertaining to the commensuration of calendrical cycles with astronomical cycles at Xultun, Guatemala; to dynastic history at

Holmul, Guatemala; to training, rites of passage, or educational or initiation content in both Naj Tunich Cave, Guatemala, and one of the eastern rooms of El Castillo acropolis, Xunantunich, Belize. A review of informal and formal pedagogical texts shows that there are multiple examples of painted or incised walls with hieroglyphs.

This chapter explores examples of Maya writing on walls of buildings with a special emphasis on little-known texts dating to near the end of the Maya Early Classic period (250–550 CE) at Balamkú. The role of these hieroglyphic texts written on walls suggests an example of a "history house." After discussing the glyphic expressions written on these walls, we consider other examples, such as the now-famous texts found at Xultun, which date to the Late Classic period (550–800 CE). Then we survey a range of other Mesoamerican examples (see table 8.1). These texts show that time was transformed into real-world physical notations, and demonstrate how sky-watching, calendars, genealogy, and agricultural practices came together in ways that documented social history and influenced future divinatory predictions (Milbrath 1999, 2013; Rice 2007, xvi).

Table 8.1. Examples of Maya painted or incised hieroglyphic texts discussed in chapter

| Site | Structure/Group/Feature | Date |
| --- | --- | --- |
| Balamkú | 1A-Sub, Grupo Central | 550–650 CE |
| Bonampak | 1 | 790 CE |
| Cacaxtla | Citadel | 650–950 CE |
| Copán | 16 | Rosalila Phase (520–655 CE) |
| Holmul | A, Group II | 593 CE |
| Naj Tunich | Cave | 750–850 CE |
| Playa del Carmen | C-1 | 1200–1519 CE |
| San Bartolo | Ixim Structure, Sub-1A, Las Pinturas Complex | 300–100 BCE |
| Uaxactún | B-VIII, B-XIII | 200–600 CE |
| Xultun | 10K-2, Los Sabios, Area A, east wall | 749 CE |
| Xunantunich | A-5, El Castillo Acropolis | Hats' Chaak Phase (670–780 CE) |

This study considers places used for producing books, for planning ritual events, and keeping days, engaging in astronomy, and interpreting calendars. These intellectual pursuits based in science, technology, education, and mathematics connected religious adepts with the natural and social world around them. Old World case studies serve as important theoretical anchors for the development of these practices. Ian Hodder (2016, 2018) has discussed the first recognized example of a communal religious structure that was used for the purpose of commemorating ancestors. Some of the Maya examples we showcase were places where ritual specialists calculated units of time, cared for sacred bundles, and recorded lines of succession and generations of those who held political power (Eberl 2015, 92; Estrada-Belli and Tokovinine 2016, 158).

## Curating Time in History Houses

Ian Hodder and colleagues (2018, 23, 25; see also Hodder and Pels 2010) have discussed history-making and history houses in the Middle East, contrasting large communal religious structures for aggregating groups at sites such as those established during the Pre-Pottery Neolithic A (PPNA; 10,000–8,800 BCE). They described tensions between history houses based on ancestry or descent and history-making structures based on sodalities and the way these places linked their inhabitants to continuity with the past or the future.

History houses at Çatalhöyük in Turkey had at least three phases of rebuilding and contained over ten burials in at least one of those phases. While history houses were often more elaborate than other buildings, at Çatalhöyük there were also elaborate structures with multiple burials without evidence of sequential rebuilding. James Mellaart (1967) characterized these multiphase buildings as shrines, noting, for example, that pairs of leopards repeated in consecutive levels VII and VIB on the north wall in Building E.44 and painted vultures repeated in the Shrine 8 sequence indicated a consistent building function after renovation. Ian Hodder's team (Regan and Taylor 2014) excavated structures such as those in the South Area's 65-56-44-10 stacked house sequence, which have been interpreted as efforts at memory- or history-making. Two forms of history-making occur:

1) repetitive social practices within the buildings resulting in distinctive deposition patterns or evidence of use;
2) object retrieval, iconographic repetition, or curation from earlier buildings for deposition in later ones.

Ian Hodder (2018, 25), referring to Çatalhöyük, states:

Gradually through time, however, a second form of history-making emerged that allowed greater and wider collaboration within segments of the community as a whole. This second type allowed crosscutting sodalities to be constructed. These sodalities probably included a diversity of forms such as hunting societies, men's houses, secret societies, and medicine societies (Mills 2014). They functioned to link people together across house-based groups. They were often exclusive and highly ritualized. But they allowed any particular individual to call upon a wider array of support in times of hardship. They allowed cross-community sharing on a larger scale while at the same time promoting difference and contestation.

It is thus inaccurate to see the increase of ritual, public monuments, and special buildings as resulting from community cohesion alone. Rather, over millennia there was a tension between house-based and sodality-based forms of history-making. These forms competed with each other, and in the end the public buildings that came to dominance in the PPNA decreased in importance and influence. Throughout, there was a competitive process of inventing and materializing histories, both between house-based and sodality-based groups and between distinct houses and sodalities. Both the house-based descent groups and the crosscutting sodalities that convened in public buildings invested in religious practices that involved history-making. Because Maya societies also are characterized by complex interplays between sodalities and residence-based kin groups, this perspective has value in refining what it was to be Maya in the context of ritual specialization, timekeeping, and the deification of dynastic founders (and by extension their successors) (McAnany and Hodder 2009).

Ian Hodder (2018, 3, 25) identifies three types of key places:

1) Places that include communal religious structures or complexes where larger groups of people congregated for religious purposes. For the Maya region, this included examples of religious precincts such as Calakmul's E Group or large platforms at sites such as Aguada Fénix.
2) Places that include houses, often in community centers, where a sense of inherited place is conveyed through burial and ancestor veneration. These include Balamkú's first-phase palace and Holmul's first-phase palace/funerary shrine.
3) Places that include smaller communal structures, where restricted access meant that only a subset of the community was welcome, in these cases more like a sodality than like a family. Xultun, Xunantunich, and San Bartolo are potential examples of this type.

Some Middle Eastern houses or structures, as indicated by the leopard reliefs duplicated through time in levels VII and VIB at Mellaart's Shrine 44 at

Çatalhöyük (Hodder 2018, 22), are places where ritual knowledge specialists passed down information.

In Mesoamerica, one can see parallels with Ian Hodder's (2018) first type of communal religious structures or complexes where sites such as Aguada Fénix (chapter 3, this volume) have large communally constructed platforms thought to be for the purpose of seasonal ritual ceremonies. The range of orientations displayed by these platforms, some with multiple mounds constructed on top, match the horizon-based astronomical patterning initially recognized by Anthony Aveni, Anne Dowd, and Ben Vining in 2003 as calendar intervals. Earlier architecture examples aligning with intervals in the 260-day count suggest the sacred round developed much earlier than written sources attest, as has long been suspected (Šprajc et al. 2023). Related E Group complexes, which are religious precincts often with astronomically oriented temple locations containing skull burials, murals, writing, and divination, calendar development or timekeeping features, may indicate concern with past and future temporal continuity—bringing place-making and historical perspectives together (A. Chase 1983; A. Chase and D. Chase 1995; Aveni et al. 2003; Dowd 2017c; Freidel et al. 2017). Group E–type complexes persisted later in time and documented both 260-day and 365-day calendars through the architectural alignment patterning (Dowd et al. 2017).

In the Maya region, the second type of ancestor or history house in the categorization of Ian Hodder and others (2016, 2; 2018; see also Hodder and Pels 2010) is perhaps seen at Structure IA-Sub at Balamkú and at Holmul. Structure 1A-Sub may have functioned as "time's house," referring to the idea that calendar adepts could have used the space for calculating mythic events in real time for the purpose of commemorating the divine acts of ancestral rulers and their successors (Dowd 2016a). The Balamkú example has at least two known construction phases and only one presumed burial, so data on the use of the building for the two types of memory making are limited. The substructure was painted with two layers of paint and then quickly remodeled into a funerary monument and buried under a taller temple construction. Other comparable examples of structures could better show points of comparison or contrast with Hodder's (2016, 2018) architectural category. But if dynastic ritual scheduling occurred and iconographic decoration situated relationships between ancestors and descendants within the cosmos, Ian Hodder's (2016, 2018) idea of a kin-based history house may apply to Structure IA-Sub at Balamkú.

The architectural function of the building in which the hieroglyphs from Balamkú were found compares well to Building A in Group II at Holmul, which was originally a palace but was also used as a burial place and mausoleum, according to information Francisco Estrada-Belli has presented on hieroglyphic inscriptions from the roof-comb frieze of the basal element of the Holmul building. Francisco Estrada-Belli and Alexandre Tokovinine (2016, 151) describe the west side of a west-facing second-to-last construction phase of Building A in Group II. Emblazoned with a painted frieze dated to 593 CE, Building A is the southeastern building in the plaza. Decorated with yellow, orange, blue, and green pigments, it was covered by a later construction, which was a south facing but never completed final phase. At Holmul, Estrada-Belli and Tokovinine (158) translated a possible name for Building A in Group II as "*tz'a(h)k/tz'akab' naah* (the house of time/sacred bundles/succession/generations)," referring to elapsed time in bundles. The relief on this structure was interpreted as the ruler reborn as a god seated in the cleft of an animate personified mountain. Thus, Structure A at Holmul shows an example of a ruler's apotheosis to a godlike status (163). In 2021, a comparable stucco frieze dated to 568 CE was excavated from Structure 105 at Chochkitam in Guatemala (Estrada-Belli and Tokovinine 2022, 719–721).

Ian Hodder's (2018) third type of smaller sodality-based communal structures is also found in Mesoamerica. One example of a hierarchical religious specialist order has been identified within a prominent priest's residence in Structure 10K-2 at Xultun, known as the Los Sabios building. If it was the home office of a leading member of the Taaj priest sodality who was concerned with affairs of both religion and state, Hodder's (2018) cross-community group form of history-making is a good fit. In addition, Structure Sub-1A at San Bartolo and Structure A-5, the El Castillo acropolis at Xunantunich, have been interpreted as schools for elite youth (Saturno et al. 2006; Saturno, Stuart et al. 2012; chapter 11, this volume). The Naj Tunich Cave may also fit this third category of sodality-based communal locations because of its isolation, the metaphor of entry into a cave as a journey or rite of passage, and the content of its hieroglyphic texts. Murals are present in colonial-period (1519–1697 CE) highland Guatemalan homes that still stand in the town of Chajul. The several-hundred-year-old wall paintings show performances such as those *cofradías* (religious brotherhoods) organized. Brotherhoods met in domestic spaces that rotated to different houses. Interestingly, modern examples also exist: the Santa Fe Institute, which was originally a ranch house, the equivalent of an elite residence in its own original cultural context, was converted to and used as a think tank for the exchange of ideas much later in time.

The glyphic content of the inscriptions at Xultun indicates mathematical and astronomical calculations of lunar cycles commensurate with periods when Jupiter, Venus, and Mars were visible related to calendar development at 749 CE. The Holmul inscriptions appear to treat dynastic history and relate to ancestor veneration in 593 CE. Given that the subject matter of the roof-comb friezes from Balamkú and Holmul have significant parallels, the scribes writing on Balamkú's interior walls at around 550–650 CE may have treated topics that can help scholars interpret how these buildings functioned. The dialectic between kin- or dynasty-based timekeeping and associated ritual- and sodality-based calendar crafting or other activities will be better understood in the future by comparing and contrasting information from locations such as these.

## Balamkú's History House

Archaeologists first explored Balamkú in the 1990s and early 2000s (García Cruz 1990, 1992, 1993–1994; Carrasco Vargas et al. 1994, 1995; Baudez 1996; Becquelin et al. 1996; Michelet et al. 1997; Arnauld et al. 1998; de Pierrebourg 2004; Boucher and Dzul Góndora 2001; García Vierna et al. 2009). During that time, Ramón Carrasco Vargas led the excavations of the Proyecto Arqueológico de la Biosfera de Calakmul, which revealed an elaborate structure, designated as Structure 1A-Sub, with a stucco façade representing the cosmos through a layered representation of space occupied by humans, animals, and deities or earth, sky, and underworld realms. This structure has hieroglyphic texts painted in a calligraphic style on walls inside the central south room of the structure that provide a point of departure for the study of Maya materialization of time.

Structure 1A-Sub is located in the Grupo Central or Group B/Plaza B of the four main groups at Balamkú—north, central, south, and southwest (Arnauld et al. 1998, 144). Two other groups, an east group and La Fortaleza (about 500 meters north of the north group), were also identified, and a large reservoir is located about 300–400 meters west of the south group (Becquelin et al. 1996, 26). An E Group–type complex is in the southwest group (Becquelin et al. 1996, 61). At approximately 25 hectares in size, Balamkú is about 47 kilometers west of the urban center of Calakmul (Folan et al. 1995) and northwest of the small hamlet of Conhuas in present-day Mexico,

Twenty-four small, hand-painted, codex-style hieroglyphs are superimposed and unevenly preserved in widely separated locations on the south and west walls of a central south-facing room of Structure 1A-Sub. They show evidence of multiple (at least three) layers of superimposed stucco. Red and black glyphs were painted on the second of these layers (Dowd 1998a, 2015a, 2016a, 2017a, 2018a). The individual hieroglyphs measure about 2.5 centimeters high and 2–3 centimeters wide. One example had a cutmark from a

194 · Anne S. Dowd and Gabrielle Vail

knife blade around an area of 8–10 square centimeters, suggesting that looters had attempted unsuccessfully to remove it. The distribution and layering of these plaster and painted remnants of the wall surface indicate that much of the wall was originally covered in texts and that the location had been written on repeatedly. This iterative use suggests that such inscriptions were used in educational practices. Erasing and rewriting texts are not just performative acts; they also help us understand how repetition of designs and temporal rhythms are closely linked.

Sketches were made of the discontinuous series of painted hieroglyphs on the south and west inside walls to the left of the central doorway as one entered the building (figs. 8.1–8.4). Radiocarbon ($^{14}$C) analysis of a wooden lintel sample from the central doorway to the structure provided a calibrated radiocarbon date of 631±30 CE (Arnauld et al. 1998, 144; R. Carrasco Vargas, personal communication, 1997). Dating estimates based on the style of the art are about 550–650 CE (Baudez 1996).

While a looter's trench had exposed an area several meters wide inside the central doorway, the interior of the room was not excavated because a full excavation would have undermined the structural stability of the temple that was later constructed above the substructure. Archaeologist Armando Paul supervised the excavation of a test unit within the front central room in the earlier substructure and uncovered at least three stucco floors about a meter under the floor of the room and above the presumed stucco floor of the plaza the platform was built on (Carrasco Vargas et al. 1994, 1995).

The substructure measured approximately 16.8 meters long. It was 6.46 meters wide at the base of walls of the room and 6.53 meters high from the floor to the top of the roof-comb. Three south-facing portals provided access to the building, and the exterior frieze was positioned on its long axis. The roof-level frieze measured 17.2 meters (reconstructed) or 16.8 meters (actual) long by 4.1 meters high (actual), including the roof-comb elements. It may have extended out from the walls 0.2 meters on each west-east end and is thought to have continued around the building (R. Carrasco Vargas, personal communication, 1995). The whole edifice, including a later construction, is about 12 meters high.

**The Façade of Balamkú Structure 1A-Sub**

In 1994, the team documented the exterior painted al fresco frieze that decorated the roof and roof-comb of the structure. In the field study series of the Instituto Nacional de Antropología e Historia (fig. 8.5), Ramón Carrasco Vargas et al. (1994, 1995) reported on the work at Balamkú's Structure 1A-Sub. Two years later, Claude-François Baudez (1996) published an iconographic

Figure 8.1. Glyphs in column texts 1, 2, and 3 in Balamkú Structure 1A-Sub. Copyright © 1995, Anne S. Dowd. All rights reserved., used with permission.

196 · Anne S. Dowd and Gabrielle Vail

Figure 8.2. Additional painted glyphs, column texts 4, 5, 6, 7, 8 in Balamkú Structure 1A-Sub. Copyright © 1995, Anne S. Dowd. All rights reserved, used with permission.

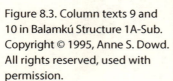

Figure 8.3. Column texts 9 and 10 in Balamkú Structure 1A-Sub. Copyright © 1995, Anne S. Dowd. All rights reserved, used with permission.

study. Using photographs Jean-Pierre Courau took and first-hand observations, Anne Dowd was responsible for documenting the roof façade, which extended upward, forming a roof-comb on the south side of the structure (Baudez 1996). Ceramic studies have also been published, as have results of the conservation work and materials analysis that took place on the exterior of the structure (Boucher and Dzul Góndora 2001; García Vierna et al. 2009).

The roof façade was painted with at least two layers of paint in three Munsell

Figure 8.4. Glyphs in column text 11 in Balamkú Structure 1A-Sub. Copyright © 1995, Anne S. Dowd. All rights reserved, used with permission.

colors, the background in red 2.5YR5/6, outlines in dusky red 10R3/4, and black 2.5YRN2.5/0 for pupils in eyes. A recent analysis of the pigments on the exterior of the substructure showed that hematite ($Fe_2O_3$) was used to produce red and coal was used to create black (Arano et al. 2020, 7, 9). The bas-relief was painted al fresco, while the plaster was still damp. Because it was covered completely by a later temple platform, it was in an excellent state of preservation.

Anne Dowd's (1998a) analysis of the roof façade showed that all of the poetic devices then known in Maya discourse analysis were present in this design. The overall interpretation is that linguistic conventions conveying highly structured prayer-like features were invoked in artistic media because this was a sacred religious space. For Maya people, poetic principles structured design and language, as they still do today: "Linguistic structures permeated other media ranging from ritual performance, to modern (ca. AD 1978) Quiche [K'ichee'] textile design, to ca. 300 BC–AD 200 site design at Cerros" (Dowd 1998a, 4). Dowd interpreted the building façade as using poetic features linked to ritual performance and the role of the art and inscriptions in repeated rhythmic social acts. Similar to numerical commensuration in Maya calendrics, poem meter and song rhythm create a pulse or a tempo for the ritual story. In the Maya worldview, connecting time with a creation myth or a cosmological beginning secures built space to a bedrock foundation and links the passage of time to deeply rooted narratives of dynastic history. The drive of humans to explain the past and anticipate the future is a cultural universal.

How did Maya people express cosmogonic principles at Balamkú? Their cosmology is expressed in stucco and stone in the façade of the main palace building. In the relief-sculptured roof façade, a bicephalic feathered serpent appears below four animate mountains, four saurian creatures, at least

Figure 8.5. Northwest view of the stucco frieze on Balamkú Structure 1A-Sub. Copyright Anne S. Dowd. All rights reserved, used with permission.

two but possibly four seated humans or gods, and three anthropomorphic jaguars or monster-headed battle beasts (Baudez 1996; D. Freidel, personal communication, August 13, 2020).[1] The serpent has significant parallels with the basal celestial serpents that situate the cosmological space in the Pinturas Building in San Bartolo, Guatemala (Saturno 2009).

The artist(s) incorporated couplets, triplets, and possibly a quatrain on the frieze of the roof façade (Dowd 1998a, 9–10). The frieze on the upper roof façade appears in three principal horizontal registers underlain by the cornice element. Besides a stratigraphic (top to bottom or bottom to top) reading, there is also a right-to-left or left-to-right reading. Across the frieze, chiasmus (mirroring) is evident, bisected by central axes (both vertical and horizontal). The triadic series unifies the composition because the jaguars face outward. The first two jaguars face in one direction and the last jaguar faces in the opposite direction, evoking a rough approximation of bilateral symmetry while still showing a progression or narrative sequence from one to another, left to right. This focus away from the center contrasts with the inward orientation of the toads and crocodiles and the comparable outward orientation of the bicephalic serpent. Although the murals were poorly preserved on the façade of the lower wall below the roof, the doorways leading into the interior rooms are a set of three, positioned directly beneath the three jaguar panels.

As Dowd (1998a, 8) has noted:

> All poetic forms known from Maya literature are displayed in the ca. 550 AD temple façade at Balamkú, Campeche, Mexico. Their existence clinches the argument that poetic structures governed both audio and visual media, and confirms the use of architecture as stage, set, or backdrop for theatrical religious or political performances. This is because architectural sculpture can be seen as a multi-dimensional exhortation device. It is designed by the artist to incite the audience to give the ritual events, framed by architecture, their utmost attention (Jones 1996). A discursive exchange is set up between the artist and/or patron and the audience. The purpose of this exchange is to illustrate the direction and placement of the ritual journey.

The tight structure of the Balamkú façade's poetic features may have complemented processions of people praying or singing, with the intensity of the poetic utterances rising to a crescendo as the building was approached or reached. This ties in well with the glyphic evidence of ritual processions and a reference to a singer within Structure IA-Sub's interior room.

Other studies that have significant correspondences with the Balamkú case

200 · Anne S. Dowd and Gabrielle Vail

include William Saturno's (2009) structural analysis of the west wall of the Pinturas Building at San Bartolo, Linda Schele and David Freidel's (1990) reading of Structure 5C-2nd at Cerros (see also Freidel and Schele 1988a; Freidel 2020), and Francisco Estrada-Belli and Alexandre Tokovinine's (2016) interpretation of the Holmul frieze. Each of these studies underscores the potential of linguistic structures to aid in understanding Maya architecture and performance.

### Interior Texts and Context at Balamkú

Equally important to our understanding of Balamkú Structure 1A-Sub are the small, hand-painted, codex-style hieroglyphs found on the south and west walls of a central south-facing room of the structure (Dowd 1998a, 2015a, 2016a, 2017a, 2018a).

Analysis of the hieroglyphic texts allows us to develop some preliminary proposals about their content. For the purposes of this analysis, the visible text has been divided into eleven subtexts based on the columns in which they appear and the size and style of the glyphs; they are labeled Texts 1–11 in the discussion that follows (figs. 8.1–8.4).

Although Text 1 is fairly legible, it remains poorly understood (fig. 8.1, left column). The first glyph block in the column is substantially eroded. It is unclear if what remains is the outline of a day glyph cartouche; if so, the coefficient appears to be missing. The glyph below this clearly belongs to the "P" (persons) category in the Macri, Looper, and Vail coding system (Macri and Looper 2003; Macri and Vail 2009; Looper et al. 2022) and may correspond to PL8 in Looper et al. (2022), which is the name of the maize deity (*'ajan*) and the number eight (*waxak*). If this identification is correct, it is possible that the dark hank of hair is a female indicator, as it is used on occasion in the codices with female deities.

The final glyph block in Text 1 includes the upper element of 32A (Macri and Vail 2009; reclassified as ZM1 in Looper et al. 2022), although it is unclear whether the syllable **ma** was intended here or if it is the upper part of the ZUK glyph (reclassified as ZRC in Looper et al. 2022), reading *noj* (right; *noh?* in Macri and Looper 2003, 244) or *nojool/nojo:l* (south; *nohol* in Macri and Vail 2009, 186). It does provide a possible date range for the inscription, however. According to John Justeson (personal communication, November 9, 1995), the **ma** form on the interior at Balamkú (A3 in Text 1) may date to Cycle 9 in the Long Count but not earlier. Cycle 9 began about 436 CE and lasted until 830 CE.

Although Texts 2 and 3 are in close proximity to each other, they appear to have been written by separate individuals (fig. 8.1). The former includes two partially eroded glyph blocks at A1-A2 that remain difficult to interpret, followed by one that has an analogue in the texts painted on the walls of the

Naj Tunich Cave, where it appears at A2 in Drawing 82 (Stone 1995, 179) (fig. 8.6). There it follows a date in the Calendar Round, a repeating 52-year cycle, and depicts a seated figure with his or her hand raised to a tumpline that supports what appears to be a glyphic representation of fire (*k'ahk'*), signifying that fire is his or her burden (*kuch*). A depiction of a female goddess with a tumpline and a fire compound occurs in the third frame of the almanac on pages 16a–17a of the Dresden Codex, where it is paired with a collocation specifying that it is her burden (fig. 8.7).

The corresponding glyph in the Balamkú text similarly shows a figure grasping a tumpline (glyph ZB2 in Looper et al. 2022). In this case, the burden is a textile bundle, the contents of which are unknown. Other examples of glyphs showing a figure grasping a tumpline and burden occur on Stela D (Altar 41 and Altar D) at Copán. The next one or two glyphs in the Balamkú text are substantially eroded and cannot be read, whereas enough remains of the one below (the final one in the column) to suggest a possible reading as ZCF (**k'o**) or ZCG (reading unknown), based on Looper et al.'s (2022) catalog of Maya hieroglyphs. If the former, it may be part of a name phrase or it may be a couplet construction based on the phrase *k'ochtaj* (is carried). Both interpretations are speculative, however, since whatever appears below the possible **k'o** syllable is eroded. It may be feasible to make a more definitive

Figure 8.6. Drawing 82 at Naj Tunich Cave. Note the figure with the tumpline and burden in the lower left of the text. Source: After Stone (1995).

202 · Anne S. Dowd and Gabrielle Vail

Figure 8.7. Dresden Codex page 17a. Source: After Förstemann (1880).

determination in the future using a greater range of recording methods than were available at the time the texts were initially recorded, if their current state of preservation allows such a possibility.

Based on what is preserved, it is clear that this text refers to the carrying of an unspecified burden. The carrying of burdens is a common theme in the Dresden Codex (Förstemann 1880), where it is most commonly associated with a young female goddess. Her burdens include various types of prognostications, including fire, and specific deities (the rain god Chahk, the death god, and various others). Deities are also identified as burdens on the yearbearer pages of the Dresden Codex (pages 25–28) in a series of rituals associated with the transition from one year—and its associated prognostications—to the next. In this context, ritual performers in the guise of opossum actors are shown carrying the burdens. There is nothing in the glyphic representation of the burden bearer at Balamkú to specify whether the actor is male or female, whether the act of carrying the bundle had ritual significance, or what the contents of the bundle might be.

In Text 3, only two glyph blocks are evident. They appear to involve a name phrase referring to a female protagonist. This is marked by the glyph at A1a, PLB (Looper et al. 2022), which is read as *'ix* or *'ixik,* the former serving as a classifier for a noun that is either female, relatively small, or relatively nonactive (Kaufman and Norman 1984, 139) and the latter meaning woman. This is followed by what we believe is a continuation of the protagonist's name or a title at A2, which begins with what we identify as PL1 (Looper et al. 2022), reading *'ixi'm* (maize) or *juun* (one), followed by a glyph that is not found in the Maya Hieroglyphic Database catalog (Looper et al. 2022). Whether this text is self-referential or refers to a woman who was important to the history of the structure is unknown.

Not enough remains of Texts 4 and 5 to allow anything definitive to be said about them at present (fig. 8.2). Text 6 includes several identifiable glyphs, including one identified as "rubber" at A1a (ZUQ in Martha Macri and Gabrielle Vail's 2009 catalog; reclassified as ZRJ in Looper et al. 2022) and *k'ay* (to sing; Tokovinine 2017, 24) or *k'ayoom* (singer) at A4 (PC5 in Macri and Looper's 2003 catalog; reclassified as PY3 in Looper et al. 2022) (fig. 8.4). The glyph at A1b is shaped like a number of different syllabic glyphs, including **chu** and **ye**, although none of them have the same markings. Based on the context, it is more likely a logograph. While it includes several features suggestive of a hand (the category "M" in the Maya Hieroglyphic Database), we have been unable to find a good match.

Instead, we would like to suggest the following as possibilities: Macri and Looper's (2003, 253) ZY3, which is a profile view of one side of a ballcourt (reclassified as ZY2 in Looper et al. 2022) or Macri and Vail's (2009, 185) ZUJ, meaning *yahx* (first) or *yaax/ya'x* (green/blue; reclassified as 1BA in Looper et al. 2022). The first interpretation receives support from a scene painted in the interior of the Naj Tunich Cave (Drawing 21), which shows the hero twin Hunahpu wearing ballgame regalia and standing in front of a stepped structure with a depiction of a rubber ball with the coefficient 9 (fig. 8.8). On page 41a in the Dresden Codex, the rain deity Chahk (also spelled Chaak) is seated next to a ballcourt with a rubber ball perched between a profile view of the two sides (Vail and Hernández 2018; Vail 2022, 198–199) (fig. 8.9). Other examples with a similar focus include Steps IV–XIII of Hieroglyphic Stairway 2, at Yaxchilan (Tate 1991, 217–218). Additional examples of the

204 · Anne S. Dowd and Gabrielle Vail

Figure 8.8. Scenes from Drawings 21–23 at Naj Tunich Cave. Source: After Stone (1995).

spiral glyph (ZRJ) can be found in the second frame of the almanac on pages 29c–30c of the Dresden Codex (fig. 8.10), which shows rubber offerings being made to cenotes. In the next frame, Chahk holds a stingray spine bloodletter in one hand and an offering of rubber incense paired with a *ya'x-k'an* compound in the other, referring to the life cycle of maize, from its immature (green) phase to its ripening (yellow). Vail (2022) suggests that this pairing signifies abundance (fig. 8.10). Rubber offerings have also been recovered archaeologically from the Cenote of Sacrifice at Chichén Itzá, where many of the offerings made were painted blue (*yaax/ya'x*) (Coggins 1984, 133, no. 161). At present it is not possible to choose between these or other possible interpretations of the glyph paired with the rubber ball or incense,

Figure 8.9. Dresden Codex page 41a. Source: After Förstemann (1880).

206 · Anne S. Dowd and Gabrielle Vail

Figure 8.10. Dresden Codex page 29c, frames 2–3. Source: After Förstemann (1880).

although the reference to a *k'ayoom* in the final visible glyph block of Text 6 suggests that a ritual context is most likely, based on comparisons with the Dresden Codex (fig. 8.11). Although we are still working to interpret the two glyphs at A2 and the suffix beneath them, which resemble the syllabic glyph **ji**, we believe this text likely relates to ballgame contests and/or rain-making rituals, both of which have clear associations with caves, cenotes, and other portals that provide access to the underworld realm.

Figure 8.11. Page 68b of the Dresden Codex includes a reference to Chahk as a possible *k'ayoom* (see Looper and Macri 1991–2022). This interpretation is based on a reading of the first part of the caption as *ayan? ti' k'ayoom chahk* (There is? Chahk as singer). Source: Förstemann (1880).

Text 7 (fig. 8.2, far right) begins with what appears to be the glyph read as *piit* (litter; Tokovinine 2017, 33; ZUA in Looper et al. 2022),[2] followed by what might be the phrase *y-otoot* (his house; *'otoot* is also used to refer to what the Spanish chroniclers called a "temple") (fig. 8.4). The glyph at A3 is too eroded to interpret. This text recalls passages from the Spanish chroniclers referring to the carrying of "statues" of deities during yearbearer ceremonies (Tozzer 1941, 141n663) and to descriptions from Late Classic period monuments describing litters or palanquin-like structures, such as those on a series of wooden lintels from Tikal. In both contexts, images or representations of deities are being resituated within the house or temple of the ruler or *principal* of the community (Tozzer 1941, 141).

The following section (Text 8; fig. 8.2, lower right) is difficult to interpret. There are what appear to be several syllabic glyphs (a possible **ya** or **ji**, followed by **jo**), after which the glyphs *aj* and *tok'* appear. This latter phrase may be a title or a name, reading "He of Flint" or "Flint Person." In the codices, flint is used for weapons, such as knives or spear points, and for bloodletting implements.

Our reading of Texts 9 and 10 likewise remains provisional (fig. 8.3). Text 9 begins with an unidentified glyph (possibly BV3 or BV5 in Looper et al. 2022) followed by HJ1 in Looper et al. 2022 (syllabic **cho**). This is followed at A2 by a prefix that remains enigmatic and what may be the syllable **ja**, or a reference to a lunar goddess (PL4 in Looper et al. 2022). This is followed by the glyph for year (*haab'/ha'b'*) at A3 with an unidentified suffix and a glyph at A4 that begins with the syllable **xa** (the remaining portion is eroded).

Text 10 begins with an eroded glyph at A1, followed at A2 by a compound that may include the glyph *'aat* (penis) or the syllable **me**, prefixed to a glyph that could have the value *k'al* or *winal* (twenty) or be the syllable **ja**, although the latter usually has three small dots rather than a single large one (J. Justeson, personal communication, April 29, 2022). Its meaning is uncertain. What occurs below at A3 is difficult to read due to erosion, as is the glyph at A4. The outline suggests the possibility that it signifies a ballcourt (ZY3 in Macri and Looper 2003; Looper et al. 2022), but this is a highly preliminary interpretation. Text 11 (fig. 8.4) is too eroded to reconstruct.

When taken together, this subject matter seems to indicate that information about a ritual and perhaps also of a dynastic nature was being recorded. Of particular interest is evidence suggesting the possibility that yearbearer rituals were one of the topics addressed, including references to burdens, rubber (a type of rubber incense was burned in the yearbearer ceremonies highlighted in the Madrid Codex), a possible litter and house or temple, and a *k'ayoom*, or ritual singer. Whether references were made to the ballgame or to lunar deities is less certain, but it does seem likely that a female name and title is highlighted in Text 3. Thus, the texts that can be read to some extent focus on carrying burdens or naming a female and/or referring to rubber (as incense or a ball), to a singer (likely a ritual performer), to a litter or palanquin, to a house or temple, and possibly to lunar deities, the 365-day *haab'/ha'b'* year, and ballcourts.

The painting of these texts on the interior walls of the central south room of Structure 1A-Sub at the Balamkú site calls to mind Diego de Landa's (Tozzer 1941, 161) description of ceremonies celebrated in the months of Ch'en or Yax in the Maya 365-day calendar. Landa notes that "they celebrated this festival every year . . . for it was the custom that each idol should have its little brazier in which they should burn their incense to it; and, if it was necessary, they rebuilt the house, or renovated it, and *they placed on the wall the memorial of these things, written in their characters*" (Tozzer 1941, 161, our emphasis). This provides another important context for painted wall texts and the types of information they might have contained, and brings us to the next section, in which we compare a range of examples from elsewhere in the Maya region that illustrate the implications of microtexts such as those from Balamkú.

## Scribal Workshops and the Materialization of Time

In earlier working group discussions at the Santa Fe Institute, David Freidel and colleagues (2014, 1–5) posed a series of questions about Maya materialization of time and about history and prophecy in a long-term perspective. Paraphrased, these are:

1) What happened to timekeeping during the Classic period among the many lowland societies that chose not to inscribe public monuments?
2) How did they relate to southern lowland societies that made public writing and calendar chronicling institutionally central?
3) Were those southern lowland societies exceptional in their historical consciousness and, if so, what difference did it make to their developmental trajectory?
4) How does one detect the impact of such an understanding of history, writing, and calendars in the archaeological record?
5) What role did timekeeping play in cultural evolution?
6) How is time interwoven with Maya cultural identity and aspirations?

These six questions frame a study of places such as room interiors and workshops for keeping time and the tools used to craft, create, or curate time. Books or codices, the boxes or storage containers to hold them, and the paper binding or paint fabrication implements to make them are all examples of the complex of material remains used for mathematical numeracy, astronomical practice, and commemorative rituals linked to calendrical cycles.

As a prestige technology, timekeeping contributed to an anthropology or an archaeology of technology in which political, religious, economic, kinship, and other systems interpenetrated one another (Lemonnier 1986; Pfaffenberger 1992; Clark and Blake 1994; Dowd 1998b, 1998c, 1998d, 2015b; Hayden 1998; Dobres 2010).[3] In the past, some scholars put forward the idea that separate writing traditions may have accompanied the institutions of religion and kingship. In a 1928 letter to Alfred V. Kidder, Frans Blom (1933) asked, "Did the ancient Maya priesthood have a hieratic language, just as now-a-days the Catholic Church uses latin freely?" (Nielsen 2003, 6). While the evidence we have suggests that religion and kingship went hand in hand, there may be linguistic markers of specialist production in texts that have not been discovered yet or that are unrecognized in the known corpus.

Meredith Paxton (1986, 21; see also Love 1994, 13) has suggested that Mayapán in Yucatán, Mexico, may have been one center of learning and the making of lime-coated screenfold books made of bark paper in the Postclassic period (1200–1519 CE). Based on finds of a certain form of codical writing of T168, 533.130 'aajaaw (ahau in the original) (Thompson [1962] 1991, 145–148) in Structure C-1 at Playa del Carmen, Mexico, dating to the Late Postclassic period, Paxton (1986, 24, 28) suggested that the east coast of Yucatán and the time period after Chichén Itzá's fall provided a broad possible source of origin and expanded the possible date range for the Dresden Codex. Paxton (1986, app. 1.1) used photographs of many interior painted texts from buildings in northern Yucatán taken in the early 1980s to make stylistic comparisons with codices.

Gabrielle Vail and colleagues (Macri and Vail 2009; Vail and Hernández 2010b, 2013; Vail 2015, 2019a), following Stone (1995, 111–112), have treated these glyphs as part of a genre that is in the style of the codices and is more equivalent to writing in books or on a pottery vessel than to enlarged painted or sculpted glyphs meant to be viewed from farther away. Hieroglyphs in codices typically measure less than 1 centimeter. Increasing our comparative information about codical texts would involve excavating more scribal workshops within elite stucco-covered masonry structures, where such texts, forming blackboard-like wall paintings, may have been preserved. Such an effort would significantly expand scholars' understanding of cultural practices related to religious rituals, timekeeping, the recording of history, and calendar developments in Mesoamerica. New work to augment the corpus of codical scripts would broadly position the development of Mesoamerican written forms in the context of established writing systems worldwide (Battles

2015) and would contribute to our understanding of how ritual knowledge was passed from one generation to another.

There are now examples of what have been identified as scribal workshops or training centers in elite palaces, temples, caves, and acropoli (e.g., at Balamkú, Aguateca, Naj Tunich, San Bartolo, Xultun, and Xunantunich). For this reason, research specifically designed to identify and study crafting loci for specialized book production or education could significantly increase the sample of texts comparable to those in the codices from the four screenfold books known for the Postclassic Maya and others similar to codex fragments from Group A, Structure A-I, Burial A6 at Uaxactun found associated with Tzakol phase ceramics (350–550 CE) that were excavated in 1932 (Smith 1937; Carter and Dobereiner 2016).[4] According to John Justeson (1978, 325):

> The most plausible instances of other types of text are those presumed to have been on codices found at a small number of highland and lowland sites. Two were reported from Uaxactun, and one each from Altun Ha, Chiapa de Corzo, Nebaj, and San Agustín Acasaguastlán. They occur only in chambers and crypts. Differential preservation could well account for this distribution; however, as noted by Thompson (1950), the presence of these codices in tombs parallels the Yucatec practice reported by Landa of burying the priests with their books.

John Justeson's synopsis brought the total number of possible codices to about nine by 1978, and remnants of more have been discovered since then. At least one codex was identified in a tomb from Structure 10L-26 at Copán, and two codices were reported from burials at Mirador in Jiquipilas, Chiapas (Reents-Budet 1994, 57; Whiting 1998, 207–208). Remains of a codex were also found in a tomb in Structure 7 at Santa Rita in Corozal (D. Chase and A. Chase 1988, 33; 2005, 115). The Códice maya de México may have been found in a cave (Turner 2022).

Among the techniques available for studying painted surfaces with uneven preservation are broad-spectrum or infrared photography and flatbed scanning techniques that can tease out details that are difficult to see using traditional photography. Advances in recovering eroded or faint texts pioneered by William Saturno (2009) and finds discussed in this chapter suggest that in the future, many more painted walls with codex-style microtexts will be found and recorded, giving archaeologists and descendant communities another way to access "time's tools," that is, books on walls, blackboard-like sets of superimposed layers, or more private settings for hand-painted inscriptions.

Significant points of comparison, such as resurfacing, repainting, and over-writing, presently exist among codex-style painted texts at Balamkú and Xul-tun and in the Uaxactun codex fragments. Based on several known examples of structures or walls with writing and painted or incised images on them that were packed with earth and buried, a pattern is emerging of intentionally preserved wall texts in contexts that may have originally been associated with book production or prophecy and thus with the creation or preservation of Maya intellectual and spiritual life.[5] By expanding the corpus of early written texts through studies such as these, we can learn more about subject matter, if not the agents or authors behind those texts (Kelly 1994).[6]

The size of the Balamkú glyphs is similar to those from Xultun and to those from the codices and codex-style vessels (672–751 CE). For example, in Area A on the east wall in residential house Structure 10K-2 at Xultun, a 5 × 48 centi-meter text shows twenty-seven columns of black bar-and-dot numerals topped by three forms of Glyph C that are less than 2 centimeters wide and date to 9.15.17.13.10 11 Ok 13 Pop, or February 13, 749, in the Julian calendar using the 584,283 correlation (Aveni et al. 2013, xliv; Bricker et al. 2014; Saturno, Rossi et al. 2017, 426; Zender and Skidmore 2012, 1). Glyph C specifies where in a cycle of six lunations (177 or 178 days, or 6 × 29.53) a particular date falls. Each lunation is named as being associated with a female (lunar) deity, the jaguar god of the underworld, or a skull. Stylistic variables suggest that dif-ferent artists were at work at both sites. Changes in the size, shape, and scale of the microtext elements at Balamkú suggest diverse authors with varying calligraphic brush-stroke techniques. Anthony Aveni (personal communica-tion, October 13, 2020) measured the dimensions of the Xultun lunar table and found that they are identical to the relevant spaces in the eclipse table on pages 51–58 of the Dresden Codex.

Characteristics present at both Xultun and Balamkú include the size of the glyphs, overwriting or overpainting, and a lack of standardization in terms of style, technique, alignment, scale, or color. These may all point to the use of some walls as if they were notebooks or blackboards used by multiple scribes. Certain of these texts may at some point have been transferred to screenfold books. For example, at both sites:

1) multiple artists' hands are represented,
2) overpainting was done repeatedly,
3) various scales of execution, column alignment, or colors were used, and
4) mixed techniques, such as incising and painting, were employed.

One notable difference is that while Xultun has both incised and painted examples, Balamkú's interior texts are painted. A comparison with the codices is likewise informative: Gunter Zimmerman (1956), Alfonso Lacadena (2000), and Nikolai Grube (2018) have recognized multiple hands in the codices, as is also the case at Balamkú.

As at Xultun, the examples at Balamkú are so small that the texts were probably not meant for many viewers because a person would have to be close to the wall in order to read them. This suggests that they likely were intended for a private audience, such as one-on-one tutelage or mentoring in small groups. This is supported by the small size of the room, which measures 9.3 meters by 1.9 meters, for a floor plan of 17.7 square meters (fig. 8.12), a space that could comfortably hold several people at one time.

Maya scribes from Balamkú and Xultun were working in residential, palace, and shrine settings, sitting on benches and standing or sitting on the floor, much in the way they are portrayed in polychrome pottery scenes (Loughmiller-Newman 2008), like that in which a scribe is pictured sitting alongside the lord on a mat (Coe 1973, 91; Justeson 1978, 334). One such vessel (AP 2004.04) from the Kimbell Art Museum is a good example of teaching and pedagogy; it depicts numbers coming out of the mouth of the older person instructing the younger one (see also Thompson 1942). The low elevation of glyphs close to the floor at Xultun shows that the artist was sitting on the floor.

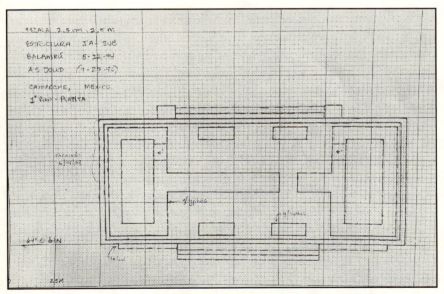

Figure 8.12. Floor plan of the interior of Balamkú Structure 1A-Sub. Field sketch map by Anne S. Dowd, used with permission, Copyright 1996, Anne S. Dowd, All rights reserved.

Scholars who have studied the Xultun murals have suggested that they provide evidence of a scribal workshop location (Saturno, Stuart et al. 2012, 714–717; Zender and Skidmore 2012, 6; chapter 9, this volume). This supposition is based on the several hundred red and black painted or incised hieroglyphs in different sizes on a section of wall surface with abundant natural light, potentially indicating more than one author. The implication is that the scribes used the walls as a writing surface to practice, as references to use in the process of painting or inscribing hieroglyphs on other surfaces, such as screenfold books, and then studying them, or as the "memorials" mentioned in the Landa quote (Tozzer 1941, 161) referred to above. The lunar table on the wall from the block in Area A has been compared to the eclipse table on Dresden Codex pages 51–58 (Aveni et al. 2013, xliv; Bricker et al. 2014). Protagonists in the murals of the north and west walls are named with the terms *itz'iin* and *sakuun,* which have been glossed as "younger same-sex sibling" and "elder same-sex sibling," in the sense of fictive kin or sodality-based relationships. Both are paired with the term Taaj, which may be a family name and may have identified the scribes in question (Stuart 1997; Zender and Skidmore 2012, 4–5; Saturno et al. 2017, 430–431).

The mural at Xultun depicts seated men wearing white circular pectorals. Mirrors were attached to clothing, suspended and worn by ranked ritual specialist orders as badges of office, and this may have been the case among the Taaj at Xultun. David Freidel, Marilyn Masson, and Michelle Rich (2016; see also chapter 15, this volume) have written about the use of mirrors with beeswax coating as tablets for writing, erasing, and rewriting and as scrying devices. One ceramic disc example is known from a burial in Structure 10K-2 at Xultun. If pyrite mosaics were originally attached to a ceramic backing, as has been previously suggested, perhaps they did not preserve well (Gallaga and Blainey 2016; Dowd et al. 2017; Dowd 2018b, 473). This evidence provides support for the idea that the building may have been where the specialists lived and worked (Rossi et al. 2015). The existence of multiple thin coats of plaster applied over existing texts to rejuvenate, cover, or clear the surface for new painted texts, as is seen at Xultun, corresponds well with the situation on the interior walls of Structure 1A-Sub at Balamkú. Might that building also have been multifunctional and perhaps have served as both a workspace and a domicile for scribes?

The very small hieroglyphs from room interiors at Balamkú and Xultun are comparable to examples from other locations, such as the Structure Sub-1A mural at the Las Pinturas Complex in San Bartolo, which three artists painted over a period of several weeks around 100 BCE (Saturno et al. 2006; O'Grady and Hurst 2011, 4–5). Sites such as Copán, Honduras, which has murals inside the Rosalila phase of Structure 16 (dated to 520–655 CE); Uaxactun, Guatemala, which has painted walls in Structures B-VIII (displaying the 260 days in the *tzolk'in*) and B-XIII (dating to 200–600 CE; Smith 1950); and Bonampak, Mexico, with its famous frescos in Structure 1 (790 CE) also have hieroglyphic inscriptions. Also worthy of mention are the approximately 500 glyphs, some 8 centimeters wide, painted on the walls of the Naj Tunich Cave (Stone 1995) and the extensive mural texts at Ek' Balam (Lacadena 2004). Some of the examples from building interiors have larger hieroglyphs and others have smaller ones, like those from Uaxactun's Structure B-XIII that Linda Schele drew after Antonio Tejeda F. in A. L. Smith (1950; Dowd 2017b, 467–468), which are 3 centimeters wide.

Craft specialists appear to have been collectively producing informal texts or images at separate workstations during the Late Classic period Hats' Chahk phase (670–780 CE) and acted as storytelling agents in the eastern room of Structure A-5 (the El Castillo acropolis) at Xunantunich (M. Kathryn Brown, personal communication, August 16, 2016; chapter 11, this volume). The decision to excavate this building was in part based on its careful burial, suggesting to researchers that the interior merited special treatment. Our discussions at the Santa Fe Institute working group meetings led to this important discovery.

## Scribal Praxis and Places of Learning

Do hieroglyphic texts contain information that can supplement our knowledge of Maya pedagogy? Bishop Diego de Landa discussed schooling or training in writing and art (Tozzer 1941). Was the material painted on walls at Balamkú used for educational purposes, perhaps as reference material or texts drawn by or for apprentice scribes? Elizabeth Boone (1985) reported that when children from central Mexico turned in their idolatrous parents, the parents were often painters. This information suggests that the role of scribes as carriers of specialist religious interpretations was an entrenched part of Mesoamerican societies that lasted at least until Indigenous peoples' contact with Europeans and likely beyond.

The act of writing, taking notes, and recording in both informal private and formal public contexts is part of the process of transferring information. Visual, auditory, and kinesthetic modes of learning were then and are now reinforced by the act of writing, seeing script, hearing words spoken, listening to and feeling rhythmic brush strokes, and using hand motions. Altogether, these actions foster memorization and provide a reference for consultation at a future date. Even artists using controlled breathing to ensure that they can draw smooth lines with minimal body movement contribute to our perspectives on kinesthetic learning. Timekeeping as a craft required specialists to become educated for that occupation, and the physical places and social contexts where training may have occurred are of interest for what they reveal. The authors of this volume had the Santa Fe Institute as a group workshop; what spaces did Maya people have for intellectual congress?

Learning, recording, mentoring, teaching, or passing down history and scientific knowledge would have taken place in classrooms or settings where rituals were planned. Repeated practice using mnemonic aids fosters visual, auditory, and kinesthetic learning. Counting out loud or listening to the sounds of dropping tokens and sticks fuses these modes of learning or memorizing numerical information. Weaving and the metaphor of time and space as interwoven in discernible patterns also demonstrates how different learning styles, like those based on eyesight or visual perception, could assist in memorizing oral histories or creating future prophecies based on patterns of past events.

Maya titles related to books and writing include *'aj kuju'un* (as in librarian), *aj tz'ihb* (scribe), and *aj wooj* (painter) (see Kaufman 2017 for a discussion of the terms for writing). The word for book is *huun,* also spelled *hun* or *hu'n* (Wichmann 2004b, 9). According to Prudence Rice (2007, 168–9), the curvilinear qualities of Maya writing suggest that it developed through painted media as opposed to stone- or wood-carving traditions. For this reason, early painted texts have much to offer scholars interested in the origins of Mesoamerican writing and timekeeping systems. Buildings encased in other buildings offer significant potential for intact and well-preserved, recoverable wall paintings that can contribute to an understanding of Maya materialization of time.[7]

A stone box was found in Hun Nal Ye Cave north of Coban in northern highland Guatemala (Woodfill et al. 2012, 102). It has been hypothesized that this was a container for a codex; however, a fragment of a tapir femur was in it at the time of its discovery in 2005 (Woodfill et al. 2006). A translation of the inscription found on the stone box reads, "Here is the dedication of the carving of the stone . . . Deer (?) House, the Moon Goddess and 30 days (the Rabbit) is the name of the carved (box) of *Yuhklaj Chan Muwaan, K'an K'uuch*" (Woodfill et al. 2012, 98). Two ceramic boxes were found with the stone archival box. The interior space within the stone box is 38 centimeters long by 21.7 centimeters wide by 10.9 centimeters high and includes a lid 2.8 centimeters thick and so could have accommodated a folding screen book similar in size to the Paris Codex, which measures about 23.5 centimeters long by 12.73 centimeters wide when folded.

A wooden box found in the Piedras Negras region of Guatemala, named as the offering container (*yotoot mayij*) of Aj K'ax B'ahlam, dates to October 14,

681 CE (9.12.9.7.12. 9 Eb' 15 Keh). It is thought to have been found in the same cave where the Códice maya de México may have been discovered. The style of the inscription and references in the text suggest that the box's owner was an official of the Tortuguero king Ik' Muyil Muwaahn II (Dunkelman 2007, 14–15). The wooden box, which measures 4.37 centimeters high by 15.3 centimeters long by 3.54 centimeters wide, may have held ritual implements, possibly even scribal tools, within its narrow interior cavity. In the Bonampak murals from Room 2, Structure 1, the box being carried off the battlefield is another example of a long narrow box (Carnegie Institution of Washington 1955).

Arks, trunks, or boxes suitable for storing sacred books or objects are known from other culture areas besides Mesoamerica (Dowd 2016b). The legendary gold-plated wooden Ark of the Covenant was said to have held sacred texts inscribed on sheepskin (one possible ark was found in King Tut's tomb in Egypt). As can be surmised from the myths that surround these ornate boxes or arks, the information or object inside them was a powerful life force with capabilities such as destroying enemy armies, causing the Red Sea to part, and other qualities, perhaps alluding to the idea that knowledge is power.

Modern Jewish religious ceremonies include large wooden boxes that contain the Torah, as Anne Dowd observed in Vail, Colorado, at a B'nai service in 2016. Containers for sacred religious texts held strong animated written words or a book, one that could not only give life but could also take it away. In this sense, it is easy to understand why places where such sacred texts were produced in the Maya region were alive. They were born, they died, and they were entombed, their secrets eternally guarded. These locations then took on the existential meaning of the intellectual achievements recorded there: they were in essence, "time's houses."

## Memorializing Ancestors and Archiving Place

Recently, a resurgence of interest in animism has become evident among Mesoamericanists. Animism is the process of assigning life qualities to what some cultures consider inanimate or at least inorganic things. David Stuart (2011) talks about living time. A 2016 Dumbarton Oaks symposium was titled "Sacred Matter: Animism and Authority in the Pre-Columbian Americas." Time is among the "fruits" of the World Tree in Robert Carlsen's (1997, 52) ethnography of the contemporary Tz'utujil Maya of Santiago Atitlan in highland Guatemala. Possibly Maya people saw cultural products such as calendars like offspring. If time was alive, then it must have had a place to live, and if that were the case, where was it housed? Creating life is a process whereby actions imbue the sacred with energy expended by the living. Places of learning, prognostication, or book production might be seen as where time itself came alive, or was born.

A culture's cosmovision may relate landscapes to cultural creation spaces in the way mountains and temples are seen as animate (Dowd 2015b). Kristin Landau (2015) linked the concept of *ichnal* to this phenomenon, referring to "a corporeal field of interaction that includes the totality of objects within view, each conceived as a participant" (Hanks 1990, 89; Houston and Taube 2000, 287). The subject of how to connect record-keeping and archiving places that are important for recalling ancestors bears scrutiny because both are significant ways of materializing time.

The centipede place or mountain Freidel et al. (2013, 243) describe could refer to such a location. What these authors refer to as "Mountain of Memories" is portrayed as a living monster mountain, or Wak Witz, with centipedes coming out of its mouth. It is a pyramid, an effigy mountain, and a portal, a place where collective dynastic memories are preserved and ancestors may be recalled or visited through vision quests. In addition to studying specific buildings and concentrations of artifacts or features within general site contexts, focusing on site planning as part of landscape-scale architectural programs to create unique political viewpoints has great potential as a research methodology in Mesoamerica (S. Sugiyama 1993; Dowd 2015b; Dowd and Milbrath 2015).

Maya people archived written records by storing codices in boxes, preserving script on the walls of rooms, on lintels, in caves, on freestanding or buried monuments, and on functionally specific buildings or complexes, some seen as effigy mountains that memorialized ancestors. These locations and the entangled rituals surrounding them connected ancient rulers and the people they led to their ancestors iconographically and through the burial of human remains or the caching of objects or texts. Maya people still revere places where past historical time and divination of the future come together.

Societies in northern lowland Classic period centers put up fewer public monuments in exterior locations than their counterparts in the southern lowlands, but Maya people there continued later to inscribe capstone murals with texts in more private interior spaces (Thompson 1973; Paxton 1986, Vail and Hernández 2010; Vail 2019a). Examples such as mural texts at Ek' Balam, writing in books, or writing on portable objets d'art such as polychrome ceramics are sources of information. Calligraphic writing genres were present in both northern and southern lowland societies, and those societies related to one another through trade, economic scheduling, and movements of populations.[8] Historical consciousness in the southern lowlands functioned to reinforce dynastic rule and played a role in a developmental trajectory that emphasized kingship. Perhaps for this reason there was a strong relationship between public monuments and dynastic succession in this region. Through architecture, art, hieroglyphic inscriptions, numerical tallies, or materials used to facilitate astronomy, mathematics, writing, and prophecy, Maya people materialized time and calendrical reckoning across the large region they occupied.

In private spaces, improvisational calligraphy or informal sketches were employed throughout the lowlands regardless of the type of political control. Formal inscriptions on sculpture may have dominated public spaces in the southern lowlands because stone media endured, reinforcing ideas about dynastic continuity and permanence. Where other forms of rule besides dynasties developed, as has been suggested for parts of the northern lowlands, public sculptured hieroglyphic texts on monuments were not used to the same degree. Nevertheless, people still used books, painted ceramics, and interior wall murals to craft time. Maya priests had roles similar to those of Franciscan friars or religious adepts in other cultures who studied, crafted, and created knowledge stored in books. Measuring time and commensuration of various cycles through astronomy, math, music, language, weaving, and artistic media were prized Maya cultural traditions, imbuing many ritual actions with their sacred character.

## Concluding Thoughts

The examples from other cultures provide valuable ideas about scribal practice in the Maya region. There are several key points to summarize regarding the spaces where literate Maya priests studied and oversaw the process of composing texts and making books.

The first point is that housing time, essentially packaging, sheltering, storing, or containing it for future generations, both protects an intellectual legacy and effectively removes it from circulation. In a way, the people who engaged in these pursuits were having the last word about historical time by emphasizing their own perspective. This housing can take many forms, such as a box, a buried chamber, an encased structure, a cave, or a tomb cavity. In the example of the walls at Balamkú, a building was covered over by a later structure. The substructure walls were largely intact. A tentative case has been made for Balamkú's Structure 1A-Sub as a short-lived history house or an ancestor shrine for kin group affiliation, following Hodder (2016, 2018). Origin houses, such as Structure 10L-16 at Copán and Structure 5 at Rio Amarillo, and textual references to them, such as on Stela B at Copán, have also been identified in the Maya region (Stuart 2000, 2004b; Eberl 2015, 92). *Sab'ak naah* and *wi(n) te' naah* (house[s]) deserve additional study along the lines presented in this chapter and volume.

A second point is that reconstructing *chaînes operatoires,* or production sequence models, involving the horizontal distribution of stages of book-making activities, is a useful enterprise. Archaeologists routinely describe the horizontally distributed (and sometimes superimposed) activity areas associated with stone tools and the quarrying and production of such tools (Dowd 1998b, 1998c, 1998d). Researchers have begun this effort to elucidate hypothetical sequences of text production that involve the artifacts and the tools needed to make them, in this case books or texts, such as bark beaters, and additional locations for making lime-coated bark paper (Ardren 2019). Distributions of bark beaters used to flatten paper pulp, polishing stones used to smooth the gesso surface of codex blanks, paint pots or palettes in modified shells or in shell effigy ceramic vessels, pecked circles and *patolli* boards (considered to be related to counting for divination and calendar reckoning), and priests' burials with specific tool kits are categories of artifacts presumably associated with the *chaîne operatoire* of activities related to producing books and the subsequent use of those books through to final deposition. William Haviland's (1974, 496; see also Justeson 1978, 33) observation that a pottery model of a stela was found in a Tikal stonecutter's workshop debris may also be relevant because the find sheds light on the detailed process of how a stone carver used a small-scale ceramic model to create a large-scale stone monument. In buildings such as Structure 1A-Sub at Balamkú's, clues about the process of how scribes made books could be apparent depending on preservation and interpretation of fragile painted surfaces and other archaeological contexts. End-stage use includes inscribed chambers as well as books and other portable objects.

Third, time and intellectual concepts have value as powerful forces that affected social evolution as active rather than passive subjects and as agents of political change and community representation. Artists' and scientists' roles in crafting original works brought ideas to life. After 1,400 years, it is fascinating that glimpses of those ideas are passed down to modern Maya people and others interested in Maya culture through archaeological study of spaces for housing historical texts. Few contemporary writers or painters dare hope that their work will have such longevity.

This study has relevance for today. People in different cultures stored information for future generations in many ways. Some people argue that printed books are no longer necessary now that electronic books exist. After having been in production for approximately 2,000 years, paper books may now be on the verge of becoming functionally obsolete. Returning to the alternatives raised earlier in this chapter about whether Balamkú's microtexts might contain information about Maya pedagogy, the education and practice of scribes, Maya science and mathematics, calendrical rituals, or dynastic themes (e.g., connecting ancestors with dynastic ruling families), the evidence most strongly suggests that they concerned ritual activities, perhaps related to honoring deities associated with the ebb and flow of cyclical time and with veneration of a revered ancestor.

In this sense, these books on walls extended and created a private social medium, a rich text of people and their books as references that existed alongside the written language in order to explain and add depth to complex subjects, to teach history and mythology, and to incubate scientific knowledge. Like the changes in technology that have pervaded modern book production, ancient authors at Balamkú had a range of media, discourse strategies, and environments, even metalanguages, for reproducing and disseminating knowledge.

Study chambers, where scholars met, were intrinsically related to the development of varied social, religious, and political institutions. Learning about the scientific laboratories ancient researchers used to explore various subjects breathes life into the roles past timekeepers, astronomers, mathematicians, and religious adepts had in connecting mythic history and ritual to primordial diurnal and seasonal rhythms of the sun, moon, and stars. The architectural cosmograms that encoded materialized time on walls provide nuanced opportunities for learning how master craftspeople fused art and science to animate time at Maya centers.

## Acknowledgments

Sincere appreciation is extended to John Justeson, Anthony Aveni, Susan Milbrath, David Freidel, and Arlen Chase, who read earlier drafts of this chapter. Heartfelt thanks also go to Santa Fe Institute past president Jeremy Sabloff and current president David Krakauer for hosting our group and to Jerry Murdock of Insight Venture Partners for graciously sponsoring the set of conferences that led to this volume.[9] Deep gratitude is extended to Ramón Carrasco Vargas of the Instituto Nacional de Antropología e Historia, who welcomed Anne Dowd's participation in the Proyecto Arqueológico de la Biosfera de Calakmul; to the late Claude-François Baudez of Centre national de la recherche scientifique; and to Armando Paul and Jean-Pierre Courau. In 1998, the Eben Demarest Trust funded Dowd's work on Balamkú.

## Notes

1 Oswaldo Chinchilla Mazariegos (2005, 2006) suggests the jaguars are stars, and Ignacio Cases Martín (2013) interprets stars as sky jewels. David Freidel (personal communication, August 13, 2020) compares these jaguars to a bas-relief from Chalcatzingo

published by David Grove (1984, 1987). Freidel says that it is one of several from Chalcatzingo and La Venta in full round sculpture and one from La Corona Panel 6 (Dallas altar) where it is part of the Teotihuacan war monster cult (Tlaloc is depicted on the back). The battle palanquin was likely captured from Tikal king Ujol Ch'aak in 679 CE when his half-brother defeated him.

2 David Stuart (2005b, 88–89) describes the glyph as a masonry throne with a pillow and back cushion, similar to what rulers are depicted seated on in scenes from polychrome ceramics. The *piit* glyph also occurs at Naj Tunich in Drawing 25, preceded with the number 9 (Stone 1995, 200).

3 Brian Hayden (1998, 1) defines prestige technology: "The aggrandizer model of prestige technology postulates that prestige items were essential elements in aggrandizer strategies and that prestige items emerged only under conditions of sustainable food surpluses and included the most important innovations of the last 30,000 years such as metal working, pottery, sophisticated art, and domesticated plants and animals."

4 Many codical researchers feel that the Grolier/Códice maya de México is not a Maya codex in the strict sense but is rather a hybrid manuscript with characteristics of Maya and highland Mexican codices.

5 The Cacaxtla murals are an example of a Mesoamerican set of paintings that was ritually cached or stored with sand packing from Central Mexico (Brittenham 2015; Matos Moctezuma 1987).

6 Common people wrote prayers to gods on wall surfaces in the manner Timothy Knowlton (2015) discussed for the Chapel of San Simón in San Andrés Izapa, Guatemala.

7 Examples exist in other cultures of writing or scribal houses where people produced or cared for books, such as a library. For example, in China, storied pavilions (*ge*) were like simple pavilions but were stacked on top of one another. They held important articles and documents and were places where educated men could gather to write articles and hold banquets. *Ge* also had impressive views due to their height. In Beijing's Forbidden City, Wenyuange was the imperial library. In the Temple of Confucius in Qufu, Shandong Province, East China, Kulwenge was used for safeguarding the books and paintings or works of calligraphy that dynastic courts had stored. A private collection of ancient books is housed in Tianyige in Ningbo, Zhejiang Province, China. Large monasteries also usually have a library built in the style of a *ge*, called *cangjingge*, for housing Buddhist sculpture collections. In some cases, multistory buildings housed a single large sculpture. See "Storeyed Pavilion (*Ge*)," China Style, n.d., http://www.chinastyle.cn/architecture/classification-by-structure/ge.htm.

8 Economic scheduling creates production efficiencies based on labor and market timing to respond to supply and demand.

9 Dowd presented versions of this chapter at four Santa Fe Institute working groups. The first two were titled "Maya Materialization of Time: History and Prophecy in Long-Term Perspective" and were held on February 13–15, 2015, and August 26–28, 2016. The third, "Telling Time: Myth, History and Everyday Life in the Ancient Maya World," was held on August 24–26, 2017. A fourth, "On Time and Being Maya," was held on August 29–30, 2018. David A. Freidel, Anne S. Dowd, and Arlen F. Chase organized the working groups.

# 9

## Scorpion Star

### Constellations, Seasons, and Convergences of Meaning in a Classic Maya Entity

FRANCO D. ROSSI

Long ago, Friar Antonio de Ciudad Real (1577) included the Maya term *sinan ek'* in his sixteenth-century vocabulary known as the *Calepino maya de Motul*. The term, literally "scorpion star," is likely the earliest European record of such a reference from the Maya area. Along with a collection of other terms detailing celestial objects, constellations, and asterisms, evidence of a vast knowledge of astronomical time and celestial cycles among pre-Columbian Maya peoples became quite clear to western scholars at an early date. Yet unlike some of the other astronomical terms provided in the Motul dictionary, the definition for *sinan ek'* (scorpion sign of the sky; my translation)[1] did not specify what celestial objects constituted this recurring "sign of the sky."

To which star or stars exactly might *sinan ek'* be referring and why were they important? This question remains an ongoing topic of discussion and debate, and this chapter briefly reviews some of the contending viewpoints. It explores different ways that scorpion stars appear in Maya imagery and discusses some of the mythical associations and layered iconographies that can be detected within the anthropological and archaeological record. Instead of lingering on questions of exact astronomical identity, I focus on considering what information particular stellar scorpion attributes might have communicated in Classic Maya artistic depictions and the relationship between such attributes and the timing/seasonality of represented acts, especially in scenes of deity impersonation. Deity impersonation scenes would commonly connect ancient or mythical events to scenes of ritual performance depicted in Classic Maya art. Such scenes often used counts of recurring calendrical and/or celestial cycles in order to bridge large spans of time in meaningful ways, serving

224 · Franco D. Rossi

to bring mythical pasts into the Classic Maya present by relying on conceptualizations of time itself to do so. In line with the theme of this volume, this chapter brings temporal and social context to ancient Maya representations of scorpion attributes so that we might better understand the broader political import such entities held in the statecraft of Classic period polities.

## Modeling a Maya Zodiac

Scholarly discussions of pre-Columbian Maya representations of star groups usually begin and end with pages 23 and 24 of the Paris Codex and the Monjas frieze at Chichén Itzá (fig. 9.1a and b). These works were among the earliest such representations Mayanist scholars recognized. Eduard Seler (1996, 269) first noted that the various creatures dangling from the skyband on the Paris Codex pages might represent constellations, comparing them to "a kindred series of animal pictures on a narrow relief band on the main front of the east wing of the Casa de las Monjas, Chichen Itza." He argued that the Monjas frieze was "evidently intended to represent conjunctions of Venus with different constellations" (Seler 1996, 269). On the Monjas frieze, each creature somehow incorporated the T510 glyph, a logogram for "star," or **EK'** in Maya glyphic script (Kelley 1976, 38–42). Notably, the scorpion in this frieze has the head of a youthful human.

Seler argued that the creatures on the Paris Codex pages were constellations, citing overlaps with the creatures of the Monjas frieze. However, Seler's interpretations also drew on increasingly available data being published by his contemporaries, including Ernst Förstemann, Alfred Maudslay, Teobert Maler, Charles Bowditch, Daniel Brinton, Alfredo Barrera Vásquez, Herbert Spinden, and Alfred M. Tozzer (Stuart 1992, 23–30).[2] Time, astronomy, and calendrics were a key topic of scholarly debate among these contemporaries, especially as high-quality facsimiles of codices, photographs of monuments, Maya language vocabularies, and other ethnohistoric documents began to circulate among them. Research undertaken on these documents collectively revealed with increasing resolution the sophisticated degree to which Indigenous Maya people tracked celestial objects.

Perhaps none of these resources proved more important for confirming Seler's Paris Codex constellation hypothesis than the *Calepino maya de Motul*, which included many astronomical references, several of which had already been noted by Daniel Brinton (1895) by the time Seler was writing. Among those entries applicable to the Paris Codex zodiac were Ac Ek (turtle star),[3] which occurs on the first page of the Motul dictionary; *tsab* (rattlesnake rattles);[4] and *sinan ek'* (scorpion star) (Ciudad Real 1577, 1:1v, 104r, 113v; for

Scorpion Star: Convergences of Meaning in a Classic Maya Entity · 225

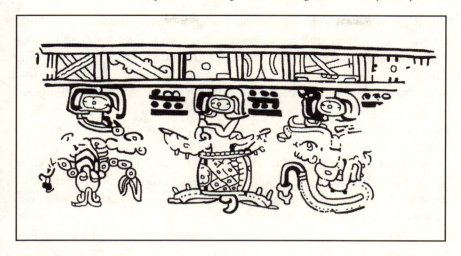

Figure 9.1. Maya "Zodiac," Paris Codex 24b (*a*); Casa de las Monjas frieze at Chichén Itzá (*b*). Drawings by F. D. Rossi.

the *sinan ek'* entry in the Motul dictionary, see note 1 below). These examples are directly comparable to the three animals depicted on page 24 of the Paris Codex. Other documents, such as Diego de Landa's *Descripción de las cosas de Yucatán,* added to these discussions with the first mention of the use of constellations, specifically the Pleiades and Gemini, as nighttime guides for the rising of Venus (Tozzer 1941, 132–133).

Subsequent research has lent further support for a "Maya Zodiac" as visualized within the Paris Codex.[5] Various functional models and theories for this "zodiac" have been developed over the years. Much of this work relied on identifying what are generally accepted as thirteen Maya constellations and/ or asterisms in the Paris Codex, placing them within sky maps, and fitting these sky map placements with the neatly ordered sequence of animals and insects within a zodiac model.

Close readings and understandings of surviving Maya codices alongside ethnographic and ethnohistorical research has proven vital to these endeavors, resulting in various models for the Paris Codex zodiacal pages (see Spinden 1916, 1924, 55–56; Kelley 1976; Bricker and Bricker 1992; see also Love 1994, 93–98; and Bricker and Bricker 2011, 708–729 for a full history of such research). Two different models for these pages demonstrate an issue, however, with regard to identifying the Scorpion constellation: the Victoria and Harvey Bricker model and the Bruce Love model. Both models rely on the positive identification of three beasts on the zodiac pages—the turtle, the rattlesnake, and the scorpion. However, only two of these three animal constellations have been confidently identified by specialists: the turtle in association with Orion (specifically the three stars of Orion's belt) and the rattlesnake in association with the Pleiades (Bricker and Bricker 1992; Lounsbury 1982, 166–167; Love 1994, 97).

Today, the Bricker model (1992; Bricker and Bricker 2011, 729–768) for the Paris Codex is most widely accepted. It posits that the ancient Maya scorpion constellation overlaps with at least part of the constellation we know of as Scorpius (Vail 1997; Milbrath 1999, 264; Rossi 2015, 58–59, 355–356). However, Susan Milbrath (1999, 264) sagely cautions that

> ethnographic accounts give varying identifications for the scorpion constellation, which include Ursa Major (Tojolabal area in Chiapas), Scorpius (Tzotzil area in Chiapas and Yucatec area in Quintana Roo), a large constellation running from Gemini to Sirius (Yucatec area southeast of Valladolid), and a constellation running from Orion to Sirius (Yalcobá in Yucatán). This variety gives us perhaps too many options to work with when interpreting Maya images of celestial scorpions.

As Milbrath mentions, several twentieth-century ethnographic accounts support the designation of the Maya scorpion constellation with at least some stars of the Scorpius constellation, including Antares (Redfield and Villa Rojas 1934, 206; Nikolai Grube, personal communication, 1992, quoted in Love 1994, 97). In fact, Evon Vogt (1997) points out that some Zinacantecos refer to the star Antares, the brightest star in Scorpius, as the "heart of the Scorpion."

Bruce Love's model draws on his own ethnographic work in Yucatán to contest the Bricker model and to support an alternative association between the scorpion constellation and the two brightest stars of Gemini, Castor and

Pollux (Love 1994, 97). Love even suggests that ethnographic associations of the scorpion constellation with Scorpius may be a result of colonial influence on such matters. Sosa (1985, 431), who also worked in Yucatán, found an Indigenous "scorpion" constellation of stars that included Castor and Pollux. The Tojolabal Maya association of the scorpion constellation with Ursa Major is an ethnographic detail that further complicates any uniform designation of the scorpion constellation as any particular star group or asterism. While Bricker and Bricker (2011, 838) remain relatively certain of its designation within the Paris Codex, they also note the uncertainty of the scorpion constellation designation more widely. In the artistic record, variations of scorpions and scorpion composites across Maya imagery and iconography might help shed light on the reasons for these variations and how we might work through them.

## Cataloging Sky Scorpions

Stellar scorpions have a deep history in the Maya area, and a variety of celestial scorpion-tailed composites appear across time in visual media. There is, of course, the representation of a scorpion constellation in the zodiac pages of the Paris Codex already discussed, but sky scorpions also occur throughout the Madrid Codex. In that codex, full-body sky scorpions are shown on the initial pages of three different "deer-trapping" almanacs (M44b, M44c, and M48c) and on page 7A, where it appears to be linked with the onset of summer rains (Vail 1997, 84–85, 91, 96, 98–100).

At Chichén Itzá, a scorpion is part of the inscription of the east doorway lintel of the Monjas structure (fig. 9.2a), a text thought to discuss the various celestial references shown separately in the Monjas frieze above (Bricker and Bricker 1992). Also at Chichén Itzá, a mural fragment from the exterior of the Temple of the Warriors depicts a scorpion floating just to the upper left of a skeletal figure who holds a severed human head (fig. 9.2b).

Such examples are not restricted to the Terminal and Postclassic periods. It has been suggested that the representation of a scorpion on a well-known Late Classic period pot called the Blowgunner Vase (K1226) was in fact a reference to a scorpion constellation. The scorpion floats in the background just above the horizon as a hunter, who is often equated with the hero twin Hun Ajaw, readies his blowgun to shoot a great bird (the avatar of Itzamnaaj, or God D) that "descends from the sky" (Bardawil 1976; Coe 1989b, 169–170; Tedlock 1992; Zender 2005).[6] Stephen Houston (2019) points out another Classic period example of the celestial scorpion on Kerr vessel 8562. In this scene, the scorpion appears twice in a dark band stretching out over a watery post-battle scene. It is interspersed with other celestial phenomena, signaling that the depicted

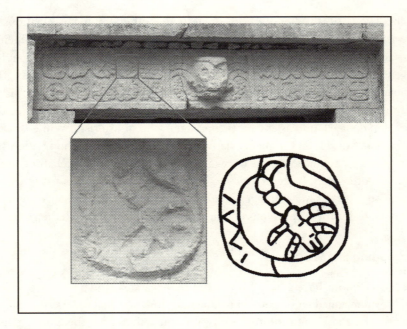

Figure 9.2. Sky scorpions: (*a*) lintel of east doorway, Casa de las Monjas, Chichén Itzá photo and drawing by author; (*b*) details of fragment from the exterior mural, north wall, Temple of the Warriors, Chichén Itzá, drawing by Linda Schele © David Schele, image courtesy Ancient Americas at LACMA, ancientamericas.org.

event occurred at night. The **EK'** (T510) or "star" logogram is visible on the scorpion's body.

Several of these examples reference acts of violence, whether hunting or war, as occurring under the auspices of a sky scorpion, an association that has not gone unnoticed. As John Carlson and Ron Cherry (1996, 153) write: "That the scorpion should be associated with hunting, warfare, and sacrifice in Maya mythology is quite understandable, considering the legendary behavior of this arthropod."

## Scorpion Composites in the Codices

Scorpions do not always appear as full bodied in Maya art. Many images are scorpion composites, like the one that appears on the Monjas frieze. There are several such entities in the Madrid Codex, including both deities and deer, in addition to the full-body scorpion representations mentioned above. All of these entities also appear throughout the codex without scorpion tails. This suggests that the scorpion tail is not a permanent characteristic of them but instead is one born of particular temporal contexts.

Several examples of deer with scorpion tails occur within the "deer-trapping" almanac, which also feature full-body representations of sky scorpions holding ensnared deer (see Madrid Codex 7a, 44b and c, and 48c). Gabrielle Vail (1997) interprets the scorpion-tailed deer as an iconographic conflation of the Maya scorpion constellation[7] and a deer constellation in late spring (correlated to late May) (fig. 9.3a). She argues that the depiction represents a seasonal moment just at the onset of the rainy season, when deer trapping is recommended and when the scorpion constellation would be particularly visible in the night sky. Vail further connects the scorpion with the onset of the rainy season by highlighting a representation of the rain deity Chahk with a scorpion tail (fig. 9.3b) and points out the water iconography of the full-bodied scorpion rendered on page 7a of the Madrid Codex.

The seasonal emphasis Vail places on scorpion imagery in the deer almanacs is supported indirectly through ethnography. Evon Vogt, working in Chiapas, mentioned stellar tracking and its relationship with seasonality. He noted that according to Zinacantecos, "when the Milky Way hits the tail of the Scorpion, it is the dry season and the frost falls. But when there is distance between the Milky Way and the tail of the Scorpion, it rains again" (Vogt 1997, 113). In this case, the scorpion constellation (in Vogt's example, the constellation Scorpius) is a hallmark of the dry season in general, but it also marks the onset of the rainy season.

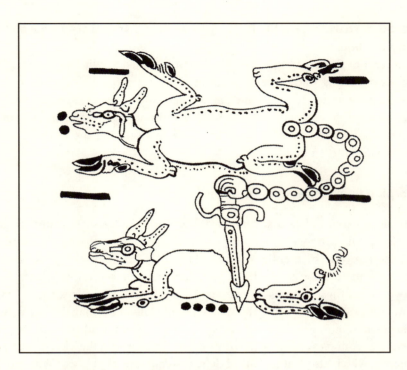

Figure 9.3. Scorpion tails in the Madrid Codex: (*a*) Scorpion-tailed deer, page 39b; (*b*) scorpion-tailed Chahk, page 31a. Drawings by F. D. Rossi.

However, the majority of scorpion-tailed figures in the codices do not seem to reference water or rain in any way, nor do they explicitly signal any other seasonal trends. Many occur in action-oriented scenes, like the deer-trapping almanac. In such instances, seasonal affiliations need to be meticulously worked out, as Vail (1997) has done. The key, Vail showed, is demonstrating a connection between the action being carried out by or performed on a scorpion-tailed entity and the months when the scorpion constellation regularly appeared in the night sky.

Other examples in the Madrid Codex include an aged goddess (fig. 9.4a) who is often referred to as Chac Chel. She is depicted with a scorpion tail on page 11a, in what Vail (1997, 94) described as a "context of an almanac with possible astronomical associations." The image is part of the first section of the Madrid eclipse almanac, which "is concerned with rain, drought, the agricultural cycle, and how these phenomena fit with eclipses" (Bricker and Bricker 2011, 351). The goddess's actual depiction occupies the central image of three pictures on page 11a. She holds a maize tamale glyph topped with seeds and wears a scorpion tail. The pictures on either side of her depict Chahk performing actions in the rain. Her image notably occurs in dry conditions.

There is also the black deity (God M), who is depicted with scorpion tail across several pages in the Madrid Codex (fig. 9.4b). God M occurs throughout the Madrid Codex and in the books of the Chilam Balam as a merchant deity with stellar links. This deity, named Ek Chuaah, was involved in katun prophecies (Seler 1904, 35–36; Roys 1967, 151; Kelley 1976, 71–74; Milbrath 1999, 264). The name Ek Chuaah closely echoes the Yukatek Ek Chuh, or "black scorcher," a type of local scorpion (Kelley 1976). Some have argued that an astronomical significance is related to the scorpion constellation due in part to the many images in which God M, a stellar deity, wears a scorpion tail (Chinchilla Mazariegos 2005, 116; Van Akkeren 2000, 261–273). In the Madrid Codex, several scenes from the almanac involving this deity are violent, including one in which God Q (Kisin), a deity with lacerations and an eccentric blade emerging from his head, spears God M (Madrid Codex 84a). These two deities appear together several times, contributing to arguments that God M is closely associated with acts of war and sacrifice (Bill 1997)—a recurring theme in scorpion-related iconography.

As is the case with images of full-bodied scorpions, the astronomical connections of scorpion composites reach back to earlier periods.[8] Oswaldo Chinchilla Mazariegos (2005) discusses three figures with stellar scorpion attributes on the Classic period Vase of the Stars in the Museo Popol Vuh in Guatemala, thinking through their potential relationship to the scorpion constellation. He writes, "It is tempting to associate Personage 2 with the

Figure 9.4. Scorpion tails in the Madrid Codex: (*a*) Scorpion-tailed goddess, page 11a; (*b*) scorpion-tailed God M, page 79a. Drawings by F. D. Rossi.

constellation, but the multiplicity of stellar beings associated with scorpion tails in this and other contexts suggests instead that the latter is a widespread attribute of celestial beings in Maya iconography" (Chinchilla Mazariegos 2005, 116). He reviews the variety of scorpion-tailed composites, including a "handsome young man with a scorpion tail" and the codex examples, then he raises a question: "Which one of all these beings, if any, corresponds with *the* scorpion constellation?" (116).

The variety of these stellar beings is intriguing. Rather than one embodying *the* scorpion constellation over the others, perhaps scorpion attributes signal a more flexible category related to the scorpion constellation's seasonal time window. Susan Milbrath (1999, 249) suggests as much: "Although we look for precise events, such as a star's heliacal rise date, most probably the Maya looked for a more general association with the season." Ethnographic evidence supports this argument. Barbara Tedlock (1992, 181–183), who worked with Maya people in Momostenango, noted the role of stellar risings for tracking seasonality. Evenly spaced "signs of the night" break up seasons and help mark appropriate timing for particular ritual events.

Taken together, these various reviews of scorpion imagery suggest that perhaps full-body scorpions referred to the scorpion constellation, while scorpion composites might have signaled affiliation with the season when the scorpion constellation was in the sky. Even when both the Bricker and Love Paris Codex zodiac models and contradictory ethnographic evidence are acknowledged, it is generally agreed that the scorpion constellation exists in the sky in close correspondence with the dry season, roughly from January into May across the Maya area.

## Scorpion-Tailed Maize Warriors

During the Classic and Terminal Classic periods, a particular scorpion composite turns up more than any other. This figure occurs in sky imagery and in scenes of royal embodiment and performance—the figure Chinchilla Mazariegos (2005) calls the "handsome young man with a scorpion tail." John Carlson refers to this figure as the "Maya Venus Scorpion man sacrificer" (Carlson and Cherry 1996, 153).[9] The most famous image of this figure occurs on a well-known bench from Las Sepulturas group at Copán (Webster et al. 1998). Included as part of the skyband that runs across the front of the bench, a figure (often glossed as "a youthful maize god") embraces an **EK'** (star) (T510) logograph (fig. 9.5a). His scorpion tail is clearly visible emerging from behind the glyph. The same scorpion-tailed youth is portrayed on a Late Classic period dish, in which the **EK'** glyph constitutes his

Figure 9.5. Scorpion-tailed maize youth: (*a*) Carved bench from the Skyband Group, Copán, after Dowd in Webster et al. (1998, 333); (*b*) detail from Late Classic polychrome bowl (K4565). Drawings by F. D. Rossi.

torso (fig. 9.5b). This figure also appears on the Monjas frieze (fig. 9.1b). Depicted as a youthful human head in profile attached to an insect-like body, it sits atop an **EK'** glyph and has a scorpion tail. Again, the text on the lintel immediately beneath contains a logograph containing a full-body scorpion within a circle (fig. 9.2a). The common appearance of the **EK'** or star glyph with this particular figure has led to various theories. Some argue that he is a representation of the scorpion constellation (Kelley 1976, 38–42; Bricker and Bricker 1992), others suggest that he is a conjunction of Venus with the scorpion constellation (Seler 1996, 269; Milbrath 1999, 264–266), and others contend that he is a representation of Venus itself (Carlson 1991, 1993; Carlson and Cherry 1996).

Two other Classic period depictions of the youthful scorpion-tailed personage are less frequently discussed. One is on the north wall of the mural at Los Sabios discovered in 2010 at Xultun, and the other is on Naranjo Stela 2 (fig. 9.6), first documented at the turn of the twentieth century but only recently recognized as an example of this entity (Rossi 2015, 354). In both examples, the ruler is dressed as the scorpion-tailed personage in the performance of a public ceremony. At Naranjo, the event depicted on Stela 2 could be associated with any of four dates inscribed on the monument. However, the event associated with the monument's opening date (B1–B8) seems the most likely to be represented in the scene. This date, the latest chronologically of the four featured in the stela text, falls on 9.14.1.3.19 3 Kawak 2 Pop (February 10, 713 CE) and marks the one-*katun*, or 20-year, anniversary of K'ahk' Tiliw Chan Chahk's accession into Naranjo kingship (Mathews n.d.; Martin and Grube 2008, 74). The scene on the front of the stela shows the ruler K'ahk Tiliw Chan Chahk (693–728 CE) holding an incense bag in one hand and the square shield and atlatl darts of a central Mexican/Teotihuacano warrior in the other (Graham and Von Euw 1975, 13–15; Martin and Grube 2008, 74–75). Inverted heads overlay his textured shoulder pads and a pectoral featuring an obsidian blade run through a skull hangs around his neck. He wears a beaded helmet, a feathered headdress, a cape, and a shell-edged skirt. Feathers with darkened tips are clearly visible emerging from his helmet. He stands on a toponymic register that features the IK' (wind) logogram as part of its name (see Stuart and Houston 1994). A scorpion tail is just visible descending between his legs in a frontal view.

The second example from the mural at Los Sabios depicts the ruler Yax W'en Chan K'inich (fig. 9.7). He is shown wearing a jester god headband and a large headdress from which a centipede head with obsidian tongue emerges at the front and a dark tipped feather extends outward from the back (the same type of feather as on Naranjo Stela 2). He is adorned with

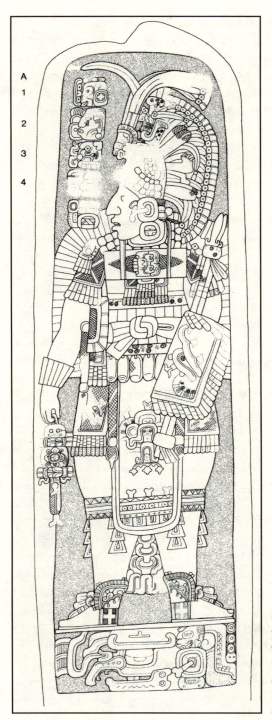

Figure 9.6. Maya ruler dressed as youthful scorpion-tailed deity, front of Stela 2, Naranjo. Drawing by Ian Graham. © President and Fellows of Harvard College, Peabody Museum of Archaeology and Ethnology, 2004.15.6.2.4.

Figure 9.7. Detail from Los Sabios mural: reconstruction painting and text of north wall niche with depiction of and caption naming Hun Ik' Ixiim ti taaj (First Wind-Maize with Obsidian) as the impersonated deity. Illustration by H. Hurst, text drawing by D. Stuart. Courtesy of the San Bartolo–Xultun Regional Archaeological Project.

earflares, a collar, anklets, and bracelets and appears in a seated position, holding an incense bag in one hand and a scepter with repeating **IK'** (wind) motifs in the other. He is also interacting with another individual, glyphically called "junior obsidian." Most important for our discussion, however, is the scorpion tail that trails down from the small of his back and out behind him.

The parallels between the two depictions are many, but at Xultun the ruler does not hold a square shield, darts, or an atlatl. However, painted on the vault above him, the lower halves of two standing warriors are preserved, as though these figures watch over the scene unfolding below from the sky above. Each of the two vault figures stands facing west and holding square shields like the one held by the ruler on Naranjo Stela 2 (shields that are commonly associated with central Mexican/Teotihuacano warriors). Like the Xultun ruler, each of these warriors has a scorpion tail (Rossi 2015, 45, fig. 1.7; Saturno, Rossi, et al. 2017, 428).

Neither depiction contains any reference to the T510 glyph, **EK'**. However, the context of the mural at Los Sabios suggests a celestial component to the painted scene. The mural was found in a high-status residence that archaeological and epigraphic data suggest was a locus of codex book production and schooling for specialized knowledge related to complex calendrics and astronomy (Rossi et al. 2015; Rossi 2018). On the east wall of the mural room, which served almost as a kind of scratchboard, zodiacal references to Orion and the Pleiades are present (Bricker et al. 2014) amid a variety of painted and incised counts known from much later codex books—including "ring" numbers (Saturno, Stuart, et al. 2012), a lunar semester table (ibid.), various distance number calculations (Rossi 2015, 345–346), and Long Rounds, or what Floyd Lounsbury (1978) called supernumbers (Saturno, Stuart, et al. 2012; Aveni et al. 2013). These calculations are separate from the main scene. In the main scene, a ranked and black-painted order of individuals, who are glyphically labeled and literally dressed as "obsidians," look directly at the ruler. The ruler himself is dressed as an invocation of the very youthful scorpion-tailed figure previously mentioned (Saturno et al. 2015). A glyphic caption details the scene at Los Sabios.

In 2015 and again in 2017, a preliminary transcription and in-depth discussion of the glyphic caption on the north wall niche at Los Sabios was published (see Rossi 2015, 353–358; Saturno, Rossi, et al. 2017). To summarize, the caption recounts a public ceremony connected to obsidian and sacrifice, the *h'aab* New Year (or 365 solar cycle), and the invocation or impersonation through costume of a deity named First Wind-Maize with Obsidian (Hun Ik' Ixiim ti taaj; Rossi 2015, 57–65; Saturno, Rossi, et al. 2017, 428–430). In Table 9.1, I present a current working transcription, which is largely the same as those previously published with the exception of a few minor details.

Table 9.1. Glyphic caption on north wall niche, Los Sabios mural

|     | Transcription |     | Transcription |
| --- | --- | --- | --- |
| A1 | 11-OOK | C1 | IHK'-T533 |
| A2 | 13-[K'AN]JAL-wa | D1 | ti-12-NAHB-ba |
| A3 | U-ba-hi | E1 | K'AHK'-HOP-*la-*ja |
| A4 | ti-? | F1 | *CHAN-*YOP-*AAT |
| A5 | k'u-?-ju-lu | F2 | YAX-WE'-*ne |
| A6 | ti-ta-ji | F3 | CHAN-K'INICH |
| A7 | U-ba[AHN]-*hi-*li-nu | F4 | BAAX-WITZ-AJAW |
| A8 | 1-IXIIM?[IK'] | F5 | ba-ka-ba |
| A9 | ti-ta-*ji | F6 | *K'UHUL-K'AB-TE'-yo-OK[K'IN] |
| B1 | *U?-*CHAHK?-li |  |  |

The reading Yax We'nel has been modified to Yax We'n in order to reflect our current thinking (see Rossi and Stuart 2020, 15n1). The potential readings at B1, E1, and F1 are tentative and serve as suggestions largely based on patterns observed in other contemporaneous texts (see Beliaev et al. 2019: 360 for E1). Rather than review every aspect of this text, which has been discussed thoroughly elsewhere (Rossi 2015; Saturno, Rossi, et al. 2017), I focus on a few relevant features.

First, the text includes a Calendar Round date at A1-A2, 11 Oc 13 Pop, which most likely corresponds to the Long Count 9.15.17.13.10, or February 12, 749 CE (Saturno et al. 2017, 426). Second, two *ubaah* constructions are consecutively introduced in the text that together shed light on what is being depicted in the scene and on the identity of the impersonated deity.

The first *ubaah* construction, at position A3, is simply *ubaah* (*u-ba-hi*; it is his image) (Houston and Stuart 1996). This common construction is often followed by the preposition *ti* in order to recount an event that took place more specifically. For example, it is used in statements such as *ubaah ti ahk'ot* (it is his image in dance) (Grube 1992), and *ubaah ti cha'nil* (it is his image in public ceremony) (Tokovinine 2003). Here, the statement connected to this construction eludes full decipherment but can provisionally be read as *ubaah ti ? k'u? jul ti taaj*, or "it is his image in ?, ? with obsidian." David Stuart (personal communication, 2015) noticed that the illegible logograph at A4 is the same glyph at position A2 on the Naranjo Stela 2, with the form of a human head in profile. On the Naranjo stela, droplets descend from the eye of the logograph; these droplets occur as darkened red streaks on the glyph at Los

240 · Franco D. Rossi

Sabios, which implies that blood, as either streaks or as droplets, is what is being represented in both contexts.

The second *ubaah* construction on the mural at Los Sabios refers to the invocation or "impersonation" event. The glyphic phrase occurs at A7, as *ubaahil ahn* (*u-ba[AHN]-\*hi-\*li-nu*), which Houston and Stuart (1996) have shown signals deity impersonation. It is typically followed by the name of the deity being impersonated (see also Stuart 1996). This phrase is important because it allows us to clearly identify the name of the youthful, scorpion-tailed maize deity during the Classic period as Hun Ik' Ixiim ti taaj, or "First Wind-Maize with Obsidian" (Saturno, Rossi, et al. 2017, 428–430).

The name "First Wind-Maize with Obsidian" paired with the associated imagery implies the impersonated deity's role was related to winds, agricultural abundance, and the sacrificial offerings and material implements necessary to achieve that abundance (obsidian). The iconography of Stela 2 at Naranjo and the mural at Los Sabios suggest that this composite contains martial themes as well, although warfare is never mentioned in explicit relation to this deity.

The decipherment of this deity's name on the mural at Los Sabios soon led to its identification in another text: that of an unprovenienced vessel (K1728) currently housed at the Museum of Fine Arts in Boston (Rossi 2015, 355). Unfortunately, no image of the impersonated deity adorns the scene painted on the vessel's surface, but Hun Ik' Ixiim ti taaj is mentioned as part of an "impersonation" statement in the dedicatory text that wraps around the top of the pot. It begins with a Calendar Round date, 7 Men 8 Mol, which corresponds to 9.17.8.9.15 or June 20, 779 CE (Tokovinine and Zender 2012, 39). It then goes through the normal dedicatory formula (see Stuart 2005c). Then, following the glyph for *ch'ok* (youth), a reference to the vessel owner, the text goes on to say that "he impersonates/invokes the divine ?, First Wind-Maize with Obsidian" (*ubaahil ahn k'uhul ?, Hun Ik' Ixiim ti taaj*). The ruler of the Ik' polity, K'inich Lamaw Ek', is then named as the ostensible impersonator.[10]

Two monuments from Piedras Negras (PNG), Stelae 8 and 35, depict rulers dressed in similar ways as those represented on Stela 2 at Naranjo and the mural at Los Sabios, though the scorpion tails are conspicuously absent (Saturno et al. 2015). Megan O'Neil (2012, 82) describes PNG Stela 8 specifically as "an enormous image of K'inich Y'onal Ahk II dressed in Teotihuacano-inspired warrior costume." Like Stela 2 at Naranjo and the mural at Los Sabios, PNG Stelae 8 (fig. 9.8a) and 35 (fig. 9.8b) show rulers with large headdresses replete with feathers, beaded collars, shell-edged skirts, obsidian tongues, dark-tipped feather imagery in the headdresses, square shields, and several other Mexican/Teotihuacano-style referents of dress, which, along with depicted captives, are suggestive of warfare. In both depictions, the protagonist holds a spear. The spear on PNG Stela 8 (fig. 9.8a) is pointed with a curved obsidian blade (marked with the "darkness" glyph) (Stone and Zender 2011, 74), and the depicted ruler wears a pectoral prominently marked with the **IK'** (wind) glyph. Also, the square shields on Piedras Negras Stela 8 and Naranjo Stela 2 have the same central icon. While these examples should not necessarily be conflated with the same scorpion-tailed entity being impersonated on Stela 2 at Naranjo and the mural at Los Sabios, the overlaps in dress are significant.

## Pondering the Dates

The time period between any constellation's arrival in the east and its setting in the west likely indicates its season in antiquity. In other words, it would be odd to expect a constellation hidden from observable view to be actively incorporated into a deity impersonation event. If we accept that the youthful scorpion-tailed personage was related to the scorpion constellation, at least in part, then the dates of its appearance should fit with the constellation's presence in the observable sky.

The dates on Naranjo Stela 2 and on the mural at Los Sabios both occur in February, and they fit neatly within the annual dry season and within the season the Bricker model set for the scorpion constellation in the Paris Codex zodiac. A published seasonal table for the Bricker zodiacal model provides the date range for each constellation in their model throughout the year and was measured at both dawn and dusk for the year 755–756 CE (Bricker and Bricker 1992, 168, table 6.4). Following this table, the Bricker model places the scorpion constellation (as Scorpius) in rising position on the eastern horizon on December 8 at sunrise. Five months later, on May 24, Scorpius appeared in the setting position on the western horizon at sunrise. Thus, the June 20 date for Vessel K1728 falls outside this model, suggesting that perhaps Classic period stellar scorpions referenced a different constellation or celestial entity or perhaps that the seasonal boundaries related to such constellations were not so rigid.

Observing the sky on June 20, 779 CE using Google's Stellarium sky program, Scorpius appears in the sky for several hours after nightfall. Also, Castor and Pollux of the Gemini constellation (Bruce Love's proposition for the scorpion constellation) would have been visible just before nightfall on the western horizon that evening. Furthermore, Ursa Major (mentioned as the scorpion constellation among Tojolabal Maya) also appeared in the sky over the course of the night. All three of these star groups—each referred to as the scorpion constellation within different but related cultural traditions and divergently embraced as the likely scorpion constellation by scholars—all overlap

Figure 9.8. (*a*) Front of Stela 8, Piedras Negras; (*b*) front of Stela 35, Piedras Negras. Drawing of Stela 8 by David Stuart © President and Fellows of Harvard College, Peabody Museum of Archaeology and Ethnology, 2004.15.6.19.23. Photograph of Stela 35 courtesy of the Peabody Museum of Archaeology and Ethnology, Harvard University, 2004.24.2659.

considerably in their visibility during the dry season, even if they do not overlap in their specific star group designation.

Another interesting feature of the three dates associated with impersonations of Hun Ik' Ixiim ti taaj is that Venus would have been on the western horizon at or slightly before dusk on all three. Perhaps Seler's (1996) initial suggestion that the Monjas frieze creatures represented constellations in conjunction with Venus was at least partially correct. John Carlson's (1991) long-standing arguments for the close connection of the scorpion-tailed youth with Venus (though not necessarily exclusively with Venus) are also supported by this evidence.

An image that both Susan Milbrath (1999, 160–161) and John Carlson (1991) have discussed further confirms this connection. In the Venus tables in the Dresden Codex (DC47), a deity with maize foliage on his head holds darts and an atlatl. A scorpion tail emerges from behind him and is tipped with a the **EK'** (star) logograph (T510) (fig. 9.9a). On the previous page of the same codex, the term *sinan* or "scorpion" is spelled out (**si-na-na**) in registers B and C in potential reference to the scorpion constellation; this text is also part of the Venus tables. Milbrath (1999) discussed this figure as an important Venus deity related to the western sky in the Dresden Codex. Visually, the parallels between this Dresden Codex Venus figure and the impersonated deity on the much earlier Naranjo Stela 2, in particular, are striking. While the depiction of the ruler dressed as First Wind-Maize with Obsidian on the mural at Los Sabios does not necessarily bear martial symbolism, the square-shielded, scorpion-tailed warriors painted on the vaulted ceiling above the scene certainly do. These warriors evoke the Naranjo Stela 2 depiction of the ruler

*a*  *b*

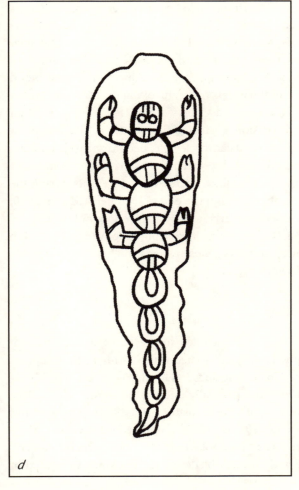

Figure 9.9. (*a*) Scorpion-tailed maize god in the Venus Table on page 47 of the Dresden Codex; (*b*) detail of Aztec carving of scorpion with an obsidian blade for its stinger (after Carlson 1991, fig. 16); (*c*) First Wind-Maize with Obsidian, from an incised obsidian blade from Tikal; (*d*) scorpion with tail ending at blade point, from an incised obsidian blade from Tikal. Drawings by F. D. Rossi.

246 · Franco D. Rossi

dressed as scorpion-tailed warrior. The tips of their tails belch fire. This immediately calls to mind the scorpion-tailed deity in the Dresden Codex whose tail is tipped with a fiery **EK'** logogram.[11]

These various threads of evidence highlight the youthful scorpion-tailed composite as a seasonal deity that embodied and was temporally bound to the visibility of both a dry-season constellation and the planet Venus in the sky. In my own thinking on this topic, I emphasize both the scorpion constellation and Venus in the west as part of this deity's identity. Evon Vogt's (1997, 113) ethnographic research shows the interesting relationships that can form between highly visible planets and constellations, highlighting specifically that in Tzotzil thought, the red star Antares in the constellation Scorpius and the planet Venus are paired conceptually as "junior elder star" and "senior elder star."

Writing that Mesoamerican scorpion-tailed entities were part of "Venus-regulated sacred warfare and sacrifice," John Carlson summarized his findings with a colleague (Carlson and Cherry 1996, 154). They write that such acts of warfare and sacrifice were "an early and pervasive pan-Mesoamerican tradition in which battle captives were taken for sacrifice, their shed blood symbolically transformed into the waters of life, invoking the forces of human and agricultural fertility" (Carlson and Cherry 1996, 154; see also Carlsen 1991, 1993 for previous discussions). However, since then, the argument that warfare was regulated by Venusian cycles has been disproven (Aldana 2005; Villaseñor 2012), and continued research shows that war was not necessarily restricted in such ways, save for a decrease in war events during the harvest months (mid-September through the end of October) (Martin 2020, 216–217). This suggests that Venus warrior iconography does not necessarily reference or record actual acts of war, even if the iconography (as on page 47b of the Dresden Venus tables) supports a close association between scorpion-tailed maize warriors and Venus cycles.

## Scorpions, Fire, and Obsidian

Neither "scorpion" nor "Venus" are included in the name of the youthful maize scorpion tailed deity, First Wind-Maize with Obsidian, as it appears on the mural at Los Sabios. A recurring question for me has been: Why obsidian? The Classic Maya word *taaj* is generally understood to mean "obsidian" (Wanyerka 2002, v; Wanyerka 2003, 86; Houston 2012, 89), but the term has also been translated as "obsidian blade" and "bloodletter." One Classic Maya glyph for the word *taaj* consists of a hooked obsidian eccentric implement. Implements such as these and obsidian blades of various kinds were used in human sacrifice and were often depicted either as darkened matter or as infixed with the **AK'AB** (darkness) logogram (Beliaev and Houston 2020). Such representations helped naturalize obsidian's common use as an instrument for various forms of sacrifice. Its linguistically related terms often mean "lancet," "bloodletter," or "knife" as well as the volcanic glass we know as obsidian. In colonial Yucatán, such sacrificial blades were known as "the hand of god" (*uk'abk'u*) (Tozzer 1941, 119). These were all tools used in ritual bloodletting events, suggesting that human sacrifice was part of the ceremonies that were captioned on Naranjo Stela 2 and the mural at Los Sabios (Rossi 2015, 101–159; Saturno, Rossi, et al. 2017).

It has been demonstrated elsewhere that on the mural at Los Sabios, the black-painted individuals—who were ranked, labeled, and depicted as "obsidians"—were part of the Classic period state infrastructures that underpinned public acts of violence (Rossi 2015; Saturno, Rossi, et al. 2017). Such events were sometimes timed astronomically, as shown in the public sacrifice scene rendered so vividly in Room 2 at Bonampak. In that scene, the sun, Venus as the morning star, and the constellations Leo (in the form of belching pigs) and Orion (in the form of the turtle) auspiciously shine overhead as captives have their fingernails pulled out, are decapitated, or are otherwise made to let blood—revealing the ways specialized celestial time and planetary cycles were used as tools of state ritual and legitimized violence (Miller 1986, 51; Bricker and Bricker 2011, 715–718; Miller and Brittenham 2013, 93–112).

In 1984, Linda Schele wrote about various forms of legitimized violence the Maya practiced, bringing artistic and epigraphic evidence to bear on Landa's sixteenth-century descriptions. The use of obsidian in such cases fits with the material's sacrificial associations, as it is commonly linked artistically, epigraphically, and archaeologically with such acts (Schele and Miller 1986; Tiesler and Cucina 2006a, 2007; Tiesler 2007; Rossi 2015; Scherer 2015, 180–207; Beliaev and Houston 2020).

A particularly interesting component of the caption of the mural at Los Sabios (fig. 9.7; Table 9.1) is its dual use of *ubaah* (it is his image/representation [in]) and *ubaahil ahn* (it is his image in impersonation/invocation of) within the same single column of text. This usage serves to describe both the action being performed and the impersonated deity with whom the act is connected. However, both the act and the deity's name contain the terms *ti taaj* (with obsidian). The question of what exactly "obsidian" refers to in these two instances is worth exploring. Why is *ti taaj* mentioned twice, once as part of the event description and once as part of the deity name?

To begin with the event description, which is read *ubaah?, k'u? jul ti taaj*, the inclusion of "with obsidian" that occurs at A6 supports the previous

248 · Franco D. Rossi

suggestion that the illegible logograph at A4 signals a violent act of some kind—a statement akin to "it is his image in sacrifice." Considering the glyph at A4 and its red diagnostic streak that runs across a human face, perhaps the term it represents signaled some kind of human or captive sacrifice rather than auto-sacrifice. A recent discussion by Beliaev and Houston (2020) surveys a category of Wound-by-Obsidian glyphs that depict an obsidian eccentric blade and a cut face as the primary signs. It is visually reminiscent of the glyphs at both A4 on the Los Sabios mural and A2 on Naranjo Stela 2 and may signal related acts of violence.

The statement that follows the potential "sacrifice glyph" at A4 on Los Sabios mural contains the syllables **k'u-ju-lu-ti-ta-ji**, which could be read as *k'ujul ti taaj*. However, when read this way, the phrase evades full decipherment since the term *k'ujul* has proven difficult to trace.[12] Considering the underspelling that is widely present throughout this caption, I wonder if this statement could be alternatively thought of as *k'u? jul ti taaj*. **JUL** has been deciphered as the transitive verbal root for "to shoot, pierce, throw (a dart or spear), hurl" and in noun form as "perforator, dart, spear" (Wanyerka 2002, 2003; Safronov et al. 2015, 37, 53). In this case, although a missing syllable prevents a confident reading of the first term of the phrase, the words *jul ti taaj* (to pierce, shoot with obsidian) might just fit. If we suspect that the first, undeciphered term functions as part of a verbal construction, the noun *jul ti taaj* (perforator, dart or spear of obsidian) also works.[13] Sacrifice by arrow or dart is an attested pre-Columbian practice that is described in colonial accounts and depicted in pre-Columbian graffiti (Trik and Kampen 1983; Schele 1984; Taube 1988a). In line with this interpretation, the Naranjo Stela 2 scorpion-tailed personage holds atlatl darts in one hand, as does the much later depiction of a scorpion-tailed god in the Venus tables of the Dresden Codex (D47).

Again, on the Los Sabios mural, both subjects of its texts' two *ubaah* phrases, action and deity agent, include *ti taaj* or "with obsidian." The layered associations of this phrase with the sacrificial verb at A4 make sense, but the redundancy of use in including *ti taaj* in the deity's name also seems significant. However, it is suspicious (though not necessarily an issue) that the scorpion-tailed deity's name, First Wind-Maize with Obsidian, does not use any documented term for scorpion in any known Mayan language (Kaufman and Norman 1984). I have often wondered whether *taaj* in this deity name context might be referring to the scorpion tail itself or to its sting.

A cognitive and aesthetic link between a dark shiny scorpion's scorching stinger that pierces skin and a dark, shiny volcanic glass that does the same would not be a large conceptual leap. As far as central Mexico, scorpion

Scorpion Star: Convergences of Meaning in a Classic Maya Entity · 249

stingers were shown as literal knives (fig. 9.9b, see Carlson 1991). Scorpion tails evoke curving obsidian blades. Scorpions appear on or as obsidian eccentric blades from Uaxactun (fig. 9.9d; for example, see Kidder 1947, figs. 69–71), Caracol (Johnson 2016, 310, fig.7-3D) and elsewhere in the Maya area. In a particularly relevant example from Tikal, the image of the scorpion-tailed maize deity, First Wind-Maize with Obsidian is etched onto the surface of a scorpion-shaped obsidian eccentric blade. Unfortunately, no **EK'** (star) glyph is visible (fig. 9.9c).

Obsidian was often represented as a material of the night and was commonly set in a kind of mythical opposition with chert, a material of the day (Agurcia Fasquelle et al. 2015). Obsidian objects were not glyphically marked as black, gray, or green in color, which would reflect an expectation in accordance with western color perspectives. Rather, they were marked with the logogram **AK'AB** (darkness). Obsidian was literally the color of night (Houston et al. 2009). These nighttime associations and even mythologized celestial origins of obsidian objects are preserved in terms such as the Tzotzil Maya phrase *tzo' k'anal* (sky shit), referring to the widespread belief that obsidian was dropped by shooting stars as they seared through the night sky (Laughlin 1975, 93). It has also been shown that shooting stars, atlatls, and comets were all associated with obsidian as the celestial fiery weapons of the gods (Taube 1992a). The *ti taaj* of the youthful scorpion-tailed Maize god's name conflates and presents these seemingly disparate ideas and objects—scorpion tails, obsidian, sacrifice, and celestial objects in the night sky.

Like obsidian, scorpion tails sting and are noted for leaving their victims with a strange feeling akin to a seemingly counterintuitive icy burning. Perhaps that is what earned the local Yucatán scorpion the name Ek Chuh (black scorcher). The term **EK'**, which can also mean "star" as well as "black," has been the subject of some confusion among scholars (see chapter 13, this volume). Oswaldo Chinchilla Mazariegos (2005, 116) touches on this term in his treatment of God M's relationship with the scorpion, suggesting, with the help of Schellhas (1904) and Seler (1996), that in the context of God M's name, **EK'** may signal "star" over color—an association that Ruud Van Akkeren (2000, 261–273) also explored. But just as we see with the term *taaj,* such ambiguities do not need to be resolved as wholly one or the other. God M often appears as a black figure, but that does not preclude him from also relating to the stars. Multiple valences of terms in Mayan languages are well attested (Hanks 1990; Hanks 2000, 221–248) and are not uncommon in Maya text. The Yukatekan Maya term *chuh* is also complex in this way. It is translated as "scorcher" here because it relates to a local scorpion type, but *chuh* is also a colonially attested term for "sacrifice," a translation that opens Linda Schele's 1984 chapter on that subject.[14] The term *chuh* specifically relates to sacrifice through burning or fire-induced injuries (Barrera Vásquez 1980). As a material born of shooting stars and comets that is associated with divine celestial weapons, obsidian conceptually aligns with fire. The vault of the mural at Los Sabios supports this link. As previously mentioned, the central Mexican/Teotihuacano warriors rendered on the northern vault at Los Sabios each have scorpion tails, but fiery plumes emerge in the place where their stingers should be. Celestial cycles and cosmological events were invariably bound up with Classic Maya conceptions of time: iconographies, terminologies, and temporal cycles overlapped in ways that could perhaps produce ambiguity but also allowed for a flexibility and wide breadth of cultural meaning.

## Scorpion Tails and the Promise of Rain

In his discussion of Classic Maya scaffold year-renewal sacrifices, Karl Taube (1988a) writes of the three themes of such rites: the hunt, planting, and captive sacrifice. He explains that during these springtime (or dry-season) events, human victims, often war captives, would be symbolically conflated with deer in public acts of killing. Such ceremonies melded hunting and war but also petitioned for rains during the dry season through blood spilled upon the earth. Taube writes, "The sacrifice seems to have had the purpose of increasing the fertility of the fields through renewal ceremonies, as well as shaming and annihilating the enemy" (359). He describes a rite in which people were burned and then doused with water in evocation of the fiery dry season and its quenching by the rains, called *tup kaak*. Unfortunately, the state of the night sky during the periods Taube discussed is left out of the article. Yet considering what is known of Maya astronomy, it is difficult to imagine that the position of celestial objects in the sky did not also play a part in these rites.

While the impersonation of First Wind-Maize with Obsidian depicted at Classic period Los Sabios was much earlier and clearly not part of the sacrificial events Taube explored, the three themes he laid out resonate with this chapter's discussion. Elsewhere, colleagues and I have discussed the parallels between the impersonation scene at Los Sabios and Landa's description of the renewal ceremonies that routinely took place during the month Pohp—the first month in the Ha'ab calendar (Rossi 2015; Saturno, Rossi, et al. 2017).

The prevalence of planting and rain-beckoning rituals across ancient societies is well attested. Many of the ceremonies described in colonial-era documents and ethnographic accounts about the Maya area are concerned with these two factors. This is no surprise, since food and water literally dictate the terms of life for human beings. Recently, Jobbová and colleagues (2018) explored Classic period Maya "bathing" and "scattering" phrases that commonly took place during 20-year period-ending celebrations; they associate these phrases with beckoning rain and planting. During the Classic period, it is likely that in any given city, a variety of celebrations and sacrificial events like the ones Jobbová and colleagues describe regularly transpired. During the dry season, these would have likely overlapped and related to the typical actions and concerns of that season. Among these, planting (and seasonal fires), hunting, and beckoning rain would have been key, as would have been success in future wars. These are concerns that implicitly undergird most ritual activities worldwide. I argue that we should add the impersonation of a scorpion-tailed, obsidian-dart-wielding, celestial maize youth to the corpus of known ceremonies focused on these concerns.

Classic Maya deities can take dramatically different forms between sites, even as they share qualities and aspects of identity (Houston and Stuart 1996; Baron 2016b). The variety of deities and entities wearing the scorpion tail is both specific and diffuse enough to warrant a flexible model for its use in loose correlation with the dry season (January to June) and renewal ceremonies more generally. First Wind-Maize with Obsidian (Hun Ik' Ixiim ti taaj) is only one of many different localized deities that were invoked during the Classic Maya dry season across the cities of central Petén. The only Classic Period examples of his name and images of his invocation occur during the eighth century, and these all seem to have some connection astronomically with Venus in the west and to agricultural practice. While many questions remain, we might finally, at the least, fit a name to a long-acknowledged Maya entity. In doing so, we can hope to reopen discussions about seasonality, celestial designations, and the many layered meanings and temporal associations that can be present in the representations of a scorpion-tailed personage.

## Notes

1 *sinan ek*: "escorpion signo del cielo" (Ciudad Real 1577, 1:104r).
2 See also Houston et al. (2001) for a thorough review of contemporaries and their notable contributions.
3 "*ac*, 1. *ac ek*: las tres estrellas juntas que estan en el signo de geminis; las quales con otras hacen forma de Tortuga" (Ciudad Real 1577, 1:1v). Floyd Lounsbury (1982, 166) explains the occurrence of the "signo de Geminis": "the term 'signo' is used in both Spanish and Maya sources for calendrical zodiacal divisions, *not for constellations*" (my emphasis). He clarifies why the "sign of Gemini" is included in the Motul definition of the constellation *ac ek* ("turtle star," known to us as Orion): "by the sixteenth century, when the Motul dictionary was being assembled, the constellation of Gemini, because of precession, was already mostly in the 'sign' of Cancer,

252 · Franco D. Rossi

and the stars in the 'sign' of Gemini included those of Orion and much of Taurus" (166–167).

4 "*tzab*: las cabrillas constelacion de siete estrellas y los cascabeles de la vibora" (Ciudad Real 1577, 1:113v).

5 I follow Bricker and Bricker's note on intended meaning and terms of use underpinning the term "Maya zodiac": "The groupings of stars, both constellations and asterisms, that we think are relevant are, in whole or in part, reasonably close to the ecliptic, but we have no expectation that all of them lie within 8° or 9° of it. We use the familiar names of Western constellations (Gemini, Scorpius, etc.) in order to specify in an approximate fashion the area of the sky to which we refer. By so doing, we do not imply, however, that the ancient Maya delimited the star groupings in the same way that we do. (With the exception of the Pleaides and perhaps the belt of Orion and possibly the scorpion constellation)" (Bricker and Bricker 2011, 729–768).

6 The scene caption reads *1 Ajaw 3 K'ank'in ehm ta chan Itzaamnaaj*, **1-AJAW-3-K'ANK'IN-EHM-\*ta-CHAN-na-ITZAM-NA-ji** (On the date 1 Ajaw 3 K'ank'in, Itamnaaj descends from the sky).

7 Vail (1997) accepts the scorpion constellation as roughly equivalent to western Scorpius, following Bricker and Bricker (1992, 2011).

8 Such scorpion composites do not seem to overlap with any Classic period composites recognized in the corpus of Maya art as *way* (pronounced "why")—a category of spiritual co-essence embodied by historical individuals that is often linked to specific late Classic period rulers or dynasties (Grube and Nahm 1992; Just 2012). While such a comparison may be possible to make, I currently do not know of any Classic period scorpion composites associated with the *uway* phrase that commonly accompany depictions of *way* composites. Rather, the glyphic phrase associated with the Classic period example of a scorpion composite I review below is *ubaahil ahn*, a phrase reserved for invoking deities, not *way*, by Classic period rulers (Houston and Stuart 1996).

9 Though I have omitted the reference here, stellar scorpion entities painted on the Cacaxtla murals in Central Mexico are another important rendering of this figure and are the subject of much of the discussion in Carlson and Cherry (1996).

10 This vessel is the last object that explicitly refers to this ruler, and on it his name is followed by a curious parentage statement that makes clear that his father, though likely royal, had not ruled the Ik' polity (Tokovinine and Zender 2012, 38–39). It is unclear if the term *ch'ok* in the dedicatory text, expressing who this vessel belonged to, refers to K'inich Lamaw Ek' or to someone else. Typically, *ch'ok* is an age-grade term reserved for young men, though it has been suggested it could also apply to unmarried men (Houston 2009). K'inich Lamaw Ek' would have acceded to the throne at least twelve years earlier (Tokovinine and Zender 2012, 38–39, 45–46). This suggests three possibilities: that he was very young when he acceded, that the term *ch'ok* does not refer to him, or, intriguingly, that he remained unmarried.

11 Depictions of rulers at Piedras Negras on Stelae 8 and 35 are similarly dressed and carry the same weapons, although they do not have scorpion tails.

12 Its similarity to the widely used adjective *k'uhul* (divine), with which it has been grouped in some epigraphic sources (see Safronov et al. 2015, 56), is intriguing but doubtful in this context.

13 Beliaev and Houston (2020) have recently identified the glyph for the verb *kup*, which signifies "heart sacrifice" in particular.

14 Shele also records the term *kup* in her opening list of sacrifice types discovered in the San Francisco dictionary. **KUP** has only recently been attested by Beliaev and Houston (2020) in the passive verb *kuhpaj* (*ku-pa-ja*; he is being cut, sawn, sacrificed).

# 10

## Time as Ordinary Practice

### A Divination Building at Chan

CYNTHIA ROBIN

> With progress in astronomy and growing skill in computation, the Maya priests burst the bounds of the baktun, and roamed further into the past: they probed with their calculations outermost time, as modern astronomers with giant telescopes penetrate to the recesses of the universe.
>
> (Thompson 1950, 149)

> A preoccupation with time is often described as basic to Maya life, and the Zinacanteco are no exception. Whereas a Navaho asks, when meeting a person, "where are you going?" and "where have you come from?" a Zinacanteco asks, "when did you arrive in Chiapas?" and "when are you returning to your country?"
>
> (Vogt 1976, 207)

As these two epigraphs illustrate, time is central for the Maya, high priests and ordinary people alike. The first quote, by J. Eric S. Thompson, highlights the role of priests and monumentality in computing celestial time. In discussing pre-Columbian ideas about time, Thompson draws on evidence about time gleaned from monuments and inscriptions and addresses time as an elite practice. The second quote, by Evon Z. Vogt, highlights the importance of time for ordinary people in the Tzotzil Maya community of Zinacantán. The challenge for pre-Columbian archaeologists who study the pervasiveness of time for all people is identifying time as an ordinary practice in the archaeological record. This can be accomplished by examining how ordinary people used everyday objects to materialize time.

In this chapter, I examine time as it is materialized through the act of divination. I present and interpret the material evidence for divination in a building at the Maya farming community of Chan, Belize. At Chan, diviners materialized both celestial and human time. The chapter concludes by comparing the Chan divination building to a divination building at Cerén, El Salvador. The Chan divination building was constructed and used from 670 to 900 CE. The Cerén divination building was buried by a volcanic eruption in 590 CE. The two divination buildings, which are remarkably similar in terms of architecture and artifacts, illustrate the central role of time as materialized through divination practices in pre-Columbian Maya farming communities. The comparability between the two divination buildings helps researchers understand pre-Columbian divination as an ordinary practice and encourages us to look for divination buildings in other small communities in the Maya area.

This chapter is also about archaeological methods. Notions of context, the place where an artifact is found, and assemblage that have long been central to the archaeologist's toolkit underlie my analysis and interpretations. I discuss a set of artifacts that at first glance seem to constitute quite mundane objects: jute (snail) shells, a spindle whorl, chert bifaces, a broken pedestal base of a ceramic vessel, a deer antler, a patolli (game) board etched into a floor, and incised designs on a wall (often referred to as graffiti in the Maya area). But when these objects are seen as part of an assemblage that occupies a context, in this case a room in a civic building in the Maya farming community of Chan, the seemingly mundane objects take on new meanings. Studies of assemblage and context are taking on new resonance in and beyond archaeology in discussions of materiality, material culture studies, and new materialism that highlight how things can gather meaning from one another through their entanglements in contexts and assemblages (e.g., DeLanda 2006; Bennett 2010; Hodder 2012; Overholtzer and Robin 2015; Hamilakis and Jones 2017).

## Contemporary Maya Divination

The practice of divination is a key part of Maya communities today. Diviners keep time, see into the future, answer questions, fill positions, and settle disputes. Time and divination are critical for the organization and operation of lives and communities (e.g., Hanks 1990; Love 1992; Tedlock 1992; Freidel et al. 1993; Brown 2000; McGraw 2016a, 2016b).

256 · Cynthia Robin

For the contemporary Quiche Maya of Momostenango and the Quiche Maya across highland Guatemala, calendrical diviners are shamans who keep the days and look into time to see the future (Tedlock 1992). The term *ajk'ij* refers to day (sun or time) keeper (Tedlock 1992, 47). Calendrical diviners were interested in both the quantitative aspects of time and the qualitative aspects of time and its significance in human life. In this sense, the Quiche term for the divinatory process is *ch'obonic* (to understand). Diviners kept the days and used divination to answer questions about the future for individuals and the community.

For the Yucatec Maya of Oxkutzcab, Mexico, shaman diviners use "illumination" (*tiíčk'aák*) to bring into visual access events and things that are otherwise imperceptible, such as future and past events, or time (Hanks 1990, 240). The purpose of illumination is to gain knowledge. Through illumination, diviners acquire knowledge about events beyond normal access and answer questions.

For the Maya diviner, time is both a quantity and a quality. It could be counted and it had meaning. Time was invested as much in celestial bodies as it was in the human body. Through divination, the diviner brought together all aspects of time: the quantitative and the qualitative, the celestial and the human. Through ritual practice and specialized paraphernalia, which were often ordinary objects, diviners materialized these symbolic aspects of time and made them meaningful for people and communities.

## Time and Divination Materialized

The places, practices, and paraphernalia of divination materialize time in ways that are observable in the archaeological record. Here I discuss three material practices associated with divination: the curation of small, often found or used, items for casting; the wearing of deer antler headdresses; and patolli boards.

In divination processes, Maya diviners used objects such as seeds, beans, crystals, shell, flint, and discarded materials for casting (Wagley 1949; Vogt 1969; Hanks 1990; Tedlock 1992; Brown 2000). Tz'utujil Maya ritual practitioners use found objects (rock, broken fragments, shell, marbles), objects that were worn, used, and curated as "direct lines of communication to the spirit world," referring to these objects as *cuentecito* in Spanish and *k'ijbal* in Tz'utujil (Brown 2000, 327; Douglas 1969, 138). Found objects might also include ritually collected pre-Columbian artifacts such as spindle whorls, whistles, ceramic sherds, and lithics (for a complete list, see Brown 2000, 330, table 3). The collection and curation of found objects for use in divination was important because "ritual reciprocity with ancestor teachers was a crucial component in gaining access to the supernatural" (Brown 2000, 326). Cast objects would be counted and would have had meaning. Gourd and ceramic bowls could be used to cast and store divination paraphernalia.

We know from ethnographies that Maya diviners used a multitude of different types of small objects in divination. What is important for the present study is that divining objects are small and could be easily cast. They are typically ordinary objects that are often made of nonperishable materials, which makes them archaeologically visible. They can be used and worn objects that diviners found and curated because of sacred properties that were visible to them. The specific object that diviners use for casting varies from place to place, based on localized understandings of which properties of materials were appropriate for use in divination.

The deer was an important supernatural being that had ritual association in Maya beliefs and divination (Miller and Taube 1993; Simmons and Sheets 2002; Brown 2009; Looper 2019; see archaeological example in D. Chase and A. Chase 2009, 221). Diego de Landa (Tozzer 1941) observed Maya diviners wearing deer antler headdresses. The Chichan (deersnake) *way* spirit of the Kaanul rulers is sometimes depicted as a man wearing deer antlers and blowing a conch trumpet on codex vases. The cache of twenty-three ceramic figures in the burial of Waka' queen Lady K'abel (Waka' Burial 39) included a figurine of a dwarf wearing a horned deer headdress and blowing through a conch (Freidel and Rich 2018; David Freidel, personal communication, April 2020). Houk and Booher (2020, 167) identify an adult female ritual specialist buried at Chan Chich, Belize, with part of a deer antler headdress, a spindle whorl, and a shell bead.

Linda Brown's (2009) ethnoarchaeological study of Tz'utujil and Kaqchikel hunting shrines around Lake Atitlan notes that community members most frequently identified the white-tailed deer as a sacred animal whose remains should be returned to animal guardians at sacred sites. For the contemporary Huichol of north-central Mexico, shamans can transform themselves into deer and deer can resurrect themselves from their bones. The deer-maize-peyote symbolic complex re-created the "original times" and the Ancient Ones from before the Spaniards invaded (Myerhoff 1970). This broad temporal and geographical review of deer and deer antlers in Mesoamerican belief illustrates broadly held ideas of deer as sacred beings associated with divination and local instantiations of how people living in different times and places drew upon deer symbolism in their sacred worlds.

Patolli is a Mesoamerican dice game played on a board that was simultaneously sacred and profane and could be used in divination (Connell 2000;

Walden and Voorhies 2017; Fitzmaurice et al. 2021; Novotny and Houk 2021). Although patolli is often associated with elites, ethnohistoric sources suggest that commoners also played it (Walden and Voorhies 2017, 198; Fitzmaurice et al. 2021, 63). In the Maya area, patolli boards are typically associated with religious architecture and are located in spatially restricted locations that may underscore their association with divination practices (Walden and Voorhies 2017). Patolli boards are often etched into plaster floors or benches. They feature cross-shaped playing squares that divide the board into four quadrants that are often oriented to the cardinal directions, thus representing the earthly plane and the quadripartite division of the cosmos and the four cardinal directions and the center; the four corners of the board represent the four corners of the world. The act of casting dice in the patolli game was parallel to the casting of the diviner in divination (Edmonson 1967, 201; Walden and Voorhies 2017, 200). Patolli was play that had a purpose (Fitzmaurice et al. 2021).

While some of the paraphernalia of the diviner were perishable items such as seeds, beans, and gourd bowls that would be difficult to identify at archaeological sites with regular preservation, much of the diviner's toolkit would have left material markers in the archaeological record. Identifying the places and materials of divination in the archaeological record is a robust way to track the importance and prevalence of time and divination in the lives of ordinary people and the organization of communities.

## The Maya Farming Community of Chan

Excavations were undertaken at Chan in the period 2002 and 2009 by a team of more than 120 archaeologists, botanists, geologists, geographers, chemists, computer scientists, artists, students, workers, and volunteers from Belize, the United States, England, Canada, and China (Robin 2012, 2013). The project team excavated a 10 percent sample of Chan's households (26 households) and associated agricultural terraces. This sample represents the temporal, socioeconomic, and vocational variability in households at the site. The project also excavated all ritual, residential, and administrative buildings at Chan's community center.

Chan is located in the upper Belize Valley region of west-central Belize in an upland area between the Mopan and Macal branches of the Belize River. Its ancient inhabitants constructed a productive landscape of agricultural terraces surrounding a community center in undulating upland terrain. This agricultural base supported Chan's residents for 2,000 years (800 BCE–1200 CE) that span the major eras of political change in Maya society: the Preclassic (1000 BCE–250 CE), Classic (250–900 CE), and Early Postclassic (900–1200 CE)

Time as Ordinary Practice: A Divination Building at Chan · 259

periods. The scale of the Chan community provides a window into the lives of people who lived in a prehistoric Maya agrarian community. Chan's deep chronology provides a way to examine over time how farmers' lives were both embedded within and significant for Maya society (Robin 2012, 2013).

The Chan community consisted of 274 households and 1,223 agricultural terraces surrounding a community center (fig. 10.1; Robin, Wyatt, et al. 2012). (The Chan research draws upon a definition of a community as both a place and a group of people who create a salient social identity based upon that place [Yaeger and Canuto 2000]). The majority of Chan's residents were farmers (Wyatt 2012). Some residents also produced chert bifaces (Hearth 2012) or limestone blocks (Kestle 2012), and leading residents, who are defined by the size and central location of their residences and their access to elaborate funerary rituals and certain luxury items, were involved in the production and

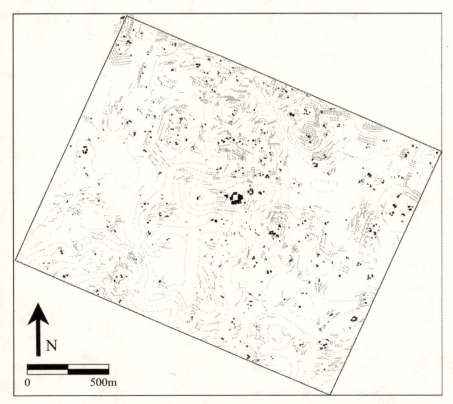

Figure 10.1. Map showing topography, settlement pattern, and agricultural terraces at Chan. Black squares are mounds and gray linear features are agricultural terraces. Ten-meter contour interval. Map created by the Chan Project and René Rivera.

procurement of marine shell and obsidian objects (Keller 2012; Meierhoff et al. 2012).

Agricultural terraces are the most ubiquitous and substantial construction at Chan. Farmers constructed terraces up and down hillslopes and across channels. Agricultural terraces surrounded the homes of farmers, making the farmsteads (or discrete residential and agricultural areas) the basic settlement unit at Chan. All of Chan's residents, from the humblest farmers to community leaders, lived in perishable buildings with thatched roofs constructed above stone substructures.

The community center is located at the spatial and geographical center of the settlement on a high point in the local topography. It consists of two adjoining plazas, the Central Plaza and the West Plaza (fig. 10.2). The Central Plaza is the largest architectural complex at Chan. It was its main location for community-level politics and ceremonial, administrative, and adjudicative events. It was also the location of a residence for Chan's leaders. The adjoining West Plaza is a largely open space that was used for political and ritual events (Cap 2012). On the east and west sides of the Central Plaza are the east and west shrines, Structures 5 and 7 (fig. 10.2). The east shrine, Structure 5, is a

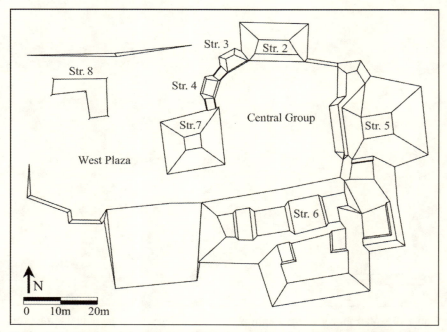

Figure 10.2. Chan's community center showing the location of Structure 6, the divination and administrative building. Map created by the Chan Project and René Rivera.

tripartite structure. The central building of the triad is the tallest structure at Chan (5.6 meters). The west shrine, Structure 7, is a single pyramidal structure. The leaders' residence (Structure 2) is located on the north side of the Central Plaza, as are two ancillary structures (Structures 3 and 4). The administrative and divination building, Structure 6, is located on the south side of the Central Plaza.

## Structure 6, Room 2: A Divination Building

Chan's administrative and divination building (Structure 6) is situated on the south edge of the Central Plaza (Robin, Meierhoff, and Kosakowsky 2012; see also fig. 10.2). The unusually well-preserved architecture and unique array of terminal deposits in the rooms of Structure 6 provide a rare glimpse into the role of divination in a Maya farming community.

This structure is the only vaulted masonry building at Chan. It consists of two buildings, Structure 6 East and Structure 6 West, that were connected by a vaulted passageway and an interior staircase (fig. 10.3). The smaller of the two buildings, Structure 6 West, was heavily looted and only salvage excavations were conducted there. The form of Structure 6 West is comparable to but smaller in scale than that of Structure 6 East. In its final late Late Classic (670–800/830 CE) form, Structure 6 East had twelve vaulted rooms (fig. 10.4). No domestic functions were associated with Structure 6. Ten of the twelve rooms formed part of a tandem-layout *audiencia* range structure with north, south, and interior doorways (Harrison's [1970, 100] type 2 range structure). The south doorways opened to a rear patio bounded by two rooms, one to the east and the other to the west. Ten of the twelve rooms were excavated. Each room contained a substantial bench that took up at least half the floor area and was elevated to a height of 60 centimeters. A patolli board was inscribed into the floors of Rooms 2 and 5, and horizontal and vertical lines, often called graffiti in the Maya area, were incised into the south wall of Room 2 (Meierhoff and Miller 2005). Additionally, five holes in a quincunx pattern were placed in the floor of Room 2 (see fig. 10.4). In Room 2, the incised wall designs are adjacent to the quincunx holes and the patolli board is east of the holes. The patolli boards are Type II cross-and-frame boards, the most common type of patolli boards in the Maya area. They consist of an exterior square frame made up of individual playing squares that encloses an interior cross marked with more playing squares. In their study of Maya patolli boards, Walden and Voorhies (2017) identified that 37% of Maya patolli boards, including the Chan examples, are associated with graffiti (incised wall designs).

Figure 10.3. Vaulted passageway and interior stair between Structure 6 east and Structure 6 west. Photo by James Meierhoff.

Figure 10.4. Structure 6 east showing six of twelve rooms. The five quincunx holes of room 2 are visible. Structure 6 west can be seen in the background. Photo by James Meierhoff.

To illustrate how Structure 6 functioned in terms of administration and divination in the Chan community, I highlight Rooms 1 and 2, its two central rooms (fig. 10.5; Meierhoff and Miller 2005). Room 1 (located in the center front of Structure 6) and Room 2 (located in the rear) are the two largest rooms in the building and are joined by a doorway that was partly filled in at some point in the history of the rooms' use. Room 1 measures 3.8 meters by 0.9 meters in its interior dimension and has three front doorways opening onto two long benches. No terminal deposits were found on the floor of Room 1. In form, Room 1 is similar to an *audiencia*—a place where Chan's leaders could have held meetings and settled disputes. Benches in other smaller rooms in Structure 6 may have served as meeting places for smaller groups of people.

Like Room 1, Room 2 of Structure 6 measures 3.8 meters by 0.9 meters in its interior dimension, but it is unique in that it is the only room in the structure that has internal divisions. Room 2 is also exceptional at Chan because of its terminal deposits, which contained an array of objects not identified in terminal deposits elsewhere at the site. At the end of its use life, Room 2 was covered with a lens of fine *sascab,* suggesting that particularly special care and attention was taken at the end of its use life to "bury" this room. The unique architecture and terminal assemblages of Room 2 identify this room as a diviner's room.

Three narrow interior masonry walls or screens divide the space of Room 2 into three areas. The floors and benches in each of the three subdivisions differed in height. Multiple interior dividing walls and differing floor and bench elevations made it more physically complex to move around in Room 2. The unique division of space and multiple levels in Room 2 may have referenced the three levels of the universe—the earth, the sky, and the underworld.

The architecture of Room 2 had both cosmological and practical implications for the movement of a person entering the room. This can be gleaned by comparing the layouts of Rooms 1 and 2 in figure 10.5. Rooms 1 and 2 have the same overall interior dimensions, 3.8 meters by 0.9 meters. Three doorways allow entry into the *audiencia,* Room 1. Once a person entered one of the doorways, they were standing on a single-level floor and the person could walk the length or breadth of the room on that surface. From the point where a person entered Room 1, regardless of which of the three doorways the person used, they could see the entirety of the room, its two benches, and any person sitting or performing an activity on one of the benches. While Rooms 1 and 2 are larger than the other rooms in Structure 6 (see figs. 10.4 and 10.5), the layout of Room 1 is comparable to the layout of other rooms in Structure 6 and to the layout of other ritual and residential rooms at Chan. In a typical interior room layout at Chan, a person would enter a single doorway

Figure 10.5. Rooms 1 and 2, the two central rooms of Structure 6 east. The east, central, and west divisions of room 2 are marked. Two of five quincunx holes are visible in the floor of the west division of room 2. Photo by James Meierhoff.

into a room into a space with no interior subdivisions and a single-level floor for the entire room.

The way the architecture of Room 2 channeled movement and vision was quite different (see fig. 10.5). There was only one doorway to Room 2. When a person entered that doorway, they immediately encountered a masonry wall on their left that would block their movement and their view of the five quincunx holes, the incised wall designs, and the patolli board, all of which were located in the west division of Room 2. In order to gain access to the west division of the room, the person would have to take two steps up to a height of 60 centimeters, walk forward, and turn to the left to maneuver past the wall.

Alternatively, the person entering Room 2 could turn to their right, where they would have full view of the central division of the room but would encounter another wall at the east side of the central division of the room that would block their view of the east division of the room. They would have to step up to enter the east division, an area that had two different floor levels. Both movement and vision are restricted in Room 2 in ways that they are not in Room 1 or in other civic, religious, and residential rooms at Chan.

The west division of Room 2 has the highest floor and bench elevations and consists almost entirely of a raised bench area. The five holes in the quincunx pattern were cut into this bench, a patolli board was etched into the bench surface east of the quincunx holes, and horizontal and vertical lines were incised into the south wall of the room adjacent to the five holes. The holes and the patolli board were oriented to the cardinal directions, representing Maya spatiotemporality on the earthly plane of the four cardinal directions plus the center, locating the points of the rising and setting of the sun on the earth and the duration of the day, invoking earthly, celestial, and cosmological time. Contextualized in association with the deposits in the central and eastern divisions of Room 2, the patolli board and incised-line designs likely formed components of a diviner's workplace. In this context, the patolli board indicates the performative aspect of the divination that took place in Room 2. It provided a fixed physical space within the west division of Room 2 to play a game associated with divination. This fixed physical space was directly associated with and adjacent to the representation of the quincunx and the incised wall designs.

The association of a patolli board and incised wall designs at Chan is intriguing because this association is also seen at the nearby polity capital of Xunantunich (Fitzmaurice et al. 2021; chapter 11, this volume) and for 37 percent of the patolli boards identified in the Maya area (Walden and Voorhies 2017). The incised wall designs at Chan consist of horizontal, vertical, and angled lines that sometimes intersect. Most of the incisions are solid lines, but some are dashed lines. The designs are geometric and indeterminate. Only a portion of the south wall of Room 2 that contained the incised wall designs was preserved. The preserved incised wall designs were presumably part of a larger group of design elements. Although we can't be sure what the incised wall designs represent at Chan, their contextual association is clear. Just as Brown and colleagues argue for the much more elaborate and extensive incised wall designs at Xunantunich (see chapter 11), the incised wall designs in Room 2 of Structure 6 at Chan may have conveyed sacred meanings. Given their contextual associations, they were certainly not doodles, as one early researcher theorized (Thompson 1954, 10).

The central division of Room 2 has the lowest floor elevation. A terminal deposit terminating the use of Room 2 that dates to the Terminal Classic period was located on the bench in this room. It consists of a pile of 548 jutes (shells of edible snails) covering a spindle whorl next to a broken pedestal base from a Roaring Creek Red vessel that had been reworked as a cord holder (fig. 10.6; Kosakowsky 2012). The jute pile, spindle whorl, and pedestal

Figure 10.6. Terminal deposit on bench floor of central division of room 2 in Structure 6 east. Jute shells are next to a pedestal base from a Roaring Creek Red vessel reworked as a cord holder. The shells are on top of a spindle whorl that is not visible in the photograph. Photo by Alexandra Miller.

base may have been part of a diviner's toolkit. At Chan, jutes not only were a source of food but were also used in ritual practices (Cap 2012; Keller 2012). The jutes in the central division of Room 2 may have been used similarly to the found seashells that Tz'utujil ritual practitioners collected as part of their ritual toolkits (Brown 2000, 327; see also Douglas 1969, 138). In Maya beliefs, God N, called Mam, inhabits a snail shell (Coe 1973; Milbrath and Walker 2016a). At Late Postclassic Santa Rita, cache vessels from Structures 36 and 216 depict jaguars and deity heads emerging from snail shells (D. Chase and A. Chase 2008).

Snail shells are potent symbols across Maya history, and at Chan there was particular ritual relevance for jute shells. Two large deposits of jute shells, a higher-density deposit roughly 100 square meters in area and a lower-density deposit roughly 125 square meters in area, were located between Chan's Central Plaza and the adjacent residences of leaders (Keller 2012, 257–260). Given the average density is 46,000 jutes per cubic meter in the deposits, Keller estimates that the entire deposit contains at least 2.7 million jutes. Using Healy and colleagues' (1990) nutritional data, the jute deposits contain roughly 23,000 meals of 500 calories each, well beyond the consumption needs of a family. Keller proposes that the jute deposits are the remains of community feasts. Ceramics associated with the jute deposits suggest that they were reworked or redeposited secondary middens placed in the location where they were identified in the Late Classic period. However, the jutes, which were intermixed with highly eroded sherds that date to the Middle to Late Preclassic, were likely originally consumed in those earlier periods (Kosakowksy 2007, 13; Keller 2012, 258). The Late Classic period when Chan's residents were undertaking the massive reworking or redepositing of the jutes, forming what Keller (2012, 259) refers to as an enormous sea of jutes, was the period when Room 2 of Structure 6 was used. Diviners at Chan may have chosen old jutes with what they deemed to be supernatural qualities for their toolkits.

Similarly, just as contemporary Maya diviners use pre-Columbian spindle whorls as divination tools, Chan's diviners may have used the spindle whorl identified with the jute shells in Room 2 as a divination tool. The broken and reworked pedestal base may also have been a divination object. Jutes, spindle whorls, and broken ceramics could have been the locally potent small objects that diviners at Chan chose for divination. Intriguingly, while diviners at Cerén curated a larger range of small items for their divination toolkits, shell, spindle whorls, and broken ceramics were among the items that Cerén's diviners included in their divination toolkits.

The east division of Room 2 has floors with two different elevations and no bench. A Terminal Classic cache containing six fragments of the antlers of white-tailed deer and two chert bifaces, one broken and one whole, was interred in the north floor in the east division of Room 2. The deer antler cached in the east division of Room 2 may have been part of a deer antler headdress worn by a diviner that used Room 2, similar to the deer antler headdresses Diego de Landa (Tozzer 1941) observed diviners wearing, the deer antler headdress of the female ritual specialist at Chan Chich (Houk and Booher 2020), the headdress seen on the Chichan (deersnake) *way* spirit of the Kaanul rulers, or the dwarf in the burial cache of the Waka' queen Lady K'abel (Freidel and Rich 2018; David Freidel, personal communication, April 2020). At the divination building at Cerén, white-tailed deer antler, interpreted as the remains of a diviner's headdress, were stored in a niche with other divination paraphernalia (Brown 2000; Simmons and Sheets 2002).

The architecture and artifact assemblages of Room 2 of Structure 6 suggest that this room was a diviner's room. The diviner working there could have communicated with the leaders who were meeting in Room 1 through the doorway that connected the two rooms. In this way, divination may have been directly tied to the resolution of issues of community interest and the settling of disputes.

## Comparing Civic and Divination Architecture at Chan and Cerén

The administrative and divinatory assemblages at Structure 6 at Chan are strikingly similar to those in Structures 3, 13, and 12 at Cerén. Room 1 of Structure 6 at Chan is comparable to Structures 3 and 13 at Cerén, which Andrea Gerstle (2002) identifies as Cerén's civic complex. Gerstle did not discern any residential functions for Structures 3 and 13. Structure 3 is the largest building at Cerén, and both structures represent uncommon constructions at the site. They feature rammed-earth wall construction, large benches in their front rooms, and few associated artifacts. Structure 12, the divination building at Cerén (Simmons and Sheets 2002), has strong parallels with Room 2 of Structure 6 at Chan.

The architecture and deposits at Structure 12 at Cerén present strong parallels to those at Chan. Just as Room 2 of Structure 6 is divided into three areas, Structure 12 at Cerén is divided into three rooms. Scott Simmons and Payson Sheets (2002) likened this unusual tripartite division to a representation of the three levels of the Maya world: the earth, sky, and underworld.

Like Room 2 of Structure 6 at Chan, Structure 12 at Cerén is one of the most architecturally complex constructions at the site. It has numerous interior walls, steps, and changing floor elevations that made physical movement more complex than within other structures. Simmons and Sheets (2002) suggest that narrow passageways and changing floor levels made the space feel like a cave, a key spiritual place in Maya sacred geography.

The artifacts in Structure 12 at Cerén constitute one of the most unusual collections of objects found anywhere at the site. There are striking similarities between the artifact assemblages at Structure 12 and in Room 2 of Structure 6 at Chan. White-tailed deer antler was found in a niche in Structure 12 along with 6 beans, 3 fragments of *Spondylus* shell, a female figurine, a ceramic animal head, and half of a ceramic double ring (Brown 2000; Simmons and Sheets 2002). Simmons and Sheets (2002) interpret the deer antler as potentially part of a diviner's headdress; it was located in a niche along with other divination material. In Structure 12, two piles of beans were found on a floor, which Simmons and Sheets (2002) liken to the beans that modern Maya shamans use in divination and curing ceremonies. The beans, preserved because of the unique conditions at Cerén, may be casting paraphernalia, like the jutes and spindle whorl in Room 2 of Structure 6. Other groupings of small objects stored in niches or elevated wall contexts in Structure 12 include obsidian tools, a greenstone disk, a miniature frog effigy, spindle whorls, a polychrome sherd, unmodified mineral crystals, *Spondylus* fragments, and two gourds (Brown 2000). Based on the use wear on all of the small objects stored in Structure 12, Linda Brown identifies them as used, worn, and chosen objects. The size of the objects in comparison to the size of the objects contemporary Maya diviners use suggests to Brown that the small worn objects stored in Structure 12 were part of a diviner's toolkit.

The identification of a female figurine and spindle whorls, textile production tools often associated with Maya women and female deities, with the deer antler at Structure 12 led Sweely (1999) and Brown and Sheets (2000) to posit that the diviner working in Structure 12 was a woman. This possibility gains further resonance in light of Houk and Booher's (2020) identification of the burial of an adult female ritual specialist at Chan Chich that included deer antler, a spindle whorl, and a shell bead. Shell was also part of the toolkit of the diviner at Structure 12. At Chan, deer antler, a spindle whorl, and shell were also associated with each other and were part of a diviner's tool kit. The association of deer antler, spindle whorls, and shell with a female burial at Chan Chich and a female figurine at Cerén prompts consideration of the gender of pre-Columbian diviners.

## Conclusions

There are remarkable parallels between the divination buildings at Chan and at Cerén. Unique and parallel aspects of architecture and artifact assemblages at Structure 6 at Chan and Structure 12 at Cerén suggest that these buildings were used for divination. These buildings were focal elements of these two farming communities. Chan's divination room directly accessed the largest meeting room—or *audiencia*—in its main civic building, linking divination and adjudication in the organization of the community. This is similar to the description Diego de Landa (Tozzer 1941) gave of a prophet in a small room next to a council meeting.

The diviners at Chan and Cerén likely wore deer antler headdresses in some of their ceremonies—just as Diego de Landa observed diviners wearing deer antler headdresses at the time of the Spanish invasion. The diviners at Chan and Cerén worked in architecturally unique and complex buildings in which interior walls, steps, and changing floor elevations made physical movement more complex than in other structures, enhancing and mysticizing the experience of the divination process for the observer.

The divination buildings at Chan and Cerén were built to encapsulate Maya models of time and the cosmological structure of the world. The tripartite division of these buildings may be representations of the three levels of the Maya world: the earth, sky, and underworld. At Chan, the five quincunx holes and the patolli board in Room 2 of Structure 6 represent another division of the Maya world into the four cardinal directions plus the center. The sun cycled across these divisions—earth, sky, and underworld and north, south, east, west, and center—and passed the days. Thus, the divination buildings at Chan and Cerén were visual representations of the Maya cosmos and Maya time. Diviners at Chan and Cerén cast small objects that were often found and already used; they could be beans, seeds, minerals, shells, spindle whorls, or broken ceramics to further materialize the time that architecturally encompassed their craft. At Chan, diviners appear to have been directly linked through a doorway to community leaders who would have met in an *audiencia*-style room, linking the craft of divination and the administration of the community.

## Acknowledgments

I thank all the members of the Chan project and Belize Institute of Archaeology for their work on the Chan research, without which this chapter would not have been possible. The Chan project was funded by a National Science

Foundation Senior Archaeology Grant (2004: BCS-0314686) and a National Science Foundation International Research Fellowship (2003: INT-0303713), a National Endowment for the Humanities Collaborative Research Grant (2007:RZ-50804-07), a National Geographic Society Grant (2002), an H. John Heinz III Fund Grant for Archaeological Field Research in Latin America (2002), two anonymous donations, three University Research Grants from Northwestern University (2002, 2005, 2009), two Alumnae Foundation Grants from Northwestern University (2002, 2006), and an AT&T Research Scholar award (2005).

# 11

## The Chamber of Secrets at Xunantunich

M. KATHRYN BROWN, LEAH MCCURDY,
AND JASON YAEGER

Sacred knowledge played a key role in ancient Maya religion and politics, providing important foundations for social differentiation and the institution of kingship. Political authority was maintained and legitimized through privileged access to sacred knowledge and was reinforced through performance, symbol-laden art programs, and written records (Freidel and Schele 1988a; Schele and Freidel 1990; Inomata 2006). Thus, ancient Maya sages, scribes, and artists played important roles in Maya civilization because of their roles as keepers of time, history, and sacred knowledge (Coe 1973; Rossi 2018; chapter 8, this volume; chapter 9, this volume). Their domain included the critical technologies of writing and symbolic representation that were required for the materialization of time and history in text and image.

In this chapter, we discuss recent discoveries from the Classic Maya site of Xunantunich, Belize. We describe a vaulted building, Structure A-5-2nd, that bears over 400 designs incised into the plastered surfaces of the exterior and interior walls and the benches of two excavated rooms. We examine the content, context, variability, and spatial patterning of this corpus of designs to argue that these designs—often called graffiti—indicate that the structure was used for specialized training of young nobles. We also suggest that Structures C-2 and C-3, just south of El Castillo, may represent the residential complex that housed the young men in training.

### Sacred Knowledge, Political Authority, and Civilization

Arcane knowledge was one of the cornerstones of ancient civilizations. The concepts and mysteries of religion—including ontologies, cosmologies, and mythologies—formed the ideological foundations of ancient political systems and social orders (Baines and Yoffee 1998; Flannery and Marcus 2012). These ideologies were expressed, legitimized, embodied, and reproduced through performances and ritual actions (Inomata 2006), and they were materialized in material culture, art, and architecture (DeMarrais et al. 1996).

To be politically efficacious in constituting a political order, some ideological aspects of religion must be widely understood and meaningful to a broad swath of society. Differential understanding and knowledge of sacra, however, can also be a key dimension of social differentiation, one that sets the possessors of certain knowledge apart from those not privy to those arcane secrets. This is true not only of the knowledge itself but also of the attendant technologies—such as writing and iconographic symbolism—that are used to materialize that knowledge and convey it to others.

In ancient societies around the world, religion was often central to the development of social hierarchies and political complexity as emerging rulers legitimized their political authority by arguing they had closer connections to more powerful forces (deities, spirits, ancestors, etc.) that influenced events in the world (Flannery and Marcus 2012). Those connections could be anchored in kinship and descent relations, control of key sacred spaces, and/or access to key materials and objects, but they were activated by knowledge of proper ritual actions and incantations. It should not be surprising that sacred knowledge was important to social differentiation as early hierarchical societies grew more complex.

In Maya civilization, religion was one of the central pillars of the authority of divine kings and queens (*ajawtaak*) (Freidel and Schele 1988a; McAnany 2001; Brown et al. 2018; Saturno et al. 2018) and of the development of divine kingship, particularly the ruler's divine nature (Houston and Stuart 1996; Stuart 1996; Freidel 2008). This authority was expressed and reinforced in elaborate imagery in public art and architecture that was dense with symbols and was often accompanied by hieroglyphic texts (e.g., Saturno 2009; Estrada-Belli 2011). These images and texts not only legitimated the authority of the current *k'uhul ajaw* but also anchored his or her rightful rulership in the line of divine kings and queens extending back to the founding of that royal house.

Artists depicted politically powerful events and histories in art and imagery. Scribes recorded important events—from contemporary and recent events to the cosmogonic acts at the dawn of time—in texts on durable and perishable media. Maya architects created sacred spaces (e.g., plazas, temples, ball courts, E Groups) in which historical events could be celebrated, important ancestors could be commemorated, and mythological events from the time of creation could be reenacted and thus reinstantiated. Through their efforts, time and history were materialized, made tangible and durable, and inscribed in objects, buildings, sites, and landscapes. As Chase et al. (chapter 1, this volume) state, "Time was something to be commemorated, to be vocationally derived through divination, or to be promulgated by leaders as prophecy."

Royal authority was also expressed and reinforced through public and private rituals. For these rituals to be effective, the participants had to enact the proper sequence of actions and incantations using the requisite materials and objects. This important information was likely guarded jealously and had to be conveyed from generation to generation.

Rituals are fleeting and ephemeral, however. That is why sages, artists, and scribes—the keepers of time, history, and sacred knowledge and the masters of technologies for inscribing them in more enduring media—played an integral role in Classic Maya royal courts. Arcane knowledge was fundamental to Maya politics and religion. It also served as a key way to distinguish the elite from the rest of society. Yet the ways this knowledge was transferred from one generation to the next remains understudied.

Specialized knowledge of Maya ideology and other sacra was likely acquired through years of schooling, and the ability to represent that knowledge materially took intensive training and practice. Given the importance of sages, scribes, and artists in Maya society, it is important we understand how this knowledge and the skills to represent it were transferred from one generation to the next. As Franco Rossi (2017, 2) asserts, "Understanding how particular forms of knowledge are created, defined, controlled and dispersed through institutions and pedagogical processes constitutes a vital anthropological approach for examining how power, systems of inequality, cultural difference and structures of violence are produced, normalized and reinforced in societies across time."

An informative analogy for formal education in pre-Columbian Mesoamerica is the Late Postclassic Aztec *calmecac* (Calnek 1988; Berdan 2014). Early Spanish chroniclers describe it as an academy where noble children and talented commoners were schooled in both sacred knowledge (religion, ritual, reading, writing, and the calendar) and military tactics (Berdan 2014).

It has been challenging to identify the spaces where instruction took place in pre-Columbian sites, however. Peter Harrison (1970) argues that several of the buildings in the Central Acropolis at Tikal likely functioned as schools to train young nobles. The recent work at the site of Xultun, Guatemala, provides a compelling archaeological example of a place of instruction (chapter 9, this volume). In that case, a room with painted murals and calendar notations incised in the walls provides very strong evidence of noble training and educational practices (Rossi 2017). Structure 1A-Sub at Balamkú, Mexico, was another space that likely functioned as a formal place of learning (chapter 8, this volume).

In this chapter, we argue that one of the vaulted buildings on the El Castillo acropolis at the Classic Maya site of Xunantunich was a space where young Maya people, presumably elite individuals, learned arcane knowledge during the Late Classic Hats' Chahk period (670–780 CE). Our excavation of two rooms of Structure A-5-2nd revealed several hundred incised images and designs that range from simple etchings to masterful renderings.

We begin by reviewing the literature on the images incised in the plaster walls of palaces and temples. These were labeled as graffiti early in the history of Maya archaeology because they are often inexpertly executed. While this enduring label may be true to the origins of the term in art history to refer to texts and images scratched into hard surfaces, it is unfortunate, as it often connotes irreverence and vandalism to modern readers. These connotations are not consistent with our understanding of Classic Maya graffiti (e.g., Haviland and de Laguna Haviland 1995; Źrałka 2014). Here, we build on arguments that Scott Hutson (2011) and other scholars have made that many of these incised images were made by children, but we further argue that in at least some contexts, graffiti reflects the transfer of arcane knowledge across generations.

We argue that Structure A-5-2nd was a place of instruction of arcane knowledge and religious symbolism. We marshal several lines of evidence to support this interpretation: (1) the nature of the incised designs, which include sacred symbols; hieroglyphs; depictions of animals, sages, warriors, and ballplayers; depictions of architecture; and depictions of sacrifice scenes and bloodletting; (2) the range of skill evinced in the execution of the designs, which vary from crude renderings of phalluses and profiles to a masterfully incised depiction of Chak Xib Chahk (Christophe Helmke, personal communication, 2017); (3) the clustered repetition of designs that may indicate practicing and copying; (4) the division of walls into gridded spaces; and (5) the fact that many of the images were marked with a gouged X, possibly an assessment or form of termination of the image. We argue that the interior walls of the rooms and the exterior surfaces of the building served as canvases for sketching, artistic training, and learned scribal expression. Of particular salience to our interpretation, an incised glyph that reads *itz'at* (wiseman or sage) was incised on the plastered wall of one of the rooms of Structure A-5-2nd (Christophe Helmke, personal communication, 2017; Helmke and Źrałka 2021; McCurdy et al. 2018) (fig. 11.1c).

We also argue that a complex in Group C, just south of El Castillo, served as the living quarters for young nobles who were being taught at El Castillo. The presence of two long, simple range structures with tall interior benches; the presence of incised images and patolli boards in the rooms; a broad plastered surface ideal for dances and drills; and an adjacent sweat bath all support this interpretation.

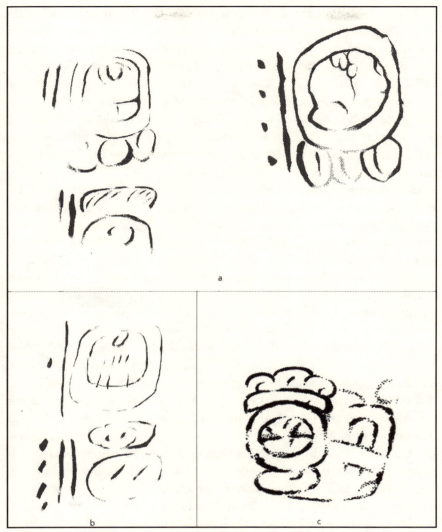

Figure 11.1. Hieroglyphs incised in Structure A-5-2nd: (*a*) Grouping including a Calendar Round date and an isolated Tzolk'in date in Room 2; (*b*) Calendar Round date in Room 2; (*c*) *itz'at* glyph in Room 1. Drawings by Christophe Helmke.

## Studies of Ancient Maya "Graffiti"

In this chapter, we use the term "graffiti" to describe a range of designs and graphic elements incised into plaster surfaces ranging from simple sketches to more formal, detailed renderings. We use the term sparingly, in part because of the negative connotations it carries. Incised designs referred to as graffiti have been documented at many sites across the Maya lowlands, including Tikal, Rio Bec, La Blanca, Nakum, Holmul, and Xunantunich. Maya graffiti have often been defined as crude or haphazard incising on plaster surfaces such as interior and exterior walls, doorjambs, and benches. Cristina Vidal Lorenzo and Gaspar Muñoz Cosme's 2009 edited volume *Los grafitos mayas* provides a comprehensive overview of graffiti in the Maya lowlands. Additionally, a recent publication by Jarosław Źrałka (2014) presents a detailed history of the documentation of ancient Maya graffiti. Here we provide a brief overview of the study of this form of expression and present a few of the ways scholars have interpreted graffiti.

Early interpretations of graffiti focused on the unrefined nature of the designs and a perceived lack of foresight or planning in their execution. Edward H. Thompson and George Dorsey (1898) suggested that graffiti was drawn by "some young idler," raising themes subsequent scholars echoed. J. Eric S. Thompson (1954, 10) suggested that graffiti was the result of "doodling" by "bored or inattentive novices" or was made by Maya novices before an initiation ceremony. These early considerations represent graffiti as unplanned, isolated renderings that were executed by individuals and were not part of a larger program or institution.

Helen Webster, an artist and staff member on the Tikal Project in 1962–1963, recorded images of graffiti at the site. Her preliminary interpretations are intriguing, especially given her perspective as a trained artist. She suggested that the graffiti were not intended to be formal wall decorations due to the variable spacing and lack of continuity of design. Webster (1963, 39) noted that on occasion, graffiti "convey an understandable story," an interpretation that resonates with our view that some graffiti may have been used to teach important historical events. She described two broad categories of graffiti, "descriptive or demonstrative drawings" and "pictorial offerings to the gods." She argued that the descriptive drawings may have been made by "priests or officials demonstrating costumes, headdresses, thrones, temples, standards, and other ceremonial regalia, as well as important dates, all of which could have been used for instruction." Although she does not elaborate on this statement, it is interesting to note that she connects the graffiti to instruction. Furthermore, she suggests that some graffiti "could have a very special and individual significance in the promulgation of magic," an interpretation with which we agree.

Another important study at Tikal resonates with our argument that some graffiti represent the transfer of arcane knowledge. Peter Harrison's (1970) study of the Central Acropolis is noteworthy because he suggested that some buildings may represent schools, based on their architectural form and the presence of graffiti. Using the Aztec analogy of the *telpochcalli*, a school for commoner male children (see Calnek 1988), Harrison suggested that some of the tandem plan structures in the Central Acropolis may have functioned as a boys' house and school. He suggested that the graffiti, which include patolli boards incised on benches, supported his interpretation that some of these buildings may have functioned as places of instruction. Harrison (1970) also examined architectural features of these buildings, including benches, to support this interpretation. Finally, he made connections between the architectural features in the Central Acropolis and the Aztec *calmecac*, a religious school for young nobles. He notes that the graffiti on the walls of these buildings have esoteric and ceremonial content.

Kampen's (1978) slightly later assessment of the graffiti from Tikal focused more on the unrefined nature of the images. He argued that at "every stage of conception and execution, the graffiti appear to lack the logical and organized principles of construction characterizing other varieties of Maya art" (167; see also Trik and Kampen 1983). He suggested that most of the Tikal graffiti were terminal acts of desecration of abandoned structures, an interpretation that is more aligned with modern connotations of the term graffiti. He argued that examples found in sealed contexts dating to the Classic period represented terminal acts after the buildings were no longer in formal use and that examples in final-phase, unfilled rooms were the work of later people who lived at the site in the Eznab phase (850–925 CE). Although this may be the case in some instances, other explanations are more compelling, given that much of the final-phase graffiti has Classic period iconography. Although Kampen (1978, 169) recognized this, he asserted that "the fact that certain themes and motifs of Late Classic art appear in the graffiti in no way proves contemporaneity."

While it is plausible that some graffiti may represent desecration by post-abandonment squatters, we do not find this to be a convincing explanation for most examples of graffiti. Furthermore, this explanation, in our opinion, is somewhat problematic because it forecloses the need for further inquiry to understand the nature of Maya graffiti.

More recent interpretations have moved beyond these early explanations. Haviland and Haviland (1995) applied a psychological lens to graffiti and its production, suggesting that the haphazard nature and inferior quality derives from the mental/psychological state of the artists. They argued that graffiti was produced as part of hallucinatory trances and was most likely created by high-status people in secluded interiors. Building on their work, Jason Yaeger (2010) suggested that some of the graffiti found in Structure A-11 in the Late Classic palace at Xunantunich were products of this type of ritual behavior.

Scott Hutson (2011) argued that scholars should consider graffiti as a subset of Maya expression. He provided a detailed summary of previous explanations that emphasized the "crudeness" of graffiti. First, he discussed the possibility that graffiti were preliminary sketches that Maya artists created as they prepared to make more formal works of art. Second, Hutson considered the arguments of Kampen (1978) and others that graffiti represented decadent art of post-abandonment squatters. Third, Hutson examined Haviland and Haviland's (1995) hypothesis that these marks were representations of hallucinations that individuals saw while in trance states. Last, Hutson focused on the possibility that the crudeness of graffiti was due to the young age of its creators, who lacked experience and/or training. Hutson favors this last hypothesis, arguing that many examples of graffiti were created by ancient Maya children. He also makes a very important observation: "People of different ages and skill levels left their marks on the same walls and . . . there was a dialogue between these different artists" (2011, 404). This interpretation is consistent with our argument. We interpret the range of skill in the execution in the corpus of graffiti in Structure A-5-2nd as a pedagogical dialogue between accomplished artists and knowledgeable sages and their less skilled pupils. Hutson's groundbreaking article and interpretations move us toward a more nuanced understanding of graffiti and a framework for more systematic analysis.

Another important and detailed recent study by Jarosław Źrałka (2014) provides a comprehensive look at graffiti across the Maya lowlands. He distinguishes four stylistic categories of Maya graffiti. His first category is "crude style graffiti," which includes rudimentary representations that are often difficult to identify. His second group are those in "classic or typical graffiti style." Although the graffiti of this group are simple, he suggests that they are typically of higher quality. His third category is "fine style graffiti," which includes examples that exhibit delicate lines and affinities to more formal art seen in other media such as painted vases, murals, and carved monuments. Graffiti in this category were made by skilled artists that had "knowledge of the canons in official codified art." Źrałka's fourth stylistic group of graffiti refers to examples that appear to be "foreign" or "Mexicanized."

Źrałka notes the variation in the kinds of graffiti, the skill levels of the producers, and the contexts in which graffiti is found. He suggests that "such diversity reflects the wide variety of the authors of graffiti: from children to old people, from well-trained and presumed artists to those who had no artistic capacities" (Źrałka 2014, 225). He further argues that graffiti constitutes personal acts of individual expression that were not meant to be widely viewed. He and other scholars have noted that much Classic Maya graffiti relates to members of the elite class and includes scenes of processions, religious ceremonies, and political meetings, themes that are also commonly depicted on painted polychrome vessels and carved monuments. These scenes demonstrate that the authors were well versed in Maya high culture.

## Xunantunich, El Castillo, and Structure A-5-2nd

The Maya site of Xunantunich is located in the Mopan River valley in the modern country of Belize. Xunantunich has a long history of occupation that ranged from the Preclassic to the Terminal Classic period (Brown 2017; LeCount and Yaeger 2010a; Brown and Yaeger 2020). The Late Classic ceremonial core covers a ridgetop overlooking the valley (fig. 11.2). Sitting at the center of the site's cruciform layout is a massive acropolis referred to as El Castillo, whose tallest structure, Structure A-6, rises 39 meters above the adjacent plaza. El Castillo is the result of a long history of occupation and construction that began in the Cunil phase around 1000 BCE (LeCount and Yaeger 2010a; Leventhal 2010; McCurdy 2016). While there is modest evidence of Preclassic and Early Classic construction, the greatest investment in architectural labor at El Castillo was made during the Late Classic Samal phase (600–670 CE) (McCurdy 2016). This marks the establishment of Xunantunich as an important political center in the Mopan Valley. It was likely a subordinate ally of the larger kingdom of Naranjo, located 14 kilometers to the northwest, and a rival of Buenavista de Cayo, located 5 kilometers farther north in the Mopan Valley (Houston et al. 1992; Taschek and Ball 1992; Leventhal and Ashmore 2004; LeCount and Yaeger 2010b; Helmke and Awe 2012, 2016b; Brown and Yaeger 2020; LeCount et al., forthcoming).

During the Samal phase, El Castillo consisted of a series of vaulted structures surrounding at least two patios that flanked a pyramidal structure, Structure A-6-3rd. These all rested on a massive elevated platform that had a footprint 80 meters by 100 meters and was 8 meters tall, forming the Medial Terrace of the acropolis (Leventhal 2010; McCurdy 2016). Leventhal (2010) has argued that this complex served as the residence of the ruler and the administrative center of the polity during this period.

During the Hats' Chaak phase (670–780 CE), El Castillo was expanded significantly. The Maya buried earlier courtyards, built new structures, and encased Structure A-6-3rd in Structure A-6-2nd (Leventhal 2010; McCurdy 2016). During this period, the ceremonial core at Xunantunich expanded significantly: the Plaza A-III palace complex was built, new pyramidal structures were built that flanked the site's main plaza, and new construction took place in Groups B, C, and D.

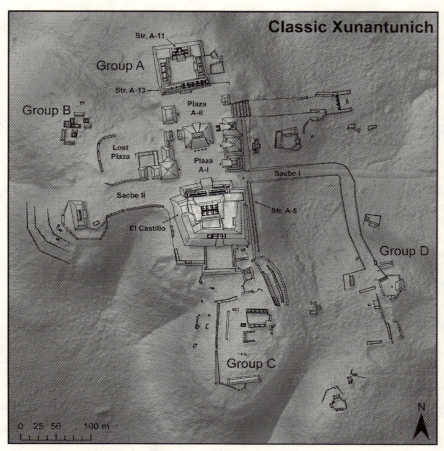

Figure 11.2. Map of Xunantunich.

LeCount and Yaeger (2010b) have argued that this rapid expansion accompanied a change in Xunantunich's relationship with Naranjo, from subordinate ally to incorporated province. In the late sixth and seventh centuries, the kings of Naranjo had forged alliances with Xunantunich, Buenavista, Cahal Pech, Baking Pot, and other polities in the Belize River Valley so they could access the products of the valley's rich alluvial soils and ensure access to a critical riverine route to the Caribbean Sea (Helmke et al. 2010; LeCount and Yaeger 2010b; Helmke and Awe 2012). By taking control of Xunantunich, Naranjo sought to solidify its control into the Mopan Valley (LeCount and Yaeger 2010b).

The new quadrangle of range structures surrounding Plaza A-III likely served as the residential and administrative focus for the new provincial

The Chamber of Secrets at Xunantunich · 283

governor (Leventhal 2010; Yaeger 2010). El Castillo likely retained important administrative functions, however. Its ideological and political importance is suggested by its central location in the site plan and the elaborate stucco frieze decorating the façade of Structure A-6-2nd (Satterthwaite 1950; Fields 2004; Brown and Yaeger 2020).

## Structure A-5-2nd

In this chapter, our focus is Structure A-5-2nd, a vaulted building located on the northeast corner of El Castillo. In the early 2000s, the remnants of the building's eastern exterior face were exposed and consolidated by the Tourism Development Project, directed by Jaime Awe, as were the building's three north-facing rooms (McCurdy 2016). Those rooms had been exposed and cleaned sometime before the Xunantunich Archaeological Project began in 1991. Any incised designs that might have been present on the plaster were not reported, and the plaster on the walls has long since eroded because the vaulted roof was not preserved on the building's northern range.

In 2012 and 2013, McCurdy (2016) exposed the southeast corner of Structure A-5-2nd, which she called the Tut Building, and followed its southern exterior face to expose the easternmost doorway, which was filled in with large, roughly stacked masonry blocks. McCurdy documented a number of incised images on the doorjambs of Structure A-5-2nd (McCurdy 2016, 633–635). She also excavated a narrow stairway that led from Structure A-5-2nd down to the terrace that runs along the east side of El Castillo. In contrast to the broad, highly visible central staircases that provided the primary access to El Castillo from Plaza A-I on its north, this small stairway was hidden from view of people in the site's main plaza, suggesting it may have had a special function (McCurdy 2016; McCurdy et al. 2018).

Over the course of three field seasons beginning in 2016, we excavated and documented the eastern (Room 1) and central (Room 2) rooms of the structure's southern range and the exterior of the building below the medial molding from its southeast corner to the western jamb of the central doorway. The architecture exposed by previous researchers and our excavations have enabled us to reconstruct Structure A-5-2nd as a masonry structure with two vaulted ranges running east-west, each with three rooms. McCurdy's excavations demonstrate that the structure was likely built early in the Hats' Chaak phase (McCurdy 2016).

Sometime later in the same ceramic phase, the rooms of this building were intentionally and carefully filled. Rough walls were erected to create construction pens that provided structural stability and the walls and vaults were left intact. Only the capstones were removed so that fill could be introduced into the rooms from above in order to eliminate any voids in the filled-in rooms. The filling of these rooms coincided with the placement of a massive fill episode in the area south of Structure A-5-2nd, which raised the surface of the acropolis up to the level of the Upper Terrace (McCurdy 2016). Structure A-5-1st was built on this surface. The incised images we discuss in this chapter were sealed and buried by the infilling of the rooms of Structure A-5-2nd, and thus they can be confidently dated very narrowly to the Late Classic Hats' Chaak phase. This is confirmed by a radiocarbon date from the fill in Room 1 that indicates that the room was filled before the end of the Hats' Chaak phase around 780 CE (PSUAMS-3853, 1260±20 BP, calibrated at the 95.4% interval to 676–774 CE).

Room 1 measures approximately 4.3 meters long (east-west) by 2.5 meters wide (north-south). Room 2 is slightly smaller, measuring approximately 3.2 meters long (east-west). The walls stand approximately 2.3 meters tall, and from that height the vaults spring to an apical height of approximately 4 meters. Both rooms contain a broad masonry bench that covers almost the entire floor area, with only a 75-centimeter area between the southern interior wall and the northern edge of the bench. The next room in the southern range of Structure A-5-2nd, inferred from the exposed architecture of the structure's northern gallery, remains unexcavated to date.

Our investigations of the interior walls and doorjambs of Rooms 1 and 2 of Structure A-5-2nd and the southern exterior wall of the building have revealed over 400 incised motifs, images, and designs, ranging from simple incised lines to legible hieroglyphs and complex, well-rendered depictions of human figures and deities. This is the largest corpus of Maya graffiti encountered in Belize, comparable in quantity and density to examples from Tikal and Rio Bec.

In documenting this remarkable corpus, we began with hand drawing in the field. In addition to creating a detailed record, this mapping strategy allowed us to study these elements in great detail. While it was time consuming, we came to many insights regarding content, style, and technique through this direct engagement with the incised designs.

We also completed a comprehensive photographic documentation of all of the exposed plaster surfaces. This was undertaken by Neil Dixon using reflectance transformation imaging (RTI), a photographic technique that uses multiple light sources to construct differentially textured composite images of surfaces and allows for high-resolution digital analysis. This enabled us to identify many new elements. The 2016 RTI analysis of the north wall of Room 1 revealed ninety-one potential new elements (McCurdy et al. 2018; see fig. 11.3). In 2017, visual inspection of the plaster surfaces revealed

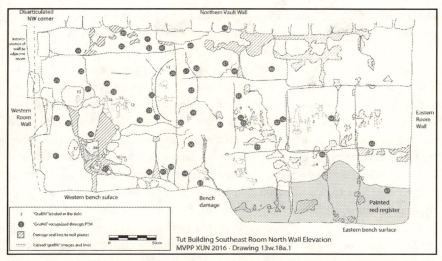

Figure 11.3. North wall of the Structure A-5-2nd Room 1, showing graffiti identified by visual inspection in the field (numbered) and reflectance transformation imaging (numbered in gray circles). Drawing by Leah McCurdy.

that fifty-six of these were incised designs that we had not recognized during our investigations in 2016. During this process, we also identified an additional seventeen elements that were not recognized during the 2016 hand drawing or RTI. These results demonstrate the importance of using multiple methods when documenting incised designs and of direct observation and engagement with the plastered surfaces bearing the designs. In the following field season, Dixon employed high-resolution photogrammetry anchored with total station shots to create precise, scaled three-dimensional georectified visualizations of our excavations of Structure A-5-2nd.

## Teaching the Noble Arts in Structure A-5-2nd

One of the unusual aspects of several of the walls in both rooms is the presence of deeply scored vertical and horizontal lines. Although the function of these gouged lines is not fully understood, our preliminary interpretation is that they were carved into the walls to create separate workspaces for artists in training. On the north wall of Room 1, the artists scored vertical lines from the level of the bench surface almost to the vault spring and horizontal lines from the northeast corner to approximately halfway across the wall (fig. 11.3). This created a series of square segments that may have been partitioned for individual artists or may represent workspaces over a certain period of time.

On the west wall, vertical panels were created by gouging a series of vertical lines across the wall that likely served the same function. Several designs were repeated on the west wall of Room 1 in one particular segmented area.

The incised designs in both Rooms 1 and 2 encompass a range of motifs. There are full-body anthropomorphic figures; anthropomorphic heads, most with embellishments such as hats, headdresses, and ear ornaments; and isolated anthropomorphic facial features (noses, profiles) and body parts. There are full zoomorphic figures, zoomorphic heads, and isolated zoomorphic body parts. Deities are represented, as are pyramidal temples and other architectural features. While there are some complex scenes that appear to be narrative in nature, simple shapes, line-based elements, and markings such as tick marks are more common. Several hieroglyphs are also present, including two full Calendar Round dates and an isolated Tzolk'in date (Helmke 2020) (figs. 11.1a and b).

Anthropomorphic heads and anthropomorphic figures are the most common images in both rooms. On the western wall of Room 2, there is one finely executed example of an anthropomorphic figure with a crocodilian head or mask. One remarkable ritual scene on the west wall of Room 1 depicts a ballplayer in an active playing stance (fig. 11.4). On the north wall of Room 1, there is a ritual scene depicting a decapitation event (fig. 11.5). In this scene,

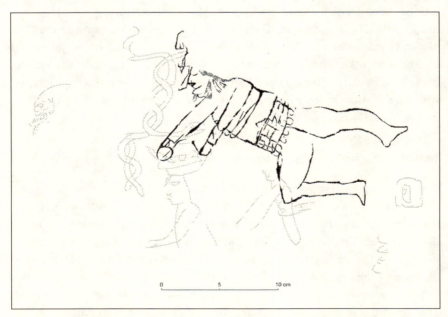

Figure 11.4. Ballplayer (bolded), twisted snakes, and other adjacent graffiti from Structure A-5-2nd Room 1. Drawing by Christophe Helmke.

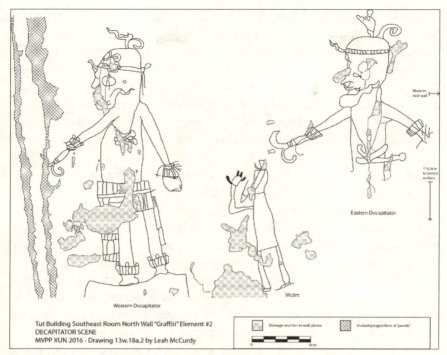

Figure 11.5. Decapitation scene from Structure A-5-2nd Room 1. Drawing by Leah McCurdy.

a pair of priests wearing masks, deer antler headdresses, and crossed-bone pendants hold a curved blade in one hand while grasping the hair of a decapitated victim in the other. A sacrificial victim missing his head is between the two priests. A similar regalia-clad priest is seen in another ritual scene on the same wall with a female figure standing nearby. These particular scenes likely represent historical events that were memorialized on the walls of the rooms.

While all interior walls retain segments of red wall paint, the north wall of Room 1 features the only graphic element painted with black pigment, likely charcoal. While it appears that this element has survived only partially, it is also possible that the image was never completed. This element is reminiscent of a large cartouche, but it does not appear to have enclosed a glyph. Helmke (personal communication, 2017) suggests that this image could represent a tribute bundle, but the preservation and/or incompleteness of the painting makes any identification difficult.

Using the categories Źrałka (2014) defined, the majority of the graffiti documented in Structure A-5-2nd fall within the category of classic or typical graffiti style with a few examples of the crude style of graffiti. Additionally, there are some excellent examples of the fine-style graffiti. Źrałka's category of foreign or Mexicanized graffiti is not present in the corpus. This is not surprising, given that this assemblage dates to the late seventh or eighth century CE.

All skill levels were represented in both rooms and on the exterior wall between the rooms. The variability suggests to us that skilled artists may have been training novices of different artistic abilities. Several lines of evidence support this suggestion. First, several groupings of graffiti consist of repeated elements, often with slight variations between each element. A series of small jaguar heads placed on flat plates (or bars) were repeated on the exterior wall between the rooms. These particular examples were about the same size as painted glyphs found on Late Classic polychrome vessels and were nicely rendered. This suggests to us that in some instances artists were practicing in multiple media, incising on plaster and likely painting on ceramic vessels. These unusual jaguar head depictions appear to have been drawn by the same hand and may reflect practice through repetition.

Another example of practice (or copying) is demonstrated on the west wall of Room 1, where four jaguar or puma heads were incised near each other, all in a section of the wall that had been delineated by vertical scoring in the plaster. Each of these drawings clearly depicts a feline head, but the formation of the ears, eyes, and mouth vary slightly (fig. 11.6). There is differential use of a curly ear versus a rounded ear as well as a slit-like eye versus a triangular eye. These differences indicate that the repetition may have been a way to practice or experiment with these features or they may have been the result of multiple hands at work (McCurdy et al. 2018). The intention was to perfect a feline head without an attempt to draw the body. Some of the heads have a large X deeply gouged through them (e.g., fig. 11.6). This marking of heads was not limited to the feline examples; it also occurs with several human figures, including an example of a well-executed slender male figure in profile wearing a loincloth and what appears to be a deer antler headdress. This figure represents an example of the fine-style graffiti, possibly drawn by a skilled artist of intermediate level. Although we do not fully understand the intention behind the gouged X mark, it may represent a method of assessment or indication of finality.

A further indication of practicing derives from series of simple elements such as profiles that appear to be unfinished (McCurdy et al. 2018; see also fig. 11.7). On the western doorjamb of Room 1, there are a series of representations of a nose in profile, one placed right next to the other. It seems that the nose in its first rendering was unsatisfactory, so the artist moved slightly over and began anew, eventually completing a full head in profile.

There is a high concentration of redrawn images on the west wall of Room 1. A more complicated example is a series of attempts to represent twisted snakes

The Chamber of Secrets at Xunantunich · 289

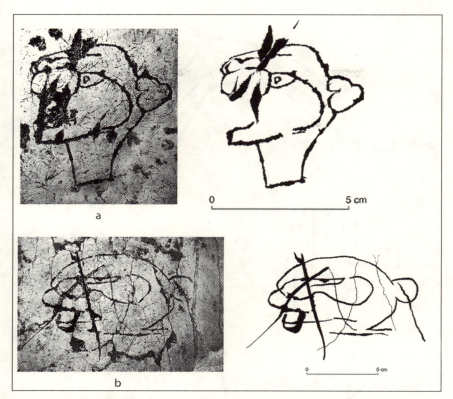

Figure 11.6. Feline heads from Structure A-5-2nd Room 1. Drawing by Lauren Nowakowski; photos by Leah McCurdy.

(fig. 11.4). The overlapping snake bodies are difficult to render without erroneously crossing lines. It appears that a novice took great pains to practice this motif so as to properly detail the crisscross pattern and realistically end with snake heads (McCurdy et al. 2018).

Consistent with the notion of wall surfaces being intentionally prepared for iterative practicing, our excavations revealed evidence of multiple plaster layers on the exterior walls, suggesting that the plaster surfaces were reused multiple times. Źrałka (2014) also documented similar re-plastering events at Nakum in several of the rooms where examples of graffiti were found.

Another interesting example of the fine graffiti style is a beautifully executed drawing on the western doorjamb of Room 1 of a full-figure profile of a man dressed in elaborate regalia with an elaborate headdress (fig. 11.8a). This representation was rendered at a scale and in a style commensurate with images of nobles painted on ceramic vases. Several examples in both rooms

Figure 11.7. Anthropomorphic profiles from Structure A-5-2nd Room 1. Gray areas indicate damaged plaster. Drawing by Lauren Nowakowski.

may represent artwork that could be of the size, style, and skill level typically represented on fine polychrome vessels. Although speculative, it is plausible that at least some skilled individuals who worked in these rooms may have also engaged in painting ceramics.

The technical qualities of incising into plaster may have transferred to other media, including incised ceramics, marine shell objects, jade, and other

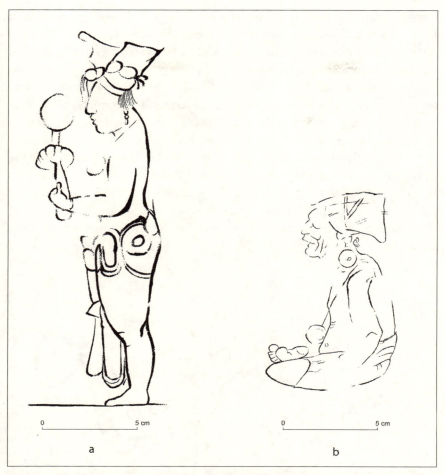

Figure 11.8. Finely executed anthropomorphic figures from Structure A-5-2nd Room 1. Drawings by Christophe Helmke.

materials. In Room 2, a small slate tablet was found that had a possible glyph or a pseudo-glyph incised on its roughly smoothed surface. Furthermore, Batún-Alpuche and Freidel (chapter 15, this volume) have argued that scribes used pointed implements to inscribe texts and images on stone tablets covered in a wax coating. It is possible that the small slate tablet from Structure A-5-2nd was used in this way. Thus, inscribing plaster may have been a natural medium for practicing these particular skills.

Stone carving would have required similar skills. Jamie Awe (personal communication, 2017) reported that the Tourism Development Project recovered a small stone block carved with a standing figure in profile (in the classic graffiti style) just south of Structure A-5-2nd. Though we are unable to directly tie this carved stone block to the rooms of Structure A-5-2nd, it is possible that it represents a discarded product from activities in this location and indicates practice on limestone.

The corpus of graffiti evinces differential skill, the presence of talented and proficient artists, and, in some cases, literate scribes. The examples of the fine-style graffiti are clearly the work of well-trained and experienced artists with specialized knowledge of iconographic and hieroglyphic form and content. A clear example of this is located on the east wall of Room 1, just above the bench surface. This graffito was finely incised with a calligraphic quality similar to the "whiplash" style of ceramic decoration that Michael Coe (1973, 91) recognized. Christophe Helmke (personal communication, 2017) identified this rendering as Chak Xib Chahk executed in a highly decorative and evocative style (fig. 11.9).

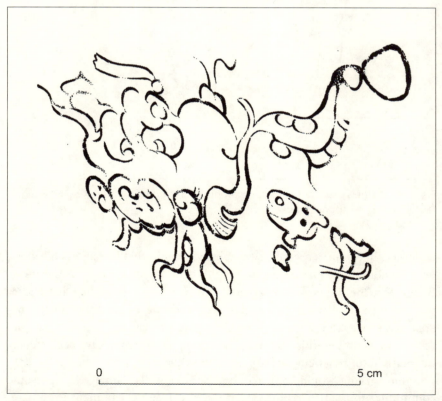

Figure 11.9. Upward-facing head of Chak Xib Chahk from Structure A-5-2nd Room 1. Drawing by Christophe Helmke.

The Chamber of Secrets at Xunantunich · 293

There were several well-executed glyphs in both rooms. In Room 2, Christophe Helmke (2020) identified two Calendar Round dates and one Tzolk'in date (fig. 11.1a and b). In light of several ritual scenes that were incised on the walls of this room, these calendric references may have memorialized time by recording important historic or mythic events that occurred on these dates (also Helmke and Źrałka 2021). In Room 1, just above the portrait of Chak Xib Chahk (fig. 11.9), a hieroglyph was expertly executed in the fine style (fig. 11.1c). This glyph represents a title very relevant to our interpretation that this room served as a training space for young nobles (McCurdy et al. 2018). Helmke (personal communication, 2017) translates this glyph as *[i]tz'a-ta* or *it'zaat* (wise man or sage). We believe that it is not a coincidence that this is the only title inscribed on the walls of the two rooms. It may refer to a person or persons who practiced in this space. In the same room, a finely executed figure (fig. 11.8b) depicts an old man with the wrapped headdress commonly worn by sages and scribes and a round pendant reminiscent of those worn by the individuals depicted in the murals at Xultun.

## The Novice Residence in Group C

Several early colonial chroniclers recorded that boys lived together away from their families while being educated. Sahagún (1978, Book 3, 305) recounts that Aztec noble boys slept and ate together in the *calmecec,* where they learned religious and military arts. Miles (1957, 769) cites early colonial documents that attest to dormitories where young boys stayed while they were going to school in contact-era Pokomam Maya towns in the highlands of Guatemala.

Landa (Tozzer 1941, 124) describes a similar institution in contact-era Maya towns in the Yucatán, a special house where boys and young men lived together prior to getting married. Landa describes these houses as places of leisure and entertainment where residents played a game with beans (presumably something akin to patolli) and the ballgame. While Landa does not mention formal schooling in reference to these buildings, it does not seem unlikely that the resident youths also received formal instruction, perhaps in the ballgame and in other skills and knowledge.

The intense level of interaction between the boys living in these contexts would have fostered strong interpersonal social bonds and robust group networks, as occurs in age-grade groups in sodalities and in modern institutions such as fraternities. Furthermore, the context of being relatively isolated from their families and communities would have facilitated the education, enculturation, and socialization at the hands of teachers and mentors that shaped their attitudes, expectations, and priorities. Similar to boarding schools and basic military training, these types of institutions provided ideal environments for producing and reproducing a shared distinct subculture.

Several archaeologists have identified structures at Classic Maya sites as atypical residences that fit the expectations for these kinds of institutions. Peter Harrison (1970) suggested that Structures 5D-62, 5D-52-lst, and 5D-50 in Tikal's Central Acropolis served as temporary residences for boys being taught in nearby structures. At Copán, Charles Cheek (2003; see also Cheek and Spink 1986) argued that Structure 10L-223 was a temporary residence associated with the education of young boys and ritual retreats for adult men. Several lines of evidence lead us to hypothesize that a complex of structures in Group C served this purpose at Xunantunich.

The Xunantunich Archaeological Project undertook excavations in Group C (Church 1996; Keller 2006). This group is located south of El Castillo and is encircled by two ditch-and-berm fortifications. The staircase to Structure A-5-2nd leads to a terrace that runs along the eastern side of El Castillo. This staircase and terrace provided access to Group C occupants.

The two largest structures in Group C are Structures C-2 and C-3. These two vaulted range structures face each other across a plastered courtyard. Both structures consist of a single range of rooms with high benches, each with its own doorway. High benches are often inferred to be sleeping benches (Harrison 1970), but the simple layout of these structures, each with a line of single rooms lacking interior doorways between the rooms, is not typical of residences.

Excavations revealed several patolli boards on the surfaces of the benches. Patolli is recognized to be both a game of chance and an instrument for divination (Walden and Voorhies 2017). It is likely that the "bean game" that Landa said was played in men's houses during the contact era was related to patolli. While patolli boards have been found in Structures A-11 and A-13 in the Hats' Chaak–phase ruler's compound at Xunantunich in Plaza A-III (Yaeger 2010; Fitzmaurice 2018), they are absent in Structure A-5-2nd. Graffiti were found in both Structures A-11 and A-13, although the density was much lower than in Structure A-5-2nd, and in these particular contexts they likely do not reflect instruction (Yaeger 2010).

The unusual layout of Group C and the presence of patolli boards on the high benches in the rooms is suggestive of a special function of some sort. We suggest that these findings are consistent with expectations for an atypical residence in which boys and/or young men were housed while they learned scribal arts in Structure A-5-2nd. The plastered plaza between the two structures would have provided a space for engaging in military drills, learning fighting skills, practicing ritual dances, and engaging in sports and other activities.

The Chamber of Secrets at Xunantunich · 295

These two buildings are associated with a sweat bath (Structure C-4). The fact that this is one of only two known sweat baths at Xunantunich is significant and suggests that purification rituals may have been particularly important for the residents of this group as they prepared themselves to learn and enact sacred knowledge.

Just south of Structure C-3 there is a modest patio group that consists of three structures (Structures C-5, C-6, and C-7) surrounding a small patio. The substructure platforms are made of cobbles and were surmounted by pole-and-thatch superstructures and thus were less formal than Structures C-2 and C-3. The combination of these observations and the fact that the artifact assemblage associated with Structures C-2 and C-3 revealed a ceramic assemblage dominated by serving vessels suggests to us that this smaller patio group was likely a servants' residence attached to the group.

While this interpretation would benefit from further investigations at Group C, the evidence presented above is consistent with our hypothesis that this unusual group served as the living quarters for novitiates while they engaged in formal training in Structure A-5-2nd.

## Conclusions

The acquisition and transfer of arcane knowledge was one of the most important aspects of ancient civilizations. These processes reproduced their cosmologies and ideologies. In ancient civilizations across the globe, access to specialized knowledge was often restricted to a subset of society, the elite class. Classic Maya royal authority was reinforced and sanctioned through scribal arts. Maya scribes, priests, and sages were the holders of sacred knowledge and were therefore a necessary and central part of the royal court. Yet how this specialized knowledge was acquired and transferred from one generation to the next is little understood.

We suggest that the practice and preparatory sketches incised on the plaster walls of Structure A-5-2nd at Xunantunich may have been educational tools and exercises to ensure that novices learned important skills, symbolism, timekeeping, and history. This new evidence from Xunantunich provides an important archaeological example of a learning space, a school of sorts for specialized training in high culture and sacred knowledge that was a key foundation of Classic Maya civilization.

# IV

## Bridging Time

# 12

# Imagery of the Yearbearers in Maya Culture and Beyond

### Susan Milbrath

Yearbearer rituals that mark the year end were an essential component of Maya timekeeping in the Late Postclassic (1250–1542 CE). Friar Diego de Landa, who consulted with Maya informants in the mid-sixteenth century, was able to record a detailed account of the five-day Uayeb ceremony at year end. The Uayeb rituals involved bloodletting and offering decapitated birds and incense to "idols" that were moved to different locations during the ceremony, followed by renewal rituals and incense offerings to these idols in the first month of the 365-day Haab (Tozzer 1941, 136–148, 152–153). Year-end ceremonies and auguries for the New Year are also represented in Maya codices. These painted books provide a context for analyzing the types of offerings and idols that were used in rituals performed at the year end and in the New Year.

The New Year was named for the yearbearer, a day sign and number combination that designates the corresponding position in the 260-day Tzolk'in. Only four of the twenty day signs could name the year; these were evenly spaced at intervals of five days in the Tzolk'in. Landa (Tozzer 1941, 136–148) noted that the Maya linked the four yearbearers with different directions, colors, and prognostications for the maize crops. The four yearbearers combined with thirteen numbers to form a cycle that repeated every fifty-two years (4 × 13).

In keeping with the theme of materialization of time, this chapter explores the iconography of the yearbearer pages in the Maya codices and their apparent links with the gods represented in the effigy censer complex. In a broader context, I examine possible relationships with yearbearer imagery in Postclassic (900–1519 CE) central Mexico and the origin of the yearbearers in Preclassic (1000 BCE–250 CE) calendrics. I also argue that the earliest yearbearers played a role in dividing the 365-day year into segments of 105 and 260 days, encoding the interval of a 260-day agrarian period that still survives in some parts of the Maya world.

## Images of Yearbearers in the Postclassic

I refer to Uayeb and New Year festivals recorded in Maya codices as yearbearer ceremonies because there is some uncertainty about whether individual scenes in the codices portray the Uayeb at year end or at the beginning of the New Year. Postclassic yearbearer imagery appears on pages 25–28 in the Dresden Codex (figs. 12.8–12.11), pages 19–20 in the Paris Codex (fig. 12.7), and pages 34–37 in the Madrid Codex (figs. 12.1–12.6) (D. Chase 1985a, 223–226; Love 1994, 73–75; Vail 2004, 223–225; Bricker and Bricker 2011, 120–142; Vail 2013, 96–103). The associated scenes are often called New Year ceremonies, but many images clearly refer to the Uayeb (see also D. Chase 1985a, 226–232).

Maya yearbearers fell on the first day of the 365-day Haab, which was divided into 20-day "months" with an added five-day Uayeb. The five-day period at year end shifted the yearbearer five days forward, rotating to the next yearbearer in the following year, and in the fifth year the calendar returned to the first yearbearer but combined with a number that had increased by four, as on Madrid Codex 35 (5 Kan + 4 years = 9 Kan) (fig. 12.1).

In the Madrid yearbearer pages (34–37), black numbers are used as coefficients for month glyphs and red numbers refer to Tzolk'in dates that appear as yearbearers and Tzolk'in dates that are sometimes paired with months in the Haab (Hernández 2004; Vail 2013, 97). The Madrid Codex uses Late Postclassic yearbearers known as the Kan set, the same set Landa recorded (Kan, Muluc Ix, and Cauac). The Kan set of yearbearers was adopted in western Yucatán from Campeche northward as early as 672 CE, or 9.12.0.0.0 in Classic Maya notation (Thompson 1972, 89). This regional innovation represents a calendar reform in the same region where Puuc-style dating in Calendar Round dates was introduced (Proskouriakoff and Thompson 1947). The Postclassic Kan yearbearers are associated with a calendar reform called the Mayapán calendar that was in use when Landa arrived in Yucatán (Bricker and Bricker 2011, 120). The Mayapán calendar is used in the Madrid Codex, the latest of the Maya codices and the calendar whose date is closest to the time of Landa's account (Vail and Aveni 2004, 6; Bricker and Bricker 2011, 95). My research suggests that the codex most likely dates to the second half of the fifteenth century (Milbrath 2017c).

The yearbearer festivals Landa recorded have counterparts in the Madrid Codex, which represents glyphs related to Landa's set of yearbearers and associated colors and directions in the upper register alongside the column of yearbearers (Bill et al. 2000, 157; Hernández 2004). Cauac is the yearbearer of the west in Landa, linked with the color black and north, as it is on Madrid page 34 (fig. 12.3). As in Landa's account, Madrid page 35 depicts the Kan yearbearers associated with the south and the color yellow (fig 12.4). Madrid page 36 links the Muluc yearbearers with the east, and the text references the red Chac of the east, as in Landa's account (Vail 2013, 101) (fig. 12.5). Madrid page 37 represents Ix yearbearers with the north and the color white, as in Landa (fig. 12.6). The only difference is that the Landa sequence begins with Kan while the Madrid begins with Cauac.

The four yearbearers Landa described that are linked with different colors and directions also relate to his account of prophecies for the maize crop in the coming year (Milbrath and Walker 2016b, table 10.1).[1] Landa (Tozzer 1941, 142, 145) notes that Kan years were generally favorable, but he records a negative outcome for maize in Muluc years because there was little rainfall after the maize sprouted. Ix years were linked with drought and a plague of locusts (146–147). Cauac years were also negative because ants and birds devoured the seeds and "hot suns" brought drought (147–148). Different deities associated with the rotation of the yearbearers can also be linked with the maize prognostications in Landa's account of the Uayeb. Landa notes that Kan (south) is affiliated with Bolon Dzacab and a good year for maize; Muluc (east) is linked with K'inich Ahau and a bad year for maize; Ix (north) is associated with Itzamna and an unfavorable year for maize; and Cauac (west) is linked with Uc Mitun Ahau and another bad year for maize. Thus, only Bolon Dzacab (God K of the codices) and the Kan yearbearers of the south were associated with a favorable year for maize.

Although the maize god (God E) is not specifically mentioned in Landa's Uayeb ceremonies, prognostications about the maize crop are associated with all four yearbearers, which seems to be why each of the Madrid Codex yearbearer pages (34–37) shows the maize god (God E) with a different yearbearer set in a column on the left of the pages. Cauac years (west) associated with Landa's negative prediction for the maize crop are confirmed by Madrid 34b (bottom of fig. 12.3). The maize god faces the death god, both seated on the Haab symbol ("year"), and the death god holds a decapitated rain god (Chac), suggesting a symbol for drought in Cauac years, as in Landa's account (Vail 2013, 97). The Haab symbol as a seat may indicate that these deities imply prognostications for the entire year. According to Vail (2013, 97), the text on this page refers to drought and warfare. In the upper and lower registers, a vessel holds maize symbols (Kan glyphs) and sprouting maize foliation. This would seem to symbolize abundant food, but the death god holds the decapitated rain god over the sprouting maize in the lower register and a burning torch is held up to the sprouting maize in the upper register. Both portrayals may refer to drought in Cauac years, as in Landa. In the

302 · Susan Milbrath

lower register, the maize god holds out empty hands and his headdress of maize foliation shows a black bird perched on top. Vail (2004, 224) relates this to Landa's account of birds devouring the seeds in Cauac years.

In Kan years (south) on Madrid page 35, the image of the maize god is similar but here he holds an object, possibly a bloodletter, recalling Landa's reference to bloodletting during the Uayeb ceremonies (fig. 12.4). The text for Kan years predicts an abundance of food and drink, and a spotted animal (a jaguar?) carries the T506 and T102 glyphs, meaning "delicious tortilla" (*waah ki*; Vail 2013, 99). A jar or olla with Kan symbols representing maize is crowned by sprouting maize in both the upper and lower registers, as on Madrid 34, but the texts and imagery seem more generally favorable, in keeping with Landa's positive auguries for maize in Kan years (Vail 2013, 99).

Although Landa says that in Muluc years there was little rainfall after the maize sprouted, Gabrielle Vail and Christine Hernández (2003, 70) identified this yearbearer as favorable based on the animal holding glyphs for maize and water on the lower left of Madrid 36 (fig. 12.5), but more recently Vail (2013, 101) has noted death auguries in the glyphic text. In Muluc years (east), this page shows a jar sprouting maize in the upper register while in the lower register the jar lacks maize sprouts. Instead, we see a black bird devouring a maize symbol held by the maize god. This bird seems to be eating maize kernels, but since the bird is a vulture, it apparently is an omen of the death of the maize god. Facing the maize god, a seated dog is attached to glyphs representing food and drink (101). He holds out a maize symbol and another bird grasps the attached maize foliation. If this is a quetzal, as some researchers have suggested (101), the symbolism is not clear. Overhead, a mammal with a flaming tail is similar to one that hovers over the dead maize god on Madrid page 24c, seeming to reinforce the negative prognostication for maize in Landa's account. Vail (2013, 74, 101) described the animal on Madrid 36 as a dog but identified a dog or opossum on Madrid 24. Both may actually depict an opossum with a burning tail. Although Madrid 37 (fig. 12.6) contains some favorable glyphic texts that allude to an abundance of food and drink in Ix years (north), these are counterbalanced with references to solar eclipse events (103). Landa's record of a negative fate for maize in Ix years correlates with Madrid page 37b, for there the sun god faces a dead maize god (Vail and Hernández 2003, 70; Vail 2004, 224). An offering of a deer haunch appears in Ix years (north), and a similar association appears on the Dresden yearbearer pages with the yearbearer of the north (see below).

Other publications (Love 1994, 73; Bricker and Bricker 2011, 137–142; Milbrath and Walker 2016b, table 10.1) have summarized further comparisons of the Madrid yearbearer imagery and Landa's account of the Uayeb, so here I will only highlight a few salient points. In addition to the correlations with maize prognostications in Landa and the Madrid Codex, these two sources share certain rituals and gods. A stilt-walking event on Madrid 36a (fig. 12.5) in Muluc years is like Landa's account of the stilt dance in the Uayeb of Muluc years (D. Chase 1985a, 229). A number of deities associated with the year-bearer rituals on Madrid pages 34–37 can also be linked with gods mentioned in Landa's Uayeb ceremonies (Milbrath and Walker 2016b, tables 10.1, 10.2). These include the Pauahtuns (God N), the death god (God A, called Sac Cimi in Landa), Itzamna (God D), and Chac (God B). The rain god is represented by the four directional Chacs in Landa's account. Although Chac appears only on one page in the Madrid yearbearer sequence, the text on each page names a Chac associated with a different color and direction (Vail 2013, 99).

Glyphs in the Madrid yearbearer pages also associate the rotation of colors and directions with a deity named Pawah-k'in, the counterpart of Landa's Pauahtun, who is represented in the upper registers by God P, seen with slightly different attire on each page (Vail 2013, 99). The Pauahtun of the west on Madrid 34a (fig. 12.3) wears a jaguar helmet and an olive shell necklace, the one on Madrid 35a (fig. 12.4), linked with the south, wears a winged headdress and olive shell necklace, and the Pauahtun of the east on 36a (fig. 12.5) wears a complete jaguar pelt. His counterpart on 37a (fig. 12.6), who is associated with the north, wears a cross-banded headdress and an *oyohualli* pendant, which is also seen on the opossum Pauahtun on Dresden Codex 26a, associated with the north (see below). All four Madrid Pauahtuns are shown planting seeds with digging sticks, recalling the planting almanacs seen on Madrid 26b (Bricker and Milbrath 2011; Vail 2013).

Haab dates referencing Pop, the month just following the Uayeb, are predominant on these pages, but other dates may allude to events that span the year (Bricker and Vail 2004, table 7.1; Bricker and Bricker 2011, figs. 6-19 to 6-22). For example, Madrid 34a (fig. 12.3) records 12 Pop, and Madrid 35a and 36a (figs. 12.4, 12.5) both show 7 Pop and 12 Pop, while Madrid 37a records 5 Pop (fig. 12.6). In Landa's time (ca. 1553), the yearbearer and its Haab date, 1 Pop, fell on July 16 (Julian; July 26 in our Gregorian calendar). Without any form of intercalation, Pop dates would fall in August during the fifteenth century (using the Gregorian calendar; Hernández and Bricker 2004, tables 10.5, 10.6). Page 36a (fig. 12.5) also clearly shows the date 1 Yaxkin, which Gabrielle Vail and Victoria Bricker (2004, table 7.1) place in December during the fifteenth century. The same date, however, would correspond to November at the end of the agricultural season during the colonial period (1519–1697 CE), as per Landa's account and the *Chilam Balam of Chumayel*, which says the maize stalks are bent over in late November during Yaxkin (Roys 1967, 85, fig. 5; Milbrath 1999, 59).

The correspondence between descriptions of Landa's Uayeb and the Madrid yearbearer pages (34–37) is compelling (D. Chase and A. Chase 1988, 73–74), but it also has been suggested that the Madrid Codex yearbearer pages relate to the ceremonies for the New Year that began on 1 Pop (Tozzer 1941, 150–151; Bricker and Bricker 2011, 137–142; Vail 2013, 97). Bruce Love (1994, 73) points out that the New Year festivities included the Uayeb and ceremonies held on the first of Pop as well as renewal rituals that took place during the month of Pop. It seems that the Madrid Codex combines the Uayeb festivals with dates and events that take place in Pop and makes predictions for events later in the year. The maize god represented on all four pages suggests that predictions about the maize crop in the coming year are important in the imagery and that Kan yearbearers were the most favorable years for maize.

In the Paris Codex, the maize god appears with all four yearbearers on pages 19 and 20, making it clear that maize was of central concern for the New Year auguries (fig. 12.7). Although the glyphs for the cardinal directions are not preserved, the directional associations of the Early Postclassic yearbearers are known from the Dresden Codex sequence and their counterparts in central Mexico (Reed, Flint, House, and Rabbit, comparable to Ben, Edznab, Akbal, and Lamat). In this series, Ben is linked with the east, Edznab with the north, Akbal with the west, and Lamat with the south.

The yearbearers sequence on Paris Codex page 19 begins with Lamat (south), now largely effaced. The imagery for Lamat years shows a vulture and a skeletal god with the maize god, suggesting a negative prediction for maize. This contrasts with Landa's prognostication of a good year for maize with the yearbearer of the south (Kan). In the next column on Paris 19, the Ben yearbearers are well preserved and there is another image of the maize god, here depicted with eyes closed in death. Love (1994, 74) has described this yearbearer as disemboweled. Here Ben years (east) have a negative maize prognostication for the yearbearer of the east, as noted in Landa. The next two columns of yearbearers (Edznab and Akbal) appear on Paris 20 with the maize god in a pose that Love (1994, 74) interprets as "woe to" the maize god; he also suggests that in Akbal years (west) the maize god is shown under attack. Because it is unlikely that all four years in the yearbearer cycle were associated with a negative outcome for maize, these interpretations of the omens for the maize god must be subject to revision.

The Paris Codex originally had all fifty-two numbers recorded alongside the columns of yearbearers, as seen in Love's reconstruction (1994, fig. 7.1), where the cycle runs from 5 Lamat to 4 Akbal. No references to the months

Imagery of the Yearbearers in Maya Culture and Beyond · 305

are preserved, and most likely the 1 Pop New Year date was implied but not represented in the Paris yearbearer pages. This Early Postclassic codex begins the year on 1 Pop, like the Late Postclassic Madrid Codex, but it uses the Akbal set of yearbearers (Bricker and Bricker 2011, 95). The Akbal set is also seen in the Dresden Codex, which Thompson dates to the thirteenth century (figs. 12.8–12.11). Thompson (1972, 89) argues that the Akbal set characterizing the Dresden Codex was also used in the Classic period (250–900 CE) (but see Stuart 2004a).

The Dresden Codex yearbearers almanac on pages 25–28 has three registers of horizontal glyphs, which include the names of different gods and directions. Unlike the Paris and Madrid yearbearer almanacs, the columns of yearbearers in the Dresden lack numbers. Here the Akbal set of yearbearers form a column alongside the two lower scenes in the following sequence: Ben (fig. 12.8), Edznab (fig. 12.9), Akbal (fig. 12.10), and Lamat (fig. 12.11), and each page is clearly associated with glyphs referencing the cardinal directions. Thompson (1972, 89) identifies the column of yearbearer glyphs alongside the lower scene as references to the first day of Pop paired with the last day of the Uayeb in a column above, but Harvey Bricker and Victoria Bricker (2011, 136) argue that the paired days are in fact the first and second days of the Uayeb. Others follow Thompson (1972, 89) in suggesting that the days are the last day of the Uayeb and first day of Pop (Vail and Looper 2015, 125–126). If this is the case, the Akbal yearbearer set shown in the two lower registers must reference the New Year and the upper set would name the last day of the Uayeb. This does not necessarily mean that the lower two registers show New Year ceremonies, for the imagery seems most closely linked with Landa's account of the Uayeb, as Bricker and Bricker (2011, 137) have pointed out.

In his discussion of the yearbearer pages on Dresden 25–28, Thompson (1972, 89–90) notes that the top third of each page represents an opossum carrying a patron of the incoming year perched on a tumpline. According to Thompson (93), page 25a (fig. 12.8) shows the opossum carrying Chac (God B), page 26a (fig. 12.9) shows the opossum bearing a jaguar, and page 27a (12.10) shows the opossum carrying the maize god (God E), whereas on page 28a (fig. 12.11) the opossum's burden is the death god (God A). Thompson (89) refers to the opossums in the upper scenes of the Dresden Codex as Bacabs bearing the idol of the incoming year, but Hernández (2004, 354) identifies the opossums as Mams bearing the gods of the New Year. However, the imagery is more closely connected with the Uayeb, and the texts in the upper register (Dresden 25a–28a) refer to the old year (Bricker and Bricker 2011, 124–125). Most likely the opossums represent the aged Pauahtuns described in Landa's account of the Uayeb ceremonies (Tozzer 1941,

306 · Susan Milbrath

135–149; Milbrath 1999, 150). These opossum Pauahtuns may be carrying Mams in the form of wooden idols that were honored during the Uayeb and discarded at year's end (Tozzer 1941, 139n646). Even today, the Tzutujil Maya bury Mam effigies as representatives of the outgoing year (Milbrath 1999, 16, 150; Christensen 2001, 182–190). The Mopan of Belize also merged the Mams with the Chacs (Taube 1992a, 97). It is noteworthy that Chac appears as one of the burdens in the yearbearer pages, reinforcing a connection between the Mams and the burden gods as representatives of the old year.

In the middle register of the Dresden Codex, gods in temples appear in the following sequence: God K, God G, God D, and God A. Thompson (1972, 89–90) interpreted the middle scenes with the temple gods and the lower scenes with gods offering decapitated birds as representations of Landa's New Year rites, but actually Landa says that birds were decapitated during the Uayeb rituals. Furthermore, Bricker and Bricker (2011, 124) see a good correspondence between Dresden 25–28 and Landa's description of the Uayeb ceremonies, an idea supported here and in studies by other scholars (e.g., Love 1994, 73–75).[2] In the bottom register, another set of gods make offerings: God G, God K, God A, and God D. They show a very good fit with Landa's Uayeb deities and their associated directions:

1. Landa's Uayeb with K'inich Ahau in the east links with God G in the east on Dresden 25c.
2. Landa's Uayeb with Bolon Dzacab in the south links with God K in the south on Dresden 26c.
3. Landa's Uayeb with the death god (Uac Mitun Ahau) in the west links to God A in the west on Dresden 27c.
4. Landa's Uayeb with Itzamna in the north links with God D in the north on Dresden 28c.

K'awiil (God K) is seated in the temple on Dresden 25b (fig. 12.8) in Ben years (east), and the lower register (25c) shows the sun god (K'inich Ahau or God G) offering a bird. The texts reference the east and prognostications of drought.[3] Here God G appears with a tree personified by Chac standing on a symbol for tun that references both the word for stone and the 360-day tun (T548). The middle scene on page 26b (fig. 12.9) shows Edznab years (north) and a temple with the sun god called *kin ahau*. Below (26c), K'awiil makes an offering to a serpent tree arising out of another tun symbol. The associated direction is south, but as Thompson (1972, 90) points out, both the glyphs and lower picture themselves are incorrectly transposed with those on 28c (fig. 12.11), which means that 26c should actually show Itzamna in the northern direction and K'awiil in the south should be on page 28c (see also Bricker and Bricker 2011, 131, table 6-1; Vail and Hernández 2013, 101, table 4.1). In Akbal years associated with the west (27b; fig. 12.10), Itzamna (God D) is housed in the temple, while the death god (God A) makes an offering to the serpent tree mounted on the glyph for tun, which can mean stone or year (27c). In Lamat years (28b; fig. 12.11), the yearbearer of the south, another variant of the death god (A′), is seated in the temple while Itzamna makes an offering to the serpent tree in the north (28c). Again, the direction and the lower picture are transposed, so K'awiil and the south should be on page 28c. The transposition of the gods in the lower registers on 26c and 28c means that the deities represented in the lower scene on each page relate to the gods depicted in the middle scene on the next page (Bricker and Bricker 2011, 131–132; Thompson 1972, 90). This suggests a rotational shift of deities during the Uayeb, like that Landa (Tozzer 1941, 139–148) described. Apparently the text also records omens for the New Year, as in Landa's account of the Uayeb (Bricker and Bricker 2011, 137).

On pages 26c–28c of Dresden, stone trees or pillars mark the four world directions. The Chac tree on Dresden 25c represents the east and snake trees sprouting vegetation representing the other three cardinal directions. The sequence of four trees positioned on the glyph for tun (or stone) relate to Landa's account of the piles of stones positioned at the four entries to the town during the Uayeb (Tozzer 1941, 139; Thompson 1972, 91).[4] The glyphic text identifies them as the "Itzamna trees" (Vail 2004, 223), and they were apparently visualized as world trees that mark the passage of time. The set of four gods standing alongside these stone pillars or trees may relate to Landa's account of the Bacabs as skybearers who represented the four yearbearers in the sequence of four Uayeb ceremonies (Tozzer 1941, 135–136). Yearbearer ceremonies shown on these pages were designed to symbolically reestablish the ordering principle of the calendar at the New Year and re-create the cosmological foundation events when the sky was raised after the flood (Taube 1989; Milbrath 1999, 227; Vail and Hernández 2013).[5] Landa (Tozzer 1941, 135–138) says that the four Bacabs were placed in four parts of the world after the great flood and that they in turn placed four trees to hold up the heavens, each associated with a different direction, color, and yearbearer. The four yearbearers are also visualized as supporting the heavens among the Maya today.[6]

We can see that the year's end is emphasized in the Dresden Codex, which shows Uayeb deities in the three registers. The Madrid Codex also seems closely related to Landa's account of the Uayeb, but Haab dates embedded in the scenes correlate with the first month of the year and some dates that fall later in the festival calendar may relate to the entire maize cycle. A number of different images of the maize god are represented in both the Madrid and Paris codices,

308 · Susan Milbrath

suggesting that these almanacs also deal with prognostications for the maize crop in the coming year, like the predictions during the Uayeb that Landa mentioned. In all three codices, the yearbearer dates must refer to the New Year, which began on 1 Pop, based on what we know of Postclassic texts. The Paris Codex uses the same set of Early Postclassic (900–1200 CE) Akbal yearbearers that are seen in the Dresden Codex, but the Madrid Codex uses the Late Postclassic Kan set Landa recorded in the mid-sixteenth century.

## Seasonal Position of the Yearbearers and the New Year

In the Late Postclassic, the yearbearer coincided with 1 Pop on July 16, marking the beginning of the annual cycle of festivals, which was also the time of the second solar zenith. This would seem to link the yearbearer drawn from the 260-day calendar to a fixed date in the Haab, but over time the yearbearer clearly shifted in relation to the true length of the solar year. For example, when Alfonso Caso (1967, table XIII) plotted the Aztec calendar, he placed the yearbearers on the 360th day, falling on the last day of the last "month" (*veintena*), and his table shows the yearbearer shifted from February 10 in 1428 to January 16 in 1531. Alfonso Caso's (1967) tables incorporate no adjustment to the festival calendar to account for the true length of the year. Regardless of whether the festival calendar was periodically adjusted, the yearbearer would always drop back in relation to the solar year because the 260-day calendar ran continuously without adjustment. In the Late Postclassic Maya and Aztec systems, the festival calendar may have been adjusted (see below), but the yearbearer would fall behind in relation to a specific date in the solar year. Even so, the Tzolk'in provided an easy way to measure the length of the year, divided into segments of 260 and 105 days, and it could also serve as a counting device that was useful in tracking seasonal events. This may be why the Tzolk'in is the principal calendar used in the Maya codices, which show almanacs representing both agricultural activities and seasonal activities such as deer hunting and beekeeping (Milbrath 1999, 141; Vail and Aveni 2004, 5; Bricker and Bricker 2011; Bricker and Milbrath 2011).

It is clear that the months of the festival calendar were related to seasonal activities in Landa's time and in later epochs of the colonial period (Roys 1967, fig. 5; Bolles 1990, 2003; Milbrath 1999, 59). Landa says the first day of Pop and the New Year always fell on July 16, which implies some form of intercalation (such as a leap year). In the nineteenth century, Pío Pérez recorded an association between the New Year and the solar zenith in Yucatán; the date for both events was July 16 in the Julian calendar (Aveni 2001, 42). The clear link between the beginning of the New Year on 1 Pop and the July 16 date in

Imagery of the Yearbearers in Maya Culture and Beyond · 309

two accounts that span many centuries would indicate an intercalation, but scholars cannot agree on whether there was a calendar adjustment to keep the festivals in a fixed relationship with the solar seasons.

During the Classic period no such adjustment was possible because the Long Count integrated larger cycles of time and the Haab clearly changed its seasonal position over time. The Long Count correlation factor, which takes into account many lines of data from colonial period documents, must be considered in any discussion of the Postclassic calendar because the Tzolk'in clearly ran continuously without adjustment (Bricker and Bricker 2011, 77–99). Weldon Lamb (personal communication, 2017) suggests that the Maya may have adopted the Julian calendar from the Europeans shortly before Landa wrote up his account of a fixed New Year around 1553. Another possibility is that there was a calendar reform in the Late Postclassic, as John Bolles (1990, 87; 2003, 2) has suggested. He proposes that the Ahau Katun integrated the solar year with a 24-year katun at some point shortly before the conquest (see also Milbrath 2017b, 126n22).

Daniel Flores Gutiérrez (1995) has developed an intriguing intercalation model. He proposes that Landa's four yearbearers and their associated colors and directions encode a way to adjust the Haab. Flores Gutiérrez argues that the Maya changed the time of day when the New Year ceremony was performed, rotating ahead one-quarter day every year. After the fourth year, a full day would have been added in a form of intercalation that left no record.[7] Such a shift of six hours each year would help explain why Landa (Tozzer 1941, 133) states that the Yucatec Maya have a year of 365 days and six hours. If the Postclassic Yucatec Maya added six hours each year by advancing the time ceremonies were performed one-quarter day every year, there is a problem in terms of the position of the yearbearer, which Landa (Tozzer 1941, 149–150) placed on the first day of the first month. The yearbearer drawn from the Tzolk'in calendar would slip back relative to the 365-day Haab by 13 days every 52 years, and after 104 years the yearbearer would be displaced by 26 days. If the Haab were adjusted to be 365.25 days long by the method Flores Gutiérrez proposed, there would still be a displacement in the yearbearer because the 260-day Tzolk'in ran continuously without any added days, shifting the position of the yearbearer relative to the New Year (Milbrath 1999, 63).

A shift in yearbearer sets between the Early Postclassic and Late Postclassic could encode a calendar adjustment to restore the New Year to a specific seasonal position. Since the yearbearer slips back 26 days in 104 years relative to any solar date, the priests could have recovered the fixed solar date of the New Year by adopting a new set of yearbearers spaced at an interval of 26 days later in the Tzolk'in. An adjustment of 26 days would move the New Year from

310 · Susan Milbrath

13 Ben used in the Dresden during the Early Postclassic to 13 Cauac used in the Madrid during the Late Postclassic (or 13 Akbal to 13 Muluc or any such shift in yearbearer dates at an interval of 26 days).

Shifting the yearbearer to a new Tzolk'in date 26 days later essentially places the yearbearer once again in the same seasonal position as it had 104 years earlier, but the directional association would be shifted (table 12.1). For example, the Akbal yearbearer linked with the west would be replaced by a Muluc yearbearer associated with the east. Thus, if the Kan set was adopted during the last 104-year period of the Late Postclassic, it would have restored the seasonal position the yearbearer had in the Early Postclassic, but the yearbearers' directional aspect would shift to the opposite direction. Presumably this form of adjustment was confined to the Late Postclassic period, when there was an apparent effort to correlate the months of the Haab with the seasonal events in the solar cycle. Earlier changes in the yearbearers probably did not reflect a desire to adjust the position of the New Year, because the Haab and the Calendar Round were firmly embedded in larger cycles of time recorded in the Long Count.[8]

Table 12.1. Last date in each trecena with a 26-day interval to the next set of yearbearers

13 Ben (east) + 26 = 13 Cauac (west)

13 Cimi

13 Cauac

13 Eb

13 Chicchan

13 Edznab (north) + 26 = 13 Kan (south)

13 Chuen

13 Kan

13 Caban

13 Oc

13 Akbal (west) + 26 = 13 Muluc (east)

13 Cib

13 Muluc

13 Ik

13 Men

13 Lamat (south) + 26 + 13 Ix (north)

13 Imix

13 Ix

13 Manik

13 Ahau

In the Classic period, the Haab began on 0 Pop, known as the seating of Pop, and the yearbearer is not easily distinguished in the texts. Thompson (1960, 127–128) notes that no glyph for the yearbearer has been identified on Initial Series monuments and no special emphasis is given to dates that began the month of Pop. He presumed that the Classic yearbearers in the southern lowlands were the Akbal set, but David Stuart (2004a) identifies some Classic period Calendar Round dates that record the Ik' set of yearbearers (Ik', Manik', Eb', Kaban), such as Naranjo Stela 18, which shows 1 Ik' and the seating of Pop (0 Pop).

The date 3 Ik' at San Bartolo was framed by a cartouche in a scene linked with yearbearer imagery (Taube et al. 2010). Stuart (2004a) interprets this date as the seating of Pop during the Late Preclassic (350 BCE–1 CE), somewhere between 131 and 27 BCE (figs. 12.12, 12.13).

Stuart (2004a, 4) proposes that the Ik' yearbearers characterize the Preclassic and the Classic period and that the Akbal set is the Early Postclassic set used in the Dresden Codex yearbearer pages, although he notes that the Dresden also shows the earlier Ik' set of yearbearers in the upper column of each page. The shift from Ik' to Akbal yearbearers may have taken place in the Terminal Classic period (800–900 CE) in some areas. Using the Akbal set of yearbearers, Stela 19 at Ceibal records 1 Ben with a partially effaced Haab inscription that John Graham (1988, 59–60) reads as 1 Pop (fig. 12.14). If Stela 19 records a Calendar Round with 1 Ben and 1 Pop, that could mean that the Akbal yearbearer set seen in the Dresden and Paris codices was introduced in the late ninth century in the southern lowlands, along with central Mexican gods, such as Ehecatl-Quetzalcoatl, who is represented on Stela 19. This could be the result of foreign influence, because the Akbal set is comparable to the set used in central Mexico (Reed = Ben, Knife = Edznab, House = Akbal, and Rabbit = Lamat). Graham reads the Ceibal Long Count date as 10.1.18.6.13 (January 6, 868 CE, in our Gregorian calendar), which would fall near the beginning of the agricultural cycle. It is noteworthy that as the Classic period came to a close, the yearbearer and the New Year assumed a seasonal position at the beginning of the agricultural cycle, and some Maya calendars surviving today show a similar seasonal link between the New Year and the beginning of the agrarian cycle.

## Modern Survival of the Yearbearer System and Festival Calendar

Although the Haab is found today in a number of communities throughout Chiapas and Guatemala (but not in Yucatán), only around thirty-four communities in northwestern Guatemala preserve both the Haab and the Tzolk'in

(Bricker 1981, 8). In some communities, the Catholic liturgical calendar has helped keep the Maya months in a fixed relationship to the solar calendar.[9] Even though Easter can shift by up to a month in date, certain Maya festival calendars have remained relatively fixed over the last 300 years, although no intercalation is formally acknowledged. Henrich Berlin's data (1967, fig. 1) show that in three different Tzotzil communities, the month Batzul begins the year, as it did in 1688 and that this 20-day month has remained relatively fixed, spanning from mid-January to early February.[10] Weldon Lamb's more comprehensive data set (2017, 248–251) shows a similar pattern in other "frozen" versions of the Maya Haab. K'iche' calendars documented in 1548 and 1688 place the Uayeb and New Year in May, indicating a fixed relationship to our solar year, but many frozen calendars begin the year closer to the beginning of the agricultural season in February (Lamb 2017, table 4.14). It seems that in certain areas where a fixed 260-day agrarian cycle is recognized, there is a preference for placing the first month of the year near the beginning of the agrarian cycle in late January or early February, as among the Ch'orti' and the Tzotzil. Although the Ch'orti' lack the Tzolk'in, they use a fixed period of 260 days for their agricultural cycle, which begins on the first crescent moon in February, and their New Year festival also takes place in February (Girard 1962, 328–342). Among the Tzotzil of Chenalhó in Chiapas, the agrarian cycle is also measured as 260 days and runs from February through October; the first month (Batzul) coincides approximately with the beginning of the agricultural cycle (Guiteras Holmes 1961, 32–35, 44–45).

The Tzolk'in is still used to measure a 260-day agricultural cycle in a number of Maya communities, including the Tzotzil, Tzeltal, and K'iche' Maya (Guiteras Holmes 1961, 33; Stross 1994, 29–31; Milbrath 1999, 15, 59–62; 2017a). The K'iche' also recognize yearbearers that gradually shift back in the calendar, for there is no apparent adjustment to make the New Year fall at a specific time of year.[11] The K'iche' cycle for valley maize begins with clearing the fields in February when the Pleiades reach the meridian around sunset and sowing is completed in March before the full moon, while the cycle for mountain maize begins in March and ends in December, and this agricultural period is said to be 260 days long (Tedlock 1992, 185, 189–190, 204). With minor adjustments to correlate with lunar phases and other astronomical cycles, the fixed 260-day agricultural count can be calculated using the Tzolk'in because whichever day begins the agrarian year will also end the cycle.

Indeed, Barbara Tedlock (1992, 93, 190) has suggested that the origin of the 260-day Tzolk'in may be found in the agricultural cycle in the Maya area and possibly also in the human gestation period. I also agree with Tedlock and Prudence Rice that the Tzolk'in may have been derived from the 260-day

Imagery of the Yearbearers in Maya Culture and Beyond · 313

agricultural cycle and the length of the human gestation period (Milbrath 1999, 30; Rice 2007, 35–36, 38–39; Milbrath 2017a, 2017b). Significantly, this connects the developing fetus with the cycle of maize (perhaps more specifically with the growing corn cob). Furthermore, the maize cycle seems to be embedded in the 260-day intervals recorded in pre-Columbian architectural orientations over a wide area in Mesoamerica, a pattern established early on at Teotihuacan and in the Maya area (Šprajc 2000; González-García and Šprajc 2016).

## The Agricultural Cycle and Middle Preclassic (1000–350 CE) Positioning of the Yearbearers

The position of the yearbearer near the start of the agricultural cycle may have been associated with the beginning of the year at a time that the Maya calendar was first developing during the Middle Preclassic. The earliest Maya calendars were probably coordinated with solar alignments that emphasized the solstices in Middle Preclassic E Groups, but very soon an interest developed in marking solar positions that measured the 260-day period of the agrarian year, spanning from February to October (Milbrath 2017a, 2017b, 97–98). The 260-day agricultural cycle is documented in early Maya alignments of architecture to the sun's horizon position in February and October, an interval of 260 days that corresponds to the agrarian cycle (González-García and Šprajc 2016, 200). Similar orientations are evident at a number of early Mesoamerican sites, suggesting that the agrarian period that spanned February to October was a significant factor when the early calendar was being developed (Rice 2007, 35–36; Šprajc and Sánchez Nava 2012; Sánchez Nava and Šprajc 2015; Milbrath 2017a; Milbrath 2017b, 106–108). The predominant orientation of east-facing architecture at Classic Lowland Maya sites shows peaks that represent intervals of 260 days; the greatest number were orientations to the sun's horizon position on February 12 and 260 days later on November 3 (Sánchez Nava and Šprajc 2015, fig. 9).

The yearbearer drawn from the 260-day Tzolk'in cycle codified a split of the 365-day year into two segments of 260 days and 105 days. This may have been coordinated at a very early time with the yearbearer cycle. The yearbearer cycle clearly predates the Long Count and can be traced back at least as far as 600 BCE in Oaxaca (Milbrath 2017a, 2017b).[12] It is likely that the Tzolk'in was initially used to measure the agricultural cycle, and even though the Haab was not recorded in the Middle Preclassic, it is likely that the twenty day names of the Tzolk'in formed 20-day sets that defined the intervals in the year that later became months in the Haab (Milbrath 2017a, 2017b).

The first month and the yearbearer fell near the beginning of the agrarian cycle in late January or early February during the Middle Preclassic, predating any known Long Count inscriptions (table 12.2). This relationship with the beginning of the agrarian period developed during Cycle 6, when the Maya calendar was in its formative stage, approximately 750 to 700 BCE.[13] This is true for both of the proposed sets of Classic period yearbearers. The Akbal set, which Thompson (1960, 127, 304) identified as Late Classic yearbearers, are paired with 1 Pop as New Year's Day, whereas the Ik' set, which Morley (1947, 301; see also Stuart 2004a) identified as Classic yearbearers, mark the New Year on 0 Pop. A New Year date equivalent to 1 Pop rather than 0 Pop would be more likely if the invention of zero was a relatively late development in the Preclassic, as John Justeson (2010, 2012) has proposed. In any case, there is a good correspondence between the yearbearer and the beginning of the agricultural cycle around 700–750 BCE (table 12.2). The pattern for both sets of yearbearers during this period coordinates the New Year with the beginning of the agricultural cycle in late January or early February, suggesting that the New Year was originally keyed to the beginning of the agrarian cycle.

Table 12.2. Middle Preclassic New Year dates on 0 Pop and 1 Pop, 750–680 BCE

| 5.19.17.16.2 | 7 Ik | 0 Pop | 750 BCE | February 1 | Gregorian |
|---|---|---|---|---|---|
| 5.19.17.16.3 | 8 Akbal | 1 Pop | 750 BCE | February 2 | Gregorian |
| 6.0.2.17.7 | 12 Manik | 0 Pop | 745 BCE | January 31 | Gregorian |
| 6.0.2.17.8 | 13 Lamat | 1 Pop | 745 BCE | February 1 | Gregorian |
| 6.0.13.1.17 | 9 Caban | 0 Pop | 735 BCE | January 28 | Gregorian |
| 6.0.13.1.18 | 10 Edznab | 1 Pop | 735 BCE | January 29 | Gregorian |
| 6.1.3.4.7 | 6 Manik | 0 Pop | 725 BCE | January 26 | Gregorian |
| 6.1.3.4.8 | 7 Lamat | 1 Pop | 725 BCE | January 27 | Gregorian |
| 6.1.4.4.12 | 7 Eb | 0 Pop | 724 BCE | January 25 | Gregorian |
| 6.1.4.4.13 | 8 Ben | 1 Pop | 724 BCE | January 26 | Gregorian |
| 6.2.8.10.12 | 5 Eb | 0 Pop | 700 BCE | January 21 | Gregorian |
| 6.2.8.10.13 | 6 Ben | 1 Pop | 700 BCE | January 20 | Gregorian |
| 6.2.18.13.2 | 2 Ik | 0 Pop | 690 BCE | January 18 | Gregorian |
| 6.2.18.13.3 | 3 Akbal | 1 Pop | 690 BCE | January 19 | Gregorian |
| 6.3.8.15.12 | 12 Eb | 0 Pop | 680 BCE | January 15 | Gregorian |
| 6.3.8.15.13 | 13 Ben | 1 Pop | 680 BCE | January 16 | Gregorian |

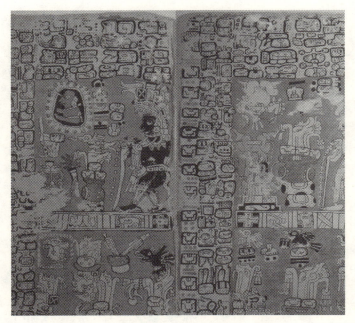

Figure 12.1. Madrid Codex pages 34–36. Source: Brasseur de Bourboug (1869–1870 edition), courtesy of Gabrielle Vail, Florida Institute for Hieroglyphic Research.

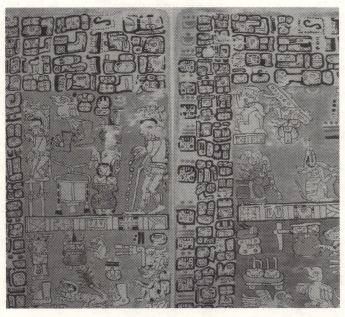

Figure 12.2. Madrid Codex pages 36–37. Source: Brasseur de Bourboug (1869–1870 edition), courtesy of Gabrielle Vail, Florida Institute for Hieroglyphic Research.

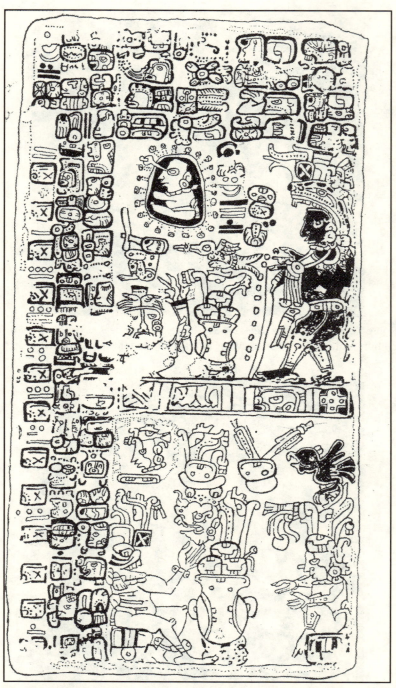

Figure 12.3. Madrid Codex page 34. Source: Villacorta and Villacorta (1976). Drawing by Carlos A. Villacorta.

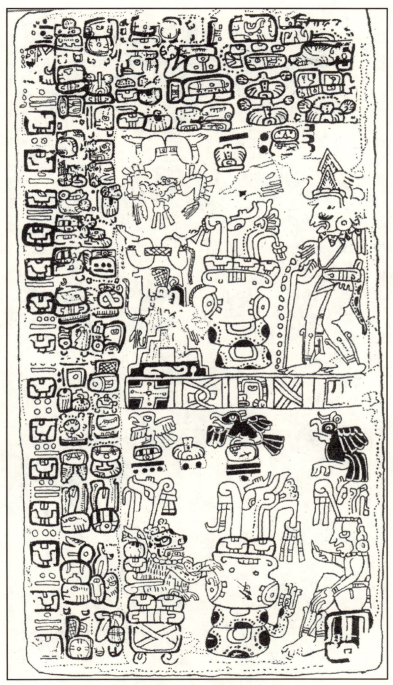

Figure 12.4. Madrid Codex page 35. Source: Villacorta and Villacorta (1976). Drawing by Carlos A. Villacorta.

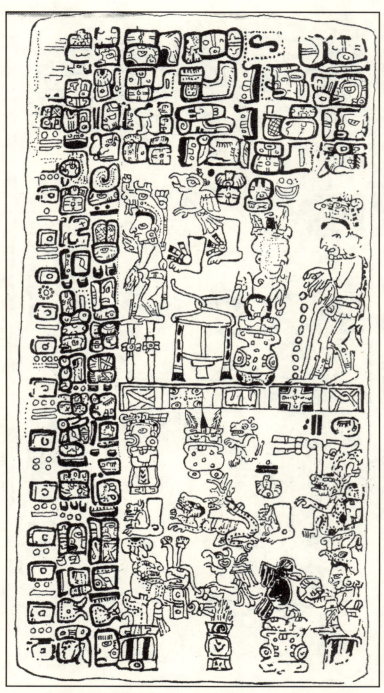

Figure 12.5. Madrid Codex page 36. Source: Villacorta and Villacorta (1976). Drawing by Carlos A. Villacorta.

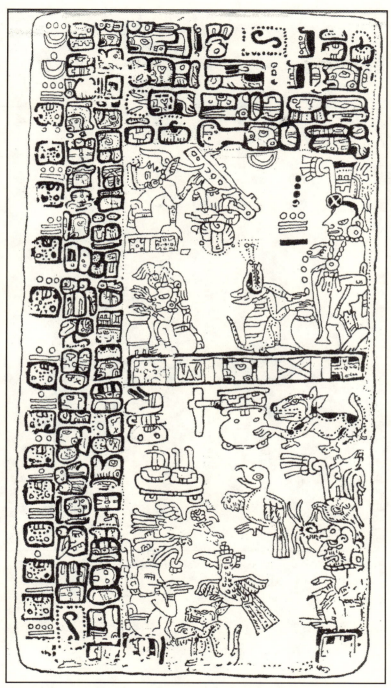

Figure 12.6. Madrid Codex page 37. Source: Villacorta and Villacorta (1976). Drawing by Carlos A. Villacorta.

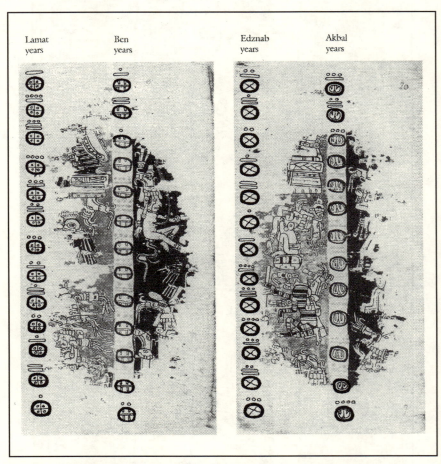

Figure 12.7. Paris Codex pages 19–20. Courtesy of Bruce Love. Source: Love (1994).

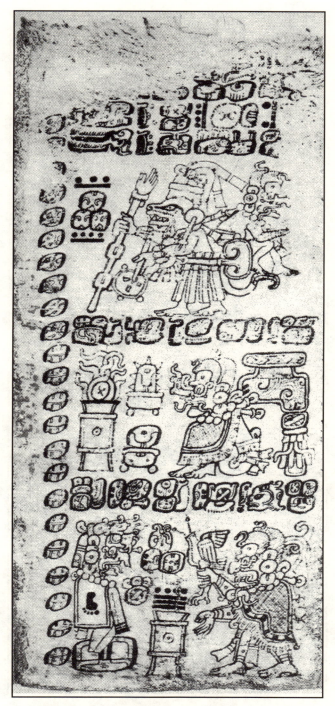

Figure 12.8. Dresden Codex page 25. Source: Förstemann (1892).

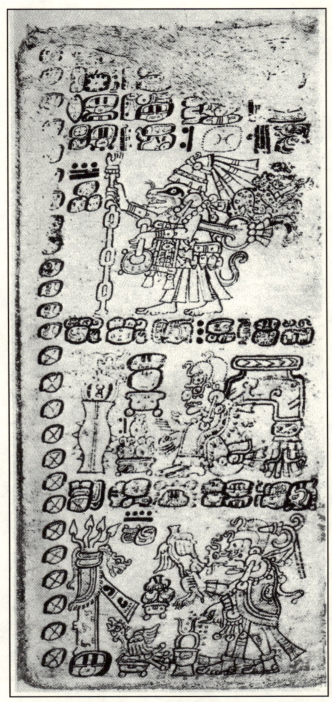

Figure 12.9. Dresden Codex page 26. Source: Förstemann (1892).

Figure 12.10. Dresden Codex page 27. Source: Förstemann (1892).

Figure 12.11. Dresden Codex page 28. Source: Förstemann (1892).

Figure 12.12. West Wall of San Bartolo mural in Structure 1. Copyrighted illustration by Heather Hurst.

Figure 12.13. Detail of West Wall of San Bartolo mural with 3 Ik glyph on right. Copyrighted illustration by Heather Hurst.

Figure 12.14. Stela 19 at Ceibal. Drawing by Ian Graham. Copyright President and Fellows of Harvard College, Peabody Museum of Archaeology and Ethnology, 2004.15.6.17.19.

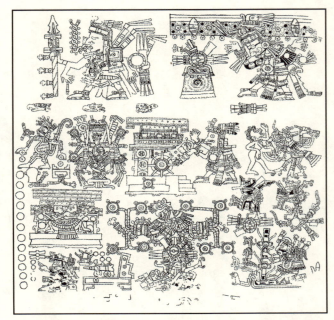

Figure 12.15. Partial reconstruction of Codex Borgia page 49. Illustration by Ian Breheny. Copyright Susan Milbrath.

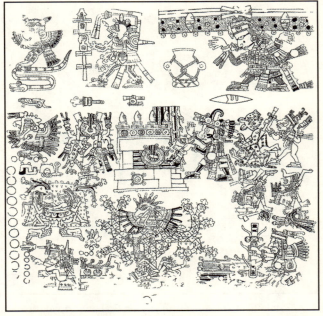

Figure 12.16. Partial reconstruction of Codex Borgia page 50. Illustration by Ian Breheny. Copyright Susan Milbrath.

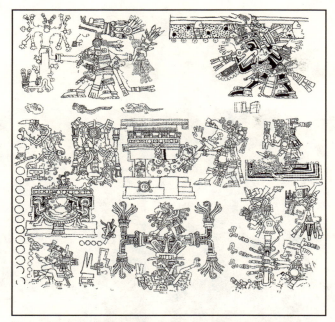

Figure 12.17. Partial reconstruction of Codex Borgia page 51. Illustration by Ian Breheny. Copyright Susan Milbrath.

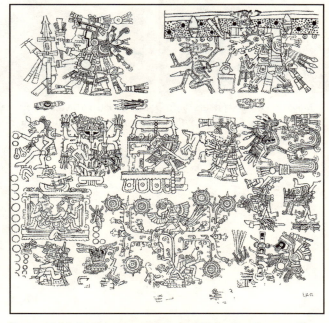

Figure 12.18. Partial reconstruction of Codex Borgia page 52. Illustration by Ian Breheny. Copyright Susan Milbrath.

Figure 12.19. Mayapán effigy censers: (*left*) Death god; (*right*) step-eyed maize god. Photos by Susan Milbrath. Courtesy of Carlos Peraza Lope, Instituto Nacional de Antropología e Historia.

Figure 12.20. Paired Mayapán effigy censers representing God N as Pauahtun. Photos by Susan Milbrath. Courtesy of Carlos Peraza Lope, Instituto Nacional de Antropología e Historia.

## San Bartolo: The Earliest Known Maya Yearbearer Images

A Late Preclassic mural on the west wall at San Bartolo in Guatemala has a 3 Ik' date in a cartouche that is considered to be an early yearbearer dating to the Late Preclassic (fig. 12.4b; Stuart 2004a). Although the site was first occupied in the Middle Preclassic, the archaeological context of the murals in Structure 1 (Las Pinturas) is Late Preclassic, circa 300 BCE–200 CE. It is worth noting that the first instance of the 3 Ik' yearbearer on the seating of Pop during Cycle 6 is January 20, 702 BCE (Gregorian), coordinating approximately with the beginning of the agrarian cycle. Most likely the San Bartolo date is much later, falling in Cycle 7, a period when the first instance of 3 Ik' 0 Pop correlated with October 24, 339 BCE, and the last with July 28, 26 CE. Stuart favors a date of 3 Ik' 0 Pop between 131 BCE and 27 BCE (September 4, 131 BCE, and August 10, 27 BCE, in the Gregorian calendar).

The San Bartolo mural depicts animal sacrifice that can be linked to imagery on the Dresden Codex yearbearer pages (Taube et al. 2010, 28). The fit is not precise, but it is compelling. Reading the mural from left to right, the first scene is a fish offering that coordinates with a similar offering for the yearbearer of the west on Dresden 27c (figs. 12.10, 12.12). The next animal offering is a deer that relates to the deer haunch on Dresden 28c as the offering of the north, which should be on Dresden 26c with the yearbearer of the north, Edznab (figs.12.9, 12.11). As the lower scenes on Dresden 26 and Dresden 28 were erroneously transposed, the images are reversed, and this is also the case with the glyph bands designating the directions. The subsequent sacrifice in the mural is a turkey that correlates with the turkey offering for the yearbearer on Dresden 26c, which is linked with the south and should be on page 28c with the yearbearer of the south, Lamat (figs. 12.9, 12.11). And the final scene coordinates with an offering that Taube and his colleagues (2010) refer to as a flower sacrifice. If this parallels Ben years (east) on Dresden 25c (fig. 12.8), it may also represent a fragrant incense offering associated with the Ik' yearbearer date at San Bartolo.

Another pattern of animal offerings is seen with the Late Postclassic yearbearers on Madrid 3a–6a. Here the column on Madrid 3a begins with Late Postclassic Kan (K'an) yearbearer, but the Edznab (Etz'nab) set appears directly below, perhaps indicating a calendrical bridge back to the Early Postclassic yearbearers. The offerings can be linked with both yearbearers. A fish offering in Kan and Edznab years on Madrid 3a is associated with the south (this directional glyph is effaced). On Madrid 4a, the offering is a turkey associated with Muluc (Muluk) and Akbal (Ak'b'al) yearbearers and the east. Madrid 5a shows Ix and Lamat yearbearers with a deer haunch offering in the

Imagery of the Yearbearers in Maya Culture and Beyond · 333

north. The last in the sequence is an iguana offering linked with the west and Cauac (Kawak) and Ben (B'en) yearbearers. The directional associations are the same as the Late Postclassic Kan yearbearers, but on Madrid 3a–6a they are paired with Early Postclassic yearbearers that represent the opposite directions (Dresden 26–28).[14]

Each scene on Madrid 3a–5a shows a serpent wrapped around a pool of water marked with the black number 18, here representing an interval that links the dates in the four scenes, as for example a count from 4 Kan to 10 Akbal (Vail 2013, 27n18; see also Dresden 31b–35b in Thompson 1972, 98–99). The serpents stand erect, recalling the serpent trees in the Dresden yearbearer pages and the trees bearing twined serpents in the San Bartolo mural. Unlike the directional yearbearers almanacs in the Dresden and Madrid codices, the mural depicts a fifth tree that seems to represent the central direction, a pattern that survives in Postclassic iconography, as seen in the sequence of five trees in the Borgia yearbearer pages, where the fifth tree represents the center.

## Central Mexican Counterparts for the Yearbearers

Comparing yearbearer rituals in the Codex Borgia pages 49–52 with those in the three Maya codices offers a fruitful line of research. Although this theme cannot be explored in any detail here, a few intriguing correspondences can be noted.[15] The sun god and the death god are featured in the yearbearer pages of the Madrid, Dresden, and Borgia codices. Borgia 49 (fig. 12.15) links the sun god with the east and Borgia 52 (fig. 12.18) links the death god with the south. The sun god appears on Madrid 37b (fig. 12.6) with the Ix yearbearers of the north, while the death god appears with Cauac yearbearers of the west on Madrid 34a (fig. 12.3). Presuming that the Dresden yearbearer directions follow the proper sequence (east, north, west, and south), the sun god in his temple is associated with the north on Dresden 26b (fig. 12.9), as in the Madrid Codex, but the death god in the temple is linked with the south on Dresden 28b (fig. 12.11), as on Borgia 52 (fig. 12.18). It should be noted that the sun god on Borgia 49 (fig. 12.15) has the yearbearer of the east overhead (the day sign Reed shown without the year sign). And on Borgia 52, the direction south is drawn from the rabbit day sign overhead (once again without the year sign).

The fire-drilling ceremonies on Borgia 49–52 (figs. 12.15–12.18) relate to the year's end in Izcalli. The imagery on these pages also incorporates the five-day nemontemi period, creating a strong parallel with the year-end Uayeb ceremonies on Dresden 25–28 (figs. 12.3a–d). All the Borgia yearbearer pages record real-time dates falling in Izcalli, the last month of the year, when new fire was drilled (Milbrath 2013, tables 2.4, 3.1).[16] The trees that are dominant on these pages evoke a link with the trees set up during Izcalli in a "solemn feast [that] ended the ceremonies of the year" (Durán 1971, 467). The vertical column of twelve red dots has generally been interpreted as the intervals used to count from one trecena to the next in the day-sign strip below each scene on individual pages. For example, there is an interval of twelve days between the day Crocodile on Borgia 49 and the day Jaguar on Borgia 50. Nonetheless, in the context of real-time events, an interval of twelve days can be associated with the Calendar Round dates shown alongside the intervals to indicate a count forward that takes the cycle from Izcalli, the eighteenth "month" of the year, through the nemontemi at year end and on to the New Year day in February (Milbrath 2013, table 2.4; 5 Grass in the year 4 Flint + 12 days = New Year's day in the year 5 House). Izcalli could be considered the beginning of the agricultural cycle for high-altitude crops that were planted during this month (Durán 1971, 465; Milbrath 2013, 20).

As with the Maya system, the yearbearers in the Aztec calendar gradually shifted position relative to the solar year. But unlike the Classic Maya calendar, the months, or *veintenas,* in the 365-day year could be adjusted because these 20-day periods were not recorded in calendar inscriptions (Milbrath 2013, 11).[17] Some form of adjustment is implied by the link between the festival cycle and the solar events that Anthony Aveni and colleagues (1988, 289–290), Johanna Broda de Casas (1969; 1982, 93), Raphael Tena (1987), and Carmen Aguilera (1989) discuss. Since the festivals did not have a fixed relationship to the Tonalpohualli, they could be moved without breaking the continuous cycle of 260 days.

Alfonso Caso (1971, 346) proposed that the yearbearer naming the year was the 360th day of the year.[18] However, around the time of the conquest in 1519–1520, the yearbearer position actually coincided with the end of the second-to-last month (Tititl) or the first of Izcalli (Milbrath 2013, tables 1.4, 1.5).[19] In the late fifteenth century, the Codex Borgia yearbearers fell in late January, and they were positioned well before the year ended with the nemontemi in February. During that time span, the yearbearer in January fell on the last of Tititl or the first day of Izcalli, the last month in the year, presuming intercalations were not made in the festival calendar. The Borgia was painted shortly before the conquest, so we can leave aside the discussion of intercalation to focus instead on the imagery, because the seasonal position of the months was close to that recorded at the time of the conquest.

The trees below the temple offerings in the Borgia recall the Itzamna trees of the Dresden. The Borgia trees can also be visualized as world trees known from creation mythology. Both codices show yearbearer images related

Imagery of the Yearbearers in Maya Culture and Beyond · 335

to ceremonies that mark the transition from one year to another (Vail and Hernández 2003, 75–76). There does not, however, seem to be any direct correlation between the types of trees represented in the Borgia and those in the Dresden. Assuming that the cardinal direction is dictated by the yearbearer day signs (without a year sign) above each scene, the east has a quetzal on a chalchihuitl tree (Borgia 49; fig. 12.15), the north has an eagle on a cactus (Borgia 50; fig. 12.16), the west has a maize tree with another raptor (probably a hawk; Borgia 51; fig. 12.17), and the tree of the south is a spiny tree with a macaw perched on top (Borgia 52; fig. 12.18). One final "tree" on Borgia 53 represents a maize plant with another quetzal and most certainly represents the center, as Eduard Seler (1963) noted long ago. The maize plant on Borgia 53 is flanked by two gods drawing blood as an offering, paralleling the gods making bloody temple offerings seen on the other yearbearer pages.

For the eastern yearbearer on Borgia 49, represented by Acatl (Reed) in a strip above the scene, we see the sun god offering a human heart to the sun in a floral temple. For the northern yearbearer on Borgia 50, represented by Tecpatl (Flint), we see Itztlacoliuhqui offering a heart to the moon in a temple crowned by flint knives. Calli (House) is the western yearbearer on Borgia 51, where a god (Xochipilli?) offers a heart to a gourd for holding tobacco in another floral temple. Tochtli (Rabbit) is the southern yearbearer on Borgia 52, where the death god Mictlantecuhtli offers a decapitated human to an owl in a bone temple.

In the upper scenes on Borgia 49a–52a, the skybearers are Tlahuizcalpantecuhtli, Xiuhtecuhtli (the fire god), Ehecatl (the wind god), and Mictlantecuhtli; each is paired with a god holding a rattle staff, suggesting comparison with the opossum Pauahtuns on the Dresden yearbearer pages, who may carry gods representing the old year. The pairing of the Borgia skybearers with the rattle staff figures also suggests Landa's pairing of the Pauahtuns and the Bacabs, who Landa refers to as skybearers. On Borgia 49, we see Xipe with the skybearer Tlahuizcalpantecuhtli; on Borgia 50, Mictlantecuhtli appears with the skybearer Xiuhtecuhtli; on Borgia 51, Xochipilli (?) appears with the skybearer Ehecatl (Quetzalcoatl); and, on Borgia 52, Centeotl is shown with the skybearer Mictlantecuhtli. This group of skybearers may be part of central Mexican year-end ceremonies that spread to the Maya area, especially at Mayapán, where there is clear evidence of contact between the two areas in the Postclassic (Chase and Rice 1985, 233; Milbrath 2005; Lacadena García-Gallo 2010; Masson and Peraza Lope 2010; Vail and Hernández 2010b, 265).

## Mayapán Effigy Censers and Yearbearer Iconography

Thompson (1957) identified a number of central Mexican gods among the Mayapán effigy censers, including Tlazolteotl, Quetzalcoatl, Xipe Totec, and the Venus god, Tlahuizcalpantecuhtli (Venus as "lord of dawn"), although he misidentified Huehueteotl, the old fire god, as Itzamna (Taube 1992a, fig. 66a). The Borgia skybearers shown in the upper registers of the yearbearer pages are comparable to these effigy censers representing foreign gods. The skybearers Tlahuizcalpantecuhtli, Xiuhtecuhtli, Ehecatl-Quetzalcoatl, and Mictlantecuhtli (the death god) all appear among the effigy censers. The first three are clearly foreign gods in the Mayapán effigy-censer complex, but the death god has similar attributes in both the Maya and central Mexican areas (see Milbrath et al. 2021). Tlazolteotl, who also represents a foreign deity in the censer complex, is prominent in the yearbearer pages of the Codex Borgia (49–52). In a marriage scene on Borgia 50b, Tlazolteotl appears with her distinctive spindle headdress, and she may also be depicted in a death aspect on all four yearbearer pages (49b–52b) in the form of a diving Cihuateteo who wears her costume but notably lacks the spindle headdress (Milbrath 2013, 54–58). Because the foreign deities among the Mayapán effigy censers can be related to yearbearer festivals shared with central Mexico, it seems possible that the Maya yearbearer ceremonies were influenced by central Mexico during the Postclassic, for central Mexican deities appear in the Early Postclassic Dresden Codex and at Late Postclassic Mayapán (Taube 1992a, 125; Milbrath 1999, 173–174; Milbrath and Peraza Lope 2013; Masson and Peraza Lope 2010, table 4).

Because a previous study explores the role of deities represented in effigy censers in the annual cycle of the Haab (Milbrath and Walker 2016b), here I focus more specifically on yearbearer festivals involving effigy censers. During the five-day Uayeb, effigy-censer rituals played an important role in ushering in the New Year (D. Chase 1986; D. Chase and A. Chase 1988, 72; Russell 2008; Milbrath and Walker 2016b). Effigy censers were also offered incense during the first month of Pop, according to Landa (Tozzer 1941, 152–153). The deities represented in the effigy-censer complex include many of the gods portrayed in the yearbearer pages of the Madrid Codex, as would be expected given the late date of this codex and the effigy-censer complex at Mayapán (1350–1450 CE). The gods and the effigy censers are shown in a combined format on Madrid 63c–64c, where a group of six gods, including God A, God N, and God D, depict effigy censers, for they have vessels attached to their bodies (Milbrath and Peraza Lope 2013, 219–220). The Dresden Codex, which dates somewhere between

1100 and 1250/1300 CE, corresponds to the Early Postclassic before Chen Mul Modeled effigy censers were produced, so these yearbearer pages illustrate composite censers from this earlier period. But the deities shown on Dresden 25–28 may be related to those seen among Mayapán's Late Postclassic effigy censers.

At least ten deities known from the codices are represented in Mayapán's effigy censers (Thompson 1957; Milbrath and Peraza Lope 2013, 217). The cast of characters in the effigy censer complex at Mayapán is certainly much broader than those found at sites to the south, where only a few Maya gods are represented (Milbrath and Walker 2016a). The most common deities among Mayapán's effigy censers are the rain god Chac (God B), the death god (God A), the maize god (God E), the merchant god (God M), and Itzamna (God D). Many of these play a role in the Uayeb festivals Landa described and the yearbearer pages in the codices (figs. 12.19a and b; Milbrath and Walker 2016b, table 10.1).

Effigy censers representing aged gods at Mayapán are most often classified as Itzamna (God D of the codices; Thompson 1957; Masson and Peraza Lope 2014, 438–442, fig. 7.3a and table 7.3). However, some of these aged gods actually represent Pauahtuns and the old fire god (Taube 1992a, 125, fig. 66a; Milbrath and Peraza Lope 2013, 217, fig. 12.1). A Mayapán effigy censer depicting God N seems to have opossum feet, suggesting that this effigy could be a counterpart for the opossum Pauahtun represented in the Uayeb ceremonies on Dresden 25–28, one of the four Pauahtuns linked with the four different yearbearers and their associated cosmic directions (figs. 12.8–12.11, 12.20; Milbrath and Walker 2016b, 197, fig. 10.4). On Madrid Codex 37, the Pauahtun associated with Ix yearbearers wears a pectoral that seems to be carved mussel shell (*oyohualli*), like the Mayapán censer representing God N (figs. 12.6, 12.20a). This Mayapán effigy wears the *oyohualli* mounted on a braided rope pectoral, a combination also seen on the opossum Pauahtun on page 26 of the Dresden Codex (fig. 12.9).

Effigy censers depicting Chac are related to representations in the codices, and Landa's (Tozzer 1941, 137–138) account of the Uayeb festivals mentions four Chacs, each associated with different yearbearers and cardinal directions and colors. On Dresden Codex 25a (fig. 12.8), Chac (God B) is a burden carried by the opossum god in the Uayeb ceremonies of Ben years that mark the eastern direction. Chac represents the tun tree in the lower register of the same page (Thompson 1972, 93). The yearbearer pages in the Madrid mention Chac repeatedly in the text. In the Madrid Codex (34b; fig. 12.3), Chac is represented as a decapitated head held by God A in the west during Cauac years, which in Landa's account (Tozzer 1941, 148) are associated with drought.

The death god (God A) appears in Cauac years on Madrid Codex 34 and is featured in Landa's (Tozzer 1941, 147–148) account of Cauac years (Milbrath and Walker 2016b, table 10.1). Vail (2004, 224) points out that the Cauac (Kawak) yearbearer images showing the death god suggest a parallel with Landa's account of the high mortality in Cauac years. Effigy censers representing the death god are not uncommon, but one exceptional example is large and shows the skeletal imagery in great detail (fig. 12.19a).

A Mayapán effigy censer representing the maize god as a youthful figure with maize foliation is the counterpart of God E in the codices (Milbrath and Peraza Lope 2013, 220–221, fig. 12.6; Milbrath and Walker 2016b, fig. 10.10) (fig. 12.19b). The unusual hollowed-out step replacing the eye evokes the "step-eyed" face paint used for the maize god in the codices, especially representations in the Madrid Codex (27a–28a, 73a–74a). The yearbearer pages in the Madrid also depict the maize god with step-eyed face paint, as do the yearbearer pages of the Paris Codex. The step-eyed face paint in the Madrid Codex images of the maize god in the yearbearer pages is also like that used for Centeotl, the maize god on Borgia 52, the last yearbearer page in the Codex Borgia (fig. 12.18). It seems likely that the Mayapán maize god censer was used in yearbearer rituals, as this god appears on the yearbearer pages in all three codices, although it appears only once in the Dresden Codex yearbearer pages (27a; fig. 12.10).

Mayapán censers were used for individual deity worship, in funerary rites associated with burials, and in calendric rituals that are evidenced in large deposits of smashed censers. At least one group of censers associated with an altar in a colonnaded hall at Mayapán was in good condition when excavated by archaeologists and the structure seems to have been in active use during the Late Postclassic period (Structure Q81; Milbrath and Peraza Lope 2013, 222–223), but other groups are missing pieces, suggesting that they were partially destroyed before being moved to their final location in altars and burials during the Late Postclassic (Thompson 1957, 602; Milbrath and Peraza Lope 2013, 209–210).[20]

Thompson (1957) recognized that the clay idols Landa mentioned were effigy censers representing deities, but he discounted Landa's statement (Tozzer 1941, 161n840) that the Maya renewed the "idols of clay and the braziers" in the festival of Oc Na, celebrated in Ch'en or Yax. Thompson (1957) argued that the braziers were renewed every 260 days on the date 1 Imix, which happened to fall in Ch'en when Landa collected his data. Nonetheless, it seems that this censer renewal in Ch'en or Yax (January 2–February 10 in the Gregorian calendar) may have been timed to coordinate with the beginning of the agricultural cycle.

The need for an annual renewal of idols and their braziers may have occurred because they were believed to have gathered negative energy throughout the year; at year's end they were disposed of in ritual dumps (D. Chase 1985b, 119, fig. 8; Russell 2000, 54–55). Smashing censers could also have been part of the fabrication process for new effigies; one colonial period source notes that censers were ground up for use in making new censer images (Chuchiak 2009, 146).[21] Since so many of the effigy censers are broken, they most likely were part of termination rituals at year's end (D. Chase 1985b, 119–121). This would make their destruction a precursor to the yearbearer ceremonies of the New Year.

Although the emphasis here is on the yearbearer cycle and effigy censers that may represent gods honored in these ceremonies, we should not underestimate the importance of effigy censers created for the katun ceremonies that were performed at approximately 20-year intervals ($20 \times 360$ days) in a katun cycle spanning 13 katuns ($13 \times 20 \times 360$ days), or about 257 years.[22] Such a pattern has been proposed for the Classic Maya composite censers at Palenque (Cuevas García and Bernal Romero 2002, 30; Rice 2004, 76–77). Temporal sequences of cache vessels at sites such as Caracol, Belize, may also be related to marking the longer cycles of time seen in the katun cycle (A. Chase and D. Chase 2013a; chapter 14, this volume).

Diane Chase (1985b, 119–121) suggests that paired effigy censers seem to follow patterns Landa described (Tozzer 1941, 168), in which one idol replaced another in the katun ceremonies. According to Landa, during the katun period, idols were used in pairs and the second one was brought in halfway through the katun. This detail may be compared with paired effigy censers found in varying stages of completion in five different structures (2, 5, 6, 17, and 81) at Santa Rita, Corozal, Belize (D. Chase 1985b, 119–121, D. Chase and A. Chase 1988, 72, 85). An effigy-censer pair has been documented at Mayapán, where an almost complete example was recovered in Structure Q-152a and a more fragmentary duplicate was found buried nearby between Q-151 and Q-152a (figs. 12.20a and b). These paired effigy censers represent Pauahtuns (God N) and possibly were used in katun ceremonies (Milbrath and Peraza Lope 2013, 217). The more complete version portrays this old god with opossum feet wearing an *oyohualli* mounted on a braided breastplate (Milbrath and Walker 2016a, fig. 10.4). The braided pectoral is fairly common throughout the corpus of Postclassic effigy censers but is only rarely seen with the *oyohualli*.[23] This unusual combination also appears on the opossum god that is one of the four Pauahtuns represented in the yearbearer imagery on Dresden 26a, raising a question about whether these effigy censers are paired gods associated with katun ceremonies or two opossum Pauahtuns like the four seen in the Dresden Codex.

340 · Susan Milbrath

In sum, it seems most likely that the foreign gods represented in the effigy-censer complex from Mayapán are images of yearbearer gods like those known from central Mexico. Maya deities represented among the effigy censers also can be found in the yearbearer pages of the Maya codices. Although effigy censers were used throughout the year, they may have been especially important in year-end ceremonies as "idols" that were rotated to different locations in Landa's account of the Uayeb ceremonies. Effigy censers representing the deities of the outgoing year may have been smashed, recalling the destruction of the Mam effigies representing the old year that López de Cogolludo (1688) described, a practice that seems to survive today among the Tzutzujil Maya in Guatemala.

## Concluding Remarks

Postclassic Maya codices provide evidence of yearbearer ceremonies, and parallel rituals are known from the central Mexican codices, especially the Codex Borgia. The scenes of gods making temple offerings on the Borgia yearbearer pages evoke comparisons with the Madrid and Dresden yearbearer pages. During the Postclassic period, extensive use of effigy censers in ritual contexts and their destruction and deposition in ritual deposits suggests an association with year-end ceremonies. Mayapán censers representing foreign gods have direct counterparts in the Borgia yearbearer pages, and those depicting Maya gods are seen in the yearbearer pages of the Maya codices.

Although Maya codices list the yearbearers naming the New Year, the imagery on these yearbearer pages seems most closely related to Landa's description of the Uayeb ceremony. However, the Madrid includes references to the first month of Pop and imagery that predicts the fortunes of the maize crop during the year. Evidence of these prophecies is also seen in Landa's Uayeb ceremonies, in the Paris yearbearer pages, and in some texts on the Dresden Codex yearbearer pages that predict drought or abundance.

Perhaps the yearbearer had an early association with the maize cycle. Prior to the development of the Long Count, the yearbearer may have initiated the year around the beginning of the agricultural cycle. Middle Preclassic patterns placed the yearbearer and the New Year on 0 Pop or 1 Pop near the beginning of the agricultural cycle, circa 750–700 BCE. The yearbearer could have marked the beginning of a 260-day agricultural count at this time. When the Long Count calendar came into use in the Late Preclassic, the yearbearers no longer correlated with the beginning of the agrarian cycle, but the 260-day period of the Tzolk'in was still used to measure the agricultural season.

After the Long Count began to fade away in the Terminal Classic, there was a renewed link between the yearbearer and the beginning of the agricultural cycle, as seen at Ceibal, Guatemala. At this time, as a result of influence from central Mexico, a new set of yearbearers (the Akbal set) repositioned the yearbearer near the beginning of the agricultural cycle. The Kan set was introduced during the Late Postclassic, perhaps to integrate the yearbearer with the New Year in July and the second planting in Yucatán. The Mayapán calendar yearbearers (the Kan set) that were adopted in the Late Postclassic helped reposition the yearbearer in relation to a fixed time of year. This adjustment was possible only because the calendar had a new emphasis on yearbearer cycles, perhaps borrowed from central Mexico.

Periodic adjustments to the festival calendar may be evident during the Late Postclassic in both the Maya region and central Mexico. In the Maya area, this adjustment also seems to have involved the adoption of the Kan set of yearbearers. Although the yearbearers no longer marked the beginning of the Maya agricultural cycle in late January or early February, the pattern seems to have been preserved in central Mexico and in some Maya calendars today. In Postclassic central Mexico, the fact that the year end and New Year fall in February in festival calendars—along with the emphasis on agricultural rituals in the *veintenas*—indicates that the festival calendar was probably adjusted periodically to keep in tune with the seasons, even though the yearbearer clearly changed position over time.

The practice of coordinating the beginning of the 260-day agricultural cycle and the New Year in late January or early February could be an ancient pattern dating to the Middle Preclassic, before the advent of the Classic Maya Long Count calendar. Originally the yearbearer played a role in subdividing the year into a 260-day agricultural period and a 105-day residual period, which helped calculate both the nine-month agrarian cycle and the 365-day year. The development of the Long Count during the Late Preclassic made the yearbearer relatively insignificant, which may be why yearbearer notations appear during the Preclassic but are not common in the Classic period.

Although the yearbearer gradually shifted away from the beginning of the agricultural cycle, a count of 260 days is built into the Tzolk'in, in which the agrarian cycle would begin and end on the same day. Today, the Maya agricultural cycle preserves a fixed 260-day agrarian period that is apparently quite ancient and may have originated as a subdivision of the 365-day year. The maize cycle probably inspired Mesoamerican calendar priests to develop a 260-day calendar coordinated with the agricultural cycle. The position of the yearbearer at the beginning of the agrarian cycle in late January or early February during the early part of the Middle Preclassic provides

## Acknowledgments

My thanks to Victoria Bricker, Weldon Lamb, and Gaby Vail for reading and commenting on an earlier draft of this paper. Also, many thanks to the Foundation for the Advancement of Mesoamerican Studies, Inc. (FAMSI), which funded my research on effigy censers.

## Notes

1  Among the Tzotzil of Chenalhó, maize prognostications are also linked to cardinal directions and colors. North is linked to the color white, west to black, south to yellow, and east to red. Three of these colors relate to scarcity of maize (famine): black represents famine related to women, red famine related to men, and white famine related to children, while yellow is a color associated with an abundance of maize, in accord with the good prognostications for maize associated with south and the color yellow associated with the Kan yearbearer in Landa's account (Tozzer 1941, 139, 142; Guiteras Holmes 1961, 287).

2  Gabrielle Vail and Christine Hernández (2013, 103) argue that the temple gods in the middle register are covered with their capes to symbolize their death as the patron of the old year. They directly equate them with the burden gods carried by the opossums, but this link remains unconvincing, for the maize god (God E), the burden god on 27a, cannot be not directly equated with Itzamna depicted in the temple below. I would also question the direct equation between the jaguar burden on 26a and K'inich Ahau in the temple on 26b and God A with the death god known as God A' (Dresden 28a). All of these gods seem to play different roles (Milbrath 1999, 81, 123–124, 135, 137, 156).

3  Thompson (1972, 92) identified the sun god offering a decapitated bird on Dresden 25c (bottom scene of fig. 12.8) as Itzamna, but he has a Roman nose, a tau-shaped tooth and the barbel of the sun god, whereas God D is clearly aged and toothless. Harvey Bricker and Victoria Bricker (2011, 124, table 6-1) identify this god as Ahau Kin, even though the typical Kin infix in the forehead associated with the sun god and the glyph compound naming the sun god are both lacking. A name with the Chac prefix above

Imagery of the Yearbearers in Maya Culture and Beyond · 343

this figure is interpreted as a reference to the red cape worn by the sun god. See also Vail and Hernández (2013, appendix 8.1), who refer to this god as K'in Ahaw.

4  The piles of stones that Landa described served as altars where images of the gods were placed during the Uayeb ceremonies. Remains of such altars can be seen at the entry to Maya towns today (Thompson 1972, 91; Bricker and Bricker 2011, 121). Thompson also notes that these stone "trees" may represent either the *acante* (set-up tree or post) or the *acatun* (set-up stone or pillar), which is mentioned in the *Ritual of the Bacabs*.

5  *The Book of Chilam Balam of Chumayel* and parallel passages in the Tizimin and Mani texts say that after the sky fell and a great flood ensued, the world order was restored when the four Bacabs set up trees of different colors to mark the cardinal directions (Roys [1933] 1967, 99–101n3). The Chumayel text specifically mentions setting up the idol of katun in this context, which Ralph Roys ([1933] 1967, 101n1) interprets as a numerical marker for the sequence of 13 katuns in the calendar cycle.

6  In the Tzotzil community of San Andrés Larráinzar, the four corners of the heavens are intercardinal directions where the *cargadores* (yearbearers) reside (Holland 1964, 16). East is white and is linked to the god of rain; north is also white but is associated with the god of maize; west is black, linked with the god of death; and south is red, linked with the god of wind. Among the Tzotzil, Lacandón, and K'iche', the yearbearer days are also linked with the skybearers who hold up the heavens at the four intercardinal directions, which apparently are associated with the sun's solstice extremes (Köhler 1980, 585–586).

7  Certain aspects of Landa's yearbearer cycle confirm the associations Flores proposed (Tozzer 1941, 147–149). Landa describes Cauac ceremonies as nocturnal events, in keeping with the model Flores proposed, and on page 34 of the Madrid Codex we find a priest-astronomer looking at the night sky in the Cauac years, indicating that the ceremony is nocturnal, in keeping with the midnight-to-dawn ceremony Flores described. On page 37, in the Ix years, the animal playing a drum has been described as a dog (Milbrath 1999, 62; Vail 2013, 103), but it also resembles what seems to be an opossum with a burning tail on Madrid 36. Be it dog or opossum, overhead there is a lunar crescent, a nocturnal image for a dusk-to-midnight ceremony, as Flores proposed. Previously, I (Milbrath 1999, 62–63) summarized the sequence as follows:

> Flores notes that in the years named Kan, which were associated with the south and the color yellow, the ceremony began at dawn and ran until noon. He proposes that the priest positioned himself to the south to observe the sun until it reached its noon position, symbolized by yellow for the resplendent sun overhead. In the next year, a Muluc year associated with the east and red, the ceremonies began at noon and ran until sunset. Now the priest positioned himself to the east and looked to the west to observe the setting sun, associated with the color red because of the red glow of sunset. Then followed an Ix year, symbolized by the north and black; the ceremony began at sunset and continued to midnight. At this time, the priest positioned himself to the north and focused his attention on the underworld, waiting for the sun to reach its lowest position at midnight. In the last year of the four-year sequence, a Cauac year represented by the west and white, the ceremony began at midnight and ended at dawn; the priest positioned himself to the west to observe the rising sun, associated with white because that is the usual color of the dawn sky.

344 · Susan Milbrath

8 There is evidence that the Ik set of yearbearers were used for a long time during the Late Preclassic and Classic (Stuart 2004a). This set of yearbearers remains in use today in the Maya area among the Ixil and K'iche' (Thompson 1960, 127).

9 In Catholic Latin America, carnival is followed by Semana Santa (Holy Week), the week from Palm Sunday to Easter Sunday. In the Tzotzil Maya community of Chamula, the five-day festival of games in February is linked with the Catholic celebration of carnival, but it also evokes a connection with the five-day period of the Uayeb that ends the year. On the fourth day of carnival, officials run back and forth along a path of burning thatch in a fire walk that dramatizes the first ascent of the sun/Christ into heaven (Gossen 1986, 229–230, 246–247, figs. 1–2). Vail (2019b; see also Vail and Hernández 2013, 102) also argues that the Mam in the Tzutzujil holy week may be linked with the Uayeb that marked the last five days of the year.

10 The correlation of the Tzotzil calendar and the European year seems to have occurred at different times, with the result that the months are sometimes positioned slightly differently in the year (V. Bricker, personal communication, August 2017).

11 The K'iche' name their solar year with the Tzolk'in day name and number combination that begins the year, which serve as yearbearers known as the Mam (Tedlock 1992, 35, 91, 99–104).

12 Early yearbearer inscriptions, dating between 600 and 400 BCE, are known from Oaxaca, but they do not make any clear reference to the corresponding position in the 20-day month (Milbrath 2017a, 2017b, 100). These early dates in Oaxaca may be like the Postclassic system in central Mexico, because the months may have operated independently in both systems.

13 Cycle 6 began with 11 Ahau (6.0.0.0.0, 11 Ahau 8 Uo, JDN 1,448,283) on February 28, 748 BCE, close to the beginning of the agrarian year (using the preferred 584,283 correlation and the Gregorian calendar). Thirteen tuns later, 11 Ahau (6.0.13.0.0 11 Ahau 8 Kayab, JDN 1,452,963) was a winter solstice date on December 22, 736 BCE, providing a link between the early calendar and the focus on winter solstice alignments in Middle Preclassic E Groups. The next tun, 6.0.14.0.0 (7 Ahau 13 Kayab, JDN 1,453,323), also approximates the winter solstice, even though it is three days earlier (December 19, 735 BCE). Although Ahau is not among the known yearbearers, it later became important as a tun and katun ending in the Long Count.

14 The Late Postclassic Kan yearbearer set is paired with the Early Postclassic Akbal set, which have opposite directional associations. For example, on Madrid 6a Cauac (west in the Kan set) appears above Ben, which symbolizes the east in the Early Postclassic Akbal set. Such a reversal in directions would be expected if a new set of yearbearers spaced at a 26-day interval were to be adopted.

15 Christine Hernández (2004, 354, fig. 11.15) compares the seated Ahuiteotl figures on Borgia pages 49–52 to the Maya Pauahtuns. I would argue that the rattle staff figures in the upper scenes on these pages make better counterparts for the opossum Pauahtuns, for they share an unusual rattle staff and there are some overlaps in the gods represented. The maize god and the death god appearing among the rattle staff figures of the Borgia are also represented as burdens of the opossums in the Dresden, perhaps depicting representatives of the old year being carried away.

16 The yearbearer festivals on Borgia 49–52 show fire-drilling rituals like those performed

in Aztec accounts of Izcalli, the last *veintena* of the year, which corresponded to February in the Late Postclassic (Gregorian calendar dates are ten days later than the Julian dates in Milbrath 2013, table 3.1). Codex Borgia shares the Aztec yearbearers, Reed (east), Flint (north), House (west), and Rabbit (south), day signs that reference both the year and day of the same name as yearbearer dates. But when they are paired with another Tonalpohualli date, they refer to different times of year. The four yearbearers and their year signs on Borgia 49b–52b are paired with Tonalpohualli dates shown nearby, all bearing the number five. The Tonalpohualli dates (5 Movement, 5 Wind, 5 Deer, 5 Grass) have two occurrences in the year, but when they are paired with the yearbearers, they mark the second occurrence in the year and consistently fall fourteen days after the yearbearer dates on these pages, as in the year 4 Flint diagramed in my Borgia book (Milbrath 2013, table 2.4). These four dates (5 House 5 Movement, 4 Rabbit 5 Wind, 4 Reed 5 Deer, and 4 Flint 5 Grass) correspond to the last festival of the year, Izcalli, during a period running from 1458 to 1497, each positioned at a thirteen-year interval, marking the beginning of a trecena that ends with the New Year in February (Milbrath 2013, 35, table 3.1). For example, on page 49b, the year 4 House is paired with the day 5 Movement to form the date 4 House 5 Movement, which correlates with February 3, 1458, and on Borgia 52 the last date is 4 Flint 5 Grass, which falls on February 7, 1497 (both dates in the Julian calendar), near the end of the 4 Flint, an exceptional year because it included a total eclipse of the sun that is recorded on Borgia 40 (Milbrath 2013, 45, tables 2.4, 3.1).

17 Year dates in the Aztec system were always recorded using the yearbearers and individual days of the 260-day calendar, a cycle of 52 years that is quite unlike the Classic Maya Calendar Round, which has a built-in link between the Haab and the 260-day Tzolk'in (Milbrath 2013, 11). In the Aztec system, periodic adjustments to reposition the festivals in relation to the seasons could be made by adding a quarter day every year, or one day every four years or thirteen days every fifty-two years. A number of ethnohistoric sources maintain that such an adjustment existed, and the festivals seem to have been correlated with seasonal events. Sahagún (1950–1982, 2, 35, 4, 144) says that an extra day was added every four years by extending the nemontemi for six days rather than five. Sahagún (1950–1982:2:35; 4:144) also suggests that a leap-year adjustment took place during a special ceremony held every four years in Izcalli, the last festival of the year.

18 Alfonso Caso (1971, 346, table 4) argued that the Aztec yearbearer had to fall in a "significant position," as the last day of the last *veintena* just before the five-day nemontemi. In order to align the yearbearer with the 360th day of the year, his model ended the year in Tititl, even though his table that compiles the actual records of calendars show that Izcalli most often ended the year (Caso 1967, table X). Henry B. Nicholson's (1971, table 4) synthesis of the festivals indicates that Izcalli ended the year and that the yearbearer was positioned very near the end of the year but was not the last day of the last *veintena* festival.

19 Ethnohistorical sources disagree about the positioning of the yearbearer. There is evidence that the yearbearer was the first day of the year in the Codex Magliabechiano and in Tlaxcala, the possible origin point of the Borgia Codex (Milbrath 2013, 3). Caso favored the 360th day, but I have proposed that the yearbearer only needed to

346 · Susan Milbrath

be positioned in the last *veintena* of the year to retain a significant position in the year (Milbrath 2013, 6–7, 10).

20 The archaeological record shows that the censers were found in a great variety of contexts at Mayapán, including civic and religious structures such as colonnaded halls, shrines, round structures, and pyramids. They also have been found in ceremonial middens, ritual caches, and burial cists but are only rarely found in burials associated with residential structures (Milbrath and Peraza Lope 2013, 210).

21 Some refuse middens contained substantial amounts of effigy-censer sherds, suggesting that these could actually be middens resulting primarily from ceremonial activities. Effigy-censer sherds tend to be so fragmentary that they probably were smashed at another location and subsequently dumped in the midden (Adams 1953, 146; Smith 1971, 111–112, table 22; Milbrath and Peraza Lope 2013, 210). Ceremonial deposits such as these are also found at Dzibanché and at some sites in Belize (Russell 2000; D. Chase and A. Chase 1988, 71–75; Nalda 2005). Freidel (1981b), D. Chase (1985b), Freidel and colleagues (1986), Walker (1990), Rice (1999), and Milbrath et al. (2008) have also noted archaeological evidence for the ancient manipulation of broken censers as part of ritual circuits within cities and pilgrimages between cities. The timing of these pilgrimage trips may show some patterning in terms of the annual cycle, which may have left a syncretic trace in the modern pilgrimage cycles, such as the Ch'orti' pilgrimage just before the rainy season to the sacred spring that is believed to be the home of a great serpent that guards the water (Girard 1962, 81, 95).

22 The Paris Codex katun cycle, the most complete known from the codices, shows a number of deities that can be recognized from the censer corpus. These include multiple images of God E wearing maize foliation and a Kan glyph signifying maize (Paris Codex 3), God N on page 6, God K on page 7, and God D on page 11. Some of these may be linked with the roster of effigy-censer deities, but God K is not among the gods known from the effigy censer complex. All of these gods also appear in the yearbearer ceremonies represented in Maya codices.

23 The braided breastplate with the *oyohualli* is not always associated with the elderly God N, and these two elements appear independently in a wider iconographic context. At Chichén Itzá, reliefs representing the elderly Pauahtun (God N) show him wearing the *oyohualli* without the braided breastplate, and the murals of Santa Rita Corozal show God M wearing an *oyohualli* pendant without the braided breastplate (Taube 1992a, figs. 45b, 46f; Schele and Mathews 1998, fig. 6.10). An effigy censer from Lamanai shows Tlaloc-Chac wearing a braided breastplate without the *oyohualli* (Milbrath et al. 2008, fig. 5).

# 13

# Lived Experience and Monumental Time in the Classic Maya Lowlands

Patricia A. McAnany

Time—whether perceived as a linear phenomenon or a corkscrewing spiral—provides a benchmark for lived experiences. The dimensionality of time—the recursivity of annual cycles arrayed against the potentialities of the future and the historicities of the past—carries heavy freight and seems to possess its own intentionality. The fact that temporality can be seated in place (or as landesque cosmography; see chapter 1, this volume) to evoke potentially recurring historicities means that time can be bent to serve the needs of humans and to bolster the fragility of political authority by recourse to temporal precedent.

This chapter considers the intersection of time and authority—the former inexorable and the latter fleeting— for the Classic (250–900 CE) Maya lowlands. For the past 100 years, countless scholars have dwelled on the complexity of Maya temporal calculations and pondered the significance of a dynastic calendar capable of calculating very large bundles of time that far surpassed the scale of human lived experience. The Long Count calendar, however, was juxtaposed with the older, so-called Calendar Round that tracked seasonality and cycles of ritual activity. This count of time that synced with human lived experience continues in use today and provides a touchstone of cultural identity (Tedlock 1983).

As US non-native archaeologists engage with Native Americans on the topic of temporality, we often are told that a linear concept of the past as a place of abandonment and a time that no longer exists is not accurate (Colwell-Chanthaphonh and Ferguson 2006). Many Indigenous people see conjunctions between the past and present as real possibilities. From this perspective, time is not an arrow but a corkscrew of considerable plasticity with pinch points along the spiraling of the corkscrew in which past and present are conjoined.

I suggest that this cosmic framework structured lived experiences—particularly in reference to ancestors—and was further deployed in the southern

348 · Patricia A. McAnany

Maya lowlands in defense of kingship. I address how and why the dynastic (Long Count) calendar became such a fundamental tool of royal courts in the southern lowlands. Although the vast majority of Long Count dates were recorded during the Late Classic period (550–800 CE), the Preclassic period (1000 BCE–250 CE)—during which large shrines began to be erected to patron deities—was crucial to the establishment and acceptance of the Long Count calendar in the Maya region. A critical and underdiscussed dimension of the Long Count calendar is its underutilization in the northern lowlands. The larger significance of this pattern is approached by reference to an anomaly that stands out against this contrastive pattern—the northern court of Ukit Kan Le'k Tok' at Ek' Balam. I discuss the combination of the underutilization of the dynastic count in the northern lowlands and the political resurgence of the north during the Postclassic period (900–1519 CE) in terms of its implications for long-term political sustainability.

## Monumental Time and Social Order

Paul Ricoeur (1984, 1985) uses the term monumental time to describe how a long-duration temporality could be hitched to structures of authority of much shorter duration to enhance their robusticity and their perceived naturalness or inevitability. In a historical sense, such structures of authority are termed "civilizations" and are conceived as triumphs of human creativity and advancement. More recently, the durability (and equability) of schemes of civilizational or monumental time has been called into question (Graeber and Wengrow 2021). Moreover, Scott (2017) and Yoffee (2019) stress the fragile character of authority structures in early states, especially those that rested upon a spectacular degree of social differentiation and hierarchy.

When deployed politically, monumental time inevitably is cross-threaded with social order. Middleton (2017) examines indigenous retrospective texts that address the end times of civilizations—many of which had a concept of royal/monumental time—such as Old Kingdom Egypt, the Akkadian Empire, and Mycenaean Greece. Middleton shows that retrospective texts—which often are considered to be akin to eyewitness accounts—generally were composed after order was restored by later political constellations that were invested in promoting the benefits of an authoritarian regime over more anarchic forms of governance.

Stuart (2011) emphasizes the role of royal courts in maintaining the order of days both calendrically and morally in the southern Maya lowlands of the Classic period. Eberl (2015, 83) develops this idea in more detail by examining the syntax and meaning of *tz'ak* (to put in order) in Classic Maya hieroglyphic texts, particularly as it was used to introduce a retrospective reference via distance numbers. Surveying Ch'olan language texts, Eberl (2015, table 5.1) finds a variety of meanings for the root *tz'ak,* which are translated variously as "fulfill," "complete," "connect," "stack one above the other," or "cure." Yucatec Mayan contains the term *tz'ak yaj,* which refers to a *curandero* (curer) or a *medico* (Martinez Huchim 2014, 238). When these variations on the theme of restorative order are coupled with the placement of *tz'ak* in a hieroglyphic text to introduce retrospective long counts, they reinforce the idea that order and political authority were closely intertwined.

In the colonial-era Maya books of Chilam Balam, calculations of time were organized around a shorter count that involved the *k'atun,* or 20-year count, but in a very different way from the Classic era Long Count (see A. Chase 1986). Within this framework, colonial Maya scribes weighed in retrospectively on problems with the construal of political authority at Chichén Itzá, again reinforcing the idea that scribes perceived the keeping of days (and thus ordering the world) as intertwined with political authority. Houston and colleagues (2003) write about the political crisis at the end of the Classic period in the southern lowlands (when the Long Count fell out of use) as a loss of moral authority—intimating that authority is ephemeral, something that over time can be gained or lost. Here I am concerned primarily with how authority was gained (and ultimately lost) through deployment of monumental time.

## Master Cultivators of Monumental Time

If time (in the larger sense of the cosmos) is perceived as durable and inevitable, then a key question is whether the passage of time will create greater order or greater entropy. A property that we equate with order seems to have been very much on the minds of Classic Maya scribes as they sought to fit the short span of human lives (especially those of rulers) into much larger folds of time. Stuart (2011) illustrates how scribes ordered time in a masterful fashion by extrapolating bundles of days to the nineteenth order, thus abstracting time into a truly monumental entity. Rulers could key into auspicious folds of monumental time (or pinches in the corkscrew of time) to emphasize how their accession to rulership, martial campaigns, or building dedications coincided with events of deep time (see also Freidel et al. 1993, 62–63). Palenque ruler K'inich Akhal Mo' Nahb did just that. His accession took place on a Tzolk'in anniversary of the earlier "accession" of the maize god in 2325 BCE and also commemorated the anniversary of the seating of one of Palenque's patron deities (GI) even earlier (Stuart 2011, 248–249). At Tikal, where the *k'atun* was the focus of much celebration and meditation,

350 · Patricia A. McAnany

the accession of Late Classic ruler Jasaw Chan K'awiil to the throne occurred precisely on the thirteen-katun anniversary of the earlier accession of Sihyaj Chan K'awiil Chak Ich'aak' (A. Chase and D. Chase 2020a, 45; see also Schele and Freidel 1990, 205–209). Tikal Stela 31, which dates to the Early Classic, depicts and describes Sihyaj Chan K'awiil Chak Ich'aak as one who tends to the *k'atun* much as one would a maize field (Stuart 2011, 274). Employing the expression *u-kabjiiy,* rulers presented themselves as tending to the spatial and temporal dimensions of their realm much in the way that a farmer cultivates a field (Houston and Inomata 2009, 145). In short, *k'uhul ajaw* were master cultivators of monumental time.

The way the royal chronicling of the Long Count meshed with the older agricultural calendar (Calendar Round) to create a complex whole indicates the importance of grounding the abstractness of the very large numbers entailed in the Long Count with the seasonal concerns of farmers who were served by the Calendar Round (fig. 13.1). The latter 52-year cycle combines a ritual/lunar (260-day) count with the annual solar cycle of 365 days. Milbrath (chapter 12, this volume) probes the Preclassic origins of the agricultural calendar and its signature yearbearers. Inomata and Triadan (chapter 3, this volume) and Stanton et al. (chapter 5, this volume) present case studies that detail how the annual passage of the sun was marked architecturally by the construction of Preclassic E Group architecture—the earliest form of non-residential architecture in the Maya lowlands (Inomata et al. 2020; McAnany 2020a). Although Classic period texts often contain a Calendar Round date that is not accompanied by the Long Count, a Long Count date rarely occurs without a Calendar Round date. They meshed together to form a totality, yet the agricultural calendar proved to be far more durable than the kingly Long Count.

The abstract quality of large numbers—particularly in reference to bundles of time—presumably would not have been very effective in mediating the social distance that stood between Classic Maya literati and their supporters. The latter likely were more invested in units of time that tracked lived experiences, including planting, harvesting, transporting heavy tumplines from place to place, and participating in the rituals and festivities that populated the ritual and solar year. The genius of sculptors who worked under the patronage of Waxaklahun Ubaah K'awiil, thirteenth ruler of Copán, was the way they connected the abstract with the practical day-to-day routine in the lives of ordinary peoples. Waxaklahun Ubaah K'awiil filled the Great Plaza of Copán with images of himself in the guise of various deities (Newsome 2001a). On the obverse of Stela D, a Long Count date is presented in full figural glyphs (fig. 13.2). Monumental time is represented as a monumental burden to be

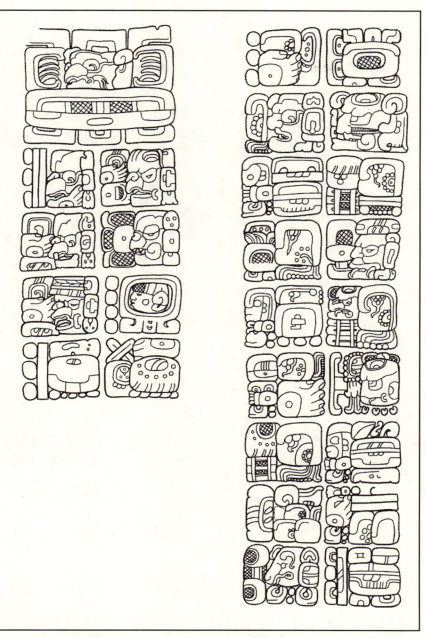

Figure 13.1. Stela C (obverse) at Quirigua; "creation" date of 3,114 BCE, or 13.0.0.0.0 in the Long Count followed by a calendar-round date of 4 Ajaw 8 Kumk'u. Source: Looper (2014). Drawing by Matthew Looper, used with his permission.

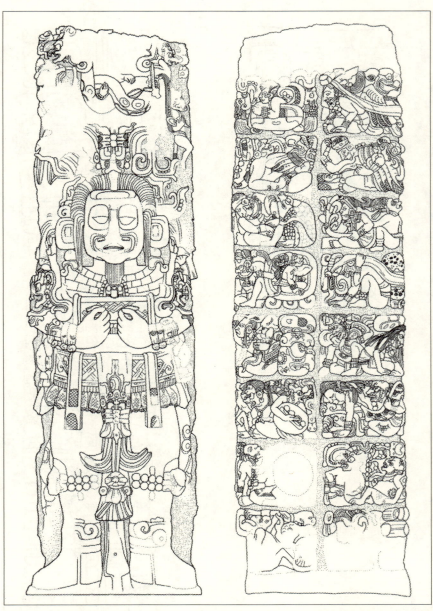

Figure 13.2. Stela D at Copán, front and back sides. A Long Count date is rendered in double-column full-figural glyphs that use the trope of deep time as a burden accepted by dynastic ruler Waxaklahun Ubaah K'awiil. Drawing by Anne Dowd, used with her permission. Source: Baudez (1994, figs. 11A–B).

borne on a tumpline, much as a harvest of maize would be borne. Rulers were "burdened with time" as Eberl (2015, 80, after Thompson 1966, 163–164) has suggested (see further discussion in Stanton et al., chapter 5). But time is different from maize; the former cargo was borne by those who had authority over (and responsibility for) the well-being of a kingdom. One cannot help but imagine that such representations strove to create an intersubjectivity or shared basis of experience between rulers and ruled. Such conventions address what Kurnick (2016, 19–20) refers to as the paradox and incongruity of governance by rulership that simultaneously reinforced social inequality (in this case by referring to the abstract Long Count) yet also promoted solidarity by suggesting that we all have burdens to bear (although for rulers it may be the abstract burden of time).

## Creating Deep-Time Narratives for Patron Deities

Patron deities were even more effective in mediating the social distance between Classic Maya literati and their supporters. Baron (2016b) emphasizes that patron deities were linked to place rather than to a royal line and thus were important to everyone, not just the royal court. Excavations at the Classic Maya royal court and community of La Corona provide supporting artifactual evidence for a broad base of propitiators around patron-deity shrines (Baron 2016b).

The popularity of patron deities across Maya social sectors foreshadowed the important role of patron saints in Catholic communities in Latin America, such as San Bartolomé at the northern lowland community of Tahcabo, Yucatán, the site of an ongoing community-engaged archaeological project (McAnany and Brown 2016; Batún-Alpuche et al. 2017; Dedrick et al. 2020). Just as patron saints can weather adversity (see Watanabe 1989) and keep on ticking, so also could patron deities, even when stolen or lost during martial activity. They were durable in a way that is parallel to the durability of monumental time and countered the precariousness of political authority.

Arlen Chase and Diane Chase (2012, 258) suggest that specific deities figured importantly in the founding of many pre-Hispanic Maya communities. In this manner, patron deities also anticipated the acceptance of patron saints. In liturgical histories of Yucatán such as that compiled by López de Cogolludo (1688, 238), the founding of a Catholic community took place when a patron saint was installed. At the *reducción* of Tahcabo, a chapel was built in 1612 to house San Bartolomé, who became the patron of the community. Despite the political violence that rocked eastern Yucatán during the latter half of the nineteenth century (and resulted in the nearly complete abandonment of Tahcabo), the new/returning population of the late nineteenth and early twentieth centuries reinstalled San Bartolomé, refurbishing his halo and sword.

During earlier times, patron deities bridged the gap between mythic time and lived experience. The Palenque Triad is probably the best-known example of patron deities with histories that extend back to primordial times, but there are many other examples (see Stuart 2011, 245–251; Baron 2016b, 173–187). Baron (2016b) discusses the confusion on the part of epigraphers between patron deities and royal persons due to strong parallels in the ways such deities are presented textually and their frequent association with the Long Count. Commencing in the Late Preclassic period (350 BCE–250 CE), Long Count dates chiseled into stone on the Pacific Slope of the Maya region are roughly coeval with the building of massive pyramid complexes at places such as the Mirador Basin of northern Guatemala or at Xocnaceh, located at the base of the Puuc in Yucatán, México (see also chapter 4, this volume). This coincidence suggests that monumental time (i.e., the Long Count) initially was created to provide deep narratives of place for patron deities and was only later adapted to the needs of hereditary rulership. After all, the tall, thin funerary pyramids of dead dynasts seldom were built before the Classic period, and the most spectacular examples date to the Late Classic period (550–800 CE).

Ringle (1999, 214) has suggested that Preclassic pyramids were community shrines that effectively integrated a burgeoning population. Writing in reference to the northern lowlands, Ringle notes that although these monumental constructions resulted in the marked social differences that were evident during the later Classic period, the shrines were not necessarily the expression of that difference. The visibility of patron deity shrines during Preclassic times may indicate the conflation of the Long Count (as an expression of mythic time) with everyday concerns of survival, fertility, good fortune, and martial victory. These concerns are dear to community life and were materialized in patron deity shrines that created a kind of landesque cosmography.

## Ancestralizing Time

How did ancestors fit into the long spiraling cycles of time in which moments of conjunctions between the past and present existed? Contemporary and Classic Maya naming practices recycle ancestral names in a patterned frequency that Bricker (2002) discusses for Yaxchilan and Stuart (2011, 280) notes for Palenque (see chapter 2, this volume, for another example from Calakmul). The historically known practice of naming grandchildren after a grandparent is well attested among highland Maya peoples (Vogt 1970; Mondloch

1980; Carlsen and Prechtel 1991; Pitarch 2010). This convention—in which a grandchild is referred to as a renewal of the ancestral form of a grandparent (Carlsen and Prechtel 1991)—indicates how short temporal cycles of inter-generational continuity can be achieved simply through naming conventions, although such conventions may be guided by deeper beliefs. Both Vogt (1970) and Pitarch (2010) suggest that among Maya peoples in the highlands of Chiapas, the soul of an ancestor can be infused into an infant. A belief in the immortality of a soul—which is also attested among Nahua peoples in the Mexican highlands (López Austin 1980)—appears to have been widespread throughout Mesoamerica during pre-Columbian times.

In some parts of Mesoamerica, beliefs regarding the soul and immortality were materialized through investments that are recoverable by archaeologists. In the southern Maya lowlands, in particular, anchoring place by reference to ancestors evolved into the iterative practice of residential burial (McAnany 2013). Recently, I have explored this practice in greater detail in reference to the thesis of residential burial as a practice related to the curation of souls (McAnany 2020b). More traditionally, residential burial—a practice that can be traced back to 1000 BCE—has been linked to founding events, renovation episodes, and sometimes closure of residential complexes in the southern low-lands (e.g., McAnany 2004). This practice continued through the Terminal Classic period. Goudiaby and Nondédéo (2020) chronicle the careful manner in which Classic period building construction and burial interment at Naach-tun were intertwined, suggesting that the practice of founding a new structure through ancestor interment had become de rigueur. The widespread distribution of this practice throughout the southern lowlands provides support for this notion.

On the other hand, ancestor interments are not found in every residential complex in the southern lowlands. Many modestly constructed domiciles do not contain subfloor burials or separate ancestor shrines. Spotlighting ancestors is a conservative practice that looks to the past as a source of inherited authority. Over time, that past may become mythic and (if linked to place) en-twined with those of a patron deity. Such a process appears to have occurred in the southern lowlands as leaders became rulers and absorbed the sacred qualities of (and entangled their pedigrees with) those of deities. Although rulers were mortal like all humans, through the construction of postmortem ancestor shrines, rulers joined deities in occupying auspicious points in the pinched spiral of monumental time.

In popular parlance, it is common to declare that something (especially a mode of social media such as Twitter) has been weaponized. While I hesi-tate to suggest that time was weaponized in the southern lowlands through

356 · Patricia A. McAnany

the invocation of ancestors, it does seem accurate to suggest that time was ancestralized. Particularly in royal contexts, ancestral time and monumental time were interlocked both conceptually and materially. The conservatism of ancestor veneration with its emphasis on inherited authority plowed a deep furrow. And there were no easy work-arounds for the tendency of ancestor veneration to create and maintain social difference.

## Monumental Time in the Northern Lowlands?

What of the northern lowlands? Ancestors certainly were/are important there, but the practice of residential burial and the presence of Classic period pyramidal shrines containing royal ancestors is understated or not present at all (but see discussion of the royal ancestor shrine at Ek' Balam below). From a purely pragmatic perspective, the thin soils of the northern lowlands created a challenge for subfloor burial, and cremation was practiced there (Tiesler 2018). In many parts of the north, residential complexes were built directly on top of bedrock outcrops, as at Sayil in the Puuc region (Carmean et al. 2011) or at Chunchucmil (Hutson 2010) on the northern Yucatec plain. In the royal complexes of the north, funerary pyramid construction is not common, although it is not completely absent (e.g., Tiesler et al. 2017). The role of ancestors was different. In the north, there was more emphasis on architectural monumentality as a way to promote group solidarity rather than to extol the virtues of a sacred ruling lineage (Gallareta Cervera 2016; see also Batún-Alpuche and Freidel's discussion of *mul meyah,* or "mountained work," in chapter 15 of this volume).

Great halls (Popol Nah) are a common feature of the Early Puuc Civic Complex and often survived for generations with only minor remodeling or floor resurfacing, while surrounding complexes underwent massive architectural changes (Gallareta Cervera 2016; Ringle et al. 2021). Popol Nah, which are not a common characteristic of southern lowland court complexes, suggest the presence of a more consultative style of governance and perhaps one with a less authoritarian style of rulership.

Although the south displays many differences from the northern region, both share a limestone substrate. However, the distinctive geomorphology, hydrology, and (perhaps most important) the circumstance of being surrounded by water on three sides meant that the north never had the insularity that cyclically was a strongly determinative characteristic of the southern lowlands. Most relevant to the study at hand—of lived experience and monumental time—is the underrepresentation of Classic period royal tombs and carved hieroglyphic texts with Long Count dates in the northern lowlands. These are the characteristics that mark the southern lowlands as distinct from the rest of pre-Hispanic Mesoamerica.

A cursory examination of stone structures built in the northern region during the Late to Terminal Classic (550–900 CE) reinforces the commonly held notion that while architectural innovations—such as the corbelled vault—may have been used extensively and perhaps earlier in the southern lowlands, these techniques of monumental construction were perfected in the northern region. Massive complexes that perhaps erroneously are called "palaces" were built across the Puuc region at places such as Sayil, Kabah, and Labna (Gallareta Négron 2013). Ringle (2020) notes that the northern emphasis on quadrilateral architectural forms is a clear divergence from the more organic arrangement of southern courts. Elaborate carved stone mosaics such as appear on the structures of the Nunnery Quadrangle at Uxmal (fig. 13.3)—the largest of the Puuc royal courts—indicate that there was no shortage of stone workers who possessed the carving skills to incise a Long Count date in limestone. Yet such dates are underrepresented at northern sites, suggesting that an explicit link between political authority and Long Count dates carved into stone monuments was not a key element of rulership in the north. Although some of the most recent Long Count dates (i.e., tenth cycle) can be found in the north (Ebert et al. 2014), eighth- and ninth-cycle dates carved on stone stelae are less common. Also scarce are tombs that established a royal line as the axis mundi of a community and—by virtue of a funerary shrine—created a place where descendants could venerate past rulers. For instance, at Piedras Negras, royal ancestors continued "to reside" at the royal court in a dynastic shrine called a "Five-Flower House," likely a reference to a paradise-filled afterlife that royals enjoyed (Taube 2004d; Eberl 2015, 92–94).

At royal courts located outside the core area of the southern lowlands—such as Copán in western Honduras—founding events were greatly emphasized, perhaps because of the intrusive character of the royal court (Helmke et al. 2019). Structure 10L-16 at Copán commemorated the establishment of dynastic structure upon the landscape (Stuart 2004b; Taube 2004d; Eberl 2015, 82). Thus, the triangulation of monumental time, dynastic place, and political authority created a totality of seeming robusticity and durability.

To the north of the core area of southern courts, a court was founded in the Late Classic at Ek' Balam—located less than 30 kilometers south of Tahcabo—where George Bey and colleagues (1998) documented a history of occupation going back to the Balam Complex (600–450 BCE) and continuing through colonial times. Recent work by Leticia Vargas de la Peña and Victor Castillo Borges (2017) on the acropolis of Ek' Balam has yielded what Alfonso Lacadena García-Gallo (2004) called the fanciest royal burial

Figure 13.3. Portion of the carved mosaic façade in the Nunnery Quadrangle at Uxmal, Yucatán. Photo by Patricia A. McAnany.

Lived Experience and Monumental Time in the Classic Maya Lowlands · 359

crypt north of Calakmul. The burial chamber contained the remains of Ukit Kan Le'k Tok', who is referred to as a *kalo'mte'* (more powerful than a *k'uhul ajaw* and possibly one who excelled in martial affairs). Also found on the acropolis is a room containing a painted mural of ninety-six hieroglyphs that opaquely describes the arrival in 770 CE of a powerful person who witnessed the accession of Ukit Kan Le'k Tok' to rulership (Vargas de la Peña and Castillo Borges 2017). Of course, Ek' Balam existed before 770 CE, but this date marks the establishment of a southern-style royal court and the founding of a kingdom known as TAL-lo (Lacadena García-Gallo 2004, 96–97). Ringle and colleagues (2021) discuss the possibility that Ukit Kan Le'k Tok' may have been a stranger-king in the sense Sahlins (2008) has formulated. At Copán, the expansion of southern-style authoritarian rulership into areas outside the southern lowlands is well documented hieroglyphically and through strontium isotopic analysis of the bones of ancestor interments (Price et al. 2010).

At Ek' Balam, hieroglyphic texts—especially painted texts—are known from five mural paintings, thirteen painted vault stones, eight stone-carved texts, one pottery vessel bearing the name of Ukit Kan Le'k Tok', a carved shell pendant with that name, and a carved human femur with the name of Ukit Kan Le'k Tok's father (Lacadena García-Gallo 2004, 3–84). By southern standards, such artifacts are to be expected in association with a sacred king, but they are not so commonly found in the northern lowlands despite the heavy investment in monumental architecture. At Ek' Balam, elements of sacred kingship seemingly were borrowed from southern courts, where the institution held a much deeper pedigree. For instance, at Palenque (~700 kilometers to the southwest), where a hieroglyphic text of equal length (the exquisite Panel of 96 Glyphs) was commissioned by a coeval Palenque ruler named K'inich K'uk' Bahlam II to celebrate his first *k'atun* of rule, the panel named several previous rulers (Martin and Grube 2008, 174), something not found in the Ek' Balam text.

The abundance of painted texts at Ek' Balam is significant because Long Count dates are more often expressed in stone. True to form, and despite all the writing at Ek' Balam, only four long counts are known (one is Stela 1, dedicated to Ukit Kan Le'k Tok'; Lacadena García-Gallo 2004, 98). The few dynastic dates exist alongside two short-count notations, four short-count plus Calendar Round dates, and twelve Calendar Round notations. Even in this dynastic context, the Long Count was used sparingly; there was a pronounced preference for the short count and, of course, for the Calendar Round, the people's calendar.

Furthermore, Lacadena García-Gallo (2004) discusses the fact that at Ek' Balam, the grammar and vocabulary of the mostly painted hieroglyphic texts is an eclectic mix of Classic Ch'olan with ancestral Yucatec conventions and word usage. Court language—so ubiquitous in the south (Houston et al. 2000)—seems here to have been used interchangeably with the local patois. Thus, the Ek' Balam royal court adopted many characteristics of southern-style rulership, including the visit of a foreign dignitary concurrent with the founding of the royal court and the spectacular tomb of Ukit Kan Le'k Tok', who may or may not have been a stranger-king.

Given the survival of Maya hieroglyphic writing into the Postclassic period in northern Yucatán, we can surmise that the scribal community at Ek' Balam was fully literate, yet only four Long Count dates are documented and the mixed linguistic composition of hieroglyphic texts departs from southern modes of expressing kingship. The final dated text from Ek' Balam (which is dated less than 100 years after the 770 CE founding date) indicates that the incorporation of southern elements of rulership at Ek' Balam was short lived and highly selective. Given the late date of the establishment of this royal court and concomitant principles of sacred rulership, Ringle et al.'s (2021) invocation of the idea that sacred rulership went to die in the north is worth considering. But over the long run, the conjunction of monumental time with political authority does not seem to have been of extreme importance in the northern lowlands. As Ringle and colleagues note, there was an indifference to dynastic history and pedigree in the north, suggesting that descent was not the central or sole consideration in matters of succession. In fact, successors to Ukit Kan Le'k Tok' chose not to portray themselves as master cultivators of monumental time.

Ek' Balam continued to be a seat of power through the Postclassic period, although construction activity diminished greatly. However, sixteenth-century *encomendero* Diego de Contreras stated in a *relación* that (before the coming of Spaniards) the people of Tahcabo gave tribute to Namon Cupul, a Late Postclassic ruler of Ek' Balam (Asensio y Toledo 1900). This evidence of durational authority at Ek' Balam suggests that at least some of the political capitals in the north exhibited more resilience than those of the south.

## Weathering Politics over the *Longue Durée*

Regardless of how succession was determined, a royal court had to weather all sorts of challenges and stresses. Elsewhere (McAnany et al. 2015; McAnany and Lamoureux-St-Hilaire 2017), I have examined the dissolution of alliance networks that knit together royal courts. This fracturing resulted in the abandonment of courts, often well before the departure of their sustaining populations. Although Ringle and colleagues (2021) emphasize the enhanced authority that came with bestowal of a title such as *kaloomte'* on a local ruler, joining "the society of kings" (Martin 2020, 383) also meant support from allied courts when facing challenges that could run the gamut from meteorological to martial. Ek' Balam, whose founding event was in 770 CE, was one of the last royal courts to be founded and to join the intricate network of court alliances that appear to have pivoted around the two influential courts located at Tikal and Calakmul. Freidel (2018, 2020) argues that statecraft differed fundamentally between those two supra-states. Calakmul, he suggests, embraced an older, councilor-based system of governance and ruler selection, while Tikal went in a different direction. Sometime during the Late Preclassic period, Tikal instituted hereditary rulership. Chains of succession were bolstered by reference to monumental time and royal ancestor shrines. Judging from the martial back-and-forth between these two heavyweights, both strategies of rulership proved effective over the short run. But emphasis on hereditary rulership in the south translated into a harder landing when the southern lowlands faced crises due to a multiplicity of factors. The emphasis on deep time—a seemingly unassailable rationale for rulership—created a path dependency that appears to have reduced resilience and dampened options for regeneration at the end of the Classic period.

The southern alliance of networks may have been effective for mitigating the effect of dry spells that periodically plagued areas of the southern lowlands. Gill (2000) and, earlier, Lowe (1985) argued that drought was the deus ex machina of the southern political dissolution. A host of archaeologists and paleo-environmentalists (Iannone 2014) have examined this theory without reaching a conclusion. Kennett and colleagues (2012, 790) argue for a concordance between proxy evidence of dry spells and archaeological data that include declining numbers of Long Count dates and other indicators that the southern courts were moving away from statecraft based on hereditary rulership. The dry spells in the period 820–870, around 930, and again in 1000–1100 CE must have stressed southern lowland populations. But when correlated with hieroglyphic accounts of martial activity and the erection of monuments with Long Count dates, the resulting pattern indicates that southern royal courts were changing—some were even abandoned—before the droughts began and certainly well before the best-documented dry spell, which commenced around 1000 CE. Rather, the dry spells appear to have blocked a resurgence in the south, one that might have reknit the highly fractured political landscape.

## Concluding Thoughts

In the southern lowlands, rulership meshed with concepts of monumental time as a paramount assumed responsibility for the "order of days." Such coupling provided a trope of durability to political authority that in reality could be ephemeral and fleeting. Because political forms codify authority through governance and the imposition of order, they are more fragile than social or religious constellations. The construction of massive shrines and the origins of the Long Count in the Late Preclassic period suggest an initial linkage between deities and deep, mythic time—a connection that southern rulers later adopted. Retrospective texts at Palenque Temple XIX in particular emphasize the important role of the sun deity K'inich Ajaw. Freidel (2017) traces this primacy back to the Late Preclassic period. Judging from the visibility of this deity in royal naming conventions and ornamentation (McAnany 2010), K'inich Ajaw, in effect, became a Classic-period patron deity of royalty.

Political arrangements tend to be finite, with a clearly defined beginning (generally a founding event) and a muddled but somewhat definitive ending. It is significant that the practice of yoking rulership to the Long Count calendar did not really catch on in the northern lowlands, an area where Spaniards found thriving populations during Late Postclassic times (1200–1519 CE). Elsewhere (McAnany 2019a), I have suggested that the practice of framing rulers in spirals of monumental time—with significant royal activities timed to coincide with conjunctions between the past and present—may have masked tacit recognition of the fragility of rulership. The northern lowlands—where leaders were less invested in hereditary rulership, although they were greatly involved with architectural monumentality—appears to have been engaged in a more integrative and less fragile political experiment and thus was able to rebound from the peninsula-wide dissolution of sacred rulership that occurred in the Maya lowlands in the ninth century. In the end, politics practiced on the scale of lived experience—as opposed to those practiced on the scale of cosmically inflected monumental time—proved to be more durable.

## Acknowledgments

This chapter benefited greatly from the productive feedback of fellow editors of the volume. However, I take full responsibility for all shortcomings of this essay. I wish to acknowledge the generosity of Jerry Murdock, who sponsored the sessions at the Santa Fe Institute that resulted in this book.

# 14

# The Materialization of Time in the Maya Archaeological Record

## Examples from Caracol and Santa Rita Corozal, Belize

DIANE Z. CHASE AND ARLEN F. CHASE

The importance of time, particularly cyclical time, among the ancient Maya has long been known and studied. This focus is readily apparent in Maya hieroglyphic writing as well as in ethnographic and ethnohistoric descriptions of the Maya. The ancient Maya also materialized time in the form of their ritual offerings. These religious deposits were representative of ancient belief systems, and while they were structured by past Maya perceptions of the world, they also served to embody that worldview in the archaeological record. Where some see offerings as predominantly dedicatory to construction of houses and burials as activities and offerings primarily that coincided with the death of individuals, we would argue that these offerings must be contextualized in Maya beliefs about their cosmos and that they are materializations of time itself; they represent ancient Maya attempts to codify beliefs about time and destiny as well as to reset the counting and prognostications of time in their favor.

We posit that the archaeological records of both Santa Rita Corozal and Caracol, Belize can be analyzed to see the importance of these temporal juxtapositions. Most likely because both centers were the ritual and political seats of broader polities, the nature and quantity of archaeologically recovered deposits from these two sites permit these interpretations to be made. In both cases, history and archaeology can be conjoined. At Santa Rita Corozal, Postclassic period ritual deposits can be compared with ethnohistoric texts. We have previously shown that Postclassic period caches were deposited in accord with annual Uayeb ceremonies, probably as part of broader temporal cycles, and that *incensarios* were used to denote sacred space and the passage of 20-year periods of time, or katuns (D. Chase 1985a; D. Chase and A. Chase 1988, 71–75; 2021). At Classic period Caracol, time is materialized in the monumental hieroglyphic record of the site and in the site's burials and caches. It was also materialized far earlier; in Caracol's epicenter in roughly 400-year baktun cycles, ritual caches were used to center the construction of an E Group beginning with the transition to the eighth baktun in 41 CE (A. Chase and D. Chase 1995, 2006). Other ritual events identifiable in the archaeological record in this E Group presumably coincided with the transitions to the ninth and tenth baktuns (A. Chase and D. Chase 2017a). The site's central monuments, particularly its Giant Ahau altars (Satterthwaite 1954; Beetz and Satterthwaite 1981), kept a record of the passage of katuns throughout the Late Classic period. But the ritual celebration of time was not restricted to Caracol's epicenter.

Archaeology in Caracol's residential groups has revealed that the general population also engaged in rituals focused on cyclical time. Plentiful ceramics that accompany household interments can be dated to show that burials were cyclically placed in residential groups, each seemingly coinciding with the passage of two katuns (D. Chase and A. Chase 2004, 2011). Similarly, the widespread caching practices found in Caracol's residential groups appear to be tied to the passage of katuns (A. Chase and D. Chase 2013a). Analysis of the archaeological contexts demonstrates that these widespread ritual offerings represent the materialization of an ancient Maya worldview concerned with cyclical time.

## Background

The archaeological concern with time has most often focused on creating chronology and documenting changes in material remains. Without a chronology that is fixed in calendric time and dating, archaeological interpretation is difficult if not impossible. Thus, from a methodological perspective archaeologists segment time into a linear form in order to gain a framework for describing and interpreting patterns in the archaeological record. Our resources for segmenting and ordering time range from methods borrowed from geology, such as those that outline the process of stratigraphy and the formation of strata (Schiffer 1987; Harris 1989), to mechanisms for seriating, ordering, and associating the material remains found in the archaeological strata, such as those based in elements of style and technology (Rowe 1961; O'Brien and Lyman 1999), to ever-refined scientific methods of using proxy elements to establish calendric time, such as radiocarbon dating and Bayesian statistics (Ramsey 2009; Bayliss 2015). Time has also been categorized as appearing in at least three different guises that are important for analytical purposes: lengthy segments of time that may last hundreds of years, segments of time that structure shorter periods of history, and time associated with events and the actions of individuals (e.g., Braudel 1980; Bintliff 1991; Bradley 1991). Bradley (1991, 212) argues that these three time scales (which he refers to as geographical, social, and individual time) "cut across the fundamental division between ritual and mundane" and are useful for investigating fundamental societal change. While these approaches to time have potential for interpretations in the field of Mesoamerican archaeology (e.g., Smith 1992; Iannone 2002; Rice 2009b), they have not yet been fully applied.

Also recognized in the historical records are two very different ways of thinking about time. For most western societies, time and history are linear and events are not expected to repeat. Events are pegged to certain dates, and while incidents may be linked, repetition is not expected. However, for the Maya, time was embedded in a series of different cycles and actions that could be expected to replicate themselves. Thus, time could be used for prognostication. Recognizing the Maya expectation of periodicity and reoccurrences of experiences and history, archaeologists working in the Maya area have attempted to link some specifically dated cycles to particular events that have been recognized in the archaeological record, such as the correlation of Katun 8 Ahau with knowledge of the impending Maya collapse (Puleston 1979; A. Chase 1991; Haviland 1992). Other researchers have even postulated that political organization in the Maya lowlands was, in fact, based on these broader temporal cycles (e.g., Rice 2004).

While Mayanists are blessed with a historic record of time that is found in hieroglyphic form on stone monuments, buildings, and smaller artifactual materials, the absolute articulation of this record of temporal events with archaeological remains has still been difficult. However, in some cases, the tombs of individual rulers who are portrayed on the monuments and are linked to specific dated events have been archaeologically identified, as at Palenque (K'inich Janaab' Pakal: Ruz Lhuillier and Mason 1953; Tiesler and Cucina 2006b), Tikal (Jasaw Chan K'awiil: Coe 1990, 851), Copán (K'inich Yax K'uk Mo': Bell et al. 2004), Pusilhá (K'ak' U ? K'awiil: Somerville et al. 2018), and Caracol (Yajaw Te' and K'an II, interred at Tikal [Burials 195 and 123]: D. Chase and A. Chase 2017, 219; A. Chase and D. Chase 2020a; A. Chase et al. 2022). The identification that Caracol (Belize) rulers were interred in the sacred center of Tikal (Guatemala) can be construed as a prime example of the stranger-king concept (A. Chase and D. Chase 2020a, 23; see also Graeber and Sahlins 2017, 5, 124, 148) in which a "foreign" ruler was accepted by local subjects and provided stability. These rulers had the ability to change that society because their cosmic power derived from other places. That the need for such stability was necessary at Tikal can be inferred from the timing of monument destruction at that city (Moholy-Nagy 2016, fig. 5). The existence of stranger-kings has also been noted in the Classic period archaeological record for the northern Maya lowlands (Ringle et al. 2021). While we do not have that many firm concordances between the archaeological and hieroglyphic records, epigraphers have amassed a wide range of temporal data about the individuals recorded in the monumental record and have detailed an interactive dynastic history for various sites through the Maya lowlands (Schele and Freidel 1990; Grube 1994a; Martin 2020; Martin and Grube 2000).

Yet mostly absent from archaeological discourses on time, be they theoretical or chronological, are discussions of the physical embedding of ritual time in the archaeological record (see chapter 5, this volume, for a discussion of embedding ritual time in Yucatán). Bradley (1991), for example, analyzed ritual time in terms of the linear history of Stonehenge, England, relating the development of that monument to the long-term changes that occurred in the society that used it. However, for the Maya area we find evidence for the continuous materialization of time itself in the archaeological record. Events in cyclical time repeated and thus could be predicted; because time was dynamic and animate (Stuart 2011), individuals could interact and endeavor to intervene with time to negotiate changed outcomes. It was possible to use ritual to attempt to augment positive outcomes and expectations as well as to alter or mitigate negative ones. Thus, time could be physically embedded in both daily life and in the archaeological record of the ancient Maya in an omnipresent and interactional way that is not typically characteristic of western cultures. Far more than modern "time capsules," which are intended to be viewed in the future but not actually interact with or impact future events, Maya offerings were intentional, prescribed negotiations with time and the course of history. The Maya used time and temporal ritual to structure their sociopolitical relationships and, in their worldview, to interact with time and impact the future. Thus, a Maya offering, such as a cache vessel, could contain the remnants of a ritual that was meant both to commemorate the present and negotiate the future. As will be shown below, this can be demonstrated in the archaeological records from a wide variety of Maya sites. The Maya embedded time in various building complexes—in E Groups, twin-pyramid groups, and other public architecture and in residential groups—both through the use of monuments, symbols, and iconography and through the physical deposition of caches, burials, and *incensarios*. This embedding of time and cosmos in their archaeological remains extended from at least the

Late Preclassic through the Late Postclassic and constitutes a hallmark of ancient Maya civilization.

## How Do We Know That the Maya Memorialized Time in the Archaeological Record?

There are two basic starting points for documenting that the Maya memorialized time in the archaeological record: the stelae and altars of the Classic period that denote fixed periods of time, and historic references to the Maya worship of ritual time for divination when the Spaniards arrived in the Yucatán (e.g., Landa; Tozzer 1941, 168). But the Maya did not actually "worship" time, as was once claimed in the popular literature (see Becker 1979 for a summary). Rather, they contracted and negotiated with time. Time to them was animate and could function as an active agent in their lives and their societies (see chapter 7, this volume, and chapter 13, this volume, on rulers as time lords). Because of the archaeological focus on linear time to reconstruct archaeological sequences, it is possible that some of the deeper and far more significant interpretations that relate to the Maya's ritual use of cyclical time have been missed. We also suspect that the Maya may not be unique and that the bonds that they attempted to establish with time may have been present in other nonwestern cultures but that these patterns are more noticeable among the ancient Maya precisely because of their focus on materializing the cyclical nature of time.

While both the Classic Maya stone monuments and their historic-era writings record periods of twenty years of time (katuns), a variety of other cycles were also counted, both longer and shorter. Simply referring to Maya time as cyclical does not capture the multitude of intersections and permutations of cycles that were followed. There were lunar cycles, yearly cycles, 819-day cycles, Uayeb cycles, katun cycles, baktun cycles, and the use of time to count into the past and into the future (Kubler 1974). Some constructions were built and modified in accord with temporal cycles. Complete architectural complexes, known as twin-pyramid groups, each built to commemorate a specific katun and temporal rituals associated with that katun, were constructed at Tikal, Guatemala for a span of approximately 150 years (n = 8 Late Classic complexes).

At Caracol, time also was clearly important to the site's ancient inhabitants. Its Late Classic period stone altars (n = 15) were predominantly carved to represent Giant Ahau day signs that were representative of katuns. Through the use of the archaeological record and radiocarbon dating, it has been possible to demonstrate that Caracol's E Group, the earliest public and ritual architecture for the site, was constructed and modified in accord with a 400-year baktun cycle (A. Chase and D. Chase 2006). Evidence of temporal ritual is also evident in the site's residential groups in the form of caching and burial practices that accorded with katun cycles (D. Chase and A. Chase 2011, 2017; A. Chase and D. Chase 2013a). It is likely that other Maya sites also employed temporal ritual as an integrative mechanism.

## Structuring Time: Classic Period Stone Monuments

Researchers have long recognized that Classic period stone monuments were erected as markers of time (Morley 1917; Proskouriakoff 1950). The stelae and altars of the Maya area record a series of expansive dating cycles that combine ritual time with mundane time. Long Count dates on these monuments are situated with cyclical time focused on baktuns (400-year periods of time) and katuns that are linked to the lunar cycle and the Nine Lords of the Night. The Long Count also is linked to a Calendar Round date (a 52-year cycle) that focuses on the vague year (365 days) and the 260-day sacred almanac cycle that in turn is linked to mundane time that corresponds to events (birth, accession, war) in an individual's life. The patterning of dates on these monuments all show a focus on the 20-year katun cycle. This cycle is actually spread over 260 years. While each katun is twenty years long, in the Postclassic era the katuns are denoted by the Ajaw day on which they start, which could only be numbered from 1 to 13, thus giving parameters to a 260-year cycle and constituting what is called the Short Count (see A. Chase 1986, 101–102).

Prudence Rice (2004) has suggested that the Maya world manifested a region-wide political organization that was organized according to katun cycles. While we do not fully agree with her premise, we do believe that ancient Maya rulers were conditioned by their relationship with time and their preordained temporal cycles. The individuals that are iconographically portrayed on their carved stone monuments are literally embedded in time and carried out rituals both associated with and mandated by the specific katuns (in many cases conducting rites on half and quarterly segments of katuns as well). Thus, the stone monuments provide a temporal frame for contextualizing rulers and are themselves imbued with ritual power (Houston and Stuart 1996; Houston et al. 2006; D. Chase and A. Chase 2009, 232; chapter 7, this volume). This may explain why many of these stone monuments were ritually destroyed in later political actions (for examples of the ritual destruction of monuments, see Satterthwaite 1958 and Harrison-Buck 2016).

Certain sites were more explicit than others about the katun focus of these stone monuments. At Caracol, Giant Ahau altars (fig. 14.1; see also Beetz and Satterthwaite 1981 and Grube 1994a) record each Late Classic katun in the

Figure 14.1. Giant Ahau Altar 19 at Caracol, representing the 9.10.0.0.0 katun. The altar was later moved and paired with Stela 11 at Caracol. Source: after Beetz and Satterthwaite (1981, fig. 26).

form of its specific day sign (one of thirteen numbered Ahaus), mimicking the system that Landa noted for the Postclassic Yucatán (Tozzer 1941, 167). Fifteen Giant Ahau altars appear at Caracol: fourteen were presumably once paired with stelae (assuming a stela was once present at Chaquistero) and the fifteenth was set to commemorate the tenth baktun on the summit of Caana (Caracol Altar 16). Other Giant Ahau altars are noted from Altar de Sacrificios (n = 2), Tikal (n = 1), Quirigua (n = 1), and from Caballo (n = 1). The cartouche containing the Ahau is often in the shape of a quatrefoil, which signifies completion, forms a ritual portal (Freidel 2017, 183), and can be associated with the shell of a turtle (see the south jamb of Temple 18 at Copán; Baudez 1994, 192) and the four corners of the Maya world. Turtles are important both in the creation of the world and in supporting the Bacabs who held up the sky (e.g., D. Chase and A. Chase 1986, 1988, 2009). Several of the Giant Ahau altars at Caracol also rested on three-stone pedestals, which were further symbolic of the three founders of the site (A. Chase and D. Chase 2012, 2017a; see also Baron 2016b for Maya patron deities) and of the Cosmic Hearth (Taube 1998; chapter 5, this volume; see also Vail and Hernández 2013 for foundation rituals in the Postclassic codices). Thus, the ties between katun ceremonies and Maya creation mythology are fairly explicit.

While many stone monuments commemorated katuns, in the Terminal Classic period some sites erected stone monuments on a quarterly system in the katun cycle. Machaquilá is a good example of this; there, seven successive stelae were erected every hotun (5 years) from 9.19.0.0.0 through 10.0.10.0.0 (Graham 1967). Caracol also appears to have followed the hotun erection cycle in the Terminal Classic, but only in relation to altars (e.g., A. Chase and D. Chase 2015). In this same Terminal Classic era, paired *incensarios* begin to appear in the archaeological record. On a front terrace of Caracol Structure B19, Altar 16, dating to 10.0.0.0.0, was associated with two flanged effigy censers, suggestive of the ethnographical evidence of the use of these artifacts as katun idols in the Postclassic period (D. Chase and A. Chase 1988, 2008).

## The Materialization of Time and Worldview in the Archaeological Record

That there was time depth to the Maya materialization of time and the Maya worldview can be seen by looking at two deposits separated by 1,300 years, one dating to approximately 41 CE and the other dating to approximately 1340 CE. One is a cache placed while Caracol Structure A6-1st was being built (fig. 14.2) and the other is a cache placed while Santa Rita Corozal Structure 213 was being constructed (fig. 14.3). Together, these deposits represent continuity in Maya ritual practice while illustrating changes in symbols and society. The Santa Rita Corozal cache is embedded in the broader residential community whereas the Caracol cache is set in a most important public building. Both caches represent the cosmological embodiment of time (e.g., D. Chase and A. Chase 2009, 226–227).

The Caracol cache, S.D. C8B-1, was placed in a specially constructed open-air pit covered by three capstones (A. Chase and D. Chase 1987, 12–13). It was deposited during a pause in laying the fills for Structure A6-1st, the central building for the site's E Group. Once the pit had been dug, various small shells (from both land and sea animals) were arranged at its bottom and then a large lidded ceramic barrel was set over the shells. When we found it in 1985, the

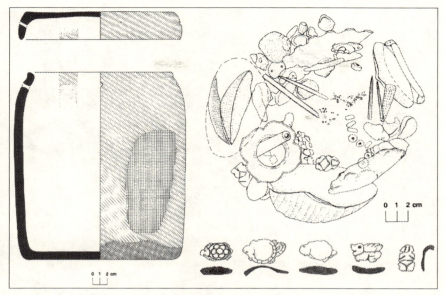

Figure 14.2. Cache (Caracol Special Deposit C8B-1) from the front core of Structure A6 dating to ca. CE 41. The lidded urn (*a*) was set in an open-air pit covered by three capstones. The upper right shows the arrangement of shells and small artifacts above malachite and mirrors (*b*). The lower right shows small shell (*d–g*) and jadeite (*c*) figures from the cache. Source: A. Chase and D. Chase (1987, fig. 8) and A. Chase and D. Chase (2006, fig. 7).

lid was intact, permitting a full understanding of the layering that occurred in the cache. Inside the urn and above the urn's lower contents, a fragile beehive had been placed that still contained some bees or wasps in the comb (see chapter 15, this volume). The beehive had been set above a layer of pine needles, some of which were still present. Although the pine needles may have been used as padding to keep the carefully positioned items in the central bottom from shifting during transport, Vogt (1969, 1976) has pointed to the sacred animating power of pine needles among the modern Tzotzil Maya. Because pine needles do not occur in the immediate vicinity of Caracol, their inclusion in this cache is suggestive of a broader purpose. Beneath the pine needles were seashells and a large jadeite earflare. The stem of upright earflare would have protruded in the center of the cache. Surrounding it were four large seashells set to cardinal directions, each properly color-coded for the appropriate Maya direction (fig. 14.2). These were bedded in a series of other objects: jadeite beads, a jadeite turtle, a jadeite "Charlie Chaplin" figure, a carved-shell fire-serpent, a pearl (possibly from the end of the earflare), four carved circular

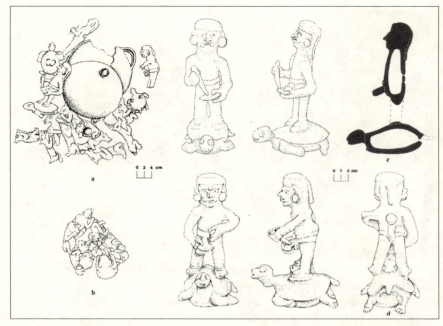

Figure 14.3. Cache (Santa Rita Corozal Special Deposit P26-3) from the core of Structure 213 dating to ca. CE 1340: overall plan of deposit in upper left (*a*); figures nested within urn lower left (*b*); two of four bacabs (*c* and *d*, each with three views of the object) on the right. Source: After D. Chase and A. Chase (1988, figs. 24 and 25).

shells with central shell inlays, four shell "Charlie Chaplin" figures, two shell turtles, worked shell points, unworked shells, pumpkin seeds, unidentifiable seeds, burnt wood, and small faunal remains. Below these items were stingray spines, stingray vertebrae, sharks' teeth, seaweed, and coral. Finally, the eroded remains of two pyrite mirrors were at the bottom. These were likely once set on wooden backings that had not survived but that had been set above a layer of malachite pebbles. Elsewhere we have suggested that this cache represented the cosmological centering of Structure A6 and functioned as a portal connecting world levels (D. Chase 1988; D. Chase and A. Chase 1998; see also Houk and Zaro 2011 for caches as ritual engineering). A second cache placed in Structure A6-2nd immediately before Structure A6-1st was built was associated with this centering. This cache (S.D. C8B-3) was placed against the rear wall of the earlier building in a sealed geode and contained a layered deposit consisting of liquid mercury on the bottom, a textile bundle containing a carved jadeite head with other beads set in a pair of *Spondylus* shells in the middle layer, and a complete jadeite earflare with stucco backing and a pearl at the top (A. Chase and D. Chase 1995, 2017a). Multiple radiocarbon dates for Structure A6-1st (including both caches) indicate that the placement of these two caches and the construction of Structure A6-1st took place at the start of baktun 8.0.0.0.0 in 41 CE (A. Chase and D. Chase 2006), securely placing this cache at the onset of an important temporal cycle.

The Santa Rita Corozal cache, S.D. P26B-2, was placed directly in the core of SRC Structure 213, a northern building in a Postclassic period residential group (see D. Chase and A. Chase 1988, 47–52; see also Badillo 2021 for other information about this structure). The cache consisted of a total of twenty-five modeled pottery figurines set around and in a lidded urn (fig. 14.3). Twelve figurines—four deer, four dogs, and four pisotes—were placed to the south of the urn. Four other bacab figurines positioned on the backs of sea turtles performing penis perforation were placed vertically at the "corners" of the urn. Within the urn were eight figurines—four male monkeys and four female creatures—arranged above a mitered individual seated upon a throne blowing on a shell trumpet. His stool or throne was located above a central piece of jadeite flanked directionally by four small shells. As in the earlier cache at Caracol, the Santa Rita Corozal Postclassic period cache represents the materialization of Maya cosmology and the Maya worldview. Because of the figurines, the iconography of the Postclassic cache is easier to understand than the more symbolically charged Preclassic period cache. That it represents a temporal ritual can be inferred from the creation mythology in the cache, from the animals represented in the cache (e.g., D. Chase 1985a, 1985b, 1988; D. Chase and A. Chase 2008), and from the two katun idols that were buried in the front step of the building and that accompanied a Postclassic period burial (fig. 14.4; D. Chase and A. Chase 1988, 51).

While similarities in caching practices can be identified over a span of 1,300 years, we are not suggesting that Maya ritual remained unchanged for this entire period of time. However, we are suggesting that the focus of ritual remained relatively constant; the consistency in structure that is seen in these caches is striking. Both the Preclassic and Postclassic buildings act as ritual containers for display. Time and the ceremony—not the building—were what were important. The caches could have acted as offerings for the buildings. However, we believe the caching and construction activities were themselves materializations of time. Thus, the broader focus is time, cosmology, and negotiation—and not the construction or destruction of a particular building episode. In both cases, the building continued to be used, as is evident at Caracol with the deposition of an Early Classic tomb at the base of Structure A6 and at Santa Rita Corozal with the deposition of two other caches and a burial in front of Structure 213.

Paired *incensarios* were recovered in association with both buildings. The ones at Santa Rita Corozal were likely placed during the katun of the cache (fig. 14.4); the ones at Caracol were placed a baktun earlier, sometime after 10.0.0.0.0 (fig. 14.5). Two paired effigy censers were recovered from the floor of the front room of Caracol Structure A6 in late Terminal Classic contexts. We suspect that these paired censers are antecedent to the Postclassic practice

Figure 14.4. Paired Postclassic incensarios from a deposit in the front stair block of Structure 213 at Santa Rita Corozal, possibly representing katun idols. Source: after D. Chase and A. Chase (1988, fig. 26).

Examples from Caracol and Santa Rita Corozal, Belize · 375

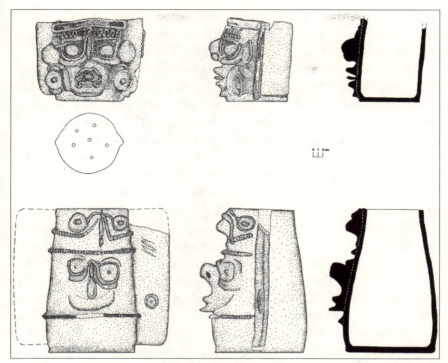

Figure 14.5. A pair of Terminal Classic incensarios that had been set on the floor in the northern part of the front room of Caracol Structure A6 (three views of each vessel; the upper incensario also has a perforated base).

of using paired effigy censers as katun idols at Santa Rita Corozal (as described below; see D. Chase 1985b, 1986, 1991; D. Chase and A. Chase 1988, 2008). Because it is likely that not all relevant ritual activities or deposits are being archaeologically encountered, even with the quantity of remains currently uncovered, we are still dealing with incomplete information.

## Idols and Earth Offerings as the Memorialization of Time

Marshall Becker (1992, 193) argued that Maya burials and caches at Tikal existed along a ritual continuum and suggested that both kinds of deposits functioned as "earth offerings" in the buildings they were associated with. In this sense, the building forms the container for the deposit. Based on our work at Caracol, we have argued that these "earth offerings" were placed according to set temporal cycles that can be related to katuns (D. Chase and A. Chase 2003, 2004, 2011, 2017; A. Chase and D. Chase 2013a). Besides caches and burials, there are other patterns in the archaeological record that can be related to temporal cycles, specifically paired-effigy *incensarios* found in both Classic and Postclassic contexts.

Paired *incensarios* have been specifically noted for their relationship to katun idols during the Postclassic period (D. Chase 1985a; Milbrath and Walker 2016a). Archaeological excavations at Santa Rita Corozal have recovered twelve separate contexts (SRC Structures 2, 5, 6, 7, 17, 25, 81, 92, 182, 183, 212, and 213) that yielded paired-effigy *incensarios* (D. Chase and A. Chase 1988, 72). Following Tozzer (1941, 166–169), who describes how katun idols were paired in order to transfer power from one to the other and thus maintain continuity in the katun cycle, we identified the archaeologically recovered *incensarios* from Santa Rita Corozal as katun idols (D. Chase 1985a, 1985b). In their temple or shrine contexts, these effigy censers literally "lived" sacred time and were ritually destroyed upon their "expiration," which presumably accounts for the archaeological contexts in which one relatively whole and one relatively partial effigy censer are recovered (fig. 14.6; see also D. Chase and A. Chase 1988, 72). The archaeological record demonstrates that these two *incensarios* and a host of other vessels holding offerings resided on the floor of their associated building for an extended period of time (A. Chase and D. Chase 2013b, 56–62). These katun idols in essence represented "living" time in that they mediated predictions and could do things to ensure the well-being of their supplicants.

The features of these *incensarios* can be used to correlate them with directionality and major Maya gods (Thompson 1957; see also chapter 13, this volume). At Mayapán, four of the ten gods that have been identified have Mexican connections (Milbrath and Walker 2016a, 213n5). Some researchers have interpreted a passage in Landa (Tozzer 1941, 161) about the creation of and renewal of idols for specific monthly rituals as referring to ceramic *incensarios* (Milbrath and Walker 2016a, 192), but Landa (Tozzer 1941, 160) had earlier made it clear that these were idols of wood. The interpretation of the "renewal" of these idols may refer to refreshing the offerings to the idols rather than to their ritual destruction (see Milbrath and Walker 2016a, 191–196). It is far more likely that the ceramic *incensarios* represented gods and prophecies for specific katuns, as Landa indicated (Tozzer 1941, 168): "The order which they used in counting their affairs and in making their divinations, by means of this computation, was this,—they had in the temple two idols dedicated to these characters [numbered katuns]." The fact that each deity had multiple aspects (Thompson 1957, 1960) and that there were thirteen different numbered katuns helps account for the diversity of Postclassic effigy *incensarios* seen in the archaeological record and the difficulty in interpreting them.

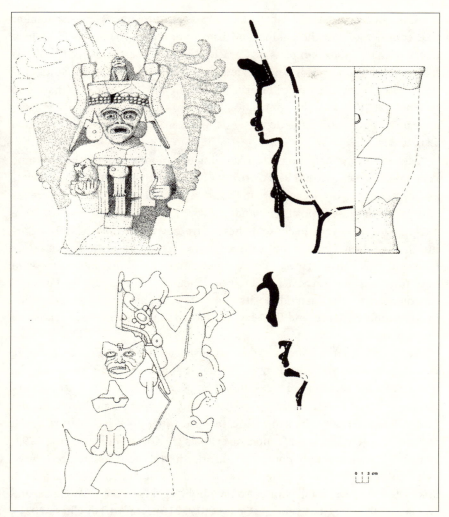

Figure 14.6. A pair of Postclassic incensarios set on the floor in front of the interior shrine in Structure 81 at Santa Rita Corozal. Source: after D. Chase and A. Chase (1988, fig. 8).

It is significant that paired *incensarios* are not only a Postclassic phenomenon. The use of effigy *incensarios* not only continued into the colonial period (Chuchiak 2009) but also extended back into the Terminal Classic period. Paired *incensarios* occur in three Terminal Classic contexts in the Maya area at Caracol. Two flanged effigy burners were located in Caracol Structure B19 and two in Caracol Structure A6. The third set is from Caracol Structure A3, but here the flanged effigy burner is paired with a large spiked brazier. One of the Caracol sets of flanged effigy *incensarios* was set with a Giant Ahau altar that commemorated the baktun and katun ending of 10.0.0.0.0. Elsewhere in the archaeological contexts of Caracol, the ritual destruction of multiple flanged effigy *incensarios* was located in two ritual deposits in residential groups that were likely placed during this same baktun shift (A. Chase and D. Chase 2010). Thus, the connection between katuns and effigy *incensarios* appears to have some time depth, going back at least as far as the Terminal Classic period.

Caches are also involved in the recording of temporal events. The elaborate Postclassic caches at Santa Rita Corozal can be directly linked to Uayeb events and cycles based on the iconography and repetition of figures that were recovered from these deposits (D. Chase 1985a, 1985b; D. Chase and A. Chase 1988, 2008). It is very likely that these Uayeb events, which occurred during the five unlucky days that ushered in the new year, were part of larger temporal cycles that formed a coordinated ritual "path" that moved through both time and space at Santa Rita Corozal, helping to integrate this Postclassic community. The cache deposits embedded specific points of ritual time in communities, space, and the Maya cosmos, and these points are evident in the archaeological record.

Although at Santa Rita Corozal Postclassic caches that served the entire community were embedded in residential groups scattered throughout the site, residential caching practices did not appear in full form at Caracol until the Late Classic period. Earlier Caracol caches from the Late Preclassic and Early Classic periods were generally associated with public architecture, and it appears that temporal and "centering" rituals (D. Chase and A. Chase 1998) were more hierarchically controlled during these eras. This changed, however, with the onset of the Late Classic period at Caracol and may have been associated with the establishment of symbolic egalitarianism (A. Chase and D. Chase 2009; D. Chase and A. Chase 2017, 215–216; Adrian Chase 2021), which coincided with the spread of the ritual domain through Caracol's residential groups.

The Late Classic period inhabitants at Caracol had access to tombs and caching practices that all levels of society shared. The caches and tombs were linked by virtue of being associated with the eastern buildings in the site's residential groups. Caching focused on two types of deposits: face caches and finger bowls (fig. 14.7). These deposits are found throughout Caracol's residential groups, often set in front of these buildings but sometimes also embedded in the structures. Late Classic caches have been recovered in eighty-seven non-epicentral residential groups at the site (D. Chase et al. 2024). The modeling of the face caches from Caracol range from crude to elaborate. Some clearly

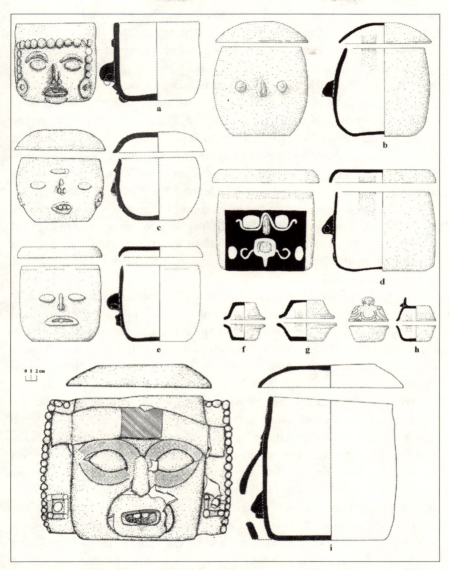

Figure 14.7. Late Classic cache containers at Caracol representing face caches (*a–e, i*) and finger bowls (*f–h*). (*a, c, e*) from Talking Trees Residential Group (Structures 3D21–3D34); (*b, f–h*) from Caana summit, buried under lower plaza floor in front of Structure B20; (*d*) from the core of Structure I28 in the Rebel Residential Group; (*i*) from Structure B34 in Northeast Acropolis, buried within an earlier stairway.

represent the Maya sun god, some a bird (Principal Bird Deity?), and others are more human in their aspects (see A. Chase 1994; D. Chase and A. Chase 1998, 2010, fig. 2; A. Chase and D. Chase 2010, fig. 2).

It was not until the excavation of extensive stratigraphic sequences from several residential groups that it proved possible to sequence the iconographic features of the face caches. The correlation of the face caches with the archaeological records of Caracol's residential groups also indicates that they were being consistently deposited over time in a cyclical fashion that appeared to correlate with katuns (A. Chase and D. Chase 2013a). Thus, we posited that Caracol's face caches were katun markers that were being used in household ceremonies (fig. 14.8). In this capacity, they were antecedent to the use of *incensarios* for katun markers that appears in the Terminal Classic period. While most face caches are empty when found in the archaeological record, some do have contents that may be indicative of their use in activities related to temporal cycles. For instance, one found in Structure I7 contained a carved limestone face of K'inich Ahau and ten eccentric obsidian blades (A. Chase and D. Chase 2010, fig.3).

Temporal cycles were also involved in the placement of interments in residential complexes at Caracol (D. Chase and A. Chase 2004, 2011). That would have been appropriate for the corporate function these deposits had of unifying the inhabitants of a given residential group. The timing of these burials was clearly significant and their placement followed a general developmental sequence. First, a tomb was built in the eastern building, often including a constructed entryway that permitted passage in and out of the chamber for some time. There are indications that while this entryway was open, the tomb may have been used, cleaned out, and then reused for various bodies. However, eventually one or more occupants were placed in the chamber and it was sealed in the core of a building. Later, additional burials were placed under the front step of the building and then even later through the front stairway or in the plaza to the front of the structure (D. Chase and A. Chase 2004, 206, fig. 1). Because more than half of Caracol's burials are accompanied by ceramic vessels (D. Chase 1998) and because six Caracol burials—all containing ceramics—are associated with hieroglyphic dates on their walls or capstones (A. Chase 1994), it is possible to gain relatively fine temporal control over the placement of the site's interments. Consistently, the ceramics in burials associated with a single structure indicated a temporal separation on the order of approximately forty years (e.g., A. Chase and D. Chase 2013a, 17, fig. 4).

Archaeological work at Tikal and Caracol has shown that only a small percentage of any residential groups' inhabitants were being buried in the group's residential area (D. Chase 1997, 25–26); most were buried somewhere

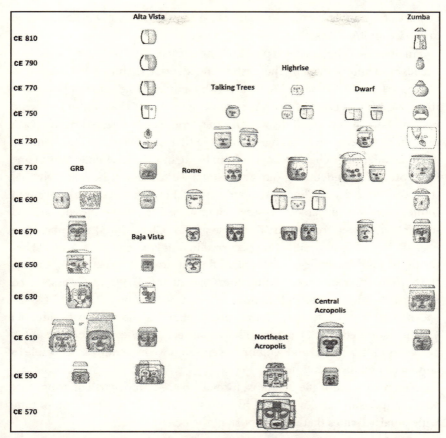

Figure 14.8. Caracol cache sequence showing use of face caches as katun markers in various residential groups. Source: A. Chase and D. Chase (2013a, fig. 5).

else. At Caracol, the six Late Classic tombs that contained recorded hieroglyphic dates indicated that the ancient Maya sought to purposefully anchor these chambers in time through the use of temporal markers. Painted textual dates in two stratigraphically sequential chambers in Caracol Structure B20 also suggested that the chambers were used based on a double katun pattern (see A. Chase and D. Chase 2017c). Because the temporal sequencing deduced from the residential group burials matches this timespan, it strongly suggests that these earth offerings were made in accord with a temporal cycle. While we originally suspected that they were being deposited in accord with a Calendar Round (52-year) cycle (D. Chase and A. Chase 2004, 221, table 1), subsequent archaeological work has strongly supported the interpretation that interments in a given residential group were made as part of a double katun (40-year) cycle (A. Chase and D. Chase 2013a; D. Chase and A. Chase 2017).

Finally, one other cache type—the finger cache—is associated with face caches and interments in the eastern residential shrines (A. Chase and D. Chase 1994; D. Chase and A. Chase 1998). Finger caches incorporate bones from one or more fingers from one or more individuals. These finger bones are placed between two small dishes, and they are usually interred in the plaza in front of the eastern building. We believe that these deposits represent the personal offerings of human fingers from living individuals in memory of one (or more) of a residential group's ancestors; we feel that it is also likely that they were offered according to temporal cycles. Finger caches usually occur in limited numbers in Caracol's residential groups. They sometimes are located in tombs that were reentered (D. Chase and A. Chase 2003) and may have been deposited episodically. That occurred in four contexts at Caracol: (1) beneath the four-meter-deep earlier plaza floor in front of Structure B20; (2) in the buried earlier summit building floors of Structure B19-2nd; (3) associated with the two-meter-deep plaza floor in front of Structure B34; and (4) associated with a constructed central plaza "altar" in the Centro Residential Group associated with Structure J13. We suspect that these episodic deposits correlate with personal and temporal events, but we have not yet been able to completely fix them in time.

In summary, we argue that most formally placed Maya earth offerings that we find in the archaeological record represent the literal conjunction of time with ritual activities that were important to ancient Maya.

## Architectural Groups and the Manifestation of Time

Two architectural groups have been specifically suggested as manifesting time in the archaeological record: E Groups and twin-pyramid groups. Both E Groups and twin-pyramid groups involve the convergence of several temporal cycles. E Groups are characterized by a western pyramid across a plaza from a long eastern platform that is usually supporting three constructions. They form the earliest versions of public architecture that can be widely recognized across the Maya southern lowlands (e.g., A. Chase and D. Chase 1995; Freidel et al. 2017) and throughout a large part of Mesoamerica (Inomata et al. 2021). Coggins (1980) specifically states that E Groups form an antecedent for twin-pyramid groups. Each E Group was involved in the cosmological founding of a Maya center (A. Chase and D. Chase 2012, 2017a) and in providing both horizon-based astronomy and a solar calendar for Maya communities (Aveni et al. 2003; Aimers and Rice 2006; Milbrath and Dowd

2015; Šprajc 2021a). At Caracol, archaeological data also demonstrate that E Groups were constructed and used in conjunction with baktun cycles of 400 years (A. Chase and D. Chase 2013a; A. Chase and D. Chase 2017a, 60). This is also explicitly visible in the architectural plans of some Maya sites such as Yaxha, Guatemala (A. Chase and D. Chase 2017a, 63).

The architectural form of twin-pyramid groups was recognized at Tikal in the 1950s (Shook 1957). They are characterized by quadrilateral pyramids on the eastern and western sides of a plaza, a nine-doorway structure on the south side of the plaza, and a roofless structure on the northern side of the plaza (fig. 14.9). These complexes were the subject of Christopher Jones's PhD dissertation (1969), in which he concluded that the complexes were built as a whole to celebrate specific katuns and to serve for yearly solar ceremonies. The complex is a perfect stage for such ceremonies, especially as the overall plan of the group incorporates multiple temporal cycles: katun (north), vague year (east and west), and lunar year (south). The twin-pyramid groups' symbolic directional focus on four sides and the central plaza (or stage) is similar to the quincunx layouts of many Maya caches (see D. Chase 1988; Mathews and Garber 2004; D. Chase and A. Chase 1998), adding to its layered meaning.

Clemency Coggins (1980, 736–737) noted that twin-pyramid groups formed a miniature version of the Maya cosmos laid on its side: the east and west pyramids were symbolic of the daily and yearly solar cycle; the nine-doored range building on the south edge of the complex represented the Nine Lords of the Night (or underworld); and the roofless northern structure housed an altar and stela that portrayed the ruler carrying out katun

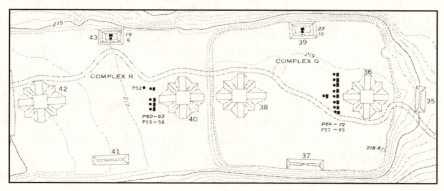

Figure 14.9. Twin-pyramid groups from Tikal: Complex R is anchored to 9.18.0.0.0 by Stela 19 and Complex Q is anchored to 9.17.0.0.0 by Stela 22. Both stelae are in the north buildings of their respective groups. Source: after the Great Plaza map sheet in Carr and Hazard (1961).

ceremonies. The Nine Lords of the Night have also long been viewed as representing the nine moons of the lunar year (coinciding with the period of human gestation; Nuttall 1904, 495, 510) and as associated with the 260-day calendar (Aveni 2001, 156–157). Wendy Ashmore (1992, 176) noted that the placement of a stela in the northern building of a twin-pyramid group "visibly and materially apotheosized" the king "by prominent placement of his portrait monument in the symbolic heavens, where he joins his divine ancestors." Other Late Classic stelae at Tikal surmount caches that usually contain nine eccentric lithics or flints, a shorthand arrangement of the architectural expression found in twin-pyramid groups Because these caches also contain sets of carved obsidian eccentrics, they also likely represent the Nine Lords of the Night (Moholy-Nagy 2008, 18, 26). An examination of other caches and deposits associated with the twin-pyramid complexes of Tikal related the katun cycle to the exhumation and reburial of deceased individuals (Weiss-Krejci 2010, 95–96; 2012).

At least eight (and possibly nine) twin-pyramid groups can be identified at Tikal, all dating to the Late Classic period. The earliest two securely identified groups are dated back to the katuns representing 9.11.0.0.0 (Group 4D-2) and 9.12.0.0.0 (Group 5B-1) but are not associated with dated stelae. Six of these groups can be dated as being erected between 9.13.0.0.0 and 9.18.0.0.0 (Groups 3D-1, 5C-1, 4D-1, 3D-2, 4E-4, and 4E-3). Jones (1969, 1996, 22) identifies a potential ninth complex beneath Tikal's East Plaza ballcourt that would have corresponded to 9.10.0.0.0 (see Moholy-Nagy 2016, 264). However, there are issues related to including these two pyramids in the series because the dating for these pyramids is Early Classic based on recovered caches and the two pyramids "are unaccountably crowded into the center of the plaza" and did not yield "the expected pit for a centerline stela between the structures." In our estimation, the Tikal pyramids beneath the East Plaza ballcourt represent a different architectural complex than a twin-pyramid group. Given the intense political connections between early Late Classic Tikal and Caracol (e.g., A. Chase and D. Chase 2020a), which is symbolically noted in the fusion of Tikal's only Giant Ahau altar with the twin-pyramid group built to celebrate 9.13.0.0.0, we see Tikal's Late Classic twin-pyramid groups as linked to Caracol's earlier focus on katun cycles and Giant Ahau altars. Twin-pyramid complexes occur at four other neighboring sites: Uolantun, Ixlu, Chalpate, and Yaxha. These four complexes represent a new emphasis on celebrating ritual time in the eastern Petén of Guatemala during the Late Classic period.

## Conclusion

Multiple temporal cycles can be found in the archaeological record. These include cycles that approximate the sacred calendar of 260 days (associated with the Nine Lords of the Night), vague year cycles of 365 days, katun cycles (which can be quartered into segments of five years, or hotuns), Calendar Round cycles of 52 years, and baktun cycles of 400 years. As the ethnohistory notes, the Maya were preoccupied with the computation of time and embedded temporal aspects in most of their activities.

Among the outcomes of this analysis is a better understanding of Maya materialization of time. Archaeological patterns codify worldview as it intertwines with time. Material remains provide a window on that relationship. Constructions, monuments, and deposits of various sorts not only memorialized the cycles of time, they also localized it clearly in physical space. As is evident in the Postclassic period caches of Santa Rita Corozal, these episodes themselves sometimes established ritual paths on the ground that provided internal connections within communities.

Classic period caches at Caracol and Postclassic period caches and incense burner deposits at Santa Rita Corozal can be analyzed to show remarkable similarities in worldview across more than 1,000 years. Although there are clear differences in specific contents and in associated buildings, the consistency in the basic conceptions of the world as directional, layered, and associated with time is unmistakable.

It is evident that individual ritual activities and deposits are most effectively viewed together rather than in isolation. When constructions, monuments, special deposits, and on-floor remains are contextually recovered through archaeological investigation, they can be used to establish meanings that are more clear (e.g., A. Chase and D. Chase 2020b). Construction and destruction of buildings may sometimes have been correlated with cycles of time. What might be viewed in isolation as only the consecration and dedication of new space or the termination of existing space might in broader view be identified as reflections of the Maya materialization of time. Thus, the Caracol E Group, with its various caches, coincides with the establishment of a new baktun. Twin-pyramid complexes at Tikal showcase the concordance of multiple temporal cycles (e.g., daily, yearly, katun) in a single architectural complex.

This work suggests that in Maya culture the human engagement with time was dynamic. While cycles of time and the events associated with them were expected to repeat, ritual activities might be used to attempt to negotiate different outcomes or paths. In essence, for the ancient Maya, time was alive and had agency. They did not passively commemorate the passage of time; they actively engaged with it to change or ensure the course of history. Viewing time, specifically cyclical time, as an agent explains the Maya preoccupation with time and provides a very different view of the ancient Maya than that derived from earlier conceptions of them as time worshippers and somewhat later visions of them as history-bound dynasties. It also provides a fuller example of how the ancient Maya contextualized, interacted with, and adapted to the complexities of their time and place.

## Acknowledgments

The research in this chapter builds on our work at the sites of Santa Rita Corozal and Caracol over more than forty-five years. We thank the Institute of Archaeology in Belize, our sponsoring universities (University of Central Florida; University of Nevada, Las Vegas; Pomona College; Claremont Graduate University; and the University of Houston), and all of the funding agencies that have enabled these investigations: the Ahau Foundation, the Alphawood Foundation, the Dart Foundation, FAMSI, the Geraldine C. and Emory M. Ford Foundation, the government of Belize, the Harry Frank Guggenheim Foundation, NASA, the National Science Foundation, the Stans Foundation, and USAID. We hope that this chapter showcases what can be gained from detailed long-term archaeological research.

# 15

# Materializing Time on Wax

## The Cozumel Maya Bee Gardens

ADOLFO IVÁN BATÚN-ALPUCHE AND DAVID A. FREIDEL

Then they swarmed, the children of the bees. Little Cuzamil (was) the honey's flower, the honey's gourd, the first apiary, the heart of the land. Kin Pahuatun was their priest. He commanded the numerous armies [army or armies?], which guarded Ah Hulneb at Tantun Cuzamil.

*Libro del Chilam Balam de Chumayel*
(Mediz Bolio [1930] 1973, 5, trans. Adolfo Batún-Alpuche)

In sixteenth-century Cozumel, bees were tamed in order to obtain honey and wax. This amazed the early Europeans who stopped at the island; their travel journals mentioned an extensive practice of beekeeping there (Las Casas in Wagner 1941, 50; Juan Diaz in García Icazbalceta 1980, 286; Gómara 1983, 31–32). Cozumel's importance as a beekeeping center is also mentioned in the *Libro del Chilam Balam de Chumayel,* which refers to Cozumel as the "first apiary" (Mediz Bolio 1973, 5). The 1582 list of towns of Yucatán mentions the two main towns in the island; San Miguel Xamancab and Santa Maria Oycib; both towns bore their Maya names after their new Spanish names. Xamancab can be translated as the northern honey or the northern bee, and Oycib means beeswax. Both names thus imply the importance of bees in those communities.

Archaeological vestiges of beekeeping in Cozumel were identified in 1978, when Henry Wallace (1978; see also Teran Silvia and Rasmussen 1994, 265–274) noted the correlation between the form of stone disks (10–12 centimeters in diameter) at several Cozumel sites[1] and the limestone disks used to plug the hollow logs modern Maya used as beehives to tame stingless bees in Yucatán. Hereafter we refer to these disks by the Maya word *maktun* (pl.

*maktunoob*). Recently Źrałka and colleagues (2018) reported the discovery at Nakum in eastern Petén, Guatemala, of a Terminal Preclassic (0–250 CE) ceramic artifact that appears to be an effigy hollow-log beehive complete with circular-disk plugs of the kind we discuss here. Batún-Alpuche carried out extensive field research at Buena Vista, the major southern site on Cozumel, and determined that this was a primary pre-Columbian town that produced honey and wax.

Why was beeswax a major commercial commodity on the east coast of Yucatán and the island of Cozumel in particular? The short answer to the last part of this question is that in addition to being an area where many people kept bees, Cozumel was a famous pilgrimage destination where the oracle of the goddess Ix Chel resided (Tozzer 1941; Freidel 1975). This goddess was patroness of diviners, and no doubt many such adepts who calculated calendar numbers and wrote prognostications lived on the island. Those activities involved waxed surfaces.

In this chapter, we situate the production of wax in the materialization of time. Since the Spanish conquest, Maya people have used beeswax primarily to fashion votive candles for religious ceremonies (Patch 2003). Among the Chan Santa Cruz Maya of the area, people used wax to make sacred votive images that are placed on and around the altars of Indigenous churches (see photographs in Everton 1991). We propose that in the pre-Columbian era, beeswax was used to cover the surfaces of writing boards and mosaic mirrors and was sometimes used to cover interior surfaces (Freidel et al. 2015; Freidel et al. 2016). Justin Kerr (mayavase.com, K5861) posted an unprovenienced Late Classic polychrome plate from Campeche or Yucatán that bears images of what we interpret as dots that represent the positions of casting tokens, possible representations of twin stepped katun pyramids (chapter 14, this volume), possible footprints (see discussion of the spatial-temporal plan of the Madrid Codex in chapter 4, this volume), cosmic quarter crosses (chapter 5, this volume), and numbered day names. It is a ceramic materialization of Maya time.[2] We suggest that this might be a painted commemoration of a waxed surface calendar divination.

Źrałka and colleagues' (2018) epigraphic and iconographic identification of possible beehives depicted on the Madrid Codex bee pages challenges our own identification (Freidel et al. 2016) of some of these yellow-painted objects as waxed writing tablets. We argue here that while what they identify as objects housed in roofed apiaries are likely hives, those objects differ from the ones we have previously discussed (Freidel et al. 2016) that were associated with gods holding writing styluses and were likely writing tablets. Writing with pointed styluses made of wood, bone, or horn, scribes and other literate sages could make provisional mathematical calculations and take glyphic notes as they prepared to write more formally with paint brushes (or quills, see Coe 1998) on permanent media such as bark-paper books, plastered walls, or ceramic containers or to carve their texts in stone, ceramic, bone, and shell. Images of this activity are illustrated on Classic (250–900 CE) painted vases and have been identified in archaeological contexts that we discuss below.

Occasionally, as in the case of the well-known calendar calculations from the Classic period Sabios building at Xultun (Saturno, Stuart, et al. 2012; Saturno et al. 2015; chapter 9, this volume), sages improvised with brushes in paint on walls and then covered their lines so they could write again, forming a palimpsest of text. As M. Kathryn Brown, Leah McCurdy and Jason Yaeger describe, at Xunantunich (chapter 11, this volume), some Classic novice sages practiced writing graffiti with sharp styluses or blades on plastered walls. Adepts in the scribal arts also wrote with pointed styluses on ceramic containers prior to firing them and on soft wall plaster before it dried (see chapters 6 and 8, this volume). However, we think that incision with styluses on waxed boards and mirror surfaces was the more common practice. There are no explicit descriptions of erasable waxed boards, but there are some close approximations. In the treatise *De Orbe Novo: The Eight Decades of Peter Martyr D'Anghera,* which describes writing among the highland Mexicans, the author declares:

> I know Your Holiness has handled some of these tablets on which sifted plaster similar to flour was sprinkled. One may write thereon whatever comes into one's mind, a sponge or cloth sufficing to rub it out, after which their tablet may be used again. The natives also used fig leaves for making small books, which the stewards of important households take with them when they go to market. They write down their purchases with a little point, and afterwards erase them when they have been entered into their books. (2:40)

Such writing boards had fallen out of favor by the colonial period (1519–1697 CE); if they had not, scholars would have documented them. Although the craft of papermaking was well established in pre-Columbian Mesoamerica, paper had both sacred and practical value, and Spanish priests systematically suppressed it in their notorious burning of books. European papermakers set up shop in the New World and Maya noble children who were trained in Spanish and Latin were no doubt strongly discouraged from using Indigenous writing practices, such as using styluses on waxed boards, that were associated with forbidden literacy in their own script. However pre-Columbian artifacts and contexts may document the practices proposed here. For example, at Yaxuná (Stanton et al. 2010; Tiesler et al. 2017), a probable scribe was buried in the Late Classic period (550–800 CE) with a shell cup suitable for work as a paint pot, a cached vessel nearby depicting a carved vessel showing a scribe wearing an appropriate turban ornamented with a tasseled brush and a bone stylus featuring a spatula on its end that would have been handy for erasing a waxed surface after calculations or writing had been transferred to a more permanent medium (fig. 15.1).

This sage was also buried with a set of blue-painted beads. Landa (Tozzer 1941, 154) describes how diviners painted their casting stones (called *am*; spiders) blue and laid them in the ritual blessings of Ix Chel. As Freidel and Schele (1988a, 559) discuss, spider casting stones were associated with pointed stone needles that we suggest may have been inscribing styluses. In the early 1960s, Aubrey Trik (1963, fig. 10) identified a bone with a spatula on one end as "awl-like artifact," but we hypothesize that it is a stylus. It was discovered in Tikal Bu 116, the tomb of King Jasaw Chan K'awiil. Incised on it is the image of a hand emerging from a centipede maw, preparing to write with a stick-shaped instrument taken to be a brush. Trik says of the Bu 116 bones: "Similar artifact forms have been classified as 'tools,' such as awls, needles, perforators, pins, but it seems more likely that the Burial 116 collection

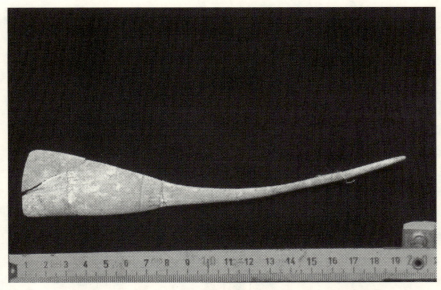

Figure 15.1. Late Classic stylus from Yaxuná featuring a spatula "eraser." Photo by Travis Stanton. Courtesy of the Selz Foundation Yaxuná Archaeological Project.

represents a type of ceremonial paraphernalia or priestly implements rather than tools in the usual sense of the word" (18).

Another stylus with a spatula end, part of a cluster of such artifacts, has been recently reported in a Classic crypt context at Cahal Pech in Belize (Novotny et al. 2018, fig. 5) in association with another shell paint pot that has preserved paints of different colors. Michelle Rich (Freidel and Rich 2018) identified elaborately carved styluses in Burial 39 at El Perú-Waka', which dates to the seventh century. These were associated with ceramic figurines depicting individuals holding writing boards painted golden yellow, the principal color of beeswax, and styluses. (There is also black beeswax in Yucatán). Those styluses were also associated with miniature spindle whorl tokens and a square mosaic mirror that was surfaced with iron pyrite.

Recent high-magnification forensic analyses of jadeite tesserae that were incorporated in the funerary mask of King K'inich Janaab Pakal of Palenque (Martinez del Campo 2010) show that beeswax was used as a binder or glue on that mosaic composition. In a recent substantial review of pre-Columbian Mesoamerican mirrors, Emiliano Gallaga (2016, 13) cites Magar and Meehan (1995) to the effect that the ancient gluing adhesive of mirror tesserae included wax and resin in the context of a turquoise mosaic mirror from the burned palace of Tula. Martinez del Campo's study and the Instituto Nacional de Antropología e Historia's Funerary Masks Project (Martínez del Campo 2010) have shown that tree resin was also used as a glue on King K'inich Janaab Pakal's mask. While more studies need to be done on preserved mosaics to see if this was a common practice, these studies indicate that beeswax was used in the fabrication of stone mosaics. In our view, the use of wax coating on mosaic surfaces was a plausible extension of this practice. On the basis of Classic painted depictions of mirrors and styluses used in the context of gifting and tribute scenes, Freidel, Masson, and Rich (2016) suggest that these mirrors were writing tablets that elite Mayans used. Mirrors coated with wax would have provided hard surfaces that were impervious to scratching. In addition, they would have reflected light, thus illuminating numbers and glyphs.

Maya mirrors and Mesoamerican mirrors generally served as instruments of divination and the discernment of the supernatural, as Karl Taube (2016) has recently underscored. This function segues comfortably to the notion that mirror surfaces could be read. As Taube writes, "Rather than passive and inert objects, ancient Mesoamerican mirrors were surely considered to be sources of information with stories to tell[,] much like reading a sacred book" (294).

But while mirrors may have served as writing tablets for high elites, as depicted in palace scenes on painted vases, it seems likely to us that such tablets would have also been made of wood or other materials. Gary Gossen

(1974) reported on a twentieth-century wooden Chamula calendar board that was used repeatedly for writing and erasing calculations. Maxime Lamoureux-St-Hilaire (personal communication, November 2018) discovered a set of ceramic palettes in a Late Classic palace at La Corona, Peten, that he identifies as writing tablets of the kind we postulate. Testing these surfaces and those of preserved mirrors for wax is a next step in research, but the ubiquity of styluses in the Maya archaeological record, which have often been identified as pins for weaving, as ornamentation for hair or clothing, or as bloodletters, is sufficient to propose that bees were kept not only to produce honey for mead but also to produce wax for writing tablets.

Historical records made after the Spaniards arrived make clear that both honey and wax were valuable pre-Columbian commodities produced on Cozumel. The research described below demonstrates that Cozumel had towns that featured apiaries and wax in the Classic period.

## Buena Vista, Cozumel

The site of Buena Vista, Cozumel is laid above a low natural ridge located 1.5 kilometers inland, parallel to the southeastern coast of the island. The site core is composed of a complex of stone platforms of irregular plan, varying in height from 2 to 7 meters, "agglutinated" (that is, the adjacent platforms share retaining walls; Freidel 1975) into a sprawling seven-hectare community. Freidel and Sabloff (1984) suggest that this unusual settlement plan facilitated secure and dry storage of valuable trade commodities, including honey, wax, salt, cotton, and cacao. These commodities have been documented as part of the centuries-old canoe commerce along the coast that was still flourishing in the early sixteenth century. In light of Batún-Alpuche's (2004) more recent research, we think that Buena Vista specialized in the production and storage of honey and wax.

The community's platform complex was constructed by artificially leveling the natural elevation. Some of the platforms have standing vestiges of masonry buildings and others have foundation braces that would have supported perishable structures. Likely many buildings that were at this site have left no observable trace on the surfaces, which are eroded and have been disturbed by trees. An interesting feature that was discovered and excavated under the direction of William Rathje in the 1973 field season was a corbel-vaulted tomb chamber containing the remains of a number of individuals (Rathje and Phillips 1975, fig. 14). This was one of four such multiple-individual tombs that were discovered and documented in that season. Human skeletal remains that Freidel observed in rock shelters in the vicinity of Buena

Vista suggest that the dead were sometimes exposed and the bones were later gathered and integrated into common graves. This ritual practice evidently reflects the collective nature of social identity in this town of beekeepers and wax and honey makers. A formal plaza group at the northern end of the community is evidence of an elite presence at Buena Vista. The assembly halls, modest palaces, and temple shrines of the formal plaza are comparable to those found in other ancient communities on the island.

A short distance from the main complex of platforms are four other groups that contain small masonry shrines that are typical of Cozumel and the nearby mainland in the era before Spaniards arrived (Freidel and Sabloff 1984). These are connected to Buena Vista with narrow stone paths or sacbes. Although modern-day looters have destroyed these shrines, they represent a common sacred encircling of community that is found at other sites on Cozumel. They also register the pilgrimage routes visitors traveled when they came to this island dedicated to Ix Chel. Several other small platforms and structures in the ambient area around Buena Vista likely represent the temporary shelters of farmers and beekeepers. Beyond them is an extensive network of field walls (*albarradas*) that vary in size from single-course limestone walls with an estimated standing height of 1 meter to massive walls with rubble and gravel cores and dry-laid masonry retainers that stand more than 2 meters high and more than 2 meters wide. Such massive and simple walls occur apparently in a random fashion and enclose many different sizes. The random arrangement argues against a defensive function for the massive walls, despite historic accounts of Indigenous pirates raiding Cozumel. It is possible that such walls served as windbreaks to protect crops and trees against major storms approaching from the windward side of the island.

From May to August 2003, Batún-Alpuche carried out archaeological survey and mapping in the Buena Vista peripheral area to study the distribution of archaeological features and the biophysical environment surrounding the site core. His survey covered a total area of 4 square kilometers centered on the site's monumental plaza. It included both the mapping of all archaeological and main topographic signatures found in his exploration of 28 kilometers of 50-meter-wide *brechas* (forest cut transects) and detailed mapping of sectors of the site. The mapped sectors were chosen because they represent different micro-environmental adaptations, as evidenced by their topography and concentrations of archaeological vestiges.

Three main micro-environmental zones were detected in the site: (1) the *akalche bajos,* which have poorly drained gleysol and vertisol soils; (2) the booxluum ridge zone with rich organic redzina soils; and (3) a transitional plain and sloping *tzekel* zone with stony lithosol soils. In addition, *rejolladas* (earth-filled sinkholes), *huayás* (shallow depressions), caves, cenotes, and *sascaberas* (shallow mines for soft limestone) were mapped throughout the survey area; these represent special ecological niches inside microenvironments. The entire area was covered by the stone-wall *albarrada* system mentioned above, and different types of mounds and circular structures were identified inside some *albarradas'* enclosures.

The peripheral area exhibited no evidence of domestic activity signatures, such as pottery, metates, or indisputable dwelling structures. However, the site core produced a considerable number of pottery sherds, shell tools, and other diagnostics of everyday life. In addition, a single substructure located above the main platform yielded a cluster of twelve metates that are representative of domestic activity. The lack of domestic materials on the periphery, where the landscape was modified as described above, suggested that the periphery was used exclusively for agrarian activities, probably by workers quartered in the site core. Of relevance to this chapter were particular circular and linear structures found at the site, which by their form and associated materials can be identified as beekeeping structures or apiaries. We now suggest a model that explains the distribution of apiaries in Buena Vista and the practical use of *albarradas* in parceling the area around them.

## Beekeeping Structures in Buena Vista

Large amounts of *maktunoob,* the limestone disk plugs, were found associated with different structures in Buena Vista. Beekeeping structures in the site were classified into three types: circular structures, half-circles, and niched walls.

### Circular Structures

Dry-laid masonry-walled circular shapes that are 5–8 meters in diameter are the most common form of beekeeping structures in the site. They are preserved to a maximum observed height of 1.5 meters and are about 1 meter thick. Sometimes these walls are composed of inner and outer retaining walls built with roughly shaped limestone blocks or slabs and with a hearting of rubble and gravel. In some cases, they were observed to have a low parapet running around the outside about 50 centimeters above ground level. These circular structures were found both isolated and in groups, sometimes next to other structures such as rectangular platforms or walls. In addition, some of them have a rectangular altar-like platform (approximately 2 × 1.7 meters) in the center and one or two associated barrel-shaped stones that are 31 centimeters tall and 18–21 centimeters in diameter. These altars have vestiges of stucco plaster. Most of these structures have no entrances, but a few located in the main platform have openings. One had a small square room attached (1.5 × 1.5 meters).

### Half-Circles

Half-circles are dry-masonry walls built with the same techniques used in circular structures. They never have outside parapets or central altars as the circular structures do, but sometimes they have a masonry wall located at their front, enclosing the half-circle. These structures were found isolated or in clusters with circular structures. Occasionally they are adjacent to large platforms or stone walls.

### Niched Walls

Niched walls are sections of dry-laid stone walls 1.5–2.0 meters wide and 1.0–1.5 meters tall, on average. Some sections of these walls have parapets up to 1.0 meters wide by 1.0 meters tall. Some of these walls have square niches that measure 1 meter on each side (on average) and are built with stone boulders and slabs. There is no indication that these niches were used for burials or as crypts or altars. Tentatively these niches have been interpreted as shelters for beehives. We discuss this further in the concluding section.

## Distribution of Beekeeping Structures in Buena Vista

As mentioned earlier, the site core is situated on a natural elevation running northeast to southwest paralleling the coast at an average distance of 1.5 kilometers. Beekeeping structures are mostly distributed on this elevated area near permanent freshwater cenotes in clusters or groups separated by 400–500 meters. In addition, as part of the beekeeping clusters, a complex field wall system divides the area around beekeeping structures into unevenly sized lots that range in area from 400 to 10,000 square meters. During survey in areas located closer to the coastline, we found no evidence of beekeeping structures.

## *Pet Kot, Tolche,* or Bee Gardens

*Kot* is the Maya word used to name the modern single-lined stone walls (*albarradas*) found in all Yucatán towns dividing *solares*, but the composed word *pet kot* is the name assigned to *albarradas* found in the forest, which modern peasants claim their ancestors constructed for the protection and cultivation of useful trees (Gómez-Pompa et al. 1987, 10).

Managing forests is a common practice among contemporary Yucatán Maya, by selecting useful species, eliminating other species, introducing useful species from outside sources, and protecting the forest from fire and destructive uses. Traditionally, Maya used a variety of techniques to keep land belts that included different forest resources around their milpas as part of an ancient forest management system known in Maya as *tolche* (Flores and Ek 1983). The *tolche* system consists of classifying and preserving forest land belts at different stages of regeneration in order to increase the diversity of plant species available at any given time (Gómez-Pompa 1991, 338).

Recent studies of the phrenology (flowering cycle of plants) of the Yucatán and its relationship with beekeeping and the honey production cycle (Poot and Bocara 1980; Chemas and Rico-Gray 1991; Porter-Bolland 1999) have demonstrated that Maya beekeepers have a specialized knowledge of the *tolche* system and the phrenology related to the distinct *tolche* stages (see also Ewell and Merrill-Sands 1987, 95–129, for the relation of milpa to beekeeping). They seek to locate their apiaries near selected plant species or to plant flowering species bees prefer close to them. In addition, they continue to plant their traditional milpa in areas not too far from their apiaries.

Some of the most important ecological factors that modern beekeepers consider when they choose an optimal place to set their apiaries are:

a) The active radius of bees (500–600 meters for stingless bees): there should be no other apiary in this radius
b) Year-round flowering: a mixture of different stages of regenerated forest is ideal because different species flower at different times of the year
c) A permanent source of water
d) An area surrounding the apiary that is not heavily bushed and does not have thick trunks because the queen could crash and die during the nuptial flight (Chemas and Rico-Gray 1991)
e) Presence of a milpa, which is important for beekeeping because just after the dry season, during the first rains when flowering species are scarce, pollen from tasseling corn is the primary stimulus for renewed colony development (Ewell and Merrill-Sands 1987, 95–129).

## Discussion and Conclusion

Identification of beekeeping structures in Buena Vista was confirmed by the discovery of associated *maktunoob* with these features and by drawing an analogy with contemporary Yucatán beekeeping practices. However, it could be wrong to identify all beekeeping structures as "bee houses" as they are pictured in modern ethnographies. Some structures in Buena Vista could have been used for storing bee products (Piña Chan 1978) or for special bee ceremonies, such as those Fray Diego de Landa described (Tozzer 1941, 193–194), which are also depicted in the Madrid Codex (Cordan 1966; Vail 1994, 37–68; Ciaramella 2002, 1–68; Źrałka et al. 2018). In addition, some *maktunoob* concentrations probably mark their place of manufacture or workshops.

Batún-Alpuche (2004) turned to the investigation of traditional beekeeping practices in other parts of Mesoamerica and elsewhere in the world after discovering that more than fifteen species of stingless bees are present in the Yucatán peninsula (Roubik et al. 1990; Roubik 1992). There is also evidence to suggest that the pre-Hispanic Cozumel Maya probably domesticated other stingless bees besides *Melipona beecheii*. If that were the case, that could provide an explanation for the different forms of beekeeping structures on Cozumel Island. We will address just one other stingless bee: *Scaptotrigonia*. This bee species has a wider distribution than *Melipona* species. They are found in tropical climates like *Melipona* bees, but they are also found in cooler latitudes such as those in central Mexico, where they were traditionally domesticated in vertical pot hives. *Scaptotrigonia* are better adapted to cool latitudes: they build vertical rather than horizontal nests, as *Melipona* species do. In most places of the world where vertical-hive bees are domesticated, the hives are protected by walled enclosures. Some of them are sheltered in niches constructed in wide stone walls called bee boles (Crane 1983, 117–162; 1999). Bee boles found elsewhere look similar to the niched walls found in Buena Vista.

We did not find *maktunoob* inside any of the wall niches we observed, perhaps because most of the wide walls in Buena Vista are totally collapsed. However, *maktunoob* were often found in association with collapsed walls at the site, and this association also has been reported for other Cozumel sites such as Aguada Grande near the northeast point of the island (Freidel and Sabloff 1984, 33). In addition, stone disks associated with collapsed walls have been recovered from excavations on several east coast sites, including a considerable number of them found among the rubbish of the large wall at Tulum (Terrones 1990, 1994).

Landscape analysis of the location and distribution of beekeeping structures resulted in the discovery that there was a marked preference for locating apiaries in a land belt located 1.0–1.5 kilometers inland above a natural elevation. Clusters of beekeeping structures were distributed at an average distance of 500 meters, surrounding or forming part of the wall system, dividing the area into parcels. This pattern of distribution left enough area between the apiaries to avoid competition among bees from different apiaries for access to flowering plants (considering the gathering radius of stingless bees).

*Pet kots,* areas that enclosed apiaries, were probably used for milpas, but most important, during fallow periods they enclosed *tolches,* thus providing bees with flowering plants throughout the year. *Pet kots* in Buena Vista most probably functioned in the past as the bee gardens of the Cozumel Mayas.

Finally, we need to consider the place of beekeeping, honey, and wax harvesting in the larger context of Cozumel as a sacred pilgrimage place. Cozumel was declared the first apiary for a reason. It seems plausible that the round structures at Buena Vista were not just practical structures for storage, work, or habitation. These structures were most likely charged with the spiritual power of bees and their wax and honey.

Bees were sacred to the pre-Columbian people of this area. Bees depicted in the Paris Codex descend onto hives (Źrałka et al. 2018), and onto waxed tablets (Freidel et al. 2016). Descending gods were part of Maya and Mesoamerican religions in depictions from the Preclassic (1000 BCE–250 CE) onward. In the Postclassic (900–1519 CE), murals at Tulum were clearly associated with the celestial cordage that linked the world of the gods and ancestors to that of human beings (Miller 1974), and a large descending bee is recorded on the wall of a Postclassic building at Xelha (Farriss et al. 1975, 9; Miller 1982). Scribes and their monkey god patrons, who are seen depicted on Classic period painted vases with writing tablets and styluses, were also linked to the otherworldly beings as they materialized time and read the numbers and words of the gods and ancestors (Freidel et al. 2016).

One of the principal descending gods of the east coast peoples was Kukulcan, the feathered serpent incarnation of Venus, diving star and avatar of the wind god. At Buena Vista, on the southwestern point of Cozumel, is a Postclassic shrine called El Caracol with the conical hat of Ehecatl-Quetzalcoatl studded with sets of four shell trumpets set to catch the wind. As Harry Pollock (1936) showed in his survey of round structures in Mesoamerica, there is a close connection between this deity complex and round structures, including, of course, the Caracol at Chichén Itzá and the famed temple of Quetzalcoatl in Tenochtitlan. When Hernan Cortez landed on Cozumel, he visited a prominent temple dedicated to Kukulkan/Quetzalcoatl in the principal leeward side town on the island, likely San Miguel Xamancab, probably where the modern town of San Miguel is situated. Buena Vista was likely the predecessor to Santa Maria Oycib, the town of wax, although by the time of Cortez that community may have shifted to the leeward locality of El Cedral. In any case, Cozumel was sacred to Ix Chel and to the descending gods and their materializing powers.

Bees were only one type of insect that the ancient Maya revered, depicted, and contemplated, but because their honey is a key ingredient in sweet fermented beverages important to rituals, that is the bee product Maya artists of the Classic period focused on most. And because the death god Akan, God A prime, presided over intoxication, bees and fermented drink are part of his rituals. However, Spanish observers made clear in their accounts that wax was also prized and commercially produced in places like Cozumel Island. Freidel and colleagues (2016) show that beeswax was also associated with the gods and depicted in the bee pages of the Madrid Codex as a surface for writing tablets the gods used. We reiterate those arguments here and we have reviewed the evidence that the Classic Maya wrote and calculated with sharp styluses on soft surfaces. We have shown why we think many of those surfaces were layers of beeswax on boards, divining plates, and scrying mirrors. Maya time calculations, as colleagues in this book show (chapters 9, 12, and 17), required intellectual agility as well as deep knowledge. Having provisional surfaces on which to initiate the materialization of time helped ensure that most of the time the final declarations carved in stone reflect their best efforts, the mathematical acumen for which the Maya are justly famous.

## Notes

1  These disks were identified during the 1972–1973 Harvard-Arizona expedition.
2  Maya plate, Kerr number 5861, Maya Vase Data Base, http://research.mayavase.com/kerrmaya_list.php?_allSearch=&hold_search=&x=28&y=11&vase_number=5861&date_added=&ms_number=&site=.

# 16

## Temporal Fusion

### Mythical and Mortal Time in Maya Art

JAMES A. DOYLE

Maya sculptors, painters, and scribes wielded their blades and brushes as tools for marking, bending, and inventing time. They demonstrated tremendous ability to comprehend the oral histories and philosophies of temporal realities and translate those complex narratives into visually compelling architecture and personal belongings for their royal patrons. Maya rulers seem to have been preoccupied with mythic glosses of dynastic events, especially in the eighth century. Contemporaneous viewers of such monuments would have understood the fusion of present, recent past, deep historical past, and mythic past (Carter 2010, 352; Houston 2011). In their quest to represent founding deities from deep time or personified natural phenomena, Maya painters and sculptors created an intimate relationship between human time and divine time that endured for centuries. They also signaled to the viewers of their creations how to find the element of mythic time using visual clues or date markers in the texts.

This chapter focuses on case studies in which Maya artists demonstrated exceptional brilliance in marking time. There are, of course, many examples when Maya sculptors fused present, past, and mythical time in the same image on stelae, altars, and architectural programs (see Stuart 2011). The use of and ceremonial enjoyment of stone monuments and mural paintings as records of the passage of time, however, are somewhat restricted because they are not portable. Because of this, my analysis thus includes painters of codex-style vessels, who fused historical time with mythic time in the late seventh or eighth century in order to connect their patrons with divine inspiration. A reexamination of individual hands in the codex style provides a window into the approaches of different scribal schools to bringing time to art. The method of materializing mythological time by painter-scribes is less systematic and may be focused on certain vases that signal an alternate scheme of timekeeping. Some of these have previously been interpreted as having intentional calendric "errors." These vessels, as codified depictions of what would have been widely known historical and mythical narratives, served as bearers of temporal meaning, mnemonics for performance, and symbols of artistic capital as diplomatic gifts.

## Sculpting as Time Traveling

The crisp low-relief detail on the platform panel from Palenque's Temple XXI surprises modern viewers upon close viewing. The beauty of the monument transports even uninformed beholders to a transcendent place. The original scene of the action is a multilayered timescape that speaks to the expansive minds of Classic Maya sculptors as much as their undeniable genius in working stone. In addition to the recent past, when it was rediscovered by archaeologists and the contemporary world in which it is currently displayed and studied, this work of art existed in many different planes of time when it was dedicated (Stuart 2005b; Finamore and Houston 2011, catalog no. 48; de la Garza 2015, catalog no. 1; Pillsbury et al. 2017, catalog no. 137). The monument is a materialization of the time spent finding and quarrying the perfect piece of dense limestone, the time artists took to measure and compose the portraits and glyphic passages, and the hours of detailed work required to gouge and incise the delicate image. Further it was carefully placed on the temple platform and painted red around its edges. In its original context, it was an act of legitimation, a dedicatory monument to a platform in Temple XXI. It also told a story of the past as part of the kingly narrative of Ahkal Mo' Nahb and his rite of passage to becoming the chosen heir to the throne of Palenque.

The scene, which was carved in 736 CE but had taken place more than fifty years earlier, shows K'inich Janaab Pakal I handing his grandson, K'inich Ahkal Mo' Nahb III, a stingray spine adorned with jade and feathers. The commissioning lord and his brother flank the larger Pakal and are seated behind his large throne as accompanying courtly attendants. The artist took special care to create detailed portraits of each man, pictured in profile as they face away from him. The choice of the artist to position Pakal's grandsons looking away from the central figure emphasizes the great ruler's importance; perhaps protocol dictated that others look away in such a ceremony. The two brothers' engagement with the peripheral characters is another technique of the artist to indicate the timing of this event: was the handing over of the ritual bloodletter a spontaneous act by Pakal? Were the brothers, who were deeply engaged in other conversations, surprised by Pakal's choice of Ahkal Mo' Nahb?

The retroactive scene, which allegedly took place over fifty years earlier, underscores time as a foundation for rulership. Pakal is not named but is noted only as the "5-k'atun Ajaw" in the caption. Pakal took on an identity in this composition that was explicitly related to linear time that celebrated his extreme old age, but the caption also specifies that he was in an act of impersonation as he donned the mantle of mythic time. He is said to be in the image of a founding patron deity of Palenque. Pakal, as the glorious protagonist, is actually reaching even farther back in the past with his headdress, which contains the name of the divine patron, probably as a jade *hu'unal* jewel.

The panel records the rite of passage of the first bloodletting Ahkal Mo' Nahb performed, presumably with the newly gifted bloodletter. This past vignette may have, in fact, fused reality with mythology in that moment with the inclusion of the characters on either end of the scene. They are either mythological beings or people donning elaborate costumes. Although the event was certainly possible given the brief overlap in the lives of Pakal and his grandson, the artist may have been complicit in creating a fictive time in which events were imagined and reinserted into the historical narrative. The fact that the similar compositions from Temple XIX show specific human individuals in historic scenes throws the unique nature of this spiritually charged retelling of the past into sharper relief.

Other sculptural ateliers in the eighth century, such as the one at Piedras Negras, achieved visual time blending through a similar technique of representing a specific monument in a retroactive historical scene supervised by patron deities. On Panel 3, a monument created in 782 CE by a team of three led by a head sculptor, a retroactive scene creates multiple time frames (Houston 2016, table 13.3). The patron, Piedras Negras Ruler 7, commissioned the sculptors to show his predecessor, Ruler 4, in an event that had happened decades earlier. The king sits on an elaborate throne and gestures toward vassal visitors from subordinate kingdoms. The sculptors reference a contemporaneous throne, however, perhaps even Ruler 7's own Throne 1, injecting the patron's identity into the historic moment. Furthermore, the patron gods of Piedras Negras, those Ruler 7 presumably honored in his courtly world, were said to supervise the gathering, merging godly time, mortal time, and past time.

Even without explicit textual or visual references to multiple time frames, Maya artists of the eighth century could combine portraits with contemporary events that were overlaid with supernatural machinations. One example that has long been known to scholars known as Laxtunich Lintel 1 has recently been reexamined by an interdisciplinary team (Houston 2021). The lintel's sculptor, named Mayuy, portrayed a fusion of cosmic bodies and political hierarchy and included a unique reference to the vernal equinox in sculpture. This lintel may be the only depiction of construction in the corpus of monumental Maya art. The overlord who commissioned the composition, Shield Jaguar IV, is shown impersonating the sun god as he is lifted into the sky on the equinox. His loyal subordinate seated across from him impersonates his divine foil, the nighttime maize god. Two other *sajal* individuals play Atlantean roles, holding up the lintel itself as a manifestation of the sky.

In the case of these roughly contemporaneous monuments, the peer sculptors created texts and headdresses to alert a viewer to the presence or impersonation of deities in cyclical time. For Pakal, it was a local founding deity and for Shield Jaguar IV, it was the all-important sun god. Such temporal fusions could perhaps be considered one of the hallmarks of Maya art from the beginning of visual culture in the Preclassic period (see chapters 3 and 5, this volume). It is clear that by the first century BCE, as seen in the West Wall of the Las Pinturas building at San Bartolo, Guatemala, artists and their patrons linked cycles of time in the lives of humans with those of deities. The main text contains a detailed hieroglyphic day sign of 3 Ik', the cartouche of which features red-painted motifs that signal dripping blood. 3 Ik' was a day name associated with yearbearers in the Classic and Postclassic periods (Taube et al. 2010, 20; chapter 12, this volume). It appears as an enlarged hieroglyph that introduces a scene in which the Principal Bird Deity descends as it is addressed by a smaller being wearing the duck-billed mask associated with later wind deities. This dramatic depiction of the 3 Ik' day name underscores the importance of marking time in early Maya art. In other words, this event could not have happened a long time ago on an unspecified day; rather, it had to be marked as the 3 Ik' event. David Stuart has suggested that this particular 3 Ik' is the seating of the month Pop in 27 BCE, 79 BCE, or 131 BCE (Stuart 2004a, 6). It also could be a date that was not fixed in the Long Count of mortal time associated with the impersonation of the duck-billed wind god.

## Unreal Time on Codex-Style Vessels

One compelling case for manipulating time in visual compositions comes from a large group of vessels created in the codex style, a polychrome tradition characterized by a cream ground, black line for figural outlines and texts, and red highlights on the rim and base (Coe 1973; for codex scribes, see Rossi et al. 2015, and chapter 9, this volume). Recent research on such

404 · James A. Doyle

vessels has demonstrated that drinking cups, plates, flasks, and other vessels had the narrative qualities of illuminated manuscripts (Doyle 2016; O'Neil 2019). The original contexts and use of these vessels are difficult to determine due to lack of archaeological provenience for the vast majority of museum holdings. Archaeological and compositional research suggests that a center of production was located around the important royal court of Calakmul, which spanned the areas surrounding southern Campeche, Mexico, and northern Petén, Guatemala (Hansen et al. 1991; García Barrios 2011a; Reents-Budet et al. 2011). The preliminary archaeological designation of a codex-style homeland around Calakmul suggests that the kings and queens of the city commissioned a small group of painters to create vessels for ceremonies or diplomatic gifts (Hansen et al. 1991; Martin 1997; Carrasco Vargas et al. 1999; García Barrios and Carrasco Vargas 2006; Delvendahl 2008; Reents-Budet et al. 2011; García Barrios 2011a, 2011b). Simon Martin (2017) argues that codex-style vases were produced in a workshop overseen by a *k'uhul chatan winik* in the Calakmul region.[1]

An analysis of the available corpus of codex-style painting strongly suggests that a small, talented group of people or workshops created scenes in the same color scheme during a limited time period in the late seventh to early eighth centuries. Several challenges, however, limit the possible conclusions about individual "hands," including the chosen methods of identification (e.g., Morellian), the lack of specific signatures or information about the length of artists' careers, and the lack of current technical analysis of the sequence of painting or microstratigraphy of specific passages. Preliminary studies in connoisseurship or thematic groupings have identified ten to twenty different artists or workshops (see Robicsek and Hales 1981; Kerr and Kerr 1988; Aimi and Tunesi 2017).

Based on a sample of approximately 275 codex-style vessels, the majority known only from rollout photographs by Justin Kerr, I suggest that the number of artists may be between a minimum of twenty-five and a maximum of more than fifty, not including related schools. My evaluation considered factors such as general composition of scenes, paleography of texts and certain glyphic compounds as parts of regalia, diversity of brush size and ink quality, and confidence of brushwork. Given that few scribes signed codex-style works, it is unclear at present how to properly distinguish hands of potters or painters, although they were likely not the same teams (see Reents-Budet 1994; Just 2012). In one rare instance in which an *itz'aat* signed his work, it is clear that one artist operated in multiple known styles. Aj Maxam excelled in both the codex style and the Holmul-style polychromes (see Herring 1996; K633; K635; K4379). Several art-historical questions remain about the codex style. For example, why did the painters actively avoid further polychrome treatments, giving scenes a monochromatic character?

The aspect of codex-style painters most pertinent to the current volume's exploration of time is that they largely focused their compositions on the actions of supernaturals rather than historical figures in real poses on listed dates, as their sculptor peers did (see chapter 7, this volume). A few of them, who are recognizable by their distinctive hands, could have been key interlocutors or spiritual advisers to the royal courts as they visually manipulated time to support courtly initiatives. The abbreviated snapshots of larger myths present on drinking cups and plates may have served as mnemonic devices for recitations, entreaties to specific deities, or performances of mythic histories. Some vessels bear dates, including some day signs highlighted in red pigment, probably a reference to blood (as seen in San Bartolo), conflating sacrifice with the progression of time (Houston et al. 2006, 89–96).

A group of vessels that Justin Kerr and Barbara Kerr have categorized as part of the Fantastic School (Robicsek and Hales's Painter 2), represents the work of a small group of painters working in a very fine line who excelled at scenes involving rain god Chahk, serpents and death gods, and *way* creatures. In one example (K1300), the painter captured a chase between a monstrous toad poised to jump and a bounding deer (fig. 16.1). The anuran or saurian creature, which is marked with the glyph for darkness, also has a spine of *yax* glyphs that mark it as a green creature, but also likely as a primordial "first" creature. The dexterity of the Fantastic School painter in the fine lines suggests with the gaze of the deer that it is fleeing, an action that would have been perpetually repeated in the turning of the vessel in one's hands. This haptic experience is another key component of manipulating time with codex-style

Figure 16.1. Rollout of a codex-style vessel attributed to the Fantastic Painter, dated to the seventh or eighth century. Ceramic. 14 centimeters tall, 12 centimeters in diameter. Photo by Justin Kerr (K1300).

drinking cups. Other examples of the Fantastic School painter's *way* creatures and Chahk's interactions with other beings also convey a sense of frenetic motion (e.g., K1001, K3450).

One of the most talented artists in creating complex scenes of mythic time was named the Princeton Painter and his school by Justin and Barbara Kerr (Robicsek and Hales's Painter 3 and Painter 5; Aimi and Tunesi's Master of Cheen K'uk', or Master of the Two Kings). These painters excelled at telling the tales of the maize god and old gods such as the creator deity and ideal ruler, Itzamnaaj, and a related trading deity known as God L. In the remarkable vessel K0511 (fig. 16.2), now in the Princeton University Art Museum (y1975-17), the old god with his harem presides over a scene in which two deities prepare to decapitate a humanlike captive (Kerr and Kerr 2005; Velásquez García 2009; Martin 2010; Houston 2017b). The date that hovers above the decapitation scene could be 13 Caban 5 Ceh. 13 Caban is known as a yearbearer from other contexts. This could be another reference to decapitation sacrifice as a precursor to the beginning of a new cycle of time, as seen in the 3 Ik' scene of the West Wall mural in the Pinturas Building at San Bartolo dated many centuries earlier (Taube et al. 2010; chapters 5 and 12, this volume). Below the old god's throne is a seated rabbit, personified as a scribe working away on a screenfold codex bound in a jaguar pelt. Perhaps in a humorous gesture, the painter transformed himself into a rabbit and inserted his scribal presence in this supernatural scene.

The Princeton painters also captured multiple sequences of events in a single vessel (K1560), illustrating the maize god with attendants dominating three other deities. From right to left, the maize god seems to capture a deity, grasping him by the arm and head. Then he and a person of small stature seem to have removed the old god's clothing and accoutrements, and finally, the maize god tramples a vanquished deity with the aid of an attendant with a physical deformity. In this scene, the painter collapsed either three different episodes of the same event or three different events altogether in one object. The owner was thus empowered to re-create these mythic events over and over with a turn of the wrist. The workshop's expert treatment of deity representations is notable in many other vessels (e.g., K1004, K2286, and K2794). On a tripod vessel (K2572), a date appears for a K'awiil-taking event, a metaphor for accession across the inscriptions. The complex mythological scene on the vessel may depict the artist's conception of the supernatural meaning of K'awiil taking.

One codex-style painter, perhaps one of the most virtuoso Maya painters from the Classic period, depicted a singular creation scene that bounces between cosmic time and the historic time of a living owner. Stephen Houston

Figure 16.2. The Princeton Vase, a codex-style vessel attributed to the Princeton Painter. Ceramic with red, cream, and black slip with remnants of painted stucco. 21.5 centimeters tall, 16.6 centimeters in diameter. Princeton University Art Museum. Museum purchase, gift of the Hans A. Widenmann, Class of 1918, and Dorothy Widenmann Foundation (y1975-17). Photograph courtesy Justin Kerr (K511).

and I recently reexamined the Cosmic Plate, the first analysis of which appeared in the *Blood of Kings* exhibition and catalog (Schele and Miller 1986, plate 122). We concluded that both the imagery and the text served to fuse the mythic and the historical in microcosmic form. Day signs on the plate divide time into two, perhaps even three frames. Above the scene is the sky, depicted as Venus signs and the frontal (to the right) and rear (to the left) parts of the Starry Deer Crocodile (Velásquez García 2006, fig. 5; Martin 2015). In the absence of a Long Count, the events in these cosmic places could have occurred sometime before the artist and his patron were alive or an even longer time before that, before the realm of humans was formed. One day sign, 4 Ceh, appears above the head of the celestial bird at the top of the scene, which may suggest that the painter is referencing an event in mythic time separate from the one pictured in the main passage of the painting (fig. 16.3).

Another fictive date, 13 Ok 8 Zotz, begins the upper text, which refers to an event in deep time, perhaps something related to "sacred milpa/planted maize water" (*k'uhul jinaj*) in primordial places: "at the black cenote, at the black water, at the five-flower house (?)." The protagonists are the "four gods of *matawil*" (4 ma-ta-K'UH), denizens of a watery paradise that appears in texts at

Figure 16.3. Main scene of the Cosmic Plate. Drawing by James Doyle.

Palenque (Stuart and Stuart 2008, 211–215). The gods include a jaguar (hi-HIX), and Chak Xib Chahk, the rain god first identified as a Classic period deity on this very plate by David Stuart (2004a). These mythic dates contrast with the unfortunately eroded day sign prefaced by the coefficient 12 and the month 6 Pohp, which we argued might be either 9.16.5.15.3 12 Ak'bal 6 Pohp (February 10, 757 CE) or 9.16.19.0.8 12 Lamat 6 Pohp (February 7, 770 CE). The historical text, however, records the "raising" of the *jawte'* (plate) by an actual historical figure associated with an *ajaw* title but whose name is unknown elsewhere (la-ch'a-TUUN-ni si-k'u-AJAW). The scribe almost seems to underscore the split in ancient and present time by misaligning the texts.

Another gifted hand identified in over a dozen codex-style creations is that of the Metropolitan Painter (Robicsek and Hales's Painter 4), who was named after a drinking cup currently in the collection of the Metropolitan Museum of Art (fig. 16.4). A sherd bearing stylistic elements of the Metropolitan Painter's workshop was found at Calakmul, underscoring the possible connections between this royal court and the most talented painters of the eighth century. The Metropolitan vessel shows a scene in which a deity is born on a mountain while Chahk faces off with a skeletal death god. This subject is repeated in the corpus of this workshop. Above the reclining baby jaguar deity is the date of 7 Muluk 7 Kayab, a day-and-month combination that is an error; it does not fit into the actual cycles of time.

The 7 Muluk day sign appears on other Metropolitan Painter works, such as the Met's small drinking cup (K1152), a drinking cup in the Dallas Museum

Figure 16.4. Rollout of a codex-style vessel attributed to the Metropolitan Painter, dated to the seventh or eighth century. Ceramic with red, cream, and black slip. 14 centimeters tall, 11.4 centimeters in diameter. The Metropolitan Museum of Art, The Michael C. Rockefeller Memorial Collection, purchase, gift of Nelson A. Rockefeller, 1968 (1978.412.206).

of Art (K1370), and a drinking cup in the Princeton University Art Museum (K1003). These cups indicate that on a 7 Muluk day, the Calakmul ruler Yuhknoom Took' K'awiil acceded to the throne, which may be an indication that the artists anchored these mythological scenes in an actual royal event (Stuart et al. 2015). This is similar to the artist's temporal fusions on the Palenque panel: the painter implied that the Calakmul king was the patron of these vessels or the ancestor of the patron who was connected to the patron deities portrayed in the scenes, conveying this through the reference to the day he took the throne. Furthermore, the hieroglyphic text above Chahk's on the Met's smaller cup specifies that this is the Chahk of the First Rain, setting the scene at the start of the rainy season but not in a particular year (Doyle 2016, 52; see also García Barrios 2008). A wider group of more than twenty-five vessels that could be considered to have been painted in the school of the Metropolitan Painter includes more versions of the Chahk story and processions of different *way* creatures.

A talented painter who was connected archaeologically and epigraphically to Calakmul is the founder of the Liner School, or Strong Glyph School, that is represented in more than sixty codex-style examples. Aimi and Tunesi (2017) have proposed approximately seven different hands associated with this workshop, including those who served under the Calakmul *chatan winik* Yopaat Bahlam. The characteristics of this school include a dedicatory text of glyphs that carry bold outlines with fine detailing and shading. Often the guide lines that frame the texts remain visible. A whole vessel used to consume "fruity chocolate" that was excavated in Tomb 1 of Structure XV at Calakmul bears a scene in which the reclining maize god is born from a monstrous seed or rhizome among a band of water (Finamore and Houston 2010, catalog no. 86; Chinchilla Mazariegos 2017, 214–218; on chocolate content, see Loughmiller-Newman 2012). Another plate possibly painted by this workshop is distinct for the painter's deployment of a deep red throughout the composition. It was excavated in Tomb 1 of Structure 2 from nearby Uxul. Because of the propensity of the Liner or Strong Glyph artists to include dedicatory texts, this group of vessels includes many unique examples of mixing mythological and mortal time. *Way* creatures (K771), feathered serpents, water birds, supernatural scribes, or deities such as Chahk and the maize god (K2068) all feature prominently in vessels raised by Maya nobles (fig. 16.5).

Some painters experimented with more shading and washes than others when portraying celestial time, such as the talented artist of two vases that each feature two sequential events involving deities (K1398, K8622). In the cylinder vessel known as the Regal Rabbit vase, one passage depicts an old god beseeching a trickster rabbit to return his clothes, which the rabbit has

Figure 16.5. Rollout of codex-style ceramic vessel attributed to the Liner School, dated to the seventh or eighth century. Red, cream, and black slip. 19 centimeters tall, 11.2 centimeters in diameter. The Metropolitan Museum of Art, gift of Justin Kerr in memory of Barbara Kerr, 2014 (2014.632.1).

presumably stolen and holds over his victim. The following scene on the other side of the vessel shows the same old god kneeling in front of the sun god and entreating him to intervene. The larcenous rabbit hides behind the solar deity, as if taunting his victim. Perhaps the same artist created a vessel now in the Kimbell Art Museum (K8622) that shows a sequence of events involving an old god riding different creatures. Itzamnaaj rides a peccary on a specific date (emphasized in red); in another instance, he rides a deer while addressing a standing elder holding a paddle.

One final group of codex-style vases that mark time deserves mention. These vessels contain texts that list historical names and actions and are completely devoid of figural representations. This departure from a focus on deities in favor of a list of historical names and acts is noteworthy within the codex style. Simon Martin (2017) has revisited the evidence of scribal "error" with respect to dates in the Dynastic Vases, a series of twelve vases whose imagery consists of a list of days, verbs, and royal names (fig. 16.6). That the authors of these vessels chose to eschew imagery and include only a time-based list of rulers underscores the primacy of time over even portraits of the rulers (for a similar case study from Belize, see Helmke et al. 2018).

Codex-style artists presented two time frames that are subtly noted in a contrast between the scene and the texts, but sometimes the artists blended time using a different strategy. Two master codex-style artists presented two different versions of an enigmatic moment in the creation of the mortal world, completely distinct from the Cosmic Plate mentioned above. These depictions build on known polychrome versions of a scene in which Itzamnaaj,

412 · James A. Doyle

Figure 16.6. Codex-style vessel from Mexico or Guatemala, southern Campeche or northern Petén region, Mirador Basin, Maya, 650–800 CE. Slip-painted ceramic. 14.29 centimeters in diameter, 16.51 centimeters tall. Los Angeles County Museum of Art, anonymous gift (M.2010.115.1).

the supreme deity of the sky, presides over a court of other deities and anthropomorphic beings (Miller and Martin 2004, plate 35). The Vase of the Seven Gods and Vase of the Eleven Gods specifically refer to the 4 Ajaw 8 Kumku date in 3114 BCE when the gods were "placed into order."[2]

The codex-style versions of mythological courts present very different narratives. The first is known as the Court of God D vessel. According to the dedicatory text, this vessel for cacao was painted by RABBIT—*bu* (T'ulub?) for a *ch'ok* (youth) associated with the Ik' polity (Boot 2008; Coe and Houston 2015, plate XVIII; Houston 2017b). In addition to the 8,000 deities of the sky and 8,000 deities of the earth pictured on polychrome scenes, chatty animal scribes—a dog, an opossum, a vulture, and four monkeys—surround the enthroned Itzamnaaj. The mythic time, though, plays out differently. The full Initial Series date is 12.10.1.13.2 9 Ik' 5 Mol (April 6, 3309 BCE), over two centuries before the 3114 BCE event depicted on the other courtly vases (Boot 2008, 20). On this date, Itzamnaaj supervised the Chahk deity's accession to the rank of *ajaw,* the same deity who was the principal subject of the Cosmic Plate. The early date was also recorded on Palenque sculpture (Lounsbury 1976). Is the artist of the Court of the God D vessel presenting the last vestiges of a previous world, before Itzamnaaj crowned Chahk, centuries before the ordering of the rest of the gods? Some clues to the scribe's beliefs about the ineptitude of the animal scribes come from the unusually recorded speech as Itzamnaaj addresses the four monkeys and from the red-painted speech scroll that seems to represent a visual tongue twister (Houston 2017a).

## Conclusion: The Boomerang of Mortality and Immortality

A Princeton School painter depicted a parallel creation scene on the masterful codex-style plate known as the Resurrection Plate, now at the Museum of Fine Arts Boston (1993.565) (fig. 16.7). Three characters appear, each named with a caption: a central maize god (Hun Ixi'm Ahiin) emerges from a turtle carapace, presumably coaxed by one son (Hun Ajaw) and watered by the other (Yax Bahlam?). Here is a primordial metaphor for maize sprouting from a cleft in the earth's surface. The birth or rebirth of the maize god would have been a pervasive story in Maya royal rhetoric, yet the artist-scribe here gives little detail other than the individuals' names.

The painter of the plate chose not to include a date, even a fictive one. The Resurrection Plate offers no textual clues about time, either mythological or contemporaneous. This choice could have been made because the date would have been obvious to a viewer or, perhaps more likely, because it had occurred deep in the mythic past and a specific date was not important in that context. The text on the rim, which is larger than the deity nominals, names the owner of the plate (*lak*) as someone from the Chatan place, another connection to the realm of Calakmul (Grube 2005). In the absence of a day sign, the scene floats in time, just as it does on the physical space of the plate. The lack of a specific day allows a user of the plate, whether they were eating off it or being inspired by its images for activation in a ceremony, to re-create the story of the maize god's birth on any day. One distinct moment that is materialized in time, however, distinguishes this plate from the other vessels: someone created a tiny, deliberate drill hole before the plate was placed in the tomb it laid in for centuries.

Figure 16.7. Codex-style ceramic plate, seventh or eighth century. Red and black on cream slip paint. 32 centimeters in diameter, depth 5.8 centimeters. Museum of Fine Arts Boston, gift of Landon T. Clay (1993.565). Photo by Justin Kerr (K1892).

Maya thinkers clearly conceived of the lives and deaths of mortal rulers as predestined and intertwined with the lives of immortals. Deities crowned each other and placed each other in order thousands of years before humans built cities like Calakmul and Tikal. These courtly models were archetypal guides for how to construct a successful royal court and in some cases, perhaps, how not to run a court. Maya artists grafted divine identities onto elite people and aspects of divine time onto special human days as a strategy for bolstering their patrons' claims to moral and godly authority within their political orbits. On monuments and large-scale paintings, these combined identities and mixing of human and godly deep time served to reinforce claims to sovereign power. With portable ceramic vessels, the effect of bolstering authority is less obvious and less public. More than the presumed performative or didactic function in ceremonial contexts, codex-style vases served as physical manifestations of the bending (that maybe even was thought of as blending or stirring) of time that artists used to emphasize the mythological underpinnings of divine kingship. Only by making oblique references to important dates and by remixing the calendar in a way that indicated that time was not quite real did artists signal to the viewers that the rain god, Itzamnaaj, the maize god, and other ruling deities were operating on a different plane a long time ago.

## Acknowledgments

Special thanks go to Stephen Houston, dutiful mentor, for his insightful discussions about the Cosmic Plate and the invitation to present some of the ideas on "hands" in the codex style at the John W. Kluge Center at the Library of Congress in 2019.

## Notes

1 See chapter 7, this volume, for, a sixth-century queen of El Perú-Waka' who holds the title *k'uhul chatan winik*. See also Aimi and Tunesi (2017) and Beliaev (2004). Interestingly, one of the individuals on Laxtunich Lintel 1 holds the same title.
2 See also the Vase of the Eleven Gods at the Los Angeles County Museum of Art, M.2010.115.14, https://collections.lacma.org/node/1903409.

# 17

# "How Much May They Not Have Written?"

## K'atuns 11 Ajaw and the Itzá

PRUDENCE M. RICE

It may be there is no meaning to it all:
It may be an error and not true as it is written.
If the real meaning is mastered entirely,
Why didn't they see it?
How much may they not have written then?
Book of Chilam Balam of Chumayel (Edmonson 1986, ll. 1615–1619)

Most Mayanists readily recognize the significance of the recurring approximately twenty Gregorian-year temporal intervals named K'atuns 8 Ajaw. But another calendrical cycle that emphasized K'atuns 11 Ajaw, was also important, particularly during the Postclassic period in the northern Yucatán Peninsula. How and why did this alternative scheme originate? And where did it originate? I address these questions by considering two interrelated topics: the highly contentious history of Chichén Itzá and the correspondences (or lack thereof) of archaeological dates compared to the events sketched in the books of the Chilam Balam, the late Indigenous literature of Yucatán. By the time these books were written, the significance of K'atun 11 Ajaw had expanded to include the mythic identification of a primordial period of world destruction and re-creation (Knowlton 2010, 53–83).

The site of Chichén Itzá is important in this regard. Unfortunately, its chronology remains a matter of fierce dispute despite nearly a century of excavations, decades of ceramic analyses, and many radiocarbon assays, thermoluminescence dates, and epigraphic readings (Volta and Braswell 2014;

Ringle 2017). I have no wish to take sides in these arguments; my interest is solely in the possible role of K'atun 11 Ajaw to the Itzá. The reasons why they chose this period to begin their calendar cycles instead of K'atuns 8 Ajaw to end them may be lost forever, or, as I propose here, circumstances related to founding and termination may have shaped this decision.

I agree with previous interpreters of the Indigenous prophetic histories who claim that Chichén Itzá was founded, in some poorly understood sense, during a K'atun 11 Ajaw in the late eighth century. But K'atuns 11 Ajaw became lasting, symbolically pivotal temporal intervals for peoples known as Itzá. Consideration of these intervals illuminates parallels between archaeological data and the Indigenous chronicles. Moreover, such attention reveals an instantiation of ~256-year cycles in lowland Maya political affairs that began in the Late Classic and continued through the Early Postclassic. These interconnections were not written in stone—that is, explicitly inscribed in Classic stone monuments. Rather, they must be teased out of coherences among multiple data sets.

## Maya Linear and Cyclical Time: A Review

The Maya, like westerners today, tracked time in both linear and cyclical formulations. Western linear timekeeping on a grand scale is based on the passage of solar (tropical) years, measured by the flow of decimal-based units of decades, centuries, and millennia. Western cyclical time is more intimate and includes the infinitely repetitive and nested sexagesimal counts of 60 seconds in a minute, 60 minutes in an hour, 24 hours in a day, 7 days in a week, and 12 months in a year. For today's western cultures, time is mostly a matter of allotting various activities to these ordered slots, giving us our anniversaries of meaningful life experiences.

The ancient lowland Maya observed similar but more complicated sets of nested and intermeshing temporal segments. Time and its units of observation were animate and toyed capriciously with the outcomes of all social, political, economic, and personal human endeavors. Maya time recording was based on counts of days that were grouped or bundled into units that were typically multiples of twenty (a vigesimal system) and/or thirteen. Classic linear timekeeping, known by scholars as the Long Count, was based on tallying the passage of days by means of these bundles, beginning with a seemingly arbitrary or mythical starting date in August 3114 BCE. The specific ways the bundles of days or units of time were named and counted varied by culture and by time period (see Edmonson 1988; Sharer with Traxler 2006).

418 · Prudence M. Rice

The Maya also registered the passage of time via several cycles that ordered everything from their quotidian world to the very continuity of the cosmos:[1]

> One cycle is the *tzolk'in* (count of days): a period of twenty named days prefixed by one of thirteen numbers. Totaling 260 days, this count constitutes the Maya version of a widespread tradition of Mesoamerican ritual calendars or sacred divinatory almanacs.

> Another cycle is a calendar based on multiples of 360-day Maya "years," or *tuns,* plus five days to create the *haab',* thus approximating the solar year of 365.24 days.

> A third cycle, observed within the *haab'* (and within the Long Count), is a bundle of twenty *tuns,* or 7,200 days (19.71 Gregorian years). This interval was called a *k'atun* in Yukatekan in the Postclassic and later Indigenous literature (but hieroglyphically "spelled" *winikhaab'*—20 *haab'*—in Ch'olan in the Classic period).

> A fourth cycle consists of 13 *k'atuns* or 260 *tuns* (93,600 days), very slightly more than 256 Gregorian years (93,504 days). This 260-*tun* interval was the basis for the Short Count, a late, abbreviated alternative to linear Long Count dating. In the Short Count, only the *k'atun* in which an event occurred was recorded, plus the day in the 260-day almanac and "month" in the 360-plus-5-day calendar. By the Postclassic, events were chronicled only with reference to an Ajaw (lord) *k'atun*-ending day and number (from the *tzolk'in*): for example, a K'atun 8 Ajaw.

My interest here centers on what is known or surmised about the practices of counting and celebrating these ~256-year/260-*tun k'atun* cycles in three Maya calendars: the Classic period Tikal calendar and two Postclassic calendars in the northern Yucatán Peninsula, one used by the lineages of the Xiw alliance in the northwest and the other by the rival Itzá alliance in the northeast.

## Postclassic Cycles of Time: Counting K'atuns

The abbreviated Short Count, or dating by *k'atun* cycles, was the scheme for chronicling events in the books of the Chilam Balam. These books are accumulations of prophecies, history, astronomy, medicine, and other lore found in hieroglyphic texts such as codices. These texts or prophetic histories were initially compiled by Maya priests and scribes in hieroglyphs and then, after the Spanish conquest, transcribed into Yukateko by educated Maya using the Latin alphabet. Copied and recopied into the eighteenth century in an obfuscating and allusive poetic style, the texts are named for the Yucatán towns in which they were found. Unfortunately, their minimal historical content is largely unanchored to the modern western (Gregorian) calendar.

## K'atuns 8 Ajaw

Mayanists are familiar with the calendar scheme of the Postclassic Xiw of the northern Yucatán Peninsula because it was essentially the same as the Classic calendar used at Tikal and various other sites (Edmonson 1988, 246–250; see also Chase 1991). This calendar was first attested in a Long Count notation registering a date corresponding to 292 CE on Tikal Stela 29. The thirteen-*k'atun* cycles of both the Classic period Maya and the Xiw began with a K'atun 6 Ajaw (hereafter abbreviated as K6A): a period of approximately twenty years ending on a day 6 Ajaw. The cycle continued through twelve more such 20-year periods, named and numbered in retrograde order as K'atuns 4 Ajaw (K4A), K2A, K13A, and so on (see Table 17.1), ending approximately 256 Gregorian years (260 *tuns*) later with a K'atun 8 Ajaw on a day 8 Ajaw. The entire cycle was named by this ending *k'atun*. Then a new cycle began with the next K6A.

Table 17.1. Gregorian dates (CE) of Late Classic through colonial-period ~256-year *k'atun* cycles

| | | Late Classic through Colonial | | | |
|---|---|---|---|---|---|
| K'atun | Early–Late Classic | Cycle 1 | Cycle 2 | Cycle 3 | Cycle 4 |
| 6 Ajaw[a] | 435–455 | 692–711 | 948–968 | 1204–1224 | 1461–1480 |
| 4 Ajaw | 455–475 | 711–731 | 968–987 | 1224–1244 | 1480–1500 |
| 2 Ajaw | 475–495 | 731–751 | 987–1007 | 1244–1263 | 1500–1520 |
| 13 Ajaw | 495–514 | 751–771 | 1007–1027 | 1263–1283 | 1520–1539 |
| 11 Ajaw | 514–534 | 771–790 | 1027–1047 | 1283–1303 | 1539[b]–1559 |
| 9 Ajaw | 534–554 | 790–810 | 1047–1066 | 1303–1323 | 1559–1579 |
| 7 Ajaw | 554–573 | 810–830 | 1066–1086 | 1323–1342 | 1579–1599 |
| 5 Ajaw | 573–593 | 830–849 | 1086–1106 | 1342–1362 | 1599–1618 |
| 3 Ajaw | 593–613 | 849–869 | 1106–1125 | 1362–1382 | 1618–1638 |
| 1 Ajaw | 613–633 | 869–889 | 1125–1145 | 1382–1401 | 1638–1658 |
| 12 Ajaw | 633–652 | 889–909 | 1145–1165 | 1401–1421 | 1658–1677 |
| 10 Ajaw | 652–672 | 909–928 | 1165–1185 | 1421–1441 | 1677–1697 |
| 8 Ajaw | 672–692 | 928–948 | 1185–1204 | 1441–1461 | 1697–1717 |

*Source:* Sharer with Traxler (2006, table A.1).

[a] This table uses the Classic or Tikal (also Xiw) calendar and cycles in the books of the *chilam b'alams*.

[b] The Mayapán calendar was inaugurated in 1539.

420 · Prudence M. Rice

For the Xiw, the cycle-ending K8As were times of turmoil and change in anticipation, in experience, and in retrospect. For example, in the Chilam Balam of Chumayel, the Itzá were reportedly driven from the homeland they occupied in a K8A (Puleston 1979, 64). Another example is the Xiw revolt against their rivals, the Kokom (an Itzá lineage) at Mayapán. This co-ruled city was the center of a political confederacy known as the League of Mayapán, which possibly began as a peace agreement among the rulers and allies of that city, Chichén Itzá, and Uxmal (Restall 1998, 24). The date of Mayapán's founding is debated. Carlos Peraza Lope and Marilyn Masson (2014, 59) conclude that it was founded and refounded several times as a result of political power struggles. One possible date is the K8A of 1185–1204 CE. The Xiw revolt against the Itzá took place, if we are to believe the Chilam Balam books, in the next K8A of 1441–1461 CE. This rebellion led to the collapse of *multepal* (crowd or joint rule) and the abandonment of the city.

The Postclassic Xiw seem to have continued some Classic Petén practices in addition to observing the Tikal calendar. For example, Classic lords ritually commemorated the termination of *k'atuns* (or halves or quarters of them, perhaps even eighths; Stuart 2005b, 43) by erecting carved, dated stone monuments in public places. Franciscan Diego de Landa (in Tozzer 1941, 38–39) reported that in the sixteenth century, the Xiw raised stelae (or wooden poles in postconquest times) every twenty years to celebrate the endings of these periods. In the 1960s, Proskouriakoff (1962, 134–136) identified thirteen carved and twenty-five plain stelae at Mayapán; two more have been discovered since then (Peraza Lope and Masson 2014, 52). Three carved monuments have dates: 1185 CE (end of a K10A), 1244 (end of a K4A), and 1283 CE (end of a K13A and beginning of a K11A) (Peraza Lope and Masson 2014, 59). The Xiw at Mayapán are not considered the most powerful of the confederated powers and the site's ceremonial architecture emulates prominent edifices of earlier international-style structures at Chichén Itzá. Nonetheless, Mayapán appears in some respects to have been essentially a Xiw-affiliated site that continued certain Terminal Classic period (e.g., late western Puuc-style) architectural traditions.

### K'atuns 11 Ajaw

Alongside the Xiw *k'atun* calendar of northwestern Yucatán, the Postclassic Itzá Maya in the northeastern peninsula observed a similar but differently counted pattern of temporal cycling. This is Munro Edmonson's (1982, 54, 197; 1986:9; 1988, 202–203) Mayapán calendar and Arlen Chase's (1986, 124–129) Itzá calendar. The Itzá cycles began with K11A, followed by 9A, 7A, 5A, 3A, and so on, ending roughly 256 years (260 *tuns*) later with a K13A (table 17.1).

The Itzá thus emphasized the ritual importance of the cycle's initial K11A, not its terminal K13A. It is currently not known when this divergent practice began, although it appears to have been pre-Columbian (Chase 1986, 128).

K11A was nicknamed the flower *k'atun,* perhaps because flower was the first day name in the Itzá 260-day almanac. The flower is the *nikte',* the sweet-scented *Plumeria. Nikte'* has many negative metaphorical meanings, including "sex, war, Xiu, and Spanish" (Edmonson 1986, 116n1856) and female sexuality, loss of virginity, and sorcerers' "love magic" (Zumbroich 2013, 345–346). The last meaning is part of the origin myth of the contact period Petén Itzá of Guatemala who, through *nikte'* enchantment, kidnapped a maiden about to be wed in the north and fled south to the central Petén lakes region (Soza 1970, 403–415). According to the Chilam Balam of Mani, a K11A is a "very erotic and evil katun whose ending will be very difficult" (Craine and Reindorp 1979, 68). The Chilam Balam of Chumayel noted that K11A was "the katun when the Maya men ceased to be called Maya [and] were called Christians" (Edmonson 1986, 59). One prophecy for a very late flower *k'atun* was the end of colonial government (Gunsenheimer 2000–2001, 281).

In summary, during the Postclassic period in the northern Maya lowlands, two calendars and sets of associated practices were in operation (Edmonson 1988; see also Chase 1986). One, which was continued from the Classic period, emphasized *k'atuns* cycling from K6A through K8A and was used primarily by the Xiw and their allies in the northwest. The Itzá and their allies in the northeast primarily used the other calendar, which emphasized *k'atuns* cycling from K11A through K13A. Presumably the adherents of each calendar would have considered it to be more efficacious than the other and their priests more adept in prophecy and ritual. Doubtless this situation caused considerable confusion as well as resentment and conflict.

Disagreements over calendrical beliefs and practices were partially resolved in 1539, when the Itzá and Xiw effected a compromise: the Mayapán (Itzá) calendar, as related in the pro-Itzá Chilam Balam of Tizimin (Edmonson 1982, 54; 1986, 11). Some of its practices were drawn from the Xiw, but this calendar followed the Itzá tradition of counting *k'atun* cycles beginning in K11A. In 1752, the Mayapán instrument was replaced by the Valladolid calendar, which formally abandoned Classic calendrical practices and was itself terminated in 1848 (Edmonson 1982, 11; 1988, 263–264).

## The Importance of K'atuns 11 Ajaw: Chichén Itzá

What evidence can be identified that attests to the singular importance of K11A to the Itzá? One point is that a possible founding date of Mayapán was in a

K11A (1283–1303 CE; Peraza Lope and Masson 2014, 59). Another concerns earlier descents or immigrations of Itzá and others into the northern Yucatán Peninsula. According to one legend, the little descent (*tz'e emal*) referred to the arrival of the Itzá by sea from Cozumel Island as they crossed the channel to Polé (P'ole) and moved inland. Their arrival is dated to a K11A, which is not anchored in the Gregorian calendar, and is told in the Chumayel as a naming of 171 towns during two counterclockwise processions through the present state of Yucatán. The meaning of this event is unclear and interpretations vary (e.g., cf. Edmonson 1986, 27, 82–91, 269–272 and Roys 1967, 70n4).

## Early Chichén Itzá and Its Founding

Chichén Itzá's location—with its sacred, water-filled well or cenote, portal to the underworld and home of the rain gods—might have been an early pilgrimage center in the northern lowlands. Preclassic through Early Classic artifacts were recovered in the cenote, along with two Late Classic jades naming rulers of Palenque (690 CE) and Piedras Negras (706 CE) (Coggins and Shane 1984, 67, 68, 134–139; Ringle and Bey 2009, 330–332). It is possible, of course, that these objects were heirlooms that were cast into the cenote considerably later. Chichén's inscriptions begin with two retrospective dates in 673–674 CE on the Circular Stone or Tenoned Disk at the Caracol structure (Boot 2005, 136).

The date of Chichén Itzá's emergence or founding as a regional political center has long been a matter of debate, partly because it has been difficult to reconcile archaeological and scanty epigraphic evidence with the dating in the Chilam B'alam books (Lincoln 1990). The texts in these Indigenous accounts are opaque, although recent scholarship suggests the possibility of greater historical accuracy (e.g., Harrison-Buck 2014, 681; Peraza Lope and Masson 2014, 101). A key event is mentioned in the Xiw-authored Chumayel[2] in a K6A (692–711 CE), with the phrase *u chictahal u chi ch'een ytza*. At issue is the meaning of *chictahal*:

> In Edmonson's translation (1986, lines 3, 13–14), it refers to the appearance of the Chichén Itzá, the definite article suggesting a gloss of "the appearance of the Itzá people [living at] the mouth of the cenote," or water-filled sinkhole.
>
> In Ralph Roys's translation (1967, 135), it is the discovery of Chichén Itzá; that is, the place. Masson (2001, 94, 95) considers the discovery of places in the Maya accounts to refer to centers that immigrant elites (re)founded at existing settlements (Boot 2005, 91–92).

Linda Schele and Peter Mathews (1998, 368n32) read *chictahal* as "to find something that one is looking for" (*hallar buscando*; Arzápalo Marín 1995, 238)—presumably, in this case, a place to found a new state.

Oddly, this momentous discovery/appearance/finding is barely noted in the pro-Itzá Tizimin and in the preceding K8A (Edmonson 1982, lines 21–26). Also, perplexingly, neither the arrival verb (*hul/jul*), which can imply coming into power, nor the foundation verb (*kaj*), which can mean arriving as much as settling (Tokovinine 2013, 80–81), were used here. Founding does not necessarily refer to a first or earliest occupation; rather, it refers to the formal initiation of a community's political ascendancy and influence. The Xiw authors of the Chumayel were apparently acknowledging but downplaying the importance of this event.

Drawing on Roys's account (1967, 73–74, 139), Schele and Mathews (1998, 363–368nn30–31) argued that the Itzá alliance was formed through a meeting of lords from the northern and southern lowlands. These lords probably represented groups that were later distinguished (and perhaps conflated) ethnopolitically as Itzá, Xiw, and others. These authors proposed that the lords come together in the northwestern corner of the peninsula at the sites now known as Dzibilchaltún or Tihoo (present-day Mérida).[3] According to their reconstruction, this meeting occurred in the K11A dated 771–790 CE.

I also favor this dating based on my review of the Indigenous texts (Rice 2018). In the immediately preceding K13A (751–771 CE), for example, the Itzá "ordered the mat" (Edmonson 1986, lines 17–18), or "the mat 'of the katun' was counted in order" (Roys 1967, 135). The "mat of the *katun*" is a metonym for the seat (woven mat, *pop*) of political authority. Its ordering is an appropriate metaphor for the activities at the end of an approximately 256-year cycle in a K13A, preparatory to founding a new political order or seating a new cycle centered on Chichén Itzá in the upcoming K11A.

In 770 CE, an important lord, Chak Jutuuw Chan Ek', visited the site of Ek' Balam, a powerful Late Classic regional center 51 kilometers to the northeast of Chichén (Bey et al. 1998, 101; Bíró 2003; Lacadena García-Gallo 2004; Ringle et al. 2004).[4] This visitor, who was possibly related to the ruler and dynastic founder of Ek' Balam, was identified by the supreme but poorly understood title *kaloomte'*. He arrived (*huli*) on the day 11 Eb'—itself a powerful southern lowland arrival meme (Stuart 2000)—a little more than nine *winals* (months) before the beginning of K11A (on October 9 of that year) (Lacadena García-Gallo 2004). Thereafter, if not before then, Ek' Balam's rulers adopted southern lowland political institutions and practices such as identifying themselves as *k'ul ajaws* (holy lords), displaying an emblem glyph, erecting

424 · Prudence M. Rice

at least one stela with a Long Count date, and carving texts in Ch'olan (with Yukateko syntax). It stretches credulity to think that the 770 CE arrival of this presumably southern-affiliated *kaloomte'* at Ek' Balam is not somehow connected to the 771–790 CE meeting of the lords and the appearance/discovery/founding/finding of that city's satellite, Chichén Itzá. It is particularly suggestive that this newcomer had a Chan/Kan Ek' appellative.

Returning to the poorly understood but textually attested K6A (692–711 CE) *chictahal* event—which the Tizimin placed in the preceding K8A (672–692 CE)—archaeological evidence for early Late Classic occupation (e.g., pottery; see Pérez de Heredia Puente 2012) is scanty in and around the city but does not contradict this date. This means that Chichén as both a place and a people was present at the time of the event. It also may help explain why the scribes copying the chronicles employed the now-ambiguous *chictahal* lexeme rather than the more definitive arrival or founding verbs.

## The Decline of Chichén Itzá

Chichén Itzá's decline is as poorly dated as its origins. The chronicles claim that Chichén was destroyed in a K8A (928–948? CE 1185–1204? CE), but archaeological data fail to support this assertion. Damage to certain buildings may be attributed to roughly contemporaneous ritual termination or to late Late Postclassic desecration that accompanied abandonment by the ruling elites and/or priests. The claim of destruction might be a Xiw self-aggrandizing conceit, a retrodiction, or simply a rhetorical device to conjoin events of Indigenous political history with Xiw calendrical cycling and prophecy. Ceramic evidence (or the absence of such evidence) has suggested broader settlement disruption in the general Puuc area, including a decline in construction and dated monuments, population loss, and perhaps political breakdown (e.g., Volta and Braswell 2014, 388, 392; cf. Ringle 2017, 131–132). A review of radiocarbon dates and environmental data from the northern lowlands supports the idea of an apparent regional collapse between 850 CE and 925 CE, linking it to droughts (Hoggarth et al. 2016).

After the late florescence of the so-called international (Toltec) architectural style at Chichén Itzá, the city ceased its monumental building program around 1050–1100 CE. This coincides with a prolonged severe drought during the eleventh century (Hoggarth et al. 2016). It is not implausible that the cessation of construction was timed to the K11A of 1027–1047 CE. Although existing structures continued to be maintained or refurbished, Chichén's political power, both ritual/symbolic and actual, may have largely dissipated. Nonetheless, the city—or the Itzá alliance in general—was still sufficiently important to share power at Late Postclassic Mayapán. Chichén Itzá perdured into the sixteenth century as a key pilgrimage destination for rain priests visiting its long-sacred cenote.

In sum, multiple lines of etic evidence—constructional, ceramic, inscriptional, climatic, radiometric—support the interpretation that the general period of Chichén Itzá's florescence extended from the late eighth century to the middle eleventh century. Within this window, it is not too much of a stretch to suggest that the Itzá leaders of the city commanded peak power from the K11A of 771–790 CE to the K11A of 1027–1047 CE. This is a cycle of ~256 years.

## Short Counts and Classic K'atun Cycling

The real or apparent recurrence of events in Yucatán in approximately 256-year cycles allowed the Maya to remember the future and anticipate the past (Farriss 1987). This Short Count cycling, as described in the late chronicles, drew Roys's attention as far back as his 1933 (1967) translation of the Chumayel. The significance of this cycling was elucidated in two subsequent publications. In one, archaeologist Dennis Puleston (1979, 67) declared that "a thirteen-katun historical cycle was recognized and was of great significance during the Classic period," noting the K11A beginnings of Tikal's sixth-century hiatus[5] and its collapse in the Terminal Classic. He also cited the observations of art historian Clemency Coggins (1975, 444) concerning the passage of 256 years between the accession of Tikal ruler Sihyaj Chan K'awiil II and that of Jasaw Chan K'awiil I, both in a K8A.

Epigraphers and archaeologists have roundly attacked the idea that such cycles were observed in the Classic period based on the absence of direct lexical references to temporal geopolitical cycling in Classic texts (Tokovinine 2008, 228; Bíró 2012; see also comments in Rice 2013). Indeed, it is not clear from textual sources what the Postclassic Maya called this cycling. Dating by the Short Count is referred to as *u kahlay katunob,* "the count or memory of the *k'atuns*" and *u tzolan/u xocan katunob* is suggested for "the ordering/counting of the katuns" (Bíró 2012, 62). The central inscription in Landa's illustration of a *k'atun* wheel (fig. 17.1), however, in Tozzer (1941, 167 n878) provides the answer: "*llaman a esta cuenta en su lengua uazlazon katun que quiere decir la gerra [sic] de los katunes*" (in their language this count is called *uazlazon* katun, which means gerra[?] of the katuns). The reference to *guerra* here is apparently a misinterpretation of the meaning of *uazlazon*: the Motul dictionary defines *uazaklon* (*wasak'lom*) as "turn, return," in the sense of "revolve, revolving, revolution." The *Diccionario Maya* (Barrera Vásquez 1991, 460, 912) gives the same sense of "turn, return" for *wasak'* and *lon* means to

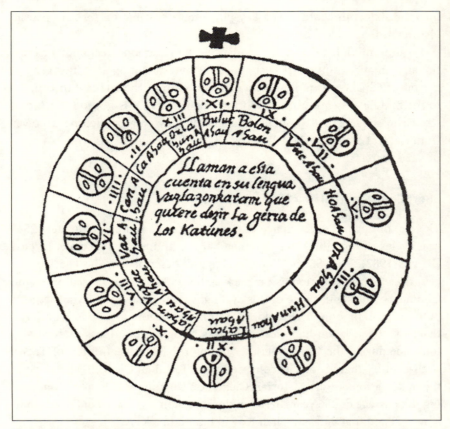

Figure 17.1. Landa's "*k'atun* wheel." The commentary in the center reads "In their language [Yukateko] they call this count Uazlazon Katun, which means the war of the Katunes." Note that K11A (or XI, *buluc ahau*) is at the top of the wheel. Source: Tozzer (1941, 167).

kneel, sometimes in reverence. The notion of cycling is implicit. The translation of war may be a misinterpretation of revolution as rebellion or warfare or it may be a double entendre.[6]

## K'atuns 11 Ajaw Elsewhere in the Lowlands

The Late Postclassic chronicles report that the approximately 256-year cycles were seated in a particular holy city, as were its thirteen constituent *k'atuns*. Archaeologist Lorraine Williams-Beck (2019) has proposed that southwest of Chichén Itzá in Campeche, a cycle was seated at Edzna after the mid-eighth century—perhaps in the K11A of 771–790 CE. According to her working

"How Much May They Not Have Written?" K'atuns 11 Ajaw and the Itzá · 427

hypotheses, this role continued until approximately 1020 CE, at which time the seat moved to nearby Acanmul (Williams-Beck 2011); note that the next K11A began in 1027 CE. Acanmul seated the cycle until the late thirteenth century (K11A, 1283–1303? CE), after which it moved to Porfía-Pa'ilbox to the south and then north to Ceiba Cabecera (Williams-Beck 2019), perhaps around the K11A beginning in 1539. The Campeche region thus provides a possible rotational sequence of four cities and *k'atun* cycles continuing over nearly a millennium.

Farther south in Petén (Guatemala), something else important happened in Itzá history in the Late Classic K11A of 771–790 CE. This occurred at or around the site of Motul de San José, the center of the Ik' polity on the northwestern shore of Lake Petén Itzá. Ik' was a Late Classic satellite—a secondary center—under Tikal. According to the reconstruction of the polity's dynastic history, ruler Yahawte' K'inich, who carried the title *kaloomte'* and has long been known to scholars by his nickname the Fat Cacique, ruled in the middle of the eighth century, possibly 738–768 (Tokovinine and Zender 2012, 45). One of his lieutenants, named K'inich Lamaw Ek' (earlier dubbed Lord Completion Star), a *baah ts'am* (head [of the] throne, perhaps a position similar to chief of staff or an heir apparent), might have been a co-ruler and then assumed the title of *kaloomte'* upon the death of the Yahawte' (Tokovinine and Zender 2012, 45).

Motul de San José Stela 2, dated approximately 771 CE (K11A) and probably commissioned by Lamaw Ek', displays the Itzá toponym as an emblem glyph, hinting at a dynastic referent. The earliest known textual mention of *itza* comes from an unprovenienced Early Classic carved black cylinder tripod, where it appears as *itza ajaw* and refers to a lord from Itzimte southwest of Lake Petén Itzá (Boot 2005, 36–37; Tokovinine and Zender 2012, 55). The final appearance of the Ik' emblem glyph occurs not at Motul de San José but on Seibal Stela 10, dated to the K5A *k'atun* ending of 10.1.0.0.0, 849 CE, with the Chan/Kan Ek' title. That name/title also appears on Flores Stela 1, probably dedicated at the next (K3A) *k'atun* ending 10.2.0.0.0 in 869 CE (Tokovinine and Zender 2012, 48).

The early dual rulership of K'inich Lamaw Ek' and the occurrence of an Itzá emblem glyph on Motul de San José Stela 2 plausibly mark the beginnings—the appearance, discovery, or founding—of an Itzá/Kan Ek' dynasty and/or an Itzá polity in the western Lake Petén Itzá region. Motul was part of the group of *chan/kan* (four) in Alexandre Tokovinine's (2008, 263) ideational landscape groupings, and I propose that this appellative was combined with Ek' (surname of Lamaw) as the new identifier of the ruler of the Itzá polity. That name/title Kan Ek' endured in the region, as did dual rulership (Rice and Rice

428 · Prudence M. Rice

2018), until the end of the seventeenth century and the Spanish conquest. A Canek patronym is still found around Lake Petén. Chan is also a widespread patronym throughout central Petén (Thompson 1977).

## Discussion and Conclusions

"How much may they not have written then?" lamented the compilers of the Chumayel Chilam B'alam. Although archaeological interpretations of the long-muddled chronology of Chichén Itzá still lack precision in many respects, today they combine ceramic and architectural data in ways that give some weight to the sketchy and even more muddled chronology presented in the Indigenous books of the Chilam B'alam. That is, if we ignore the prevailing Xiw K8A-based cycling and instead work with Itzá cycles based on K11As, the dates in Gregorian years mesh satisfactorily with gross archaeological intervals of ceramic complexes and monumental construction at Chichén. The chronicles are given very little credence as factual, western-style histories, which of course they do not purport to be. But if we endeavor to move away from our ethnocentric decimal rounding of Gregorian dates in terms of 50 or 100 years and try to interpret Maya history in terms of their own vigesimal calendars and temporal units—~20-year *k'atuns* as well as the approximately 256-year cycles, or *wazak'lom k'atun*—we might get a different (and possibly more accurate) picture of political rises and falls.

One important question out of all of this is when the alternate Itzá pattern of dating—distinct from the Classic Tikal (or Xiw) calendar in terms of the *k'atun* emphasized—and initial versus terminal dating began and why. Surely it is not mere coincidence that the proposed foundings of Chichén Itzá and of an Itzá ethnopolity in the Petén began in the same Late Classic K11A. But at the same time, it is difficult to believe that a K11A was deliberately and independently selected as the time for the Late Classic meeting of northern and southern lords, unless these two events are closely connected.

It is possible that the new *k'atun* cycling was a Maya adaptation related to a host of calendrical innovations introduced to the lowlands from the Mexican highlands in the Late Classic.[7] For example, the so-called Campeche calendar or Puuc-style dating began to be used in the Puuc area and the western lowlands in the late seventh and early eighth centuries. This dating may refer not to a new calendar per se but rather to a way of recording events based on beginning the day in the morning or at night (P. Mathews 2001; Stuart 2004c). Other interpretations suggest ties to Mexico in the counting of days, beginning with 1 rather than 0 (seating) (Prager et al. 2014, 296–298). A Palenque calendar appeared at about the same time and named the year terminally (the

"How Much May They Not Have Written?" K'atuns 11 Ajaw and the Itzá · 429

Campeche calendar also may have done so), which is not a Maya practice (Maya years are named by their first, yearbearer days). It and the Puuc calendar variants are said to evidence some Mixtec or Zapotec characteristics (Edmonson 1988, 148). A Mixtec calendar-based notation also has been identified on a lintel in the east wing of the Monjas structure at Chichén Itzá, dated 877 CE (Edmonson 2005, 170–171).

Alongside these Late and Terminal Classic calendrical innovations, aberrant day-sign glyphs with square cartouches appear in the southern lowlands and may have Gulf Coast origins (Justeson et al. 1985, 53–54, 69; Edmonson 1988, 229–230). Alfonso Lacadena García-Gallo (2010, 384–387) proposed that some of the common elements, including a particular sequence of day glyphs, mark the entry of a highland Mexican calendar to the Maya region, chronicling the heliacal rising of Venus and complex associations with the emerging Quetzalcoatl cult.

*K'atuns* and cycles based on *k'atuns* were not part of western Mexican calendrical praxis, of course. But it is not impossible that some of the innovations mentioned above along with use of the Short Count/period-ending recording system were unevenly adopted throughout the lowlands, along with an emphasis on K11A instead of K8A cycling. This system may have begun at Tikal and its realm by 692 CE (end of a K8A and beginning of a K6A) on Tikal Altar 14 and Stela 30. Perhaps the K11A dates in the Chilam B'alam books were retrodicted by later scribes copying the books, which admits the possibility that all subsequent K11A anniversaries in the prophetic histories were also retrodicted and thus factually or historically meaningless. But this possibility is contraindicated by reconstructions of the periods of Chichén's rise and fall and of dynastic events at Motul de San José.

The emphasis on K11As for the Postclassic Itzá suggests that the cycling of these *k'atuns* possessed cosmopolitical gravitas equivalent to the K8As for the Xiw. These canonical intervals structured monumental time for the Postclassic and colonial period lowland Maya and might have been in operation in the late Late Classic. If events didn't actually occur at these times, they should have occurred then, according to Maya prophetic history, epistemology, and ontology.

## Acknowledgments

Arlen Chase read a much earlier version of this paper and suggested contributing it to the Santa Fe discussion. I am grateful to Lorraine Williams-Beck for sharing published and unpublished papers and for her interest in *k'atun* cycling in southwest Campeche.

## Notes

1 These cycles begin with 18 named "months," or *winals*, and move to larger cycles—besides those mentioned in the text—of 65 days, 819 days, 18,980 days (approximately 52 years), and approximately 400 years (a *bak'tun*). There are also numerous lunar cycles.

2 Gunsenheimer (2006, 43) suggests that in the late eighteenth century, Juan Josef Hoil not only copied and signed the Chumayel but also completely revised it.

3 Dzibilchaltún, which has a large cenote on the edge of its civic-ceremonial core, may have been the site of a first, earlier *chi-ch'en* (L. Williams-Beck, personal communication, August 2, 2017).

4 Nikolai Grube and Ruth Krochok (2011, 184) suggested that Chich'en might have begun as a satellite of that early center.

5 Martin and Grube (2008, 40) date Tikal's hiatus to 562–692 CE, a half-cycle of 130 years, and theorize that it began with a defeat by Calakmul. I have long suspected that the conflicts between Tikal and Calakmul (and the Kanu'l) and the latter's network of allies (Caracol, Naranjo, Edzna) were based, at least in part, on more than material concerns and worldly competition: that is, on cosmopolitical issues of calendrical cycling, efficacy, and power.

6 By the colonial period, the lexeme *k'atun* referred not only to a period of twenty years but also to the nouns "soldier, army, warrior" and the verbs "fight, [make] war, combat, conquer" (Barrera Vásquez 1991, 385–386; Arzápalo Marín 1995, 413). An association between *k'atuns* and war might have grown from disagreements about the counting and naming—the ordering—of these 20-year periods by initial versus terminal dates and about the counting/naming of the longer cycles.

7 Stephen Houston (2000, 144, 146, table 1), following Nikolai Grube (1994b, 184–185), identifies the period 650–700 CE as one of great scribal innovation and increase in the number of new signs.

# V

## Materializing Mesoamerican Chronoscapes

# 18

# The Ideas and Images of Cities and Centers

## Teotihuacan and the Lowland Maya

DAVID A. FREIDEL, SABURO SUGIYAMA, AND NAWA SUGIYAMA

Teotihuacan was clearly a powerful and inspiring ritual center (Cowgill 1997), and while its design and scale were unprecedented and revolutionary in the Valley of Mexico (Millon 1973), it emerged in the context of a long history of sedentary agrarian settlement (Sanders et al. 1979). While sedentism and subsistence agriculture may have fostered the dynamics of urban aggregation and nucleation at Teotihuacan and the earliest Maya lowland ceremonial centers, revolutionary religious vision and political ideology mobilized the labor that built the ceremonial center (Millon 1981, 1992, 1993). Persuasive ideas and beliefs evidently drove the establishment of Teotihuacan in the Valley of Mexico as an orthogonally designed ceremonial center and metropolitan city whose plan was formalized by the third century CE (Millon 1992; see also Sugiyama and Sugiyama 2021). Here we argue that the dramatic construction of a ceremonial core (fig. 18.1) that guided the development of a gridded city at Teotihuacan may have materialized time as an expression of rulership and dynastic succession in ways analogous to and perhaps historically linked to the coeval innovation of the Classic Maya stela cult that celebrated dynastic succession in the southern lowlands. In many ways, Teotihuacan's ceremonial core expressed a pan-Mesoamerican worldview that compiled many fundamental concepts of time and space that has precedence in lowland Maya sites (Sugiyama and Sugiyama 2020). Extensive review of the timing of Teotihuacan and lowland Maya contacts in conjunction with the material evidence of their world views helps us decipher the complex and intensive interaction history among early Mesoamerican cities, all of which shared innovating ideas that converted some cities to cosmograms that expressed sophisticated astronomical knowledge in the built landscape.

434 · David A. Freidel, Saburo Sugiyama, and Nawa Sugiyama

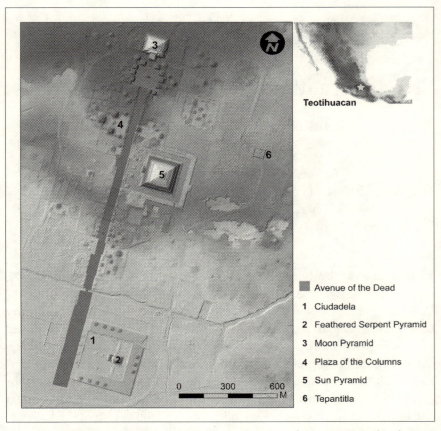

Figure 18.1. Lidar map of Teotihuacan indicating location of sites mentioned in the text. Copyright Project Plaza of the Columns Complex.

Recent discoveries in southwestern Petén at Ceibal (Inomata et al. 2015; Inomata 2017b), located at the confluence of the Usumacinta and San Pedro Mártir Rivers at Aguada Fénix (chapter 3, this volume), and at Nixtun Ch'ich' in the lake district of Petén (Pugh and Rice 2017; Rice 2018; chapter 2, this volume), among other ancient sites, challenge the notion that a gradual evolution of sedentary settlement drove the initial establishment of ceremonial centers. At the sites of Ceibal and Aguada Fénix, monumental structures appeared by 1000 BCE in the midst of possibly ephemeral settlements that housed populations that may have still been partly mobile. The small, nucleated, and gridded city of Nixtun Ch'ich' rose by 800 BCE, when subsistence maize agriculture was just establishing its hold in the middle of the lowland Maya region. The site anticipated Teotihuacan, which previously was known as the first urban-gridded Mesoamerican city, by many centuries. In the middle of the site stood an E Group analogous to the pervasive early Maya E Group solar commemorative ceremonial centers in the southern lowlands (chapter 2, this volume; Doyle 2012; Freidel et al. 2017). Rice (chapter 2, this volume) suggests that this grid design replicated the scutes of a crocodile and that the community was a giant cosmic crocodile facing east. In some important ways ideas and beliefs were driving monumental centralization in southeastern Mesoamerica, followed by or immediately accompanied by sedentism and staple maize agriculture. We believe that the grid pattern at Teotihuacan, emanating from the design of the ceremonial center radically imposed in the first several centuries CE (S. Sugiyama 2017a) may have had guidance from a similarly emic source: the world tree axis of the cosmos linking the underworld, middle world, and upper world, an in-line triad principle we will discuss further. At the same time, the Classic southern lowland Maya began raising great stones referencing the same time-bound axis. The sequence of early and enduring center setting and orthogonality seems to reverse generations of evolutionary modeling by archaeologists (Childe 1950; Sherratt 1990; Dietrich et al. 2012; Rosenswig 2012).

Explicit evidence of early Maya-Teotihuacan interactions shows parallel expressions of "city as cosmogram" between vastly distant centers, potentially explaining these linkages as a direct outcome of the interpersonal exchange of ideas and beliefs. Connections between Teotihuacan and Tikal have been discussed for many years (see Coe 1972; Coggins 1975). Laporte and Fialko (1995) report massive tableros that embellished the western radial building of the Lost World Pyramid E Group at Tikal by the third century CE. Sarah Clayton's (2005, 445) NAA analysis of Maya ceramics in Teotihuacan concurred that there was significant interaction with the ancient Maya for a period of some 500 years, and early contact is documented archaeologically in the Maya for Altun Ha between 150 and 200 CE (Pendergast 1971) and for Caracol before 350 CE (A. Chase and D. Chase 2011). Recent excavations by Edwin Roman R. and colleagues (Houston et al. 2021) have confirmed lidar identification of a Teotihuacan-style Ciudadela complex south of the Lost World Pyramid E Group. Excavated material so far dates to the Early Classic and shows Teotihuacan symbolism. It is significant that radiocarbon dates from the Plaza of the Columns Complex confirm clear connections with Maya personages by the third century CE (Sugiyama et al. 2020). Early evidence of imported engraved conch shells and greenstone objects in the ancient tunnel below the Feathered Serpent Pyramid indicate that foreign dignitaries, including Maya ones, participated in the most sacred rituals early in Teotihuacan's establishment as a monumental center (Gómez Chávez and Robb 2017).

436 · David A. Freidel, Saburo Sugiyama, and Nawa Sugiyama

We think that similar to layout of Preclassic (1000 BCE–250 CE) cities in the Maya lowlands, the planned coeval construction of the Pyramid of the Moon (Phase 4), the Pyramid of the Sun, and the Ciudadela was aligned to the central axis of the Avenue of the Dead to form a monumental linear triad. In Teotihuacan iconography, this triad was expressed as three dots, sometimes embellished with flower petals, in a horizontal row that is usually interpreted as the superior component of an abbreviated insignia of the storm god when accompanied by a downturned basin-shaped element that Langley (1992, 249–250) terms a "mustache" (see also Nielsen and Helmke 2017, plates 13 and 26). Freidel does not see this in-line triad motif as an abbreviated variant on the pervasively fang-mouthed storm god, which is more frequently depicted by a linearly configured face with two circles representing its goggle eyes that frame the central nose (Robb 2017a, plate 70). Instead, the in-line triad is clearly an independent insignia, sometimes depicted alone as a headpiece element crowning important deities and human figures (e.g., Yaxha Stela 11 in the Maya lowlands; Langley 1992, fig. 14).

The famous Tepantitla mural depicts a composite deity image. The in-line triad over the groin area surmounts the downturned basin from which liquid and shells pour out of this fertile source. The main protagonist has been identified as a moon goddess (the predecessor of Xochiquetzal) (Pasztory 1973, 151–152) and as a great goddess (Berlo 1992, 147, 158); more recently, Robb (2017b, 156) has identified it as a water goddess. She stands on the upper panel, looming over a water mountain with frolicking little people on the lower panel. Milbrath (2000, 44–47) identifies the basin as the crescent moon and as an early form of the Aztec moon goddess Yacametzli. If that reading is accurate, then the overall insignia in Teotihuacan symbolism references a moon goddess qualified by the in-line triad. It would be redundant for this composite motif to represent the storm god here, for the Tepantitla deity is already wearing the fangs and goggle eyes of the storm god over the face area. In fact, the in-line triad/downturned basin is positioned over the genital area. Berlo (1992) and Headrick (2002, 94), among other experts, identify the downturned basin as a female womb or vagina, and this reading makes sense of the liquids pouring from it.

The in-line triad motif likely expressed the city as a cosmogram. It represented the city center itself on completion of the cosmographic plan from 200 CE to 250 CE (see discussion below of monument dates). Together with the watery cave/basin, the postulated abbreviated storm god insignia represented the city plan and its goddess. The Pyramid of the Moon embodied that water goddess (N. Sugiyama 2014; S. Sugiyama 2017a). That pyramid is also an effigy of Cerro Gordo, the *altepetl* (water mountain) of the city and the realm (N. Sugiyama 2014). The *altepetl* is the symbol of the state and dominion among later peoples of the Valley of Mexico (Hirth 2003; López Austin and López Luján 2009), and we suggest that the Teotihuacanos used it before them. Certainly, the idea of a water mountain was in place by Middle Preclassic (1000–350 BCE) times throughout Mesoamerica, including the Maya lowlands (Ortíz and Rodríguez 1999, 2000). In our view, this in-line triad/basin insignia of the Teotihuacan state was as clear to all contemporaries as the insignia SPQR (Senate and People of Rome) was in the time of the Romans—and that, like it, sometimes people put it on a staff as a banner.

## Materializing Time at Teotihuacan and in the Maya Lowlands

Perhaps one of the most fascinating outcomes of S. Sugiyama's (1992, 2010) long-term application of the Teotihuacan Measurement Unit (TMU) is that the layout of the city includes not just the location and orientations of building, plazas, and streets but also the specific dimensions and distances between each architectural feature, explicitly materializing a cosmogram and encoding in Teotihuacan's built landscape how its founders comprehended time and the world order. Bayesian statistical models of radiocarbon samples from within the Pyramid of the Moon, the Pyramid of the Sun, and the Feathered Serpent Pyramid confirm that state monumentality was established in a brief window of time and all at once during the early third century CE (S. Sugiyama 1998, 2017; Sugiyama and Cabrera Castro 2007; N. Sugiyama, S. Sugiyama, et al. 2013). The original layout of the ingeniously engineered ritual precinct expressed an integrated materialization of major calendars that included the 365-day solar year, the 260-day sacred almanac, and the Venusian cycle (S. Sugiyama 2010). The orientation of the entire cosmic city to 15.5 degrees east of north divided the year between two days in which the sun sets along this path, April 29 and August 12 (Malmström 1981; Šprajc 2000; S. Sugiyama 2017a). The calendric year was thus separated into a period of 260 days when the sun passes southward and 105 days when the sun moves northward (Aveni 2000, 254). This, in turn, marked the transition between two fundamental seasons of the year: the rainy season, when the sun passes north of this alignment (lower cosmos), and the dry season, when the sun passes to the south (higher cosmos). The division of the ceremonial center into northern and southern sectors marked the passage of time through recording the seasons that dictated their agrarian cycle.

While there is no direct evidence of the Maya Long Count at Teotihuacan, we believe that their astronomers were likely cognizant of this calendric system. The east-west orientation of the pyramids and the orientation of virtually all east-west walls of the city to sunset on August 12 (between 11 and 13), corresponding to the Creation Day in the Long Count calendar, cannot be a coincidence (see also Malmström 1981, 1997). The Long Count integrates major calendars, including the 260-day sacred almanac, the 365-day solar year, and the Venus count. S. Sugiyama (2010) has demonstrated that all of these day counts were expressed in the TMU calculations that correspond to the dimensions of the Pyramid of the Sun, the sum of the dimensions of that pyramid and Pyramid of the Moon (Phase 4), and the dimensions of the Ciudadela. Thus, sky watchers, who harmonized complex calendric and astrological phenomena in monumental works must have established Teotihuacan's layout. The distribution of pecked crosses and underground observatories in the city likely alludes to the places where such observances were made. Interestingly, Anthony Aveni and colleagues (Aveni et al. 1978) have shown that the wide distribution of Teotihuacan-style pecked crosses appeared at various lowland Maya sites during the Classic period (250–900 CE), such as Uaxactun and Alta Vista near the Tropic of Cancer, and, more recently, at Alta Verapaz (Woodfill 2014). These engraved figures were likely used for calendar calculations and therefore reinforce a coherent and widespread calendric system (Aveni and Dowd 2017).

We are exploring the prospect that the lowland Maya adoption of Long Count inscribed stelae in the third century CE might be linked to the rapid establishment of the Teotihuacan central mind frame through elite interaction and to political coordination of a novel principle: dynastic succession of monarchs (Cowgill 1997).[1] Cosmographically, the ruler as a crocodile tree was a Preclassic trope in southeastern Mesoamerica that carried over into the lowland Classic understanding of stelae (Schele and Mathews 1998, 141–144; Taube 2005; chapter 2, this volume; Reilly and Freidel forthcoming). At the Feathered Serpent Pyramid at Teotihuacan, the head of the Primordial Crocodile (known as Cipactli during Aztec periods) is depicted as a headdress carried on the serpentine body (S. Sugiyama 2017b). Worn at Teotihuacan as a headdress or crown, this crocodile head was a Teotihuacan-style crown among the lowland Maya rulers of the Early and Late Classic periods (Taube 2003a), beginning with the entrada of Sihyaj K'ahk'. King Yax Nuun Ahiin is depicted as wearing it on Stela 31 at Tikal (Stuart 2000). This headdress likely represented royal power at Teotihuacan as well, even if warriors were usually depicted wearing it (for the crocodilian warrior headdress, see S. Sugiyama 1992; Taube 1992b). The proposed Teotihuacan royal crown often features the heads of raptors (Headrick 2007).

Major discoveries of complex ritual deposits in the nucleus of the Pyramid of the Moon (Phase 4) (Sugiyama and López Luján 2007; N. Sugiyama 2014,

The Ideas and Images of Cities and Centers: Teotihuacan and the Lowland Maya · 439

2017) and the Pyramid of the Sun (N. Sugiyama et al. 2014; Sarabia Gonzalez and Nunez Rendon 2017) as well as the extraordinary discovery of the artificial cave and offerings 15 meters under the Feathered Serpent Pyramid in the Ciudadela (Gómez Chávez 2017b) invite further consideration of the in-line triad Teotihuacan cosmogram as not only a materialization of time but also an expression of the city center.

This image, which represents a celestial World Tree that integrated the major gods of the realm, resonates with political power. In her lucid and brilliant dissertation on the Tepantitla murals, Esther Pasztory (1976, 146–156) reviews the significance of the trees emerging above the Tepantitla image now identified as the water goddess as representations of the World Tree and the axis mundi. Annabeth Headrick (2002) reaffirms this identification and advances the hypothesis that Teotihuacanos raised World Trees of the great goddess image in the plaza of the Pyramid of the Moon. Saburo Sugiyama (2005) and Nawa Sugiyama (2014, 2017; N. Sugiyama, Sugiyama et al. 2013), in particular, examined the spatial arrangements of sacrifices and offerings in the Pyramid of the Moon, the Pyramid of the Sun, and the Feathered Serpent Pyramid, demonstrating unequivocally that the people of Teotihuacan practiced tableau macabre in ways that can be interpreted ideologically and cosmographically. Below we advance a new contextual analysis of the massive ritual offering termed Burial 6 in the central locality of Phase 4 of the Pyramid of the Moon and discuss the working hypothesis that the Avenue of the Dead was cosmographically the World Tree anchored in the goddess's mountain-self, Cerro Gordo (fig. 18.1). We propose that the city of Teotihuacan was a tree cosmogram with the Pyramid of the Moon as the great mountain effigy base, the Pyramid of the Sun as its heart, and the Feathered Serpent Pyramid with a crocodilian crown as its summit.

Alongside its reference to the three prevailing monuments, the in-line triad at Teotihuacan could also have referenced the belt stars of the constellation of Orion, the most conspicuous asterism in the night sky. While neither the alignment of the three buildings nor that of the stars forms a perfectly straight line, both express the motif. The Avenue of the Dead makes very clear the connection between the buildings, as does the exquisitely expressed math of the architectural planning (S. Sugiyama 2017a). Milbrath (2017b, 97) notes that at Uaxactun, which was tied to Teotihuacan by the presence of pecked cross circles (Aveni et al. 1978; Aveni 2000), and elsewhere in the Maya lowlands, the equinoxes are linked to the horizon position of Orion. She suggests that the appearance and disappearance of the belt stars may have related to maize seeds and stalks: at the summer solstice, the belt stars rise vertically at dawn like maize stalks and they set horizontally before dawn like planted seeds (Milbrath 2017b, 97; Susan Milbrath, personal communication to David Freidel, April 30, 2019). Clearly the orientation of the center and the city grid to 15.5 degrees east of north shows cosmographic reference to the celestial bodies and the agrarian year (S. Sugiyama 2017a), as discussed below. The in-line triad with the downturned basin (mustache) insignia, which Helmke and Nielsen (2017) identified as an abbreviated storm god face, often appears within a cartouche; that is why it is identified as an insignia (Langley 1991). But this icon is not always in a cartouche, and in one appearance there is richly symbolic contextual information that suggests a different reading.

There are linkages between Maya complex ritual deposits and those at Teotihuacan. For instance, at Yaxuná, Mexico, Burial 24 (fig. 18.2) can be related to Teotihuacan deposits (Suhler and Freidel 1998). The relationship with Teotihuacan is not only contemporary, dating to the late fourth century CE when Building 6 of the Pyramid of the Moon would have been constructed, it is also underscored by a unique, Teotihuacan-influenced ceramic effigy of a moon/mountain goddess marked with rain cloud glyphs on her arms (fig. 18.3).

Yaxuná Burial 24 formed a tableau macabre (Tiesler et al. 2017, 204–214) in which, as in the case of Burial 6 in the Pyramid of the Moon, some individuals at the chamber's southern limit were carefully arranged while others in the northern extent were tossed in a pile. Freidel has argued that the Yaxuná tableau macabre represents the horizontal depiction of a mountain with its peak in the south and its base in the north. The chamber's southern orientation is underscored by the positioning of the ceramic effigy of the moon/mountain goddess, whose head is oriented to the south. The partially burned remains of a ruler whose white shell headband segments were also burned and are accompanied by a name diadem jewel in the form of a quetzal bird profile head are also in the south. Two men accompany that ruler, one in the southeast corner of the chamber and one directly north of him. There is a plate painted with the image of a ruler wearing a triple-tailed scarlet macaw costume that was characteristic of Teotihuacano warriors. Freidel (2018) has interpreted this depiction as a conquest scene in which the intruder has sacrificed the ruler and his entourage. In Maya cosmology, the scarlet macaw is the conceptual armature of the Principal Bird Deity, the solar avatar of the creator deity Itzamnaaj (see chapter 6, this volume). Thus, south in this tableau represents the masculine, fire/heat, and the sun. The central and northern arranged bodies are female. They include the queen, who is identified by a headband crown embellished with polished white conch-shell beads embellishing and a cut-seashell cache-sexe. She is adjacent to the moon/mountain/cloud goddess and to an older woman with a headdress ornamented with

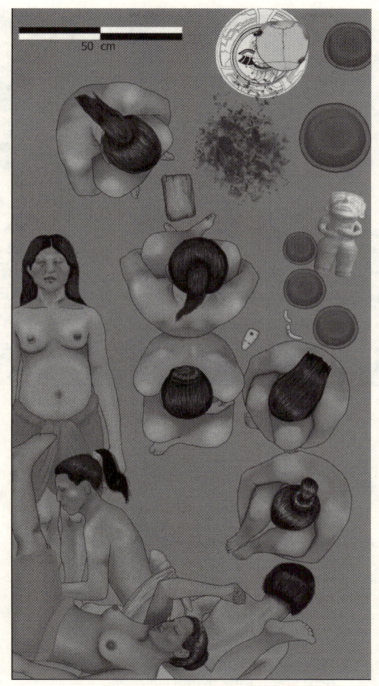

Figure 18.2. Reconstruction drawing of Yaxuná Burial 24 by Vera Tiesler, with her permission and that of the Selz Foundation Yaxuná Project.

Figure 18.3. Teotihuacan-style ceramic figurine from Burial 24 at Yaxuná. Photo by Travis Stanton. Courtesy of the Selz Foundation Yaxuná Archaeological Project.

sticks of coral pierced for suspension and a clay rabbit effigy figurine painted red. To the east is a supine pregnant young woman with a pectoral consisting of a bed of white olive shells containing three jade jewels arranged in a line: an in-line triad. North is thus associated with women, the moon, water, fecundity, and rain. Northeast of the arranged bodies is a pile of women and youths. Freidel interprets this apparently jumbled arrangement as the base of a symbolic mountain made of human beings. If that is true, then the tableau macabre in Yaxuná Burial 24 is a cosmogram that replicates in design the cosmogram discernible in Burial 6 that dedicated Building 4 of the Pyramid of the Moon at Teotihuacan.

In Burial 6 of the Pyramid of the Moon at Teotihuacan, the roughly triangular pile of ten decapitated bodies on the northwest corner of the enclosure (Sugiyama and López Luján 2007) constitutes the pyramidal base of the cosmographic mountain that is analogous to the pile of people discerned in

Yaxuná Burial 24. To the south, at the peak of this mountain in Burial 6, is a large iron pyrite mosaic mirror. In his review of mirrors at Teotihuacan, Taube (1992b) argues cogently that these can represent both fire and water. Here the mirror references fire, as it is in the south and that direction in the city cosmogram registers fire and the sun.

Reinforcing this identification of the summit locale of the mountain is the nimbus of nine pairs of obsidian eccentrics in a circle. Nine black eccentrics represent the Feathered Serpent and nine red ones are undulating elements we can identify as fire feathers. Together they register the number eighteen. The solar year is composed of eighteen months of twenty days plus a five-day interregnum, so we suggest that this is a reference to the solar year, analogous to the eighteen images of the Feathered Serpent on the west face of the Feathered Serpent Pyramid (Sugiyama 2005). This was a critical numeral lowland Maya used to express their calendric cycle; it appeared repeatedly in offertory complexes. Nawa Sugiyama (2017) reports that the dedicatory act necessitated eighteen golden eagles, which were acquired by aggregating chicks raised in captivity and even some prepared taxidermically. Similarly, the bundle of rattlesnakes sacrificed in a basket in this interment likely included a minimum number of eighteen (between sixteen and twenty-two, based on MRI imagery) (N. Sugiyama 2014).

Above the proposed sun disk mirror in Burial 6, ritualists placed a unique figurine made of greenstone tesserae. Unlike the clearly female central figurine in Burial 2 of the Pyramid of the Moon, the sex of this figurine cannot be identified. The mosaic body, however, suggests that it is an incarnation of the crocodilian creature that is borne on the back of the legendary Feathered Serpent in the southern monument.

That sculptured stone head has the goggles of the storm god and fangs of the crocodile. López Austin and colleagues (1991) have identified this mythological being as the Primordial Crocodile and as representing the Feathered Serpent's arrival bearing a new era on its back. Saburo Sugiyama (2005, 2017b) sees this image as likely heralding a royal accession scene, further associating the Feathered Serpent Pyramid with the military powers of the Teotihuacan state. The central offering of the Feathered Serpent Pyramid is a deposit, Burial 14, that consists of anonymous human beings pointing to the east, the direction of the rising sun: another mountain. We suggest in this case that the figurine emerging above the sun portal mirror in Burial 6 might represent the primordial crocodilian nature and military might of the mountain goddess as an embodiment of the city. This aspect is registered in the depiction of the water goddess in the Tepantitla mural: the goggles and fangs of the storm god are on a green face that is painted to look like it

444 · David A. Freidel, Saburo Sugiyama, and Nawa Sugiyama

is made of mosaic tesserae, shown directly below the goggles. The mosaic figure in Burial 6 is flanked by two human sacrifices whose bodies are intact. These individuals are adorned with precious insignia, suggesting that they are worshippers, analogous to the two elaborately dressed individuals that flank the water goddess on the Tepantitla mural.

The mountains of people in Burial 6 and in the center of the tableau macabre inside the Feathered Serpent Pyramid resonate with the water mountain (also called the fountain; Pasztory 1976) painted on the talud below the water goddess scene on the Tepantitla mural. It may be coincidental, but just as ten sacrificial victims compose the mountain in Burial 6, ten small figures frolic in the water mountain on the Tepantitla mural talud scene of Tlalocan. Nawa Sugiyama (2014, 29) has identified the Pyramid of the Moon as an *altepetl,* the Nahuatl term for water mountain; the Aztecs and other peoples of highland Mexico used the term to mean dominion or realm. Along with the clear association of the water goddess with the cosmic water mountain at Teotihuacan (Pasztory 1976; Robb 2017b), the charismatic animals sacrificed and carefully arranged in multiple ritual offerings in the Pyramid of the Moon accord with the widespread Mesoamerican beliefs that animal gods and their animal spirit companions dwell in sacred mountains. Evon Z. Vogt's (1969, 1976) analyses of the Zinacanteco Maya of highland Chiapas have substantiated this belief ethnographically. We offer an additional potential clue to this identification on the Tepantitla talud depiction of the water mountain. Eight distinctive fronds emanate from the mountain, perhaps referencing the cardinal and intercardinal positions (mirroring the deliberate deposit of charismatic animals in Burial 6; N. Sugiyama 2017). These perhaps have natural counterparts as aquatic or terrestrial plants, but they are remarkably similar to the highland Mexican symbol *atl,* water spray, that is used to denote *altepetl.* The chronological gap between Classic (200–600 CE) Teotihuacan and the Postclassic (900–1519 CE) Aztec occupations is significant, but scholars of Teotihuacan have been analogically bridging that gap in symbolism and meaning productively for some time. It is possible that this enigmatic frond reads *atl* and identifies the Tepantitla mountain as an *altepetl.* That mountain is clearly associated with the water goddess on the mural above, an effigy of the Mother of Stone (the Aztec name), Cerro Gordo, and her human-made counterpart, the Pyramid of the Moon.

The same distinctive frond element frames the base of the greenstone carvings called cones (Juan Carlos Meléndez, personal communication to David Freidel, 2019) discovered among the offerings in the central ritual complex deposited in the Feathered Serpent Pyramid, identified above as another mountain of sacrificial bodies (Burial 14). Eighteen of these cones were found

The Ideas and Images of Cities and Centers: Teotihuacan and the Lowland Maya · 445

concentrated together in association with one individual in that pile of people. Eighteen is the number of Feathered Serpents sculpted on the western façade of the Feathered Serpent Pyramid, the number of obsidian eccentrics framing the mirror in Burial 6, and possibly the number of snakes in the basket next to that mirror. If the cones read as *altepetl,* they could reference the Feathered Serpent Pyramid as the dominion mountain where time (the solar year) began (Sugiyama 2005). The arrangements reviewed here underscore the inference that the Teotihuacano planned the Pyramid of the Moon and its frontal plaza to be both horizontal and vertical effigies of the mountain goddess, with the Avenue of the Dead as the World Tree growing southward from the pyramid. Esther Pasztory's (1976) review of the World Tree in Mesoamerica notes the visual correspondences between the Tepantitla deity from which trees emanate and the lowland Maya World Trees that emerge above deity masks (or from the bodies of crocodiles in the case of Izapa stelae). Stone stelae in southeastern Mesoamerica had World Tree connotations from Middle Formative (850–500 BCE) Olmec times (Reilly 1987; Reilly and Freidel forthcoming), and the lowland Maya began erecting stone stelae by the beginning of the Late Preclassic period (350 BCE–1 CE) (chapter 6, this volume). But Tikal Stela 29, which has a Long Count calendar date of 292 CE (Jones and Satterthwaite 1982), is the earliest dated lowland Maya stela depicting an ancestor in the heavens over a king who wears the regalia of a holy lord of Tikal, K'uhul Mutal Ajaw. Although the calendar date of the unprovenienced miniature Hauberg stela is contested (Schele 1985; Stuart 2008), it is stylistically third century CE. It depicts a young ajaw masked as GI, Hun Yeh Winik, the sun who brings the rains (Stuart 2005b). He is cradling a vision serpent and is making the offering gesture over a tree-marked, sprocketed element that carries the upper halves of three sacrificed individuals and alludes to the primordial reptilian creature that in sacrifice makes the earth (Taube 2010) (fig. 18.4).

This downward image is reified elsewhere as the Cosmic Crocodile Tree (Taube 2005; chapter 2, this volume; Reilly and Freidel forthcoming). Wearing the mask of Hun Yeh Winik (Stuart 2005b; see also chapter 6, this volume), the Hauberg personage is performing as the axis mundi and appealing to an ancestor in the heavens, who emerges from the maw of a serpent named Six Sky, "stood-up sky." At the outset of the Classic, the lowland Maya used stelae to establish calendric time (Thompson 1950) and the placement of rulers in sacred time (Stuart 1996, 2011). These monuments denoted the loci of the axis mundi. Reilly and Freidel (forthcoming) suggest that World Trees and in some cases crocodile trees were already being depicted by the third century CE.

Figure 18.4. Hauberg Stela. Drawing by Linda Schele. Copyright David Schele. Courtesy of Ancient Americas at LACMA (ancientamericas.org).

The Ideas and Images of Cities and Centers: Teotihuacan and the Lowland Maya · 447

Despite later (fifth century) lowland Maya dynasties' retrospective claims to have originated during the first millennium BCE (Martin 2016, 533), both archaeology and epigraphy show that the first known historical, dynastic founder is King Yax Ehb Xook of Tikal, whose first century CE tomb, Tikal Burial 85 (Coe and McGinn 1963), lay under a frontal platform in the patio of the early North Acropolis (Martin and Grube 2000). That small stuccoed platform had four postholes, suggesting that it was used for a perishable structure. Freidel (Freidel and Reilly 2010; see also Taube 1988a; Reilly 2002) identifies these postholes as remaining from a scaffold accession throne, similar to the one in the depiction of a coronation ceremony for a human king two centuries earlier on the west wall mural of the Pinturas Building at San Bartolo (Saturno 2009; Taube et al. 2010). A fuchsite mask depicting the king wearing the trefoil sprout crown of rulership accompanied the bundled remains of this Tikal king (Coe 1965; Schele and Freidel 1990, 133–134). This mask is not in the Olmec style of some Late Preclassic lowland Maya masks (Schele and Miller 1986; A. Chase and D. Chase 2017a, fig. 2.8). Rather, the Tikal Burial 85 mask is more similar in style to funerary masks from Teotihuacan (Headrick 1999). This is also the case for an early Early Classic mask from El Perú-Waka' Burial 80 (fig. 18.5), home of another first century CE dynasty in the lowlands. These two masks resemble the greenstone mask (fig. 18.6) in the first century CE central dedicatory offering in the Pyramid of the Sun (N. Sugiyama, S. Sugiyama, et al. 2013).

Freidel (2018) has proposed that Yax Ehb Xook innovated dynastic succession in the Maya lowlands and that other Late Preclassic Maya kings were not dynastic but rather were elected by counsels and inducted into the status of holy lord by an initiation that involved simulated sacrifice and resurrection. If that was the case, then collective or collaborative political power was preeminent in Preclassic lowland Maya royal realms (Freidel 2018). This royal cycle is depicted on the west wall of the Pinturas Building, where it is performed by the maize god (Saturno 2009). If this hypothesis is correct, then the Classic period practice of raising calendrical stelae that situated kings in Long Count time began at Tikal in the third century CE and was primarily designed to establish legitimate succession in rule from lineage predecessors (and ultimately from the founder, Yax Ehb Xook). It is not coincidental that the earliest Classic Maya stela is Tikal Stela 29, which was dedicated at the end of the third century CE. The interactions the ancient Maya had with Teotihuacan beginning in the Late Preclassic era may have motivated the innovation of dynastic succession in both central Mexico and the Petén of Guatemala.

The practice of raising calendar-dated stelae emerged slowly in the Maya lowlands. Again, some southern lowland dynasties recorded their founding

Figure 18.5. Ancestor bundle mask from Burial 80, El Perú-Waka'. Photo by Juan Carlos Pérez. Courtesy of Proyecto Arqueológico Waka' and the Ministry of Culture and Sports, Guatemala.

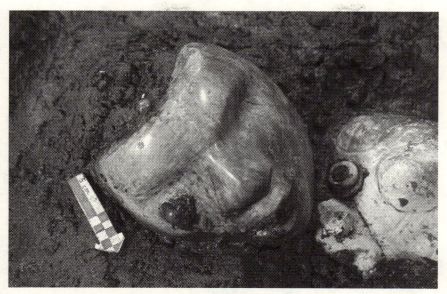

Figure 18.6. Early Classic greenstone mask from Offering 2, Pyramid of the Sun. Photo by Saburo Sugiyama. Copyright Pyramid of the Sun Project.

in the Preclassic period in retrospective histories, but actually dynasties came into focus in the fourth and fifth centuries CE. The multiple desecrations and rebuildings of the North Acropolis of Tikal during the late first, second, and third centuries CE—including the trenching during that era of the accession platform over the tomb of the founder, Burial 85 (Coe 1990)—suggests that there was significant resistance to the idea of dynastic succession among adversaries of Tikal's founder and his progeny. In the repeated rebuilding and transformation of the North Acropolis, we can see that the institutionalization of dynastic rulership was continuously reaffirmed. In Freidel's (2018) view, the turning point came with a change in strategy from eliminating dynastic rulership to co-opting it by inserting usurpers who were loyal to the sodality-based hegemons Tikal had rebelled against. A subsequent stela with identifiable calendric dates at Tikal is Stela 39, which was dedicated in 376 CE. This mutilated monument depicts the lower half of King Chak Tok Ich'aak I in profile celebrating the ending of a period with a sacrificial victim. King Sihyaj Chan K'awiil II noted the same period-ending celebration in the middle of the fifth century on Tikal Stela 31. He mentions Chak Tok Ich'aak I in the context of telling how that earlier king had "died" (or, presumably, was deposed and killed) in 378 CE upon the arrival of the presumed Teotihuacano lord Kaloomte' Sihyaj K'ahk' (Stuart 2000, Laporte

450 · David A. Freidel, Saburo Sugiyama, and Nawa Sugiyama

and Fialko 1994). By then, Maya stelae were not only placing dynasts in calendar time but were also relating historical events. In the absence of deciphered writing systems at Teotihuacan, we can hardly understand exactly what happened in the city where the Maya elites interacted during this politically transformative period. But there is unquestionable archaeological evidence of desecration activities and tomb looting at the Feathered Serpent Pyramid in Teotihuacan, evidently indicating a suppression of succession history in Teotihuacan during the fourth century CE (Millon 1992; S. Sugiyama 1992, 1998, 2005). We will return to this pivotal historical moment at Teotihuacan and in the Maya lowlands in our concluding thoughts.

## Altepetl in the Maya Lowlands: The Entrada and Rendezvous with Destiny of Sihyaj K'ahk'

One candidate for the second-oldest documented dynasty in the lowlands is that of the Wak (Centipede) kings of El Perú-Waka' (Guenter 2005, 2014). There, a fragment of El Perú Stela 28 that can be stylistically dated to around 600 CE declares that the king is the twenty-fourth in the line. Conservatively calculating lengths of reign (as ca. twenty-two years; Martin 2016), it is possible that the dynastic founder lived in the first century CE (Chak Tok Ich'aak I of Tikal was the fourteenth successor of Yax Ehb Xook in the late fourth century CE and by the early seventh century twenty-four kings had reigned at Tikal). An early fourth century CE king has been discovered in Burial 80 in the Palace Acropolis at El Perú-Waka' (Freidel et al. 2018). This king could be a ruler nicknamed Te' Chan Ahk, whose epithets include a bird and a turtle carapace (Kelly 2020). According to retrospective history on El Perú Stela 15, this early king presided over the period ending in 317 CE. Like Yax Ehb Xook in Burial 85 at Tikal, this king was interred with a greenstone mask (fig. 18.5) that is distinctly non-Olmec in style and is closer to the Teotihuacan style. This young king was interred with a shell pectoral depicting a crocodile with a skull on its tail. The skull has a sagittal crest and falls in the Late Preclassic goggle-eyed bib-head royal diadem jewel category that James Garber identified as the severed head of the maize god (Garber and Awe 2009; Reilly and Freidel forthcoming). Thus, even prior to definitive evidence of stela erection at El Perú-Waka', rulers were embodying the Crocodile World Tree (fig. 18.7).

By the fifth century CE, Wak kings were raising large stelae that celebrated both their dynasty and their alliance with Kaloomte' Sihyaj K'ahk', the Teotihuacano warrior (Stuart 2000; Freidel et al. 2007). Sihyaj K'ahk', emissary of a dynastic king nicknamed Spearthrower Owl, arrived at Wak on 3 Kan (January 9, 378 CE) and carried out a ritual at or with an object called a Wiinte'(?),

Figure 18.7. Crocodile Tree shell pectoral from Burial 80, El Perú-Waka'. Photo by Juan Carlos Pérez. Courtesy of Proyecto Arqueológico Waka' and the Ministry of Culture and Sports, Guatemala.

very likely referencing the existence of a Wiinte' Naah fire shrine that emulated the primary one at Teotihuacan. David Stuart (2004b) reads Altar Q at Copán as retrospectively describing the accession of the dynastic founder at the Wiinte' Naah. Because of the length of time of that king's journey and the clear association of Yax K'uk' Mo' with the Teotihuacan-inspired New Order in the

452 · David A. Freidel, Saburo Sugiyama, and Nawa Sugiyama

Maya lowlands, he places that Wiinte' Naah at Teotihuacan. William Fash and colleagues (2009) postulate that this was on the frontal platform of the Pyramid of the Sun because of the fire iconography on sculpture there. However, we think that the Feathered Serpent Pyramid, which we argue was the accession place of the city (S. Sugiyama 1992, 2005), was more likely the primary Wiinte' Naah. According to retrospective history on Tikal Stela 31, this same lord arrived at Tikal on 11 Eb' (January 15, 378 CE). That is the day the Tikal king died.

Less than a year later, Sihyaj K'ahk' placed a youth named Yax Nuun Ahiin (First Stranger Crocodile; chapter 2, this volume), on the throne. This king portrayed himself as a Teotihuacano on Tikal Stela 4, which depicts a frontal blocky depiction of his head in keeping with Teotihuacan sculptural conventions. Yax Nuun Ahiin wore the Teotihuacano headdress of a jaguar with feathered ears. Retrospectively, his son, Sihyaj Chan K'awiil II, portrayed his father on Stela 31 dressed as a Teotihuacano warrior and wearing a mosaic headdress, possibly representing a Teotihuacan mosaic feline deity that was later featured on a battle palanquin carved in a lintel of Tikal Temple I. This time, however, the profile matched the convention Tikal's carvers used. Although Yax Nuun Ahiin's father was a presumed Teotihuacano known as the overlord of Sihyaj K'ahk', Yax Nuun Ahiin was recorded as being a vassal to Sihyaj K'ahk', an interesting historical development. Two major events coincide with this apparently direct military presence of Teotihuacanos in the Maya region: the Feathered Serpent Pyramid's principal façade was desecrated and buried below the *adosada* platform circa 350±50 CE (S. Sugiyama 1998) and splendid Maya style murals were demolished and heaped in the plaza fill at the Plaza of the Columns complex at approximately the same time (N. Sugiyama et al. 2016, 2020). Despite this major sociopolitical restructuring at Teotihuacan, Teotihuacano dynasts continued to exist into the fourth and fifth centuries CE, as recounted at Tikal.

In his bold vision of what has come to be known as the entrada in 378 CE, David Stuart (2000) argued that Sihyaj K'ahk' arrived at El Perú-Waka' first because he was marching east from Teotihuacan to Tikal. From the vantage point of the Waka' rulers and people, the entrada was a transformative event that shaped all subsequent history, and we suspect that many other lowland Maya regarded it that way. The earliest known all-text Maya calendar stela is El Perú-Waka' Stela 15, which was dedicated in 416 CE. It celebrates the 378 CE arrival of Sihyaj K'ahk' on 3 Kan, clearly preceding by eight days his conquest of Tikal on 11 Eb'. It also celebrates the reign of his vassal Wak king K'inich Bahlam I and implicates the Wiinte' Naah of the city. These events are framed in Wak dynastic history, going back to King Leaf Chan Ahk in

The Ideas and Images of Cities and Centers: Teotihuacan and the Lowland Maya · 453

317 CE. In 470 CE, the grandson of K'inich Bahlam I dedicated El Perú-Waka' Stela 16, which has the only certain posthumous portrait of Sihyaj K'ahk'. On that monument, Sihyaj K'ahk' carries the ceremonial fire bundle of the Wiinte' Naah cult and a throwing stick symbolizing his overlord Spearthrower Owl (Freidel et al. 2007). El Perú-Waka' Stela 10 portrays a Teotihuacano lord or a Wak king emulating one wearing the feathered jaguar headdress and carrying a fire bundle. El Perú-Waka' Stela 14, a head fragment, depicts another individual dressed as a Teotihuacano with the eye goggles and buccal mask of the storm god (like Stela 16). From Stela 16 onward, the carving convention at El Perú-Waka' was frontal depiction in contrast to the profile convention used at Tikal and other cities such as Uaxactun that were raising stelae in the fourth and fifth centuries CE (fig. 18.8). El Perú-Waka' stelae are notably large. El Perú-Waka' Stela 27 likely was five meters tall based on the dimensions of the preserved carved facial fragment, and El Perú-Waka' Stela 9, which depicted a king at the beginning of the sixth century, is estimated to have had three meters of carved surface. On El Perú-Waka' Stela 9, a king stands on a fire mountain and the finely engraved text next to the leg of the king mentions a Wiinte' Naah (see chapter 7, this volume). Why was El Perú-Waka' important to Sihyaj K'ahk', who would soon be overlord of Tikal, the greatest Early Classic royal capital?

Freidel (2018) hypothesizes that El Perú-Waka' followed Tikal into the practice of dynastic succession, as did other kingdoms in the core of the southern lowlands, including Uaxactun, El Zotz, and Bejucal. These kingdoms came under attack from kingdoms that adhered to sodality election, the general Preclassic practice in the Maya lowlands. The early major state of the region was centered in the Mirador Basin and the Early Classic heartland was in the central peninsular region and adjacent parts of Campeche and Quintana Roo (Martin 2016, Martin and Velásquez 2016; Freidel 2018). That alliance of sodality kingdoms, the Snake Regime, thrived in the Classic period under the banner of Kaanul. In this interpretation, when Sihyaj K'ahk' came into the lowlands he was not a conqueror but rather a liberator for these early dynastic kingdoms, relieving them of usurpers and quislings put in power by Kaanul and its allies. Having failed to stop dynastic succession by repeatedly destroying the North Acropolis of Yax Ehb Xook and his descendants during the second and third centuries CE, the Kaanul lords devised a regional strategy of placing vassals on the dynastic thrones of the rebels. Tikal king Chak Tok Ich'aak I and his father King Muwaan Jol were such usurpers (Freidel et al. 2003); their regime was overthrown by Sihyaj K'ahk'.

While Sihyaj K'ahk' may have been marching into Petén from the west, there is another reason he came to Waka'. At the eastern end of this citadel

Figure 18.8. Stela 16 at El Perú-Waka' portraying Sihyaj K'ahk'. Drawing by Sarah Sage. Photo by Juan Carlos Pérez. Courtesy of Proyecto Arqueológico Waka' and the Ministry of Culture and Sports, Guatemala.

The Ideas and Images of Cities and Centers: Teotihuacan and the Lowland Maya · 455

city, some 100 meters above the San Juan River (a strategic tributary of the great San Pedro Mártir River), El Mirador hill towers another 40 meters. This natural promontory and adjacent ridge were terraformed in three sacred localities in the Late Preclassic period (chapter 2, this volume). By the Early Classic period, there were two pyramids and a sacred summit on the hill. A grand stairway gave access to the sacred summit from the end of a broad stone causeway that linked this temple acropolis to the city's main temple, Structure M13-1, the Fire Shrine and probable place of Sihyaj K'ahk's Wiinte' Naah. The causeway crossed a reservoir constructed at the foot of El Mirador hill, clearly signaling its status as a water mountain.

We postulate that for the Teotihuacanos, the in-line triad represented the belt stars of Orion, just as it did for the Maya (Freidel et al. 1993, figs 2.14–2.17). That constellation also represented the carapace of the Cosmic Turtle (chapter 2, this volume), the womb and portal of emergence for the resurrected maize god. As Karl Taube (2005) discerned, one famous Classic painting of the maize god emerging from the turtle carapace shows him wearing the pendant Crocodile Tree. We have argued that the in-line triad over the upturned basin insignia represents the water goddess mountain, Cerro Gordo, and that the tree axis mundi represents the Avenue of the Dead. Together, these icons represent the insignia of Teotihuacan, especially in the Maya lowlands. El Mirador hill was an existing expression of that insignia, the place for Sihyaj K'ahk' to proclaim *altepetl* dominion in the name of his Teotihuacano lord.

In front of the center temple on El Mirador hill, under a frontal platform such as those found at Teotihuacan, Michelle Rich (Rich et al. 2006; Rich 2011, 230–258) discovered a tomb dating from the time of the entrada, complete with a Teotihuacano-style tableau macabre: two young women, one pregnant, arranged one on top of the other. The arms of one of them suggest a dancing pose. The turtle carapace resurrection scene depicted on Classic Maya ceramics regularly shows the maize god being helped by two nude young women. At El Mirador hill, three lidded vessels were placed at the foot of the women, arranged in a triangle. One of the vessels has three red circles on the lid (fig. 18.9).

Within each of the three circles is a profile depiction of Witz (water spray serpent; Stuart 2010), the god of the number 13 (S. Houston, personal communication to Juan Carlos Meléndez, November 2005). This god is likely the Maya equivalent of the Nahuatl concept of Atl. In the debris of the final shrine built on the frontal platform, which dates to the seventh century CE, Michelle Rich and colleagues (2006) discovered a larger-than-life stucco head of a Teotihuacano lord. This lord had the goggles of the storm god in his headdress, goggles around his eyes, and a buccal mask. This ritual location witnessed many other pivotal events after 378 CE. Clearly the kings and

Figure 18.9. Vessel from tomb at El Perú-Waka'. Photo by Ricky Lopez. Courtesy of Proyecto Arqueológico Waka' and the Ministry of Culture and Sports, Guatemala.

queens of Waka' remembered Sihyaj K'ahk' and his entrada to the end of history; their mountain materialized time and destiny for them.

## Concluding Remarks

In the late nineteenth century, the great buildings of Teotihuacan and the ornate calendar stelae of the lowland Maya captured the interest and imagination of scholars and the public. They were fascinated by the architectural and mathematical accomplishments and practices of the ancient Mesoamericans. Here we have proposed that these masterworks, so different in form and scale, may have had a common inspiration in the desire of their patron rulers to

The Ideas and Images of Cities and Centers: Teotihuacan and the Lowland Maya · 457

place themselves and their peoples in models of the cosmos that compellingly explained and legitimized dynastic succession. We appreciate the fact that many thoughtful experts on Teotihuacan argue that self-effacing rulers must have held power through the auspices of great councils (see Cowgill 1983; Carballo and Feinman 2016; Carballo 2020), institutional arrangements that would have been more amenable to collective rule and perhaps the election of leaders (rather than dynastic succession). But to us, the extraordinary establishment of the center of Teotihuacan as a calendar-inspired axis mundi in a matter of a few generations points to the rise of a powerful and charismatic dynastic family that located itself in cosmic time like the patrons on Maya stelae. The extreme concentration of exclusive, precious, and finely crafted exotic goods that are accompanied by abundant sacrificial retainers that are deposited in the hearts of Teotihuacan's major pyramids supports the idea of despotic rulers declaring divine authority inherited by bloodline and presiding over a hierarchically stratified society. The analogy to the Aztec emperors and their Templo Mayor offerings is not far fetched.

Similarly, most experts on the ancient Maya assume that kingship was always and everywhere dynastic in the lowlands. Here we propose that Maya dynastic succession was the historical invention of a remarkable family at Tikal who built the North Acropolis as a royal seat and moved away from pervasive sodality-based elective kingship (perhaps centered at Tikal in the Lost World Pyramid Group, the ancient E Group where the earliest concentration of royal dynastic interments occurs) (see A. Chase and D. Chase 1995, 100; 2017a). This new dynastic institution was successfully emulated and adopted principally in the southern lowlands; it never took hold in the northern lowlands. Calendar-reckoning stelae, raised primarily to legitimize dynastic succession in the south, were never so popular in the north, where they were raised only by exemplary individual rulers to celebrate their accomplishments (Freidel 2018; McAnany 2019a).

To make our case we have to move away from the idea that the Maya materialization of time is knowable mainly through the study of calendar texts and that in the absence of calendar texts, as at Teotihuacan, timekeeping is knowable only through such distinctive features as the pecked circles made famous by Anthony Aveni (2000) and the architectural alignments they inform. A focus on Maya E Groups has demonstrated that it is possible to study the materialization of time through a specific architectural configuration (Freidel et al. 2017). Saburo Sugiyama has advanced the study of time and calendrics at Teotihuacan through the mathematics of architecture and urban planning. His work resonates with that undertaken and published by Aveni and others (1978) on the Caracol, the Castillo, and other buildings at Chichén Itzá in the northern lowlands. Maya archaeoastronomers and other archaeologists will no doubt continue to apply such methods systematically. Hopefully they will discern measuring units in Maya architecture as S. Sugiyama has for Teotihuacan, perhaps elucidating the record of kingship and timekeeping in architecture in those regions of the Maya world where rulers rarely raised inscribed calendar stelae. We will let our other methods and arguments speak for themselves. We think they are grounded in careful documentation of complex ritual deposits and iconographically explicit imagery.

The cultural historical implications of our arguments are that the partisans of dynasty at Teotihuacan and the lowland Maya who chose to collaborate closely with them between the second and fifth centuries CE were bent on establishing a New Order, as the historians of the lowland Maya, Simon Martin and Nikolai Grube (2008), have called the time between the arrival of Sihyaj K'ahk' in 378 CE and the burning of Teotihuacan's center in 500 CE. But it was not a hegemonic imposition from highland Mexico on the lowland Maya; it was very probably an alliance, at least initially. In our view, it was a revolutionary effort on the part of extraordinary leaders to span the sun-path breadth of this world—to define it (or perhaps renew it) as a world and to advocate for the benefits of that common understanding. Those leaders defined themselves as the first of their kind who would be followed by people they had given life to as their successors. They used military force and fear to advance their vision, and their power over life and death is well documented in their sacrificial offerings. But clearly it was devotion and other factors rather than fear that inspired people to build and dwell in Teotihuacan and the dynastic royal capitals of the lowland Maya. The economic prosperity and social cohesion of those urban places is undeniable in the archaeological record. Whatever the flaws and failures of that world-spanning alliance, it remained legendary for the rest of pre-Columbian history, and the idea was revived in the era of Tula Hidalgo and Chichén Itzá. Together, these dynasts not only materialized time but also determined destiny.

Yet the dynasts of Teotihuacan and their partisans were probably only one of several powerful factions in that city and state. The people who desecrated the probable royal burials in the Feathered Serpent Pyramid and defaced sculptures on that building were careful not to disturb the sacrificial offerings there. The attack was more focused on the probable rulers in those tombs than on the effigy mountain of the people representing the state, a decisively collective symbol. Moreover, despite the defacement of sculptures there, the Feathered Serpent and the storm god endured as city gods of widespread renown and influence in Mesoamerica through the time of the Spanish arrival. It seems likely that the timing of the attack on the Ciudadela and the Plaza of the Columns manifests a common source of collective pushback against the dynasts who had presided over the design of the city center. A great struggle for power occurred at Teotihuacan in the fourth century CE and very likely continued until the burning of the city center generations later.

Such factional partisan struggle at Teotihuacan could make sense of what we can discern in the archaeological record of the Maya lowlands. Although we are confident of the historical alliance between the dynasts at Tikal and those at Teotihuacan, it is also true that the Early Classic capital of the Kaanul regime, Dzibanché in Quintana Roo, evinces clear archaeological evidence of alliance with Teotihuacanos. This evidence takes the form of shared architecture in the form of panel/slope (talud-tablero) architectural façades on major buildings (similar to those reported for Tikal; see Laporte 1987, 2003), exquisite jade jewels fashioned as Teotihuacano lords discovered in tombs, and Teotihuacan-style mountains with flowers fashioned in stucco reliefs on buildings (Nalda and Balanzario 2014). It seems possible to us that a great Mesoamerica-wide political contest was taking place during the Early Classic period in which factions that favored collective power and elective rulership competed with factions that favored dynastic rulership and succession in bloodlines. Such a scenario, should it prove to be supported by the weight of evidence, would demonstrate that ancient Mesoamerica was in the same arena as great powers the world over, in antiquity and today, struggling over the nature of state power.

## Acknowledgments

We are grateful for the long-term initial funding the Jerry Jerome Glick Foundation provided for the Proyecto Arqueológico Waka'. We also acknowledge Jerry Murdock for his support of the Santa Fe Institute of the Maya Working Group, an exceptional experience for all of those involved. We are grateful for the inspiration and mentorship of George Cowgill, a great human being and a formidable specialist in the archaeology of Teotihuacan. We appreciate the support of our colleagues, including Richard Meadow and William Fash of Harvard, and our partners from INAH, especially Ruben Cabrera Castro, Alfredo López Austin, Leonardo López Luján, and Sergio Gómez Chávez. We also thank the archaeologists of the Proyecto Arqueológico Waka': Juan Carlos Pérez, Juan Carlos Meléndez, Griselda Pérez, Michelle Rich, Olivia Navarro-Farr, Stanley Guenter, Mary Kate Kelly, and Damien Marken.

## Note

1  See Sugiyama (2005) for a discussion of possible royal tombs and dynasty in the Feathered Serpent Pyramid deposits.

# 19

## Epilogue

### Architects of Time

ANNE S. DOWD

Just as earth time is almost always originally rooted in the materiality of astronomical cycles, human time is originally rooted in the materiality of the body.

(Robb 2020, 5)

The Maya base 20 partly vigesimal calendar system, which incorporates units of 0, 1, and 20, has been envisioned as counting on 10 fingers and 10 toes (Stuart 2012a; Aveni n.d.). It is connected to the human body, as Robb notes above. Maya kings and queens embodied time; they bore or carried it, spiraling forward and back. This chapter explores the thesis that analogies with human physiography, counting units, time management, astronomical movements, and calendar use were expanded into or distilled out of larger sky and earthscapes to create cosmoscapes. As the authors of preceding chapters have shown, cosmoscapes materialize time.

One reason for emphasizing this theme is the exploration of the idea that mobile groups who coalesced seasonally as hunter-gatherer-fisher and horticultural populations or emerging agricultural groups came together to form centers around nuclei of outdoor religious precincts (see especially chapter 3, but also 1 and 18). This interpretation completely overturns previous evolutionary theories about cities forming through ever-denser populations in places occupied by sedentary farmers.

The discovery of spacious platforms of up to 140 acres (n = 478; Inomata et al. 2021, 1487), some with twenty mounded edges, and further E Group research (n = 93) has expanded the sample of 163 religious precincts the Santa Fe Institute working group explored in the volume *Maya E Groups: Calendars, Astronomy, and Urbanism in the Early Lowlands* (Freidel et al. 2017) to at least 734 examples (Dowd 2017c, 570), an increase of 350 percent (see also Chase et al. 2017 14; Dowd et al. 2017; Inomata et al. 2021, 1487). These platforms date to 1100–750 BCE and are aligned with pairs of dates such as those matching azimuths of sunrise or sunset. The span of days bracketed by these date pairs can be separated into day bundle intervals divisible by 13 or 20, similar to units marked in E Group complex alignment patterning across the region (Aveni et al. 2003; Dowd et al. 2017, 560; Freidel et al. 2017; Dowd 2017c; Inomata et al. 2021). Measuring time using the human body as the source for vigesimal counting and multiplying these units around compass-like arcs along the line of the horizon is one powerful example of the microcosmos as macrocosmos, connecting human to earth time.

These ideals are framed in the notion of landesque cosmography (chapter 2, this volume). David Freidel combined the terms "landesque," meaning distinctive landscapes, and "cosmography," representing the cosmos, to describe polity integration where outlying religious edifices mark the four quarters and merge territory with chronology, community, ancestors, and gods. The idea of landesque cosmography is similar to cosmovision as Johanna Broda (1982) used it (see also Freidel et al. 1993; Ashmore and Sabloff 2000; Ashmore 2015; Dowd 2015b, 2017b). The authors of this volume have drawn on over 4,198 square kilometers of available high-density and 85,000 square kilometers of lower-density lidar imagery, for a total of 89,198 square kilometers, to investigate ideas related to the Maya cosmos. Working with this methodological advance, archaeologists have produced many of the exciting results described in the preceding chapters, and there is much more to accomplish. As David Freidel (personal communication) has phrased it: "For archaeologists, the revolution in lidar imagery is to space what radiocarbon dating was to time."

The Maya invention or discovery of zero-like null units positioned and centered humans within their universe and contributed to their worldview, intertwining ideas of absence and totality that many of the authors in this volume investigate (see chapters 1, 4, 5, 10, and 14). Human digits provide metaphors for counting units and show how the human body is a microcosm of the universe (see chapters 3, 7, 9, 12, 13, 16, and 17). Spatial referents such as planetary movements in the sky framed by the horizon line are considered in discussions that deal with the Maya macrocosmos (see chapters 2, 3, 4, 5, 6, and 18). The idea of crafting cosmography is explored in chapters 1, 8, 11, and 15, and in this epilogue, I summarize the interplay between ideas about the cosmos and the physical world around us. In the next section, a discussion of

462 · Anne S. Dowd

how complex time and the invention (or discovery) of a zero-like concept reinforced regional innovations in calendars, architectural standardization, and astronomy provide a basis for integrating the chapter authors' contributions. The cultural chronology of this volume is presented in table 19.1.

Table 19.1. Chronological overview of the Maya area

| Sequence | Period | Major Events |
|---|---|---|
| 1958–2000 CE | After International Geophysical Year[a] | International Geophysical Year Earth system observations |
| 1920–1958 CE | Modern | Carnegie Institution of Washington research using instrumental observation |
| 1697–1920 CE | Historic | Maya integrated into modern nation-states |
| 1519–1697 CE | Colonial | Euro-American colonial occupation of Maya region |
| 1200–1519 CE | Late Postclassic | Northern lowlands heavily occupied |
| 900–1200 CE | Early Postclassic | Florescence of eastern Yucatán coastal sites |
| 800–900 CE | Terminal Classic | Political collapse in the southern lowlands |
| 550–800 CE | Late Classic | Widespread regional polities, urban settlements |
| 250–550 CE | Early Classic | Transition to stratified regional polities, use of vaulted buildings, and widespread appearance of polychrome ceramics. Concept of zero or null in place by 357 CE. Teotihuacanos from Central Mexico enter Maya area 378 CE. |
| 1–250 CE | Terminal Preclassic | Changes potentially reflective of a mini-collapse |
| 350 BCE–1 CE | Late Preclassic | Large vertical monumental constructions, E Groups proliferate. Evidence of full-time religious specialists. Writing began by 400–200 BCE. Long Count established by 35 BCE. Settlements coalesce into cities. |
| 1000–350 BCE | Middle Preclassic | Large horizontal monumental constructions, E Groups are built, evidence for 365-day calendar |
| 2000–1000 BCE | Late Archaic | First recognizably Maya peoples, large horizontal monumental constructions by 1100 BCE, evidence for 260-day calendar |
| 7500–2000 BCE | Middle Archaic | Archaic lithic assemblages, ceramics rare |
| 11600–7500 BCE | Paleoindian | Paleoindian lithic assemblages |

*Source:* Modified after Chase, Chase, et al. (2014, 14); Chase et al. (2017, 4).

[a] July 1957–December 1958.

## The History of the Maya (and Possibly Epi-Olmec) Invention of a Null or Zero Concept

By 35 BCE, using positional notation, Maya and imaginably also Epi-Olmec mathematicians set the stage for a concept of zero (Justeson 2010, 47), an intellectual accomplishment that was pivotal in the world's history of arithmetic.[1] Native Mesoamerican scholars accomplished this independently from contact with other cultures. Maya people expressed their interest in numbers at least in part due to an intense concern with ranked heredity measured in deep time through connections with gods and world creation. Tracking agricultural and congruent ritual cycles using a sophisticated calendar yielded these calculations. Religious adepts materialized time in physical representations of calendar dates for historical records. Specialist daykeepers produced Long Count timelines that connected real-world dynastic relationships and events with creation stories and supernatural protagonists.

As early texts at San Bartolo, Guatemala, attest, Maya writing began by around 400–200 BCE and persisted until at least 1695 CE among the Itzá of Tayasal in Petén (Fray Andrés de Avendaño y Loyola in Means 1917). Early skywatching in the region was accomplished on massive rectangular platforms and in smaller E Groups, with architectural complexes showing evidence of commensuration of multi-day intervals such as the $13 \times 20 = 260$-day Tzolk'in sacred almanac and $18 \times 20 + 5 = 365$-day *h'aab* solar calendars marked with horizon-based astronomical alignments (Aveni et al. 2003; Dowd et al. 2017; Dowd 2017c; Inomata et al. 2021).

John Justeson (2010, 44), citing Joseph Greenberg (1987, 255), emphasizes "a view that *zero is not an innate element of human numerical cognition,* but rather has appeared as an extension or addition to the conception of number in some mathematical traditions [Justeson's italics]." Justeson (2010, 44) says, "A number zero must have its source in an *extension* of the concept of number. That source can be identified in the conscious practices of mathematical specialists working with mathematical notation—in particular, with positional notation [Justeson's italics]." The timing of the discovery of zero implies that its function within the Long Count may have been connected to a tradition of rulership that emerged in the period 35 BCE to 357 CE (because positional notation used in the Long Count was developed by 35 BCE and zero was written by 357 CE) (Justeson 2010, 45, 48; Marcus 1976, fig. 6). Before 200 CE, the longest length of time a distance number recorded did not exceed $13 \times 360$ days $= 4{,}680$ days (12.82 Julian years of 365 days) on the La Mojarra Stela, an interval that fit well within a person's lifespan. The longest span of time recorded on an individual text works out to 14.65 Julian

464 · Anne S. Dowd

years (also on the La Mojarra Stela) (Kaufman and Justeson 2001, 2.71–2.74; Justeson 2010, 48).

Justeson (2001; 2010, 49) has convincingly argued that placing Long Count katun-ending dates firmly within the oratory and high-impact rhetorical tradition of repetition of a series by *naming* the null placeholder position may have yielded a concept of zero that was reinterpreted as a numerical construction. The *mi* adjective (possibly signifying zero in Mayan or perhaps simply indicating a placeholder position) indicated "lacking" or "no" when it preceded a noun (Kaufman and Justeson 2002–2003, 1553).[2] To illustrate this, Justeson (2010, 49) suggests comparing the impact of 8.16.0.0.0 3 Ahau 8 Kankin (357 CE) written on Uaxactun Stela 18 with and without the zero placeholder position:

[There were] 8 baktuns [8 × 144,000 days = 1,152,000 days]
[There were] 16 katuns [16 × 7,200 days = 115,200 days]
There were no years [0 × 360 days = 0 days]
There were no months [0 × 20 days = 0 days]
There were no days [0 × 1 days = 0 days]
[when] on 3 Lord . . . occurred.

Rhetorically, repetition would have lent weight and gravitas to the Long Count date. Prior to the time when the Long Count came into use, in positional notations, numbers alone in a sequence without baktun, katun, year, month, and day signs skipped a null case, or left a space in the zero position. Earlier in Cycle 8, Stela 5 from Tak'alik Ab'aj shows a positional notation in which a blank in the text indicates any number of *winal*, and the later of the two dates on the stela (8.3.2[0.]10 and 8.4.5[0.]17) is the seating (or 365th day) of the year (Justeson 2001, 988) (fig. 19.1). The formula on the Dumbarton Oaks celt is different both visually and rhetorically. It stamps or punctuates the time statement to read: 1) completion (verb), 2) 8 baktuns stated explicitly, 3) completion (verb), 4) 4 katuns, stated explicitly (Justeson 2001, 988). Nothing is mentioned about years, *winals*, or days.

During the Middle Preclassic period (1000–350 BCE) and possibly much earlier in the Late Archaic period (2000–1000 BCE), the Mesoamerican bar-and-dot (five and one, respectively) system of mathematical notation was in use for the 260-day *tzolk'in* calendar (Justeson 2010, 47; Lounsbury 1978). For example, by 300–200 BCE, an early San Bartolo text showed day signs. Earlier, 500 BCE lunar day count names appeared on monoliths 12–14 of the Danzante building at Monte Albán (Justeson 2012, 831–832). A day name may be present at San Jose Mogote in 600 BCE, and a day name (and possibly the owner's name) is present on a Guerrero jade paint/ink palette. The dating

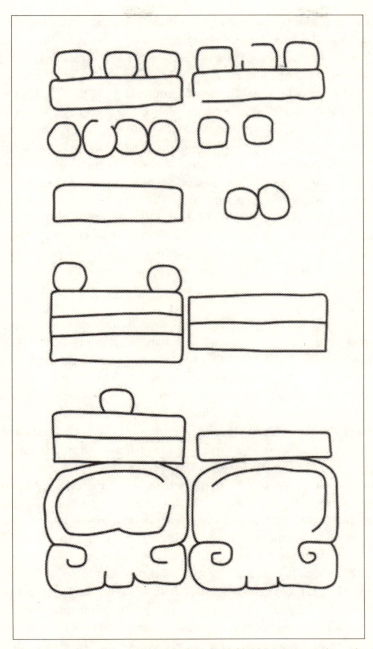

Figure 19.1. Part of the Stela 5 text from Tak'alik Ab'aj, Guatemala, with no zero digit: 8 4 5 17, 11 Quake for 8.4.5.(0).17 (*top*), 11 Quake (365th day or seating of the year in Yucatec) (*middle*), and 8 3 2 10, 5 Dog for 8.3.2.(0).10, 5 Dog (*bottom*). Source: Justeson (2001, 988), drawing by John Justeson.

466 · Anne S. Dowd

of this item is more difficult due to its likely heirloom status, but it potentially dates to the Late Archaic (2000–1000 BCE) through Middle Preclassic (fig. 19.2) (Covarrubias 1946, fig. 24; Marcus and Flannery [1983] 2003; Saturno et al. 2006; Justeson 2012, 831–832; Turner 2020).

In the Late and Terminal Preclassic periods (350 BCE–250 CE), time intervals in days, months of 20 days, or years of 360/365 days, were counted through distance numbers (Justeson 2010, 47–48). By 357 CE, however, Maya sculptors at Uaxactun, Guatemala, were carving hieroglyphs that are almost universally referred to as zero on Stelae 18 and 19 in the tun, *winal*, and *k'in* positions for the 8.16.0.0.0 Long Count. Spanning millennia and connecting human lives with mythic events and using T173 prefixes, Long Count inscriptions endured for 144,000 + 8 × 7,200 days (Justeson 2001, 989; Justeson 2010, 48; Blume 2011, 58).[3] Until 909 CE, when a date of 10.4.0.0.0 was inscribed on Tonina Monument 101 (according to the Gregorian or Julian calendars 552 years later), the same glyph form was used to denote "lacking," "there is no," "there are no," or "not" (Blume 2011, 59; J. Justeson, personal communication, April 26, 2022).

On Quirigua Stela F, the black water place, *ik' najb' naal*, was referenced as a time and a place of creation, like a primordial sea (Looper 2003, 125, 219; Blume 2011, 61). The syllabic sign **mi**, the *mi-hi* form, and the logogram *MIH*—"there is/are no"—are also found on Stela 63 at Copán (Grube and Nahm 1990, 16; 1994, 699; Stuart et al. 1999, II-35; Carrasco et al. 2009: 19248; Justeson 2010, 51; Blume 2011, 63; Stuart 2018). The syllabic sign **ma** spells "no" or "not." In Classic period (250–900 CE) texts, zeros or null units may be shown as a three-petal, half-flower, or quatrefoil T173; a shell T17; or 713a (fig. 19.3a–d) or the head variant with a human profile combined with a hand or a bony snake mandible T1085 (fig. 19.4a and b). In contrast, texts from the walls on Structure 10K-2 at Xultun display an oblong oval form with a small interior circle and a border along the upper edge and the codices display a stylized *Oliva* shell (Tozzer and Allen 1910, 297; Grube and Nahm 1990, 16; Grube and Nahm 1994, 699; Stuart et al. 1999, II-35; Justeson 2001, 989; Kaufman and Justeson 2002–2003, 1533; Blume 2011, 63; Saturno, Stuart et al. 2012; Bricker et al. 2014). David Stuart (2012, fig. 3) interprets this as a possible informal notation for zero used for mathematical computation, comparable to Pomoná Panel 7 in the Dallas Museum of Art and to examples in the Dresden Codex. David Freidel (personal communication, May 2021) interprets an Early Classic (250–550 CE) shell pectoral—a pierced giant limpet the Aztec called Oyohualli—as meaning *tep' pet,* "to wrap" or "to envelop," in the sense of "complete" (fig. 19.5).

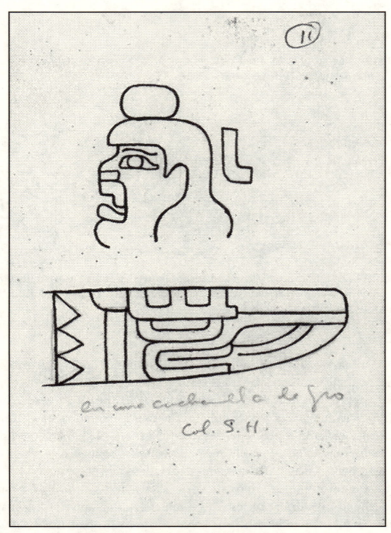

Figure 19.2. (*a*) possible day sign, after A. Turner (2020, fig. 12), (*b*) Covarrubias wrote "Col. S. H." on the original sketch, which was the first published image of a jade wing oyster-shell skeuomorph pendant/paint pot with a possible profile-head day sign, produced in 900–400 BCE. Source: Covarrubias (1946, fig. 24), drawing by Miguel Covarrubias.

468 · Anne S. Dowd

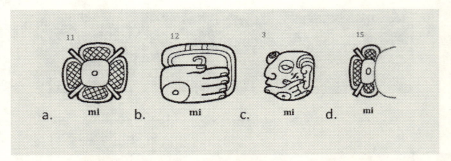

Figure 19.3. Hieroglyphic signs for (*a*) the syllable **mi**, (*b*) "no, not," (*c*) zero, and (*d*) "lacking." Source: Blume (2011), drawing by Ana Blume.

Figure 19.4. Detail from Stela D at Copán: (*a*) position A-3, meaning "0" *winal*; (*b*) position B-3 (*b*), meaning "0" *k'in*. Both use the glyph form shown in Figure 19.3c. Source: Baudez (1994), drawing by Anne S. Dowd.

Given Maya mathematicians' interest in bundling time using groups of commensurate numbers that are rhythmic, synchronizing multiples of different integers (Aveni et al. 1995; Lounsbury 1978), the idea of zero as both nothing and totality is intriguing. This nested numeration has zeroing, balancing, and summing properties that the Maya equated with harmonious beginnings and endings of time periods. These contrived, aesthetically pleasing, poetic, mathematical frameworks, based on the principle of the least common multiple, imposed order, beauty, and symmetry on astronomical and calendrical cycles. The commensuration concept has spatial correlates that the authors of this volume express in their discussions of materializing time. There is a unifying theme of cosmic centrality in the quincunx metaphor for Maya settlement (Hanks 1990; chapter 4, this volume). This idea may also have a connection to the physical representation in the hieroglyphic record for zero, which is especially relevant if the idea of

Epilogue: Architects of Time · 469

Figure 19.5. The Toltec Kislak Oyohualli pendant. Source: Urschel (2009).

complete is another gloss for the meaning of a null value in Maya linguistics and mathematics.[4]

The authors of this volume directly engage the reader in Maya materialization of time; that is, in the ways that people imprinted their temporal worldview on the surrounding landscape through the use of the cosmological metaphors that surrounded them. These concepts came from peoples' careful observations of the natural world. In Maya cultures, people from ritual specialists to

470 · Anne S. Dowd

laymen and laywomen observed the movement of the sun across the horizon. The motion of other astronomical bodies and groups of stars structured alignments of viewing platforms or other architecture in the region.

To understand the need for zero, especially as a way of heightening drama in the recitation of the katun-ending dates that Maya kings celebrated, it is helpful to understand the activities of the rulers on such dates. New work by Anthony Aveni (personal communication, 2021) and Mary Miller strives to amplify rulers' perceptions and uses of time through seasonal patterning in the birth dates of rulers of Piedras Negras. Furthermore, locating the places where rituals occurred sets the stage for a more comprehensive interpretation of how time morphed linguistically and conceptually from a single human generation to greater time depths that represented many generations, if not cosmic time. The authors of this volume have collectively made such an effort.

Many scholars describe a "four parts around a center" urban plan that alluded to world directions with an axis mundi (for example, see Freidel et al. 1993, 123–172; Dowd and Milbrath 2015, 12, 61, 78, 109; Wolf 2022, 239; chapter 5, this volume). Ritual circuits from centers to peripheries are thought to have helped map time onto urban and community spaces. The zero concept came into spatial constructs in the sense of an owned, finished, or bound territory.

As Diane Chase and Arlen Chase document in chapter 14 and as Cynthia Robin asserts in chapter 10, common people also had their own routes and practices, albeit on a smaller scale that included adjudication alongside divination in cavern-like chambers. At Caracol, in modern-day Belize, people were commemorating past time through 20-year katun cycles with Giant Ahau altars or face caches and 40-year two-katun cycles of burials or caching in residential groups. Also in Belize, in Structure 6, Rooms 1 and 2 at Chan, future divination was integrated with leaders' resolutions of disputes or decisions about issues related to community planning. In chapter 14, Diane Chase and Arlen Chase have made a strong case for periodic site rejuvenation as an integrative mechanism that linked people, their built environment, and nested time periods at Caracol. At Chan, as Cynthia Robin describes in chapter 10, a five-hole quincunx pattern on a bench and a patolli board inscribed on a floor related to the Maya divisions of the world into four directions and a center in a room partitioned into three sections, like the levels of earth, sky, and underworld. The diviner's Room 2 in Structure 6 at Chan on the south side of the Central Group also contained incised horizontal and vertical lines on the south wall, perhaps representing a nonfunctional reference to a patolli board that may have been used for education or training.

These examples are just a sample of many possible time-fashioning trends in Maya cultures. Evolutionary processes are not implied because materially represented time could and did serve a variety of sociopolitical purposes and varied from site to site and time period to time period depending on the goals of the agents and actors. Nevertheless, considering how a Maya king celebrated katun endings in Copán, Honduras, where stelae illustrated the regal processional routes at period-ending dates in 578–652 CE, has value (Schele and Mathews 1998; Newsome 2001b, 2003; Bíró 2017, 50). The ruler modeled the specific ritual regalia for these events on the stelae. Examples are Stelae 7 and P, which K'ahk' Uti' Chan Yopat, erected in 9.9.0.0.0 (613 CE), and 9.10.0.0.0 (623 CE) to celebrate individual ritual circuits, and the eight stelae (E, 3, 2, 12, 10, 19, 13, and 23) that K'ahk' Uti' Witz' K'awiil erected to commemorate a single tour of his realm in 9.13.0.0.0 (652 CE). This tour of space can also be envisioned as a seasonal round, perhaps modeled after the routes farmers took to their milpas to plant, cultivate, tend, and harvest.

The rituals took place in different locales as a way of engendering the gods and animating the community. For example, a ruler conjured the gods through blood offerings and then breathed life into them (Bíró 2017, 38). At Copán, the ruler and the manifested gods then visited the ruler's formed stone which represented the first snake dynasty, at Wintik city; the cornfield; and the dwelling of the twelfth successor of the three-mountain water lord, K'inich Yax K'uk' Mo' in the house of the ruler. The ruler nourished the gods with maize kernels during the period-ending ceremony (Bíró 2017, 38). Wearing insignia that represented the gods that participated and headdresses that alluded to ancestry, the ruler circumnavigated the community, shedding blood, breathing life into gods, nourishing them with corn, and purifying them with incense. In this way, the ruler bundled the katun and tied the community together through actions meant to cultivate and tend.[5] The ruler planted, grew, and harvested time in the sense of growing plants from seeds. The small cast objects diviners used for counting may have been thought of as seeding time.

Some scholars (Wichmann 2004a; Bíró 2005, 13; Bíró 2017, 29) see the paddler gods as lords of time, specifically dusk and dawn, suggesting that the paddle strokes of these deities were like a metronome beating out a temporal rhythm as daylight faded into dark night skies and then brightened again to repeat the cycle. Temporal adverbs include *sahm-iiy* or *sa-mi-ya* (earlier today) and *'ak'ab'-iiy* (yesterday or the night before) (Stuart et al. 1999, II-35; Stuart 2020a). A theme in several chapters in this volume is the different interpretations of when a temporal cycle began or ended. If zero is also read as totality or completion, it is spatially central and punctuates procession in a repeated return to the center using routes around quadripartite spaces analogous to the way temporal calculation collected or bundled days into completed cycles (Stuart 1996; Guernsey and Reilly 2006; chapter 4, this volume). One

472 · Anne S. Dowd

imagines stepped rhythmic processions to a drum beat as a way of precisely timing actions: encapsulating, claiming, or enclosing space, monuments, and the ruler who acted as a movable axis for centered community focus (Aveni 2011, 187–216). Classic (250–900 CE) and colonial period (1519–1697 CE) processions are discussed below in a summary of chapter 4.

## Human Time

Human time brings together calendars, time measurement, and timekeeping, weaving the threads of peoples' existence into the rhythms of temporal units and astronomical bodies. The combination of physical notations of how timekeeping was practiced and theoretical literature or chronological history about time materialized from the record of a person's lifespan provides examples of the human scale in thinking about time. Using predictions about what would happen in the future based on past events was one connection Maya people made between ancestors and succeeding generations.

In chapter 12, Susan Milbrath describes actors moving idols, like those depicted on effigy censors for burning incense, through space or rotating them to different locations during ceremonies such as those associated with the first month of the 365-day *haab'/ha'b'*. Bloodletting, incense, and decapitated bird offerings are part of the five-day Uayeb year-end rituals. These can be compared to zero and the pivot of the northern night sky because they occur in a liminal time/space between the manifested human-form, vigesimal day bundles. There was an east, north, west, and south sequence for rotating yearbearers. As Milbrath notes, "The Akbal set, which Thompson (1960, 127) identified as Classic yearbearers, are paired with 1 Pop as New Year's Day." There is no *mi* or *mi-hi* preceding a month name in calendrical texts; rather, the new year and each new month are seated on the last day of the preceding month, making the seating of Pop identical to 5 Uayeb. The years are all named for the divinatory calendar date 1 Pop.

The timing of the invention of a zero-like concept coincides with state-level institutionalization in the Maya region. One measure of the degree and emergence of full-time religious specialists, who undoubtedly were skilled mathematicians and astronomers, has been analyzed using the size of interior spaces in E Group temples as a proxy for changing bureaucratic scale during the Preclassic to Classic transition at least 2,000 years ago. The results show that a 1-σ standard deviation of 49.83 square meters from the size of pre-state buildings characterizes state-level requirements for institutional space (Dowd 2017c, 545). The construction of pre-state religious precincts at centers where skywatching and calendar development occurred on mounded edge platforms and other examples of standardized architecture began to appear during the Archaic to Preclassic transition at least 3,000 years ago.

Patricia McAnany promotes the idea of rulers as cultivators of deep monumental time in chapter 13. The lack of choice about who would succeed rulers in hereditary institutions made those systems especially fragile; talent was not a prerequisite. Perhaps anchoring rulership in calendrical timekeeping was a way of affirming the selection and stabilizing political succession, whether it was accomplished by council choice or heredity. Accession ceremonies incorporated binding and bundling the king, just as time was bundled and transformed into null, zero, or fulfilled units. It is interesting to consider the possibility that connecting cyclical movements with ritual may have extended farther back into horticultural or hunter-gatherer-fisher lifestyles patterned on seasonal rounds. Moving to the ethnographic present, McAnany extends time and temporality as expressed in Indigenous thought and culture into contemporary Maya life.

In chapter 7, David Freidel and Olivia Navarro-Farr discuss the function of Structure M13-1 at El Perú-Waka' as a possible E Group during the Late Preclassic period (350 BCE–1 CE), prior to its transformation into a Wiinte' Naah fire shrine. It was certainly the central—and centering—temple of the city where rulers performed as embodiments of cosmic totalities. The idea of stelae as agentive, standing in for ruler power, was embraced: remnants of burned and defaced fragments were planted as though they were heirloom seeds. As agents, the stelae multiplied and concentrated the power of a place through human recollection, repeating and reinforcing history-making and the materialization of time. Time was made physical when relics were placed into special, highly evocative places and in the process, rulers became personified, sentient, and agentive time.

In chapter 9, Franco Rossi discussed the meaning of scorpion-tailed young men and the reigning king's impersonation of a star deity named First Wind-Maize with Obsidian (Hun Ik' Ixiim ti taaj) in the Los Sabios murals of Xultun, Guatemala. The protagonists resemble a full-figure hieroglyph example from the Sepulturas Bench, position E-1, at Copán, Honduras. The idea of stinging with an obsidian eccentric may explain why the image of a scorpion is conflated with the name that incorporates raw materials for stone tools. Rossi suggested that seasonal sacrifices were carried out by the *taaj* priestly sodality related to agricultural success at the end of the dry season. If Rossi's theory is correct, the ritual specialist nature of a *taaj* sodality would imply a tighter focus on and special power directed at materializing time in a culturally particular manner. Moreover, certain office holders were seated through tying or wrapping events, as at the installation of rulers into office, but this evidence has not been demonstrated for the *taaj* order (Saturno et al. 2017, 436). Instead, Rossi in Chapter 9 and earlier, with colleagues (Saturno, Rossi, et al. 2017), has demonstrated correlations between political or religious guilds and their celestial counterparts at Xultun that anchored a hierarchical cosmic polity (Graeber and Sahlins 2017).

In chapter 16, James Doyle described fictive and real time, wherein the artist who carved the stone Platform Panel at Temple XXI in Palenque eloquently expressed immortal myths and mortal histories. The codex-style vessels from the Calakmul region celebrate time at court. This 180-degree departure from the interpretation when some of these vessels were studied in the 1970s that illiterate painters did not know how to write dates correctly follows Michael Coe's (1973) rebuttal. Future residue analysis should assess the contents of these containers because attempts to connect with mythical time may have happened in a number of different ways, including the use of psychotropic substances, entheogens.

## Earth Time

Time and space are centered in community and urban plans at multiple scales, including those connected to land and skyscapes. As Robb (2020, 5) reminds us, earth time is almost always rooted in the materiality of astronomical cycles. From an individual human body in a burial chamber or pit to a larger scale that encompasses the layout of an entire city, directionality and centrality are continually reinforced through patterned placement of objects, buildings, and open spaces. These directions and sightlines refer to horizon-based astronomical principles (Dowd and Milbrath 2015).

In chapter 18, David A. Freidel, Saburo Sugiyama, and Nawa Sugiyama delve into the entrada of Sihyaj K'ahk' in 378 CE. They consider a debate about an alternative timing of this event in which scholars wish to learn when and under what circumstances Teotihuacanos first ventured into the Maya region. The authors describe mounded and compositionally emplaced human offerings within temple mounds. They interpret Burial 24 from Yaxuná in cosmogonic terms and compare it with Burial 6 in the Temple of the Moon at Teotihuacan. Both interments are thought to date to the late fourth century CE.

These examples have a parallel in a primary extended burial recovered from the Citadel at La Quemada in Zacatecas, Mexico. While it postdates the other two examples by several hundred years (ca. 750–800 CE), the concept of orienting, centering, and staging a tableau of an *altepetl* mountain within a mountain temple is a strong thematic link. The interment at La Quemada included a mosaic-encrusted mirror that likely featured one large and four small green obsidian chips surmounting a quincunx diagram of an olla and four goblets over a youth with one severed leg crossed over the other. The dedicatory burial was vertically positioned at the center of the pyramid and the crossed femurs were within 7 centimeters of the central axis. The structure's main staircase was aligned with the winter solstice of December 21, when the shortest day and longest night of the solar year could be anticipated. The excavator, Achim Lelgemann (1999; 2016, 169–173) interpreted the individual at the center of the tableau as Tezcatlipoca's northwest Mexico antecedent, which has associations with mirrors, north, winter, and the night sky. Another burial linked to the Tezcatlipoca cult was recovered at the Hall of the Columns in Alta Vista (Holien and Pickering 1978). These comparisons show that centering or aligning the temple mound to materialize a solar event created symbolically charged cosmoscapes or chronoscapes.

In chapter 4, Kathryn Reese-Taylor, Veronica Vázquez López, Shawn G. Morton, Meghan M. Peuramaki-Brown, Sarah Bednar, F. C. Atasta Flores Esquivel, Debra S. Walker, Armando Anaya Hernández, and Nicholas P. Dunning examine Yaxnohcah processions as a way of bundling space (like bundling time) and fusing time and space to underscore concepts of cosmovision, using the sequence of events across vignettes in the San Bartolo murals as a point of departure. They liken progress through days in directional almanacs to the movement of space and time in other examples, including the Codex Fejérváry-Mayer, the Tudela Codex, Aubin Manuscript No. 20, the Madrid Codex, and the Dresden Codex. Sequences of east, north, west, south, and center describe a quincunx pattern that was used since the Middle Preclassic in the Maya area for processions and burning (Baron 2016b; Guernsey 2010b, 84–85). Recall that four parts around a center is interpreted as completion. This is a model the chapter 4 authors use to interpret the city plan and associated processional routes at Yaxnohcah. Contemporary and traditional practices were juxtaposed along circuits named *tzol peten* (naming places according to the *tzolk'in* 260-day count), and *tzol pictun* (counting land markers that delimit space—surveying owned property). Reese-Taylor and colleagues see the rotation of *regidor* offices during Uayeb at Tekanto, Yucatán, and the placement of statues of K'awiil at Quirigua, Guatemala, as parallel patterns to the rituals at Yaxnohcah that marked time, founded communities, and claimed territory.

In chapter 17, Prudence Rice contrasts the 20-year katun canonical interval that cycled between Classic Xiw katuns 8 Ahau in northwest Yucatán to Postclassic (900–1519 CE) Itzá katuns 11 Ajaw in northeast Yucatán. In chapter 2, David Freidel and Prudence Rice describe structures or communities shaped into animal forms such as the geoglyphs and effigy mounds that are known from other parts of the world. Some of these have been interpreted as having cosmological significance. The early crocodile-shaped gridded layout preserved through nearly three millennia of occupation into the present at Nixtun Ch'ich' is a materialization of Maya creation time. The alignment of the city matches the alignment of the two E Groups (Šprajc 2021a). Recent excavations have shown that a Nixtun Ch'ich' E Group in Sector Y had one-room or larger temples on its platform. The poor preservation of the walls on the eastern Uaxactun-type range structure, however, did not permit identification of the number or size of temple rooms (T. W. Pugh, personal communication, May 2021). The authors of chapter 17 liken the emergence of land in creation to the emergence of rulership. Prudence Rice and Timothy Pugh (2017; Rice et al. 2019) have further argued that this is a place where the sun rose in a play of light and shadow that occurred close to the autumn equinox or three quarter-year mark, when the dawning sun appears to rise out of Fosa Y, a deep natural depression, as observed from the west. This is the height of the rainy season and a time of intense maize cultivation in Petén (Milbrath 1999, 2013, 2017b).

In chapter 3, Takeshi Inomata, Daniela Triadan, Rodrigo Liendo, and Keiko Teranishi explore how building time into place began in the Middle Preclassic and started with broad horizontal expressions of public ritual space. Long rectangular platforms at sites such as Aguada Fénix in 1100 BCE may have held large gatherings of people whose social organization is thought to have mimicked the flatter, hierarchical structure that is congruent with pre-state sociopolitical organization among complex hunter-fisher-gatherer-horticulturalists. Inomata and colleagues hypothesize that vertical hierarchical social divisions and their accompanying temporal worldview were documented in the higher-profile E Group architecture. This interpretation is congruent with the pattern of temples of one room or more in E Groups (religious precincts associated with sky watching) that demonstrate an institutionalization of religion that was characteristic of increasingly hierarchical social organization, particularly in comparison to platforms or mounds that did not have temples that enclosed rooms at their summits (Dowd 2017c, 553). The origins of the Aguada Fénix plaza and center in the context of nearby contemporaneous sites built by the Maya/Chiapas people, who were part of a larger Olmec horizon, provide evidence of a 260-day calendar in place linked to points in the growing season. Analyses of the astronomical orientations of the east-west alignments of the platforms compare favorably to the goal of Maya astronomers of discovering commensurate relationships among calendar periods, astronomical cycles, and nonastronomical cycles (Bricker et al. 2014). Because these data point to a sacred almanac that was established earlier than it appeared in written records, it would also be interesting to learn if or when irrigation systems for staple crop production are first associated with the sites where large elevated platforms are found.

Chapter 5's authors, Travis Stanton, Karl Taube, and Ryan Collins, contrast civilized, domesticated, temporally ordered community centers with wild, chaotic, temporally disorganized peripheries (Turner 1970, 1974, 1982). The theme of zero relates to this chapter because it is a product of an orderly center and possibly functioned to begin/complete the settlement process. Stanton and colleagues theorize that "arrowing" was tantamount to establishing the corners of the central place (see also Baudot 1995, 207).

Community architecture was built first in the form of an E Group at Yaxuná. Stanton and colleagues interpret E Group centers as places where community-founding rituals happened and were repeated to order time and space into four parts. During these rituals, references were also made to a central ancestral mountain, a water source, cave, a fire altar, a maize field, and astronomical (especially solar) movements. Like related discussions in chapters 4 and 12, the authors of chapter 5 provide an overview of processional movements and cargo rotations. In chapter 5, Travis Stanton, Karl Taube, and Ryan Collins describe research on the act of seating Pop as beginning the first month of the year and note how Maya scribes used the logograph *chum* to articulate both the seating day of the month and accession to rulership, another important beginning. Markus Eberl (2015, 85) also discusses the fact that Copán ruler Yax Pasaj is highlighted on the text of the bench in Structure 21a text as seated "*ti* 6 Kaban" or "on 6 Kaban"—in other words in *time,* as opposed to in *office,* as the earlier phrasing of accession statements said: "*chumwan ti ajawlel*" or "(s)he is seated in rulership."

In chapter 6, Francisco Estrada-Belli and David Freidel connect rain, or Chahk, with western temples and sun gods with eastern temples within E Groups. They explore how gnomons may have been used in these standardized ceremonial complexes. A tree trunk post installed during the Middle Preclassic as a single gnomon referencing the World Tree is thought to have showcased the zenith passage of the sun, which is observable May 6–9 and again on August 2–5 at Cival (17° 21′ 30″N, 89° 14′ 59″W). The zenith passage would mark the disappearance of the shadow and literally manifest nothing, zero, or the absence of shadow, a centering of the sun along an axis mundi. Francisco Estrada-Belli and David Freidel also examine the performance known ethnographically among the Totonac of Veracruz and other groups as *los voladores* ("the flyers"; López de Llano 2019). They suggest that one or more masked bird dancers may have been suspended from a rope attached to the pole. A solar bird perched in a World Tree is similar to what is

478 · Anne S. Dowd

seen in the San Bartolo murals. This chapter has points in common with Maria C. Pineda de Carías and colleagues' (2017) study of Stela D as a gnomon in Copán, Honduras. Estrada-Belli and Freidel describe a Late Preclassic set of three posts nearly 1 meter thick possibly referencing "hearth stone" stars in an Orion constellation, which was in the same location at the E Group at Cival and above the earlier gnomon. The posts aligned with solar movement on March 22 and September 21, likely commemorating the quarter days of the year, which fall to within one or two days of the spring or fall equinox.

## Crafting Cosmography

Crafting cosmos by illustrating the spatial relationships among earth, sky, and underworld connected people to the land and the changing seasons. Daykeepers and religious adepts were the craft specialists whose knowledge of mathematics, astronomy, and scientific principles was passed down in educational settings using books, waxed tablets, and plastered walls for drawing and writing. Conveying the rich and vibrant perspectives on how the world worked and the societal values for sustaining moral ideals on proper behavior is part of what has given Maya culture its resiliency over so many generations.

In chapter 8, Anne Dowd and Gabrielle Vail describe a setting for gathering and processing esoteric data, possibly for producing books or preparing rituals, such as making preparations in advance of a ruler who provided nourishment for the gods in the form of maize seeds as part of a period-ending ceremony. Examples of the period-ending dates that may have related to the Balamkú structure could have been 9.8.0.0.0 (603 CE), 9.9.0.0.0 (613 CE), 9.9.5.0.0 (617 CE), or 9.10.0.0.0 (623 CE). The structure was on the north side of the site center. "Sprout-tree-house" is the metaphorical name for lineages (Schele 1992b), and an apotheosis theme is hypothesized at Balamkú, Mexico, and has been interpreted for a building with a similar frieze from Holmul, Guatemala, in which the building is named "*tz'a(h)k/ tz'akab' naah*" (the house of time/sacred bundles/succession/generations) (Estrada-Belli and Tokovinine 2016). Another frieze is known from Chochkitam (Estrada-Belli and Tokovinine 2022). This chapter uses Ian Hodder's analyses of history houses at Çatalhöyük in Turkey as a theoretical point of departure (Hodder 2016; 2018, 23, 25; see also Hodder and Pels 2010). As Franco Rossi does in chapter 9, Dowd and Vail hypothesize that priests were literate craft specialists who were adept at mathematics, astronomy, and tracking time with calendars. Using information from Dowd's drawings of the small codex-style hieroglyphs inside Structure 1A-Sub at Balamkú,

Dowd and Vail present the broader implications of scribes working inside buildings with blackboard-like wall texts to explore literacy and specialist training at 550–650 CE (fig. 19.6).

In chapter 11, M. Kathryn Brown, Leah McCurdy, and Jason Yaeger describe Structure A-5-2nd at Xunantunich, Belize, which has a calibrated radiocarbon date of 676–774 CE, as a school associated with the residential and Group C complex south of El Castillo, where over 480 images have been identified on exterior and interior walls or floor surfaces. These have been analyzed using reflectance transformation imaging. Brown and colleagues interpret these images as pedagogical tools, suggesting that the walls were used as drawing surfaces for educating youth and passing on sacred knowledge to them. An interesting potential connection with Adolfo Batún-Alpuche and David Freidel's work in chapter 15 is the find of a small slate tablet in the south-central room in Structure A-5-2nd with an incised glyph or pseudo-glyph on its surface. Batún-Alpuche and Freidel argue that tablets may have functioned as devices for writing. Another hieroglyph, translated as *[i]tz'a-ta*, or *itz'at* (alternate spelling *itz'aat*), meaning "wise man" or "sage," was identified on a room wall, supporting the authors' interpretation of this structure as

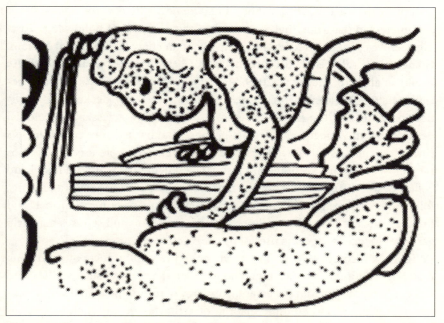

Figure 19.6. Woman scribe from polychrome vessel K6020. Source: Kerr (1997, 823), drawing by Markus Eberl.

480 · Anne S. Dowd

a school for young nobles. A possible comparative example of a men's house, Structure XIX, was excavated at Calakmul (Dowd 1995).

In chapter 1, Arlen Chase, Anne Dowd, David Freidel, and Jerry Murdock focus on the idea of Maya space-time, comparing it to western thought on theories of temporal relativity and charting the book's unveiling of community building, knowledge transfer, kingship, and a Maya life of the mind. Like the E Groups, many early ceremonial centers were associated with nighttime astronomical skywatching functions in the lowland Maya zone. Orientations of large early (1400–750 BCE) platforms with some along an east-of-north axis are found throughout Chiapas and the Gulf Coast of Mexico. Central sunken courts at Tiwanaku and other South American sites also had a nocturnal place-making role for observing the Mayu, a celestial river akin to the Milky Way, and Yacana, a llama-shaped dark cloud constellation with the stars Alpha and Beta Centauri as the llama's eyes (Urton 1981a, 1981b; Vranich and Smith 2016). These standardized ceremonial complexes suggest processes of religious and political institutionalization comparable to that found in the Maya region.

Adolfo Iván Batún-Alpuche and David Freidel build on Batún-Alpuche's original research on apiaries in the Yucatán of Mexico in chapter 15 to open the door to future analyses of this understudied industry centered on the island of Cozumel. The identification of *maktuuno'b'*, circular stone disks 10–12 centimeters in diameter, that were used to plug the ends of hollow logs hosting beehives, is supported by the discovery of an effigy beehive from Nakum, Guatemala (Źrałka et al. 2014; Bianco et al. 2017, 95; Paris et al. 2018, 8–10; Źrałka et al. 2018; Rice et al. 2019, 561) and the disks' associations with specialized stone beekeeping structures. The time range for beekeeping activities spans at least the Late Preclassic through the Postclassic and colonial periods. Batún-Alpuche and Freidel propose that backed wax-coated tablets (including mirrors, shallow plates, and writing boards) were used for temporary, erasable record keeping with a stylus, following the work of Freidel and colleagues in 2016. This technique may have been used to tally trade items, following a suggestion by Michael Coe (personal communication to David Freidel). The use of residue analyses on mirror surfaces and styluses may help garner evidence for specific uses of beeswax in these contexts.

There is theoretical value in studying the practical aspects of producing materials relating to timekeeping and associated activities: such studies lead to a deeper understanding of an anthropology of technology—the social, economic, religious, and cultural shaping of artifacts and production systems (Pfaffenberger 1988; Lemonnier 1992, 2018). For example, the location of mirror elements in settings that were used for rituals related to prognostication, divination, or other religious activities is evidence for assigning many of these artifacts to sacred rather than mundane roles, at least for certain social groups. Counting with tokens or by notation may have bridged ritual and economic spheres. For example, see Prudence Rice's (2015) innovative analysis of the Las Bocas mirror as a reflective, calendrical, or abacus-like calculation device.[6] A recent chapter on stick counters that signified five is also worthy of mention (Tokovinine 2020).

In cosmological imagery, portals, depicted as mirrors, caves, pools, or decorated four-part frames, penetrated below the earth's surface to a shadowy inverted watery realm or reached toward the sky to a flowery solar bower along a centered axis mundi to access deep time. Recall that a three-petaled flower is one way the Maya wrote zero: a portal with a fourth invisible petal. One might speculate that a negative space between materialized realms is represented. Mirrors may have had absence-like qualities if zero is conceived of as a space in time. Whether mirrors provided writing surfaces or reflections, directed the viewer up through the heavens or down beneath the earth, provided insight into the soul or revealed what is sacred, they were powerful instruments for human perception. This quality of reflecting and recording new information pertaining to an alternate or supernatural reality—akin to metaphorical mirroring, or chiasmus, a feature of poetry that inverts the order of elements of syntax—has shaped Mesoamerican thought and culture in profound ways (Dowd 2018a).

## Summary

David Krakauer (2019), the current Santa Fe Institute (SFI) president, has eloquently articulated his program's goal regarding time: "We are very interested in partnering with individuals or laboratories or institutions that have highly resolved temporal data, that contain some signature of the arrows of time. . . . For example . . . what is the relationship between the perception of time and the structure of our society?"[7] This volume has explored complex time. The authors have sought to identify examples of how Maya people materialized time. In doing so, they have made a major discovery: before sedentary agricultural life became the norm, pre-Maya, mixed-economy mobile communities formed centers where populations congregated in religious precincts that were laid out according to calendar principles and marked horizon-based astronomical observations of sunrise and sunset measured in calendar units from the passage of the sun. These centers persisted for over 2,000 years (1000 BCE to 1000 CE). This new work sheds light on the origins of urban life and centralization in ways that were not appreciated before SFI sponsored the

Maya Working Group's synergistic research over the past decade (see Sabloff 1986; Sabloff and Marcus 2008; and Sabloff and Sabloff 2018 for additional research directions SFI has pursued).

When sedentism took hold and political and religious institutions developed to support specialists, Maya material expressions of calendar development and time records were shown in codices and on building walls in rooms where daykeepers authored books and planned ceremonies (or trained colleagues to do so) and were encoded in patterned building alignments oriented with the rise and set of astronomical bodies on the horizon, principally the sun. Astronomer-mathematicians were the agents behind innovations in counting, recording, and refining diurnal, seasonal, and planetary cycles of time. Excellent preservation, for example at Xultun, Guatemala; Balamkú, Mexico; and, Xunantunich, Belize, has provided scholars with biographical information about these Indigenous scientists, elevated members of Maya society, who achieved prestige and recognition for their numerological skills, which included the independent invention of what we now refer to as "big data" in their use of large units of time. Our SFI working group research and publications contribute to cross-cultural understandings of science, technology, engineering, and math. Ideas such as the concept of a zero-like null placeholder or numerical equivalent, which the Maya had invented independently by 357 CE, demonstrate the rich intellectual life Maya mathematicians claimed.

Maya thought and culture exemplify expressions that connect earth time to the materiality of the human body (Aveni and Brotherston 1983; López Austin 1988; Aveni 1989, 1998, 2006, 2015, 2021; Justeson 2010, 45). At small scales, the Maya related time to numbers of human digits, signals hands make, the length of time required to grow a fetus, a human generation, or a human lifespan. At medium scales, they connected time to annual seasons and diurnal day or night patterns on Earth. At large scales, they related time to the movements of astronomical bodies along the horizon over multiple generations in the context of the universe. In circumstances where social structure supported the activities of specialists, they made predictions about broader patterns, including eclipses, and relationships among other astronomical bodies emerged as part of the process of crafting sophisticated calendars. Through the staging of burials and the creation of geoglyphs, earth art, effigy mounds, and city plans—as well as standardized ceremonial complexes with skywatching functions—architects of time connected people with the places where they lived.

Maya rulers re-created the universe to replace, reaffirm, and reestablish cosmographic principles such as majesty, authority, or *k'awiil* at period endings (Helmke and Awe 2016a, 14). These processes addressed the concept of zero, null, lacking, or absence. Consider the term *ch'ab'-ak'ab,* which is glossed as "removed is creation, removed is darkness," describing the inchoate obscure liminality prior to world illumination through a ruler's efforts (Nájera Coronado 2019, 7). The story of creation is frequently recounted as a time when no light, no land, no plants, no people, and no animals existed. Therefore, to begin or recharge a community through ritual meant replacing nothing with everything. As the contributions of this volume on materializing time show, the Maya crafted landesque cosmographies and imprinted their collective cosmovision in the archaeological record of the past through concepts of null, zero, and absence merged with wrapping, bundling, and completing units of time.

## Acknowledgments

Jerry A. Sabloff's able leadership has steered the Maya Working Group along a productive course for ten years. For this reason, it is appropriate that we dedicate this volume to him, with our sincere appreciation. I would also like to thank our talented volume contributors. This chapter has significantly benefited from the astute comments of my coeditors, David Freidel and Arlen Chase. John Justeson commented on the text and carefully explained his research on the Maya concept of a zero-like null unit, calendar development, and numerical literacy. Anthony Aveni commented on the epilogue and has patiently guided my explorations in cultural astronomy. I thank Ramón Carrasco Vargas, who invited me to join the archaeological team Proyecto Arqueológico de la Biosfera de Calakmul, which supported documentation of the façade of Structure 1A-Sub at Balamkú through a subproject led by Claude-François Baudez. The Eben Demarest Trust has funded my work on Balamkú. Jerry Murdock has sponsored the series of SFI working groups reported on here, which has given us time, a very precious commodity, to think through complex ideas. David Krakauer has provided strong and consistent institutional support.

## Notes

1 According to John Justeson (personal communication, April 25, 2022), it is not clear that Epi-Olmec mathematicians had a practice relating to zero or to absence because none of the eight known Epi-Olmec long counts has or calls for a zero digit. This is a very small sample size and is not evidence that they did not have a placeholder or a zero construct. The chance of missing 0 in all four trailing digits is $17/18 \times 19/20^3 \approx$ 0.80974. This means because we have only eight expressed Epi-Olmec long counts, the chance of missing a zero digit if it had been in use would be 18.48 percent and it

would take $k = 15$ long counts or more for $0.80974^k$ for the absence to be statistically significant at the 0.05 level.

2  Eric Boot (2009, 224) interprets nothing, "zero," as *mih*, *mi*.

3  Stela 19 at Uaxactun is an innovation related to rulership, expressed in the T533AM1 *'ajaw* "Lord, Ruler" logogram (Mora-Marin 2021).

4  Zero is also shown in Xultun calligraphic writing as PET, possibly translated as totality or grouping (Stuart 2012):

> One alternative I have considered regarding the forms of the Xultun zeroes is that they are calligraphic variants of the very similar-looking logogram read PET, a sign deciphered many years ago by Nikolai Grube. This root, meaning "circular" in proto-Ch'olan, appears in a variety of settings in the inscriptions, such as PET-ne, *peten* (island), or the verb written PET-ta-ja, *pet-aj* (become round or be encircled). It is interesting to note that in the *Calepino Motul* dictionary of colonial Yucatec, *pet* is the basis of a derived noun *petel* meaning "totality" or "grouping." Conceivably this might be an appropriate marker for a number position that has reached its totality. However, I prefer for now to see the Xultun zeroes simply as calligraphic forms derived from the more complex and familiar sign of the stone inscriptions.

5  John Justeson (2010, 45) discusses how container metaphors are prevalent in higher-number semantic bases for words like 400 or 8,000: "Even some less widely distributed words for '20' were derived from words for containers; a semantically distinct but related case is Mayan *tahb'* 'tumpline', which is used in carrying a bundle." The container term in Zoque, Zapotec, Nahua, and early Ch'olan for "duffel bag" (meaning a closed-up skirt) was used to describe storage bags for cacao kernels and was the source for the highest numerical unit, 8,000.

6  It is difficult to resist comparing the mirrored tablets so frequently found with decorated backs to the cases available today for smart phones and tablets. The iridescent reflective surfaces of smart devices, the fact that users employ a special text language to communicate with formerly unseen but now more often visible colleagues, the mirror or light source properties that are used for selfies and flashlights, the undeniable prestige value of these cases, and the concept of planning for the future with internet, calculator, and calendar features are points of comparison with the social roles of iron ore, mica, mother-of-pearl, and obsidian mirrors—and later, gold, copper, or tin and mercury coatings for glass mirrors.

7  Complex Time: A SFI/JSMF Research Theme, YouTube video, 2019, https://www.santafe.edu/research/themes/complex-time.

# References

Acuña, Mary Jane. 2013. Art, Ideology, and Politics at El Achiotal: A Late Preclassic Frontier Site in Northwestern Petén, Guatemala. PhD diss., Graduate School of Arts and Sciences of Washington University in St. Louis.

Acuña Smith, Mary Jane. 2014. Royal Death, Tombs, and Cosmic Landscapes: Early Classic Maya Tomb Murals from Río Azul, Guatemala. *Maya Archaeology* 3: 168–185.

Adams, Robert M., Jr. 1953. Some Small Ceremonial Structures at Mayapán. *Carnegie Institution of Washington Current Reports* 9: 144–179.

Agrinier, Pierre. 1975. *Mound 1A, Chiapa de Corzo, Chiapas, Mexico: A Late Preclassic Architectural Complex*. Papers of the New World Archaeological Foundation vol. 37. New World Archaeological Foundation, Brigham Young University, Provo, Utah.

———. 2000. *Mound 27 and the Middle Preclassic Period at Mirador, Chiapas, Mexico*. Papers of the New World Archaeological Foundation, no. 58, Brigham Young University, Provo, Utah.

Aguilera, Carmen. 1989. Templo Mayor: Dual Symbol of the Passing of Time. In *The Imagination of Matter: Religion and Ecology in Mesoamerican Traditions,* ed. Davíd Carrasco, 129–135. BAR International Series 515, Oxford.

Agurcia Fasquelle, Ricardo, Payson Sheets, and Karl A. Taube. 2015. *Protecting Sacred Space: Rosalila's Eccentric Chert Cache at Copan and Eccentrics among the Ancient Maya*. San Francisco, CA: Precolumbia Mesoweb Press.

Aimers, James J., and Prudence M. Rice. 2006. Astronomy, Ritual, and the Interpretation of Maya "E-Group" Architectural Assemblages. *Ancient Mesoamerica* 17 (1): 79–96.

Aimi, Antonio, and Raphael Tunesi. 2017. Notas sobre unos nuevos grandes artistas de los Sagrados Hombres de Chatahn. *Glyph Dwellers* 54.

Alcina Franch, José. 1993. *Calendario y Religión entre los Zapotecos*. Universidad Nacional Autónoma de México, Mexico City.

Aldana, Gerardo. 2005. "Agency and the 'Star War' Glyph: A Historical Reassessment of Classic Maya Astrology and Warfare." *Ancient Mesoamerica* 16: 305–320.

Alonso, Ana M. 1994. The Politics of Space, Time and Substance: State Formation, Nationalism, and Ethnicity. *Annual Review of Anthropology* 23 (1): 379–405.

Ames, Kenneth M. 2012. On the Evolution of the Human Capacity for Inequality and/or Egalitarianism. In *Pathways to Power: New Perspectives on the Emergence of Social Inequality,* ed. T. D. Price and Gary M. Feinman, 15–44. New York: Springer.

Anaya Hernández, Armando. 2002. *The Pomoná Kingdom and Its Hinterland*. Report presented to FAMSI, Crystal City, FL.

486 · References

Anaya Hernández, Armando, Meaghan Peuramaki-Brown, and Kathryn Reese-Taylor. 2016. *Proyecto Arqueológico Yaxnohcah, informe de las 2014 y 2015 temporadas de investigaciones*. Report submitted to the Instituto Nacional de Antropología e Historia, Mexico City.

Anaya Hernández, Armando, and Kathryn Reese-Taylor. 2017. *Proyecto Arqueológico Yaxnohcah, informe de la 2016 temporada de investigaciones*. Report submitted to the Instituto Nacional de Antropología e Historia, Mexico City.

Andrews, E. Wyllys, IV. 1943. *The Archaeology of Southwestern Campeche*. Contributions to American Anthropology and History Vol. 8, no. 40, Washington, DC: Carnegie Institution of Washington.

Aoyama, Kazuo, Takeshi Inomata, Flory Pinzón, and Juan Manuel Palomo. 2017. Polished Greenstone Celt Caches from Ceibal: The Development of Maya Public Ritual. *Antiquity* 91 (357): 701–717.

Arano, Diana, Patricia Quintana, Leticia Jiménez, F. Camacho, Y. Espinosa, and J. Reyes. 2020. Chromatic Palette Studies in Sculptural Architectonical Elements of Maya Buildings in the South of Campeche, Mexico. *STAR: Science & Technology of Archaeological Research*, 1–13. https://doi.org/10.1080/20548923.2020.1735144.

Ardren, Traci. 2019. Bark Beaters and Cloth Production in the Classic Maya Area. Paper presented at the 84th Annual Meeting of the Society for American Archaeology, Albuquerque.

Argyle, Craig J., and Richard D. Hansen. 2016. The Preclassic Frieze of the Great Central Acropolis at El Mirador: Resource Allocation and Myth Recounted in Stucco. In *Mirador: Investigación y conservación en el antiguo Reino Kaan. Research and Conservation in the Ancient Kaan Kingdom*, ed. R. Hansen and E. Zuyuc, 131–152. Guatemala City: Perenco, FARES.

Arieta Baizabal, Virginia, and Ann Cyphers. 2017. Densidad Poblacional En La Capital Olmeca De San Lorenzo, Veracruz. *Ancient Mesoamerica* 28 (1): 61–73.

Arnauld, Charlotte, Marie France Fauvet-Berthelet, Dominque Michelet, and Pierre Becquelin. 1998. Balamkú, Campeche, México: Historia del Grupo Sur. In *XI Simposio de Investigaciones Arqueológicas en Guatemala, 1997,* ed. J. P. Laporte and H. Escobedo, 144–161. Guatemala City: Museo Nacional de Arqueología y Etnología.

Arnold, Philip J., III. 1999. Tecomates, Residential Mobility, and Early Formative Occupation in Coastal Lowland Mesoamerica. In *Pottery and People: A Dynamic Interaction,* ed. James M. Skibo, and Gary M. Feinman, 159–170. Salt Lake City: University of Utah Press.

———. 2000. Sociopolitical Complexity and the Gulf Coast Olmecs: A View from the Tuxtla Mountains, Veracruz, Mexico. In *Olmec Art and Archaeology in Mesoamerica,* ed. John E. Clark and Mary E. Pye, 117–135. Washington, DC: National Gallery of Art.

———. 2007. Ceramic Production at La Joya, Veracruz: Early Formative Techno Logics and Error Loads. In *Pottery Economics in Mesoamerica,* ed. C. A. Pool and G. J. Bey III, 86–113. Tucson: University of Arizona Press.

———. 2009. Settlement and Subsistence among the Early Formative Gulf Olmec. *Journal of Anthropological Archaeology* 28: 397–411.

Arzápalo Marín, Ramón. 1995. *Calepino de Motul*. Mexico City: Instituto de Investigaciones Antropológicas, Dirección General de Asuntos del Personal Académico UNAM.

Asensio y Toledo, José María, ed. 1900. *Relaciones histórico-geográficas de las provincias de Yucatán*. Vol. 2. Madrid: Tip. "sucesores de Rivadeneyra."

Ashmore, Wendy. 1991. Site-Planning Principles and Concepts of Directionality Among the Ancient Maya. *Latin American Antiquity* 2 (3): 199–226.

———. 1992. Deciphering Maya Architectural Plans. In *New Theories on the Ancient Maya,* ed. Elin C. Danien and Robert J. Sharer, 173–184. University Museum Monograph 77. Philadelphia: The University Museum, University of Pennsylvania.

———. 2002. "Decisions and Dispositions": Socializing Spatial Archaeology. *American Anthropologist* 104 (4): 1172–1183.

———. 2015. Lived Experiences of Space, Time, and Cosmovision. *Cambridge Archaeological Journal* 25 (1): 293–297.

Ashmore, Wendy, and Jeremy A. Sabloff. 2000. El orden de espacio en los planes cívicos mayas. In *Arquitectura e ideología de los antiguos mayas: Memoria de la Segunda Mesa Redonda de Palenque,* ed. S. Tejo, 15–34. Instituto Nacional de Antropología e Historia, Mexico City.

———. 2002. Spatial Orders in Maya Civic Plans. *Latin American Antiquity* 13: 201–215.

———. 2003. Interpreting Ancient Maya Civic Plans: Reply to Smith. *Latin American Antiquity* 14: 229–236.

Aveni, Anthony. 1989. *Empires of Time: Calendars, Clocks, and Cultures*. New York: Basic Books.

———. 1998. Time. In *Critical Terms for Religious Studies,* ed. M. Taylor, 314–333. Chicago: University of Chicago Press.

———. 2000. Out of Teotihuacan: Origins of the Celestial Canon in Mesoamerica. In *Mesoamerica's Classic Heritage,* ed. David Carrasco, Lindsay Jones, and Scott Sessions, 253–268. Boulder: University of Colorado Press.

———. 2001. *Skywatchers: A Revised and Updated Version of Skywatchers of Ancient Mexico*. Austin: University of Texas Press.

———. 2003. Archaeoastronomy in the Ancient Americas. *Journal of Archaeological Research*. 11 (2): 149–191.

———. 2006. *Uncommon Sense: Understanding Nature's Truths Across Time and Culture*. Boulder: University Press of Colorado.

———. 2011. Maya Numerology. *Cambridge Archaeological Journal* 21 (2): 187–216.

———. 2021. *Creation Stories: Landscapes and the Human Imagination*. New Haven, CT: Yale University Press.

———. n.d. Introduction to Mesoamerican Mathematics. *Mesolore*. http://mesolore.org/scholars/lectures/19/Mesoamerican-Mathematics-by-Anthony-Aveni.

Aveni, Anthony F. editor. 2015. *The Measure and Meaning of Time in Mesoamerica and the Andes*. Washington, DC: Dumbarton Oaks Research Library and Collection.

Aveni, Anthony F., and G. Brotherston, eds. 1983. *Calendars in Mesoamerica and Peru: Native Computations of Time*. British Archaeological Reports, International Series, No. 174. Oxford, UK.

Aveni, Anthony F., Edward E. Calnek, and Horst Hartung. 1988. Myth, Environment and the Orientation of the Templo Mayor of Tenochtitlan. *Antiquity* 53 (2): 287–309.

Aveni, Anthony F., and Anne S. Dowd. 2017. E Groups, Astronomy, Alignments, and Maya Cosmology. In *Maya E Groups: Calendars, Astronomy, and Urbanism in the Early*

488 · References

*Lowlands,* ed. David A. Freidel, Arlen F. Chase, Anne S. Dowd, and J. Murdock, 75–94. Gainesville: University Press of Florida.

Aveni, Anthony, Anne S. Dowd, and Benjamin Vining. 1978. Astronomy in Ancient Mesoamerica. In *In Search of Ancient Astronomies,* ed. E. Krupp, 165–202. New York: Doubleday.

——. 2003. Maya Calendar Reform? Evidence from Orientations of Specialized Architectural Assemblages. *Latin American Antiquity* 14 (2): 159–178.

Aveni, Anthony, and Horst Hartung. 1986. *Maya City Planning and the Calendar.* Philadelphia: American Philosophical Society.

——. 1989. Uaxactun, Guatemala, Group E and Similar Assemblages: Archaeoastronomical Reconsideration. In *World Archaeoastronomy,* ed. Anthony Aveni, 441–461. Cambridge: Cambridge University Press.

——. 2000. Water, Mountain, Sky: The Evolution of Site Orientations in Southeastern Mesoamerica. In *Chalchihuitl in Quetzalli = Precious Greenstone, Precious Feather: Mesoamerican Studies in Honor of Doris Heyden,* ed. Eloise Quiñones Keber, 55–65. Lancaster: Labyrinthos.

Aveni, Anthony F., Horst Hartung, and Beth Buckingham. 1978. The Pecked Cross Symbol in Ancient Mesoamerica. *Science* 202: 267–269.

Aveni, Anthony F., Stephen J. Morandi, and Polly A. Peterson. 1995. The Maya Number of Time: Intervalic Time Reckoning in the Maya Codices. *Archaeoastronomy: Supplement to the Journal for the History of Astronomy* 20:S1–S28 (Part 1); 21:S1–S32 (Part II).

Aveni, Anthony F., William A. Saturno, and David Stuart. 2013. Astronomical Implications of Maya Hieroglyphic Notations at Xultun. *Journal for the History of Astronomy* 44: 1–16.

Awe, Jaime J., Nikolai Grube, and David Cheetham. 2009. Cahal Pech Stela 9: A Preclassic Monument from the Belize Valley. *Research Reports in Belizean Archaeology* 6: 179–189.

Bachand, Bruce R., and Lynneth S. Lowe. 2012. Chiapa de Corzo's Mound 11 Tomb and the Middle Formative Olmec. In *Arqueología Reciente de Chiapas: Contribuciones del Encuentro Celebrado en el 60o Aniversario de la Fundación Arqueológica Nuevo Mundo,* ed. Lynneth S. Lowe and Mary E. Pye, 45–68. Provo, UT: Brigham Young University.

Bachand, Bruce R., Lynneth S. Lowe, and Emiliano Gallaga Murieta. 2008. Un Reencuentro con Chiapa de Corzo: Rescatando y Aumentando los Datos de un Centro Mayor Mesoamericano. Paper Presented at the Simposio De Arqueología Guatemalteca, Guatemala.

Badillo, Melissa. 2021. Investigating Ancient Maya Late Postclassic Period Households and the Associated Function of Buildings at Santa Rita Corozal, Belize. PhD diss., University of Nevada, Las Vegas.

Baines, John, and Norman Yoffee. 1998. Order, Legitimacy, and Wealth in Ancient Egypt and Mesopotamia. In *Archaic States,* ed. Gary M. Feinman and Joyce Marcus, 199–260. School of American Research Press, Santa Fe.

Banning, E. B. 2011. So Fair a House: Göbekli Tepe and the Identification of Temples in the Pre-Pottery Neolithic of the Near East. *Current Anthropology* 52 (5): 619–660.

Bardawil, Lawrence. 1976. The Principal Bird Deity in Maya Art: An Iconographic Study of Form and Meaning. In *The Art, Iconography, and Dynastic History of Palenque, Part III: Proceedings of the Segunda Mesa Redonda de Palenque, December 14–21, 1974—Palenque,* ed. Merle Greene Robertson, 195–209. Pebble Beach, CA: Precolumbian Art Research Institute, Robert Louis Stevenson School.

Barnard, Alan, and James Woodburn. 1988. Property, Power and Ideology in Hunter-Gathering Societies: An Introduction. In *Hunters and Gatherers,* vol. 2, *Property, Power and Ideology,* ed. Timothy Ingold, David Riches and James Woodburn, 4–32. Oxford: Berg.

Baron, Joanne P. 2006. *Patron Gods and Patron Lords: The Semiotics of Classic Maya Community Cults.* University Press of Colorado, Boulder.

———. 2016a. Patron Deities and Politics among the Classic Maya. In *Political Strategies in Pre-Columbian Mesoamerica,* ed. Sarah Kurnick, and Joanne Baron, 121–152. Boulder: University Press of Colorado.

———. 2016b. *Patron Gods and Patron Lords: The Semiotics of Classic Maya Community Cults.* Boulder: University Press of Colorado.

Barrera Vásquez, Alfredo. 1980. *Diccionario Maya Cordemex: Maya-Español, Español-Maya.* Mexico City: Editorial Porrua.

———. 1991. *Diccionario Maya, Maya-Español, Español Maya.* Mexico City: Editorial Porrua.

———. 1984. *Documento n. 1 del deslinde de tierras en Yaxkukul, Yucatan.* Mexico City: Instituto Nacional de Antropología e Historia, Centro Regional del Sureste.

Bassie-Sweet, Karen. 2008. *Maya Sacred Geography and the Creator Deities.* Norman: University of Oklahoma Press.

Bassie-Sweet, Karen, and Nicholas A. Hopkins. 2021. Predatory Birds of the Popol Vuh. In *The Myths of the Popol Vuh in Cosmology, Art and Ritual,* ed. Holley Moyes, Allen Christensen, and Frauke Sachse, 222–248. Louisville, CO: University Press of Colorado.

Battles, Matthew. 2015. *Palimpsest: A History of the Written Word.* New York: W. W. Norton & Company.

Batún-Alpuche, Adolfo Iván. 2004. *Maya Settlement Patterns and Land Use in Buena Vista, Cozumel, México.* Report on file at the Foundation for the Advancement of Mesoamerican Studies, Inc. (FAMSI), Crystal River, Florida.

Batún-Alpuche, Adolfo Iván, Patricia A. McAnany, and Maia Dedrick. 2017. Tiempo y Paisaje en Tahcabo. *Arqueología Mexicana* 25 (145): 66–71.

Baudez, Claude-François. 1994. *Maya Sculpture of Copan: The Iconography.* Norman: University of Oklahoma Press.

———. 1996. La Casa de los Cuatro Reyes de Balamkú. *Arqueología Mexicana* 3 (18): 36–41.

Baudot, Georges. 1995. *Utopia and History in Mexico: The First Chroniclers of Mexican Civilization (1520–1569).* Boulder: University Press of Colorado.

Bayliss, Alex. 2015. Quality in Bayesian Chronological Models in Archaeology. *World Archaeology* 47 (4): 677–700.

Becker, Marshall. 1979. Priests, Peasants, and Ceremonial Centers: The Intellectual History of a Model. In *Maya Archaeology and Ethnohistory,* ed. Norman Hammond and Gordon R. Willey, 3–20. Austin: University of Texas Press.

———. 1992. Burials as Caches; Caches as Burials: A New Interpretation of the Meaning

490 · References

of Ritual Deposits among the Classic Period Lowland Maya. In *New Theories on the Ancient Maya,* ed. Elin C. Danien and Robert J. Sharer, 185–196. University Museum Monograph 77. Philadelphia: The University Museum, University of Pennsylvania.

Becquelin, Pierre, Dominique Michelet, Charlotte Arnauld, and Eric Taladoire. 1996. *Proyecto de investigación arqueológica Del Clásico Temprano al Clásico Receinte en Balamku (Hopelchen, Campeche).* Report of the field work carried out from February 5 to March 29, 1996, presented by CEMCA to the Instituto Nacional de Antropología e Historia, México, D.F.

Beetz, Carl P., and Linton Satterthwaite. 1981. *The Monuments and Inscriptions of Caracol, Belize.* University Museum Monograph 45. Philadelphia: The University Museum, University of Pennsylvania.

Beliaev, Dmitri D. 2004. Wayaab' Title in Maya Hieroglyphic Inscriptions: On the Problem of Religious Specialization in Classic Maya Society. In *Maya Religious Practices: Processes of Change and Adaptation,* ed. Daniel Graña Behrens, Nikolai Grube, Christian Prager, Frauke Sachse, Stefanie Teufel, and Elisabeth Wagner, 121–130. Acta Mesoamericana 14. Markt Schwaben: Verlag Anton Saurwein.

Beliaev, Dmitri D., Albert Davletshin, and Sergei Vepretskii. 2018. New Glyphic Appellatives of the Rain God. In *Tiempo detenido, tiempo suficiente: Ensayos y narraciones mesoamericanistas en homenaje a Alfonso Lacadena García-Gallo,* ed. Harri Kettunen, Verónica Amellali Vázquez López, Felix Kupprat, Cristina Vidal Lorenzo, Gaspar Muñoz Cosme, and María Josefa Iglesias Ponce de León, 351–371. Couvin: WAYEB

Beliaev, Dmitri, and Stephen Houston. 2020. A Sacrificial Sign in Maya Writing. *Maya Decipherment: Ideas on Ancient Maya Writing and Iconography,* June 20. https://mayadecipherment.com/2020/06/20/a-sacrificial-sign-in-maya-writing/.

Bell, Ellen E., Robert J. Sharer, Loa P. Traxler, David W. Sedat, Christine W. Carrelli, and Lynn A. Grant. 2004. Tombs and Burials in the Early Classic Acropolis at Copan. In *Understanding Early Classic Copan,* ed. Ellen E. Bell, Marcello A. Canuto, and Robert J. Sharer, 131–158. Philadelphia: University of Pennsylvania Museum of Archaeology and Anthropology.

Bennett, Jane. 2010. *Vibrant Matter: A Political Ecology of Things.* Durham, NC: Duke University Press.

Berdan, Frances F. 2014. *Aztec Archaeology and Ethnohistory.* New York: Cambridge University Press.

Berlin, Brent, Dennis E. Breedlove, and Peter H. Raven. 1974. *Principles of Tzeltal Plant Classification: An Introduction to the Botanical Ethnography of a Mayan-Speaking People of Highland Chiapas.* New York: Academic Press.

Berlin, Heinrich. 1967. The Calendar of the Tzotzil Indians. In *The Civilizations of Ancient America: Selected Papers of the 29th International Congress of Americanists,* ed. Sol Tax, 155–164. New York: Cooper Square Publishers.

Berlin, Heinrich, and David Kelley. 1961. *The 819-Day Count and Color-Direction Symbolism among the Classic Maya.* Middle American Research Series 26. New Orleans, LA: Middle American Research Institute, Tulane University.

Berlo, Janet C. 1992. Icons and Ideologies at Teotihuacan: The Great Goddess Reconsidered.

In *Art, Ideology, and the City of Teotihuacan,* ed. Janet C. Berlo 129–168. Washington, DC: Dumbarton Oaks.

Bernal, Ignacio. 1969. *The Olmec World.* Translated from the Spanish edition by Doris Heyden and Fernando Horcasitas. Berkeley: University of California Press.

Bernal, Stephen Castillo. 2014. La Lítica Tallada De Moral-Reforma, Tabasco: Primeros Acercamientos. *Arqueología* 47: 160–181.

Bernal Romero, Guillermo. 2014. El fuego, el taladro y el tlacuache. Ritos de *Joch K'ahk'* y otras ceremonias de fuego en el Clásico. *Arqueología Mexicana* 128: 66–71.

———. 2016. The 63-Day Cycle in Maya Culture: Discovery of a New Calendric Factor. In *The Role of Archaeoastronomy in the Maya World: The Case Study of the Island of Cozumel,* ed. UNESCO Office Mexico, 111–123. Paris: The United Nations Educational, Scientific and Cultural Organization and Mexico City: UNESCO Office.

Bey, George J., III, Tara M. Bond, William M. Ringle, Craig A. Hanson, Charles W. Houck, and Carlos Peraza Lope. 1998. The Ceramic Chronology of Ek Balam, Yucatan, Mexico. *Ancient Mesoamerica* 9: 101–120.

Bianco, B., R. T. Alexander, and G. Rayson. 2017. Beekeeping Practices in Modern and Ancient Yucatán. In *The Value of Things: Prehistoric to Contemporary Commodities in the Maya Region,* ed. J. P. Mathews, and T. H. Guderjan, 87–103. Tucson: University of Arizona Press.

Bierhorst, John. 1988. *The Mythology of Mexico and Central America.* Oxford: Oxford University Press.

———. 1992. *History and Mythology of the Aztecs: Codex Chimalpopoca.* Tucson: University of Arizona Press.

Bill, Cassandra. 1997. The Roles and Relationships of God M and Other Black Gods in the Codices, with Specific Reference to Pages 50–56 of the Madrid Codex. In *Papers on the Madrid Codex,* ed. Victoria Bricker and Gabrielle Vail, 111–145. New Orleans, LA: Middle American Research Institute.

Bill, Cassandra R., Christine L. Hernández, and Victoria R. Bricker. 2000. The Relationship between Early Colonial Maya New Year's Ceremonies and Some Almanacs in the *Madrid Codex. Ancient Mesoamerica* 11: 149–168.

Bintliff, John, ed. 1991. *The Annales of School and Archaeology.* Leicester: Leicester University Press.

Bíró, Péter. 2003. The Inscriptions on Two Lintels of Ikil and the Realm of Ek' Bahlam. Unpublished paper. www.mesoweb.com/features/biro/Ikil.pdf.

———. 2005. Sak Tz'i' in the Classic Period Hieroglyphic Inscriptions. *Mesoweb Publications.* http://www.mesoweb.com/articles/biro/SakTzi.pdf.

———. 2012. The Non-Existent May Cycle: Methods, Colonial Texts and Epigraphy. *Journal de la Société des américanistes* 98: 33–57.

———. 2017. A New Teotiwa Lord of the South: K'ahk' Uti' Chan Yopat (578–628 C.E.) and the Renaissance of Copan. *Glyph Dwellers* 57: 1–64.

Blake, Michael. 1991. An Emerging Formative Chiefdom at Paso De La Amada, Chiapas, Mexico. In *The Formation of Complex Society in Southeastern Mesoamerica,* ed. William L. Fowler, 27–46. Boca Raton, FL: CRC Press.

———. 2015. *Maize for the Gods: Unearthing the 9,000-Year History of Corn.* University of California Press, Oakland, California.

492 · References

Blake, Michael, John E. Clark, Barbara Voorhies, Michael W. Love, and Brian S. Chisholm. 1992. Prehistoric Subsistence in the Soconusco Region. *Current Anthropology* 33 (1): 83–94.

Bloch, Maurice. 1977. The Past and the Present in the Present. *Man* 12 (2): 278–292.

Blom, Frans. 1933. Maya Books and Sciences. *The Library Quarterly* 3 (4): 408–420.

Blume, Anna. 2011. Maya Concepts of Zero. *Proceedings of the American Philosophical Society* 155 (1): 51–88.

Bolles, David M. 1990. The Mayan Calendar: The Solar-Agricultural Year and Correlation Questions. *Mexicon* 12 (5): 85–89.

———. 2003. *Post Conquest Mayan Literature: Based on Pre-Columbian Sources*. Lancaster, CA: Labyrinthos.

Boone, Elizabeth Hill. 1985. The Color of Mesoamerican Architecture and Sculpture. In *Painted Architecture and Polychrome Monumental Sculpture in Mesoamerica*, ed. E. H. Boone, 173–186. Washington, DC: Dumbarton Oaks.

———. 2007. *Cycles of Time and Meaning in the Mexican Books of Fate*. Austin: University of Texas Press.

Boot, Erik. 2005. *Continuity and Change in Text and Image at Chichén Itzá, Yucatán, Mexico*. Leiden: CNWS Publications.

———. 2008. At the Court of Itzam Nah Yax Kokaj Mut Preliminary Iconographic and Epigraphic Analysis of a Late Classic Vessel. Unpublished paper. http://www.mayavase.com/God-D-Court-Vessel.pdf.

———. 2009. The Updated Preliminary Classic Maya-English, English-Classic Maya Vocabulary of Hieroglyphic Readings. *Mesoweb Publications*. https://www.mesoweb.com/resources/vocabulary/Vocabulary-2009.01.pdf.

———. 2019. The Itza Maya Migration Narratives: Historic Reality, Myth, or . . . Weighing the Idea of Migrations in Light of New Research. In *Migrations in Late Mesoamerica*, ed. Christopher S. Beekman, 241–284. Gainesville: University Press of Florida.

Borstein, Joshua A. 2001. Tripping over Colossal Heads: Settlement Patterns and Population Development in the Upland Olmec Heartland. PhD diss., Pennsylvania State University, University Park.

Boucher, Sylviane, and Sara Dzul Góndora. 2001. Las sequencias constructiva y céramica de la Estructura 1, Plaza B, del Grupo Central de Balamkú, Campeche, Mexico. *Los Investigadores de la Cultura Maya* 9 (1): 40–54.

Boucher, Sylviane, and Yoly Palomo Carillo. 2005. Cerámica del Preclásico Medio y Tardío en depósitos sellados del sitio de Tzubil, Yucatán. *Temas Antropológicos* 27: 153–188.

Bradley, Richard. 1991. Ritual, Time and History. *World Archaeology* 23 (2): 209–219.

———. 1998. *The Significance of Monuments*. London: Routledge.

Braudel, F. 1980. *On History*. Trans. S. Matthews. Chicago: University of Chicago Press.

Brecher, Kenneth, and William G. Haag. 1983. Astronomical Alignments at Poverty Point. *American Antiquity* 48 (1): 161–163.

Bricker, Harvey M., and Victoria R. Bricker. 1992. Zodiacal References in the Maya Codices. In *The Sky in Mayan Literature*, ed. Anthony Aveni, 148–183. Oxford: Oxford University Press.

———. 2007. When Was the Dresden Venus Table Efficacious? In *Skywatching in the*

*Ancient New World: New Perspectives in Cultural Astronomy,* ed. Clive Ruggles and Gary Urton, 95–119. Boulder: University Press of Colorado.

———. 2011. *Astronomy in the Maya Codices.* Philadelphia: American Philosophical Society.

Bricker, Victoria R. 1981. *The Indian Christ, the Indian King: The Historical Substrate of Maya Myth and Ritual.* Austin: University of Texas Press.

———. 2002. Evidencia de Doble Descendencia en las inscripciones de Yaxchilán y Piedras Negras. In *La Organización Social entre los Mayas Prehispánicos, Coloniales y Modernos: Memoria de la Tercera Mesa Redonda de Palenque,* vol. 1, ed. V. Tiesler Blos, R. Cobos, and M. G. Robertson, 125–145. Mexico City: Instituto Nacional de Antropología e Historia and Universidad Autónoma de Yucatán.

Bricker, Victoria, Anthony F. Aveni, and Harvey Bricker. 2014. Deciphering the Handwriting on the Wall: Some Astronomical Interpretations of the Recent Discoveries at Xultun, Guatemala. *Latin American Antiquity* 25 (2): 152–169.

Bricker, Victoria R., and Susan Milbrath. 2011. Thematic and Chronological Ties between Borgia and Madrid Codices Based on Records of Agricultural Pests in the Planting Almanacs. *Journal of Anthropological Research* 67 (4): 497–531.

Bricker, Victoria R., and Gabrielle Vail. 2004. *Haab* Dates in the Madrid Codex. In *The Madrid Codex: New Approaches to Understanding an Ancient Maya Manuscript,* ed. Gabrielle Vail and Anthony F. Aveni, 171–214. Boulder: University Press of Colorado.

Brittenham, Claudia. 2015. *The Murals of Cacaxtla: The Power of Painting in Ancient Central Mexico.* Austin: University of Texas Press.

Broda de Casas, Johanna. 1982. Astronomy, Cosmovision, and Ideology in Pre-Hispanic Mesoamerica. In *Ethnoastronomy and Archaeoastronomy in the American Tropics,* ed. A. F. Aveni and G. Urton, 81–110. New York: New York Academy of Sciences.

———. 1987. Zenith Observations and the Conceptualization of the Geographical Latitude in Ancient Mesoamerica: A Historical Interdisciplinary Approach. In *Viewing the Sky through Past and Present Cultures. Oxford Seventh International Conference on Archaeoastronomy,* ed. T. W. Bostwick and B. Bates, 183–212. Pueblo Grande Museum, Anthropological Papers No. 15. Phoenix, AZ: Pueblo Grande Museum.

Brown, Linda. 2000. From Discard to Divination: Demarcating the Sacred through the Collection and Curation of Discarded Objects. *Latin American Antiquity* 11 (4): 319–333.

———. 2009. Communal and Personal Hunting Shrines around Lake Atitlan, Guatemala. *Maya Archaeology* 1: 36–59.

Brown, Linda, and Payson Sheets. 2000. Distinguishing Domestic from Ceremonial Structures in Southern Mesoamerica: Suggestions from Cerén, El Salvador. *Mayab* 13: 11–21.

Brown, M. Kathryn. 2017. E Groups and Ancestors: The Sunrise of Complexity at Xunantunich, Belize. In *Maya E Groups: Calendars, Astronomy, and Urbanism in the Early Lowlands,* ed. David A. Freidel, Arlen F. Chase, Anne S. Dowd, and Jerry Murdock, 386–411. Gainesville: University Press of Florida.

Brown, M. Kathryn, Jaime J. Awe, and James F. Garber. 2018. The Role of Ideology, Religion, and Ritual in the Foundation of Social Complexity in the Belize River Valley. In *Pathways to Complexity: A View from the Maya Lowlands,* ed. M. Kathryn Brown and George J. Bey III, 87–116. Gainesville: University Press of Florida.

494 · References

Brown, M. Kathryn, and George J. Bey III, eds. 2018. *Pathways to Complexity: A View from the Maya Lowlands*. Gainesville: University Press of Florida.

Brown, M. Kathryn, and Jason Yaeger. 2020. Monumental Landscapes, Changing Ideologies, and Political Histories in the Mopan Valley. In *Approaches to Monumental Landscapes of the Ancient Maya*, ed. B. A. Houk, B. Arroyo, and T. G. Powis, 290–312. Gainesville: University Press of Florida.

Brumley, John H. 1988. *Medicine Wheel on the Northern Plains: A Summary and Appraisal*. Archaeological Survey of Alberta Manuscript Series no. 12. Edmonton: Alberta Culture and Multiculturalism Historical Resources Division.

Brunton, Ron. 1989. The Cultural Instability of Egalitarian Societies. *Man* 24: 673–681.

Buikstra, Jane E., and Douglas K. Charles. 1999. Centering the Ancestors: Cemeteries, Mounds, and Sacred Landscapes in the Ancient North American Midcontinent. In *Archaeologies of Landscape: Contemporary Perspectives,* ed. Wendy Ashmore and A. Bernard Knapp, 201–228. Oxford: Blackwell.

Burger, Richard L., and Lucy C. Salazar. 2012. Monumental Public Complexes and Agricultural Expansion on Peru's Central Coast during the Second Millennium BC. In *Early New World Monumentality,* ed. Richard L. Burger and Robert M. Rosenswig, 399–430. Gainesville: University Press of Florida.

Butler, Judith. 2011. *Bodies that Matter: On the Discursive Limits of Sex*. New York: Taylor & Francis.

Calnek, Edward. 1988. The Calmecac and Telpochcalli in Pre-Conquest Tenochtitlan. In *The Work of Bernardino de Sahagun: Pioneer Ethnographer of the Sixteenth-Century Aztec Mexico,* ed. Jorge J. Klor de Alva, Henry B. Nicholson, and Eloise Quiñones Keber, 169–177. Albany: Institute for Mesoamerican Studies, University at Albany, State University of New York.

Campbell, Paul D. 1992. *The Humbolt Celt: Key to the Lost Olmec World*. Laguna Hills, CA: Aegean Park Press, Laguna Hills.

Canuto, Marcello. 2016. Middle Preclassic Maya Society: Tilting at Windmills or Giants of Civilization. In *The Origins of Maya States,* ed. Loa Traxler and Robert J. Sharer, 461–506. Philadelphia: University Museum, University of Pennsylvania.

Cap, Bernadette. 2012. "Empty" Spaces and Public Places: A Microscopic View of Chan's West Plaza. In *Chan: An Ancient Maya Farming Community,* ed. Cynthia Robin, 150–172. Gainesville: University Press of Florida.

Carballo, David M. 2020. Politics, Power and Governance at Teotihuacan. In *Teotihuacan: The World Beyond the City,* ed. Kenneth G. Hirth, David M. Carballo, and Barbara Arroyo, 57–95. Washington, DC: Dumbarton Oaks.

Carballo, David M., and Gary M. Feinman. 2016. Cooperation, Collective Action, and the Archaeology of Large-Scale Societies. *Evolutionary Anthropology* 25: 288–296.

Carlsen, Robert S. 1997. *The War for the Heart and Soul of a Highland Maya Town*. Austin: University of Texas Press.

Carlsen, Robert S., and Martin Prechtel. 1991. The Flowering of the Dead: An Interpretation of Highland Maya Culture. *Man* 26: 23–42.

Carlson, John. 1991. *Venus-Regulated Warfare and Ritual Sacrifice in Mesoamerica: Teotihuacan and the Cacaxtla "Star Wars" Connection*. Technical Publication 7. College Park, MD: Center for Archaeoastronomy.

————. 1993. Venus-Regulated Warfare and Ritual Sacrifice in Mesoamerica. In *Astronomies and Cultures,* ed. Clive L. N. Ruggles and Nicholas J. Saunders, 202–252. Boulder: University Press of Colorado.

Carlson, John, and Ron Cherry. 1996. Arthropods in Astronomy: Cases in "Western" and Mesoamerican Ethnoentomology. *American Entomologist* 42: 149–158.

Carmean, Kelli, Patricia A. McAnany, and Jeremy A. Sabloff. 2011. People Who Lived in Stone Houses: Local Knowledge and Social Difference in the Classic Maya Puuc Region of Yucatan, Mexico. *Latin American Antiquity* 22 (2): 143–158.

Carnegie Institution of Washington. 1955. *Ancient Maya Paintings of Bonampak Mexico.* Supplemental Publication 46. Richmond, VA: William Byrd Press.

Carr, Robert F., and James E. Hazard. 1961. *Map of the Ruins of Tikal, El Peten, Guatemala.* Philadelphia: University Museum, University of Pennsylvania.

Carrasco, Michael D. 2010. From Field to Hearth: An Earthly Interpretation of Maya and Other Mesoamerican Creation Myths. In *Pre-Columbian Foodways: Interdisciplinary Approaches to Food, Culture, and Markets in Ancient Mesoamerica,* ed. J. E. Staller and M. D. Carrasco, 601–634. New York: Springer.

Carrasco Vargas, Ramón. 2012. Religion. In *Calakmul. Patrimonio de la humanidad,* ed. Regina Martínez Vera, 89–95. Mexico City: Grupo Azabache.

Carrasco Vargas, Ramón, Sylviane Boucher, Paula Alvarez González, Vera Tiesler Blos, Valeria García Vierna, Renata García Moreno, and Javier Vázquez Negrete. 1999. A Dynastic Tomb from Campeche, Mexico: New Evidence on Jaguar Paw, a Ruler of Calakmul. *Latin American Antiquity* 10 (1): 47–58.

Carrasco Vargas, Ramón, Sylviane Boucher, Anne S. Dowd, Armando Paul, Emyly González G., and Maria Elena Garcia. 1994. Informe preliminaire del Proyecto Arqueológico de la Biosfera de Calakmul. Unpublished manuscript on file at the Consejo de Arqueología, Instituto Nacional de Antropología e Historía, Merida, MX.

————. 1995. Informe sobre el Proyecto Arqueológico de la Biosfera de Calakmul. Unpublished manuscript on file at the Consejo de Arqueología, Instituto Nacional de Antropología e Historía, Merida, MX.

Carrasco Vargas, Ramón, Verónica A. Vázquez López, and Simon Martin. 2009. Daily Life of the Ancient Maya Recorded on Murals at Calakmul, Mexico. *Proceedings of the National Academy of Sciences* 46: 19245–19249.

Carson, John Francis, Bronwen S. Whitney, Francis E. Mayle, José Iriarte, Heiko Prümers, J. Daniel Soto, and Jennifer Watling. 2014. Environmental Impact of Geometric Earthwork Construction in Pre-Columbian Amazonia. *Proceedings of the National Academy of Sciences* 111 (29): 10497–10502.

Carter, Nicholas P. 2010. Sources and Scales of Classic Maya History. In *Thinking, Recording, and Writing History in the Ancient World,* ed. Kurt A. Raaflaub, 340–371. Oxford: Wiley-Blackwell.

Carter, Nicholas P., and Jeffery Dobereiner. 2016. Multispectral Imaging of an Early Classic Codex Fragment from Uaxactún, Guatemala. *Antiquity* 90 (351): 711–725.

Casas, Johanna Broda de. 1969. The Mexican Calendar as Compared to Other Mesoamerican Systems. Part of author's diss., Vienna, published in 1967 under title: Der mexikanische Kalender und eine Analyse der Jahresfeste bei Diego Duran.

Cases Martín, Juan Ignacio. 2013. A Sky of Jewels: Cosmographic Elements in the Context

496 · References

of Classic Maya Lunar Series. Paper presented at the 78th Meeting of the Society of American Archaeology, Honolulu.

Caso, Alfonso. 1967. *Los Calendarios Prehispanicos*. Mexico City: Universidad Nacional Autónoma de México.

———. 1971. Calendric Systems of Central Mexico. In *Archaeology of Northern Mesoamerica*, Part 1, ed. Gordon Ekholm and Ignacio Bernal, 333–348. *Handbook of Middle American Indians*, vol. 10. Austin: University of Texas Press.

Castañeda, José Francisco. 2011. Registro Fotogramétrico de la Estela 1 del Perú-Waka'. In *Proyecto Arqueológico Waka': Informe No. 9: Temporada 2011,* ed. Mary Jane Acuña, 40–46. Report delivered to the General Directorate of Cultural and Natural Heritage of Guatemala, Guatemala City.

———. 2014. Operacion Wk17: Excavaciones en la Plaza 2 y Estela 7. In *Proyecto Arqueológico Waka': Informe No. 12: Temporada 2014,* ed. Juan Carlos Pérez, Griselda Pérez, and David Freidel, 85–103. Report delivered to the General Directorate of Cultural and Natural Heritage of Guatemala, Guatemala City.

Catherwood, Fredrick. 1844. *Views of Ancient Monuments of Central America, Chiapas, and Yucatan*. London: F. Catherwood.

Chase, Adrian S. Z. 2021. Urban Life at Caracol, Belize: Neighborhoods, Inequality, Infrastructure, and Governance. PhD diss., Arizona State University, Tempe.

Chase, Arlen F. 1983. A Contextual Consideration of the Tayasal-Paxcaman Zone, El Petén, Guatemala. PhD diss., University of Pennsylvania, Philadelphia.

———. 1986. Time Depth or Vacuum: The 11.3.0.0.0 Correlation and the Lowland Maya Postclassic. In *Late Lowland Maya Civilization: Classic to Postclassic,* ed. J. A. Sabloff and E. W. Andrews V, 99–140. Santa Fe: School for Advanced Research Press.

———. 1991. Cycles of Time: Caracol in the Maya Realm. In *Sixth Palenque Round Table, 1986,* vol. 7, ed. Merle Green Robertson, 32–42. Norman: University of Oklahoma Press.

———. 1994. A Contextual Approach to the Ceramics of Caracol, Belize. In *Studies in the Archaeology of Caracol, Belize,* ed. Diane Z. Chase and Arlen F. Chase, 157–182. Monograph 7. San Francisco: Pre-Columbian Art Research Institute.

———. 2020. Contextualizing the Archaeology of Pacbitun, Belize: An Epilogue. In *An Archaeological Reconstruction of Ancient Maya Life at Pacbitun, Belize,* ed. Terry G. Powis, Sheldon Skaggs, and George J. Micheletti, 201–204. BAR International Series 2970. Oxford: BAR Publishing.

Chase, Arlen F. and Diane Z. Chase. 1987. *Investigations at the Classic Maya City of Caracol, Belize: 1985–1987*. Monograph 3. San Francisco: Pre-Columbian Art Research Institute.

———. 1994. Maya Veneration of the Dead at Caracol, Belize. In Seventh Palenque Round Table, 1989, ed. Merle Green Robertson and Virginia Fields, 55–62. San Francisco: Pre-Columbian Art Research Institute.

———. 1995. External Impetus, Internal Synthesis, and Standardization: E-Group Assemblages and the Crystallization of Classic Maya Society in the Southern Lowlands. *Acta Mesoamericana* 8: 87–101.

———. 2006. Before the Boom: Caracol's Preclassic Era. *Research Reports in Belizean Archaeology* 3: 41–67.

———. 2009. Symbolic Egalitarianism and Homogenized Distributions in the Archaeological Record at Caracol, Belize: Method, Theory, and Complexity. *Research Reports in Belizean Archaeology* 6: 15–24.

———. 2010. The Context of Ritual: Examining the Archaeological Record at Caracol, Belize. *Research Reports in Belizean Archaeology* 7: 3–15.

———. 2011. Status and Power: Caracol, Teotihuacan, and the Early Classic Maya World. *Research Reports in Belizean Archaeology* 8: 3–18.

———. 2012. Complex Societies in the Southern Maya Lowlands: Their Development and Florescence in the Archaeological Record. In *Oxford Handbook of Mesoamerican Archaeology,* ed. Debora L. Nichols and Christopher A. Pool, 255–267. Oxford: Oxford University Press.

———. 2013a. Temporal Cycles in the Archaeology of Maya Residential Groups from Caracol, Belize. *Research Reports in Belizean Archaeology* 10: 13–23.

———. 2013b. Interpreting Form and Context: Ceramic Subcomplexes at Caracol, Nohmul, and Santa Rita Corozal, Belize. In *Ancient Maya Pottery: Classification, Analysis, and Interpretation,* ed. James Aimers, 46–73. Gainesville: University Press of Florida.

———. 2015. A New Terminal Classic Carved Altar from Caracol, Belize. *Mexicon* 37 (2): 47–49.

———. 2016. Urbanism and Anthropogenic Landscapes. *Annual Review of Anthropology* 45: 361–376.

———. 2017a. E Groups and the Rise of Complexity in the Southeastern Maya Lowlands. In *Maya E Groups: Calendars, Astronomy, and Urbanism in the Early Lowlands,* ed. David A. Freidel, Arlen F. Chase, Anne Dowd, and Jerry Murdock, 31–71. Gainesville: University Press of Florida.

———. 2017b. Detection of Maya Ruins by LiDAR: Applications, Case Study, and Issues. *Geotechnologies and the Environment* 16: 455–468.

———. 2017c. Ancient Maya Architecture and Spatial Layouts: Contextualizing Caana at Caracol, Belize. *Research Reports in Belizean Archaeology* 14: 13–22.

———. 2020a. The Materialization of Classic Period Maya Warfare: Caracol Stranger-Kings at Tikal. In *A Forest of History: The Maya after the Emergence of Divine Kingship,* ed. Travis W. Stanton and M. Kathryn Brown, 20–48. Boulder: University Press of Colorado.

———. 2020b. Final Moments: Contextualizing On-Floor Archaeological Materials from Caracol, Belize. *Ancient Mesoamerica* 31 (1): 77–87.

Chase, Arlen F., Diane Z. Chase, Jaime Awe, John Weishampel, Gyles Iannone, Holley Moyes, Jason Yaeger, and M. Kathryn Brown. 2014. The Use of LiDAR in Understanding the Ancient Maya Landscape. *Advances in Archaeological Practice* 2 (3): 208–221.

Chase, Arlen F., Diane Z. Chase, and Adrian S. Z. Chase. 2022. Caracol, Belize and Tikal, Guatemala: Ancient Human-Nature Relationships in Their Socio-Political Context. In *Sustainability and Water Management in the Maya World and Beyond,* ed. Jean Larmon, Lisa Lucero, and Fred Valdez. Boulder: University Press of Colorado.

Chase, Arlen F., Diane Z. Chase, C. T. Fisher, S. J. Leisz, and J. F. Weishampel. 2012. Geospatial Revolution and Remote Sensing LiDAR in Mesoamerican Archaeology.

498 · References

Proceedings of the National Academy of Sciences of the United States of America. 109 (32): 12916–12921.

Chase, Arlen F., Diane Z. Chase, John M. Morris, Jaime J. Awe, and Adrian S. Z. Chase. 2020. Archaeology and Heritage Management in the Maya Area: History and Practice at Caracol, Belize. *Heritage* 3 (2): 436–456.

Chase, Arlen F., Diane Z. Chase, John F. Weishampel, Jason B. Drake, Ramesh L. Shrestha, K. Clint Slatton, Jaime J. Awe, and William E. Carter. 2011. Airborne LiDAR, Archaeology, and the Ancient Maya Landscape at Caracol, Belize. *Journal of Archaeological Science* 38 (2): 387–398.

Chase, Arlen F., Anne S. Dowd, and David A. Freidel. 2017. The Distribution and Significance of E Groups: A Historical Background and Introduction. In *Maya E Groups: Calendars, Astronomy, and Urbanism in the Early Lowlands,* ed. David A. Freidel, Arlen F. Chase, Anne S. Dowd, and Jerry Murdock, 3–30. Gainesville: University Press of Florida.

Chase, Arlen F., Lisa J. Lucero, Vernon Scarborough, Diane Z. Chase, Rafael Cobos, Nicholas Dunning, Joel Gunn, Scott Fedick, Vilma Fialko, Michelle Hegmon, Gyles Iannone, David L. Lentz, Rodrigo Liendo, Keith Prufer, Jeremy A. Sabloff, Joseph Tainter, Fred Valdez Jr., and Sander van der Leeuw. 2014. Tropical Landscapes and the Ancient Maya: Diversity in Time and Space. In *Resilience and Vulnerability of Ancient Landscapes: Transforming Maya Archaeology through IHOPE,* ed. A. F. Chase and V. L. Scarborough, 11–29. Hoboken, NJ: John Wiley & Sons.

Chase, Arlen F., and Prudence M. Rice, eds. 1985. *The Lowland Maya Postclassic.* Austin: University of Texas Press.

Chase, Diane Z. 1985a. Between Earth and Sky: Idols, Images, and Postclassic Cosmology. In *Fifth Palenque Round Table, 1983,* vol. 7, ed. Merle Greene Robertson and Virginia M. Fields, 223–233. San Francisco: Pre-Columbian Art Research Institute.

———. 1985b. Ganned but Not Forgotten: Late Postclassic Archaeology and Ritual at Santa Rita Corozal, Belize. In *The Lowland Maya Postclassic,* ed. Arlen F. Chase and Prudence M. Rice, 104–125. Austin: University of Texas Press.

———. 1986. Social and Political Organization in the Land of Cacao and Honey. In *Late Lowland Maya Civilization,* ed. Jeremy Sabloff and E. Wyllis Andrews, 347–377. Albuquerque: University of New Mexico Press.

———. 1988. Caches and Censerwares: Meaning from Maya Pottery. In *A Pot for All Reasons: Ceramic Ecology Revisited,* ed. Louana Lackey and Charles Kolb, 81–104. Philadelphia: Laboratory of Anthropology, Temple University.

———. 1991. Lifeline to the Gods: Ritual Bloodletting at Santa Rita Corozal. In *Sixth Palenque Round Table, 1986,* ed. Merle Greene Robertson and Virginia M. Fields, 86–96. Norman: University of Oklahoma Press.

———. 1997. Southern Lowland Maya Archaeology and Human Skeletal Remains: Interpretations from Caracol (Belize), Santa Rita Corozal (Belize), and Tayasal (Guatemala). In *Bones of the Maya: Studies of Ancient Skeletons,* ed. Stephen C. Whittington and David M. Reed, 15–27. Washington, DC: Smithsonian Institution Press.

———. 1998. Albergando a los Muertos en Caracol, Belice. *Los Investigadores de la Cultura Maya* 6 (1): 9–25.

Chase, Diane Z., and Arlen F. Chase. 1986. *Offerings to the Gods: Maya Archaeology at Santa Rita Corozal.* Orlando: University of Central Florida.

———. 1988. *A Postclassic Perspective: Excavations at the Maya Site of Santa Rita Corozal, Belize.* Monograph 4. San Francisco: Pre-Columbian Art Research Institute.

———. 1998. The Architectural Context of Caches, Burials, and Other Ritual Activities for the Classic Period Maya (as Reflected at Caracol, Belize). In *Function and Meaning in Classic Maya Architecture,* ed. Stephen D. Houston, 239–332. Washington, DC: Dumbarton Oaks.

———. 2003. Secular, sagrado y revisitado: La profanación, alteración y reconsagración de los antiguos entierros Mayas. In *Antropología de la eternidad: la muerte en la cultura maya,* ed. Andres Ciudad Ruiz, Maria J. Ruz Sosa, and Maria J. Iglesias Ponce de Leon, 255–277. Publicación 7. Madrid: Sociedad de los Estudios Mayas.

———. 2004. Patrones de enterramiento y ciclos residenciales en Caracol, Belice. In *Culto funerario en la sociedad Maya: Memoria de la cuarta mesa redonda de Palenque,* ed. Rafael Cobos, 203–230. Mexico City: Instituto Nacional de Antropología e Historia.

———. 2005. The Early Classic Period at Santa Rita Corozal: Issues of Hierarchy, Heterarchy, and Stratification in Northern Belize. *Research Reports in Belizean Archaeology* 2: 111–129.

———. 2008. Late Postclassic Ritual at Santa Rita Corozal, Belize: Understanding the Archaeology of a Maya Capital City. *Research Reports in Belizean Archaeology* 5: 79–92.

———. 2009. Changes in Maya Religious Worldview: Liminality and the Archaeological Record. In *Maya Worldviews at Conquest,* ed. Leslie G. Cecil and Timothy W. Pugh, 219–237. Boulder: University Press of Colorado.

———. 2010. Rituales mezclados: analizando comportamientos públicos y privados en el Registro Arqueológico de Caracol. In *El ritual en el mundo maya: de lo privado a lo público,* ed. Andres Ciudad Ruiz, Maria J. Iglesias Ponce de Leon, and M. Sorroche, 107–128. Publication 9. Madrid: Sociedad Española de Estudios Mayas; Granada: Grupo de Investigación Andalucía-América; Mérida: Patrimonio Cultural y Relaciones Artísticas (PAI: HUM-806); Yucatán: Centro Peninsular en Humanidades y Ciencias Sociales, UNAM.

———. 2011. Ghosts amid the Ruins: Analyzing Relationships between the Living and the Dead among the Ancient Maya at Caracol, Belize. In *Living with the Dead: Mortuary Ritual in Mesoamerica,* ed. James Fitzsimmons and Izumi Shimada, 78–101. Tucson: University of Arizona Press.

———. 2017. Caracol, Belize, and Changing Perceptions of Ancient Maya Society. *Journal of Archaeological Research* 25: 185–249.

Chase, Diane Z., Arlen F. Chase, and Adrian S. Z. Chase. 2024. Economic and Socio-Political Change during the Classic and Terminal Classic Periods at Caracol, Belize. In *Ancient Maya Embedded Economies,* ed. Bernadette Cap and Rachel Horowitz. Louisville, CO: University Press of Colorado.

Cheek, Charles D. 2003. Maya Community Buildings: Two Late Classic Popol Nahs at Copan, Honduras. *Ancient Mesoamerica* 14 (1): 131–138.

Cheek, Charles D., and Mary L. Spink. 1986. Excavaciones en el Grupo 3, Estructura 223

500 · References

(Operación VI). In *Excavaciones en el área urbana de Copan,* vol. 1, ed. William T. Sanders, 27–154. Tegucigalpa: Instituto Hondureño de Antropología e Historia.

Cheetham, David. 2010. America's First Colony: Olmec Materiality and Ethnicity at Canton Corralito, Chiapas, Mexico. PhD diss., Arizona State University, Tempe.

Chemas, A., and V. Rico-Gray. 1991. Apiculture and Management of Associated Vegetation by the Maya of Tixcacaltuyub, Yucatán, México. *Agroforestry Systems* 13: 13–25.

Childe, V. Gordon. 1950. The Urban Revolution. *The Town Planning Review* 21 (1): 3–17.

Chinchilla Mazariegos, Oswaldo. 2005. Cosmos and Warfare on a Classic Maya Vase. *Res: Anthropology and Aesthetics* 47: 107–134.

———. 2006. The Stars of the Palenque Sarcophagus. *Res: Anthropology and Aesthetics* 49–50: 40–58.

———. 2017. *Art and Myth of the Ancient Maya.* New Haven, CT: Yale University Press.

Chisholm, Brian S., and Michael Blake. 2006. Diet in Prehistoric Soconusco. In *Histories of Maize: Multidisciplinary Approaches to the Prehistory, Linguistics, Biogeography, Domestication, and Evolution of Maize,* ed. John E. Staller, Robert H. Tykot and Bruce F. Benz, 161–172. New York: Academic Press.

Christensen, Allen J. 2001. *Art and Society in a Highland Maya Community: The Altarpiece of Santiago Atitlán.* Austin: University of Texas Press.

———. 2016. *The Burden of the Ancients: Maya Ceremonies of World Renewal from the Pre-Columbian Period to the Present.* Austin: University of Texas Press.

Chuchiak, John F. 2009. De descriptio idolorum: An Ethnohistorical Examination of the Production, Imagery, and Functions of Colonial Yucatec Maya Idols and Effigy Censers, 1550–1750. In *Maya Worldviews at Conquest,* ed. Leslie Cecil and Timothy Pugh, 135–158. Boulder: University of Colorado Press.

Church, Minette C. 1996. Excavations at Group C and at Structure A-32. In *Xunantunich Archaeological Project: 1996 Field Season,* ed. Richard M. Leventhal, 40–58. Report on file with the Belize Institute of Archaeology, Belmopan, Belize.

Ciaramella, Mary A. 2002. *The Bee-Keepers in the Madrid Codex.* Washington, DC: Center for Maya Research.

Ciudad Real, Antonio de. 1577. *Diccionario de Motul: Maya-Español.* Motul, Mexico.

Clark, John E. 2016. Western Kingdoms of the Middle Preclassic. In *The Origins of Maya States,* ed. Loa P. Traxler and Robert J. Sharer, 123–224. Philadelphia: University of Pennsylvania Museum of Archaeology and Anthropology.

Clark, John E., and Michael Blake. 1994. The Power of Prestige: Competitive Generosity and the Emergence of Rank Societies in Lowland Mesoamerica. In *Factional Competition and Political Development in the New World,* ed. E. Brumfiel and J. Fox, 17–30. New York: Cambridge University Press.

Clark, John E., and David Cheetham. 2002. Mesoamerica's Tribal Foundations. In *The Archaeology of Tribal Societies,* ed. W. A. Parkinson, 278–339. Ann Arbor, MI: International Monographs in Prehistory.

Clark, John E., and Richard D. Hansen. 2001. Architecture of Early Kingship: Comparative Perspectives on the Origins of the Maya Royal Court. In *Royal Courts of the Ancient Maya,* vol. 2, *Data and Case Studies,* ed. Takeshi Inomata and Stephen D. Houston, 1–45. Boulder, CO: Westview Press.

Clark, John E., and John G. Hodgson. 2021. Wetland Villages in Soconusco, 6000–2000 BCE:

A New Interpretation of Archaic Shell Mounds. In *Preceramic Mesoamerica,* ed. Jon C. Lohse, Aleksander Borejsza, and Arthur A. Joyce, 420–447. New York: Routledge.

Clark, John E., Mary E. Pye, and D. C. Gosser. 2007. Thermolithics and Corn Dependency in Mesoamerica. In *Archaeology, Art, and Ethnogenesis in Mesoamerican Prehistory: Papers in Honor of Gareth W. Lowe,* ed. Lynneth S. Lowe and Mary E. Pye, 23–42. Provo, UT: Brigham Young University.

Clayton, Sarah C. 2005. Interregional Relationships in Mesoamerica: Interpreting Maya Ceramics at Teotihuacan. *Latin American Antiquity* 16 (4): 427–448.

Coe, Michael D. 1965. A Model of Ancient Community Structure in the Maya Lowlands. *Southwestern Journal of Anthropology* 21 (2): 97–114.

———. 1973. *The Maya Scribe and His World.* New York: Grolier Club.

———. 1989a. *Mexico.* London: Thames & Hudson.

———. 1989b. The Hero Twins: Myth and Image. In *The Maya Vase Book: A Corpus of Rollout Photographs of Maya Vases,* vol. 1, ed. Justin Kerr, 161–184. New York: Kerr Associates.

———. 1998. *The Art of the Maya Scribe.* New York: Henry N. Abrams.

———. 2013. CA Comment. *Current Anthropology* 54 (5): 593–594.

Coe, Michael D., and Richard Diehl. 1980. *In the Land of the Olmec.* 2 vols. Austin: University of Texas Press.

Coe, Michael D., and Stephen Houston. 2015. *The Maya.* 9th ed. New York: Thames & Hudson.

Coe, William R. 1965. Tikal, Guatemala, and Emergent Maya Civilization. *Science* 147 (3664): 1401–1419.

———. 1972. Cultural Contact between the Lowland Maya and Teotihuacan as Seen from Tikal. In *Teotihuacan: XI Mesa Redonda,* vol. 2, 257–271. Mexico City: Sociedad Mexicana de Antropología.

———. 1990. *Excavations in the Great Plaza, North Terrace, and North Acropolis of Tikal.* Tikal Report 14. Philadelphia: University of Pennsylvania Museum of Archaeology and Anthropology.

Coe, William R., and John McGinn. 1963. Tikal: The North Acropolis and an Early Tomb. *Expedition* 5 (2): 24–32.

Coggins, Clemency C. 1975. Painting and Drawing Styles at Tikal: An Historical and Iconographic Reconstruction. PhD diss., Peabody Museum of Archaeology and Ethnology, Harvard University.

———. 1980. The Shape of Time: Some Political Implications of a Four-Part Figure. *American Antiquity* 45: 727–739.

———. 1984. The Cenote of Sacrifice: Catalog. In *Cenote of Sacrifice: Maya Treasures from the Sacred Well at Chichén Itzá,* ed. Clemency Chase Coggins and Orrin C. Shane III, 23–166. Austin: University of Texas Press.

Coggins, Clemency Chase, and Orrin C. Shane III. 1984. *Cenote of Sacrifice: Maya Treasures from the Sacred Well at Chichén Itzá.* Austin: University of Texas Press.

Collins, Ryan H., and Travis W. Stanton. Forthcoming. The Monumentality of the Early Maya North: A View from Yaxuná, Yucatan, Mexico (1000 to 350 BCE). In *The Preclassic Maya: The Making of a Lowland Civilization,* ed. F. Estrada-Belli and A. Runggaldier. New York: Routledge.

502 · References

Colwell-Chanthaphonh, Chip, and T. J. Ferguson. 2006. Rethinking Abandonment in Archaeological Contexts. *The SAA Archaeological Record,* January: 37–41.

Connell, Samuel V. 2000. Were They Well Connected? An Exploration of Ancient Maya Regional Integration from the Middle-Level Perspective of Chaa Creek, Belize. PhD diss., University of California, Los Angeles.

Cordan, Wolfgang. 1966. La Fiesta de las Abejas del Códice de Madrid. *Revista de la Universidad de Yucatán* 8 (43): 88–96.

Covarrubias, Miguel. 1946. El arte "Olmeca" o de La Venta. *Cuadernos Americanos* 4: 153–179.

Cowgill, George L. 1983. Rulership and the Ciudadela: Political Inferences from Teotihuacan Architecture. In *Civilization in the Ancient Americas: Essays in Honor of Gordon R. Willey,* ed. Richard Leventhal and Alan Kolata, 313–343. Albuquerque: University of New Mexico Press and the Peabody Museum of Archaeology and Ethnology, Harvard.

———. 1997. State and Society at Teotihuacan, Mexico. *Annual Review of Anthropology* 26: 129–161.

———. 2015. *Ancient Teotihuacan: Early Urbanism in Central Mexico.* New York: Cambridge University Press.

Craine, Eugene R., and Reginald C. Reindorp, ed. 1979. *The Codex Pérez and the Book of the Chilam Balam of Maní.* Trans. Eugene R. Craine and Reginald C. Reindorp. Norman: University of Oklahoma Press.

Crane, Eva. 1983. *The Archaeology of Beekeeping.* Ithaca, NY: Cornell University Press.

———. 1999. *The World History of Beekeeping and Honey Hunting.* New York: Routledge.

Cuevas García, Martha, and Guillermo Bernal Romero. 2002. La función ritual de los incensarios compuestos del Grupo de las Cruces de Palenque. *Estudios de Cultura Maya* 22: 13–32.

Culbert, T. Patrick, and Laura J. Kosakowsky. 2019. *The Ceramic Sequence of Tikal.* Tikal Report 25B. Philadelphia: University of Pennsylvania Press.

Cyphers, Ann. 1997. Olmec Architecture at San Lorenzo. In *Olmec to Aztec: Settlement Patterns in the Ancient Gulf Lowlands,* ed. Barbara L. Stark and Philip J. Arnold III, 96–114. Tucson: University of Arizona Press.

———. 2016. The Early Preclassic Olmec: An Overview. In *The Origins of Maya States,* ed. Loa P. Traxler and Robert J. Sharer, 83–122. Philadelphia: University of Pennsylvania Museum of Archaeology and Anthropology.

Cyphers, Ann, and Anna Di Castro. 2009. Early Olmec Architecture and Imagery. In *Art of Urbanism: How Mesoamerican Kingdoms Represented Themselves in Architecture and Imagery,* ed. William L. Fash and Leonardo López Luján, 21–52. Washington, DC: Dumbarton Oaks.

Cyphers, Ann, and Timothy Murtha. 2014. Early Olmec Open Spaces at San Lorenzo, Veracruz. In *Mesoamerican Plazas: Arenas of Community and Power,* ed. Kenichiro Tsukamoto and Takeshi Inomata, 71–89. Tucson: University of Arizona Press.

Cyphers, Ann, and Judith Zurita-Noguera. 2012. Early Olmec Wetland Mounds: Investing Energy to Produce Energy. In *Early New World Monumentality,* ed. Richard L. Burger and Robert M. Rosenswig, 138–173. Gainesville: University Press of Florida.

d'Anghiera, Pietro Martire. 1912. *De Orbe Novo: The Eight Decades of Peter Martyr D'Anghera*. Vol. 2. Trans. Francis Augustus MacNutt. New York: G. P. Putnam's Sons.

Davis, Wade. 2008. TED Talk: The Worldwide Web of Belief and Ritual. https://www.ted.com/talks/wade_davis_the_worldwide_web_of_belief_and_ritual?language=en. Transcript, 10:16.

de la Cruz, Victor. 2002. Las creencias y prácticas religiosas de los descendientes de los binnigula'sa.' In *La religión de los binnigula'sa,'* ed. V. De la Cruz and M. Winter, 275–341. Oaxaca: Fondo Editorial.

de la Garza, Mercedes, ed. 2015. *Mayas: Revelación de un tiempo sin fin*. Mexico: Instituto Nacional de Antropología e Historia.

de Pierrebourg, Fabienne. 2004. Secuencia cerámica preliminaire de Balamku, Campeche, México. In *XVII Simposio de Investigaciones Arqueológicas en Guatemala, 2003*, ed. J. P. Laporte, B. Arroyo, H. Escobedo, and H. Mejía, 340–356. Guatemala City: Museo Nacional de Arqueología y Etnología.

Dedrick, Maia, Elizabeth A. Webb, Patricia A. McAnany, José Miguel Kanxoc Kumul, John G. Jones, Adolfo Iván Batún Alpuche, Carly Pope, and Morgan Russell. 2020. Influential Landscapes: Temporal Trends in the Agricultural Use of *rejolladas* at Tahcabo, Yucatán, Mexico. *Journal of Anthropological Archaeology* 59: 101175.

DeLanda, Manuel. 2006. *A New Philosophy of Society. Assemblage Theory and Social Complexity*. London: Bloomsbury.

Delvendahl, Kai. 2008. *Calakmul in Sight: History and Archaeology of an Ancient Maya City*. Mérida: Unas Letras Industria Editorial.

DeMarrais, Elizabeth, Luis Jaime Castillo, and Timothy Earle. 1996. Ideology, Materialization, and Power Strategies. *Current Anthropology* 37 (1): 15–31.

Denbow, James R., and Edwin N. Wilmsen. 1986. Advent and Course of Pastoralism in the Kalahari. *Science* 234: 1509–1515.

Diehl, Richard A. 2004. *The Olmecs: America's First Civilization*. London: Thames & Hudson.

Dietrich, Oliver, Manfred Heun, Jens Notroff, Klaus Schmidt, and Martin Zarnkow. 2012. The Role of Cult and Feasting in the Emergence of Neolithic Communities: New Evidence from Göbekli Tepe, South-Eastern Turkey. *Antiquity* 86 (333): 674–695.

DiSalle, Robert. 2006. *Understanding Space-Time: The Philosophical Development of Physics from Newton to Einstein*. New York: Cambridge University Press.

Dobres, Marcia-Anne. 2010. Archaeologies of Technology. *Cambridge Journal of Economics* 34: 103–114.

Douglas, Bill. 1969. Illness and Curing in Santiago Atitlán, A Tz'utujil-Maya Community in the Southern Highlands of Guatemala. PhD diss., Stanford University.

Dowd, Anne S. 1995. Informe Técnico (Final) para el Consejo de Arqueología del Instituto Nacional de Antropología e Historia: Estructura XIX, La Gran Acrópolis, Calakmul, Campeche, México. In *Informe Preliminaire del Proyecto Arqueológico de la Biosfera de Calakmul,* ed. Ramon Carrasco V., 1–31. Mérida: Instituto Nacional de Antropología e Historia.

———. 1998a. A Poetic Approach to Maya Iconography. Paper presented at the 97th Annual Meeting of the American Anthropological Association, Philadelphia.

504 · References

———. 1998b. Lithic Procurement and Social Complexity in New York's Hudson River Valley. PhD diss., Brown University.

———. 1998c. Biface Standardization Accompanying Organized Chert Quarrying Efforts: An Argument for Intensifying Lithic Production. In *Craft Specialization: Operational Sequences and Beyond: Papers from the European Association of Archaeologists Third Annual Meeting at Ravenna 1997*, vol. 4, ed. S. Milliken and M. Vidale, 69–75. BAR International Series 720. Oxford: Archaeopress.

———. 1998d. Operationalizing an Anthropology of Technology: Lithic Procurement and Tool Production among North American Hunter-Gatherers. In *Lithic Technology: From Raw Material Procurement to Tool Production: Proceedings of the Workshop No. 12 of the XIII International Congress of Prehistoric and Protohistoric Sciences*, ed. S. Milliken and M. Peresani, 109–113. Forlí: M. A. C.

———. 2015a. Time's Tools: "Notebooks on Walls," "Blackboards," or Calligraphic Inscriptions for Private Audiences in Maya Interior Spaces. Presentation at Maya Materialization of Time: History and Prophecy in Long-term Perspective I, 3rd Working Group, Santa Fe Institute, Santa Fe, New Mexico, February 14.

———. 2015b. Cosmovision in New World Ritual Landscapes: An Introduction. *Cambridge Archaeological Journal* 25 (1): 211–218.

———. 2016a. Time's House: Mayan Books on Walls. Presentation at Maya Materialization of Time: History and Prophecy in Long-Term Perspective II, 4th Working Group, Santa Fe Institute, Santa Fe, New Mexico, August 26–28.

———. 2016b. *Archaeological Feasibility Study and Preliminary Scope of Work for Mount Nebo, Jordan*. Vail, CO: ArchæoLOGIC USA.

———. 2017a. Time's House: Mayan Books on Walls, Founding Dynastic History, and Seeing Future Prophecy. Presentation at Telling Time: Myth, History and Everyday Life in the Ancient Maya World, 5th Working Group, Santa Fe Institute, Santa Fe, New Mexico, August 25.

———. 2017b. Cycles of Death and Rebirth in Mesoamerican Cultural Astronomy and the Calendar. *Ancient Mesoamerica* 28: 465–473.

———. 2017c. More than Smoke and Mirrors: Maya Temple Precincts and the Emergence of Religious Institutions in Mesoamerica. In *Maya E Groups: Calendars, Astronomy, and Urbanism in the Early Lowlands*, ed. David A. Freidel, Arlen F. Chase, Anne S. Dowd, and Jerry Murdock, 517–577. Gainesville: University Press of Florida.

———. 2018a. Review of "Manufactured Light: Mirrors in the Mesoamerican Realm." *Technology and Culture* 59: 473–475.

———. 2018b. The Primordial Rhythms of Mythic Time. Presentation at On Time and Being Maya, 6th Working Group, Santa Fe Institute, Santa Fe, New Mexico, August 30.

Dowd, Anne S., Anthony F. Aveni, and Ramón Carrasco Vargas. 2017. Solar Observatory or Allegory? Calakmul's Group E-Type Complex Form and Function. *Ancient Mesoamerica* 28 (2): 559–583.

Dowd, Anne S., and Susan Milbrath, eds. 2015. *Cosmology, Calendars, and Horizon-Based Astronomy in Ancient Mesoamerica*. Boulder: University Press of Colorado.

Doyle, James A. 2012. Re-Group on "E Groups": Monumentality and Early Centers in the Middle Preclassic Maya Lowlands. *Latin American Antiquity* 23 (4): 355–379.

———. 2013a. The First Maya "Collapse": The End of the Preclassic Period at El Palmar, Petén, Guatemala. PhD diss., Brown University.

———. 2013b. Early Maya Geometric Planning Conventions at El Palmar, Guatemala. *Journal of Archaeological Science* 40 (2): 793–798.

———. 2016. Creation Narratives on Ancient Maya Codex-Style Ceramics in the Metropolitan Museum. *The Metropolitan Museum Journal* 50: 42–63.

———. 2017. A Tale of Two E Groups: El Palmar and Tikal, Peten. In *Early Maya E-Groups, Solar Calendars, and the Role of Astronomy in the Rise of Lowland Maya Urbanism,* ed. David A. Freidel, Arlen F. Chase, Anne Dowd, and Jerry Murdock, 251–288. Gainesville: University Press of Florida.

Doyle, James A., and Stephen D. Houston. 2012. A Watery Tableau at El Mirador, Guatemala. *Maya Decipherment,* April 9. https://mayadecipherment.com/2012/04/09/a-watery-tableau-at-el-mirador-guatemala/.

———. 2017. The Universe in a Maya Plate. *Maya Decipherment,* March 4. https://decipherment.wordpress.com/2017/03/04/the-universe-in-a-maya-plate/.

Dunkelman, Arthur. 2007. *The Jay I. Kislak Collection at the Library of Congress: A Catalog of the Gift of the Jay I. Kislak Foundation to the Library of Congress.* Washington, DC: Library of Congress.

Dunning, Nicholas P., Vernon Scarborough, Fred Valdez, Sheryl Luzzadder-Beach, and Timothy Beach. 1999. Temple Mountains, Sacred Lakes, and Fertile Fields: Ancient Maya Landscapes in Northwestern Belize. *Antiquity* 73 (281): 650–660.

Durán, Diego. 1971. *Book of the Gods and Rites and the Ancient Calendar.* Trans. D. Heyden and F. Horcasitas. Norman: University of Oklahoma Press.

Eberl, Markus. 2015. To Put in Order: Classic Maya Concepts of Time and Space. In *The Measure and Meaning of Time in the Americas,* ed. A. Aveni, 79–104. Washington, DC: Dumbarton Oaks.

———. 2017. *War Owl Falling: Innovation, Creativity, and Culture Change in Ancient Maya Society.* Gainesville: University Press of Florida.

Eberl, Markus, and Daniel Graña-Behrens. 2004. Proper Names and Throne Names: On the Naming Practice of Classic Maya. In *Continuity and Change: Maya Religious Practices in Temporal Perspective.* 5th European Maya Conference, University of Bonn, December 2000, ed. D. Graña-Behrens, N. Grube, C. M. Prager, F. Sachse, S. Teufel, and E. Wagner, 101–120. Verlag Anton Sauerwein, Markt Schwaben, Germany.

Ebert, Claire E., Keith M. Prufer, Martha J. Macri, Bruce Winterhalder, and Douglas J. Kennett. 2014. Terminal Long Count Dates and the Disintegration of Classic Period Maya Polities. *Ancient Mesoamerica* 25: 337–356.

Edmonson, Munro S. 1967. Play: Games, Gossip, and Humor. In *Handbook of Middle American Indians,* vol. 6, Social Anthropology, ed. Manning Nash, 191–206. Austin: University of Texas Press.

———. 1982. *The Ancient Future of the Itza: The Book of Chilam Balam of Tizimin.* Austin: University of Texas Press.

———. 1986. *Heaven Born Merida and Its Destiny: The Book of Chilam Balam of Chumayel.* Austin: University of Texas Press.

———. 1988. *The Book of the Year: Middle American Calendars.* Salt Lake City: University of Utah Press.

506 · References

———. 2005. The Toltec Countdown. In *Painted Books and Indigenous Knowledge in Mesoamerica: Manuscript Studies in Honor of Mary Elizabeth Smith,* ed. Elizabeth Hill Boone, 161–179. New Orleans, LA: Middle American Research Institute, Tulane University.

Eliade, Mircea. 1959. *The Sacred and the Profane: The Nature of Religion.* New York: Harvest Books.

Elson, Christina M., and Michael E. Smith. 2001. Archaeological Deposits from the Aztec New Fire Ceremony. *Ancient Mesoamerica* 12: 157–174.

Eppich, Keith, and Emily Haney. 2017. Operación Wk-13: Excavaciones en el Grupo Chok, Estructura N13-6. In *Proyecto Arqueológico Waka': Informe No. 15: Temporada 2017,* ed. Juan Carlos Pérez, Griselda Pérez, and David Freidel, 20–83. Guatemala City: Informe entregado a la Dirección General del Patrimonio Cultural y Natural de Guatemala.

Eppich, Keith, and David Mixter. 2013. *Excavaciones en Patios Residenciales, 2013 Proyecto Arqueológico Waka',* ed. Juan Carlos Pérez and David A. Freidel, 34–62. Informe no. 11, Temporada 2013. Report submitted to the Dirección General del Patrimonio Cultural y Natural de Guatemala, Guatemala City.

Erickson, Clark L. 2000. An Artificial Landscape-Scale Fishery in the Bolivian Amazon. *Nature* 408 (6809): 190–193.

Estrada-Belli, Francisco. 2001. Maya Kingship at Holmul, Guatemala. *Antiquity* 75 (290): 685–686.

———. 2006. Lightning Sky, Rain, and the Maize God: The Ideology of Preclassic Maya Rulers at Cival, Peten, Guatemala. *Ancient Mesoamerica* 17 (1): 57–78.

———. 2007. *Investigaciones Arqueologicas en la region de Holmul, Peten: Holmul, Cival, La Sufricaya, y K'o.* Informe Preliminar de la Temporada 2007. Nashville, TN: Vanderbilt University.

———. 2009. *Investigaciones arqueologicas en la region de Holmul, Peten: Holmul y Hamontun.* 2009 season report. Boston University. http://www.bu.edu/holmul/reports/informe_09_layout.pdf.

———. 2011. *The First Maya Civilization: Ritual and Power before the Classic Period.* London: Routledge.

———. 2012. Early Civilization in the Maya Lowlands, Monumentality, and Place Making: A View from the Holmul Region. In *Early New World Monumentality,* ed. Richard L. Burger and Robert M. Rosenswig, 198–230. Gainesville: University Press of Florida.

———. 2014. *Investigaciones arqueológicas en la región de Holmul, Petén: Holmul y Cival. Informe preliminar de la temporada 2014.* Boston University. http://www.bu.edu/holmul/reports/informe_2014_layout.pdf.

———. 2017. The History, Function and Meaning of Preclassic E Groups in the Cival Region. In *Maya E Groups: Calendars, Astronomy, and Urbanism in the Early Lowlands,* ed. David A. Freidel, Arlen F. Chase, Anne S. Dowd and Jerry Murdock, 293–328. Gainesville: University Press of Florida.

Estrada-Belli, Francisco, Jeremy Bauer, Molly Morgan, and Angel Chavez. 2003. Symbols of early Maya kingship at Cival, Petén, Guatemala. *Antiquity* 77 (298). http://antiquity.ac.uk/projgall/estrada_belli298/.

Estrada-Belli, Francisco, Nikolai Grube, M. Wolf, K. Gardella, and C. Guerra-Librero. 2003. Preclassic Maya Monuments and Temples at Cival, Petén, Guatemala. *Antiquity* 77 (296). http://antiquity.ac.uk/projgall/belli296/.

Estrada-Belli, Francisco, and Alexandre Tokavinine. 2016. A King's Apotheosis: Iconography, Text, and Politics from a Classic Maya Temple at Holmul. *Latin American Antiquity* 27: 149–168.

——. 2022. Chochkitam: A New Classic Maya Dynasty and the Rise of the Kaanu'l (Snake) Kingdom. *Latin American Antiquity* 33 (4): 713–732.

Everton, Macduff. 1991. *The Modern Maya: A Culture in Transition.* Albuquerque: University of New Mexico Press.

Ewell, Peter T., and Deborah Merrill-Sands. 1987. Milpa in Yucatan: A Long-Fallow Maize System and Its Alternatives in the Maya Peasant Economy. In *Comparative Farming Systems,* ed. B. L. Turner and Stephen B. Brush, 95–129. New York: Guilford Press.

Farriss, Nancy M., Arthur G. Miller, and Arlen F. Chase. 1975. Late Maya Mural Paintings from Quintana Roo, Mexico. *Journal of Field Archaeology* 2: 5–10.

——. 1987. Remembering the Future, Anticipating the Past: History, Time, and Cosmology among the Maya of Yucatán. *Comparative Studies in Society and History* 29: 566–593.

Fash, William L. 1991. *Scribes, Warriors and Kings: The City of Copan and the Ancient Maya.* New York: Thames & Hudson.

Fash, William L., Alexandre Tokovinine, and Barbara Fash. 2009. The House of New Fire at Teotihuacan and Its Legacy in Mesoamerica. In *The Art of Urbanism: How Mesoamerican Kingdoms Represented Themselves in Architecture and Imagery,* ed. William L. Fash and Leonardo López Luján, 201–229. Washington, DC: Dumbarton Oaks.

Faulkner, William. 1951. *Requiem for a Nun.* New York: Random House.

Fernandez-Diaz, Juan Carlos, William E. Carter, Craig Glennie, Ramesh L. Shrestha, Zhigang Pan, Nima Ekhtari, Abhinav Singhania, Darren Hauser, and Michael Sartori. 2016. Capability Assessment and Performance Metrics for the Titan Multispectral Mapping Lidar. *Remote Sensing* 8 (11): 936.

Fields, Virginia. 2004. The Royal Charter at Xunantunich. In *The Ancient Maya of the Belize Valley: Half a Century of Archaeological Research,* ed. James F. Garber, 180–190. Gainesville: University Press of Florida.

Finamore, Daniel, and Stephen Houston, eds. 2010. *Fiery Pool: The Maya and the Mythic Sea.* Salem, MA: Peabody Essex Museum.

Fish, Paul R., Suzanne K. Fish, Paulo DeBlasis, and Maria Dulce Gaspar. 2013. Monumental Shell Mounds as Persistent Places in Southern Coastal Brazil. In *The Archaeology and Historical Ecology of Small Scale Economies,* ed. Victor D. Thompson and James C. Waggoner Jr., 120–140. Gainesville: University Press of Florida.

Fitzmaurice, Rosamund. 2018. Pre-Columbian Maya Graffiti: New Insights from Xunantunich, Belize. MA thesis, Institute of Archaeology, University College London.

Fitzmaurice, Rosamund, Tia Watkins, and Jaime Awe. 2021. Play and Purpose: The Relationship between Patolli and Graffiti at Xunantunich, Belize. *Papers from the Institute of Archaeology* 31 (1): 60–92.

508 · References

Fitzsimmons, James L. 2009. *Death and the Classic Maya Kings.* Austin: University of Texas Press.

Flannery, Kent V., and Joyce Marcus. 2000. Formative Mexican Chiefdoms and the Myth of the "Mother Culture." *Journal of Anthropological Archaeology* 19: 1–37.

———. 2012. *The Creation of Inequality: How Our Prehistoric Ancestors Set the Stage for Monarchy, Slavery, and Empire.* Cambridge, MA: Harvard University Press.

Fletcher, Roland. 2019. Trajectories to Low-Density Settlements Past and Present: Paradox and Outcomes. *Frontiers in Digital Humanities* 6: 14.

Flores, J. S., and E. Ucan Ek. 1983. Nombres usados por los Mayas para designar la vegetación. *Cuadernos de Divulgación INIREB* 10: 1–33.

Flores Esquivel, F. C. Atasta, and Ivan Šprajc. 2008. Reconocimiento arqueológico en el sur de Campeche: nuevos hallazgos y contribuciones para una visión regional. *Estudios de Cultura Maya* 32: 17–38.

Flores Gutiérrez, Daniel. 1995. En el problema del inicio del año y el origen del calendario mesoamericano: Un punto de vista astronómico. In *Coloquio Cantos de Mesoamérica: Metodologías científicas en la búsqueda del conocimiento prehispánico,* ed. Daniel Flores, 119–132. Mexico City: Instituto de Astronomía, Facultad de Ciencias, Universidad Nacional Autónoma de México.

Folan, William J., Joyce Marcus, Sophia Pinceman, María del Rosario Domínguez Carrasco, Lorraine Anne Fletcher, and Abel Morales López. 1995. Calakmul: New Data from an Ancient Capital in Campeche, Mexico. *Latin American Antiquity* 6: 310–334.

Förstemann, Ernst. 1880. *Die Maya Handschrift der Königlichen öffentlichen Bibliothek zu Dresden.* Leipzig: Verlag der A. Naumannschen Lichtdruckeret.

Foucault, Michel. 1977. *Discipline and Punish: The Birth of the Prison.* New York: Pantheon.

———. 1978. *The History of Sexuality. Volume 1: An Introduction.* New York: Pantheon.

Freidel, David A. 1975. The Ix Chel Shrine and Other Temples of Talking Idols. In *Changing Pre-Columbian Commercial Systems: The 1972–1973 Seasons at Cozumel, Mexico,* ed. Jeremy A. Sabloff and William L. Rathje, 107–113. Monographs of the Peabody Museum No.3. Cambridge, MA: Peabody Museum of Archaeology and Ethnology, Harvard University.

———. 1979. Culture Areas and Interaction Spheres: Contrasting Approaches to the Emergence of Civilization in the Maya Lowlands. *American Antiquity* 44: 36–54.

———. 1981a. Civilization as a State of Mind: The Cultural Evolution of the Lowland Maya. In *The Transition to Statehood in the New World,* ed. Grant D. Jones and Robert Kautz, 188–227. Cambridge, MA: Cambridge University Press.

———. 1981b. The Political Economics of Residential Dispersion among the Lowland Maya. In *Lowland Maya Settlement Patterns,* ed. Wendy Ashmore, 371–384. Albuquerque: University of New Mexico Press.

———. 1985. Polychrome Facades of the Lowland Maya Preclassic. In *Painted Architecture and Polychrome Monumental Sculpture in Mesoamerica,* ed. E. Boone, 5–30. Washington, DC: Dumbarton Oaks.

———. 1986. The Monumental Architecture. In *Archaeology at Cerros, Belize, Central America,* vol. 1, *An Interim Report,* ed. Robin A. Robertson and David A. Freidel, 1–22. Dallas, TX: Southern Methodist University Press.

———. 1988. The Late Preclassic Antecedents of Classic Maya Discourse. In "Maya Linguistics,

Hieroglyphics, and Discourse," ed. K. Josserand and A. Hofling, special issue, *Journal of Mayan Linguistics* 6: 23–46.

———. 2000. Mystery of the Maya Façade. *Archaeology* 53 (5): 24–28.

———. 2008. Maya Divine Kingship. In *Religion and Power: Divine Kingship in the Ancient World and Beyond,* ed. Nicole Brisch, 191–206. Oriental Institute Seminars Number 4. Chicago, IL: Oriental Institute of the University of Chicago.

———. 2017. E Groups, Cosmology, and the Origins of Maya Rulership. In *Early Maya E-Groups, Solar Calendars, and the Role of Astronomy in the Rise of Lowland Maya Urbanism,* ed. David A. Freidel, Arlen F. Chase, Anne Dowd, and Jerry Murdock, 177–211. Gainesville: University Press of Florida.

———. 2018. Maya and the Idea of Empire. In *Pathways to Complexity: A View from the Maya Lowlands,* ed. M. Kathryn Brown and George J. Bey III, 363–386. Gainesville: University Press of Florida.

———. 2020. Into the Woods: Archaeology, Epigraphy and Iconography in Maya Studies. In *A Forest of History: The Maya after the Emergence of Divine Kingship,* ed. Travis W. Stanton and M. Kathryn Brown, 248–259. Boulder: University of Colorado Press.

———. 2022. Eternal Performance: Mesoamerican and Mississippian Tableaux in Comparative Perspective. In *Archaeologies of Cosmoscapes in the Americas,* ed. J. Grant Stauffer, Bretton T. Giles, and Shawn P. Lambert, 229–250. Oxford: Oxbow Books.

———. Forthcoming. Rulers, Relatives and Royal Courts: Excavating the Foundations of Classic Maya Alliance and Conflict. In *Faces of Rulership in the Maya Region,* ed. Patricia McAnany and Marilyn Masson. Washington, DC: Dumbarton Oaks.

Freidel, David A., Mary Jane Acuña, Carlos Chiriboga, and Michelle Rich. 2022. "Water Trails and Water Mountains: The View from Northwest Petén." In *Sustainability and Water Management in the Maya World and Beyond*, ed. J. Larmon, L. Lucero, and F. Valdez Jr., 119–124. University of Colorado Press: Boulder.

Freidel, David A., and Francisco Castañeda. 2015. Operacion WK17: Excavaciones en la Plaza 2 y Estela 7. In *Proyecto Arqueológico Waka',* ed. Juan Carlos Pérez, Griselda Pérez, and David A. Freidel, 83–101. Informe no. 12, Temporada 2014. Report submitted to the Dirección General del Patrimonio Cultural y Natural de Guatemala, Guatemala City. www.mesoweb.com/resources/informes/Waka2014 .html.

Freidel, David A., Arlen F. Chase, Anne S. Dowd, and Jerry Murdock, eds. 2017. *Maya E Groups: Calendars, Astronomy, and Urbanism in the Early Lowlands*. Gainesville: University Press of Florida.

Freidel, David A., and Héctor L. Escobedo. 2014. Stelae, Buildings and People: Reflections on Ritual in the Archaeological Record at El Peru-Waka'. In *Archaeology at El Perú-Waka': Ancient Maya Performances of Ritual, Memory, and Power,* ed. Olivia C. Navarro-Farr and Michelle E. Rich, 18–33. Tucson: University of Arizona Press.

Freidel, David A., Héctor L. Escobedo, and Stanley P. Guenter. 2007. A Crossroads of Conquerors: Waka' and Gordon Willey's "Rehearsal for the Collapse" Hypothesis. In *Gordon R. Willey and American Archaeology: Contemporary Perspectives,* ed. Jeremy A. Sabloff and William Fash, 187–208. Norman: University of Oklahoma Press.

510 · References

Freidel, David A., Héctor L. Escobedo, and Juan Carlos Meléndez. 2013. Mountains of Memories: Structure M12-32 at El Peru. In *Millenary Maya Societies: Past Crises and Resilience,* ed. M. Charlotte Arnauld and Alain Breton, 235–247. Mesoweb On Line Publications. http://www.mesoweb.com/publications/MMS/index.html.

Freidel, David A., and Stanley P. Guenter. 2003. Bearers of War and Creation: A Site Q Monument in the Dallas Museum of Art Is Changing Our View of Ancient Maya Royal Women. *Archaeology Magazine,* January 23.

———. 2006. Soul Bundle Caches, Tombs, and Cenotaphs: Creating the Places of Resurrection and Accession in Maya Kingship. In *Sacred Bindings of the Cosmos: Ritual Acts of Bundling and Wrapping in Mesoamerica,* ed. Julia Guernsey and F. Kent Reilly, 59–79. Barnardsville, NC: Boundary End Archaeology Research Center.

Freidel, David A., Marilyn A. Masson, and Michelle Rich. 2016. Imagining a Complex Maya Political Economy: Counting Tokens and Currencies in Image, Text and the Archaeological Record. *Cambridge Archaeological Journal* 27 (1): 1–26.

Freidel, David, Maria Masucci, Susan Jaeger, and Robin Robertson. 1986. The Bearer, the Burden and the Burnt: The Stacking Principle in the Iconography of the Late Preclassic Maya Lowlands. In *Sixth Palenque Round Table, 1986,* ed. Merle G. Robertson, 175–183. Norman: University of Oklahoma Press.

Freidel, David A., Olivia Navarro-Farr, Juan Carlos Pérez, Griselda Pérez, and Michelle Rich. Forthcoming. Birthing Gods: Queen K'abel's Mirrors, Plates, Writing Tablets. *Ancient Mesoamerica.*

Freidel, David A., Griselda Pérez, and Juan Carlos Pérez. 2016. Operacion WK01, Intervenciones de consolidacion e investigaciones arqueologicas en la Estructura M13-1. In *Proyecto Arqueológico Waka', Informe No. 13, Temporada 2015,* ed. Juan Carlos Pérez, and Griselda Pérez, 18–49. Report submitted to the Dirección General del Patrimonio Cultural y Natural de Guatemala.

Freidel, David A., Juan Carlos Pérez, and Griselda Pérez. 2018. Palace of the Maya Time Lords: Excavations in the Royal Acropolis at El Peru-Waka', Peten, Guatemala. *Current World Archaeology* 8 (5): 24–30.

Freidel, David A., Kathryn Reese-Taylor, and David Mora-Marin. 2002. The Shell Game: Commodity, Treasure and Kingship in the Origins of Classic Maya Civilization. In *Ancient Maya Political Economies,* ed. M. Masson and D. A. Freidel, 41–86. Walnut Creek, CA: AltaMira Press.

Freidel, David A., and F. Kent Reilly III. 2010. The Flesh of God: Cosmology, Food, and the Origins of Political Power in Southeastern Mesoamerica. In *Pre-Columbian Foodways: Interdisciplinary Approaches to Food, Culture, and Markets in Ancient Mesoamerica,* ed. John E. Staller and Michael D. Carrasco, 635–679. New York: Springer.

Freidel, David A., and Michelle E. Rich. 2018. Maya Sacred Play: The View from El Peru-Waka'. In *Ritual, Play and Belief in Evolution and Early Human Societies,* ed. Colin Renfrew, Iain Morley, and Michael Boyd, 101–115. New York: Cambridge University Press.

Freidel, David A., Michelle E. Rich, and Marilyn Masson. 2015. Pecked Circles and Divining Boards: Calculating Instruments in Ancient Mesoamerica. In *Cosmology, Calendars, and Horizon-Based Astronomy in Ancient Mesoamerica,* ed. Anne Dowd and Susan Milbrath, 249–264. Boulder: University Press of Colorado.

Freidel, David A., Michelle Rich, and F. Kent Reilly III. 2010. Resurrecting the Maize King, Figurines from a Maya Tomb Bring a Royal Funeral to Life. *Archaeology* 63(5):42–45.

Freidel, David A., and Jeremy A. Sabloff. 1984. *Cozumel: Late Maya Settlement Patterns.* New York: Academic Press.

Freidel, David A., Jeremy A. Sabloff, and Jerry Murdock. 2014. Maya Materialization of Time: History and Prophecy in Long-Term Perspective. Working Group Description, Santa Fe Institute, Santa Fe.

Freidel, David A., and Linda Schele. 1988a. Kingship in the Late Preclassic Lowlands: The Instruments and Places of Ritual Power. *American Anthropologist* 90 (3): 547–567.

———. 1988b. Symbol and Power: A History of the Lowland Maya Cosmogram. In *Maya Iconography,* ed. Elizabeth Benson and Gilette Griffin, 44–93. Princeton, NJ: Princeton University Press.

Freidel, David, Linda Schele, and Joy Parker. 1993. *Maya Cosmos: Three Thousand Years on the Shaman's Path.* New York: William Morrow and Company.

Freidel, David A., and Charles K. Suhler. 1995. Crown of Creation: The Development of the Maya Royal Diadems in the Late Preclassic and Early Classic Periods. In *The Emergence of Lowland Maya Civilization: The Transition from the Preclassic to the Early Classic,* ed. Nikolai Grube, 137–150. Acta Mesoamericana 8. Möckmühl: Verlag Anton Sauerwein.

———. 1998. Visiones serpentinas y laberintos mayas. *Arqueología Mexicana* 6 (34): 28–37.

———. 1999. The Path of Life: Towards a Functional Analysis of Ancient Maya Architecture. In *Mesoamerican Architecture as a Cultural Symbol,* ed. Jeff Karl Kowalski, 250–275. Oxford: Oxford University Press.

Freidel, David A., Charles K. Suhler, George J. Bey III, F. Kent Reilly III, Travis W. Stanton, Tara Bond-Freeman, and Fernando Robles Castellano. 2020. Early Royal Accession Platforms at Yaxuná, Yucatán, Mexico: Possible Further Evidence of Olmec Inspiration for Maya Divine Kingship. In *A Forest of History: The Maya before the Emergence of Divine Kingship,* ed. M. Kathryn Brown and Travis Stanton. Boulder: University Press of Colorado.

Fuchs, Peter R., Renate Patzschke, Claudia Schmitz, Germán Yenque, and Jesús Briceño. 2006. Investigaciones arqueológicas en el sitio de Sechín Bajo, Casma. *Boletín De Arqueología PUCP* 10: 111–135.

Fuchs, Peter R., Renate Patzschke, Germán Yenque, and Jesús Briceño. 2009. Del Arcaico Tardío al Formativo Temprano: Las investigaciones en Sechín Bajo, Valle De Casma. *Boletín De Arqueología PUCP* 13: 55–86.

Gallareta Cervera, Tomás. 2016. The Archaeology of Monumental Architecture and the Social Construction of Authority at the Northern Maya Puuc Site of Kiuic. PhD diss., University of North Carolina, Chapel Hill.

Gallareta Negrón, Tomás. 2013. The Social Organization of Labna, a Classic Maya Community in the Puuc Region of Yucatan, Mexico. PhD diss., Tulane University, New Orleans, LA.

Gallaga M., Emiliano. 2016. Introduction. In *Manufactured Light: Mirrors in the Mesoamerican Realm*, ed. Emiliano Gallaga M. and Marc G. Blainey, 3–24. Boulder: University Press of Colorado.

512 · References

Gallaga M., Emiliano, and Marc G. Blainey, eds. 2016. *Manufactured Light: Mirrors in the Mesoamerican Realm*. Boulder: University Press of Colorado.

Garber, James F., and Jaime J. Awe. 2009. A Terminal Early Formative Symbol System in the Maya Lowlands: The Iconography of the Cunil Phase (1100–900 BC) at Cahal Pech. *Research Reports in Belizean Archaeology* 6: 151–159.

Garber, James F., Jennifer L. Cochran, and Jaime J. Awe. 2007. The Middle Formative Ideological Foundations of Kingship: The Case from Cahal Pech, Belize. *Research Reports in Belizean Archaeology* 4: 169–175.

García Barrios, Ana. 2008. Chaahk, el dios de la lluvia, en el período clásico maya: aspectos religiosos y políticos. Doctoral thesis, Madrid, Universidad Complutense.

———. 2011a. Análisis iconográfico preliminar de fragmentos de las vasijas estilo códice procedentes de Calakmul. *Estudios de Cultura Maya* 37: 67–97.

———. 2011b. Chaahk en los mitos de las vasijas estilo códice. *Arqueología Mexicana* 106: 70–75.

García Barrios, Ana, and Ramón Carrasco Vargas. 2006. Nuevos hallazgos de cerámica Estilo Códice en Calakmul. *Los Investigadores de la Cultura Maya* 14 (1): 125–136.

García Cruz, Florentino. 1990. Balamku: Un sitio arqueológico Maya en Campeche. *Arqueología* 4: 129–134.

———. 1992. Al encuentro de Balamku. *Mexico Desconocido* 183: 31–35.

———. 1993–1994. Balamkú: Un sito Maya de Campeche. *Arqueología Mexicana* 1 (5): 59–60.

García Icazbalceta, Joaquín. 1980. *Colección de documentos para la historia de México*. Mexico City: Editorial Porrua.

García Vierna, Valeria Amparo, Yarelí Jáidar Benavides, and María Christina Ruiz Martin. 2009. Recuperando una historia: Una década de trabajos de preservación en el friso de la Casa de los Reyes, Balamkú, Campeche. In *Conservación de bienes culturales: acciones y reflexiones*, ed. L. F. G. Baca, 121–153. Mexico City: Conservación del Patrimonio Arqueológico CNCPC-INAH. http://mediateca.inah.gob.mx/islandora _74/islandora/object/libro%3A401.

García Zambrano, Ángel J. 1994. Early Colonial Evidence of Pre-Columbian Rituals of Foundation. In *Seventh Palenque Round Table, 1989,* ed. Merle Greene Robertson, 217–227. San Francisco: The Pre-Columbian Art Research Institute.

Gardner, P. M. 1972. The Paliyans. In *Hunters and Gatherers Today,* ed. M. Bicchieri, 404–447. New York: Holt, Rinehart and Winston.

Garibay, Angel Maria. 1979. *Teogonía e historia de los mexicanos: tres opúsculos del siglo XVI*. 3rd ed. Mexico City: Editorial Porrua.

Garrison, Thomas G., and Stephen Houston, eds. 2019. *An Inconstant Landscape: The Maya Kingdom of El Zotz, Guatemala*. Boulder: University Press of Colorado.

Gell, Alfred. 1992. *The Anthropology of Time: Cultural Constructions of Temporal Maps and Images*. Oxford: Berg.

Gerstle, Andrea I. 2002. The Civic Complex. In *Before the Volcano Erupted: The Ancient Cerén Village in Central America,* ed. Payson Sheets, 83–88. Austin: University of Texas Press.

Gill, Richardson B. 2000. *The Great Maya Droughts: Water, Life, and Death*. Albuquerque: University of New Mexico Press.

References · 513

Girard, Rafael. 1962. *Los Mayas eternos*. Mexico City: Libro México.

———. 1966. *Los Mayas. Su civilización, su historia, sus vinculaciones continentales*. Mexico City: Libro México.

Gómara, Francisco López de. 1983. *Historia General de las Indias: Conquista de México, segunda parte*. Barcelona: Ediciones Orbis.

Gómez Chávez, Sergio. 2017a. 38 Standing Figure, 200–250. In *Teotihuacan: City of Water, City of Fire,* ed. Matthew H. Robb, 249. San Francisco: Fine Arts Museum of San Francisco in association with University of California Press.

———. 2017b. The Underworld at Teotihuacan: The Sacred Cave under the Feathered Serpent Pyramid. In *Teotihuacan: City of Water, City of Fire*, ed. Matthew H. Robb, 48–55. San Francisco: Fine Arts Museum of San Francisco in association with University of California Press.

Gómez Chávez, Sergio, and Nikolai Grube. 2017. 45 Incised Shell, 150–250. In *Teotihuacan: City of Water, City of Fire,* ed. Matthew H. Robb, 249. San Francisco: Fine Arts Museums of San Francisco in association with University of California Press.

Gómez Chávez, Sergio, and M. Robb. 2017. The Underworld at Teotihuacan: The Sacred Cave under the Feathered Serpent Pyramid. In *Teotihuacan: City of Water, City of Fire,* ed. Matthew H. Robb, 48–55. San Francisco: Fine Arts Museum of San Francisco in association with University of California Press.

Gómez-Pompa, Arturo. 1991. Learning from Traditional Ecological Knowledge: Insights from Maya Silviculture. In *Rain Forest Regeneration and Management,* ed. A. Gomez-Pompa, T. C. Whitmore, and M. Hadley, 335–341. Paris: UNESCO and Parthenon Publishing Group.

Gómez-Pompa, Arturo, José Salvador Flores, and Victoria Sosa. 1987. The "Pet Kot": A Man-Made Tropical Forest of the Maya. *Interciencia* 12 (1): 10–15.

González-García, A. César, and Ivan Šprajc. 2016. Astronomical Significance of Architectural Orientations in the Maya Lowlands: A Statistical Approach. *Journal of Archaeological Science: Reports* 9: 191–202.

Gossen, Gary. 1974. *Chamulas in the World of the Sun: Time and Space in a Maya Oral Narrative*. Cambridge, MA: Harvard University Press.

Gossen, Gary H. 1986. The Chamula Festival of Games: Native Macroanalysis and Social Commentary in a Maya Carnival. In *Symbol and Meaning beyond the Closed Community: Essays in Mesoamerican Ideas,* ed. Gary H. Gossen, 173–184. Studies in Culture and Society, vol. 1. Albany: Institute for Mesoamerican Studies, State University of New York at Albany.

Goudiaby, Hemmamuthé, and Philippe Nondédeo. 2020. The Funerary and Architectural History of an Ancient Maya Residential Group: Group 5N6, Naachtun, Guatemala. *Journal de la Société des américanistes* 106 (1): 19–64.

Graeber, David, and Marshall Sahlins. 2017. *On Kings*. Chicago: University of Chicago Press.

Graeber, David, and David Wengrow. 2021. *The Dawn of Everything: A New History of Humanity*. New York: Farrar, Straus and Giroux.

Graham, Ian. 1967. *Archaeological Explorations in El Peten, Guatemala*. Publication 33. New Orleans, LA: Middle American Research Institute, Tulane University.

———. 1988. Homeless Hieroglyphs. *Antiquity* 62 (234): 122–126.

514 · References

Graham, Ian, and Eric Von Euw. 1975. *Corpus of Maya Hieroglyphic Inscriptions*. Vol. 2, Part 1, *Naranjo*. Cambridge, MA: Peabody Museum of Archaeology and Ethnology, Harvard University.

Graham, John A. 1988. Monumental Sculpture and Hieroglyphic Inscriptions. In *Excavations at Seibal Department of Peten, Guatemala,* ed. Gordon R. Willey, 1–79. Cambridge, MA: Harvard University Press.

Graña-Behrens, Daniel. 2009. *Die Maya-inschriften aus Nordwestyukatan, Mexiko. Kalenderangaben, Chronologie und Kulturgeschichtliche Interpretation*. 2 vols. Saarbrücken: Südwestdeutscher Verlag für Hochschulschriften.

Greenberg, Joseph H., ed. 1987. Generalizations about Numeral Systems. In *Universals of Human Language,* vol. 3: *Word Structure,* eds. J. F. Greenberg, C. A. Ferguson, and E. A. Moravcsik, 249–295. Stanford, CA: Stanford University Press.

Grove, David C. 1984. *Chalcatzingo: Excavations on the Olmec Frontier*. London: Thames & Hudson UK.

Grove, David C., ed. 1987. *Ancient Chalcatzingo*. Austin: University of Texas Press.

Grube, Nikolai. 1992. Classic Maya Dance: Evidence from Hieroglyphs and Iconography. *Ancient Mesoamerica* 3: 201–218.

———. 1994a. Epigraphic Research at Caracol, Belize. In *Studies in the Archaeology of Caracol, Belize,* ed. Diane Z. Chase and Arlen F. Chase, 83–122. Monograph 7. San Francisco: Pre-Columbian Art Research Institute.

———. 1994b. Observations on the History of Maya Hieroglyphic Writing. In *Seventh Palenque Round Table, 1989,* ed. Merle Greene Robertson and Virginia M. Fields, 177–186. San Francisco: Pre-Columbian Art Research Institute.

———. 2000. Fire Rituals in the Context of Classic Maya Initial Series. In *The Sacred and the Profane. Architecture and Identity in the Maya Lowlands,* ed. Pierre Robert Colas, Kai Delvendahl, Marcus Kuhnert, and Annette Schubart, 93–109. Acta Mesoamerica 10. Markt Schwaben: Verlag Anton Saurwein.

———. 2005. Toponyms, Emblem Glyphs, and the Political Geography of Southern Campeche. *Anthropological Notebooks* 11: 89–102.

———. 2018. El Códice de Dresde: Obra Colectiva de un Taller de Escribas, Conferencia Magistral, VI Encuentro Internacional de Bibliologí: Los Códices Mayas de Debate. *Estudios Interdisciplinarios sobre Escritura, Imagen y Materialidad*. Biblioteca nacional de México, September 5–6.

Grube, Nikolai, and Ruth Krochok. 2011. Reading between the Lines: Hieroglyphic Texts from Chichén Itzá and Its Neighbors. In *Twin Tollans: Chichén Itzá, Tula, and the Epiclassic to Early Postclassic Mesoamerican World,* ed. Jeff Karl Kowalski and Cynthia Kristan-Graham, 157–193. Rev. ed. Washington, DC: Dumbarton Oaks.

Grube, Nikolai, and Werner Nahm. 1990. *A Sign for the Syllable mi*. Research Reports on Ancient Maya Writing 33. Washington, DC: Center for Maya Research.

———. 1992. "A Census of Xibalba: A Complete Inventory of *Way* Characters on Maya Ceramics." In *The Maya Vase Book,* vol. 4, ed. Barbara and Justin Kerr, 686–715. New York: Kerr Associates.

———. 1994. A Census of Xibalba: A Complete Inventory of WAY Characters on Maya Ceramics. In *The Maya Vase Book: A Corpus of Rollout Photographs of Maya Vases,* ed. Justin Kerr, 686–715. New York: Kerr Associates.

References · 515

Guenter, Stanley P. 2003. The Inscriptions of Dos Pilas Associated with B'ajlaj Chan K'awiil. *Mesoweb.* www.mesoweb.com/features/guenter/DosPilas.html.

———. 2005. Informe preliminar de la epigrafia de el Peru. In *Proyecto Arqueológico Waka': Informe no. 2, Temporada 2004,* ed. Héctor L. Escobedo and David Freidel, 351–398. Report submitted to the Dirección General del Patrimonio Cultural y Natural de Guatemala, Guatemala City.

———. 2014. The Epigraphy of El Peru-Waka. In *Archaeology at El Perú-Waka': Ancient Maya Performances of Ritual, Memory, and Power,* ed. Olivia C. Navarro-Farr and Michelle E. Rich, 147–166. Tucson: University of Arizona Press.

Guenter, Stanley P., and Michelle E. Rich. 2004. WK-04: Excavaciones en la Estructura L13–22. *Proyecto Arqueológico Waka': Informe No. 1, Temporada 2003,* ed. Héctor L. Escobedo and David A. Freidel, 93–108. Report submitted to the Dirección General del Patrimonio Cultural y Natural de Guatemala, Guatemala City.

Guernsey, Julia. 2006. *Ritual and Power in Stone: The Performance of Rulership in Mesoamerican Izapan Style Art.* Austin: University of Texas Press.

———. 2010a. *Ritual and Power in Stone: The Performance of Rulership in Mesoamerican Izapan Style Art.* Austin: University of Texas Press.

———. 2010b. A Consideration of the Quatrefoil Motif in Preclassic Mesoamerica. *Res: Anthropology and Aesthetics* 57–58: 75–96.

———. 2021. Beyond the "Myth or Politics" Debate: Reconsidering Late Preclassic Sculpture, the Principal Bird Deity, and the Popol Vuh. In *The Myths of the Popol Vuh in Cosmology, Art and Ritual,* ed. Holley Moyes, Allen Christensen, and Frauke Sachse, 268–294. Louisville: University Press of Colorado.

Guernsey, Julia F., and F. Kent Reilly. 2006. *Sacred Bundles: Ritual Acts of Wrapping and Bundling in Mesoamerica.* Barnardsville NC: Boundary End Archaeological Research Center.

Guiteras Holmes, Calixta. 1961. *Perils of the Soul: The World View of a Tzotzil Indian.* New York: Free Press of Glencoe.

Gunsenheimer, Antje. 2000–2001. La historia de Don Andrés Cocom en los libros del Chilam Balam. *Indiana* 17–18: 269–288.

———. 2006. Out of the Historical Darkness: A Methodological Approach to Uncover the Hidden History of Ethnohistorical Sources. *Indiana* 23: 15–49.

Håkansson, N. Thomas, and Mats Widgren, eds. 2014. *Landesque Capital: The Historical Ecology of Enduring Landscape Modifications.* Walnut Creek, CA: Left Coast Press.

Hamilakis, Yannis, and Andrew M. Jones. 2017. Archaeology and Assemblage. *Cambridge Archaeological Journal* 27 (1): 77–84.

Hanks, William F. 1987. Discourse Genres in a Theory of Practice. *American Ethnologist* 14 (4): 668–692.

———. 1988. Grammar, Style, and Meaning in a Maya Manuscript. *International Journal of American Linguistics* 54 (3): 331–364.

———. 1989. Elements of Maya Style. In *World and Image in Maya Culture. Explorations in Language, Writing, and Representation,* ed. William F. Hanks and Don S. Rice, 72–111. Salt Lake City: University of Utah Press.

516 · References

——. 1990. *Referential Practice: Language and Lived Space among the Maya*. Chicago: University of Chicago Press.

——. 2000a. Copresence and Alterity in Maya Ritual Practice. In *Intertexts: Writings on Language, Utterance, and Context*, 221–248. Lanham, MD: Rowman and Littlefield.

——. 2010. *Converting Words. Maya in the Age of the Cross*. Berkeley: University of California Press.

Hanks, William F., ed. 2000. *Intertexts: Writings on Language, Utterance, and Context*. Rowman and Littlefield Publishers, New York.

Hansen, Richard. 1998. Continuity and Disjunction: Preclassic Antecedents of Classic Maya Architecture. In *Function and Meaning in Classic Maya Architecture*, ed. Stephen D. Houston, 49–122. Washington, DC: Dumbarton Oaks.

——. 2001. The First Cities: The Beginnings of Urbanization and State Formation in the Maya Lowlands. In *Maya: Divine Kings of the Rainforest*, ed. Nikolai Grube, 51–65. Könnemann: John Wilson, distributor.

——. 2016. Cultural and Environmental Components of the First Maya States: A Perspective from the Central and Southern Maya Lowlands. In *The Origins of Maya States*, ed. Loa P. Traxler and Robert J. Sharer, 329–416. Philadelphia: University of Pennsylvania Museum of Archaeology and Anthropology.

Hansen, Richard, Ronald L. Bishop, and Federico Fahsen. 1991. Notes on Maya Codex-Style Ceramics from Nakbe, Peten, Guatemala. *Ancient Mesoamerica* 2 (2): 225–243.

Hansen, Richard D., Edgar Zuyuc Ley, and Héctor E. Mejía. 2011. Resultados de la temporada de investigaciones 2009: Proyecto Cuenca Mirador. In *XXIV Simposio de Investigaciones Arqueológicas en Guatemala, 2010*, ed. Barbara Arroyo, L. Paiz Aragón, A. Linares Palma, and A. L. Arroyave, 187–204. Guatemala City: Museo Nacional de Arqueología y Etnología.

Harris, Edward. 1989. *Principles of Archaeological Stratigraphy*. 2nd ed. London: Academic Press.

Harrison, Peter D. 1970. The Central Acropolis, Tikal, Guatemala: A Preliminary Study of the Functions of Its Structural Components during the Late Classic Period. PhD diss., University of Pennsylvania, Philadelphia.

——. 2008. Animales como nombres de familias reales en Tikal y algunas consideraciones sobre Calakmul. *Mayab* 20: 109–124.

Harrison-Buck, Eleanor. 2014. Reevaluating Chronology and Historical Content in the Maya Books of Chilam Balam. *Ethnohistory* 6 (4): 681–713.

——. 2016. Killing the "Kings of Stone": The Defacement of Classic Maya Monuments. In *Ritual, Violence, and the Fall of the Classic Maya Kings*, ed. Gyles Iannone, Brett A. Houk, and Sonja A. Schwake, 61–88. Gainesville: University Press of Florida.

Harrison-Buck, Eleanor, Astrid Runggaldier, and Alex Gantos. 2018. It's the Journey Not the Destination: Maya New Year's Pilgrimage and Self-Sacrifice as Regenerative Power. *Journal of Social Archaeology* 18 (3): 25–47.

Hart, Thomas. 2008. *The Ancient Spirituality of the Modern Maya*. Albuquerque: University of New Mexico Press.

Haviland, William A. 1974. Occupational Specialization at Tikal, Guatemala: Stoneworking-Monument Carving. *American Antiquity* 39: 494–496.

———. 1992. From Double Bird to Ah Cacao: Dynastic Troubles and the Cycle of Katuns at Tikal, Guatemala. In *New Theories on the Ancient Maya,* ed. E. C. Danien and R. J. Sharer, 71–80. Philadelphia: The University Museum, University of Pennsylvania.

Haviland, William, and Anita de Laguna Haviland. 1995. Glimpses of the Supernatural: Altered States of Consciousness and the Graffiti of Tikal, Guatemala. *Latin American Antiquity* 6: 295–309.

Hayden, Brian. 1998. Practical and Prestige Technologies: The Evolution of Material Systems. *Journal of Archaeological Method and Theory* 5: 1–55.

Headrick, Annabeth. 1999. The Street of the Dead: It Really Was. *Ancient Mesoamerica* 10 (1): 69–85.

———. 2002. Gardening with the Great Goddess at Teotihuacan. In *Heart of Creation: The Mesoamerican World and the Legacy of Linda Schele,* ed. Andrea Stone, 83–100. Tuscaloosa: University of Alabama Press.

———. 2007. *The Teotihuacan Trinity: The Sociopolitical Structure of an Ancient Mesoamerican City.* Austin: University of Texas Press.

Healy, Paul F., Kitty F. Emery, and Lori E. Wright. 1990. Ancient and Modern Maya Exploitation of the Jute Snail (Pachychilus). *Latin American Antiquity* 1 (2): 170–183.

Hearth, Nicholas F. 2012. Organization of Chert Tool Economy during the Late and Terminal Classic Periods at Chan: Preliminary Thoughts Based upon Debitage Analysis. In *Chan: An Ancient Maya Farming Community,* ed. Cynthia Robin, 192–206. Gainesville: University Press of Florida.

Heckenberger, Michael J., J. Christian Russell, Carlos Fausto, Joshua R. Toney, Morgan J. Schmidt, Edithe Pereira, Bruna Franchetto, and Afukaka Kuikuro. 2008. Pre-Columbian Urbanism, Anthropogenic Landscapes, and the Future of the Amazon. *Science* 321 (5893): 1214–1217.

Hellmuth, Nicholas M. 1972. Excavations Begin at a Maya Site in Guatemala. *Archaeology* 25: 148–149.

Helmke, Christophe. 2013. Mesoamerican Lexical Calques in Ancient Maya Writing and Imagery. *PARI Journal* 14 (2): 1–15.

———. 2020. Comments on the Hieroglyphic Graffiti of the Tut Building (Structure A-5-2nd), El Castillo, Xunantunich. Unpublished paper in possession of M. Kathryn Brown.

Helmke, Christophe, and Jaime J. Awe. 2012. Ancient Maya Territorial Organisation of Central Belize: Confluence of Archaeological and Epigraphic Data. *Contributions in New World Archaeology* 4: 59–90.

———. 2016a. Sharper than a Serpent's Tooth: A Tale of the Snake-Head Dynasty as Recounted on Xunantunich Panel 4. *The PARI Journal* 17 (2): 1–22.

———. 2016b. Death Becomes Her: An Analysis of Panel 3, Xunantunich, Belize. *The PARI Journal* 16 (4): 1–14.

Helmke, Christophe G., Jaime J. Awe, and Nikolai Grube. 2010. The Carved Monuments and Inscriptions of Xunantunich. In *Classic Maya Provincial Politics: Xunantunich and Its Hinterlands,* ed. Lisa J. LeCount and Jason Yaeger, 97–121. Tucson: University of Arizona Press.

Helmke, Christophe, Arlen F. Chase, and Diane Z. Chase. 2019. Another Look at Stela 2 of Caracol, Belize. *Mexicon* 41 (1): 97–104.

518 · References

Helmke, Christophe, Julie A. Hoggarth, and Jaime J. Awe. 2018. *A Reading of the Komkom Vase Discovered at Baking Pot, Belize*. San Francisco: Precolumbia Mesoweb Press.

Helmke, Christophe, and Jesper Nielsen. 2015. The Defeat of the Great Bird in Myth and Royal Pageantry: A Mesoamerican Myth in a Comparative Perspective. *Comparative Mythology* 1 (1): 23–60.

———. 2017. Of Gods and Rituals: The Religion of Teotihuacan. In *Teotihuacan: City of Water, City of Fire*, ed. Matthew H. Robb, 130–137. San Francisco: Fine Arts Museums of San Francisco and University of California Press.

Helmke, Christophe G., and Jarosław Źrałka. 2021. Writing amidst the Scribbles: The Role and Place of Writing in Ancient Maya Graffiti. *Papers from the Institute of Archaeology* 31 (1): 93–120.

Hernández, Christine. 2004. "Yearbearer Pages" and Their Connection to Planting Almanacs in the Borgia Codex. In *The Madrid Codex: New Approaches to Understanding an Ancient Maya Manuscript,* ed. Gabrielle Vail and Anthony F. Aveni, 321–366. Boulder: University Press of Colorado.

Hernández, Christine, and Victoria R. Bricker. 2004. The Inauguration of Planting in the Borgia and Madrid Codices. In *The Madrid Codex: New Approaches to Understanding an Ancient Maya Manuscript,* ed. Gabrielle Vail and Anthony F. Aveni, 277–320. Boulder: University of Colorado Press.

Hernández Ayala, Martha Ivón. 1981. Cronología y periodificación de la región Del Río San Pedro Mártir, Tabasco. PhD diss., Escuela Nacional de Antropología e Historia, Mexico, D.F.

Herring, Adam. 1996. A Royal Artist at Naranjo: Notes on a Late Classic Maya Cylinder Vessel. *Yale University Art Gallery Bulletin* (1995–1996): 35–47.

Hicks, Frederick, and Charles E. Rosaire. 1960. *Mound 13, Chiapa de Corzo, Chiapas, Mexico*. Papers of the New World Archaeological Foundation no. 10, Provo, UT: Brigham Young University.

Hinton, Thomas B. 1964. The Cora Village: A Civil Religious Hierarchy in Northern Mexico. In *Culture Change and Stability: Essays in Memory of Olive Ruth Barker and George C. Baker Jr.*, 44–62. Berkeley: University of California Press.

Hirth, Kenneth G. 2003. The Altepetl and Urban Structure in Prehispanic Mesoamerica. In *El urbanismo en Mesoamerica/Urbanism in Mesoamerica*, ed. William T. Sanders, Alba Guadalupe Mestache, and Robert H. Cobean, 21–42. Mexico City: Instituto Nacional de Antropología y Historia, and University Park: Pennsylvania State University.

Hodder, Ian. 2007. Çatalhöyük in the Context of the Middle Eastern Neolithic. *Annual Review of Anthropology* 36: 105–120.

———. 2012. *Entangled: An Archaeology of the Relationships between Humans and Things*. London: Wiley-Blackwell.

———. 2016. More on History Houses at Çatalhöyük: A Response to Carleton et al. *Journal of Archaeological Science* 67: 1–6.

———. 2018. Introduction: Two Forms of History Making in the Neolithic of the Middle East. In *Religion, History, and Place in the Origin of Settled Life,* ed. Ian Hodder, 3–32. Boulder: University Press of Colorado.

Hodder, Ian, and Peter Pels. 2010. History Houses: A New Interpretation of Architectural

Elaboration at Çatalhöyük. In *Religion in the Emergence of Civilization: Çatalhöyük as a Case Study,* ed. Ian Hodder, 163–186. New York: Cambridge University Press.

Hodgson, John G., John G. Clark, and Emiliano Gallaga Murrieta. 2010. Ojo De Agua Monument 3: A New Olmec-Style Sculpture from Ojo De Agua, Chiapas, Mexico. *Mexicon* 32: 139–144.

Hoggarth, Julie A., Sebastian F. M. Breitenbach, Brendan J. Culleton, Claire E. Ebert, Marilyn A. Masson, and Douglas J. Kennett. 2016. The Political Collapse of Chichén Itzá in Climatic and Cultural Context. *Global and Planetary Change* 138: 25–42.

Holien, Thomas, and Robert B. Pickering. 1978. Analogues in a Chalchihuites Culture Sacrificial Burial to Late Mesoamerican Ceremonialism. In *Middle Classic Mesoamerica: A.D. 400–700,* ed. Ester Pasztory, 145–157. New York: Columbia University Press.

Holland, William R. 1964. Contemporary Tzotzil Cosmological Concepts as a Basis for Interpreting Prehistoric Maya Civilization. *American Antiquity* 29 (3): 301–306.

Houk, Brett, and Ashley Booher. 2020. All the World's a Stage: The Late Classic Built Environment of Chan Chich, Belize. In *Approaches to Monumental Landscapes of the Ancient Maya,* ed. Brett Houk, Barbara Arroyo, and Terry Powis, 152–170. Gainesville: University Press of Florida.

Houk, Brett A., and Gregory Zaro. 2011. Evidence for Ritual Engineering in the Late/Terminal Classic Site Plan of La Milpa, Belize. *Latin American Antiquity* 22 (2): 178–198.

Houston, Stephen D. 2000. Into the Minds of Ancients: Advances in Maya Glyph Studies. *Journal of World Prehistory* 14 (2): 121–201.

———. 2009. A Splendid Predicament: Young Men in Classic Maya Society. *Cambridge Archaeological Journal* 19 (2): 149–178.

———. 2011. Bending Time among the Maya. *Maya Decipherment,* June 24. https://mayadecipherment.com/2011/06/24/bending-time-among-the-maya/.

———. 2012. The Best of All Things: Beauty, Materials, and Society among the Classic Maya. In *Ancient Maya Art at Dumbarton Oaks,* ed. Joanne Pillsbury, Miriam Doutriaux, Raiko Ishihara-Brito, and Alexander Tokovinine, 86–99. Washington, DC: Dumbarton Oaks.

———. 2016. Crafting Credit: Authorship among Classic Maya Painters and Sculptors. In *Making Value, Making Meaning: Techné in the Pre-Columbian World,* ed. Cathy Lynne Costin, 391–431. Washington, DC: Dumbarton Oaks Research Library and Collection.

———. 2017a. Puzzle Writing. *Maya Decipherment,* February 13. https://decipherment.wordpress.com/2017/02/13/puzzle-writing/.

———. 2017b. Essential Luxuries: On Pleasing and Powerful Things among the Maya. In *Golden Kingdoms: Luxury Arts in the Ancient Americas,* ed. Joanne Pillsbury, Timothy Potts, and Kim N. Richter, 79–90. Los Angeles: J. Paul Getty Museum.

———. 2019. Watery War. Maya Decipherment: Ideas on Ancient Maya Writing and Iconography. *Maya Decipherment,* June 17. https://mayadecipherment.com/?s=Watery+War.

Houston, Stephen, ed. 2021. *A Maya Universe in Stone.* Los Angeles: The Getty Research Institute.

520 · References

Houston, Stephen D., Claudia Brittenham, Cassandra Mesick, Alexandre Tokovinine, and Christina Warinner. 2009. *Veiled Brightness: A History of Ancient Maya Color*. William and Bettye Nowlin Series in Art, History, and Culture of the Western Hemisphere. Austin: University of Texas Press.

Houston, Stephen D., Oswaldo Chinchilla Mazariegos, and David Stuart, eds. 2001. *The Decipherment of Ancient Maya Writing*. Norman: University of Oklahoma Press.

Houston, Stephen, Héctor Escobedo, Mark Child, Charles W. Golden, and René Muñoz. 2003. The Moral Community: Maya Settlement Transformation at Piedras Negras, Guatemala. In *The Social Construction of Ancient Cities*, ed. M. L. Smith, 212–253. Washington, DC: Smithsonian Books.

Houston, Stephen D., and Takeshi Inomata. 2009. *The Classic Maya*. New York: Cambridge University Press.

Houston, Stephen D., Edwin Román Ramírez, Thomas G. Garrison, David Stuart, Héctor Escobedo Ayala, and Pamela Rosales. 2021. A Teotihuacan Complex at the Classic Maya City of Tikal, Guatemala. *Antiquity* 95 (384): e32.

Houston, Stephen D., John Robertson, and David Stuart. 2000. The Language of Classic Maya Inscriptions. *Current Anthropology* 41: 321–356.

Houston, Stephen D., and David Stuart. 1996. Of Gods, Glyphs and Kings: Divinity and Rulership among the Classic Maya. *Antiquity* 70 (268): 289–312.

———. 1998. The Ancient Maya Self: Personhood and Portraiture in the Classic Period. *Res: Anthropology and Aesthetics* 33: 73–101.

Houston, Stephen, David Stuart, and Karl Taube. 1992. Image and Text on the "Jauncy Vase." In *The Maya Vase Book*, vol. 3, ed. Justin Kerr, 498–512. New York: Kerr Associates.

———. 2006. *The Memory of Bones: Body, Being, and Experience among the Classic Maya*. Austin: University of Texas Press.

Houston, S. D., and K. A. Taube. 2000. An Archaeology of the Senses: Perception and Cultural Expression in Ancient Mesoamerica. *Cambridge Archaeological Journal* 10 (2): 261–294.

Howe, Leopold E. A. 1981. The Social Determination of Knowledge: Maurice Bloch and Balinese Time. *Man* 16 (2): 220–234.

Hruby, Zachary X., and Gene Ware. 2009. Painted Lithic Artifacts from Piedras Negras, Guatemala. In *Maya Archaeology 1*, ed. Charles Golden, Stephen Houston, and Joel Skidmore, 76–85. San Francisco, CA: Precolumbia Mesoweb Press.

Hull, Kerry M. 2011. Ritual and Cosmological Landscapes of the Ch'orti' Maya. In *Ecology, Power, and Religion in Maya Landscapes*, ed. Christian Isendahl and Bodil Liljefors Persson, 159–166. Acta MesoAmericana 23. Markt Schwaben: Verlag Anton Saurwein.

———. 2017. Marking Time among the Ch'orti' Maya: An Expressive Act of Culture. *Maya Times* 2017: 429–450.

Hull, Kerry M., and Michael D. Carrasco. 2004. MAK-"Portal" Rituals Uncovered: An Approach to Interpreting Symbolic Architecture and the Creation of Sacred Space. In *Continuity and Change: Maya Religious Practices in Temporal Perspective*, ed. Daniel Graña Behrens, Nikolai Grube, Christian M. Prager, Frauke Sachse, Stefanie Teufel, and Elisabeth Wagner, 134–140. Acta Mesoamericana 15. Markt Schwaben: Verlag Anton Saurwein.

Hutson, Scott R. 2010. *Dwelling, Identity, and the Maya: Relational Archaeology at Chunchucmil*. Lanham, MD: AltaMira Press.

———. 2011. The Art of Becoming: The Graffiti of Tikal, Guatemala. *Latin American Antiquity* 22 (4): 403–426.

———. 2015. Adapting LiDAR Data for Regional Variation in the Tropics: A Case Study from the Northern Maya Lowlands. *Journal of Archaeological Science: Reports* 4: 252–263.

Hutson, Scott R., Aline Magnoni, and Travis W. Stanton. 2012. "All that is solid . . .": Sacbes, Settlement, and Semiotics at Tzacauil, Yucatan. *Ancient Mesoamerica* 23: 297–311.

Iannone, Gyles. 2002. Annales History and the Ancient Maya State: Some Observations on the "Dynamic Model." *American Anthropologist* 104: 68–78.

Iannone, Gyles, ed. 2014. *The Great Maya Droughts in Cultural Context: Case Studies in Resilience and Vulnerability*. Boulder: University Press of Colorado.

Ingold, Timothy. 1993. The Temporality of the Landscape. *World Archaeology* 25 (2): 152–174.

———. 1999. On the Social Relations of the Hunter-Gatherer Band. In *The Cambridge Encyclopedia of Hunters and Gathers,* ed. Richard B. Lee and Richard Daly, 399–440. Cambridge: Cambridge University Press.

Inomata, Takeshi. 2006. Plazas, Performers, and Spectators: Political Theaters of the Classic Maya. *Current Anthropology* 47 (5): 805–842.

———. 2017a. The Emergence of Standardized Spatial Plans in Southern Mesoamerica: Chronology and Interregional Interactions Viewed from Ceibal, Guatemala. *Ancient Mesoamerica* 28 (1): 329–355.

———. 2017b. The Isthmian Origins of the E Group and Its Adoption in the Maya Lowlands. In *Maya E Groups: Calendars, Astronomy, and Urbanism in the Early Lowlands,* ed. David A. Freidel, Arlen F. Chase, Anne S. Dowd, and Jerry Murdock, 215–252. Gainesville: University Press of Florida.

Inomata, Takeshi, and Laurence S. Coben, eds. 2006. *The Archaeology of Performance, Theaters of Power, Community and Performance*. Lanham, MD: AltaMira Press.

Inomata, Takeshi, Juan Carlos Fernandez-Diaz, Daniela Triadan, Miguel García Mollinedo, Flory Pinzón, Melina García Hernández, Atasta Flores, Ashley Sharpe, Timothy Beach, Gregory W. L. Hodgins, Juan Javier Durón Díaz, Antonio Guerra Luna, Luis Guerrero Chaves, María de Lourdes Hernández Jiménez, and Manuel Moreno Díaz. 2021. Origins and Spread of Formal Ceremonial Complexes in the Olmec and Maya Regions Revealed by Airborne Lidar. *Nature Human Behaviour* 5: 1–15.

Inomata, Takeshi, Jessica MacLellan, and Melissa Burham. 2015. The Construction of Public and Domestic Spheres in the Preclassic Maya Lowlands. *American Anthropologist* 117 (3): 519–534.

Inomata, Takeshi, Jessica MacLellan, Daniela Triadan, Jessica Munson, Melissa Burham, Kazuo Aoyama, Hiroo Nasu, Flory Pinzón, and Hitoshi Yonenobu. 2015. Development of Sedentary Communities in the Maya Lowlands: Coexisting Mobile Groups and Public Ceremonies at Ceibal, Guatemala. *Proceedings of the National Academy of Sciences of the United States of America* 112 (14): 4268–4273.

Inomata, Takeshi, Flory Pinzón, Juan Manuel Palomo, Ashley Sharpe, Raúl Ortiz, María Belén Méndez, and Otto Román. 2017. Public Ritual and Interregional Interactions:

Excavations of the Central Plaza of Group A, Ceibal. *Ancient Mesoamerica* 28 (1): 203–232.

Inomata, Takeshi, Flory Pinzón, José Luis Ranchos, Tsuyoshi Haraguchi, Hiroo Nasu, Juan Carlos Fernandez-Diaz, Kazuo Aoyama, and Hitoshi Yonenobu. 2017. Archaeological Application of Airborne LiDAR with Object-Based Vegetation Classification and Visualization Techniques at the Lowland Maya Site of Ceibal, Guatemala. *Remote Sensing* 9 (6): 563.

Inomata, Takeshi, and Daniela Triadan. 2016. Middle Preclassic Caches from Ceibal, Guatemala. *Maya Archaeology* 3: 56–91.

Inomata, Takeshi, Daniela Triadan, and Kazuo Aoyama. 2017. After 40 Years: Revisiting Ceibal to Investigate the Origins of Lowland Maya Civilization. *Ancient Mesoamerica* 28 (1): 187–201.

Inomata, Takeshi, Daniela Triadan, Kazuo Aoyama, Victor Castillo, and Hitoshi Yonenobu. 2013. Early Ceremonial Constructions at Ceibal, Guatemala, and the Origins of Lowland Maya Civilization. *Science* 340 (6131): 467–471.

Inomata, Takeshi, Daniela Triadan, Flory Pinzón, Melissa Burham, José Luis Ranchos, Kazuo Aoyama, and Tsuyoshi Haraguchi. 2018. Archaeological Application of Airborne LiDAR to Examine Social Changes in the Ceibal Region of the Maya Lowlands. *PLOS ONE* 13 (2): e0191619.

Inomata, Takeshi, Daniela Triadan, Verónica A. Vázquez López, Juan Carlos Fernandez-Diaz, Takayuki Omori, María Belén Méndez Bauer, Melina García Hernández, Timothy Beach, Clarissa Cagnato, Kazuo Aoyama, and Hiroo Nasu. 2020. Monumental Architecture at Aguada Fenix and the Rise of Maya Civilization. *Nature* 582 (7813): 530–533.

Ixtlilxochitl, Fernando de Alva. 1975. *Obras históricas*. Mexico City: Universidad Nacional Autónoma de México.

Izumi, Seiichi, and Toshihiko Sono. 1963. *Andes 2: Excavations at Kotosh, Peru*. Tokyo: Kadokawa.

Jobbová, Eva, Christophe Helmke, and Andrew Bevan. 2018. Ritual Responses to Drought: An Examination of Ritual Expressions in Classic Maya Written Sources. *Human Ecology* 46: 759–781.

Johnson, Lucas R. Martindale. 2016. Toward an Itinerary of Stone: Investigating the Movement, Crafting, and Use of Obsidian from Caracol, Belize. PhD diss., University of Florida, Gainesville.

Jones, Christopher. 1969. The Twin Pyramid Group Pattern: A Classic Maya Architectural Assemblage at Tikal, Guatemala. PhD diss., University of Pennsylvania, Philadelphia.

———. 1996. *Excavations in the East Plaza of Tikal*. University Museum Monographs 92. Philadelphia: University of Pennsylvania.

Jones, Christopher, and Linton Satterthwaite Jr. 1982. *The Monuments and Inscriptions of Tikal: The Carved Monuments*. Philadelphia: University Museum of Archaeology and Anthropology.

Just, Bryan. 2012. *Dancing into Dreams: Maya Vase Painting of the Ik' Kingdom*. Princeton, NJ: Princeton University Art Museum.

Justeson, John S. 1978. Mayan Scribal Practice in the Classic Period: A Test-Case of an Explanatory Approach. PhD diss., Stanford University.

———. 2001. Practiche di Calcolo nell'antica Mesomamerica. In *Storia della Scienza,* vol. 2, ed. A. F. Aveni, 976–990. Rome: Istituto della Enciclopedia Italiana, Fondata da Giovanni Treccani.

———. 2010. Numerical Cognition and the Development of 'Zero' in Mesoamerica. In *The Archaeology of Measurement: Comprehending Heaven, Earth and Time in Ancient Societies,* ed. Iain Morely and Colin Renfrew, 43–53. Cambridge: Cambridge University Press.

———. 2012. Early Mesoamerican Writing Systems. In *Oxford Handbook of Mesoamerican Archaeology,* ed. Deborah L. Nichols and Christopher A. Pool, 830–844. Oxford: Oxford University Press.

Justeson, John S., William M. Norman, Lyle Campbell, and Terrence Kaufman. 1985. *The Foreign Impact on Lowland Mayan Language and Script.* Publication 53. New Orleans, LA: Middle American Research Institute, Tulane University.

Justeson, John, and David Tavárez. 2007. The Correlation between the Colonial Northern Zapotec and Gregorian Calendars. In *Cultural Astronomy in New and Old World Cosmologies,* ed. C. Ruggles and G. Urton, 17–81. Boulder: University Press of Colorado.

Kampen, Michael. 1978. The Graffiti of Tikal. *Estudios de Cultura Maya* 11: 155–179.

Kaufman, Terrence. 2017. Aspects of the Lexicon of Proto-Mayan and Its Earliest Descendants. In *The Mayan Languages,* ed. J. Aissen, N. C. England, and R. Zavala Maldonado, 62–111. London: Routledge/Taylor & Francis Group.

Kaufman, Terrence, and John S. Justeson. 2001. *Epi-Olmec Hieroglyphic Writing and Texts.* Part Three of *Notebook for the XXVth Maya Hieroglyphic Forum at Texas.* Austin: University of Texas. https://www.albany.edu/ims/pdlma/EOTEXTS.pdf.

Kaufman, Terrence S., with the assistance of John S. Justeson. 2002–2003. A Preliminary Mayan Etymological Dictionary. Unpublished document. http://www.famsi.org/reports/01051/pmed.pdf.

Kaufman, Terrence, and William M. Norman. 1984. An Outline of Proto-Cholan Phonology, Morphology, and Vocabulary. *In Phoneticism in Mayan Hieroglyphic Writing,* ed. John S. Justeson and Lyle Campbell, 77–166. Institute for Mesoamerican Studies Publication 9. Albany: State University of New York at Albany.

Keller, Angela H. 2006. Roads to the Center: The Design, Use, and Meaning of the Roads of Xunantunich, Belize. PhD diss., University of Pennsylvania, Philadelphia.

———. 2012. Creating Community with Shell. In *Chan: An Ancient Maya Farming Community,* ed. Cynthia Robin, 253–270. Gainesville: University Press of Florida.

Kelley, David H. 1976. *Deciphering the Maya Script.* Austin: University of Texas Press.

Kelly, Mary Kate. 2019. Documentación epigráfica: Ilustración de inscripciones jeroglíficas de El Perú-Waka'. In *Proyecto Arqueológico Waka',* ed. Juan Carlos Pérez, Griselda Pérez, and Damien Marken, 349–361. Informe no. 16, Temporada 2018. Report delivered to the General Directorate of Cultural and Natural Heritage Ministry of Culture and Sports, Guatemala, Guatemala City.

———. 2020. Epigraphy of El Peru-Waka'. Manuscript for El Peru-Waka Project. In possession of David A. Freidel.

Kelly, Robert L. 1994. Mesoamerican Codices: Where Did Their Authors Come From? *University of Louisville Library Review* 44: 7–15.

524 · References

Kennett, Douglas J., Sebastian F. M. Breitenbach, Valorie V. Aquino, Yemane Asmerom, Jaime Awe, James U. L. Baldini, Patrick Bartlein, Brendan J. Culleton, Claire Ebert, Christopher Jazwa, Martha J. Macri, Norbert Marwan, Victor Polyak, Keith M. Prufer, Harriet E. Ridley, Harald Sodemann, Bruce Winterhalder, and Gerald H. Haug. 2012. Development and Disintegration of Maya Political Systems in Response to Climate Change. *Science* 338 (6108): 788–791.

Kennett, Douglas J., Keith M. Prufer, Brendan J. Culleton, Richard J. George, Mark Robinson, Willa R. Trask, Gina M. Buckley, Emily Moes, Emily J. Kate, Thomas K. Harper, Lexi O'Donnell, Erin E. Ray, Ethan C. Hill, Asia Alsgaard, Christopher Merriman, Clayton Meredith, Heather J. H. Edgar, Jaime J. Awe, and Said M. Gutierrez. 2020. Early Isotopic Evidence for Maize as a Staple Grain in the Americas. *Science Advances* 6 (23): eaba3245.

Kennett, Douglas J., Heather B. Thakar, Amber M. VanDerwarker, David L. Webster, Brendan J. Culleton, Thomas K. Harper, Logan Kistler, Timothy E. Scheffler, and Kenneth Hirth. 2017. High-Precision Chronology for Central American Maize Diversification from El Gigante Rockshelter, Honduras. *Proceedings of the National Academy of Sciences of the United States of America* 114 (34): 9026–9031.

Kerr, Barbara, and Justin Kerr. 2005. The *Way* of God L: The Princeton Vase Revisited. *Record of the Princeton Art Museum* 64: 71–79.

Kerr, Justin. 1997. *The Maya Vase Book: A Corpus of Rollout Photographs of Maya Vases*. Vol. 5. New York: Kerr Associates.

Kerr, Justin, and Barbara Kerr. 1988. Some Observations on Maya Vase Painters. In *Maya Iconography,* ed. Elizabeth P. Benson and Gillett G. Griffin, 236–59. Princeton, NJ: Princeton University Press.

Kestle, Caleb. 2012. Limestone Quarrying and Household Organization at Chan. In *Chan: An Ancient Maya Farming Community,* ed. Cynthia Robin, 207–230. Gainesville: University Press of Florida.

Kettunen, Hari, and Christophe Helmke. 2013. Water in Maya Imagery and Writing. *Contributions in New World Archaeology* 5:17–38.

Kidder, Alfred V. 1947. *The Artifacts of Uaxactun, Guatemala*. Publication 576. Washington, DC: Carnegie Institution of Washington.

Kidder, Tristan R. 2011. Transforming Hunter-Gatherer History at Poverty Point. In *Hunter-Gatherer Archaeology as Historical Process,* ed. Kenneth E. Sassaman and Donald H. Holly, 95–119. Tucson: University of Arizona Press.

Killion, Thomas W. 2013. Nonagricultural Cultivation and Social Complexity: The Olmec, Their Ancestors, and Mexico's Southern Gulf Coast Lowlands. *Current Anthropology* 54 (5).

Killsback, Leo. 2013. Indigenous Perceptions of Time: Decolonizing Theory, World History, and the Fates of Human Societies. *American Indian Culture and Research Journal* 37 (4): 85–113.

Kirchhoff, Paul. 1943. Mesoamérica, sus límites geográficos, composición étnica y caracteres culturales. *Acta Americana* 1: 92–107.

Kirk, Geoffrey S. 1970. *Myth: Its Meaning and Functions in Ancient and Other Cultures*. Sather Classical Lectures vol. 40. Berkeley: University of California Press.

Kistler, Logan, S. Yoshi Maezumi, Jonas Gregorio De Souza, Natalia A. S. Przelomska,

Flaviane Malaquias Costa, Oliver Smith, Hope Loiselle, Jazmín Ramos-Madrigal, Nathan Wales, and Eduardo Rivail Ribeiro. 2018. Multiproxy Evidence Highlights a Complex Evolutionary Legacy of Maize in South America. *Science* 362 (6420): 1309–1313.

Kistler, Logan, Heather B. Thakar, Amber M. VanDerwarker, Alejandra Domic, Anders Bergström, Richard J. George, Thomas K. Harper, Robin G. Allaby, Kenneth Hirth, and Douglas J. Kennett. 2020. Archaeological Central American Maize Genomes Suggest Ancient Gene Flow from South America. *Proceedings of the National Academy of Sciences* 117 (52): 33124–33129.

Knapp, A. Bernard, and Wendy Ashmore. 1999. Archaeological Landscapes: Constructed, Conceptualized, and Ideational. In *Archaeologies of Landscape: Contemporary Perspectives,* ed. Wendy Ashmore and A. Bernard Knapp, 1–32. Oxford: Blackwell Publishers.

Knowlton, Timothy W. 2010. *Maya Creation Myths: Words and Worlds of the Chilam Balam.* Boulder: University Press of Colorado.

———. 2012. Some Historical Continuities in Lowland Maya Magical Speech Genres: Keying Shamanic Performance. In *Parallel Worlds: Genre, Discourse, and Poetics in Contemporary, Colonial, and Classic Period Maya Literature,* ed. Kerry M. Hull and Michael D. Carrasco, 253–269. Boulder: University Press of Colorado.

———. 2015. Inscribing the Miraculous Place: Writing and Ritual Communication in the Chapel of a Guatemalan Popular Saint. *Journal of Linguistic Anthropology* 25 (3): 239–255.

Köhler, Ulrich. 1980. Cosmovisión indígena e interpretación europea en estudios mesoamericanistas. In *La antropología americanista en la actualidad: Homenaje a Raphael Girard,* vol. 1, 583–596. Mexico City: Editores Mexicanos Unidos.

Kosakowsky, Laura J. 2007. "Preliminary Report on the Analysis of the Ceramics from the Chan Project: 2007 Laboratory Season." In *The Chan Project Report: 2007 Season,* ed. C. Robin, 3–24. Report submitted to the Belize Institute of Archaeology, Belmopan.

———. 2012. Ceramics and Chronology at Chan. In *Chan: An Ancient Maya Farming Community,* ed. Cynthia Robin, 42–70. Gainesville: University Press of Florida.

Krakauer, David C. 2019. SFI Video, https://www.youtube.com/watch?v=ThX2ABAsEck &list=RDCMUC9rHXgUE9pikzYcGrAujMXQ&index=2, accessed Sept. 3, 2021.

Kubler, George. 1974. Mythological Ancestries in Classic Maya Inscriptions. In *Primera Mesa Redonda de Palenque,* part II, ed. Merle Greene Robertson, 23–43. Pebble Beach, CA: Pre-Columbian Art Research Institute.

Kupprat, Felix A., Kathryn Reese-Taylor, Debra Walker, Armando Anaya Hernandez, Matthew Longstaffe, Max Seidita, and Joshuah Lockett-Harris. Forthcoming. La transición del Preclásico al Clásico en Yaxnohcah. In *Sociedades tempranas y urbanismo en el periodo Preclásico (1000 A.C.–200 D.C.): Yaxnohcah y la region del Usumacinto medio,* ed. Verónica A. Vázquez López. UNAM.

Kurnick, Sarah. 2016. Paradoxical Politics: Negotiating the Contradictions of Political Authority. In *Political Strategies in Pre-Columbian Mesoamerica,* ed. S. Kurnick and J. P. Baron, 3–36. Boulder: University Press of Colorado.

Lacadena García-Gallo, Alfonso. 2000. Los escribas del Códice de Madrid: metodología paleográfica. *Revista Española de Antropología Americana* 30: 27–85.

526 · References

———. 2004. *The Glyphic Corpus from Ek' Balam*. Trans. Alex Lomónaco. Unpublished report. http://www.famsi.org/reports/01057/01057LacadenaGarciaGallo01.pdf.

———. 2010. Highland Mexican and Maya Intellectual Exchange in the Late Postclassic: Some Thoughts on the Origin of Shared Elements and Methods of Interaction. In *Astronomers, Scribes, and Priests: Intellectual Interchange between the Northern Maya Lowlands and Highland Mexico in the Late Postclassic Period,* ed. Gabrielle Vail and Christine Hernández, 383–406. Washington, DC: Dumbarton Oaks.

Lamb, Weldon W. 2017. *The Maya Calendar: A Book of Months, 400–2000 CE*. Norman: University of Oklahoma Press.

Landau, Kristin. 2015. Spatial Logic and Maya City Planning. *Cambridge Archaeological Journal* 25 (1): 275–292.

Landon, Amanda J. 2011. *Identifying the Trees in the West Wall Mural in Room 1 of the Pyramid of Las Pinturas at San Bartolo, Petén, Guatemala*. Report to the Mesoamerica Laboratory and Library at Washington State University in St. Louis. http://blm.academia.edu/AmandaJLandon/Papers/742711/Identifying_the_Trees_in_the_West_Wall_Mural_in_Room_1_of_the_Pyramid_of_Las_Pinturas_at_San_Bartolo_Peten_Guatemala.

Langley, James C. 1991. The Forms and Usage of Notation at Teotihuacan. *Ancient Mesoamerica* 2 (2): 285–298.

———. 1992. Teotihuacan Sign Clusters: Emblem or Articulation? In *Art, Ideology, and the City of Teotihuacan,* ed. Janet C. Berlo, 247–280. Washington, DC: Dumbarton Oaks.

Laporte, Juan Pedro. 1987. El "talud-tablero" en Tikal, Petén: Nuevos datos. In *Homenaje a Román Piña Chan,* ed. B. Dahlgren, C. Navarrete, L. Ochoa, M. C. Serra Puche, and Y. Sugiera, 265–316. Mexico City: UNAM.

———. 2003. Thirty Years Later: Some Results of Recent Investigations in Tikal. In *Tikal: Dynasties, Foreigners, and Affairs of State,* ed. Jeremy A. Sabloff, 281–318. Santa Fe, NM: School of American Research Press.

Laporte, Juan Pedro, and Vilma Fialko. 1994. Mundo Perdido, Tikal: Los enunciados actuals. In *VII simposio de investigaciones arqueológicas en Guatemala, 1993,* ed. Juan Pedro Laporte and Héctor Escobedo, 335–348. Guatemala City: Museo Nacional de Arqueología y Etnología.

———. 1995. Reencuentro con mundo Perdido, Tikal, Guatemala. *Ancient Mesoamerica* 6: 41–94.

Laughlin, Robert. 1975. *The Great Tzotzil Dictionary of San Lorenzo Zinacantán*. Smithsonian Contributions to Anthropology 19. Washington, DC: Smithsonian Institution.

Layton, Robert. 1986. Political and Territorial Structures among Hunter-Gatherers. *Man* 21 (1): 18–33.

LeCount, Lisa J., and Jason Yaeger. 2010a. A Brief Description of Xunantunich. In *Classic Maya Provincial Politics: Xunantunich and Its Hinterlands,* ed. Lisa J. LeCount and Jason Yaeger, 67–78. Tucson: University of Arizona Press.

———. 2010b. Provincial Politics and Current Models of the Maya State. In *Classic Maya Provincial Politics: Xunantunich and Its Hinterlands,* ed. Lisa J. LeCount and Jason Yaeger, 20–45. Tucson: University of Arizona Press.

LeCount, Lisa J., Jason Yaeger, Bernadette Cap, and Borislava Simova. Forthcoming. Tangled Web: The Pragmatics of Maya Political Integration in Mopan River Valley

Regimes. In *Regimes of the Classic Maya,* ed. Marcello A. Canuto and Maxime Lamoureux-St-Hilaire. Cambridge: Cambridge University Press.

Lee, David F. 2012. Approaching the End: Royal Ritual in the Palace Group at El Peru-Waka', Peten, Guatemala. PhD diss., Southern Methodist University, Dallas, TX.

Lee, David F., and Stanley Guenter. 2010. Ballgame Panels from El Peru-Waka' in Regional Perspective. Paper presented at the 75th Annual Meeting of the Society for American Archaeology, 14–18 April, St. Louis, MO.

Lee, David Henry, and Laura Gámez. 2006. Wk06: Excavaciones en el Complejo Palaciego Noroeste. Resultados de la temporada de campo de 2006. In *Proyecto Arqueológico Waka',* ed. Héctor Escobedo and David A. Freidel, 103–130. Informe no. 3, Temporada 2006. Informe entregado a la Dirección General del Patrimonio Cultural y Natural de Guatemala, Guatemala City.

Lee, Richard B. 1979. *The !Kung San: Men, Women, and Work in a Foraging Society.* Cambridge: Cambridge University Press.

Lefort, Genevieve. 2000. La royauté sacrée chez les Mayas de l'époque classique (200–900 ap. J.-C.). Thèse de Doctorat, Université Libre de Bruxelles, France.

Lelgemann, Achim. 1999. *Die Zitadelle von La Quemada, Zacatecas: Archäologische Untersuchungen in einem spätklassischen Patio-Komplex der nordwestlichen Peripherie Mesoamerikas.* Berlin: Freie Universität Berlin.

———. 2016. Pre-Hispanic Iron-Ore Mirrors and Mosaics from Zacatecas. In *Manufactured Light: Mirrors in the Mesoamerican Realm,* ed. E. Gallaga, and M. G. Blainey, 161–178. Boulder: University Press of Colorado.

Lemonnier, Pierre. 1986. The Study of Material Culture Today: Toward an Anthropology of Technical Systems. *Journal of Anthropological Archaeology* 5: 147–186.

———. 1992. *Elements for an Anthropology of Technology.* Anthropological Papers of the Museum of Anthropology 88. Ann Arbor: Museum of Anthropology, University of Michigan.

———. 2018. Shall We Just Call Them Sociomaterial Black Boxes or Take a Peek Inside? An Anthropologist's Impressionist Remarks. In *Materiality and Managerial Techniques,* ed. N. Mitev, A. Morgan-Thomas, P. Lorino, F.-X. de Vaujany, and Y. Nama, 167–192. New York: Palgrave Macmillan.

León Portilla, Miguel. 1988. *Time and Reality in the Thought of the Maya.* 2nd ed. The Civilization of the American Indian Series vol. 190. Norman: University of Oklahoma Press.

Lesure, Richard G., R. J. Sinensky, and Thomas A. Wake. 2021. The End of the Archaic in the Soconusco Region of Mesoamerica: A Tipping Point in the Local Trajectory toward Agricultural Village Life. In *Preceramic Mesoamerica,* ed. Jon C. Lohse, Aleksander Borejsza, and Arthur A. Joyce, 481–504. New York: Routledge.

Lesure, Richard G., and Thomas A. Wake. 2011. Archaic to Formative in Soconusco: The Adaptive and Organizational Transformation. In *Early Mesoamerican Social Transformations: Archaic and Formative Lifeways in the Soconusco Region,* ed. Richard G. Lesure, 67–93. Berkeley: University of California Press.

Leventhal, Richard M. 2010. Changing Places: The Castillo and the Structure of Power at Xunantunich. In *Classic Maya Provincial Politics: Xunantunich and Its Hinterlands,* ed. Lisa J. LeCount and Jason Yaeger, 79–96. Tucson: University of Arizona Press.

528 · References

Leventhal, Richard M., and Wendy Ashmore. 2004. Xunantunich in a Belize Valley Context. In *The Ancient Maya of the Belize Valley: Half a Century of Archaeological Research,* ed. James F. Garber, 168–179. Gainesville: University Press of Florida.

Lévi-Strauss, Claude. 1967. The Social and Psychological Aspects of Chieftainship in a Primitive Tribe: the Nambikuara of Northwestern Mato Grosso. In *Comparative Political Systems,* ed. R. Cohen and J. Middleton, 45–62. Austin: University of Texas Press.

Limón Olvera, Silvia. 2001. El dios del fuego y la regeneración del mundo. *Estudios de Cultura Náhuatl* 32: 51–68.

Lincoln, Charles E. 1990. Ethnicity and Social Organization at Chichen Itza, Yucatan, Mexico. PhD diss., Peabody Museum of Archaeology and Ethnology, Harvard University.

Lincoln, J. Steward. 1942. *The Maya Calendar of the Ixil of Guatemala.* Contributions to American Anthropology and History 38. Washington, DC: Carnegie Institution of Washington.

Lind, Michael. 2015. *Ancient Zapotec Religion: An Ethnohistorical and Archaeological Perspective.* Boulder: University Press of Colorado.

Lohse, Jon C. 2010. Archaic Origins of the Lowland Maya. *Latin American Antiquity* 21 (3): 312–352.

Lohse, Jon C., Aleksander Borejsza, and Arthur A. Joyce, eds. 2021. *Preceramic Mesoamerica.* New York: Routledge.

Long, R. C. E. 1923. The Burner Period of the Mayas. *Man* 23 (108): 73–176.

Looper, Matthew G. 1995. The Three Stones of Maya Creation Mythology at Quiriguá. *Mexicon* 17 (2): 24–30.

———. 2003. *Lightning Warrior: Maya Art and Kingship at Quirigua.* Austin: University of Texas Press.

———. 2014. *Lightning Warrior: Maya Art and Kingship at Quirigua.* The Linda Schele Series in Maya and Pre-Columbian Studies. Austin: University of Texas Press.

———. 2019. *The Beast Between: Deer Imagery in Ancient Maya Art.* Austin: University of Texas Press.

Looper, Matthew G., and Martha J. Macri. 1991–2022. Maya Hieroglyphic Database. Department of Art and Art History, California State University, Chico. www.mayadatabase.org.

Looper, Matthew, Martha Macri, Yuriy Polyukhovych, and Gabrielle Vail. 2022. Maya Hieroglyphic Database Reference Materials 1: Preliminary Revised Glyph Catalog. *Glyph Dwellers* 71.

López Austin, Alfredo. 1980. *Cuerpo humano e ideología: las concepciones de los antiguos Nahuas.* Mexico City: Universidad Nacional Autónoma de México.

———. 1988. *The Human Body and Ideology: Concepts of the Ancient Nahuas.* Salt Lake City: University of Utah Press.

López Austin, Alfredo, and Leonardo López-Luján. 2009. *Monte sagrado: Templo Mayor.* Mexico City: Instituto Nacional de Antropología e Historia/Instituto de Investigaciones Antropológicas-UNAM.

López Austin, Alfredo, Saburo Sugiyama, and Alfredo López Luján. 1991. The Temple of Quetzalcoatl at Teotihuacan: Its Possible Ideological Significance. *Ancient Mesoamerica* 2: 93–105.

López de Cogolludo, Juan. 1688. *Historia de la Provincia de Yucatan*. Madrid: Juan Garcia Infanzon.

López de Llano, Héctor. 2019. *Los voladores de Papantla: Una Mirada desde la ethnomusicología*. Universidad Nacional Autónoma de México, México, D.F.

Loughmiller-Newman, Jennifer A. 2008. Canons of Maya Painting: A Spatial Analysis of Classic Period Polychromes. *Ancient Mesoamerica* 19: 29–42.

———. 2012. The Analytic Reconciliation of Classic Mayan Elite Pottery: Squaring Pottery Function with Form, Adornment, and Residual Contents. PhD diss., State University of New York, Albany.

Lounsbury, Floyd G. 1976. A Rationale for the Initial Date of the Temple of the Cross at Palenque. In *The Art, Iconography, and Dynastic History of Palenque, Part III: Proceedings of the Segunda Mesa Redonda de Palenque, December 14–21, 1974—Palenque,* ed. M. G. Robertson, 211–224. Pebble Beach, CA: Robert Louis Stevenson School.

———. 1978. *Maya Numeration, Computation, and Calendrical Astronomy*. New York: Charles Scribner and Sons.

———. 1982. Astronomical Knowledge and Its Uses at Bonampak, Mexico. In *Archaeoastronomy in the New World,* ed. Anthony Aveni, 143–168. Cambridge, MA: Cambridge University Press.

Love, Bruce. 1992. Divination and Prophecy in Yucatan. In *New Theories on the Ancient Maya,* ed. Elin C. Danien and Robert J. Sharer, 205–216. Philadelphia: University of Pennsylvania Press.

———. 1994. *The Paris Codex: Handbook for a Maya Priest*. Austin: University of Texas Press.

Love, Michael W. 1999. Ideology, Material Culture, and Daily Practice in Pre-Classic Mesoamerica: A Pacific Coast Perspective. In *Social Patterns in Pre-Classic Mesoamerica,* ed. David C. Grove and Rosemary A. Joyce, 127–153. Washington, DC: Dumbarton Oaks.

Low, Setha M., and Denise Lawrence-Zúñiga, eds. 2003. *The Anthropology of Space and Place: Locating Culture*. Blackwell, Malden, MA.

Lowe, Gareth W. 1962. *Mound 5 and Minor Excavations, Chiapa de Corzo, Chiapas, Mexico*. Papers of the New World Archaeological Foundation no. 12, Provo, UT: Brigham Young University.

———. 1977. The Mixe-Zoque as Competing Neighbors of the Early Lowland Maya. In *The Origins of Maya Civilization,* ed. Richard E. W. Adams, 197–248. Albuquerque: University of New Mexico Press.

———. 1981. Olmec Horizon Defined in Mound 20, San Isidro, Chiapas. In *The Olmec and Their Neighbors,* ed. Michael D. Coe and David Grove, 231–256. Washington, DC: Dumbarton Oaks.

———. 1989. The Heartland Olmec: Evolution of Material Culture. In *Regional Perspectives on the Olmec,* ed. Robert J. Sharer and David C. Grove, 33–67. Cambridge: Cambridge University Press.

———. 2007. Early Formative Chiapas: The Beginnings of Civilization in the Central Depression of Chiapas. In *Archaeology, Art, and Ethnogenesis in Mesoamerican Prehistory: Papers in Honor of Gareth W. Lowe,* ed. Lynneth S. Lowe and Mary E. Pye, 63–108. Provo, UT: Brigham Young University.

530 · References

Lowe, Gareth W., and Pierre Agrinier. 1960. *Mound 1, Chiapa de Corzo, Chiapas, Mexico.* Papers of the New World Archaeological Foundation no. 8. Provo, UT: Brigham Young University.

Lowe, John W. G. 1985. *The Dynamics of Apocalypse: A Systems Simulation of the Classic Maya Collapse.* Albuquerque: University of New Mexico Press.

Lowie, Robert H. 1948. Some Aspects of Political Organization among the American Aborigines. *The Journal of the Royal Anthropological Institute of Great Britain and Ireland* 78 (1–2): 11–24.

Macri, Martha J., and Matthew G. Looper. 2003. *The New Catalog of Maya Hieroglyphs.* Vol. 1, *The Classic Period Inscriptions.* Norman: University of Oklahoma Press.

Macri, Martha J., and Gabrielle Vail. 2009. *The New Catalog of Maya Hieroglyphs.* Vol. 2, *Codical Texts.* Norman: University of Oklahoma Press.

Magar, Valerie, and Patricia Meehan. 1995. Investigación para la interpretación y la conservación de un disco de mosaico de turquesa. Licenciatura tesis. ENR-Churubusco, Mexico, D.F.

Malmström, Vincent H. 1981. Architecture, Astronomy, and Calendrics in Precolumbian Mesoamerica. In *Archaeoastronomy in the Americas,* ed. R. A. Williamson, 249–261. Los Altos, CA: Ballena Press.

———. 1997. *Cycles of the Sun, Mysteries of the Moon: The Calendar in Mesoamerican Civilization.* Austin: University of Texas Press.

Marcus, Joyce. 1976. Origins of Mesoamerican Writing. *Annual Review of Anthropology* 5: 35–67.

Marcus, Joyce, and Kent V. Flannery. (1983) 2003. *The Cloud People: Divergent Evolution of the Zapotec and Mixtec Civilizations.* Bristol, CT: Percheron Press/Eliot Werner Publications.

Martin, Simon. 1997. The Painted King List: A Commentary on Codex-Style Dynastic Vases. In *The Maya Vase Book: A Corpus of Rollout Photographs of Maya Vases,* vol. 5, ed. Barbara Kerr and Justin Kerr, 847–867. New York: Kerr Associates.

———. 2000. Nuevos datos epigraficos sobre la Guerra Maya del Classico. In *La guerra entre los antiguos Mayas: Memoria de la Primera Mesa Redonda de Palenque 1995,* ed. Silvia Trejo, 105–124. Mexico City: INAH.

———. 2005. Caracol Altar 21 Revisited: More Data on Double-Bird and Tikal's Wars of the Mid-Sixth Century. *The PARI Journal* 6 (1): 1–9.

———. 2008. Wives and Daughters on the Dallas Altar. www.mesoweb.com/articles/martin/Wives&Daughters.pdf.

———. 2010. The Dark Lord of Maya Trade. In *Fiery Pool: The Maya and the Mythic Sea,* ed. Daniel Finamore and Stephen Houston, 160–162. Salem, MA: Peabody Essex Museum.

———. 2014. Early Classic Co-Rulers on Tikal Temple VI. *Maya Decipherment,* November 22. https://mayadecipherment.com/2014/11/22/early-classic-co-rulers-on-tikal-temple-vi/.

———. 2015. The Old Man of the Maya Universe: A Unitary Dimension to Ancient Maya Religion. In *Maya Archaeology 3,* ed. Charles Golden, Stephen Houston, and Joel Skidmore, 186–227. San Francisco: Precolumbia Mesoweb Press.

———. 2016. Ideology and the Early Maya Polity. In *Origins of Maya States,* ed. Loa Traxler and Robert J. Sharer, 507–544. Philadelphia: University of Pennsylvania Museum.

———. 2017. Secrets of the Painted King List: Recovering the Early History of the Snake Dynasty. *Maya Decipherment,* May 5, 2017. https://decipherment.wordpress.com/2017/05/05/secrets-of-the-painted-king-list-recovering-the-early-history-of-the-snake-dynasty/.

———. 2020. *Ancient Maya Politics: A Political Anthropology of the Classic Period 150–900 CE.* Cambridge: Cambridge University Press.

Martin, Simon, and Demetri Beliaev. 2017. K'ahk' Ti' Chi'ch': A New Snake King from the Early Classic. *The PARI Journal* 17 (3): 1–7.

Martin, Simon, and Nikolai Grube. 2000. *Chronicle of the Maya Kings and Queens: Deciphering the Dynasties of the Ancient Maya.* New York: Thames & Hudson.

———. 2008. *Chronicle of the Maya Kings and Queens: Deciphering the Dynasties of the Ancient Maya.* 2nd ed. London: Thames & Hudson.

Martin, Simon, and Erik Velásquez García. 2016. Polities and Places: Tracing the Toponyms of the Snake Dynasty. *The PARI Journal* 17 (2): 23–33.

Martínez del Campo, Sofía. 2010. *Rostros de la divinidad: los mosaicos Mayas de Piedra Verde.* Mexico City: Instituto Nacional de Antropología e Historia.

Martinez Huchim, Ana Patricia. 2014. *Diccionario Maya.* Mérida: Editorial Dante.

Mason, J. Alden. 1960. *Mound 12, Chiapa de Corzo, Chiapas, Mexico.* Papers of the New World Archaeological Foundation no. 9, Provo, UT: Brigham Young University.

Masson, Marilyn A. 2001. Segmentary Political Cycles and Elite Migration Myths in the Postclassic Archaeology of Northern Belize. In *The Past and Present Maya: Essays in Honor of Robert M. Carmack,* ed. John M. Weeks, 89–103. Lancaster, CA: Labyrinthos.

Masson, Marilyn A., and Carlos Peraza Lope. 2010. Evidence for Maya-Mexican Interaction in the Archaeological Record of Mayapán. In *Astronomers, Scribes, and Priests: Intellectual Interchange between the Northern Maya Lowlands and Highland Mexico in the Late Postclassic Period,* ed. Gabrielle Vail and Christine Hernández, 77–114. Washington, DC: Dumbarton Oaks.

———. 2014. *Kukulcan's Realm: Urban Life at Ancient Mayapán.* Boulder: University Press of Colorado.

Matheny, Ray T., Dianne L. Gurr, Donald W. Forsyth, and F. Richard Hauck. 1983. *Investigations at Edzná, Campeche, Mexico.* Vol. 1, Part 1, *The Hydraulic System.* Provo, UT: New World Archaeological Foundation, Brigham Young University.

Mathews, Jennifer P., and James F. Garber. 2004. Models of Cosmic Order: Physical Expression of Sacred Space among the Ancient Maya. *Ancient Mesoamerica* 15: 49–59.

Mathews, Nancy M. 2001. *Paul Gauguin: An Erotic Life.* New Haven, CT: Yale University Press.

Mathews, Peter. 2001. Notes on the Inscriptions on the Back of Dos Pilas Stela B. In *The Decipherment of Ancient Maya Writing,* ed. Stephen Houston, Oswaldo Chinchilla Mazariegos, and David Stuart, 394–415. Norman: University of Oklahoma Press.

———. N.d. Maya Dates: Complete List of Long Count Dates, Arranged in Chronological Order. Manuscript in possession of Franco Rossi.

Matos Moctezuma, Eduardo. 1987. *Cacaxtla.* Mexico City: Citicorp.

———. 1988. *The Great Temple of the Aztecs: Treasures of Tenochtitlan.* New Aspects of Antiquity. New York: Thames & Hudson.

532 · References

McAnany, Patricia A. 1995. *Living with the Ancestors: Kinship and Kingship in Ancient Maya Society*. Austin: University of Texas Press.

———. 1998. Ancestors and the Classic Maya Built Environment. In *Function and Meaning in Classic Maya Architecture,* ed. Stephen D. Houston, 271–298. Washington, DC: Dumbarton Oaks.

———. 2001. Cosmology and the Institutionalization of Hierarchy in the Maya Region. In *From Leaders to Rulers,* ed. Jonathan Haas, 125–150. New York: Kluwer Academic/ Plenum Publishers.

———. 2010. *Ancestral Maya Economies in Archaeological Perspective*. New York: Cambridge University Press.

———. 2013. *Living with the Ancestors: Kinship and Kingship in Ancient Maya Society*. 2nd edition. New York: Cambridge University Press.

———. 2019a. Fragile Authority in Monumental Time: Political Experimentation in the Classic Maya Lowlands. In *The Evolution of Fragility: Setting the Terms,* ed. N. Yoffee, 47–59. Cambridge: McDonald Institute Conversations.

———. 2019b. *Living with the Ancestors: Kinship and Kingship in Ancient Maya Society*. 3rd ed. Cambridge: Cambridge University Press.

———. 2020a. Large-Scale Early Maya Sites Revealed by Lidar. *Nature,* June 3. https://doi .org/10.1038/d41586-020-01570-8.

———. 2020b. Soul Proprietors: Durable Ontologies of Maya Deep Time. In *Sacred Matters: Animacy and Authority in Pre-Columbian America,* ed. S. Kosiba, T. B. F. Cummins, and J. W. Janusek, 71–104. Washington, DC: Dumbarton Oaks.

McAnany, Patricia A., ed. 2004. *K'axob: Ritual, Work and Family in an Ancient Maya Village*. Monumenta Archaeologica 22. Los Angeles: Cotsen Institute of Archaeology at UCLA.

McAnany, Patricia A., and Linda A. Brown. 2016. Perceptions of the Past within Tz'utujil Ontologies and Yucatec Hybridities. *Antiquity* 90: 487–503.

McAnany, Patricia, and Ian Hodder. 2009. Thinking about Stratigraphic Sequence in Social Terms. *Archaeological Dialogues* 16 (1): 1–22.

McAnany, Patricia A., and Maxime Lamoureux-St-Hilaire. 2017. The Fragility of Political Experimentation from the Perspective of Classic Maya Cities. In *Crisis to Collapse: The Archaeology of Social Breakdown,* ed. T. Cunningham and J. Driessen, 305–314. Louvain-la-Neuve: Presses Universitaires de Louvain.

McAnany, Patricia A., Jeremy A. Sabloff, Maxime Lamoureux-St-Hilaire, and Gyles Iannone. 2015. Leaving Classic Maya Cities: Agent-Based Modeling and the Dynamics of Diaspora. In *Social Theory in Archaeology and Ancient History: The Present and Future of Counternarratives,* ed. G. Emberling, 259–288. New York: Cambridge University Press.

McCormack, Valerie. 2012. Fluctuating Community Organization: Formation and Dissolution of Multifamily Corporate Groups at La Joya, Veracruz, Mexico. In *Ancient Households of Americas: Conceptualizing what Households Do,* ed. John G. Douglass and Nancy Gonlin, 325–352. Boulder: University Press of Colorado.

McCurdy, Leah. 2016. Building Xunantunich: Public in an Ancient Maya Community. PhD diss., University of Texas at San Antonio.

McCurdy, Leah, M. Kathryn Brown, and Neil Dixon. 2018. Tagged Walls: The Discovery of Ancient Maya Graffiti at El Castillo, Xunantunich. *Research Reports in Belizean Archaeology* 15: 181–194.

McDonald, Andrew J. 1983. *Tzutzuculi: A Middle-Preclassic Site on the Pacific Coast of Chiapas, Mexico.* Papers of The New World Archaeological Foundation 47. Provo, UT: New World Archaeological Foundation, Brigham Young University.

———. 1999. Middle Formative Pyramidal Platform Complexes in Southern Chiapas, Mexico: Structure and Meaning. PhD diss., University of Texas, Austin.

McGovern, James O. 2004. Monumental Ceremonial Architecture and Political Autonomy at the Ancient Maya City of Actuncan, Belize. PhD diss., University of California, Los Angeles.

McGraw, John J. 2016a. Stones of Light: The Use of Crystals in Maya Divination. In *Manufactured Light: Mirrors in the Mesoamerican Realm,* ed. Emiliano Gallaga and Marc Blainey, 207–228. Boulder: University Press of Colorado.

———. 2016b. Maya Divination: Ritual Techniques of Distributed Cognition. *Journal of Cognition and Culture* 16 (3–4): 177–198.

Means, Philip Ainsworth. 1917. *History of Spanish Conquest of Yucatan and the Itzas.* Cambridge, MA: Museum Collection Americana.

Mediz Bolio, Antonio. (1930) 1973. *Libro del Chilam Balam de Chumayel.* México: Biblioteca del Estudiante Universitario, UNAM.

Meierhoff, James, Mark Golitko, and James D. Morris. 2012. Obsidian Acquisition, Trade, and Regional Interaction at Chan. In *Chan: An Ancient Maya Farming Community,* ed. Cynthia Robin, 271–288. Gainesville: University Press of Florida.

Meierhoff, James, and Alexandra Miller. 2005. Operations 11 and 12, C-001: South Range Structure. In *The Chan Project Report: 2005 Season,* ed. Cynthia Robin, 25–32. Report submitted to the Belize Institute of Archaeology.

Meillassoux, Claude. 1972. From Reproduction to Production. *Economy and Society* 1: 93–105.

Meléndez, Juan Carlos. 2019. A Contextual and Technological Study of Ancient Maya Greenstone Mosaic Masks. PhD diss., Washington University in St. Louis, MO.

Mellaart, James. 1967. *Çatalhöyük, A Neolithic Town in Anatolia.* New York: McGraw-Hill.

Michelet, Dominque, M. Charlotte Arnaud, Pierre Becquelin, Marie-France Fauvet-Berthelot, Philippe Nondédéo, Fabienne de Pierrebourg, and Eric Taladoire. 1997. Le Groupe Sud de Balamku (Campeche, Mexique): Éléments d'une histoire architecturale mouvementée. *Journal de la Société des américanistes* 83: 229–249.

Middleton, Guy D. 2017. *Understanding Collapse: Ancient History and Modern Myths.* Cambridge: Cambridge University Press.

Milbrath, Susan. 1999. *Star Gods of the Maya: Astronomy in Art, Folklore, and Calendars.* Austin: University of Texas Press.

———. 2000. Xochiquetzal and the Lunar Cult of Central Mexico, In *Chalchihuitl in Quetzalli = Precious Greenstone, Precious Feather: Mesoamerican Studies in Honor of Doris Heyden,* ed. Elizabeth Quiñones Keber, 31–55. Lancaster, CA: Labyrinthos.

———. 2005. The Last Great Capital of the Maya. *Archaeology* 58 (2): 27–30.

———. 2013. *Heaven and Earth in Ancient Mexico: Astronomy, Seasonal Cycles, and Religious Rituals in the Codex Borgia.* Austin: University of Texas Press.

534 · References

——. 2017a. The Role of Solar Observations in Developing the Preclassic Maya Calendar. *Latin American Antiquity* 28 (1): 88–104.

——. 2017b. The Legacy of Preclassic Calendars and Solar Observations in Mesoamerica's Magic Latitude. In *Maya E Groups: Calendars, Astronomy, and Urbanism in the Early Lowlands,* ed. David A. Freidel, Arlen F. Chase, Anne S. Dowd, and Jerry Murdock, 95–134. Gainesville: University Press of Florida.

——. 2017c. Maya Astronomical Observations and the Agricultural Cycle in the Postclassic Madrid Codex. *Ancient Mesoamerica* 28 (2): 489–505.

——. 2019. Yearbearer Imagery in the Postclassic Codices: Thresholds of Time and Space. Paper presented in the Symposium on Painted Books of Pre-Hispanic Mexico: New Discoveries. College Art Association Annual Conference, New York City.

Milbrath, Susan, James Aimers, Carlos Peraza Lope, and Lynda Florey Folan. 2008. Effigy Censers of the Chen Mul Modeled System and Their Implications for Late Postclassic Maya Interregional Interaction. *Mexicon* 30 (5): 104–112.

Milbrath, Susan, and Anne S. Dowd. 2015. An Interdisciplinary Approach to Cosmology, Calendars, and Horizon-Based Astronomy. In *Cosmology, Calendars, and Horizon-Based Astronomy in Ancient Mesoamerica,* ed. Anne S. Dowd and Susan Milbrath, 3–16. Boulder: University Press of Colorado.

Milbrath, Susan, and Carlos Peraza Lope. 2013. Mayapán's Chen Mul Modeled Effigy Censers: Iconography and Archaeological Context. In *Maya Ceramic Exchange and Stylistic Interaction,* ed. James Aimers, 203–228. Gainesville: University of Florida Press.

Milbrath, Susan, and Debra S. Walker. 2016a. Regional Expressions of the Postclassic Effigy Censer System in the Chetumal Bay Area. In *Perspectives on the Ancient Maya of Chetumal Bay,* ed. Debra S. Walker, 186–213. Gainesville: University Press of Florida.

——. 2016b. Workshops for Postclassic Effigy Censers in the Chetumal Area. In *Investigations in the Land of Chocolate and Honey: Recent Archaeological Research on Chetumal Bay,* ed. Debra Walker, 186–213. Gainesville: University Press of Florida.

Milbrath, Susan, Debra Walker, and Carlos Peraza Lope. 2021 Postclassic Effigy Censers of Mayapán: Context, Iconography, and External Connections. In *Settlement, Economy, and Society at a Postclassic Maya City: Mayapán, Yucatan, Mexico,* ed. Marilyn A. Masson, Timothy S. Hare, Carlos Peraza Lope, and Bradley W. Russell, 293–313. Pittsburgh: University of Pittsburgh Press.

Miles, Susan. 1957. The Sixteenth Century Pokomam Maya: Documentary Analysis of Social Structure and Archaeological Setting. *Transactions of the American Philosophical Society* 47: 731–781.

Miller, Arthur G. 1974. The Iconography of the Painting in the Temple of the Diving God, Tulum, Quintana Roo, Mexico: The Twisted Cords. In *Mesoamerican Archaeology: New Approaches,* ed. Norman Hammond, 167–186. London: Duckworth.

——. 1982. *On the Edge of the Sea: Mural Painting at Tancah-Tulum, Quintana Roo, Mexico.* Washington, DC: Dumbarton Oaks.

Miller, Donald E. 2014. *Excavations at La Libertad, a Middle Formative Ceremonial Center in Chiapas, Mexico.* Papers of the New World Archaeological Foundation no. 64. Provo, UT: Brigham Young University.

Miller, Mary Ellen. 1986. *The Murals of Bonampak*. Princeton, NJ: Princeton University Press.

Miller, Mary Ellen, and Claudia Brittenham. 2013. *The Spectacle of the Late Maya Court: Reflections on the Murals of Bonampak*. Austin: University of Texas Press.

Miller, Mary Ellen, and Simon Martin. 2004. *Courtly Art of the Ancient Maya*. London: Thames & Hudson.

Miller, Mary Ellen, and Karl Taube. 1993. *The Gods and Symbols of Ancient Mexico and the Maya*. London: Thames & Hudson.

Millon, Rene. 1973. *Urbanization at Teotihuacan, Mexico*. Austin: University of Texas Press.

———. 1981. Teotihuacan: City, State, and Civilization. In *Supplement to the Handbook of Middle American Indians*. Vol. 1, *Archaeology*, ed. Jeremy A. Sabloff, 198–243. Austin: University of Texas Press.

———. 1992. Teotihuacan Studies: From 1950 to 1990 and Beyond. In *Art, Ideology, and the City of Teotihuacan*, ed. Janet C. Berlo, 339–419. Washington, DC: Dumbarton Oaks.

———. 1993. The Place Where Time Began: An Archaeologist's Interpretation of What Happened in Teotihuacan History. In *Teotihuacan: Art from the City of the Gods*, ed. Kathleen Berrin and Esther Pasztory, 17–43. San Francisco: Thames & Hudson and the Fine Arts Museum of San Francisco.

Mills, Barbara J. 2014. Relational Networks and Religious Sodalities at Çatalhöyük. In *Religion at Work in a Neolithic Society: Vital Matters*, ed. Ian Hodder, 159–86. Cambridge: Cambridge University Press.

Moholy-Nagy, Hattula. 2008. *The Artifacts of Tikal: Ornamental and Ceremonial Artifacts and Unworked Material*. Tikal Report 27A. Philadelphia: University of Pennsylvania Museum of Archaeology and Anthropology.

———. 2016. Set in Stone: Hiatuses and Dynastic Politics at Tikal, Guatemala. *Ancient Mesoamerica* 27: 255–266.

Mondloch, James L. 1980. K'e?š: Quiché Naming. *Journal of Mayan Linguistics* 1 (2): 9–25.

Montgomery, John. 2001. The John Montgomery Drawing Collection. http://www.famsi .org/research/montgomery/.

Mora-Marin, David. 2021. The Iconographic Origin of the T533/AM1 *?AJAW* 'Lord, Ruler' Logogram. *Note 15*, February 21. https://davidmm.web.unc.edu/2021/02/21/note -15/.

Moreiras Reynaga, Diana K. 2013. Pre-Columbian Diets in the Soconusco Revisited: A Dietary Study through Stable Isotopic Analysis. MA thesis, Anthropology, University of British Columbia, Vancouver.

Morley, Iain, and Colin Renfrew, eds. 2010. *Archaeology of Measurement: Comprehending Heaven, Earth and Time in Ancient Societies*. Cambridge: Cambridge University Press.

Morley, Sylvanus G. 1915. *An Introduction to the Study of the Maya Hieroglyphs*. Bulletin 57. Washington, DC: Bureau of American Ethnology, Smithsonian Institution.

———. 1917. The Hotun as the Principal Chronological Unit of the Old Maya Empire. In *Proceedings of the 19th International Congress of Americanists, Held at Washington, December 27–31, 1915*, ed. F. W. Hodge, 195–201. Washington, DC.

———. 1947. *The Ancient Maya*. Stanford, CA: Stanford University Press.

536 · References

Morris, Brian. 1976. Whither the Savage Mind? Notes on the Natural Taxonomies of a Hunting and Gathering People. *Man* 11 (4): 542–556.

———. 1982. *Forest Traders: A Socio-Economic Study of the Hill Pandaram*. Oxford: Berg Publishers.

Munn, Nancy D. 1992. The Cultural Anthropology of Time: A Critical Essay. *Annual Review of Anthropology* 93–123.

Myerhoff, Barbara. 1970. The Deer-Maize-Peyote Symbol Complex among the Huichol Indians of Mexico. *Anthropological Quarterly* 43 (2): 64–78.

Nájera Coronado, Martha Ilia. 2019. El lenguaje ritual del fuego en los mayas del periodo Clásico: Un acercamiento. *Estudios de Cultura Maya* 54: 91–127.

Nalda, Enrique. 2005. Kohunlich and Dzibanché: Parallel Histories. In *Quintana Roo Archaeology,* ed. Justine M. Shaw and Jennifer P Matthews, 228–244. Tucson: University of Arizona Press.

Nalda, Enrique, and Sandra Balanzario. 2014. El estilo Río Bec visto desde Dzibanché y Kohunlich. *Journal de la Société des américanistes* 100 (100–102): 179–209.

Nations, J. D. and R. B. Nigh. 1980. The Evolutionary Potential of Lacandon Maya Sustained-Yield Tropical Forest Agriculture. *Journal of Anthropological Research* 36 (1): 1–30.

Navarro-Farr, Olivia C. 2009. Ritual, Process, and Continuity in the Late to Terminal Classic Transition: Investigations at Structure M13–1 in the Ancient Maya Site of El Perú-Waka', Petén, Guatemala. PhD diss., Southern Methodist University, Dallas TX.

Navarro-Farr, Olivia C., Keith Eppich, Griselda Pérez Robles, and David A. Freidel. 2020. Ancient Maya Queenship: Generations of Crafting State Politics and Alliance Building from Kaanul to Waka'. In *Approaches to Monumental Landscapes of the Ancient Maya,* ed. Brett A. Houk, Barbara Arroyo, and Terry G. Powis, 196–217. Gainesville: University Press of Florida.

Navarro-Farr, Olivia C., David A. Freidel, and Ana Lucia Arroyave. 2008. Manipulating Memory in the Wake of Dynastic Decline at El Perú-Waka': Termination Deposits at Abandoned Structure M13-1. In *Ruins of the Past: The Use and Perception of Abandoned Structures in the Maya Lowlands,* ed. Travis W. Stanton and Aline Magnoni, 113–145. Boulder: University Press of Colorado.

Navarro-Farr, Olivia, Griselda Pérez Robles, and Damaris Menendez Bolanos. 2013. Excavaciones en la Estructura M13-1. *Proyecto Arqueológico Waka',* ed. Juan Carlos Pérez, 3–91. Informe no. 10, Temporada 2012. Informe Entegrado a la Dirección General del Patrimonio Cultural y Natural de Guatemala, Guatemala City.

Navarro-Farr, Olivia, and Michelle E. Rich, eds. 2014. *Archaeology at El Perú-Waka': Ancient Maya Performances of Ritual, Memory, and Power*. Tucson: University of Arizona Press.

Negrín, Juan. 1975. *The Huichol Creation of the World*. Sacramento, CA: E. B. Crocker Art Gallery.

Nielsen, Jesper. 2003. Frans Blom and the Decipherment of Maya Writing. *The PARI Journal* 4 (2): 4–9.

———. 2006. The Coming of the Torch: Observations on Teotihuacan Iconography in

Early Classic Tikal. In *Maya Ethnicity: The Construction of Ethnic Identity from Preclassic to Modern Times: Proceedings of the 9th European Maya Conference, Bonn, December 10–12, 2004,* ed. Frauke Sachse, 19–30. Markt Schwaben: Verlag Anton Saurwein.

Newsome, Elizabeth A. 2001. *Trees of Paradise and Pillars of the World: The Serial Stela Cycle of "18-Rabbit-God K," King of Copan.* Austin: University of Texas Press.

———. 2003. *The "Bundle" Altars of Copan: A New Perspective on Their Meaning and Archaeological Contexts.* Barnardsville, NC: Center for Ancient American Studies.

Nicholson, Henry B. 1971. Religion in Pre-Hispanic Central Mexico. In *Archaeology of Northern Mesoamerica,* Part 1, ed. Gordon F. Ekholm and Ignacio Bernal, 395–446. *Handbook of Middle American Indians,* vol. 10. Austin: University of Texas Press.

Nielsen, Jesper, and Christophe Helmke. 2017. The Storm God: Lord of Rain and Ravage. In *City of Water, City of Fire, Teotihuacan,* ed. Matthew H. Robb, 138–143. San Francisco: Fine Arts Museum of San Francisco in association with University of California Press.

Nieves Zedeño, Maria, Jesse A. M. Ballenger, and John R. Murray. 2014. Landscape Engineering and Organizational Complexity among Late Prehistoric Bison Hunters of the Northwestern Plains. *Current Anthropology* 55 (1): 23–58.

Nolan, Suzanne. 2015. Late Classic Politics and Ideology: A Case Study of Hieroglyphic Stairway 2 at Yaxchilan, Chiapas, Mexico. PhD diss., University of Essex, UK.

Norman, Garth V. 1973. *Izapa Sculpture.* Part 1, *Album.* Provo, UT: Brigham Young University.

Novotny, Anna C., Jaime J. Awe, Catharina E. Santasilla, and Kelly J. Knudson. 2018. Ritual Emulation of Ancient Maya Elite Mortuary Traditions during the Classic Period (AD 250–900) at Cahal Pech, Belize. *Latin American Antiquity* 29 (4): 641–659.

Novotny, Claire, and Brett A. Houk. 2021. Ancient Maya Patolli from Gallon Jug, Belize. *Latin American Antiquity* 32 (3): 647–654.

Nuttall, Zelia. 1904. The Periodical Adjustments of the Ancient Mexican Calendar. *American Anthropologist* 6: 486–500.

Oakes, Maude. 1951. *The Two Crosses of Todos Santos: Survivals of Mayan Religious Ritual.* New York: Pantheon Books.

O'Brien, Michael J., and R. Lee Lyman. 1999. *Seriation, Stratigraphy, and Index Fossils: The Backbone of Archaeological Dating.* New York: Kluwer/Plenum Academic Publishers.

Obrist-Farner, Jonathan, and Prudence M. Rice. 2019. Nixtun-Ch'ich' and Its Environmental Impact: Sedimentological and Archaeological Correlates in a Core from Lake Petén Itzá, Guatemala. *Journal of Archaeological Science: Reports* 26: 101868.

O'Grady, Caitlin R., and Heather Hurst. 2011. *Lost Walls/Murals Rebuilt: Interdisciplinary Approaches to the Conservation of Preclassic Maya Wall Paintings from San Bartolo, Guatemala.* Lisbon: ICOM-CC Publications.

Okoshi, Tsubasa, Arlen F. Chase, Philippe Nondedeo, and M. Charlotte Arnauld, eds. 2021. *Maya Kingship: Rupture and Transformation from Classic to Postclassic Times.* Gainesville: University Press of Florida.

O'Neil, Megan E. 2012. *Engaging Maya Sculpture at Piedras Negras, Guatemala.* Norman: University of Oklahoma Press.

538 · References

———. 2013. Marked Faces, Displaced Bodies: Monumental Breakage and Reuse among the Classic-Period Maya. In *Striking Images, Iconoclasms Past and Present,* ed. Stacy Boldrick, Leslie Brubaker, and Richard Clay, 47–64. Ashgate Publishing.

———. 2019. The Painter's Line on Paper and Clay: Maya Codices and Codex-Style Vessels, from the Seventh to Sixteenth Centuries. In *Toward a Global Middle Ages: Encountering the World through Illuminated Manuscripts,* ed. Bryan C. Keene, 125–136. Los Angeles: Getty Museum.

Onuki, Yoshio, ed. 1995. *Kuntur Wasi y Cerro Blanco.* Tokyo: Hokusen-sha.

Ortiz C., Ponciano, and María del Carmen Rodríguez. 1999. Olmec Ritual Behavior at El Manatee, an Olmec Sacred Space. In *Social Patterns in Pre-Classic Mesoamerica,* ed. David C. Grove and Rosemary A. Joyce, 225–254. Washington, DC: Dumbarton Oaks.

———. 2000. The Sacred Hill of El Manatí: A Preliminary Discussion of the Site's Ritual Paraphernalia. In *Olmec Art and Archaeology in Mesoamerica,* ed. John E. Clark and Mary E. Pye, 75–91. Washington, DC: National Gallery of Art.

Overholtzer, Lisa, and Cynthia Robin. 2015. The Materiality of Everyday Life: An Introduction. In *The Materiality of Everyday Life,* ed. Lisa Overholtzer and Cynthia Robin, 1–9. Archaeological Papers of the American Anthropological Association 26. Hoboken, NJ: Wiley.

Paris, Elizabeth H., C. Peraza Lope, M. A. Masson, P. C. Delgado Kú, and B. C. Escamilla Ojeda. 2018. The Organization of Stingless Beekeeping (Meliponiculture) at Mayapán, Yucatan, Mexico. *Journal of Anthropological Archaeology* 52: 1–22.

Parker Pearson, Mike, Joshua Pollard, Colin Richards, Julian Thomas, Christopher Tilley, Katherine Welham, and Umberto Albarella. 2006. Materializing Stonehenge: The Stonehenge Riverside Project and New Discoveries. *Journal of Material Culture* 11 (1): 227–261.

Parsons, Lee A. 1986. *The Origins of Maya Art: Monumental Sculpture of Kaminaljuyú, Guatemala and the Southern Pacific Coast.* Studies in Pre-Columbian Art and Archaeology no. 22. Washington, DC: Dumbarton Oaks.

Pärssinen, Martti, Denise Schaan, and Alceu Ranzi. 2009. Columbian Geometric Earthworks in the Upper Purús: A Complex Society in Western Amazonia. *Antiquity* 83 (322): 1084–1095.

Pasztory, Esther. 1973. The Gods of Teotihuacan: A Synthetic Approach in Teotihuacan Iconography. In *Atti del XL Congresso Internazionale degli Americanisti,* vol. 1, 147–159. Rome: ICA.

———. 1976. *The Murals of Tepantitla, Teotihuacan.* New York: Garland Press.

Patch, Robert W. 2003. The Almost Forgotten Plants of Yucatan. In *The Lowland Maya Area: Three Millennia at the Human-Wildland Interface,* ed. Arturo Gomez-Pompa, Michael F. Allen, Scott Fedick, and Juan J. Jemenez-Osornio, 561–569. Binghamton, NY: Food Products Press.

Paxton, Meredith Daniel. 1986. Codex Dresden: Stylistic and Iconographic Analysis of a Maya Manuscript. PhD diss., University of New Mexico, Albuquerque.

———. 2001. *The Cosmos of the Yucatec Maya: Cycles and Steps from the Madrid Codex.* Albuquerque: University of New Mexico Press.

———. 2010. Solar Based Cartographic Traditions of the Yucatec Maya. In *Astronomers,*

*Scribes, and Priests. Intellectual Interchange between the Northern Maya Lowlands and Highland Mexico in the Late Postclassic Period,* ed. Gabrielle Vail and Christine Hernandez, 279–308. Washington, DC: Dumbarton Oaks.

Pendergast, David M. 1971. Evidence of Early Teotihuacan–Lowland Maya Contact at Altun Ha. *American Antiquity* 36: 455–460.

Peraza Lope, Carlos, and Marilyn A. Masson. 2014. Politics and Monumental Legacies. In *Kukulcan's Realm: Urban Life at Ancient Mayapán,* ed. Marilyn A. Masson and Carlos Peraza Lope, 39–104. Boulder: University Press of Colorado.

Pérez de Heredia Puente, Eduardo J. 2012. The Yabnal-Motul Ceramic Complex of the Late Classic Period at Chichen Itza. *Ancient Mesoamerica* 23: 379–402.

Pérez Aguilera, Abigail. 2017. The Tangibility of Maize: Indigenous Literature, Blood, and Violence in Mexico. In *Ecocriticism and Indigenous Studies: Conversations from Earth to Cosmos,* ed. Salma Monani and Joni Adamson, 204–222. New York: Routledge.

Pérez Robles, Griselda, Juan Carlos Pérez, and David A. Freidel. 2019. "Hoja" Chan Ahk: El descubrimiento de la tumba de un rey del Clásico Temprano en el Palacio Real de El Perú-Waka', Guatemala. *Anales del Museo de América* 27: 76–94.

———. Forthcoming. Te Chan Ak: El descubrimiento de la tumba de un Rey del Clásico Temprano en el palacio real de el Perú-Waka', Guatemala. *Anales del Museo de América.*

Pérez Robles, Griselda, Juan Carlos Pérez, Damaris Menéndez, and David A. Freidel. 2018. Operación Wk18. Excavaciones en la acrópolis y el palacio real de Waka'. In *Proyecto Arqueológico Waka',* ed. Juan Carlos Pérez, Griselda Pérez Robles, and David A. Freidel, 84–129. Informe no. 15, Temporada 2017. Informe entregado a la Dirección General del Patrimonio Cultural y Natural de Guatemala, Guatemala City.

Pfaffenberger, Bryan. 1988. Fetished Objects and Humanized Nature: Toward an Anthropology of Technology. *Man* 23: 236–252.

———. 1992. Social Anthropology of Technology. *Annual Review of Anthropology* 21: 491–516.

Pharo, Lars Kirkhusmo. 2014. *The Ritual Practice of Time: Philosophy and Sociopolitics of Mesoamerican Calendars.* London: Brill.

Piehl, Jennifer C., and Stanley P. Guenter. 2005. Wk-10, Excavaciones en la Estructura L11–33, La Escalinata Jeroglifica. In *Proyecto Arqueológico Waka',* ed. Héctor L. Escobedo and David A. Freidel, 209–251. Informe no. 2, Temporada 2004. Informe Entegrado a la Dirección General del Patrimonio Cultural y Natural de Guatemala, Guatemala City.

Pillsbury, Joanne, Timothy Potts, and Kim N. Richter, eds. 2017. *Golden Kingdoms: Luxury Arts in the Ancient Americas.* Los Angeles, CA: J. Paul Getty Museum.

Piña Chan, Roman. 1978. Commerce in the Yucatan Peninsula: The Conquest and the Colonial Period. In *Mesoamerican Communication Routes and Cultural Contacts,* ed. T. A. Lee and C. Navarrete, 37–48. Provo, UT: New World Archaeological Foundation, Brigham Young University.

Pineda de Carías, Maria C., Nohemy Rivera, and Christina Margarita Agueta. 2017. Stela D: A Sun Dial at Copan, Honduras. *Ancient Mesoamerica* 28 (2): 543–557.

540 · References

Pineda de Carías, Maria C., Vito Véliz, and Ricardo Agurcia Fasquelle. 2009. Estela D: Reloj Solar de la plaza del Sol del Parque Arqueológico de Copán Ruinas, Honduras. *Yaxkin* 25 (2): 111–138.

Piperno, Dolores R., Anthony J. Ranere, Irene Holst, Jose Iriarte, and Ruth Dickau. 2009. Starch Grain and Phytolith Evidence for Early Ninth Millennium BP Maize from the Central Balsas River Valley, Mexico. *Proceedings of the National Academy of Sciences* 106 (13): 5019–5024.

Pitarch, Pedro. 2010. *The Jaguar and the Priest: An Ethnography of Tzeltal Souls*. Austin: University of Texas Press.

Pollock, Harry E. D. 1936. *Round Structures of Aboriginal Middle America*. Publication 471. Washington, DC: Carnegie Institution of Washington.

Poot, Tec, and Michel Bocara. 1980. Abejas y hombres de la tierra Maya. *Boletín de la Escuela de Ciencias Antropológicas de la Universidad de Yucatán* 7 (2): 2–24.

Pope, Kevin O., Mary E. D. Pohl, John G. Jones, David L. Lentz, Christopher L. von Nagy, Francisco J. Vega, and Irv Quitmeyer. 2001. Origin and Environmental Setting of Ancient Agriculture in the Lowlands of Mesoamerica. *Science* 292 (5520): 1370–1372.

Popper, Karl. 1962. *Conjectures and Refutations: The Growth of Scientific Knowledge*. New York: Harper & Row.

Porter-Bolland, Luciana. 1999. Landscape Ecology of Apiculture en the Maya Area of la Montaña, Campeche, Mexico. PhD diss., University of Florida, Gainesville.

Prager, Christian M., Beniamino Volta, and Geoffrey E. Braswell. 2014. The Dynastic History and Archaeology of Pusilha, Belize. In *The Maya and Their Central American Neighbors: Settlement Patterns, Architecture, Hieroglyphic Texts, and Ceramics*, ed. Geoffrey E. Braswell, 245–307. New York: Routledge.

Price, T. Douglas, James H. Burton, Robert J. Sharer, Jane E. Buikstra, Lori E. Wright, Loa P. Traxler, and Katherine A. Miller. 2010. Kings and Commoners at Copan: Isotopic Evidence for Origins and Movement in the Classic Maya Period. *Journal of Anthropological Archaeology* 29 (1): 15–32.

Proskouriakoff, Tatiana. 1950. *A Study of Classic Maya Sculpture*. Publication 593. Washington, DC: Carnegie Institution of Washington.

———. 1962. Civic and Religious Structures of Mayapan. In *Mayapan, Yucatan, Mexico*, ed. H. E. D. Pollock, Ralph L. Roys, Tatiana Proskouriakoff, and A. Ledyard Smith, 87–163. Publication 619. Washington, DC: Carnegie Institution of Washington.

———. 1993. *Maya History*. Austin: University of Texas Press.

Proskouriakoff, Tatiana, and J. Eric S. Thompson. 1947. Maya Calendar Round Dates Such as 9 Ahau 17 Mol. *Carnegie Institution of Washington Notes on Middle American Archaeology and Ethnography* 79: 312–315.

Pugh, Timothy W. 2019. From the Streets: Public and Private Space in an Early Maya City. *Journal of Archaeological Method and Theory* 26 (3): 967–997.

Pugh, Timothy W., Evelyn M. Chan Nieto, and Gabriela W. Zygadło. 2019. Faceless Hierarchy at Nixtun-Ch'ich', Peten, Guatemala. *Ancient Mesoamerica* 30: 1–13.

Pugh, Timothy W., and Prudence M. Rice. 2017. Early Urban Planning, Spatial Strategies, and the Maya Gridded City of Nixtun-Ch'ich', Petén, Guatemala. *Current Anthropology* 58 (5): 576–603.

Puleston, Dennis. 1979. An Epistemological Pathology and the Collapse, or Why the Maya Kept the Short Count. In *Maya Archaeology and Ethnohistory*, ed. Norman Hammond and Gordon R. Willey, 63–71. Austin: University of Texas Press.

Quirarte, Jacinto. 1973. Izapan-Style Art: A Study of Its Form and Meaning. *Studies in Pre-Columbian Art and Archaeology* (10): 1–47.

Rabinow, Paul. 1995. *French Modern: Norms and Forms of the Social Environment*. Chicago: University of Chicago Press.

Ramsey, Christopher B. 2009. Bayesian Analysis of Radiocarbon Dates. *Radiocarbon* 51 (1): 337–360.

Ranere, Anthony J., Dolores R. Piperno, Irene Holst, Ruth Dickau, and Jose Iriarte. 2009. The Cultural and Chronological Context of Early Holocene Maize and Squash Domestication in the Central Balsas River Valley, Mexico. *Proceedings of the National Academy of Sciences* 106 (13): 5014–5018.

Rathje, William L., and David Phillips. 1975. The Ruins of Buena Vista. In *A Study of Changing Pre-Columbian Commercial Systems: The 1972–1973 Seasons at Cozumel, Mexico, a Preliminary Report*, ed. Jeremy A. Sabloff and William L. Rathje, 77–87. Monographs of the Peabody Museum 3. Cambridge, MA: Peabody Museum of Archaeology and Ethnology, Harvard University.

Redfield, Robert, and Alfonso Villa Rojas. 1934. *Chan Kom: A Maya Village*. Carnegie Institution of Washington Pub. 448. Washington, DC: Carnegie Institution of Washington.

Reed, Nelson A. 2001. *The Caste War of Yucatán*. Rev. ed. Stanford, CA: Stanford University Press.

Reents-Budet, Dorie. 1994. *Painting the Maya Universe: Royal Ceramics of the Classic Period*. Durham, NC: Duke University Press.

Reents-Budet, Dorie, Sylviane Boucher, Yoly Palomo, Ronald Bishop, and James Blackman. 2011. Cerámica de estilo códice: nuevos datos de producción y patrones de distribución. In *XXIV Simposio de Investigaciones Arqueológicas en Guatemala, 2010*, ed. Bárbara Arroyo, Lorena Paíz, Adrián Linares, and Ana Lucia Arroyave, 832–846. Guatemala City: Museo Nacional de Arqueología y Etnología.

Reese, Kathryn. 1995. Narrative and Sacred Landscape: The Ethnopoetics of the Public Architectural Programs at Cerros, Belize. Paper presented at the 94th Annual Meeting of the American Anthropological Association, Washington, DC.

———. 1996. Narratives of Power: Late Formative Public Architecture and Civic Center Design at Cerros, Belize. PhD diss., University of Texas, Austin.

Reese-Taylor, Kathryn. 2002. Ritual Circuits as Key Elements in Maya Civic Center Design. In *Heart of Creation: The Mesoamerican World and the Legacy of Linda Schele*, ed. A. Stone, 143–165. Tuscaloosa: University of Alabama Press.

———. 2017. Founding Landscapes in the Central Karstic Uplands. In *Maya E Groups: Calendars, Astronomy, and Urbanism in the Early Lowlands*, ed. David A. Freidel, Arlen F. Chase, Anne S. Dowd, and Jerry Murdock, 480–513. Gainesville: University Press of Florida.

Reese-Taylor, Kathryn, and Armando Anaya Hernández. 2013. *Proyecto Arqueológico Yaxnohcah, informe de la primera 2011 temporada de investigaciones*. Report submitted to the Instituto Nacional de Antropología e Historia, Mexico City, D.F.

542 · References

Reese-Taylor, Kathryn, Armando Anaya Hernández, Kelly Monteleone, F. C. Atasta Flores Esquivel, Christopher Carr, Alejandro J. Uriarte Torres, Helga Geovannini Acuña, Meaghan Peuramaki-Brown, Nicholas Dunning, and Juan Carlos Fernández. 2016. Boots on the Ground at Yaxnohcah: Ground-Truthing Lidar in a Complex Tropical Landscape. *Advances in Archaeological Practice* 4 (3): 314–338.

Reese-Taylor, Kathryn, and Debra S. Walker. 2002. The Passage of the Late Preclassic into the Early Classic. In *Ancient Maya Political Economies,* ed. Marilyn A. Masson and David A. Freidel, 87–122. Walnut Creek, CA: AltaMira Press.

Regan, Roddy, and James Taylor. 2014. The Sequence of Buildings 75, 65, 56, 69, 44 and 10 and External Spaces 119, 129, 130, 144, 299, 314, 319, 329, 333, 339, 367, 371 and 427. In *Çatalhöyük Excavations: The 2000–2008 Seasons,* ed. I. Hodder, 35–52. London: British Institute at Ankara and Los Angeles: Cotsen Institute of Archaeology, University of California.

Reid, Genevieve, and Renee Sieber. 2015. What Is Time? Indigenous Conceptualizations of Time and the Geoweb. Paper presented at the Spatial Knowledge Information Canada Conference, February 27–March 1. Banff, Canada.

Reilly, F. Kent, III. 1987. The Ecological Origin of Olmec Symbols of Rulership. MA thesis University of Texas at Austin.

———. 1996. Art, Ritual, and Rulership in the Olmec World. In *The Olmec World, Ritual and Rulership,* ed. Jill Guthrie, 27–46. Princeton, NJ: The Art Museum, Princeton University and Harry N. Abrams, Inc.

———. 2002. The Landscape of Creation: Architecture, Tomb, and Monument Placement at the Olmec Site of La Venta. In *Heart of Creation: The Mesoamerican World and the Legacy of Linda Schele,* ed. Andrea Stone, 34–65. Tuscaloosa: University of Alabama Press.

Reilly, F. Kent, III, and David A. Freidel. Forthcoming. Seeds, Sprouts and Cosmic Trees: Reflections on a Mesoamerican Metaphor. In *A Forest of History: The Maya before the Emergence of Divine Kingship,* ed. M. Kathryn Brown and Travis Stanton. Boulder: University of Colorado Press.

Restall, Matthew. 1998. *Maya Conquistador*. Boston: Beacon.

Rice, Prudence M. 1999. Rethinking Classic Lowland Maya Pottery Censers. *Ancient Mesoamerica* 10 (1): 25–50.

———. 2004. *Maya Political Science: Time, Astronomy, and the Cosmos*. Austin: University of Texas Press.

———. 2007. *Maya Calendar Origins: Monuments, Mythistory, and the Materialization of Time*. Austin: University of Texas Press.

———. 2009a. Mound ZZ1, Nixtun-Ch'ich', Petén, Guatemala: Rescue Operations at a Long-Lived Structure in the Maya Lowlands. *Journal of Field Archaeology* 34 (4): 403–422.

———. 2009b. Time, History, Worldview. In *Maya Worldviews at Conquest,* ed. Leslie G. Cecil and Timothy W. Pugh, 61–82. Boulder: University Press of Colorado.

———. 2013. Texts and the Cities: Modeling Maya Political Organization. *Current Anthropology* 54 (6): 684–715.

———. 2018. Maya Crocodilians: Intersections of Myth and the Natural World at Early

Nixtun-Ch'ich', Peten, Guatemala. *Journal of Archaeological Method and Theory* 25 (3): 705–738.

———. 2019. Early Pottery and Construction at Nixtun-Ch'ich', Petén, Guatemala: Preliminary Observations. *Latin American Antiquity* 30 (3): 471–489.

———. 2021. In Search of Middle Preclassic Lowland Maya Ideologies. *Journal of Archaeological Research* 29: 1–46.

Rice, Prudence M., and Timothy W. Pugh. 2017. Water, Centering, and the Beginning of Time at Middle Preclassic Nixtun-Ch'ich', Petén, Guatemala. *Journal of Anthropological Archaeology* 48: 1–16.

Rice, Prudence M., Timothy W. Pugh, and Evelyn M. Chan Nieto. 2019. Early Construction of a Maya Sacred Landscape: The Sector Y "E-Group" of Nixtun-Ch'ich' (Petén, Guatemala). *Journal of Field Archaeology* 44 (8): 550–564.

Rice, Prudence M., and Don S. Rice. 2018. Classic-to-Contact Period Continuities in Maya Governance in Central Peten, Guatemala. *Ethnohistory* 65 (1): 25–50.

Rich, Michelle E. 2011. Ritual, Royalty, and Classic Period Politics: The Archaeology of the Mirador Group at El Peru-Waka', Peten, Guatemala. PhD diss., Southern Methodist University, Dallas, TX.

———. 2013. Operacion WK-15: Excavaciones en la Estructura P13–5. In *Proyecto Arqueológico Waka'*, ed. Juan Carlos Pérez Calderon, 175. Informe no. 10, Temporada 2012. Informe entregado a la Dirección General del Patrimonio Cultural y Natural de Guatemala, Guatemala City.

Rich, Michelle E., David A. Freidel, F. Kent Reilly III, and Keith Eppich. 2010. An Olmec Style Figurine from El Peru-Waka', Peten, Guatemala: A Preliminary Report. *Mexicon* 17 (5): 115–122.

Rich, Michelle E., and Varinia Matute. 2014. The Power of the Past: Crafting Meaning at a Royal Funerary Pyramid. In *Archaeology at El Perú-Waka': Ancient Maya Performances of Ritual, Memory, and Power*, ed. Olivia Navarro-Farr and Michelle E. Rich, 66–84. Tucson: University of Arizona Press.

Rich, Michelle E., Varinia Matute, and Jennifer Piehl. 2007. WK-11: Excavaciones en la Estructura 014-04. In *Proyecto Arqueológico Waka'*, ed. Héctor L. Escobedo and David A. Freidel, 217–257. Informe no. 4, Temporada 2006. Informe entregado a la Dirección General del Patrimonio Cultural y Natural de Guatemala, Guatemala City.

Rich, Michelle, Jennifer Piehl, and Varinia Matute. 2006. WK-11A: Continuacion de las excavaciones en el Complejo El Mirador, Estructura O14-04. In *Proyecto Arqueológico Waka'*, ed. Héctor L. Escobedo and David A. Freidel, 225–273. Informe no. 3, Temporada 2005. Informe Entegrado a la Dirección General del Patrimonio Cultural y Natural de Guatemala, Guatemala City.

Ricketson, Oliver Garrison, and Edith Bayles Ricketson. 1937. *Uaxactun, Guatemala. Group E—1926–1931*. Carnegie Institution of Washington Publication 477. Washington, DC: Carnegie Institution of Washington.

Ricoeur, Paul. 1984. *Time and Narrative*. Vol. 1. Trans. K. McLaughlin and D. Pellauer. Chicago: University of Chicago Press.

———. 1985. *Time and Narrative*. Vol. 2. Trans. K. McLaughlin and D. Pellauer. Chicago: University of Chicago Press.

544 · References

Rigden, John S. 2005. *Einstein 1905: The Standard of Greatness.* Cambridge, MA: Harvard University Press.

Ringle, William M. 1999. Pre-Classic Cityscapes: Ritual Politics among the Early Lowland Maya. In *Social Patterns in Pre-Classic Mesoamerica,* ed. D. C. Grove and R. A. Joyce, 183–223. Washington, DC: Dumbarton Oaks Research Library and Collection.

———. 2017. Debating Chichen Itza. *Ancient Mesoamerica* 28 (1): 119–136.

———. 2020. The Northern Maya Tollans. In *The Maya World,* ed. S. Hutson and T. Ardren, 752–772. London: Routledge.

Ringle, William M., and George J. Bey III. 2009. The Face of the Itzas. In *The Art of Urbanism: How Mesoamerican Kingdoms Represented Themselves in Architecture and Imagery,* ed. William L. Fash and Leonardo López Luján, 329–383. Washington, DC: Dumbarton Oaks.

Ringle, William M., George J. Bey III, Tara Bond Freeman, Craig A. Hanson, Charles W. Houck, and J. Gregory Smith. 2004. The Decline of the East: The Classic to Postclassic Transition at Ek Balam, Yucatán. In *The Terminal Classic in the Maya Lowlands: Collapse, Transition, and Transformation,* ed. Arthur A. Demarest, Prudence M. Rice, and Don S. Rice, 485–516. Boulder: University Press of Colorado.

Ringle, William M., Tomás Gallareta Negrón, and George Bey III. 2021. Stranger Kings in Northern Yucatan. In *Maya Kingship: Rupture and Transformation from Classic to Postclassic Times,* ed. Tsubasa Okoshi, Arlen F. Chase, Philippe Nondédéo, and M. Charlotte Arnauld, 249–268. Gainesville: University Press of Florida.

Robb, John. 2020. Material Time. In *The Oxford Handbook of History and Material Culture,* ed. I. Gaskell and S. A. Carter, 1–18. Oxford: Oxford University Press.

Robb, Matthew H., ed. 2017a. *Teotihuacan: City of Water, City of Fire.* San Francisco: Fine Arts Museum of San Francisco in association with University of California Press.

———. 2017b. The Water Goddess. In *Teotihuacan: City of Water, City of Fire,* ed. Matthew H. Robb, 154–57. San Francisco: Fine Arts Museum of San Francisco in association with University of California Press.

Robertson, Merle Greene. 1974. The Quadripartite Badge—A Badge of Rulership. In *Primera Mesa Redonda de Palenque,* Part 1, ed. Merle G. Robertson, 129–137. Pebble Beach, CA: Robert Louis Stevenson School.

Robicsek, Francis, and Donald M. Hales. 1981. *The Maya Book of the Dead: The Ceramic Codex. The Corpus of Codex Style Ceramics of the Late Classic Period.* Charlottesville: University of Virginia Art Museum.

Robin, Cynthia. 2013. *Everyday Life Matters: Maya Farmers at Chan.* Gainesville: University Press of Florida.

———. 2017. Ordinary People and East-West Symbolism. In *Maya E Groups: Calendars, Astronomy, and Urbanism in the Early Lowlands,* ed. David A. Freidel, Arlen F. Chase, Anne S. Dowd, and Jerry Murdock, 361–385. Gainesville: University Press of Florida.

Robin, Cynthia, ed. 2012. *Chan: An Ancient Maya Farming Community.* Gainesville: University Press of Florida.

Robin, Cynthia, James Meierhoff, and Laura J. Kosakowsky. 2012. Nonroyal Governance at Chan's Community Center. In *Chan: An Ancient Maya Farming Community,* ed. Cynthia Robin, 133–149. Gainesville: University Press of Florida.

Robin, Cynthia, Andrew R. Wyatt, Laura J. Kosakowsky, Santiago Juarez, Ethan Kalosky, and Elise Enterkin. 2012. A Changing Cultural Landscape: Settlement Survey and GIS at Chan. In *Chan: An Ancient Maya Farming Community,* ed. Cynthia Robin, 19–41. Gainesville: University Press of Florida.

Rodríguez, María de Carmen, and Ponciano Ortíz. 2000. A Massive Offering of Axes at La Merced, Hidalgotitlán, Veracruz, Mexico. In *Olmec Art and Archaeology in Mesoamerica,* ed. John E. Clark and Mary E. Pye, 155–167. Washington, DC: National Gallery of Art.

Rosal, Marco A., Juan Antonio Valdés, and Juan Pedro Laporte. 1993. Nuevas Exploraciones En El Grupo E, Uaxactún. In *Tikal y Uaxactún en el Preclásico,* ed. Juan P. Laporte and Juan A. Valdés, 70–91. Mexico City: Universidad Nacional Autónoma de México.

Rosaldo, Renato. 1968. Metaphors of Hierarchy in a Mayan Ritual. *American Anthropologist* 70: 524–536.

Rosenswig, Robert M. 2010. *The Beginnings of Mesoamerican Civilization: Inter-Regional Interaction and the Olmec.* Cambridge: Cambridge University Press.

———. 2011. An Early Mesoamerican Archipelago of Complexity. In *Early Mesoamerican Social Transformations: Archaic and Formative Lifeways in the Soconusco Region,* ed. Richard G. Lesure, 242–271. Berkeley: University of California Press.

———. 2012. Agriculture and Monumentality in the Soconusco Region of Chiapas, Mexico. In *Early New World Monumentality,* ed. Richard Burger and Robert M. Rosenswig, 111–137. Gainesville: University Press of Florida.

———. 2015. A Mosaic of Adaptation: The Archaeological Record for Mesoamerica's Archaic Period. *Journal of Archaeological Research* 23 (2): 115–162.

Rosenswig, Robert M., Brendan J. Culleton, Douglas J. Kennett, Rosemary Lieske, Rebecca R. Mendelsohn, and Yahaira Núñez-Cortésa. 2018. The Early Izapa Kingdom: Recent Excavations, New Dating, and Middle Formative Ceramic Analyses. *Ancient Mesoamerica* (29): 373–393.

Rosenswig, Robert M., Ricardo López-Torrijos, Caroline E. Antonelli, and Rebecca R. Mendelsohn. 2013. Lidar Mapping and Surface Survey of the Izapa State on the Tropical Piedmont of Chiapas, Mexico. *Journal of Archaeological Science* 40 (3): 1493–1507.

Rosenswig, Robert M., Amber M. VanDerwarker, Brendan J. Culleton, and Douglas J. Kennett. 2015. Is it Agriculture Yet? Intensified Maize-Use at 1000cal BC in the Soconusco and Mesoamerica. *Journal of Anthropological Archaeology* 40: 89–108.

Rossi, Franco D. 2015. The Brothers Taaj: Orders and the Politics of Expertise in the Late Maya State. PhD diss., Boston University.

———. 2017. Pedagogy and State: An Archaeological Inquiry into Classic Maya Educational Practice. *Cambridge Archaeological Journal* 28 (1): 1–18.

———. 2018. Pedagogy and State: An Archaeological Inquiry into Classic Maya Educational Practice. *Cambridge Archaeological Journal* 28 (1): 85–102.

Rossi, Franco D., William A. Saturno, and Heather Hurst. 2015. Maya Codex Book Production and the Politics of Expertise: Archaeology of a Classic Period Household at Xultun, Guatemala. *American Anthropologist* 117 (1): 116–132.

Rossi, Franco D., and David Stuart. 2020. Stela 30: A New Window into Eighth Century Xultun. *Mexicon* 42 (1): 12–15.

## References

Roubik, D. W. 1992. Stingless Bees: A Guide to Panamanian and Mesoamerican Species and Their Nests. In *Insects of Panama and Mesoamerica: Selected Studies,* ed. D. Quintero and A. Aiello, 495–524. Oxford: Oxford University Press.

Roubik, D. W., R. G. Villanueva, E. Francisco Cabrera Cano, and W. Colli Ucan. 1990. Abejas Nativas de la Reserva de la Biosfera de Sian Ka'an. In *Diversidad biológica en la reserva de la biosfera de Sian Ka'an, Quintana Roo, México,* ed. D. Navarro and J. Robinson, 317–320. Quintana Roo: Centro de Investigaciones de Quintana Roo.

Rowe, John H. 1961. Stratigraphy and Seriation. *American Antiquity* 26: 324–330.

Rowley-Conwy, Peter. 2001. Time, Change and the Archaeology of Hunter-Gatherers: How Original Is the "Original Affluent Society"? In *Hunter-Gatherers: An Interdisciplinary Perspective,* ed. Catherine Panter-Brick, Robert H. Layton, and Peter Rowley-Conwy, 39–72. Cambridge: Cambridge University Press.

Roys, Ralph L. 1933. *Book of Chilam Balam of Chumayel.* Publication 438. Washington, DC: Carnegie Institution of Washington.

———. (1933) 1967. *The Book of Chilam Balam of Chumayel.* Norman: University of Oklahoma Press.

Russell, Bradley W. 2000. Pottery Censers: Form, Function, and Symbolism. MA thesis. State University of New York, Albany.

———. 2008. Postclassic Maya Settlement on the Rural-Urban Fringe of Mayapán, Yucatán, Mexico Results of the Mayapán Periphery Project. PhD diss., State University of New York, Albany.

Ruz Lhuillier, Alberto, and J. Alden Mason. 1953. The Mystery of the Temple of the Inscriptions. *Archaeology* 6 (1): 3–11.

Sabloff, Jeremy A. 1986. Interaction among Classic Maya Polities: A Preliminary Examination. In *Peer Polity Interaction and Socio-Political Change,* ed. C. Renfrew and J. F. Cherry, 109–116. Cambridge: Cambridge University Press.

———. 2019. How Maya Archaeologists Discovered the 99% through the Study of Settlement Patterns. *Annual Review of Anthropology* 48 (1): 1–16.

Sabloff, Jeremy A., and J. Marcus, eds. 2008. *The Ancient City: New Perspectives on Urbanism in the Old and New World.* Santa Fe, NM: SAR Press.

Sabloff, Jeremy A., and Paula Sabloff, eds. 2018. *The Emergence of Premodern States: New Perspectives on the Development of Complex Societies.* Santa Fe: SFI Press.

Safronov, Alexander, Ivan Savchenko, and Magdalena Rusek, eds. 2015. *Workshop Materials for Sacral Maya Rituals and Ceremonies in Classic Texts and Images.* Cracow: Jagiellonian University.

Sahagún, Bernardino de. 1950–1982. *Florentine Codex: General History of the Things of New Spain.* 12 vols. Introduction and translated by Arthur J. O. Anderson and Charles E. Dibble. Santa Fe, NM: School for American Research.

———. 1978. *The Florentine Codex.* Book 3, *The Origin of the Gods.* Trans. C. E. Dibble and A. J. O. Anderson. Santa Fe, NM: SAR Press.

———. 1982. *Florentine Codex: General History of the Things of New Spain, Introductions and Indices.* Trans. J. O. Anderson and Charles Dibble. Salt Lake City: University of Utah Press.

Sahlins, Marshall. 2008. The Stranger-King or, Elementary Forms of the Politics of Life. *Indonesia & the Malay World.* 36 (105): 177–199.

Salazar Lama, Daniel. 2017. Maya Lords and the Recreation of Mythical Episodes on Sculptural Programs Integrated in Architecture. *Estudios de Cultura Maya* 49: 165–199.

Sánchez Nava, Pedro Francisco, and Ivan Šprajc. 2015. *Orientaciones astronómicas en la arquitectura maya de las tierras bajas.* Mexico City: INAH.

Sanders, William T., Jeffrey R. Parsons, and Robert S. Santley. 1979. *The Basin of Mexico.* New York: Academic Press.

Sarabia González, Alejandro, and Nelly Zoé Núñez Rendón. 2017. The Sun Pyramid Architectural Complex in Teotihuacan: Vestiges of Worship and Veneration. In *Teotihuacan: City of Water, City of Fire,* ed. Mathew H. Robb, 62–73. San Francisco: Fine Arts Museum of San Francisco in association with University of California Press.

Sassaman, Kenneth E. 2004. Complex Hunter-Gatherers in Evolution and History: A North American Perspective. *Journal of Archaeological Research* 12: 227–280.

Sassaman, Kenneth E., and Michael J. Heckenberger. 2004. Crossing the Symbolic Rubicon in the Southeast. In *Signs of Power: The Rise of Cultural Complexity in the Southeast,* ed. Jon L. Gibson and Philip J. Carr, 214–233. Tuscaloosa: University of Alabama Press.

Sassaman, Kenneth E., and Donald H. Holly, eds. 2011. *Hunter-Gatherer Archaeology as Historical Process.* Tucson: University of Arizona Press.

Satterthwaite, Linton. 1950. Plastic Art on a Maya Palace. *Archaeology* 3 (4): 215–222.

———. 1954. Sculptured Monuments from Caracol, British Honduras. *University Museum Bulletin* 18: 1–45.

———. 1958. The Problem of Abnormal Stela Placements at Tikal and Elsewhere. In *Tikal Reports Numbers 1–4,* ed. Edward M. Shook, William R. Coe, Vivian L. Broman, and Linton Satterthwaite, 61–83. Philadelphia: The University Museum, University of Pennsylvania.

Saturno, William A. 2009. Centering the King: Maya Creation and Legitimization at San Bartolo. In *The Art of Urbanism: How Mesoamerican Kingdoms Represented Themselves in Architecture and Imagery,* ed. William L. Fash and Leonardo López Luján, 111–134. Washington, DC: Dumbarton Oaks.

Saturno, William A., Anthony Aveni, David Stuart, and Franco D. Rossi. 2012. Ancient Maya Calendrical Tables from Xultun, Guatemala. *Science* 33: 714–717.

Saturno, William A., Boris Beltrán, and Franco D. Rossi. 2017. Celestial Observation and Appropriation among the Early Maya. In *Maya E Groups: Calendars, Astronomy, and Urbanism in the Early Lowlands,* ed. David A. Freidel, Arlen F. Chase, Anne S. Dowd, and Jerry Murdock, 328–360. Gainesville: University Press of Florida.

Saturno, William A., Heather Hurst, Franco D. Rossi, and David Stuart. 2015. To Set Before the King: Residential Mural Painting at Xultun, Guatemala. *Antiquity* 89 (343): 122–136.

Saturno, William, Franco Rossi, and Boris Beltrán. 2018. Changing Stages: Royal Legitimacy and the Architectural Development of the Pinturas Complex at San Bartolo, Guatemala. In *Pathways to Complexity: A View from the Maya Lowlands,* ed. M. Kathryn Brown and George Bey III. Gainesville: University Press of Florida.

Saturno, William A., Franco D. Rossi, David Stuart, and Heather Hurst. 2017. A Maya *Curía Regis:* Evidence for a Hierarchical Specialist Order at Xultun, Guatemala. *Ancient Mesoamerica* 28 (2): 423–440.

Saturno, William A., David Stuart, Anthony F. Aveni, and Franco D. Rossi. 2012. Ancient Maya Astronomical Tables from Xultun, Guatemala. *Science* 336 (6082): 714–717.

Saturno, William A., David Stuart, and Boris Beltrán. 2006. Early Maya Writing at San Bartolo, Guatemala. *Science* 311: 1281–1283.

Saturno, William A., Karl A. Taube, and David Stuart. 2005. *The Murals of San Bartolo, El Petén, Guatemala*. Part 1, *The North Wall*. Ancient America 7. Bernardsville, NC: Boundary End Archaeological Research Center.

Saunders, Joe W., Rolfe D. Mandel, Roger T. Saucier, E. Thurman Allen, C. T. Hallmark, Jay K. Johnson, Edwin H. Jackson, Charles M. Allen, Gary L. Stringer, Douglas S. Frink, James K. Feathers, Stephen Williams, Kristen J. Gremillion, Malcolm F. Vidrine, and Reca Jones. 1997. A Mound Complex in Louisiana at 5400–5000 Years before the Present. *Science* 277 (5333): 1796–1799.

Schele, Linda. 1984. "Human Sacrifice among the Classic Maya." In *Ritual Human Sacrifice in Mesoamerica,* ed. Elizabeth Hill Boone, 6–48. Washington, DC: Dumbarton Oaks Research Library and Collection.

———. 1985. The Hauberg Stela: Bloodletting and Mythos of Classic Maya Rulership. In *Fifth Palenque Round Table, 1983,* vol. 7, Virginia M. Fields, 135–151. San Francisco: Pre-Columbian Art Research Institute.

———. 1992a. *Workbook for the XVIth Maya Hieroglyphic Workshop at Texas, with Commentary on the Group of the Cross at Palenque*. Austin: Department of Art and Art History, University of Texas.

———. 1992b. The Founders of Lineages at Copan and other Maya Sites. *Ancient Mesoamerica* 3 (1): 135–144.

Schele, Linda, and David A. Freidel. 1990. *A Forest of Kings: The Untold Story of the Ancient Maya*. New York: William Morrow.

Schele, Linda, and Peter Mathews. 1998. *The Code of Kings: The Language of Seven Sacred Maya Temples and Tombs*. Scribner, New York.

Schele, Linda, and Mary E. Miller. 1986. *The Bloods of Kings: Ritual and Dynasty in Maya Art*. New York: George Braziller, Inc.

Schellhas, Paul. 1904. *Representations of Deities of the Maya Manuscripts*. Vol. 1. Papers of the Peabody Museum of American Archaeology and Ethnology no. 4. Cambridge, MA: Peabody Museum of Archaeology and Ethnology.

Scherer, Andrew. 2015. *Mortuary Landscapes of the Classic Maya: Rituals of Body and Soul*. Austin: University of Texas Press.

Schieber de Lavarreda, Christa, and Miguel Orrego Corzo. 2013. *Tak'alik ab'aj, la ciudad "puente" entre la cultura olmec y maya: 1700 anos de historia y su permanencia hasta la acutalidad*. In *Millenary Maya Societies: Past Crises and Resilience,* ed. M.-Charlotte Arnauld and Alain Breton, 187–198. https://www.mesoweb.com/publications/MMS/12_Schieber-Orrego.pdf.

Schiffer, Michael B. 1987. *Formation Processes of the Archaeological Record*. Albuquerque: University of New Mexico Press.

Schmidt, Klaus. 2010. Göbekli Tepe—The Stone Age Sanctuaries: New Results of Ongoing Excavations with a Special Focus on Sculptures and High Reliefs. *Documenta Praehistorica* 37: 239–255.

Schmidt, Peter. 2007. Birds, Ceramics, and Cacao: New Excavations at Chichén Itzá, Yucatan.

In *Twin Tollans: Chichén Itzá, Tula, and the Epiclassic to Early Postclassic Mesoamerican World,* ed. Jeff Karl Kowalski and Cynthia Kristan-Graham, 151–203. Washington, DC: Dumbarton Oaks.

Schon, Robert. 2015. Weight Sets: Identification and Analysis. *Cambridge Archaeological Journal* 25 (2): 477–494.

Scott, James C. 1998. *Seeing Like a State: How Certain Schemes to Improve the Human Condition Have Failed.* New Haven, CT: Yale University Press.

———. 2017. *Against the Grain: A Deep History of the Earliest States.* New Haven, CT: Yale University Press.

Seler, Eduard. 1904. The Mexican Chronology with Special Reference to the Zapotec Calendar. *Bureau of American Ethnology Bulletin* 28: 11–55.

———. 1996. The Animal Pictures of the Mexican and Maya Manuscripts. In *Collected Works in Mesoamerican Linguistics and Archaeology,* vol. 5, ed. J. Eric. S. Thompson and Francis B. Richardson, 167–340. Lancaster, CA: Labyrinthos.

———. 1963. *Comentarios al Códice Borgia.* 3 vols. Mexico City: Fondo de Cultura Económica.

Shady Solis, Ruth, Jonathan Haas, and Winifred Creamer. 2001. Dating Caral, a Preceramic Site in the Supe Valley on the Central Coast of Peru. *Science* 292 (5517): 723–726.

Sharer, Robert J., with Loa Traxler. 2006. *The Ancient Maya.* 6th ed. Stanford, CA: Stanford University Press.

Sherratt, Andrew. 1990. The Genesis of Megaliths: Monumentality, Ethnicity and Social Complexity in Neolithic North-West Europe. *World Archaeology* 22 (2): 147–167.

Sheseña Hernández, Alejandro. 2015. *Joyaj ti Ajawlel: La ascensión al poder entre los Mayas Clásicos.* Chiapas: Universidad de Ciencias y Artes de Chiapas.

Shook, Edwin. 1957. The Tikal Project. *University Museum Bulletin* 21 (3).

———. 1958. The Temple of the Red Stela. *Expedition* 1 (1): 26–33.

Simmons, Scott E., and Payson D. Sheets. 2002. Divination at Cerén: The Evidence from Structure 12. In *Before the Volcano Erupted,* ed. Payson D. Sheets, 104–114. Austin: University of Texas Press.

Smith, A. Ledyard. 1950. *Guatemala: Excavations of 1931–1937.* Publication 588. Washington, DC: Carnegie Institution of Washington.

———. 1977. Patolli at the Ruins of Seibal, Peten, Guatemala. In *Social Process in Maya Prehistory,* ed. Norman Hammond, 349–363. London: Academic Press.

———. 1982. *Major Architecture and Caches.* Memoirs of the Peabody Museum of Archaeology and Ethnology vol. 15, no. 1. Cambridge, MA: Peabody Museum of Archaeology and Ethnology, Harvard University.

Smith, Mary Elizabeth. 1973. *Picture Writing from Ancient Southern Mexico: Mixtec Place Signs and Maps.* Norman: University of Oklahoma Press.

Smith, Michael E. 1992. Braudel's Temporal Rhythms and Chronology Theory in Archaeology. In *Annales, Archaeology, and Ethnohistory,* ed. A. Bernard Knapp, 25–36. Cambridge: Cambridge University Press.

Smith, Monica L. 2015. The Origins of the Sustainability Concept: Risk Perception and Resource Management in Early Urban Centers. In *Climate Change, Culture and Economics: Anthropological Investigations,* ed. Donald C. Wood, 215–238. Research in Economic Anthropology vol. 35. Chicago: Emerald Group Publishing.

Smith, Robert. 1937. *A Study of Structure A-I Complex at Uaxactún, Petén, Guatemala.*

Publication 456, Contributions to American Archaeology 19. Washington, DC: Carnegie Institution of Washington.

Soja, Edward W. 1996. *Thirdspace: Journeys to Los Angeles and Other Real-and-Imagined Places*. Cambridge, MA: Blackwell Publishing.

Somerville, Andrew D., Christian M. Prager, and Geoffrey E. Braswell. 2018. King K'ak (U Ti'?) Chan K'awil of Pusilha: An Ancient Maya King. *Research Reports in Belizean Archaeology* 15: 287–295.

Sosa, John R. 1985. The Maya Sky, the Maya World: A Symbolic Analysis of Yucatec Maya Cosmology. PhD diss., State University of New York, Albany.

South, Katherine E., and Prudence M. Rice. Forthcoming. Dynamics of Early Pottery from the Petén Lakes Area. In *Pre-Mamom Pottery Variation and the Preclassic Origins of the Lowland Maya,* ed. Debra Walker. Boulder: University Press of Colorado.

Soza, José María. 1970. *Monografía del departamento de El Petén*. Vol. 2. 2nd ed. Guatemala City: Editorial José de Pineda Ibarra.

Spinden, Herbert. 1916. The Question of the Zodiac in America. *American Anthropologist* 18: 53–80.

———. 1924. *The Reduction of Mayan Dates*. Papers of the Peabody Museum of American Archaeology and Ethnology 6. Cambridge, MA: Peabody Museum of Archaeology and Ethnology.

Šprajc, Ivan. 2000. Astronomical Alignments at Teotihuacan, Mexico. *Latin American Antiquity* 11 (4): 403–405.

———. 2001. *Orientaciones astronómicas en la arquitectura prehispánica del centro de México*. Mexico City: Instituto Nacional de Antropología e Historia.

———. 2008. *Reconocimiento arqueológico en el sureste del estado de Campeche, Mexico: 1996–2005*. BAR International Series 1742. Oxford: Archaeopress.

———. 2009. Astronomical and Cosmological Aspects of Maya Architecture and Urbanism. In *Cosmology across Cultures: Proceedings of a Workshop Held at Parque de las Ciencias, Granada, Spain, 8–12 September 2008,* ed. J. A. Rubiño-Martín, J. A. Belmonte, F. Prada, and A. Alberdi, 303–314. Andalucia: SEAC.

———. 2018. Astronomy, Architecture, and Landscape in Prehispanic Mesoamerica. *Journal of Archaeological Research* 26: 197–251.

———. 2020. *Lost Maya Cities: Archaeological Quests in the Mexican Jungle*. College Station: Texas A&M University Press.

———. 2021a. Astronomical Aspects of Group E-Type Complexes and Implications for Understanding Ancient Maya Architecture and Urban Planning. *PLOS ONE* 16 (4): e0250785.

———. 2021b. Equinoctial Sun and Astronomical Alignments in Mesoamerican Architecture: Fiction and Fact. *Ancient Mesoamerica*:1–17.

Šprajc, Ivan, Takeshi Inomata, and Anthony F. Aveni. 2023. Origins of Mesoamerican Astronomy and Calendar: Evidence from the Olmec and Maya Regions. *Science Advances* 9 (1): 1–15.

Šprajc, Ivan, and Pedro Francisco Sánchez Nava. 2012. Orientaciones astronómicas en la arquitectura maya de las tierras bajas: Nuevos datos e interpretaciones. In *XXV Simposio de Investigaciones Arqueológicas en Guatemala,* vol. 2, ed. Bárbara Arroyo,

Lorena Paiz, and Héctor Mejía, 977–996. Guatemala City: Museo Nacional de Arqueología y Etnología.

Stanish, Charles. 2017. *The Evolution of Human Co-operation: Ritual and Social Complexity in Stateless Societies*. Cambridge: Cambridge University Press.

Stanton, Travis W. 2017. The Founding of Yaxuná: Place and Trade in Preclassic Yucatán. In *Maya E Groups: Calendars, Astronomy, and Urbanism in the Early Lowlands,* ed. David A. Freidel, Arlen F. Chase, Anne S. Dowd, and Jerry Murdock, 450–479. Gainesville: University Press of Florida.

Stanton, Travis W., and Traci Arden. 2005. The Middle Formative of Yucatan in Context: The View from Yaxuna. *Ancient Mesoamerica* 16 (2): 213–228.

Stanton, Travis W., and Ryan H. Collins. 2017. Los orígenes de los mayas del norte: investigaciones en el Grupo E de Yaxuná. *Arqueología Mexicana* 145: 32–37.

———. 2021. The Role of Middle Preclassic Placemaking in the Creation of Late Formative Yucatecan Cities: The Foundations of Yaxuná. In *Early Mesoamerican Urbanism,* ed. M. Love and Julia Guernsey. Cambridge: Cambridge University Press.

Stanton, Travis W., and David A. Freidel. 2003. Ideological Lock-In and the Dynamics of Formative Religions in Mesoamerica. *Mayab* 16: 5–14.

———. 2005. Placing the Centre, Centring the Place: The Influence of Formative Sacbeob in Classic Site Design at Yaxuná, Yucatán. *Cambridge Archaeological Journal* 15 (2): 225–249.

Stanton, Travis W., Sara Dzul Góngora, Ryan H. Collins, and Rodrigo Martín Morales. Forthcoming. Pottery and Society during the Formative Period at Yaxuná, Yucatán. In *Crafting the Complex: Material Culture and the Rise of Complexity in Formative Mesoamerica,* ed. L. DeLance. Austin: University of Texas Press.

Stanton, Travis W., David A. Freidel, Charles K. Suhler, Traci Ardren, James N. Ambrosino, Justine M. Shaw, and Sharon Bennett. 2010. *Excavations at Yaxuná, Yucatán, Mexico*. BAR International Series. Oxford: Archaeopress.

Stanton, Travis W., and Aline Magnoni, eds. 2008. *Ruins of the Past: The Use and Perception of Abandoned Structures in the Maya Lowlands*. Boulder: University of Colorado Press.

Stavrakis-Pulston, Olga. 2015. *Settlement and Subsistence at Tikal: The Work of Dennis E. Puleston (Field research 1961–1972)*. Paris Monographs in Archaeology 43, BAR International Series. Oxford: Archaeopress.

Stephens, John L. 1841. *Incidents of Travel in Central America, Chiapas, and Yucatan*. Vol. 2. New York: Harper and Brothers.

Stevens, Chris J., and Dorian Q. Fuller. 2012. Did Neolithic Farming Fail? The Case for a Bronze Age Agricultural Revolution in the British Isles. *Antiquity* 86 (333): 707–722.

Stone, Andrea J. 1995. *Images from the Underworld: Naj Tunich and the Tradition of Maya Cave Painting*. Austin: University of Texas Press.

Stone, Andrea, and Marc Zender. 2011. *Reading Maya Art: A Hieroglyphic Guide to Ancient Maya Painting and Sculpture*. London: Thames & Hudson.

Stross, Brian. 1994. Maize and Fish: The Iconography of Power in the Late Formative. *Res: Anthropology and Aesthetics* 25: 9–35.

Stuart, David. 1987. The Paintings of Tomb 12, Río Azul. In *Río Azul Reports, No. 3: The 1985 Season,* ed. Richard E. W. Adams, 161–167. San Antonio: Center for Archaeological Research, University of Texas.

---. 1996. Kings of Stone: A Consideration of Stelae in Ancient Maya Ritual and Representation. *Res: Anthropology and Aesthetics* 29/30: 148–171.

---. 1997. Kinship Terms in Maya Inscriptions. In *The Language of Maya Hieroglyphs*, ed. Martha J. Macri and Anabel Ford, 1–11. San Francisco, CA: Pre-Columbian Art Research Institute.

---. 1998a. Fire Enters His House: Architecture and Ritual in Classic Maya Texts. In *Function and Meaning in Classic Maya Architecture*, ed. Stephen D. Houston, 373–425. Washington, DC: Dumbarton Oaks.

---. 1998b. The Jade Hearth: Centrality, Rulership, and the Classic Maya Temple. In *Function and Meaning in Classic Maya Architecture*, ed. Stephen D. Houston, 427–478. Washington, DC: Dumbarton Oaks.

---. 2000. "The Arrival of Strangers": Teotihuacan and Tollan in Classic Maya History. In *Mesoamerica's Classic Heritage*, ed. David Carrasco, Lindsay Jones, and Scott Sessions, 465–513. Boulder: University Press of Colorado.

---. 2003. A Cosmological Throne at Palenque. Unpublished paper. www.mesoweb.com/stuart/notes/Throne.pdf.

---. 2004a. New Year Records in Classic Maya Inscriptions. *PARI Journal* 5 (2): 1–6.

---. 2004b. The Beginnings of the Copan Dynasty: A Review of the Hieroglyphic and Historical Evidence. In *Understanding Early Classic Copan*, ed. Ellen E. Bell, Marcello A. Canuto, and Robert J. Sharer, 215–247. Philadelphia: University of Pennsylvania Museum of Archaeology and Anthropology.

---. 2004c. The Entering of the Day: An Unusual Date from Northern Campeche. Unpublished paper. www.mesoweb.com/stuart/notes/EnteringDay.pdf.

---. 2005a. *Sourcebook for the 29th Maya Hieroglyph Forum, March 11–16, 2005*. Austin, TX: Maya Workshop Foundation.

---. 2005b. *The Inscriptions from Temple XIX at Palenque*. San Francisco, CA: Pre-Columbian Art Research Institute.

---. 2005c. Glyphs on Pots: Decoding Classic Maya Ceramics. In *Sourcebook for the 29th Maya Meetings at Texas*. Austin: University of Texas.

---. 2008. A Childhood Ritual on the Hauberg Stela. *Maya Decipherment,* March 27. https://mayadecipherment.com/2008/03/27/a-childhood-ritual-on-the-hauberg-stela/.

---. 2010. Shining Stones: Observations on the Ritual Meaning of Early Maya Stelae. In *The Place of Stone Monuments: Context, Use, and Meaning in Mesoamerica's Preclassic Transition*, ed. Julia Guernsey, John E. Clark, and Barbara Arroyo, 283–298. Washington, DC: Dumbarton Oaks.

---. 2011. *The Order of Days: The Maya World and the Truth about 2012*. New York: Harmony Books.

---. 2012a. The Calligraphic Zero. *Maya Decipherment,* June 15. https://mayadecipherment.com/2012/06/15/the-calligraphic-zero/.

---. 2012b. On Effigies of Ancestors and Gods. *Maya Decipherment,* January 20. https://mayadecipherment.com/2012/01/20/on-effigies-of-ancestors-and-gods/.

---. 2015. The Royal Headband: A Pan-Mesoamerican Hieroglyph. *Maya Decipherment,* January 26. https://mayadecipherment.com/2015/01/26.

---. 2017. A Note on the Sign for TZ'IHB, "Writing, Painting." *Maya Decipherment,*

May 1. https://mayadecipherment.com/2017/05/01/a-note-on-the-sign-for-tzihb
-writing-painting/.

———. 2018. Finding the Founder: Old Notes on the Identification of K'inich Yax K'uk'
Mo' of Copan. *Maya Decipherment,* April 24. https://mayadecipherment.com/
2018/04/.

———. 2020a. Yesterday's Moon: A Decipherment of the Classic Mayan Adverb *ak'biiy.*
*Maya Decipherment,* August 1. https://mayadecipherment.com/2020/08/01/
yesterdays-moon-a-decipherment-of-the-classic-mayan-adverb-akbiiy/.

———. 2020b. A New Variant of the Syllable k'o in Maya Writing. *Maya Decipherment,*
June 5. https://mayadecipherment.com/2020/06/05/a-new-variant-of-the-syllable
-ko-in-maya-writing/.

———. 2020c. A Note on the Sign for TZ'IHB, "Writing, Painting." *Maya Decipherment,*
May 1. https://mayadecipherment.com/2017/05/01/a-note-on-the-sign-for-tzihb
-writing-painting/.

Stuart, David, Marcello Canuto, Tomás Barrientos, and Alejandro Gonzales. 2018. A Preliminary Analysis of Altar 5 from La Corona. *PARI Journal* 19 (2): 1–13.

Stuart, David, Marcello A. Canuto, Tomás Barrientos Q., Jocelyne Ponce, and Joanne Baron. 2015. Death of the Defeated: New Historical Data on Block 4 of La Corona's Hieroglyphic Stairway 2. *La Corona Notes* 1 (3): 1–7.

Stuart, David, and Stephen D. Houston. 1994. *Classic Maya Place Names.* Studies in Pre-Columbian Art and Archaeology 33. Washington, DC: Dumbarton Oaks.

Stuart, David, S. Houston, and J. Robertson. 1999. Recovering the Past: Classic Mayan Language and Classic Maya Gods. In *Notebook for the XXIIIrd Linda Schele Forum on Maya Hieroglyphic Writing: March 13–14, 1999.* Austin: University of Texas.

Stuart, David, and George E. Stuart. 2008. *Palenque: Eternal City of the Maya.* New York: Thames & Hudson.

Stuart, George. 1992. Quest for Decipherment: A Historical and Biographical Survey of Maya Hieroglyphic Investigation. In *New Theories on the Ancient Maya,* ed. Elin Danien and Robert J. Sharer, 1–64. University Museum Symposium Series. Philadelphia, PA: University Museum of Archaeology and Anthropology.

Sugiyama, Nawa. 2014. Animals and Sacred Mountains: How Ritualized Performances Materialized State-Ideologies as Teotihuacan, Mexico. PhD diss., Peabody Museum of Archaeology and Ethnology, Harvard University.

———. 2017. Pumas Eating Human Hearts? Animal Sacrifices and Captivity at the Moon Pyramid. In *Teotihuacan: City of Water, City of Fire,* ed. Mathew H. Robb, 90–93. San Francisco: Fine Arts Museum of San Francisco in association with University of California Press.

Sugiyama, Nawa, William L. Fash, Barbara W. Fash, and Saburo Sugiyama. 2020. The Maya at Teotihuacan? New Insights into Teotihuacan-Maya Interactions from the Plaza of the Columns Complex, in *Teotihuacan: The World Beyond the City,* ed. Kenneth G. Hirth, David M. Carballo, and Barbara Arroyo, 139–171. Washington, DC: Dumbarton Oaks.

Sugiyama, Nawa, Gilberto Pérez-Roldan, Bernardo Rodriguez, Fabiola Torres, and Raul Valadez. 2014. Animals and the State: The Role of Animals in State-Level Rituals

554 · References

in Mesoamerica. In *Animals and Inequality in the Ancient World,* ed. Sue Ann McCarty and Benjamin Arbuckle, 11–31. Boulder: University Press of Colorado.

Sugiyama, Nawa, Saburo Sugiyama, Verónica Ortega, and William Fash. 2016. ¿Artistas mayas en Teotihuacan? *Arqueología Mexicana* 24 (142): 8.

Sugiyama, Nawa, Saburo Sugiyama, and Alejandro Sarabia G. 2013. Inside the Sun Pyramid at Teotihuacan, Mexico: 2008–2011 Excavations and Preliminary Results. *Latin American Antiquity* 24 (4): 403–432.

Sugiyama, Saburo. 1992. Rulership, Warfare, and Human Sacrifice at the Ciudadela: An Iconographic Study of Feathered Serpent Representations. In *Art, Ideology, and the City of Teotihuacan,* ed. Janet C. Berlo, 204–230. Washington, DC: Dumbarton Oaks.

———. 1993. Worldview Materialized at Teotihuacan, Mexico. *Latin American Antiquity* 4 (2): 103–129.

———. 1998. Termination Rituals and Prehispanic Looting at the Feathered Serpent Pyramid in Teotihuacan, Mexico, In *The Sowing and the Dawning: Termination, Dedication, and Transformation in the Archaeological and Ethnographic Record of Mesoamerica,* ed. Shirley B. Mock, 147–164. Albuquerque: University of New Mexico Press.

———. 2005. *Human Sacrifice, Militarism, and Rulership: Materialization of State Ideology at the Feathered Serpent Pyramid, Teotihuacan.* Cambridge: Cambridge University Press.

———. 2010. Teotihuacan City Layout as a Cosmogram: Preliminary Results of the 2007 Measurement Unit Study. In *The Archaeology of Measurement: Comprehending Heaven, Earth and Time in Ancient Societies,* ed. Iain Morley and Colin Renfrew, 130–149. Cambridge: Cambridge University Press.

———. 2014. The Nature of Early Urbanism in Teotihuacan. Paper presented at Society for American Archaeology 79th Annual Meetings, Austin, Texas.

———. 2017a. Teotihuacan: Planned City with Cosmic Pyramids. In *Teotihuacan: City of Water, City of Fire,* ed. Matthew H. Robb, 28–37. San Francisco: Fine Arts Museum of San Francisco in association with University of California Press.

———. 2017b. The Feathered Serpent Pyramid at Teotihuacan: Monumentality and Sacrificial Burials. In *Teotihuacan: City of Water, City of Fire,* ed. Matthew H. Robb, 54–61. San Francisco: Fine Arts Museum of San Francisco in association with University of California Press.

Sugiyama, Saburo, and Ruben Cabrera Castro. 2007. The Moon Pyramid Project and the Teotihuacan State Polity: A Brief Summary of the 1998–2004 Excavations. *Ancient Mesoamerica* 18 (1): 109–125.

———. 2017. The Moon Pyramid and the Ancient State of Teotihuacan. In *Teotihuacan: City of Water, City of Fire,* ed. Matthew H. Robb, 74–80. San Francisco: Fine Arts Museum of San Francisco in association with University of California Press.

Sugiyama, Saburo, and Leonardo López Luján. 2007. Dedicatory Burial/Offering Complexes at the Moon Pyramid, Teotihuacan: A Preliminary Report of the 1998–2004 Explorations. *Ancient Mesoamerica* 18: 127–146.

Sugiyama, Saburo, and Nawa Sugiyama. 2020. Interactions between Ancient Teotihuacan and the Maya World. In *The Maya World,* ed. Scott R. Hutson and Traci Ardren, 689–708. New York: Routledge.

———. 2021. Monumental Cityscape and Polity at Teotihuacan. In *Mesoamerican Archaeology: Theory and Practice,* 2nd ed., ed. Julia A. Hendon, Lisa Overholtzer, and Rosemary A. Joyce, 98–128. Hoboken, NJ: Wiley-Blackwell.

Suhler, Charles K. 1996. Excavations at the North Acropolis, Yaxuna, Yucatan, Mexico. PhD diss., Department of Anthropology, Southern Methodist University, Dallas TX.

Suhler, Charles K., and David A. Freidel. 1998. Life and Death in a Maya War Zone. *Archaeology* 51 (3): 28–34.

Sweely, Tracy. 1999. Gender, Space, People, and Power at Cerén, El Salvador. In *Manifesting Power: Gender and the Interpretation of Power in Archaeology,* ed. Tracy Sweely, 155–171. London: Routledge.

Symonds, Stacey, Ann Cyphers, and Roberto Lunagómez. 2002. *Asentamiento prehispánico en San Lorenzo Tenochtitlán.* Serie San Lorenzo, vol. 2. Mexico City: Universidad Nacional Autónoma de México, Instituto de Investigaciones Antropológicas Dirección General de Asuntos del Personal Académico-Universidad Nacional Autónoma de México.

Taschek, Jennifer, and Joseph W. Ball. 1992. Lord Smoke-Squirrel's Cacao Cup: The Archaeological Context and Socio-Historical Significance of the Buenavista "Jauncy Vase." In *The Maya Vase Book,* vol. 3, ed. Justin Kerr, 490–497. New York: Kerr Associates.

Tate, Carolyn. 1991. *Yaxchilan, Design of a Maya Ceremonial Center.* Austin: University of Texas Press.

Taube, Karl A. 1985. The Classic Maya Maize God: A Reappraisal. In *Fifth Palenque Round Table, 1983,* ed. Merle Greene Robertson, 171–181. San Francisco, CA: Pre-Columbian Art Research Institute.

———. 1988a. A Study of Classic Maya Scaffold Sacrifice. In *Maya Iconography,* ed. Elizabeth P. Benson and Gillett G. Griffin, 331–351. Princeton, NJ: Princeton University Press.

———. 1988b. A Prehispanic Maya Katun Wheel. *Journal of Anthropological Research* 44 (2): 183–203.

———. 1989. *Itzam Kab Ain: Caimans, Cosmology, and Calendrics in Postclassic Yucatán.* Research reports on ancient Maya writing 26 and 27. Washington, DC: Center for Maya Research.

———. 1992a. *The Major Gods of Ancient Yucatan.* Studies in Pre-Columbian Art and Archaeology 32. Washington, DC: Dumbarton Oaks.

———. 1992b. The Iconography of Mirrors at Teotihuacan. In *Art, Ideology, and the City of Teotihuacan,* ed. Janet C. Berlo, 169–204. Washington, DC: Dumbarton Oaks.

———. 1996. The Olmec Maize God: The Face of Corn in Formative Mesoamerica. *Res: Anthropology and Aesthetics* 29–30: 39–81.

———. 1998. The Jade Hearth: Centrality, Rulership, and the Classic Maya Temple. In *Function and Meaning in Classic Maya Architecture,* ed. S. D. Houston. 427–478. Washington, DC: Dumbarton Oaks.

———. 2000. Lightning Celts and Corn Fetishes: The Formative Olmec and the Development of Maize Symbolism in Mesoamerica and the American Southwest. In *Olmec Art and Archaeology in Mesoamerica,* ed. John E. Clark and Mary E. Pye, 297–337. Washington, DC: National Gallery of Art.

———. 2001. The Breath of Life: The Symbolism of Wind in Mesoamerica and the American

Southwest. In *The Road to Aztlan: Art from a Mythic Homeland,* ed. Virginia M. Fields and Victor Zamudio-Taylor, 102–123. Los Angeles, CA: Los Angeles County Museum of Art.

———. 2003a. Ancient and Contemporary Maya Conceptions about Field and Forest. In *The Lowland Maya Area: Three Millennia at the Human-Wildland Interface,* ed. A. Gómez-Pompa, M. F. Allen, S. L. Fedick, and J. J. Jiménez-Osornio, 461–492. Binghamton, NY: Food Products Press.

———. 2003b. Maws of Heaven and Hell: The Symbolism of the Centipede and the Serpent in Classic Maya Religion. In *Antropología de la eternidad: la muerte en la cultura maya,* ed. Andres Ciudad Ruiz, Mario Humberto Ruiz Sosa, and Josefa Iglesias Ponce de Leon, 405–442. Mexico City: Sociedad Espaniola de Estudios Maya, Centro de Estudios Maya, Centro de Investigaciones Filologicas, UNAM.

———. 2004a. *Olmec Art at Dumbarton Oaks.* Pre-Columbian Art at Dumbarton Oaks no. 2. Washington, DC: Dumbarton Oaks.

———. 2004b. Aztec Religion: Creation, Sacrifice, and Renewal. In *The Aztec Empire,* ed. E. H. Boone, 168–177. New York: Guggenheim Museum.

———. 2004c. Structure 10L-16 and Its Early Classic Antecedents: Fire and the Evocation and Resurrection of K'inich Yax K'uk' Mo'. In *Understanding Early Classic Copan,* ed. Ellen E. Bell, Marcello A. Canuto, and Robert J. Sharer, 265–295. Philadelphia: University of Pennsylvania Museum of Archaeology and Anthropology.

———. 2004d. Flower Mountain: Concepts of Life, Beauty, and Paradise among the Classic Maya. *Res: Anthropology and Aesthetics* 45: 69–98.

———. 2005. The Symbolism of Jade in Classic Maya Religion. *Ancient Mesoamerica* 16: 23–50.

———. 2009. The Maize God and Mythic Origins of Dance. In *The Maya and Their Sacred Narratives: Text and Context in Maya Mythologies,* ed. Genevieve Le Fort, Raphael Gardiol, Sebastian Matteo, and Christophe Helmke, 41–52. Acta Mesoamericana 20. Markt Schwaben: Verlag Anton Saurwein.

———. 2010. Where Earth and Sky Meet: The Sea in Ancient and Contemporary Maya Cosmology. In *Fiery Pool: The Maya and the Mythic Sea,* ed. Daniel Finamore and Stephen D. Houston, 202–219. New Haven, CT: Peabody Essex Museum in association with Yale University Press.

———. 2013. The Classic Maya Temple: Centrality, Cosmology and Sacred Geography in Ancient Mesoamerica. In *Heaven on Earth: Temples, Ritual and Cosmic Symbolism in the Ancient World,* ed. Deena Ragavan, 89–125. Chicago: Oriental Institute, University of Chicago.

———. 2016. Through a Glass, Brightly: Recent Investigations Concerning Mirrors and Scrying in Ancient and Contemporary Mesoamerica. In *Manufactured Light: Mirrors in the Mesoamerican Realm,* ed. Emiliano Gallaga M. and Marc G. Blainey, 285–313. Boulder: University Press of Colorado.

———. 2017. Pillars of the World: Cosmic Trees in Ancient Maya Thought. In *Del saber ha hecho su razón de ser: Homenaje a Alfredo López Austin,* ed. E. Matos Moctezuma and Ángel Ochoa, 269–302. Mexico City: Universidad Nacional Autónoma de México.

Taube, Karl A., William A. Saturno, David Stuart, and Heather Hurst. 2010. *The Murals of*

*San Bartolo, El Petén, Guatemala*. Part 2, *The West Wall*. Ancient America 10. Bernardsville, NC: Boundary End Archaeological Research Center.

Taube, Karl A., Travis W. Stanton, José Francisco Osorio León, Francisco Pérez Ruiz, María Rocio González de la Mata, and Jeremy D. Coltman. 2020. *The Initial Series Group at Chichen Itza, Yucatan: Archaeological Investigations and Iconographic Interpretations*. San Francisco: Precolumbia Mesoweb Press.

Tedlock, Barbara. 1983. *Time and the Highland Maya*. Albuquerque: University of New Mexico Press.

———. 1992. *Time and the Highland Maya*. 2nd ed. Albuquerque: University of New Mexico Press.

Tedlock, Barbara, and Dennis Tedlock. 1985. Text and Textile: Language and Technology in the Arts of the Quiché Maya. *Journal of Anthropological Research* 41: 121–146.

Tedlock, Dennis. 1996. *Popul Vuh: The Definitive Edition of the Mayan Book of the Dawn of Life and the Glories of Gods and Kings*. 2nd ed. New York: Touchstone Press.

Tena, Rafael. 1987. *El calendario mexica y la cronografía*. Mexico City: Instituto Nacional de Antropología e Historia, Serie Historia.

Terada, Kazuo, and Yoshio Onuki, eds. 1988. *Las excavaciones en Cerro Blanco y Huacaloma, Cajamarca, Perú, 1985*. Tokyo: Andes Chosashitsu, Departamento de Antropología Cultural, Universidad de Tokio.

Teran Silvia, and Christian Rasmussen. 1994. *La milpa de los Mayas*. Mérida: Gobierno del Estado de Yucatán.

Terrones Gonzáles, Enrique. 1990. Proyecto Salvamento Arqueológico Rancho Ina, Quintana Roo. In *Mexicon* 12 (5): 89–92.

———. 1994. Apiarios prehispánicos. *Boletín de la Escuela de Ciencias Antropológicas* 20 (117): 43–57.

Thompson, Edward H., and George A. Dorsey. 1898. *Ruins of Xkickmook, Yucatan*. Field Columbian Museum Publication 28, Anthropological Series vol. II, no. 3. Chicago: Field Columbian Museum.

Thompson, J. Eric S. 1942. Maya Arithmetic. *Contributions to American Anthropology and History* 36: 37–62.

———. 1950. *Maya Hieroglyphic Writing: An Introduction*. Publication 589. Washington, DC: Carnegie Institution of Washington.

———. 1954. *The Rise and Fall of Maya Civilization*. Norman: University of Oklahoma Press.

———. 1957. *Deities Portrayed on Censers at Mayapán*. Current Reports no. 40. Washington, DC: Carnegie Institution of Washington Department of Archaeology.

———. 1960. *Maya Hieroglyphic Writing: An Introduction*. 3rd ed. Norman: University of Oklahoma Press.

———. (1962) 1991. *A Catalog of Maya Hieroglyphs*. Norman: University of Oklahoma Press.

———. 1966. *The Rise and Fall of Maya Civilization*. 2nd ed. Norman: University of Oklahoma Press.

———. 1972. *A Commentary on the Dresden Codex: A Maya Hieroglyphic Book*. Philadelphia, PA: American Philosophical Society.

558 · References

———. 1973. The Painted Capstone at Sacnicte, Yucatan, and Two Others at Uxmal. *Indiana* 1: 59–63.

———. 1977. A Proposal for Constituting a Maya Subgroup, Cultural and Linguistic, in the Petén and Adjacent Regions. In *Anthropology and History in Yucatán,* ed. Grant D. Jones, 3–42. Austin: University of Texas Press.

Thompson, Philip C. 1985. Structure of the Civil Hierarchy in Tekanto, Yucatán, 1785–1820. *Estudios de Cultura Maya* 16: 183–205.

Thomson, Belinda, ed. 2011. *Gauguin: Maker of Myth*. Princeton, NJ: Princeton University Press.

Tichy, Franz. 1991. *Die geordnete Welt indianischer Völker: Ein Beispiel von Raumordnung nd Zeitordnung im vorkolumbischen Mexiko*. Das Mexiko-Projekt der Deutschen Forschungsgemeinschaft 21. Stuttgart: Franz Steiner Verlag.

Tiesler, Vera. 2007. Funerary or Nonfunerary? New References in Identifying Ancient Maya Sacrificial and Postsacrificial Behaviors from Human Assemblages. In *New Perspectives on Human Sacrifice and Ritual Body Treatments in Ancient Maya Society,* ed. Vera Tiesler and Andrea Cucina, 14–44. New York: Springer.

———. 2018. The Fiery Dead: Igniting Human Bodies in the Maya Northern Lowlands. In *Smoke, Flames, and the Human Body in Mesoamerican Ritual Practice,* ed. Vera Tiesler and Andrew Scherer, 205–250. Washington, DC: Dumbarton Oaks.

Tiesler, Vera, and Andrea Cucina. 2006a. Procedures in Human Heart Extraction and Ritual Meaning: A Taphonomic Assessment of Anthropologenic Marks in Classic Maya Skeletons. *Latin American Antiquity* 17 (4): 493–510.

———. 2006b. *Janaab' Pacal of Palenque: Reconstructing the Life and Death of a Maya Ruler*. Tucson: University of Arizona Press.

Tiesler, Vera, and Andrea Cucina, eds. 2007. *New Perspectives on Human Sacrifice and Ritual Body Treatments in Ancient Maya Society*. New York: Springer.

Tiesler, Vera, Andrea Cucina, Travis W. Stanton, and David A. Freidel. 2017. *Before Kukulkan: Maya Life, Death, and Identity at Classic Period Yaxuna, Yucatan, Mexico*. Tucson: University of Arizona Press.

Tokovinine, Alexandre. 2003. A Classic Maya Term for Public Performance. Unpublished paper. https://www.mesoweb.com/features/tokovinine/Performance.pdf.

———. 2008. The Power of Place: Political Landscape and Identity in Classic Maya Inscriptions, Imagery, and Architecture. PhD diss., Peabody Museum of Archaeology and Ethnology, Harvard University.

———. 2013. *Place and Identity in Classic Maya Narratives*. Studies in Pre-Columbian Art and Archaeology no. 37. Washington, DC: Dumbarton Oaks.

———. 2017. *Beginner's Visual Catalog of Maya Hieroglyphs*. https://www.mesoweb.com/resources/catalog/Tokovinine_Catalog.pdf.

———. 2020. Bundling the Sticks: A Case for Classic Maya Tallies. In *The Real Business of Ancient Maya Economies: From Farmers' Fields to Rulers' Realms,* ed. M. Masson, D. Freidel, and A. Demarest, 276–295. Gainesville: University Press of Florida.

Tokovinine, Alexander, and Marc Zender. 2012. Lords of Windy Water: The Royal Court of Motul de San José in Classic Maya Inscriptions. In *Motul de San José: Politics, History, and Economy in a Classic Maya Polity,* ed. Antonia E. Foias and Kitty F. Emery, 30–66. Gainesville: University Press of Florida.

Tozzer, Alfred M. 1941. *Landa's Relación de las cosas de Yucatan*. Papers of the Peabody Museum of American Archaeology and Ethnology vol. 18. Cambridge, MA: Peabody Museum of Archaeology and Ethnology, Harvard University.

Tozzer, Alfred M., and Glover M. Allen. 1910. *Animal Figures in the Maya Codices*. Papers of the Peabody Museum of American Archaeology and Ethnology vol. 4, no. 3. Cambridge, MA: Peabody Museum of Archaeology and Ethnology, Harvard University.

Treat, Raymond. 1986. *Early and Middle Formative Sub-Mound Refuse Deposits at Vistahermosa, Chiapas*. Notes of the New World Archaeological Foundation, no. 2. Provo, UT: Brigham Young University.

Triadan, Daniela, Victor Castillo, Takeshi Inomata, Juan Manuel Palomo, María Belén Méndez, Mónica Cortave, Jessica MacLellan, Melissa Burham, and Erick Ponciano. 2017. Social Transformation in a Middle Preclassic Community: Elite Residential Complexes at Ceibal. *Ancient Mesoamerica* 28 (1): 233–264.

Trik, Aubrey S. 1963. The Splendid Tomb of Temple I at Tikal, Guatemala. *Expedition Magazine* 6 (1): 3–17.

Trik, Helen, and Michael E. Kampen. 1983. *The Graffiti of Tikal*. Tikal Report 31. Philadelphia University Museum of Archaeology and Anthropology.

Tsukamoto, Kenichiro, Javier López Camacho, Luz Evelia Campaña Valenzuela, Hirokazu Kotegawa, and Octavio Q. Esparza Olguín. 2015. Political Interactions among Social Actors: Spatial Organization at the Classic Maya Polity of El Palmar, Campeche, Mexico. *Latin American Antiquity* 26 (2): 200–220.

Turnbull, C. M. 1966. *Wayward Servants*. London: Athlone Press.

Turner, Andrew D. 2020. The Olmec Spoon Reconsidered: Material Meanings of Jade, Nacreous Shells and Pearls in Ancient Mesoamerica. *Ancient Mesoamerica* 33 (2) 261–277.

Turner, Andrew D., ed. 2022. *Códice Maya de México: Understanding the Oldest Surviving Book of the Americas*. Los Angeles: Getty Research Institute.

Turner, Victor W. 1970. *The Forest of Symbols: Aspects of Ndembu Ritual*. Ithaca, NY: Cornell University Press.

———. 1974. *Dramas, Fields, and Metaphors: Symbolic Action in Human Society*. Ithaca, NY: Cornell University Press.

———. 1982. *From Ritual to Theater: The Human Seriousness of Play*. New York: PAJ Publications, A Division of Performing Arts Journal.

Uriarte Torres, Alejandro Jesús. 2016. Sondeo preliminar en el Complejo Eva. *Proyecto Arqueológico Yaxnohcah, informe de las 2014 y 2015 temporadas de investigaciones*, ed. Armando Anaya Hernández, Meaghan Peuramaki-Brown, and Kathryn Reese-Taylor, 42–50. Report presented to the Instituto Nacional de Antropología e Historia, Mexico City.

Urschel, Donna. 2009. Love & War: Shell Pendant Reveals Clues to Ancient Toltec Culture. *Library of Congress Information Bulletin* 68 (6). https://www.loc.gov/loc/lcib/0906/toltecs.html.

Urton, Gary. 1981a. *At the Crossroads of Earth and Sky: An Andean Cosmology*. Austin: University of Texas Press.

———. 1981b. Animals and Astronomy in the Quechua Universe. *Proceedings of the American Philosophical Society* 125 (2): 110–127.

560 · References

Vadala, Jeffrey, and Susan Milbrath. 2014. Astronomy, Landscape, and Ideological Transmissions at the Coastal site of Cerros, Belize. *Journal of Caribbean Archaeology* 14: 1–21.

Vail, Gabrielle. 1994. A Commentary on the Bee Almanacs in Codex Madrid. In *Codices y Documentos Sobre México, Primer Simposio,* ed. Constanza Vegas Sosa, 37–68. INAH, México D.F.

———. 1997. The Deer-Trapping Almanacs in the Madrid Codex. In *Papers on the Madrid Codex,* ed. Victoria Bricker and Gabrielle Vail, 73–110. New Orleans, LA: Middle American Research Institute.

———. 2004. A Reinterpretation of the *Tzol'kin* Almanacs in the Madrid Codex. In *The Madrid Codex: New Approaches to Understanding an Ancient Maya Manuscript,* ed. Gabrielle Vail and Anthony F. Aveni, 215–254. Boulder: University Press of Colorado.

———. 2006. The Maya Codices. *Annual Review of Anthropology* 35: 497–519.

———. 2013. *Códice de Madrid*. Guatemala City: Universidad Mesoamericana.

———. 2015. Scribal Interaction and the Transmission of Traditional Knowledge: A Postclassic Maya Perspective. *Ethnohistory* 62 (3): 445–468.

———. 2019a. Reconstruyendo rituales de la élite maya en las Tierras Bajas del norte. Una mirada desde los códices mayas y Ek' Balam. *Revista Española de Antropología Americana* 49: 241–263.

———. 2019b. The Serpent Within: Birth Rituals and Midwifery Practices in Pre-Hispanic and Colonial Mesoamerican Cultures. *Ethnohistory* 66 (4): 689–719.

———. 2022. *Códice de Dresde*. Guatemala: Universidad Mesamericana.

Vail, Gabrielle, and Anthony Aveni, eds. 2004. *The Madrid Codex: New Approaches to Understanding an Ancient Maya Manuscript*. Boulder: University Press of Colorado.

Vail, Gabrielle, and Victoria R. Bricker. 2004. *Haab* Dates in the Madrid Codex. In *The Madrid Codex: New Approaches to Understanding an Ancient Maya Manuscript,* ed. Gabrielle Vail and Anthony F. Aveni, 171–214. Boulder: University Press of Colorado.

Vail, Gabrielle, and Christine Hernández. 2003. Fire Drilling, Bloodletting, and Sacrifice: Yearbearer Rituals in the Maya and Borgia Group Codices. In *Sacred Books, Sacred Languages: Two Thousand Years of Ritual and Religious Maya Literature, Eighth European Maya Conference,* ed. Rogelio Valencia Rivera and Geneviève Le Fort, 65–79. Markt Schwaben: Verlag Anton Saurwein.

———. 2010a. Introduction: Part III, Archaeoastronomy, Codices, and Cosmologies. In *Astronomers, Scribes, and Priests: Intellectual Interchange between the Northern Maya Lowlands and Highland Mexico in the Late Postclassic Period,* ed. Gabrielle Vail and Christine Hernandez, 263–278. Washington, DC: Dumbarton Oaks.

———. 2013. *Re-Creating Primordial Time: Foundation Rituals and Mythology in the Postclassic Maya Codices*. Boulder: University Press of Colorado.

———. 2018. *The Maya Codices Database, Version 5.0.* http://www.mayacodices.org/.

Vail, Gabrielle, and Christine Hernández, eds. 2010b. *Astronomers, Scribes, and Priests: Intellectual Interchange between the Northern Maya Lowlands and Highland Mexico in the Late Postclassic Period*. Washington, DC: Dumbarton Oaks.

Vail, Gabrielle, and Matthew G. Looper. 2015. World Renewal Rituals among the Postclassic

Yucatec Maya and Contemporary Ch'orti' Maya. *Estudios de Cultura Maya* 45: 121–140.

Valdés, Juan Antonio. 1988. Los mascarones preclassicos de Uaxactun: el caso del Grupo H. In *Primer simposio mundial sobre epigraphia maya,* ed. Juan Pedro Laporte, 161–181. Guatemala City: Asociación Tikal.

———. 1995. Desarrollo cultural y señales de alarma entre los Mayas: El Preclásico Tardío y la transición hacia el Clásico Temprano. In *Emergence of Lowland Maya Civilization: The Transition from the Preclassic to the Early Classic,* ed. Nikolai Grube, 71–85. Möckmühl: Verlag Anton Saurwein.

Valencia Rivera, Rogelio. 2019. K'awiil y el Calendario Maya de 819 días. *Estudios de Cultura Maya* 53: 103–138.

Van Akkeren, Ruud. 2000. *Place of the Lord's Daughter: Rab'inaal, Its History, Its Dance-Drama.* Leiden: Research School CNWS.

———. 2006. Tzuywa, Place of the Gourd. *Ancient America* 9: 36–73.

VanDerwarker, Amber M. 2010. *Farming, Hunting, and Fishing in the Olmec World.* Austin: University of Texas Press.

VanDerwarker, Amber M., and Robert P. Kruger. 2012. Regional Variation in the Importance and Uses of Maize in the Early and Middle Formative Olmec Heartland: New Archaeobotanical Data from the San Carlos Homestead, Southern Veracruz. *Latin American Antiquity* 23 (4): 509–532.

Vargas de la Pena, Leticia, and Victor Castillo Borges. 2000. El Mausoleo de "Ukit Kan Le'k Tok." Paper presented at the 10th Encuentro de Investigadores del Area Maya. Campeche, Mexico, November 14–17.

———. 2017. Ek' Balam y el Reino de Talol. *Arqueología Mexicana* 25 (145): 38–44.

Vázquez López, Verónica A. 2017. La excavación en el Complejo Grazia. In *Proyecto Arqueológico Yaxnohcah, informe de la 2016 temporada de investigaciones,* ed. Armando Anaya Herneandez and Kathryn Reese-Taylor, 15–43. Report submitted to the Instituto Nacional de Antropología e Historia, Mexico City.

Velásquez García, Erik. 2006. The Maya Flood Myth and the Decapitation of the Cosmic Caiman. *PARI Journal* 7 (1): 1–10.

———. 2009. Reflections on the Codex Style and the Princeton Vessel. *PARI Journal* 10 (1): 1–16.

Vidal Lorenzo, Cristina, and Gaspar Muñoz Cosme, eds. 2009. *Los grafitos mayas.* Cuadernos de arquitectura y arqueología maya no. 2. Valencia: Editorial Universitat Politècnica de València.

Villacorta C., J. Antonio, and Carlos A. Villacorta. 1976. *Códices mayas.* 2nd ed. Guatemala City: Tipografía Nacional.

Villela, Khristaan D., and Linda Schele. 1996. Astronomy and Iconography among the Classic and Colonial Period Maya. In *Eighth Palenque Round Table, 1993,* ed. Merle Greene Robertson, Martha J. Macri, and Jan McHargue, 31–44. San Francisco, CA: Pre-Columbian Art Research Institute.

Villaseñor, Rafael E. 2012. Estrella y las guerras del Clásico Maya. *Kin Kaban* 1 (1):27–43. https://ceicum.org/wp-content/uploads/Rafael-Villasen%CC%83or_k1.pdf.

Vogt, Evon Z. 1964. The Genetic Model and Maya Cultural Development. In *Desarrollo*

562 · References

*cultural de los Mayas*, ed. Evon Z. Vogt and Alberto Ruz L., 9–48. Mexico City: Universidad Autónoma de Mexico.

———. 1969. *Zinacantan: A Maya Community in the Highlands of Chiapas*. Cambridge, MA: Harvard University Press.

———. 1970. Human Souls and Animal Spirits in Zinacantan. In *Echanges et communications: Mélanges offerts à Lévi-Strauss à l'occasion de son 60ème anniversaire*, ed. J. Pouillon and P. Maranda, 1148–1167. The Hague: Mouton.

———. 1976. *Tortillas for the Gods: A Symbolic Analysis of Zinacanteco Rituals*. Cambridge, MA: Harvard University Press.

———. 1993. *Tortillas for the Gods: A Symbolic Analysis of Zinacanteco Rituals*. 2nd ed. Norman: University of Oklahoma Press.

———. 1997. Zinacanteco Astronomy. *Mexicon* 19 (6): 110–117.

Volta, Beniamino, and Geoffrey E. Braswell. 2014. Alternative Narratives and Missing Data: Refining the Chronology of Chichen Itza. In *The Maya and Their Central American Neighbors: Settlement Patterns, Architecture, Hieroglyphic Texts, and Ceramics*, ed. Geoffrey E. Braswell, 356–402. New York: Routledge.

Voorhies, Barbara. 2004. *Coastal Collectors in the Holocene: The Chantuto People of Southwest Mexico*. Gainesville: University Press of Florida.

———. 2015. *An Archaic Mexican Shellmound and Its Entombed Floors*. Monograph; 80, Los Angeles: Cotsen Institute of Archaeology Press, UCLA.

Voorhies, Barbara, and Douglas J. Kennett. 2021. Preceramic Lifeways on the Mesoamerican South Pacific Coast. In *Preceramic Mesoamerica*, ed. Jon C. Lohse, Aleksander Borejsza, and Arthur A. Joyce, 397–419. New York: Routledge.

Vranich, Alexei, and Scott Smith. 2016. Nighttime Sky and Early Urbanism in the High Andes. In *Archaeology of the Night*, ed. Nancy Gonlin and April Nowell, 121–138. Boulder: University Press of Colorado.

Wagley, Charles. 1949. *The Social and Religious Life of a Guatemalan Village*. American Anthropological Association Memoir 71. Menasha, MN: American Anthropological Association.

Wagner, Henry R. 1942. Statement of Responsibility by Francisco Hernández de Córdoba; a translation of the original texts with an introduction and notes by Henry R. Wagner. *Documents and Narratives Concerning the Discovery and Conquest of Latin America*. Cortes Society, new series; no. 1.

Wagner, Logan, Hal Box, and Susan Kline Morehead. 2013. *Ancient Origins of the Mexican Plaza from Primordial Sea to Public Space*. Austin: University of Texas Press.

Walden, John P., and Barbara Voorhies. 2017. Ancient Maya Patolli. In *Prehistoric Games of North American Indians: Subarctic to Mesoamerica*, ed. Barbara Voorhies, 197–218. Salt Lake City: University of Utah Press.

Walker, Debra S. 1990. Cerros Revisited: Ceramic Indicators of Terminal Classic and Postclassic Settlement and Pilgrimage in Northern Belize. PhD diss., Southern Methodist University, Dallas.

Wallace, Henry. 1978. The Strange Case of the Panucho Plugs: Evidence of Pre-Columbian Apiculture on Cozumel. Unpublished paper on file at the Department of Anthropology, University of Arizona, Tucson.

Wanyerka, Phil, ed. 2002. Notebook for the 26th Maya Hieroglyphic Forum at Texas:

Palenque and Its Neighbors. In *The Proceedings of the Maya Hieroglyphic Workshop*. Austin: University of Texas at Austin.

———. 2003. Notebook for the 27th Maya Hieroglyphic Forum at Texas: Palenque and Its Neighbors. In *The Proceedings of the Maya Hieroglyphic Workshop*. Austin: University of Texas at Austin.

Watanabe, John M. 1989. Elusive Essences: Souls and Social Identity in Two Highland Maya Communities. In *Ethnographic Encounters in Southern Mesoamerica: Essays in Honor of Evon Zartman Vogt, Jr.*, ed. Victoria R. Bricker and Gary H. Gossen, 263–74. Albany: Institute of Mesoamerican Studies, State University of New York at Albany.

Watkins, Trevor. 2010. New Light on Neolithic Revolution in South-West Asia. *Antiquity* 84: 621–634.

Webster, David L. 2011. Backward Bottlenecks: Ancient Teosinte/Maize Selection. *Current Anthropology*. 52 (1): 77–104.

Webster, David L., Barbara Fash, Randolph J. Widmer, and Scott Zeleznik. 1998. The Skyband Group: Investigation of a Classic Maya Elite Residential Complex at Copan. *Journal of Field Archaeology* 25: 319–343.

Webster, Helen T. 1963. Tikal Graffiti. *Expedition* 6 (1): 36–47.

Weiss-Krejci, Estella. 2010. Depositos rituales en los complejos de Piramides Gemelas de Tikal. In *El ritual en el mundo maya: de lo privado a lo público*, ed. Andres Ciudad Ruiz, Maria J. Iglesias Ponce de Leon, and M. Sorroche, 83–105. Publication 9. Madrid: Grupo de Investigación Andalucia-America and Mérida: CEPHIS-UNAM.

———. 2011. The Role of Dead Bodies in Late Classic Maya Politics: Cross-Cultural Reflections on the Meaning of Tikal Altar 5. In *Living with the Dead: Mortuary Ritual in Mesoamerica*, ed. James Fitzsimmons and Izumi Shimada, 17–52. Tucson: University of Arizona Press.

———. 2012. Allspice as Template for the Classic Maya K'an Sign. *PARI Journal* 17 (4): 1–6.

Wendt, Carl J. 2003. Early Formative Domestic Organization and Community Patterning in the San Lorenzo Tenochtitlán Region, Veracruz, Mexico. PhD diss., Pennsylvania State University, State College PA.

Wengrow, David, and David Graeber. 2015. Farewell to the "Childhood of Man": Ritual, Seasonality, and the Origins of Inequality. *Journal of the Royal Anthropological Institute* 21 (3): 597–619.

Whiting, Thomas A. Lee. 1998. The Maya Civilization. In *Maya*, ed. Peter Schmidt, Mercedes de la Garza, and Enrique Nalda, 206–215. New York: Rizzoli.

Wichmann, Søren, ed. 2004a. *The Linguistics of Maya Writing*. Salt Lake City: University of Utah Press.

———. 2004b. The Linguistic Epigraphy of Maya Writing: Recent Advances and Questions for Future Research. In *The Linguistics of Maya Writing*, ed. S. Wichmann, 1–11. Salt Lake City: University of Utah Press.

Williams-Beck, Lorraine A. 2011. Rivers of Ritual and Power in the Northwestern Maya Lowlands. In *Ecology, Power, and Religion in Maya Landscapes*, ed. C. Isendahl and B. Liljefors Persson, 69–90. Markt Schwaben: Verlag Anton Saurwein.

———. 2019. The Center as Cosmos in Pre-Hispanic and Early Colonial Period Campeche. In *Maya Cosmology: Terrestrial and Celestial Landscapes*, ed. Milan Kovac, Harri

Kettunen, and Guido Krempel, Acta Americana vol. 29. Munich: Verlag Anton Saurwein.

Wilmsen, Edwin N. 1989. *Land Filled with Flies: A Political Economy of the Kalahari*. Chicago: University of Chicago Press.

Wisdom, Charles. 1940. *The Chorti Indians of Guatemala*. Chicago: University of Chicago Press.

Wolf, Marc. 2022. Landscape, Settlement, and Community: The Natural, Human, and Sacred Geography of Classic Maya Civilization in West Central Guatemala. PhD diss., City University of New York Graduate Center.

Woodburn, James C. 1980. Hunters and Gatherers Today and Reconstruction of the Past. In *Soviet and Western Anthropology*, ed. E. Gellner, 95–117. London: Duckworth.

———. 1982. Egalitarian Societies. *Man* 17 (3): 431–451.

Woodfill, Brent K. S. 2014. Interpreting an Early Classic Pecked Cross in the Candelaria Caves, Guatemala: Archaeological and Indigenous Perspectives. *Ethnoarchaeology* 6 (2): 103–120.

Woodfill, Brent K. S., Frederico Fahsen, and Mirza Monterroso. 2006. Nuevas evidencias de intercambio de larga distancia en Alta Verapaz, Guatemala. *XIX Simposio de Investigaciones Arqueológicas en Guatemala*, 1044–1057. Guatemala City: Ministry of Culture and Sports.

Woodfill, Brent K. S., Stanley Guenter, and Mirza Monterroso. 2012. Changing Patterns of Ritual Activity in an Unlooted Cave in Central Guatemala. *Latin American Antiquity* 23 (1): 93–119.

Wright, Lori. 2005. In Search of Yax Nuun Ayiin I: Revisiting the Tikal Project's Burial 10. *Ancient Mesoamerica* 16 (1): 89–100.

Wyatt, Andrew R. 2012. Agricultural Practices at Chan: Farming and Political Economy in an Ancient Maya Community. In *Chan: An Ancient Maya Farming Community*, ed. Cynthia Robin, 71–88. Gainesville: University Press of Florida.

Yaeger, Jason. 2010. Shifting Political Dynamics as Seen from the Xunantunich Palace. In *Classic Maya Provincial Politics: Xunantunich and Its Hinterlands*, ed. Lisa J. LeCount and Jason Yaeger, 145–160. Tucson: University of Arizona Press.

Yaeger, Jason, and Marcello-Andrea Canuto. 2000. Introducing an Archaeology of Communities. In *An Archaeology of Communities: A New World Perspective*, ed. M.-A. Canuto and J. Yaeger, 1–15. London: Routledge.

Yoffee, Norman. 2019. Introducing the Conference: There Are No Innocent Terms. In *The Evolution of Fragility: Setting the Terms*, ed. Norman Yoffee, 1–7. Cambridge, UK: McDonald Institute Conversations.

———. 2022. Experimental Cities? In *Early Mesoamerican Cities: Urbanism and Urbanization in the Formative Period*, ed. M. Love, 238–246. Cambridge: Cambridge University Press.

Zaro, Greg, and Jon Lohse. 2005. Agricultural Rhythms and Rituals: Ancient Maya Solar Observation in Hinterland Blue Creek, Northwestern Belize. *Latin American Antiquity* 16 (1): 81–98.

Zedeño, Maria Nieves, Jesse A. M. Ballenger, and John R. Murray. 2014. Landscape Engineering and Organizational Complexity among Late Prehistoric Bison Hunters of the Northwestern Plains. *Current Anthropology* 55 (1): 23–58.

Zender, Marc. 2005. The Raccoon Glyph in Classic Maya Writing. *PARI Journal* 5 (4): 6–16.

Zender, Marc, and Joel Skidmore. 2012. Unearthing the Heavens: Classic Maya Murals and Astronomical Tables at Xultun, Guatemala. Unpublished paper. http://www.mesoweb.com/reports/Xultun.pdf.

Zimmermann, Gunter. 1956. *Die Hieroglyphen der Maya-Handschriften*. Hamburg: De Gruyter.

Źrałka, Jarosław. 2014. *Pre-Columbian Maya Graffiti: Context, Dating and Function*. Oxford: Archaeopress.

Źrałka, Jarosław, Christophe Helmke, Laura Sutelo, and Wieslaw Koszkul. 2018. The Discovery of a Beehive and the Identification of Apiaries among Ancient Maya. *Latin American Antiquity* 29 (3): 514–531.

Źrałka, J., W. Koszkul, K. Radnicka, L. E. Sotelo Santos, and B. Hermes. 2014. Excavations in Nakum Structure 99: New Data on Protoclassic Rituals and Precolumbian Maya Beekeeping. *Estudios de Cultura Maya* 44: 85–117.

Zumbroich, Thomas J. 2013. "Plumerias the Color of Roseate Spoonbills": Continuity and Transition in the Symbolism of *Plumeria* L. in Mesoamerica. *Ethnobotany Research and Applications* 11: 341–363.

# Contributors

Armando Anaya Hernández is professor and investigator at the Universidad Autónoma de Campeche in Campeche, Mexico.

F. C. Atasta Flores Esquivel is Primera Red Mexicana para Profesionales de la Arqueología y Disciplinas Afines, Mexico D.F.

Adolfo Iván Batún-Alpuche is professor and investigator at the Universidad de Oriente in Valladolid, Yucatán, Mexico.

Sarah E. Bednar is a graduate student at the University of Calgary, Canada.

M. Kathryn Brown is Lutcher Brown Endowed Professor of anthropology at the University of Texas, San Antonio.

Arlen F. Chase is professor of anthropology in the Department of Comparative Cultural Studies at the University of Houston, Houston, Texas.

Diane Z. Chase is senior vice president for academic affairs and provost at the University of Houston and senior vice chancellor for academic affairs for the University of Houston System, Houston, Texas.

Ryan H. Collins is Neukom Fellow at the Department of Anthropology at Dartmouth College in Hanover, New Hampshire.

Anne S. Dowd is the forest archaeologist, Heritage Program manager, and tribal liaison with the Ochoco National Forest and Crooked River National Grassland at the U.S. Forest Service based in Oregon.

James A. Doyle is director of the Matson Museum of Anthropology and associate research professor of anthropology at Penn State University in State College, Pennsylvania.

568 · Contributors

Nicholas P. Dunning is professor of geography at the University of Cincinnati in Ohio.

Francisco Estrada-Belli is a Research Professor at the Middle American Research Institute at Tulane University in New Orleans, Louisiana.

David A. Freidel is professor of anthropology at Washington University of St. Louis in Missouri.

Takeshi Inomata is professor of anthropology at the University of Arizona in Tucson.

Patricia A. McAnany is Kenan Eminent Professor of anthropology at the University of North Carolina in Chapel Hill.

Leah McCurdy is senior lecturer in art history at the University of Texas at Arlington.

Susan Milbrath is curator emeritus of Latin American art and archaeology at the Florida Museum of Natural History in Gainesville.

Shawn G. Morton is adjunct assistant professor of anthropology at the University of Calgary in Canada.

Jerry Murdock is cofounder of Insight Venture Partners and a member of the board of the Santa Fe Institute in New Mexico.

Olivia Navarro-Farr is associate professor of anthropology at the College of Wooster in Ohio.

Meaghan M. Peuramaki-Brown is adjunct associate professor of anthropology at Athabasca University in Canada.

Kathryn Reese-Taylor is associate professor of archaeology at the University of Calgary in Canada.

Prudence M. Rice is emeritus professor of anthropology from Southern Illinois University at Carbondale.

Michelle E. Rich is the Ellen and Harry S. Parker Assistant Curator of the Arts of the Americas at the Dallas Museum of Art in Texas.

Cynthia Robin is professor of anthropology at Northwestern University in Illinois.

Franco D. Rossi is postdoctoral fellow in the Department of the History of Art at Johns Hopkins University.

Travis W. Stanton is professor of anthropology at the University of California, Riverside.

Nawa Sugiyama is assistant professor of anthropology at the University of California, Riverside.

Saburo Sugiyama is research professor at the School of Human Evolution and Social Change at Arizona State University (half-time) and a professor emeritus of Aichi Prefectural University in Japan.

Karl A. Taube is distinguished professor of anthropology at the University of California, Riverside.

Daniela Triadan is professor of anthropology at the University of Arizona in Tucson.

Gabrielle Vail is research collaborator with the Department of Anthropology at University of North Carolina, Chapel Hill, and research associate with the Script Encoding Initiative, University of California, Berkeley.

Verónica A. Vázquez López is a graduate student in Estudios Mesoamericanos at the Universidad Nacional Autónoma de México, Mexico, D.F.

Debra S. Walker is research curator at the Florida Museum of Natural History, University of Florida, Gainesville.

Jason Yaeger is UTSA President's Endowed Professor of Anthropology at the University of Texas, San Antonio.

# Index

Please note that italicized page numbers in this index refer to illustrative material.

Actuncan stelae (Belize), 151

Acuña, Mary Jane, 44

agriculture: agrarian cycles, 19, 313–14, 341; calendrical systems and concepts of time, 74–76, 77–79; farming community, Chan, 258–61, *259, 260*; milpa fields, 114, 120–21, 396; and property rights, 56–57; terraces, 25, 26, 43, 258–60, *259. See also* maize cultivation

Aguada Fénix site, 37–38, 51, 67–70, 74, 76, 191, 435, 477

Aguilera, Carmen, 334

Ah Macan Pech, 86

Aimers, James J., 133

Aimi, Antonio, 410

Aj K'ax B'ahlam, 216–17

Aj Maxam, 404

Aj Yax Chow Pat, 49, 50

Akan Yaxaj, 160

Alba complex (Yaxnohcah), 93–95, 100, 102

*altepetl,* 44–45, 46, 438, 445, 475

Anaya Hernández, Armando, 476

ancestor veneration, 217–19, 354–56; ancestor bundle masks, *449*

animism, 217–18

Antares (star), 226, 246

anthropomorphic figures, 136, 141, 199, 286, *290, 291,* 412

archaeological methods, 255, 364–65

architecture: civic, in Yaxnohcah, 100–103; civic contrasted with divination, 269–71; divination buildings, 261–69; divine embodiment in, 149–54, 458–59; large scale, 150–51; monumental plazas, 7–8; as reflective of calendar, 7. *See also* E Group assemblages

archival work, 217–19

Ark of the Covenant, 217

artifacts: in context, 255; divination tools, 16–17, 255, 269–70; incorporated into newer construction, 6, 167

Ashmore, Wendy, 26, 384

Ateteco sages (Guatemala), 19

Aubin Manuscript No. 20, 81–82

Aveni, Anthony, 75, 191, 212, 334, 439, 458, 471

Avenue of the Dead (Teotihuacan), 147, 437, 440, 446, 456

Awe, Jaime, 283

Ayala, Hernández, 71

Aztec *calmecac* schools, 275, 279, 293

Aztec infant sacrifice, 119

Bahlam Tz'am, 50

Bajo Laberinto, 93, 97

Bajo Tomatal, 93

Balamkú site (Mexico): background and overview, 17, 187–89, 219–21, 275; Balamkú as history house, 193–209; "history houses," 188, 189–93; interior texts, 200–209, *201–2, 204–7;* scribal workshops, 209–18; Structure 1A-Sub, 193, 194–200, *195, 196, 197, 198,* 219–20

ballgame rituals, 48, 175, 203, 206, 293

Baron, Joanne P., 353, 354

Barrera Vásquez, Alfredo, 224

Bassie-Sweet, Karen, 168

Batún-Alpuche, Adolfo, 291, 388, 392, 393, 397, 480, 481

Baudez, Claude-François, 194, 196

Becker, Marshall, 375

Bednar, Sarah, 476

572 · Index

beekeeping, 387–99; bee gardens, 395–98;
beekeeping structures, 394–95; beeswax as
commodity, 388
Beliaev, Dmitri, 248
Beltran, Boris, 135
Berlin, Henrich, 312
Berlo, Janet C., 437
Bernal, Ignacio, 41
Bey, George, 357
Binding of Years (fire ceremony), 89
Bird Jaguar IV (Yaxchilan king), 174
Bloch, Maurice, 58–59
Blom, Frans, 210
bloodletting, 135, 247, 302, 402, 473
*Blood of Kings* exhibition, 408
blood sacrifice, 88
Blowgunner Vase, 227
Blue Creek site (Belize), 84–85
body, human, and timekeeping, 461–62
Bolles, John, 309
Bonampak, Mexico, 215
Booher, Ashley, 257, 270
Book of Council (K'iche'), 22
books: as artifacts, 209–10; bark-paper, 389;
boxes for book storage, 216–17; production
sequence models, 220; screenfold books,
210, 216
Boone, Elizabeth, 215
Bowditch, Charles, 224
Bradley, Richard, 56, 59, 365, 366
Bricker, Harvey, 226, 227, 305, 306
Bricker, Victoria, 226, 227, 303, 305, 306
Bricker model, 224, 239
Brinton, Daniel, 224
Brisa complex (Yaxnohcah), 95, 100–101, 102,
104
Broda de Casas, Johanna, 334, 462
Brown, Linda, 257, 270
Brown, M. Kathryn, 17–18, 389, 480
Buena Vista (Cozumel, Mexico), 392–98
burdens, symbolism of, 21, 34, 108, 128–29, 201,
202–3, 306, 353
burial practices. *See* tombs
burner ceremonies, 89–91
Butler, Judith, 60

caches: Caracol cache, 370–73; cruciform,
118–19; finger caches, 382; Santa Rita Corozal cache, 373–74

Cahal Pech (Belize), 391
Calakmul royal court, 361, 404, 413
calendars: Calendar Round contrasted with
Long Count, 350, *351–52,* 368; Calendar
Round dates, 286; Campeche calendar,
428–29; 819 day cycles, 88, 124; 52-year
cycles, 89, 106n1, 115, 125, 128, 350; Haab,
123, 209, 299–303, 309–13; k'atun (20-year)
counts, 349, 368; K'atuns 11 Ajaw cycle, Chichén Itzá, 416–29; Lajuntun, 159; and lived
experience, 350, 353; lunisolar, 58; Puuc-
style dating, 428–29; Short Count cycling,
20, 21, 425–26; 365-day years, 124; 260-day
calendars, 74–75, 81–82, 89–90, 104–5, 120,
123, 191, 312–13, 341–42; Tzolk'in, 299, 300,
308, 309, 311, 312–13, 340–42; utility of, 3;
vigesimal counting, 461, 462. *See also* Long
Count calendars
*Calepino maya de Motul* (Ciudad Real), 223, 224
*calmecac* instruction, 275, 279, 293
camera lucida illustrations (Catherwood), 5
Candelaria Peninsula (Nixtun Chi'ch' site),
31, 33
Cantón Corralito site, 64
Caracol site, 364–73, *369, 371, 375,* 377–82, *379,
381,* 385, 471
Caral, Peru, 61
cardinal directions, 81–82, 124; and burner
ceremonies, 90; intercardinal directions,
84; and maize prognostication, 342n1; New
Year rites, 125; in Paris Codex, 304; in *tzol
peten* ritual, 86–87; in Wayeb (New Year
ceremonies), 87
Carlsen, Robert, 19–20, 22, 217
Carlson, John, 229, 233, 244, 246
Carmela complex (Yaxnohcah), 93–95, 100,
102
Carrasco Vargas, Ramón, 89, 193, 194
Casa de las Monjas, Chichén Itzá, 224
Caso, Alfonso, 308, 334, 345n18
Caste War (1948), 76
Castillo, Xunantunich, Belize, 17–18
Castillo Borges, Victor, 357
Çatalhöyük, Turkey, 189–91
Catherwood, Frederick, 5
Catholic traditions: liturgical calendar and
Maya months, 312; syncretism with Mayan
tradition, 6
Cauac ceremonies, 300–302, 337–38, 343n7

## Index · 573

Ceibal plaza site, 11, 64, 65, 110, 113, 118–19, 435; stela 19, *327*

cenote sites, 9, 110, 204, 394, 422

centipede place/mountain, 14, 142, 218, 235

ceremonial complexes, standardized, 63–66; spread of, 71–73. *See also* Middle Usumacinta Archaeological Project

Cerén, El Salvador, 255, 269–71. *See also* divination architecture

Cerro Maya site (Belize), 33, 34–35, 36–37, 47–48, 119, 132–33, 136; solar deity masks, *142,* 141–42; Structure 5C-2nd, *137,* 136–37, *138,* 152–53

Chac Chel (goddess), 231

Chahk (rain deity), 203–4, 229, *230*

Chajul, Guatemala, wall paintings, 192

Chak Jutuuw Chan Ek', 423

Chak Tok Ich'aak, Wak king, 165–68, 172, 180, 181

Chak Tok Ich'aak I, 172, 175–81, 450

Chak Tok Ich'aak II, 170–71, 173, 180

Chak Tok Ich'aak Sak Wayis, 178

Chak Xib Chahk, 292, 293

Chan (Belize), 15–16, 255; civic vs. divination architecture, 269–71; farming community, 258–61, *259, 260;* Structure 6, 261–69, *262, 263, 265, 267. See also* divination architecture

Chan K'awiil Chak Ich'aak', 350

Chan Yopaat, 156, 159, 172

Chase, Arlen, 18, 20–21, 80, 275, 353, 420, 471, 481

Chase, Diane, 18, 20–21, 339, 353, 471

Cheek, Charles, 294

Cheets, Payson, 269–70

Cherry, Ron, 229

chert bifaces, 255, 259, 269

Chiapa de Corzo site (Mexico), 64, 67, 70

Chiapas Grijalva River region, 64

Chichén Itzá, 20, 122, 125, 182, 204; decline of, 424–25; K'atuns 11 Ajaw calendrical cycle, 416–29; Monjas frieze, 224, *225,* 227, *228*

Chichicastenango (Guatemala), 6

*Chilam Balam of Chumayel, Book of:* calculations of time, 349; ceremonial quartering of communities, 125; ceremonies recorded in, 85–87, 91, 303–4, 387; meaning of, 416; political confederacies, 420; shortcomings of, 428; translations, 422–23

Chinchilla-Mazariegos, Oswaldo, 231, 233, 249

Christensen, Allen J., 88

*Chronicle of Yaxkukul* (1554), 86–87

Chunchucmil, Yucatec plain (Mexico), 356

Ch'olan language, 349

Ch'orti' peoples, 81, 104, 114

city design/planning: civic plan of Yaxnohcah, 95–103, *96, 98, 101;* cruciform plan, 10; Teotihuacan as cosmogram, 437–38; Teotihuacan layout, 438–41. *See also* urbanization

Ciudad Real, Antonio de, 223

Cival plaza site (Guatemala), 11, 12–13, 110, 133–35, 141; Cival cache, 118, 120; rain god Chahk mask, 143–45, *143, 144;* and sun-bird king, 134–36

Clark, John, 61–62, 64, 66

Clayton, Sarah, 436

Codex Borbonicus, 89

Codex Borgia, 91, 120, *328–39,* 333–35, 344–45n16

Codex Chimalpopoca, 115

Codex Fejérváry-Mayer, 81, 91, 104, 123

Codex Pérez, 91

codex-style vessels, 22, 403–13, *405, 407, 412*

Codex Tudela, 81

Codex Vaticano (Vaticanus) B, 91, 120

Códice maya de México, 187

Coe, Michael, 41, 66, 68–69, 87, 125–28, 292, 475, 481

Coggins, Clemency, 132, 382, 383, 425

Collins, Ryan, 10, 478

constellations, 224–27. *See also* scorpion stars

contemporary Maya: Cora of Nayarit, 127; Danza de los Voladores performances, 141; divination, 255–56; education of youth, 6; Huichol of Nayarit, 109–10; Ixil, 124, 125, 126, 127–28; K'iche', 124, 128; K'iche' fire altars, 115; poetic principles and language, 197; Quiche of Momostenango, 256; Tzeltal Maya, 114; Tzotzil Maya, 128; Tzutujil of Santiago Atitlan, 217; yearbearer systems, 311–13; Yukatek shamans, 109

Contreras, Diego de, 360

Copán site (Honduras), 5, 119, 215–16, 294; Copán Stelae, 467, *469,* 472; Sepulturas Bench, 474

Cortez, Hernan, 398

Cosmic Crocodile Tree, 446

Cosmic Hearth symbolism, 26, 41, 133

Cosmic Monster, 35

574 · Index

Cosmic Plate, *408*, 408–9

Cosmic Turtle, 456

cosmographic animals: crocodiles at Nixtun Chi'ch' site, 28–40, *29, 32*; turtles at El Perú-Waka' site, 41–51

cosmological orientations on landscape: east-west axes, 8, 10, 32, 84, 438–39; north-south axes, 8, 11, 13, 17, 69, 84, 122

Courau, Jean-Pierre, 196

Cowgill, George, 38

Cozumel Island Archaeological Project, 25

Cozumel Maya bee gardens, 387–99

Creation Mountain in Pinturas murals, 36

creation stories: in Codex Fejérváry-Mayer, 123; contemporary Huichol of Nayarit, 109; crocodile sacrifice, 31; expressed in E Group assemblages, 121, 123; and founding of ritual centers, 108; and katun ceremonies, 370; Long Count calendar, 5, 8, 19, 439, 464; in Paris Codex, 31; and space-time, 129; three-stone hearth, 13; and world tree imagery, 334

Crisóforo Chiñas site, 67–68

crocodile imagery, 436; El Perú-Waka' site, *34*; Nixtun Chi'ch' site, 28–40, *29, 32*; Primordial Crocodile, 444

Crocodile World Tree, 451, *452*

cross symbolism, 11, 121; cruciform caches, 118–19; cruciform civic plans, 10

Cyphers, Ann, 66, 68

Danzante building (Monte Albán), 465

death: death god, 160, 181, 301, 307, *330,* 333, 336–38; mortality and immortality, 355, 413–15; of mortal rulers, 414; and resurrection, simulation of, 18, 19, 22, 29, 140–41. *See also* sacrifice

decapitation sacrifice, 286, *287,* 406

deep-time narratives, 353–54

deer: antlers, 269, 270; scorpion-tailed, 229, *230*; as supernatural beings, 257

deities. *See* gods

deity impersonation scenes, 223–24

*De Orbe Novo: The Eight Decades of Peter Martyr D'Anghera,* 389

*Descripción de las cosas de Yucatán* (Landa), 225

*Diccionario Maya* (Barrera Vásquez), 416

Diehl, Richard, 68, 69

directional almanacs, 81–83, 90–91

divination, 255–56; beads, 390; Chan (Belize)

divination building, 261–69, *262, 263, 265, 267*; and materialization of time, 256–58; objects used, 256–57

divination architecture: background, 254–55, 271; compared with civic architecture, 269–71; contemporary divination, 255–56; farming communities, 258–61; materialization of time, 256–58; Structure 6 Room 2 (Chan), 261–69

divinity of kings and queens, 274–75

Dixon, Neil, 284–85

Dorsey, George, 278

Dowd, Anne, 17, 23–24, 191, 196, 197, 199, 217, 479–80, 481

Doyle, James, 21, 22, 26, 145, 475

Dragon Jaguar (Wak ruler), 161

Dresden Codex, 11, 88, 91, 124, 128, 187, 201–4, *205–7,* 305–7, *321–24*

Dresden New Year, 123, 124, 126

droughts and dry spells, 231, 301, 337, 361, 424

Dumbarton Oaks celt, 465

Dunning, Nicholas P., 476

earth offerings, 375–82

earth time, 475–79

east-west axis, 8, 10, 32, 84, 438–39

Eberl, Markus, 6, 9, 348–49, 353, 478

Edmondson, Munro, 420, 422

effigy censers, *330–31,* 336–40, 346n21; Caracol/Santa Rita Corozal caches, 374–75

E Group assemblages, 7–9, 67, 74; and agrarian year, 19; astronomical orientations, 191; Brisa complex (Yaxnohcah), 95, 100; Cival sites, 9–10; maize fields, 121; and manifestation of time, 382–83; plazas as symbolic maize fields, 115; and solar spatial orientation, 25; and standardized time-keeping, 149–50; Structure E-VII-sub (Uaxactun), 132–48; Teotihuacan, 436; time/space ordering, 478; Yaxuná, 110, 117–22; Yaxuná sites, 10. *See also* Middle Formative Chiapas (MFC) pattern

819 day cycle, 88, 124

Eight House of the North, 97, 104

Einstein, Albert, 4

Ek' Balam site (Mexico), 92, 122, 123, 357, 359–60, 361, 423–24

Ek' Naah, 170

El Castillo acropolis. *See* Xunantunich site (Belize)

El Chuaah (deity), 231
Eliade, Mircea, 58
El Macabil site, 75, 76
El Manatí site, 64, 119
El Mirador site (Guatemala), 64, 70. *See also* El Perú-Waka' site (Guatemala)
El Perú-Waka' site (Guatemala), 6, 12, 14–15, 41–51, *42, 45, 46,* 391, 451–56, *455;* background, 154–55; Chak Tok Ich'aak, Wak king, 165–68, 172, 180; dynasty, 451–57; Stela 22, 175–78, *176–77;* Stela 26, *171, 172–73;* Stela 44, tunnel connecting with, 166–68; Stela 44 transcription and transliteration, 178–81; Stela 45, 168–69; Stela 45, desecration of, 170–75; stelae as active artifacts, 153–54; stone images of Chak Tok Ich'aak, 175–81; Wiinte' Naah fire shrine (Structure M13-1), *155,* 155–65, *157, 158, 160, 162, 163, 164*
El Tiradero site, 66, 67, 70–71. *See also* Middle Usumacinta Archaeological Project
Eppich, Keith, 50–51
Esma complex (Yaxnohcah), 93–95, 100, 102
Estrada-Belli, Francisco: El Mirador Central Acropolis facade, 146; interpretation of glyphs at Holmul site, 192, 200; royal authority and materialization of time, 152; symbolism of deities, 119–20; World Tree symbolism, 133; Yaxuná E Group assemblage interpretation, 13, 18, 26, 37, 40, 478–79

Fantastic School, codex-style painting, 405–6
farming. *See* agriculture
Fash, William, 89, 453
Faulkner, William, 6
Feathered Serpent Pyramid (Teotihuacan), 147–48, 436, 438, 440, 444–46, 453, 459
Fernandez-Diaz, Juan Carlos, 68
Fialko, Vilma, 436
Fidelia civic group, 95, *96,* 97, 100–101, 102, 104
Fields, Virginia, 18
52-year cycles, 89, 106n1, 115, 125, 128, 350. *See also* calendars
Finca Acapulco site, 64
Fire Mountain fire shrine (El Perú-Waka' site, Guatemala), *155,* 155–65, *157, 158, 160, 162, 163, 164*
fire rituals, 89–92, 109; fire altars, 120; Teotihuacan, 147–48

First Wind-Maize deity, 246, 248–49, 250, 474
five-part ordering, 83–84, 100
five-part ordering of space/time, 83–85
Five Sky place, 18
"flame-eyebrow" motif, 30, 144
Flores Esquivel, F. C. Atasta, 476
Flores Gutiérrez, Daniel, 309
foragers: collective ceremonial rituals and vacant centers, 70; concepts of time, 55–60, 77–79; seasonal power fluctuations, 74; shift to agriculture, 55–57. *See also* hunter-gatherers
Förstemann, Ernst, 224
Foucault, Michel, 60
Freidel, David A.: centipede mountain, 218; Group E assemblages, 25, 40, 41; E Group assemblages Yaxuná, 113, 129, 441, 443; interpretation of glyphs on structures, 18, 136, 140, 146, 200, 437, 446, 467, 474, 475, 478–79; on landesque cosmography, 11–12, 28, 462; materialization of time, 9, 209; on royal authority and calendars, 23, 29, 151–53, 361, 362, 448, 450, 454; on scribal practices, 214, 291, 390, 391, 399, 480; on settlement plans, 392; on three-stone hearth, 13; time and sacred spaces, 107; time materialized in stelae, 14–15

Gallaga, Emiliano, 391
Gamez, Laura, 49
Garber, James, 33, 47, 451
García Zambrano, Ángel Julián, 87–88, 108, 109, 110, 114, 115, 122
Gauguin, Paul, 4–5
Gemini (constellation), 226–27, 241
Gerstle, Andrea, 269
Gill, Richardson B., 361
Girard, Raphael, 75, 85, 104
glyphic content: on codex-style painting, 410; in fire rituals, 91; glyph blocks in tomb murals, 83–84; glyphic writing, 10, 239–40; stelae carvings, 159; on wall inscriptions, 192–93; Wound-by-Obsidian glyphs, 248; Xunantunich site (Belize), 293
gnomon effect, 133–34, 146, 478–79
Göbekli Tepe, 61
Gossen, Gary, 128, 391–92
Goudiaby, Hemmamuthé, 355
gourd babies, 80, 83

576 · Index

Graeber, David, 58, 74
graffiti (incised wall designs), 16, 18, 261, 276, 277–81
Graham, Ian, 155
Graham, John, 311
Grazia civic group, 95, *96,* 97–98, *98,* 100–101, 102, 104, 105
Greenberg, Joseph, 464
greenstone axes, 64
greenstone celts/objects, 118, 119, 167, 270, 436, 445, 451
grid plans: design in planned cities, 28; and rulership, 38; Teotihuacan, 436
Grijalva River region, 67, 70
Grube, Nikolai, 91, 92, 151, 213, 459
Guenter, Stanley, 154, 155, 163, 170, 172, 180

Haab calendar, 3, 123, 209, 250, 299–303, 309–13
Hanks, William F., 81, 85–86, 87, 104, 109, 121
Hansen, Richard, 37
Harrison, Peter, 275, 278–79, 294
Harrison-Buck, Eleanor, 88
Hats' Chaak phase (670–780 CE), 281, 283–84
Hauberg Stela, 152–53, 446, *447*
Haviland, Anita de Laguna, 279, 280
Haviland, William, 279, 280
Headrick, Annabeth, 437, 440
Healy, Paul F., 268
hearths: cache, Yaxnohcah, 99; ceremonies, 92; monumental, 157; three-stone arrangements, 13, 113. *See also* Cosmic Hearth symbolism
Helmke, Christophe, 140, 287, 292, 293, 441
Hernández, Anaya, 67–68
Hernández, Christine, 302, 305
hieroglyphs: Balamkú, Mexico, 193–94, 200–209; Classic Maya texts, 348–49; in codices, 210–11; coding systems, 200; Maya Hieroglyphic Database, 203; for null-like zero, *469;* survival into Postclassic period, 360; texts, 187–88
Hinton, Thomas, 127
*Historia de los Mexicanos por sus pinturas,* 120, 123
history and linear time, 365–66
history houses, 188, 189–93; Balamkú site, 193–209, *195–99, 201–2, 204–7*
Hodder, Ian, 57, 189–91, 192, 219, 479
Hodgson, John, 61–62

Holmul temple site (Guatemala), 13, 14, 18, 188, 191–92, 193, 200, 278
Houk, Brett, 257, 270
Houston, Stephen, 14, 145, 153, 171, 227, 248, 349, 406, 408
Huichol of Nayarit, 109–10
Hull, Kerry M., 89
human body and timekeeping, 461–62
human gestation period and timekeeping, 312–13
human time, 473–75
Humboldt Celt, 10
Hun Nal ye Cave, 216
hunter-gatherers, 57. *See also* foragers
Hun Yeh Winik, 142–43, 145, 446
Hutson, Scott, 276, 280

Ikoom Sak Wayis, 173, 181
Ikoom Sak Wayis K'uhul Chatan Winik, 178
Ik' Muyil Muwaahn II, 217
immortality of the soul, 13, 14, 355
incensarios, paired-effigy, 370, *375,* 376–77, *377*
*Incidents of Travel in Central America, Chiapas and Yucatan* (Stephens), 5
infant sacrifice, 119
Ingold, Timothy, 80
Inomata, Takeshi, 7–9, 28, 38, 51, 66, 75, 150–51, 350, 477
Instituto Nacional de Estadística y Geografía (INEGI) models, 67, 68
Itzam Kab Ayiin, 123
Itzamnaaj (creator deity), 441; depicted on vase, 411–12
Ix Chel, 388, 390, 393, 398
Izapa people, 29–30
Izapa site, 64, 113; Stela 4, 134–35

Jacinta civic group, 95, *96,* 97, 104
jaguar deity/imagery, 288, 409
*jalolkexol,* 19–20
Jasaw Chan K'awiil, 350, 390
Jasaw Chan K'awiil I, 425
Jobbová, Eva, 250–51
Jones, Christopher, 383
Jupiter, 92
Justeson, John, 211, 314, 464–65
jute snail shell tokens, 16

Kabah site, Puuc region (Mexico), 357
Kaloomte' Sihyaj K'ahk', 44, 450–57

Index · 577

Kaminaljuyu Stela 11, 134
Kampen, Michael, 279, 280
Kan cross, 10, 26, 182
Kan yearbearers, 300–302, 341
katun calendar/prophecies, 21, 23, 231, 346n22, 368, 376
Kaua, Chilam Balam of, 91
Keller, Angela H., 268
Kelly, Mary Kate, 155, 178
Kennett, Douglas J., 361
Kerr, Barbara, 405, 406
Kerr, Justin, 388, 404, 405, 406
Kidder, Alfred V., 210
Kimbell Art Museum, 213
knowledge: dissemination of, 221, 238; esoteric knowledge, and power, 58, 76, 108, 273–76, 295; ritual knowledge, 191, 211
Kotosh (Peru), 60
Krakauer, David, 482
!Kung peoples, 57
Kurnick, Sarah, 353
K'abel, Queen, 47–49, 156, 160, 161, 163, 164, 174
K'ahk Tiliw Chan Chahk, 235
K'ahk Uti' Witz' K'awiil, 472
K'ahk' Ti' Chi'ch', 170, 181
K'ahk' Uti' Chan Yopat, 472
K'akh' Witz fire shrine (El Perú-Waka' site, Guatemala), 155, 155–65, 157, 158, 160, 162, 163, 164
K'an Chitam, 172
k'an cross, 117
K'atuns 8 Ajaw, 419–20
K'atuns 11 Ajaw cycle, Chichén Itzá, 416–29
k'atun time cycles, 31, 123, 418–21; k'atun wheel, 426
K'iche' people, 6, 115; agrarian cycles, 19; contact period Popul Vuh, 121
K'inich Ahkal Mo' Nahb III, 401–2
K'inich Ajaw, 362
K'inich Akhal Mo' Nahb, 349
K'inich Bahlam I, 159, 160, 169, 454
K'inich Bahlam II, 46–47, 48, 49, 50, 156, 163, 164, 168, 174
K'inich Janaab Pakal, 391
K'inich Janaab Pakal I, 401–2
K'inich Lamaw Ek', 427
K'inich Uax K'uk' Mo', 159
K'inich Yax K'uk' Mo', 472

K'inich Yook, 180
K'inich Y'onal Ahk II, 240
K'uhul Mutal Ajaw, 446

La Blanca site, 278
Labna site, Puuc region (Mexico), 357
Lacadena García-Gallo, Alfonso, 213, 357, 359, 429
La Carmelita site, 66. *See also* Middle Usumacinta Archaeological Project
Lake Petén Itzá, 12, 31
La Libertad site, 64, 70
Lamb, Weldon, 309, 312
La Merced site, 64
La Mojarra Stela, 464–65
Lamoureux-St-Hilaire, Maxime, 392
Landa, Diego de: on bee ceremonies, 397; *Descripción de las cosas de Yucatán,* 225; on divination, 257, 269, 271, 390; on scribal education, 215, 293, 294; yearbearer ceremony account, 87, 88, 89, 91, 125, 126, 209, 299, 300–304, 306–9, 337–38, 376, 420, 425
Landau, Kristin, 218
landesque cosmography, 11–12, 462; derived from landesque capitalism, 26; El Perú-Waka' site, 41–51, 42; Nixtun Chi'ch' site, 28–40, 29, 32; overview, 25–26; water-mountain theme, 32, 43–44
land ownership. *See* property rights
landscapes: civic landscape of Yaxnohcah, 92–103; temporality of, 81–85
Langley, James C., 437
language. *See* linguistic structures
Laporte, Juan Pedro, 436
La Quemada (Zacatecas, Mexico), 475–76
Las Pinturas murals, San Bartolo. *See* San Bartolo murals
Las Sepulturas group, Copan, 233–35, 234
La Venta site (Mexico), 64, 70, 118
Laxtunich site, 92; Lintel 1, 402–3
Leaf Chan Ahk, 50, 453–54
LeCount, Lisa J., 282
Lee, David, 49
Lelgemann, Achim, 476
Leonora civic group, 95, 96, 99–100, 104
Leventhal, Richard M., 281
*Libro del Chilam Balam de Chumayel. See Chilam Balam de Chumayel*
lidar imagery/mapping, 66–68, 93, 99, 462

578 · Index

Liendo Stuardo, Rodrigo, 66, 477
*Lienzo de Tlaxcala,* 127
Liner School of codex-style painting, 410, *411*
linguistic structures: hieratic language and Maya priesthood, 210; poetic principles, 197–98, 199; and valences of terms, 249–50
*Living with the Ancestors* (McAnany), 57
Lohse, Jon C., 84–85
Long, R.C.E., 91
Long Count calendars, 5, 8–9, 123, 152, 309, 340; creation day, 5, 8; dates, northern lowlands, 357; decline of, 361; and null placeholders, 465–67, *466;* and successions of rulers, 23; Teotihuacan, 438–39; and time-keeping, 417. *See also* calendars
Long Rounds (supernumbers), 238
Looper, Matthew, 200, 201, 203
Lopez Austin, Alfredo, 444
López de Cogolludo, Diego, 340, 353
*Los grafitos mayas* (Vidal Lorenzo & Muñoz Cosme), 278
Los Sabios site (Xultun), 16–17, 235, *237,* 238, *239,* 240, 247, 250
Lounsbury, Floyd, 238
Love, Bruce, 226–27, 241, 304
Lowe, Gareth, 64, 361
lunar tables, 212, 214, 238
lunisolar calendars, 58

Macri, Martha J., 200, 203
Madrid Codex: bee pages, 397, 399; burner ceremonies, 91; images of yearbearers, 300–304, *315–19;* scorpion composites, 229, 231; solar cartography and calendars, 82, 85, 87, 104, 105, 123; step-eyed face paint, 338; yearbearer pages, 300; zodiac pages, 227, 229, 231
Magar, Valerie, 391
maize cultivation, 9, 13, 62–63; agricultural cycle of solar year, 40; and cross symbolism, 121; E Group plazas as symbolic fields, 115; and establishment of rituals, 108; four-cornered fields, 114; and mobility of populations, 62–63; rain deities, 120; as symbol in art, 10; and 260-day calendar, 75; yearbearer rituals, 340–41; and yearbearer rituals, 301–2. *See also* agriculture
maize symbolism: deities, 18, 26, 38–40, 136–46; maize warriors, scorpion-tailed, 233–41; in

Paris Codex, 304; in San Bartolo murals, 36; sprouting metaphor, 413
Maler, Teoberto, 224
Martin, Simon, 76, 151, 404, 411, 459
masks, burial, *449–50*
Masson, Marilyn, 214, 391, 420
materialization of time, 256–58; in archaeological record, 363–68; and architectural complexes, 382–86; architectural complexes and maize farming, 9; on codex-style vessels, 403–13, *405, 407, 412;* cosmology in architecture, 197–199; cyclicality expressed in built environment, 4; idols and earth offerings, 375–82; mortality/immortality depicted on ceramic vessels, 413–15; mythical/mortal fusion, 400–403, 413–15; processions and ceremonies, 85–92; and ritual, 275; in stone monuments, 368–75; Teotihuacan, 438–51, 457–60; of time in scribal workshops, 209–17
Mathews, Peter, 423
Maudslay, Alfred, 224
*Maya Cosmos* (Freidel, Schele & Parker), 9, 41
*Maya E Groups* (Freidel et al.), 462
Maya Hieroglyphic Database, 203
Maya North orientation, 7–8, 160
Mayapán: calendar, 300; effigy censers, *330–31,* 336–40; League of Mayapán, 420
Maya Working Group, 482–83
McAnany, Patricia, 22, 23, 57, 474
McCurdy, Leah, 283, 389, 480
McDonald, Andrew, 64
Meehan, Patricia, 391
Meillassoux, Claude, 56
Mellaart, James, 189
Metropolitan Painter, *409,* 409–10
Middle Formative Chiapas (MFC) pattern, 64–65, 70
Middle Formative Gulf (MFG) pattern, 70
Middleton, Guy D., 348
Middle Usumacinta Archaeological Project, 63–64, 66–71; analysis of, 71–77; Middle Formative Usumacinta (MFU) patterns, 67–68, 69–70
Milbrath, Susan: on agrarian cycles and calendars, 75, 103, 136, 140, 233, 350, 473; gnomon effect, 40, 133–34; interpretation of glyphs on structures, 18–19, 34–35, 226, 244, 437, 440–41
Miles, Arthur, 293

Index · 579

Miller, Arthur, 141
Miller, Mary, 471
milpa fields, 114, 120–21, 396
mirror imagery, 391, 444, 481–82
Momostenango rituals, 90, 233; yearbearers, 128
monuments: as astronomical markers, 77; early
     monuments and mixed subsistence groups,
     60–63; emergence of, and worldviews,
     56; as materialization of history, 181–82;
     monumental posts and time-telling, 133–34;
     solar commemorative, 7–8; temporality of
     monument building, 73–77
moon: and agrarian cycles, 19; lunar tables, 212,
     214, 238; lunisolar calendars, 58
Mopan River Valley, 281, 282. See also Xunantu-
     nich site (Belize)
Mopila, Yucatán, 6
Morley, Sylvanus G., 314
mortality and immortality, 355, 413–15. See also
     death
Morton, Shawn G., 476
Motul de San José site, 92
Muluc yearbearers, 301–2, 310
Muñoz Cosme, Gaspar, 278
Murdock, Jerry, 481
Murtha, Timothy, 68

"Nah Ho Chan," 18
Naj Tunich Cave (Guatemala), 188, 192, 201,
     203, 204, 215
Nakbe stelae, 151
Nakum site (Petén, Guatemala), 278, 388
naming: of locations, 86, 422, 476; naming tradi-
     tions and ancestors, 354–55, 362; toponymic
     place-names, 10, 84, 86, 109, 235, 427; year-
     bearers naming the year, 124, 334, 340
Namon Cupul, 360
Naranjo Stelae, 30, 124, 235, 236, 238, 239–41,
     244, 246, 248
National Center for Airborne Laser Mapping
     (NCALM), 66–67
Navarro-Farr, Olivia, 14–15, 50, 474
New Fire ceremonies, 89
New Year ceremonies, 87–88
Nielsen, Jesper, 140, 441
Nine Lords of the Night, 368, 383–84
Nixtun Ch'ich' site, 12, 28–40, 435–36; east-west
     axis, 32; Fosa Y depression, 32, 39–40; and
     materialization of creation time, 477

Nolan, Susan, 174, 175
Nondédeo, Philippe, 355
north-south axis, 11, 13, 17, 69; Cerro Maya
     (Belize), 132; unity of time and space, 84; in
     Yaxuná, 122
Nunnery Quadrangle, Uxmal, 357, 358
Nuun Ujol Chaak, 174, 180, 181

obsidian: artifacts, 16–17; blades and human
     sacrifice, 246–48; First Wind-Maize with
     Obsidian, 240, 246, 248–49, 250; nighttime
     symbolism, 249; in opposition with chert,
     249; ritual dress as, 238
Ojo de Agua site, 65, 70
ollas (water jars), 114, 120
Olmecs: crocodile symbolism, 29; motifs, 30;
     San Lorenzo, 9
O'Neil, Megan, 240
opossum imagery, 302, 305–6, 337, 339, 343n7
Order of Days and royal counts, 6, 348–49, 362
Orion constellation, 13, 102–3, 105, 134, 238,
     247, 456
orthogonal design, 37, 51, 434, 436
oyohualli pendants, 303, 337, 339, 346n23, 467,
     470

Pajonal site, 70
Palenque site, 92, 422; Palace Throne, 128;
     Temple XIX, 362; Temple XXI, 401; Temple
     XXI Platform Panel, 475; Triad, 354
palo jiote trees, 126
papermaking, 389. See also books
Paris Codex, 31, 124, 187, 224–26, 227, 304–5,
     320
Parker, Joy, 9
Pascual Abaj (effigy), 6
Paso de la Amada site, 64
Pasztory, Esther, 440, 446
patolli board game, 15–16, 220, 257–50, 261,
     266–67, 294
patron deities, 353–54
Paul, Armando, 194
"paw-wing" motif, 30
Paxton, Meredith, 82–83, 86, 87, 210
penis perforation, 119, 135, 373
Peraza Lope, Carlos, 420
Pérez, Don Juan, 91
Pérez, Juan Carlos, 48, 154
Pérez Robles, Griselda, 48, 50, 154

580 · Index

*pet kots,* 395, 397–98. *See also* beekeeping
Peuramaki-Brown, Meghan M., 476
Piedras Negras (Mexico), 240–41, *243–44,* 357, 402, 422, 471
Pineda de Carías, Maria C., 479
Pinturas Shrine murals. *See* San Bartolo murals
Pío Pérez, Juan, 308
Pitarch, Pedro, 355
platforms: Buena Vista, Cozumel, 392–93; at Cival, 12; in E Group assemblages, 461–62, 464; El Mirador hill, 41–42, 43; El Perú-Waka', 166–69, 180; La Carmelita, 66–67; San Lorenzo plateau, 68–69; Yaxnohcah, 93–100; Yaxuná, 121–22
Pleiades constellation, 89, 238
Pollock, Harry, 398
polynomial texture mapping (PTM), 284–85
Pomoná Panel, 124–25, 128
Popol Nah (great halls), 356
Popol Vuh, 3, 121
Poverty Point site (Louisiana, US), 61, 77
power: accession ceremonies, 474; concepts of, 60; political authority and monumental time, 347–62; seasonal fluctuations for foragers, 74
Prechtel, Martin, 19–20, 22
Pre-Pottery Neolithic A period, 61, 189, 190
Pre-Pottery Neolithic B period, 61
*Primeros Memoriales,* 119
Princeton School painting, 406, *407,* 413
Principal Bird Deity, 37, 135, 137–38, *139,* 403, 441; masks, 140–41
property rights, 56–58
Proskouriakoff, Tatiana, 22, 173, 420
Prufer, Keith, 63
Pugh, Timothy, 28, 477
Puleston, Dennis, 425
Pyramid of the Moon (Teotihuacan), 120, 437, 439–40, 443–44, 446
Pyramid of the Sun (Teotihuacan), 147–48, 156, 440

quadripartite time-space frame, 107, 108–9, 115, 117; quadripartite deities, 11, 83, 107–8, 117, 124–25
quincunx patterns/metaphors, 11, 83, 102, 114, 266, 469
Quirigua Stelae, 84, 88, *351,* 467

rain deities, 120, 145–46, *145,* 229; rain god impersonators, 145
rainy/dry seasons, 229, 250–51, 438
Rancho Zaragoza site, 70–71
Rathje, William "Bill," 25, 392
rebirth metaphors, 5, 17–18, 22, 140, 180, 413
Redfield, Robert, 126
Reese-Taylor, Kathryn, 11, 12, 35, 476
Regal Rabbit vase, 410–11
Reilly, Kent, 10, 38, 41, 446
reincarnation of souls, 19, 22. *See also* rebirth metaphors
*Relación de las cosas de Yucatán* (Landa), 125
resurrection: of gods, 21–22, 36, 146; of human rulers as gods, 46, 48, 448
Resurrection Plate, 413
Rice, Prudence: on agrarian cycles, 312–13; on burner ceremonies, 91; on crocodile imagery, 29–30, 35, 38, 39, 40; on gnomon effects, 133–34; on landesque cosmography, 12; on Las Bocas mirror, 482; on political organization/katun cycles, 368, 476–77; on Short Count/Long Count calendars, 20, 21; on urban design, 28, 37, 436; on writing vs. wood-carving, 216
Rich, Michelle, 12, 26, 42–44, 46, 214, 391, 456
Ricoeur, Paul, 348
Ringle, William M., 354, 357, 360–61
Rio Azul tomb murals, 83, 104
Rio Bec site, 278
rituals: agrarian, 107–8; fire rituals, 50, 89–92, 105–6, 115; founding rituals, 108–9, 115; house-based vs. sodality-based, 190; and materialization of time, 275; yearbearer rituals, 299, 303
Roaring Creek Red vessels, *267*
Robb, John, 461, 475
Robb, Mathew H., 437
Robin, Cynthia, 15–16, 25, 150, 471
Román Ramírez, Edwin, 436
Romero, Bernal, 91–92
Rossi, Franco D., 17, 135, 275, 474–75, 479
Rowley-Conwy, Peter, 57
Roy, Ralph, 422, 423
royal authority, 274–75, 295

Sabloff, Jerry, 25
sacrifice, 135; decapitation, 286, *287,* 406; human, 246–47; infant, 119; sacrifice glyphs, 248;

Index · 581

sacrificial bloodletting, 119; year-renewal, 250, 299, 300. *See also* death

sages. *See* scribes

Sahagún, Bernardino de, 89, 293

Sahlins, Marshall, 359

Sak Wayis (Ikoom), *165,* 165–68, 179, 180

San Bartolo murals: descending god motif, 146; fire rituals, 92; gourd babies, 80, 83; inscriptions, 15, 22; materialization of time, 11, 13, 18, 36, 80; New Year ceremonies, 88; Pinturas Shrine, 110; Principal Bird Deity, 135; Structure Sub-1A, 192; West Wall mural, *131, 325–26*

San Isidro site, 64, 118

San Jose Mogote, 465

San Lorenzo Olmec center, 9, 41, 62–66, 68–69

San Miguel Xamancab (Cozumel, Mexico), 387

San Pedro Mártir River, 8, 9, 41–42, 150, 435

Santa Fe Institute (SFI), 24, 192, 209, 215, 462, 482

Santa Maria Oycib (Cozumel, Mexico), 387

Santa Rita Corozal site (Belize), 88, 363–64, 370, *372,* 373–74, *374,* 376, 380

Sassaman, Kenneth, 57

Saturn in fire rituals, 91–92

Saturno, William, 15, 35, 37, 135, 200, 211

Sayil site, Puuc region (Mexico), 356, 357

Sa'atun Sat structure, 122

Schele, Linda: cosmological orientation of spaces, 7–8, 9, 18, 35, 41, 133; on cultural transformation, 152–53; interpretation of glyphs on structures, 200, 215, 390, 423; on ritualized violence, 247, 249

Schellhas, Paul, 249

scorpion stars: as composites in the codices, 229–33, *232;* date ranges, 241–46; Mayan history, 227–29; Maya zodiac, 224–27, *225;* overview, 223–24; rain, 250–51; scorpion-tailed maize warriors, 233–41; scorpion tails, 249–50

Scott, James C., 348

scribes: burial of, 389–91; Classic period Maya, ordering of time, 349–53; and court language, 359–60; emergence in first millennium BCE, 15; glyphic notes on, 389; improvisational calligraphy, 218–19; and Maya pedagogy, 215–17; scribal workshops, 209–17; styluses, 388–91, *390*

sculpture: Classic Maya, 401–3; MFU complexes, 72

Sechín Bajo, Peru, 60–61

sedentism and urbanization, 24, 55, 57, 65, 79, 149, 434, 482–83

Seler, Eduard, 224, 244, 249, 335

serpent symbolism, 199, 333, 446; serpent trees, 306–7. *See also* Feathered Serpent Pyramid (Teotihuacan)

shamans: contemporary, 18, 109, 257, 270; shaman-priest, 156, 159; spaces for, 16

Sheets, Payson, 269, 270

shell mounds/tokens, 16, 61–62, 270, 372

Sihyaj Chan K'awiil Chak Ich'aak, 350

Sihyaj Chan K'awiil II, 425, 450, 453

Sihyaj K'ahk', 46–47, 49, 159–60, 169–72, 439, 453–56, *455,* 459, 475

Simmons, Scott, 269–70

sinan ek' (scorpion star), 223, 244. *See also* scorpion stars

six-step stairways, 173–75

Smith, Monica, 25, 26, 28

snail shells, 16, 268

solar bird deity, 37, 40, 135, 136, 137–38, 140, 140–41, 151, 478. *See also* Principal Bird Deity

solar cycle/orientation: Cerro Maya Structure 6B, 34–35; and fire rituals, 109; in maize cycle, 40; and monumental posts at Cival site, 133–34; Structure E-VII-sub (Uaxactun), 132–48; sun as sentient entity, 21–22

solar deities, 135–36, 342n3

solar deity masks, *142,* 141–42

solstices, 74, 77, 82, 83, 85, 102, 103

Sosa, John, 126, 227

space: ceremonial spaces, 78–79; domesticated vs. wild, 114, 115, 121, 129; and fire rituals, 89; five-part ordering, 83–85, 100; private vs. public, 218–19; space-time fusion, 4, 80–81, 85, 107–9, 129, 473, 476

Spinden, Herbert, 224

*Spondylus* shells, 143, 144, 181, 270, 372

Šprajc, Ivan, 75

sprout-tree-house metaphor, 479

Stanish, Charles, 74, 77

Stanton, Travis, 10, 26, 41, 113, 350, 478

Starry Deer Crocodile, 31, 35, 39, 408

stelae: as active artifacts, 153–54; defacement of, 161, *162–63,* 179–80

Stephens, John L., 5

Stone, Andrea, 124, 210

582 · Index

Stonehenge site, 77, 366
Strong Glyph School of codex-style painting, 410
Structural Marxist theory, 56
Stuart, David: carved stelae, 14; crocodile imagery, 29; fire ceremonies, 90, 92; Humboldt Celt, 10; interpretation of texts/glyphs on structures, 38, 39, 89, 123–25, 142–43, 149, 239, 311, 332, 403, 409, 452, 453, 467; "Order of Days," 6; on performance in sacred spaces, 150, 152, 153, 171; role of royal courts, 348; San Bartolo murals, 19; Starry Deer Crocodile, 35; time-space fusion in structures, 159, 217, 349; *witz* (mountain), 28
styluses, 388–91, *390*
Sugiyama, Nawa, 8–9, 23, 440, 444, 445, 475
Sugiyama, Saburo, 23, 38, 438, 439, 440, 444, 458–59, 475
Suhler, Charles, 41
sun. *See* solar cycle/orientation
supernumbers, 238
sweat baths, 276, 295
Sweely, Tracy, 270

Tahitian concepts of time, 4–5
Tah priests, 16–17
Takutsi Nakawe (earth goddess), 109
Tak'alik Ab'aj, 465, *466*
Tapir Chan Ahk, 160
Taube, Karl: crocodile imagery, 29, 35; on divination, 391, 444; domesticated vs. wild spaces, 478; on Feathered Serpent, 147, 250; Kan cross, 10; maize gods/goddesses, 36, 38–39, 40, 456; on milpa fields, 121; on Olmec and human body, 114–15; on Principal Bird Deity, 135, 137–38
Tedlock, Barbara, 133, 233, 312
Tedlock, Dennis, 133
Temple of the Crossed Arms, 60
Tena, Raphael, 334
Tenochtitlan, founding of, 115
Teotihuacan, 147–48; connections to Tikal, 436; materialization of time, 438–51, 457–60; origins and layout, 434–38, *435;* Pyramid of the Moon, 120; Pyramid of the Sun, 156
Teotihuacan Measurement Unit (TMU), 438
Tepantitla mural, 437
Teranishi Castillo, Keiko, 66, 477
Tezcatlipoca cult, 476

Te' Chan Ahk, 451
Thompson, Edward H., 278
Thompson, J. Eric S., 24, 128, 254, 278, 305–6, 311, 314, 336, 338, 473
Tikal (Guatemala), 21, 278; connections with Teotihuacan, 436; Great Plaza, 147; royal court/sacred center, 361, 365–66; Tikal gods, 156–57; Tikal Project, 278; Tikal Stela 31, 350; twin-pyramid groups, 383
time: agentive, embodied in stelae, 159; birth of, in landscape, 217–19; as burden, 128–29; and ceremonies/festivals, 76; concepts of, 58–60; cyclical, importance of, 363, 367–68; cyclical concept of, 3–4; cyclical ritual time, 59; deep-time narratives, 353–54; earth time, 475–79; embodied in stelae, 159; five-part ordering of space/time, 83–85; forager vs. agriculturalist concepts, 77–79; human, 473–75; before humans, in Popol Vuh, 3; linear, 365–66; linear contrasted with cyclical, 417–18; linear mundane time, 59; and lived experience, 350, 353; Long Count of days, 19; long-term vs. short-term cycles, 19; Maya relationship with, 367; modern linear concept of, 3; monumental, in Classic period Maya lowlands, 347–62; past and present conjoined, 347–48; and space, fusion, 4, 80–81, 85, 107–9, 129, 473, 476; standardization of measurement, 59–60; as symbolic burden, 21, 34, 108, 128–29, 201, 202–3, 306, 353; temporality of monument building, 73–77
Tokovinine, Alexandre, 192, 200, 427
*tolche* systems, 395–96. *See also* beekeeping
tombs, 50, 151, 380–82
Tonina Monument 101, 467
toponymic place-names, 10, 84, 86, 109, 235, 427
Tozzer, Alfred M., 224, 376, 425
*trecenas* (13 day groups), 81–82
tree imagery, 307. *See also* World Tree imagery
Triadan, Daniela, 7, 38, 51, 66, 150, 350, 477
Trik, Aubrey, 390–91
Tunesi, Raphael, 410
Tun K'ab Hiix, 170
Tupp Kak fire ceremony, 91
turtle imagery, 13, 122; effigy turtle platforms, 26, *27*, 28; El Perú-Waka' site, 41–51; as symbol in art, 10, 369–70
twin-pyramid groups, 21, 147, 366, 367, 382–84, *383*, 388

260-day calendars, 81–82, 89–90, 104–5, 120, 123, 191, 312–13, 341–42
Tzolk'in calendar, 3, 19, 286, 418
*tzol peten* (counting out ceremony), 85–87, 103
Tzotzil astronomy, 246
Tzotzil Maya, 254
Tzutzuculi site, 64

Uaxactun site, 215; monumental posts and maize god, 136–46, *139;* monumental posts and time-telling, 133–34; solar bird/maize god, 135–36; Stela 18, 465, 467; Structure E-VII, 132–48
Uayeb rituals, 299–308, 337, 340, 378, 473
Ucanhá site, 123
Ukit Kan Le'k Tok', 359–60
urbanization: establishment of Teotihuacan, 434–38, *435;* grid design, 28; and landesque capital, 26, 28; and landscape capital, 25–26; low-density urbanism, 37; population centers before sedentary agriculture, 482–83; urban landscape and 260-day calendar, 104–5; in Yaxuná, 122–29
Ursa Major, 241
Usumacinta River, 8, 9, 150, 435

Vadala, Jeffrey, 34–35, 40, 136
Vail, Gabrielle, 17, 200, 210, 229, 231, 301, 302, 303, 479–80
Valencia Rivera, Rogelio, 88
Van Akkeren, Ruud, 83, 249
Vargas de la Peña, Leticia, 357
Vase of the Eleven Gods, 412
Vase of the Seven Gods, 412
Vase of the Stars, 231, 233
vases, Late Classic codex-style, 22
Vásquez López, Veronica, 476
Venus (planet), 244, 247; Venus calendar, 3
Vepretskii, Sergei, 170
Veracruz Ceremonial (VC) complexes, 69
Vidal Lorenzo, Cristina, 278
vigesimal counting systems, 461, 462
Villa Rojas, Alfonso, 126
Vining, Ben, 191
Vistahermosa site, 64
Vogt, Evon Z., 9, 89, 226, 229, 246, 254, 355, 371, 445
Voorhies, Barbara, 261

Wak Chan K'awiil, 170, 172, 178
Wak dynasty, 14, 44
Walden, John P., 261
Walker, Debra S., 35, 476
Wallace, Henry, 387
water-mountain theme, 32, 43–44, 445
Watson Brake site (Louisiana, US), 61
Waxaklahun Ubaah K'awiil, 84, 159, 350
Wayeb (New Year ceremonies), 82, 87–88
Wa'oom Uchab Ahk, 178, 181
Webster, Helen, 278
Wengrow, David, 58, 74
Wiinte' Naah fire shrine (El Perú-Waka' site, Guatemala), *155,* 155–65, *157, 158, 160, 162, 163, 164,* 452–53, 454
Williams-Beck, Lorraine, 41, 426–27
Wilmsen, Edwin, 57
Wisdom, Charles, 126
*witz* (mountain), 28, 33, 456
World Tree imagery, 13, 17, 40, 440, 446; axis of cosmos, 436; cosmic stones, 135; cosmic world trees, 126; crocodile as, 30; symbolism, 26, 133
Wright, Lori, 30

Xultun site (Guatemala), 16–17, 187, 188, 192–93, 235, 275; glyphs, 212–13; Sabios building, 389; scribal techniques, 213–15
Xunantunich Archaeological Project, 294
Xunantunich site (Belize), 17–18, 123, 188, 267; background, 273–76; El Castillo acropolis, 192; map, *282;* novice residence, 293–95; Structure A-5-2nd, 281–93, *285, 286, 287, 289, 290, 291, 292;* Tourism Development Project, 283, 291; wall graffiti, 276, 277–81

Yacametzli (moon goddess), 437
Yaeger, Jason, 279, 282, 389, 480
Yahawte' K'inich, 427
Yajaw Te' K'inich II, 170
Yaxchilan site (Mexico), 92
Yax Ehb Xook, 151, 154, 170, 448, 451
Yaxha site (Guatemala), 123
Yax K'uk' Mo', 452–53
Yaxnohcah site (Mexico), 11; Central Precinct, 93–95, *94;* civic landscape, 92–103; civic plan, 100–103, *101;* generative acts of landscape ordering, 103–6; intercardinal civic groups, 95–100, *96, 98;* processional routes, 476

584 · Index

Yax Nuun Ahiin, 30, 439, 453
Yax Pasaj, 477
Yaxuná sites, 10, 26, *27,* 28; Burial 6, 444–45;
Burial 24, 441–44, *442–43;* directionality,
110–17; E group, 110, 117–22; founding of
centers, 108–10; lidar imaging, *111;* overview, 107–8; time in urban Yaxuná, 122–29
Yax W'en Chan K'inich, 235, 237
yearbearer rituals, 299; (Reed/Flint/House/
Rabbit), 124, 125; and agricultural cycle,
313–14; Aztec counterparts, 333–35; during
contact period, 126–27; contemporary Ixil/
K'iche', 127–28; Kan, 300–302; Mayapán
effigy censers, *330–31,* 336–40; modern
survival of, 311–13; Postclassic period imagery, 300–308; San Bartolo murals, *325–26,*
332–33; seasonal positions of yearbearers,
308–11; Year Bearer dates, 19
Yik'in Chan K'awiil, 50
Yoffee, Norman, 348

Yopaat Bahlam, 410
Yucatán Peninsula. *See* Yaxnohcah
Yuhknoom Ch'een the Great, 47, 49, 164
Yuhknoom Ti', 48
Yuhknoom Took' K'awiil, 410
Yuhknoom Yich'aak K'ahk', 48, 49, 163, 174
Y'ajaw Te' K'inich II, 178

Zaro, Gregory, 84–85
Zedeño, Nieves, 57–58
Zender, Marc, 124
zero-like null units and timekeeping, 23–24,
464–73, *466*
Zimmerman, Gunter, 213
Zinacantán (Tzotzil Maya community), 254
zodiac, Mayan, 224–27, *225. See also* scorpion
stars
zoomorphic figures, 286
Źrałka, Jarosław, 278, 280–81, 287–88, 289,
388

*Maya Studies*

## Edited by Diane Z. Chase and Arlen F. Chase

*Salt: White Gold of the Ancient Maya,* by Heather McKillop (2002)

*Archaeology and Ethnohistory of Iximché,* by C. Roger Nance, Stephen L. Whittington, and Barbara E. Borg (2003)

*The Ancient Maya of the Belize Valley: Half a Century of Archaeological Research,* edited by James F. Garber (2004; first paperback edition, 2011)

*Unconquered Lacandon Maya: Ethnohistory and Archaeology of Indigenous Culture Change,* by Joel W. Palka (2005)

*Chocolate in Mesoamerica: A Cultural History of Cacao,* edited by Cameron L. McNeil (2006; first paperback edition, 2009)

*Maya Christians and Their Churches in Sixteenth-Century Belize,* by Elizabeth Graham (2011; first paperback edition, 2020)

*Chan: An Ancient Maya Farming Community,* edited by Cynthia Robin (2012; first paperback edition, 2013)

*Motul de San José: Politics, History, and Economy in a Classic Maya Polity,* edited by Antonia E. Foias and Kitty F. Emery (2012; first paperback edition, 2015)

*Ancient Maya Pottery: Classification, Analysis, and Interpretation,* edited by James John Aimers (2013; first paperback edition, 2014)

*Ancient Maya Political Dynamics,* by Antonia E. Foias (2013; first paperback edition, 2014)

*Ritual, Violence, and the Fall of the Classic Maya Kings,* edited by Gyles Iannone, Brett A. Houk, and Sonja A. Schwake (2016; first paperback edition, 2018)

*Perspectives on the Ancient Maya of Chetumal Bay,* edited by Debra S. Walker (2016)

*Maya E Groups: Calendars, Astronomy, and Urbanism in the Early Lowlands,* edited by David A. Freidel, Arlen F. Chase, Anne S. Dowd, and Jerry Murdock (2017; first paperback edition, 2020)

*War Owl Falling: Innovation, Creativity, and Culture Change in Ancient Maya Society,* by Markus Eberl (2017)

*Pathways to Complexity: A View from the Maya Lowlands,* edited by M. Kathryn Brown and George J. Bey III (2018; first paperback edition, 2021)

*Water, Cacao, and the Early Maya of Chocolá,* by Jonathan Kaplan and Federico Paredes Umaña (2018)

*Maya Salt Works,* by Heather McKillop (2019)

*The Market for Mesoamerica: Reflections on the Sale of Pre-Columbian Antiquities,* edited by Cara G. Tremain and Donna Yates (2019)

*Migrations in Late Mesoamerica,* edited by Christopher S. Beekman (2019)

*Approaches to Monumental Landscapes of the Ancient Maya,* edited by Brett A. Houk, Barbara Arroyo, and Terry G. Powis (2020)

*The Real Business of Ancient Maya Economies: From Farmers' Fields to Rulers' Realms,* edited by Marilyn A. Masson, David A. Freidel, and Arthur A. Demarest (2020)

*Maya Kingship: Rupture and Transformation from Classic to Postclassic Times,* edited by Tsubasa Okoshi, Arlen F. Chase, Philippe Nondédéo, and M. Charlotte Arnauld (2021)

*Lacandón Maya in the Twenty-First Century: Indigenous Knowledge and Conservation in Mexico's Tropical Rainforest,* by James D. Nations (2023)

*The Materialization of Time in the Ancient Maya World: Mythic History and Ritual Order,* edited by David A. Freidel, Arlen F. Chase, Anne S. Dowd, and Jerry Murdock (2024)